The UK Space
Resources, Environment and the Future

The UK Space
Resources, Environment and the Future

Edited by
J.W. House

Professor of Geography,
University of Newcastle-upon-Tyne

Weidenfeld and Nicolson

London

ISBN 0 297 76648 1   cased
ISBN 0 297 76649 X   paperback
Printed by
Redwood Press Limited
Trowbridge Wiltshire

Contributors

Chapter 1
>J. W. House, *M.A. (Oxon.)*
>*Professor of Geography, University of Newcastle-upon-Tyne*

Chapter 2
>R. Lawton, *M.A. (Liverpool)*
>*Professor of Geography, University of Liverpool*

Chapter 3
>L.W. Hanna, *M.Sc. Ph.D. (Belfast)*
>*Lecturer in Geography, University of Newcastle-upon-Tyne*

Chapter 4
>G. Humphrys, *B.A. (Bristol), M.A. (McGill), Ph.D. (Wales)*
>*Senior Lecturer in Geography, University College of Swansea*

Chapter 5
>N.R. Elliott, *B.A., Ph.D. (Dunelm)*
>*Senior Lecturer in Geography, University of Edinburgh*

>and

>B. Fullerton, *M.A. (London)*
>*Senior Lecturer in Geography, University of Newcastle-upon-Tyne*

Chapter 6
>The Contributors

Contents

Page

Contents

Figures

Page

Chapter 3

Chapter 4

Chapter 5

Figures 1.14, 2.6, 2.8, 2.9, 2.14, 2.22, 2.23 and 3.2 are produced by kind
kind permission of the Controller of Her Majesty's Stationery Office.

Tables

Preface

In the early 1970s the UK stands critically poised in several respects. One generation on from the Second World War her international role and status have by now been somewhat painfully adjusted and will need further redefinition in our early years in the EEC. At home fundamental issues of our economy, society and polity need to be re-examined, in the light of a rising national population, the great debate on the merits and prospects in economic growth, the environmental question, and the pursuit of greater social justice and regional equilibrium.

This book seeks to contribute to the need for a national stock-taking, an evaluation of resources, both natural and human. It does so through a geographical interpretation, to be set distinctively alongside those by economists, sociologists or political scientists. To the common concern the geographer adds his perspective on the UK space, a sensitivity to the differences, trends and problems arising from the characteristics of people and places. These are set within the context of post-war changes and the shifting framework of key policies and decisions, both public and private. The interpretation covers the constituent parts of the UK, and much of the material is focused at the level of the economic planning region or the sub-nation. This is increasingly a valid scale for planning and also for the expression of a rising sense of provincially-based regionalism within the complex urban society of the UK. The exposition is by review of the essentials, highlighting of the trends, survey of policies and assessment of their spatial effects. This is in other words a set of considered judgements rather than the opening of new research frontiers, towards which the full bibliographies to each chapter provide an essential indication.

With the Commission on the British Constitution expected to report imminently, and with the importance of regional planning at last recognised, it seemed right to start from the regional perspective (chapter 1). This reflects the essential and striking diversities of people and resources, of heritage, problems and aspirations at work in the UK today. In one sense these are focused meaningfully through the regional planning mechanism and the formulation of strategies for the remaining years of this century.

The people themselves come next (chapter 2), their distribution, structure, trends and the spatial implications of demographic change. Since the management of patterns of employment has played such a key role in public policy in the post-war UK, this links people and their work, with mobility between residence and workplace a most sensitive indicator of change and, at the same time, of the effects of urbanisation. A proper evaluation of the UK environment is overdue (chapter 3) and has often been neglected in planning and policy-making in the past. The key questions concern land, its use and potential, the resources offered in turn by climate, soils and vegetation. The total environment implies many management and conservation problems, illustrated by water, forests and all the implications of environment for those living in our towns and cities.

In an urban industrial society in the throes of rapid technological change the range and cost of alternative energy sources vies with the manufacturing and services sector in critical importance in economic growth and transformation (chapter 4). Mobility through the diverse media of the transport network (chapter 5) is a key to the practability and profitability of redeploying people or productive resources. The spatial potential unlocked by technological change in the transport fields bids fair to outrival all others before the end of the century.

The ambition of the book is to review spatially the tides, currents and trends of economic, social and political change in the post-war UK. Carrying an important part of the message, the line-drawings are a valuable contribution by cartographers in the Geography Departments at Edinburgh, Liverpool, Newcastle upon Tyne and Swansea. The help of all those who have kindly typed the manuscript or checked proofs is also gratefully acknowledged.

University of Newcastle upon Tyne   J.W. HOUSE
January 1973

1

Regions and the System

I THE UK IN THE POST-WAR WORLD

I.1 General assessment

By tradition geographical interpretation starts logically from the characteristics, location and pattern of all resources, including people, and studies their changes over time, using both systematic (or sector) and regional methods of analysis. Standard texts[1] traditionally have favoured a long perspective in time, with a preferred objective of explaining the present in terms of the past. Less ambitious and more selective in conventional terms, this chapter adds a further dimension: concern for the future. It starts by reviewing the major economic and social changes differentiating the UK space since the end of the Second World War. It then seeks to evaluate the manifold and diverse forces affecting, and affected in their turn by the conditions of the UK space, the impact but also the resultant modification of policies, both public and private, relating to regions, areas and localities. After this preliminary context the greater part of the chapter attempts to look ahead, with an assessment and critique of the strategy proposals for each of the eight economic planning regions of England, together with those for Wales, Scotland and Northern Ireland, in the light of their present problems, current trends and the declared intentions of policy-makers. This can only be an interim stocktaking, since regional strategies are neither fully nor uniformly elaborated as yet, and scarcely interrelated, whilst interregional relationships, flows and accounts, remain imperfectly understood. Furthermore, no comprehensive regional policy has yet been advanced by any post-war British government and there has been continuing reluctance in official circles to see the spatial dimension in its rightful perspective in economic, social or even physical planning. Finally, the economic planning regions and the national units, upon which this interpretation necessarily rests at this time, though not altogether satisfactory units, are hopefully the basis upon which more comprehensive regional planning, and even a measure of political devolution will develop during the next decade.

Observers of the post-war UK are likely to agree that economic and social growth have both been substantial since 1945, though slower and perhaps more fitful than among our European neighbours, that profound and on the whole beneficial structural changes have taken place in British economy and society, and that in this transformation successive governments have been substantially, continuously, even increasingly, involved. External influences have often imposed powerful constraints on growth, in volume and direction, but the UK has emerged as a wealthy country with rising living standards, in spite of persistent and persisting inability to sustain economic growth without unacceptable inflation. The indicators are clear: a gross national product (GNP) of £47.9 thousand millions in 1971, representing almost one-third rise in real terms even since 1960; alternatively gross domestic product (GDP) at constant factor cost, a general barometer of economic growth, of 73.5 in 1951 (100 in 1963), and 121.9 in 1971. In the late 1960s the government was habitually the biggest spender in the economy, at 38 per cent of GNP. Little wonder that Rostow spoke of the stage of high mass consumption society being reached in Britain in the late 1940s, whilst others referred to a consumer-oriented society emerging in the 1950s, with virtual satiation in consumer durables reached for an increasing number of citizens during the following decade.

Yet progress has been uneven, in time and space, as well as between social and economic groups throughout the UK, with important, at times disturbing, implications for the development of the regions. As an accompaniment to monetary and fiscal policies to restrain demand, Keynesian policies to minimise the effects of the trade cycle, intermittent and on the whole unsuccessful action on prices and incomes, together with direct action on the balance of payments, governments sought to mitigate the effects of change upon the economically and socially less-favoured regions. Criteria such as unemployment level, rate of new job provision, real income per capita or new factory floor space occupied illustrate both fluctuations throughout the UK economy, but also its regional variations. In particular there were persistent differentials between the more affluent and the less affluent regions, to the continuing social as well as economic disadvantage of the latter. Elaborated later, these differences have been diminished in degree rather than in kind by the measures referred to in section 1.III.

The sum total of public and private achievements, development and change in the UK space since the war has also been the result of a complex balance involving internal changes, both planned for and unexpected, and externalities, particularly those arising from repercussions of the international trading and monetary system. Among the more formative internal changes have been those due to new technologies, leading to structural changes in the composition of the employed population, with decline in some sectors not quite matched by new job provision elsewhere; the rise of the services economy; the emergence of the conglomerate, the large firm and the large factory; automation of processes, in both industry and communications; and proliferation of consumer demand. In policy terms the burgeoning of the mixed (state-private enterprise) economy has been paralleled by the growth of the welfare state, with priorities for full employment and an intermittently growing public social concern, not least in the housing sector, slum clearance and universal provision of basic amenities.

These internal changes, involving at times painful adjustments, regionally and locally as well as nationally, were in part the inevitable outcome of economic growth and transformation, but also the product of the changed and diminished political and economic role and status of the UK in the post-war world. The Empire had become the Commonwealth, former Dominions and Colonies independent; despite its world currency status sterling showed built-in weaknesses; the balance of payments remained characteristically adverse and competition from other industrial trading nations became pronounced. On balance, to our disadvantage, these changes were somewhat mollified by the growth of international economic cooperation. Perhaps most significantly, a reinterpretation of the geographical position of the UK saw a shifting balance among policy perspectives: with limited horizons, self-contained and insular, facing the North Sea lands and Europe; or world-wide, the open-seas policy towards the Commonwealth, the North Atlantic basin and the trading world.

I.2   International Trade

Since the UK still ranks as the world's third trading nation (7 per cent overall; 9 per cent primary product imports; 11 per cent world manufactured exports) her transformed post-war economic role is seen most clearly in the volume, direction, composition and balance of her trade. Furthermore since the nature of UK resources and the characteristics of its space traditionally have had much to do with exports and the conversion of imports the impact of changes in trade were dramatic at the regional level. This was particularly so in areas like North East England, Scotland, South Wales, and Northern Ireland which had developed product specialisation in the export trade.

UK TRADE 1970, by percentages

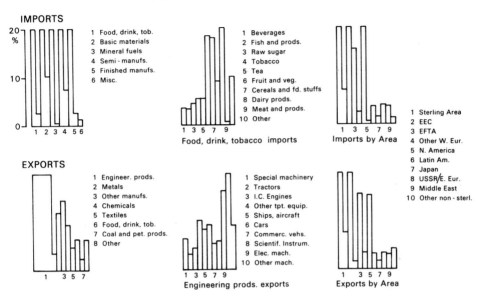

Figure 1.1   Trade, UK, 1970.

Figure 1.1 shows the composition of exports and imports for 1970, with a breakdown of the key sectors of food, drink and tobacco imports and engineering exports, together with origin and destination by major trading areas. There have been striking changes in post-war years: a decline in food (39-23 per cent) and basic raw materials imports (30-15 per cent), with sharp rises in crude petroleum and imports of both manufactures (7-23 per cent) and semi-manufactures. Following tradition, more than five-sixths of exports by value are manufactured goods, with 44 per cent attributable to engineering products; export of chemical products has risen perceptibly whilst textiles have fallen away (from 18 per cent to less than 5 per cent by value of all exports).

In direction of trade there have been notable declines in trade with the primary producing areas, the Commonwealth and other sterling area countries (exports: 42 per cent, 1958; 27 per cent, 1970), whilst trade with western Europe has risen (exports: 28 per cent, 1958, 41 per cent, 1970), already exceeding that with the sterling area by 1962. There has been an increase in trade with the communist world and with Japan, but trade with North America has remained stable.

The spatial effects of these structural changes in trade have been felt adversely in the coal mining and heavy industrial regions which powered the industrial revolution in the nineteenth century, and in the north country, Welsh and Irish ports serving them. Conversely the Midlands and South East, with an industrial structure suited to the exports in rising demand and with associated ports in London, on the south coast and the Bristol Channel received a marked growth stimulus. Industrial location policies in post-war years have not changed the essentials of this basic contrast in regional growth potential, which indeed has become sharpened in more recent times.

I.3   Economy and Society

Table 1.1 shows the basic economic and social changes during the post-war period, by the use of selected indicators, a brief commentary upon which must suffice. The UK continues to be, and to suffer from being, a highly urbanised country with a population (fifth in

TABLE 1.1

Post-war Economic and Social Change, UK, 1951-70

	1951	1961	1970
Home-based population (million)	50.2	52.7	55.3
Dwellers in: major conurbations (%)	44.9	45.9	46.4
rural districts (%)	21.1	21.6	23.1
The young, 0-14 years (%)	24.1	23.4	23.4
old, 65+ years (%)	10.9	11.7	12.2
Affluent Britain: SE, E and W Midlands (%)	44.9	45.9	46.4
Poorer Britain: North, Scotland, Wales and Ulster (%)	24.1	23.7	22.9
Working population (million): male	15.9	16.7	16.4
female	7.3	8.5	9.2
Workers (%) in: agriculture, mining	9.0	7.2	3.5
manufacturing	39.3	37.2	38.9
services	51.7	55.6	57.6
Median income before tax (£)	320	620	1170
Average weekly earnings, male manual workers (£)	8.30	14.99	23.78
Activity rates (%): male	87.2	86.8	81.0
female	37.1	40.6	41.8
Registered unemployed (100,000)	2.1	3.0	7.6
Gross industrial output (£1,000 million): all industries	18.7	25.4	46.3
manufactures	15.9	20.7	36.9
Power consumed (million ton coal equivalent)	224	263	328
Large industrial establishments (% with > 1,000 workers)	33.7	34.9 (1963)	–
Rail track milleage (1,000 miles)	52.9	48.8	31.6
Goods transport (1,000 million ton miles)	No inf.	63.8	83.3
Road vehicles with current licence (million)	4.7	10.1	15.3
Housing completed (1,000)	201	303	362
University students (1,000)	103	135	251
Offences known to the police (1,000)	615	925	1748
Juvenile delinquency (1,000 found guilty)	87	127	133
% Total public expenditure on: social security	12.1	15.8	18.1
NHS	8.4	9.0	9.7
education	6.8	9.8	12.0
housing	6.9	5.4	5.6

Source: Annual Abstract of Statistics, (HMSO 1971); and various

density in the world)[2] still rising, albeit on a decreasing tempo, with implications for congestion, overcrowding, matching of jobs with the numbers entering employment, and so forth. The concentration of almost half the population in conurbations, all with tendencies to decay at the core and growth on the fringes, illustrates a peculiarly British variant of an international problem; in addition, north country conurbations have for some decades tended to stagnate, whilst in London, the West Midlands and the Pennine towns the influx of immigrants implanted the social problem of racial minorities during the 1960s. The

quarter of the UK population classified as living in rural districts is somewhat illusory
since many of these are almost urban in character, as on parts of the coalfields; nevertheless the truly rural population, perhaps 6 per cent in all, faces difficult problems through
the rundown of employment in agriculture, the decaying social and transport provision in
outlying areas and recreational pressures from the town upon land in the countryside.
The perceptible rise in the aged conceals the welfare problem likely to escalate during the
last decades of this century, whilst the quasi-stability in numbers of the young will alarm
some but comfort those who believe in a move towards 'zero population growth'. Alarming
to all surely is the proportion still living in less prosperous areas, a product of differentially
more rapid growth by natural increase, in spite of traditional outmigration, and compounded
by an immobility nurtured by local community bias and, perhaps, fear of the unknown
elsewhere.

The value of gross industrial output has clearly accelerated during the 1960s, even
taking inflation into account, whilst the index of power consumed tells a similar story.
The working population, however, has not increased in like ratio: male employment is
even slightly down, the effect of rising unemployment, but in some contrast the sharp
rise in female employment, and in activity rate, indicates something of a 'petticoat'
industrial revolution; the rise is indeed as marked in manufacturing as in the understand-
ably more female preserve of service industries. There has been an improvement in real
income per capita during the past decade, even allowing for changing price levels, with
earnings growing somewhat faster than prices; in particular, the real income of the younger
manually unskilled increased more rapidly than that of non-manual employees. The growth
in the volume and proportion of unemployed, and the more severe incidence of this problem
in the development areas, is both dramatic, tragic and all too well-known. Overall, however,
the post-war period has seen an improvement in general living standards, indicated by an
increase in the volume of domestic consumption per capita of something like two per cent
per annum.

Properly the subject matter of chapters 2 and 4, table 1.2 gives a preliminary indication
of the principal shifts in industrial production since the mid-1950s, identifying the six
principal lead and lag sectors, in terms of output by value.

TABLE 1.2

Post-war Change in Industrial Production, UK, 1954-70

Index change, ± national mean, 6 ranked lead and lag sectors

>5 per cent over national mean	1954-60	1960-7	1963-70
Chemicals	+ 24.9	+ 38.2	+ 33.8
Electrical engineering	+ 24.2	+ 26.4	+ 24.4
Other manufactures	+ 14.0	+ 21.3	+ 21.5
Gas, water, electricity	+ 12.8	+ 23.0	+ 19.7
Glass, etc	–	+ 15.3	+ 11.1
Mechanical engineering	–	+ 16.2	+ 10.8
>5 per cent below national mean			
Mining and quarrying	– 31.2	– 47.9	– 45.8
Shipbuilding	– 28.4	– 59.5	– 38.0
Leather, etc	– 31.1	– 44.2	– 31.2
Clothing/footwear	–	– 10.9	– 21.0
Timber/furniture	– 17.1	– 9.1	– 10.5
Metals	–	– 15.5	– 9.3

Source: Central Statistical Office (CSO) data

Contemporary with economic changes the face of society has altered: class divisions have become blurred and earning power has to some extent replaced life style or habits as the prime means of class differentiation; in particular, manual/non-manual differences are much less identifiable than in the early post-war years. The housing stock has visibly improved, with 2.5 millions rehoused since the war, mainly by slum clearance programmes; yet in 1969, 37 per cent of houses were still pre-1919, 25 per cent were built between 1919 and 1944 and only 38 per cent were post-war. Of the 19.4 million dwellings in 1971, half were owner-occupied and almost one-third were rented from local authorities. Drudgery for the housewife has been greatly reduced and ownership of consumer durables has become remarkably widespread; moreover, standards of nutrition are now high and still rising.

Educational provision has greatly increased: for example in 1968-9 40 per cent of 16 year-olds were in full-time education compared to less than 29 per cent only 5 years earlier, whilst the university population has more than doubled since 1951. More than half the population takes an annual holiday of more than three weeks, compared to the one per cent who did so in 1951. Sensitivity to environmental problems, their management and improvement has become a watchword of the late 1960s, although for the under-privileged minorities the quality of life, expressed in urban ghettoes, inadequate housing, congestion, noise and squalor, has deteriorated further. This in spite of the increasing proportion of public expenditure seen to be devoted to housing, social security, the health service and education. On the distaff side the poor have become poorer and society to that extent more polarised; the figures for the increase in juvenile delinquency and in offences known to the police speak for themselves.

A final factor of change since the war has been the increased potential for mobility, and this in spite of the manifest decline in the rail network and the withdrawal of public bus services in outlying areas. The boom in road vehicles with current licences stands out in table 1.1, whilst infrastructure improvement in the creation of motorways, a better trunk road network and internal air routes are other striking features. Commuting has become a way of life for hundreds of thousands, perception and mental images of space have widened and there has been a rising demand for more personal space and access to more public recreational space. Interregional gross migration flows have been building up, though net balances are still small in comparison with gross residential populations for most regions. The paradox of immobility preferences in less privileged areas has already been commented upon, perhaps a surprising tribute to the strength of communities, even in an age of greater movement potential. The facilities for greater mobility and the technological changes in transport are the subject matter of chapter 5.

1.4 Land

Change and flux in economy and society inevitably has repercussions on the land, its use and misuse.[3] Of the 59.5 million acres (24.0 million ha) of UK land (1970) the 5.0 million (2.0 million ha) built upon are the most valuable, congested (chapter 5) and in striking contrast to no less than 16.6 million almost deserted acres (6.7 million ha) under rough grazings. With a population density over 800 persons per sq. mile (309 per km^2), expected to rise to perhaps 1000 per sq. mile (386 per km^2) by the year 2000 and a loss of farmland running at about 40,000 acres (16,187 ha) per annum in the period 1960-70 it is not surprising that there is widespread concern for conservation and careful husbanding of land (table 1.3). With agriculture doubling its output since the war whilst using no more labour and even suffering a reduction of the improved land surface this concern may at first sight seem misplaced. That it is not so is well indicated by the mounting pressures for alternative or multiple uses of land and the uniquely high priority rightly given to land use allocation in post-war economic and social planning in the UK, though the very high rate of increase in land values during the 1960s threatens to imperil these achievements.

Potential land use conflicts, severe in the urban cores, around the business district perimeter, where town meets country, and in major estuarine tracts, are spreading to even the remoter rural areas, where there may be a need to harmonise farming, forestry, tourism, water policies and access for the townsman. With perhaps the most sophisticated town and country planning mechanism in operation anywhere the UK still lacks the comprehensive interrelated central policies for space allocations at the *regional* level, with appropriate priorities assigned to what have all too often seemed to be conflicting strands of public policies.

TABLE 1.3

Land Use Change, UK, 1950-2000

1000 ha	1950	1965	1950-65 change	% change p.a.	est. 2000	1965-2000 est. ch.	% change p.a.
Agricultural	20,254	19,623	− 631	− 0.2	18,122	− 1,502	− 0.2
Forest	1,532	1,816	+ 284	+ 1.2	2,617	+ 800	+ 1.2
Urban	1,773	2,043	+ 270	+ 1.0	2,745	+ 702	+ 1.0
Other	532	608	+ 76	+ 0.9	608	0	0
Total land	24,092	24,092	0	0	24,092	0	0

Source: A.G. Champion (1973)

I.5   Decisions and Policies

Because governments spend the most sizeable part of GNP these days it is logical to give precedence to public policy objectives as these affect the UK space. Certainly the spatial perspective in UK policy-making is the least developed, hitherto poorly-esteemed and neglected, though almost all economic and social policies necessarily have and have had a spatial outcome, not infrequently without clearly-defined spatial intentions. Among the principal public policy objectives since the war, which have had important spatial implications, the following might be listed:

(a) maximisation of sustained national economic growth without an unacceptable level of inflation, success in which continues to prove elusive. The role of regional or spatial policies in meeting this objective is contested but it seems clear that successive inflationary bouts have been escalated by the scarcities of land and labour in affluent areas, with differentially higher costs there, whilst untapped or under-utilised resources continue to characterise the North, Wales, Scotland and Northern Ireland. The diminishing of this contrast in living standards and opportunities would thus contribute to the goals of social justice but, as the ill-fated National Plan of 1964 recognised, might also have added significantly to the solution of national economic growth with least inflation.

(b) balance as between the regions, sometimes referred to as 'the need to rectify imbalance' and interpreted to refer to equality of living environment, adequacy and choice of employment, equitable dissemination of growth, prosperity and the full realisation of economic potential. This objective logically relates to that above but, in view of the disparity of resources, both human and natural, the uneven way in which these have been developed through time, and the varied regional legacies of problems which have resulted, true equalisation seems to be totally impracticable; a reduction in the present growing inequality, on the other hand, seems both feasible and desirable.

The objective of regional balance and equilibrium is the opposite of the centre-periphery concept, to whose diminution so much thinking on regional policy in France was devoted during the 1960s. It may also be related to the search for greater political devolution, the accommodation, or even the neutralisation of regionalist or nationalist sentiments, which gained widespread momentum during the past decade.

(c) social justice, including the full employment policy, relief of unemployment and improvement of the activity rate, spread of welfare particularly to the lower-paid and underprivileged, income and wealth redistribution, equality of access to education, health and housing opportunities.

(d) improvement in the balance of payments, to provide the basis for and reinforcement of economic growth in the UK, and to strengthen participation in world economy, society and polity.

(e) increasingly during the late 1960s, the consciousness of the imperative need for conservation of scarce national assets in the landscape and townscape heritage and safeguarding of threatened aspects of the quality of life.

Among this amalgam of policies, whose mix and priorities varied with the political complexion of governments, deliberate priority for coordinated action at regional, area or locality level remained rare, though economic first aid policies have matured into the latest, more constructive growth promotion and aid programmes for the assisted areas (1972). The block grant financing for local authorities has increasing, if still inadequate, regard for local problems and needs, whilst acceptance of regional priorities may be detected in a rising number of key central decisions on communications, major new industrial projects or the decentralisation of some government or nationalised industry establishments. It is only during the past decade, however, that governments have shown effective concern for longer-term and coherent analysis, forecasting and strategy formulation at the regional level. This has coincided with, but in large measure also stimulated, the flow of research by social scientists and geographers, being joined by regional economists, sociologists and political scientists; and the development of relevant analytical techniques, which had been lacking hitherto.[4]

As yet regional analysis, forecasting and programming is scarcely beyond its infancy in the UK and, not least, the complex nature of development itself remains imperfectly understood. Policies by central or local government must be examined alongside the decision-taking of countless entrepreneurs, firms and corporations, whilst the actions and intentions of multifarious groups and key individuals may also need to be taken into account. All or some of these non-public actions may work in directions or at a tempo contrary to the intentions of public policy. Through the complex interactions which result the UK space is further differentiated, the characteristics of regions or subsystems evolve and change, their interrelationships are modified. It is difficult indeed to measure, much less predict, the spatial outcome of public policies and they are in turn variously susceptible to change by events, constraints of the time or new political controls or thinking. Such process of change has accelerated during the post-war years, threatening even basic interpretations of the regional economic and social geography of the UK. The next step must thus be to look at the changing identity, and the role of the variegated and variously-defined regions making up the national space.

II   REGIONS: IDENTITY, SIGNIFICANCE AND FUNCTIONS

II.1   A Perspective on Regions

To many Americans the notion of a regional breakdown of so small a unit as the UK might seem absurd, even for the purposes of an analysis, much less as the basis for more effective overall planning. To many citizens of the UK, on the other hand, if the evidence of the Royal Commission on Local Government in England[5] is to be accepted, even the provincial level of regionalism is an unfamiliar, perhaps unwelcome extension of their

concept of home area, which is characteristically and parochially expressed as a parish or
an urban ward. For some economists regional identities are impediments to more effective
use of national resources and space, but for most geographers, at least until recently,
regions in their infinite diversity have been both a key tool of analysis and the prime
means of interpreting the use of resources and space. More importantly, the spatial
organisation of economy and society expresses itself in discernable and interrelated, if
complex, entities, whilst in a practical sense governments, both central and local, work
through networks of units, not always the same territorial entities for all purposes, and
by this means help to reinforce the identities of particular areas.

Though few today are likely to accept that the UK space may be unambiguously
divided into universal-type regions, which will commend widespread acceptance, there
is likely to be greater coincidence of views on the first-stage, or national/provincial level
of identity. In reviewing regions the many types, their utility and validity, may first be
considered briefly; then the region-forming or -disintegrating forces; the flows and interregional linkages, of which presently so little is ascertainable; the hierarchy, network or
subsystem aspects of regions; and, finally, the significance of regions within the organisation
of the national space. All this is an essential prelude to a consideration of the current *de
facto* regions, the eight economic planning regions of England, together with Wales,
Scotland and Northern Ireland, their differentiation, problems and prospects. The criteria
for regional identity include some dominant or interrelated set of attributes; utility in
terms of economy, efficiency or convenience; administrative role, popular recognition or
representation; and, in a practical sense, the extent to which the area identified may
serve effectively as the territorial basis for understanding or promoting economic and
social advancement.

II.2   Types of Region

Given a potential infinity of regions, in scale level or characteristics, some priority ordering
is necessary. Conventionally, geographers have identified sets of systematic regions, starting with those derived from the physical environment, followed by those with historical,
economic, social or politically dominant attributes. Thereafter re-grouping of regions to
multi-factor identities in space has been the prelude to a regionalisation of the total UK
space as near universal in character as possible. The weaknesses of such an approach are
allegedly that subjectivity creeps in early, there is unacceptable abstraction from reality
in the process and that the end-product risks being no more than academic, and may have
neither practical utility, nor reflect the long-felt territorial loyalties of the people.

It cannot be gainsaid that the traditional divisions of the UK space into uplands and
lowlands, with as complex a differentiation according to geological history, morphological
character and present surface or drainage characteristics, as in any area of comparable
size of the world, remain an essential prelude to further regional differentiation. Likewise
climatic, soil and vegetation characteristics diversify the physiographic units, are as fundamental as ever to an understanding of land quality and potential, and establish a framework
for the range, flexibility and profitability of its uses. Yet even in an increasingly environ-
mentally-conscious age the physical nature of the UK is likely to take second place, in
official eyes, to regionalisation derived from economic, social or political attributes, in so
far as these may be adequately disentangled.

Determination of priorities as between economic, social or political regional nets is
likely to vary with the analyst, and the purpose. It involves basically a choice between
dominant or spatially interrelated forms of production, incomes, consumption or marketing in the case of economic issues; the spatial structure of society, regional, urban and
local life styles, class, mobility or social pathology among social criteria; effective political
voice, democratic representation, national and sub-national recognition, or efficiency of

government, in political terms.[6] All such factors tend to be inextricably interrelated and it may be that the nearest approach to collective identity is that of regional units with a common problem-mix, a related social or cultural identity and a sufficiently coherent and forceful political voice to seek redress or power improvements.

From a planning point of view since the war there has been some priority for identifying and studying urban regions,[7] or town-country relationships expressed in space, with special emphasis on circulation or activity spaces; mobility evidence, including journey to work, shopping, entertainments and so forth, affords the prime data. The provincial level of region has consistently been favoured by geographers,[8] from as far back as the pioneering work of Fawcett in 1919, but has variably found an echo in local government reform proposals.

II.3   Region-forming/Region-disintegrating Forces

The seemingly well-defined, if not entirely static, regions beloved of geographers in this and other European countries earlier in this century, are more difficult to sustain these days. If planning is to work in the direction of fulfilling regionalist aspirations in economy, society or polity it is important to interpret, guide and work with the forces for change, not all of which are likely to be within planning control, and many of which are at times in conflict with each other. Regional identities by some criteria are dissolving, but in others being steadily reinforced; overall the possibility exists for fashioning and developing new kinds of identity suited to a wider range of aspirations during the remaining decades of this century.

Among the balance of forces operating on the differentiation of regions at the present the centrifugal or disintegrating tendencies may be thought by some to be in the ascendant, though very unevenly over the UK space. Moreover the process has very far to go before identities are lost. Such fluidity of change is not new, but has been greatly accelerated in recent times, by: concentration of decision-taking, both political and economic, at or near the metropolis; economies of scale in production, concentrating upon fewer, larger, more nodal sites, whether these be for factories, farms, ports or profitable rail lines; urbanisation, trending persistently towards larger-scale units, concentration within national growth areas and away from the less privileged regions or, within those regions, away from the sparsely settled hinterlands. These urbanising tendencies have been counteracted, but only partially, by suburban and commuting spread and sprawl; the basic contrast of polarisation from larger regional tracts remains.[9] Rising interregional mobility of population, culminating in the peak net southward flows in the depression years of the early 1930s supply the most dramatic evidence, offset but only in limited measure by the regional aid policies of successive governments to the present time.

Less apparent than the mass flows of people in search of betterment but equally indicative of some loss of regional differentiation is the spread of common urban life styles and aspirations, matched by consumer demand, and the uniformity fostered by advertising and the media. Yet against the dictates of such standardisation, gravity model economics or the working of Zipf's Principle of Least Effort there has been a marked, perhaps rising reaction. Apart from the Royal Commission evidence that people think in terms of a very localised, not to say parochial 'home area' there is mounting and widespread evidence of a built-in reluctance to migrate in search of opportunity, even though greater means of mobility and better knowledge of the market make this possible. The strength of Welsh, Scottish or Ulster feelings on the matter of political devolution from Whitehall is a nationalist expression, weighted by sizeable populations, resources and problems, which finds echoes in less dramatic but equally heartfelt ways in the less privileged regions of England. Indeed the forceful presentation of regional needs through the economic planning councils is an indication of such feelings. Furthermore to some extent the greater mobility of the townsmen, allied with aspirations of the countryman, is reducing urban-rural distinctions and the gradient in living standards and attitudes between the two milieu. To the extent that policies of economic balance between the regions progress, the provincial metropoli can help stabilise their hinterlands and act as the political, economic or social foci of either freshly-defined or reinforced regional iconographies.

It is appropriate to add that effective regional planning may be the most powerful of forces for stabilising and developing new forms of regionalism. To be effective such planning needs to be applied to base populations and resources of adequate, even optimal size. Currently a population of around three millions is thought desirable for regional economic planning, whilst not less than 250,000 persons is thought preferable for any first-tier local government unit in the future. Likewise for New Towns target populations have been progressively revised upwards to 250,000 and beyond for the latest generation. The need to bear these norms in mind implies a large measure of compromise in any redefinition of regions for the UK space, not only in terms of scale, or as between possibly conflicting economic, social or political purposes, but also in respect of regions and their national context.

II.4 Flows and Linkages

The study of these cardinal region-forming and disintegrating forces has hitherto been greatly limited by lack of adequate data, and the absence of a sufficient framework of interregional accounts.[10] These short-comings have led some to interpret regions as more clear-cut or self-contained than is justifiable. This failing leads through directly into current regional economic planning, where the strategies for individual regions often inadequately take into account proposals for even adjacent regions, and in sum total do not add up to a coherent national strategy for space.

Migration of population, both in gross flows and in the net interchange over a period of time, is probably the most useful general purpose indicator of regional differences in job prospects and living environment (chapter 2). Though net flows may be only a small proportion of total resident population there is a trend towards increased gross mobility as an outcome of rising affluence. If the assisted areas are to build up their populations, they will need to do this by attracting residents of other areas as well as by seeking to retain more of their own citizens.

Flows of passenger or freight traffic by the various transport media, including the interchange of telecommunications, further indicate both the state of interregional linkages, but also the sinews upon which further growth is likely to be generated (chapter 5). The traditional importance of the radial network of roads and railways based upon London has been reinforced in the motorway and air ages. The lack of adequate alternative axial routeways not only gave rise, between the wars, to the great industrial belt (axial zone)[11] from Yorkshire-Lancashire through the Midlands to the metropolis, but has also ensured that the national economic skeleton has changed so little since that time. Recent work[12] indicates that freight rate costs are not such a significant charge on production in a wide diversity of manufacturing that plants are tied to a restricted range of locations. That there is so little voluntary movement of plants and firms, least of all to the assisted areas, has much to do with the immobilities engendered by earlier location decisions, allied with strong adverse perceptions of the risks or inconvenience that added distance might create.

Clearly the study of both flows and linkages between regions, of people, commodities, wealth and investment, should have a high priority among operational planners and social scientists. Of these topics that of linkages is likely to prove the more difficult, but on a correct evaluation of essential linkages between regions,[13] not only at the anlaysis

stage but, more formatively, at the subsequent stages of monitoring and management
of regional change, ultimately rests the entire regional planning process.

II.5   Regional Context

The interpretation of flows and linkages leads logically to the identification of scale order
relationships between units within the framework of the UK space. Techniques for the
analysis of these relationships are still in active evolution and most work so far has been
confined to urban hierarchies and to circulation space. Somewhat surprisingly, there is
no substantive work on regions and their component subregions, where officialdom still
creates units for administrative purposes, on occasion almost arbitrarily, and then
studies their characteristics and problems, rather than the more creative reverse process.

Early work on the urban hierarchy by Smailes[14] during the immediate post-war years,
identified indicators of the economic and social status of settlements, mapping their
hinterlands and describing the resultant hierarchy of interrelationships. This was followed
up by Green[15] in pioneering work on the pattern of urban hinterlands through an analysis
of public bus services, again a useful general-purpose barometer of individual and collective
needs for circulation space. Carruthers studied service centres in Greater London and in
England and Wales,[16] establishing a more sophisticated urban hierarchy. Moser and Scott[17]
made a comprehensive statistical analysis of British towns and more recently Hall[18] has
made a novel interpretation of city regions and standard metropolitan labour areas.

A clearer understanding of the way in which units of various types relate to one another
and nest within units of larger size, to make up a network or hierarchy, or a functioning
subsystem within the UK space, is obviously very important in regional planning. Yet
there is little indication that this type of research is being given adequate priority. For the
lack of such knowledge many subregional plans necessarily have to be formulated for ill-
defined units, and the outcome risks lacking wider context or applicability.

II.6   Development Concepts

Wide subscription to a doctrine of promoting greater regional balance implies that there
are undesirable (or politically inconvenient) inequalities, even distortions in the UK space,
which might be reduced or removed by effective public action through urban and regional
planning.[19] A simple centre-periphery model is inappropriate to explain the differentiation
of these islands, but there are nevertheless markedly differing economic and social conditions and problems between the regions. There is sufficient concentration of affluence in
the Midlands and the South East to provide a sharp and coherent contrast to the less
favoured regions in the North, Wales, Scotland and in Northern Ireland, at the opposite
end of the scale. Characteristically the less favoured areas are located on the outer margins
of the UK space but they also have common problems arising from an industrial structure
related to the use of coal, steam-power and the establishment of a range of traditional
nineteenth-century manufactures. These have been increasingly affected during this
century by competition from other products or from new centres of production in other
countries. The tribulations of coal mining, the heavy metallurgical industries or textiles lie
at the heart of problems of industrial re-structuring in the assisted areas of the UK, but
in what proportion their regional problems are an outcome of unfavourable location as
against outdated or narrow industrial structure remains a matter for conjecture. Both
conditions illustrate marginality[20] and point up the need to overcome a dual adversity,
a task which cannot but be made more problematical as the UK enters Europe and its
outer areas risk becoming even more perimeter in character within a European context.

Doubt might well be cast on the reality of creating ultimate balance or equilibrium
between the economic regions of the UK, if such a state is to mean effective equalisation
of job opportunity, living standards, environmental conditions. The fundamental diversities

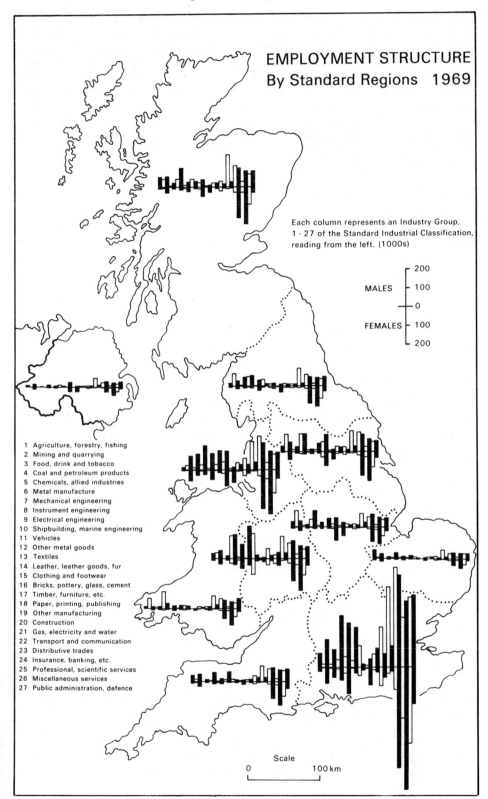

EMPLOYMENT STRUCTURE
By Standard Regions   1969

Each column represents an Industry Group,
1 - 27 of the Standard Industrial Classification,
reading from the left. (1000s)

MALES

FEMALES

200
100
0
100
200

1   Agriculture, forestry, fishing
2   Mining and quarrying
3   Food, drink and tobacco
4   Coal and petroleum products
5   Chemicals, allied industries
6   Metal manufacture
7   Mechanical engineering
8   Instrument engineering
9   Electrical engineering
10 Shipbuilding, marine engineering
11 Vehicles
12 Other metal goods
13 Textiles
14 Leather, leather goods, fur
15 Clothing and footwear
16 Bricks, pottery, glass, cement
17 Timber, furniture, etc.
18 Paper, printing, publishing
19 Other manufacturing
20 Construction
21 Gas, electricity and water
22 Transport and communication
23 Distributive trades
24 Insurance, banking, etc.
25 Professional, scientific services
26 Miscellaneous services
27 Public administration, defence

Scale
0   100 km

Figure 1.2   Employment structure, UK, 1969.

of the UK preclude such an achievement, no matter the aggregate cost to public funds or the distortion of logical investment decisions which may prove acceptable. An intermediate, realisable and worthwhile target, however, is to move towards the earliest possible achievement of self-sustaining economic growth in the less favoured regions, adjusting, by any necessary public action, growth pressures in other regions of the UK space in the interim. A firmer economic base might thereby be implanted and developed in the assisted areas, their resources of man-power, land and social capital more fully utilised. With a growth-oriented strategy, building upon the most logical economic growth localities and employment sectors, whilst accepting, even programming for decline in the least favoured places, the assisted areas might then move to a more competitive status within the European Common Market as well as within the UK (chapter 6, section I).

II.7 Economic Health and Deprivation[21]

Figures 1.2, 1.3 and 1.4 taken together permit an introductory visual assessment of the essential characteristics and problems of the economic planning regions of the UK. These economic planning regions correspond broadly to the major provincial or subnational entities which have emerged over the post-war years as a reasonable compromise for the first-stage breakdown of the UK space. Their boundaries and detailed composition may be criticised, most of all around the fluid northern borderlands of the South East, but they contain the core territories and are in number the same as found in most schemes for first-stage breakdown by geographers. In any event they are the regions for which economic planning councils and boards have been responsible since the mid-1960s and for which formulation of regional strategies has been actively, if variously prosecuted. Whatever the criticisms of the units as the optimal first-stage regions there is a sense in which they are generating and consolidating their identity, through their continuing use for policy-making and its applications.

Figure 1.2 shows the volume and structure of employment and allows quick assessment of the relationship between regional space and the quantum of its labour force, the absolute numbers in any industry group in any one region and its relative importance compared with other regions, the degree of diversification and, in particular, a comparison of the numbers in service industries (orders **XX-XXVII**, 1968 Standard Industrial Classification) with those in manufacturing or extractive occupations. It further graphically illustrates the proportionate and absolute importance of male and female contributions to the labour force in each region. In essence the contrast, more fully developed later, between four zones is hinted at: the least-favoured or development regions: the North, Scotland, Wales and Ulster;[22] the less-favoured or intermediate regions: Yorkshire and Humberside, the North West; the zones of mixed trends: the South West and East Anglia; and the more affluent, diversified and balanced growth regions of the East and West Midlands and the South East.

This categorisation is reinforced by consideration of the evidence on figure 1.3. The indicators of economic health and deprivation, mapped as deviations from the national mean, have been chosen and grouped to give a representative impression of the essential contrasts; certain indicators were not available for Northern Ireland. The combination of a high proportion in fast decline industries, as defined by job reduction 1965-9, with an above average ratio of unskilled male manual workers, high unemployment and lower than average activity rates, and a high ratio of men earning less than £17 per week in 1968 or with lower mean annual earnings, identifies the same problem development regions. This adverse picture is further reinforced by the evidence on retail turnover, household expenditure, whilst the social malaise is equally highlighted by the outmigration rate, the low ratio of pupils staying on at school after 15 years, the volume of male sickness benefit and, finally, the higher mortality rates. The situation in the three most affluent areas is not quite a mirror image, though positive and favourable aspects emerge on almost

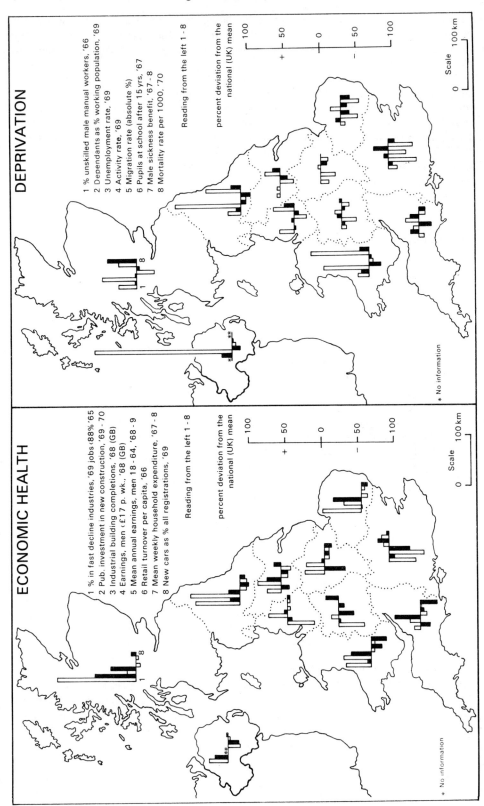

DEPRIVATION

1 % unskilled male manual workers, '66
2 Dependants as % working population, '69
3 Unemployment rate, '69
4 Activity rate, '69
5 Migration rate (absolute %)
6 Pupils at school after 15 yrs, '67
7 Male sickness benefit, '67 - 8
8 Mortality rate per 1000, '70

Reading from the left 1 - 8

percent deviation from the national (UK) mean

100
50
+
0
50
−
100

0   Scale   100 km

* No information

ECONOMIC HEALTH

1 % in fast decline industries, '69 jobs ‹88%'65
2 Pub. investment in new construction, '69 - 70
3 Industrial building completions, '68 (GB)
4 Earnings, men ‹£17 p. wk., '68 (GB)
5 Mean annual earnings, men 18 - 64, '68 - 9
6 Retail turnover per capita, '66
7 Mean weekly household expenditure, '67 - 8
8 New cars as % all registrations, '69

Reading from the left 1 - 8

percent deviation from the national (UK) mean

100
50
+
0
50
−
100

0   Scale   100 km

* No information

Figure 1.3   Economic health and deprivation, UK, 1960s.

all counts. Remedial action by government is shown by the above-average public investment in new construction in the assisted areas and the volume of industrial building completions there in a recent year, in comparison with the markedly negative indications on both counts for the South East.

Figure 1.4 shows the pattern of assisted areas 1972, referred to in the next section and analysed in chapter 4, in terms of the impact on manufactures and services. Suffice it for the moment to comment on the striking, but not surprising, coincidence between the assisted areas and those already seen to be suffering the most pronounced economic and social hardships. In the assisted areas, the special development areas (SDAs), created in 1967, form a hard core of localities with severe problems, set within development areas (DAs) covering the North, Scotland, most of Wales, Ulster and much of Cornwall. The intermediate areas (1969) are well-represented in the economic planning regions on the southern or eastern borders of the development areas.

III ˋ PUBLIC POLICIES ON THE REGIONS

III.1 An Outline Assessment

General public policy objectives with spatial implications were mentioned in section 1.I.5. Since the war the need for such policies has varied with the state of the national economy and both the policy mix and the extent of its enforcement have shifted according to the economic, social and political objectives of successive governments.[23] Nevertheless there has been a general political consensus on the continuing importance of full employment, industrial location policy, regional aid, the extension of welfare through the social services, population redistribution measures, the improvement of both the national infrastructure, particularly communications and housing, the total living environment and the need for local government reform. Priorities within all these policies have characteristically been given to distressed or development areas or districts, under a wide range of changing definitions and locations through time. Political differences between the parties have related to the extent of public involvement, the balance between inducements and controls, the definition, range and degree of enforcement of particular policies. Such policies for the UK space have required a planning mechanism, in the economic and social fields, and in physical terms for town and country, of great diversity and complexity, more wide-ranging in its nature than for any other western country. Yet the region came late into planning and even today there is no more than a set of policy objectives for the eleven economic planning regions of the UK, with an approved strategic plan only for the South East (1970). The interim verdict must be that though public policies have proliferated they have rarely been consistently applied for long enough and have been insufficiently related, with a particular gap between the objectives and achievements respectively of physical, economic and social aspects of planning, at either national or regional level. Cumulatively, however, the effects have been considerable in terms of industry, both manufacturing and services; other key economic sectors, including coal, electricity, gas, oil and natural gas; communications, rail, road, air, ports and tele-communications; the conurbations, cities and towns; and prospectively in the immediate future, on local government units or functions, and also the status of the national groups within the UK. At times governments have acted directly through particular policies and institutions, but almost as frequently influence has been indirect, often hard to trace. For this and other reasons it is difficult to make more than a general assessment of the impact of such policies on the UK space; that collectively and cumulatively these effects have been significant, even dramatic, there can be no doubt.[24]

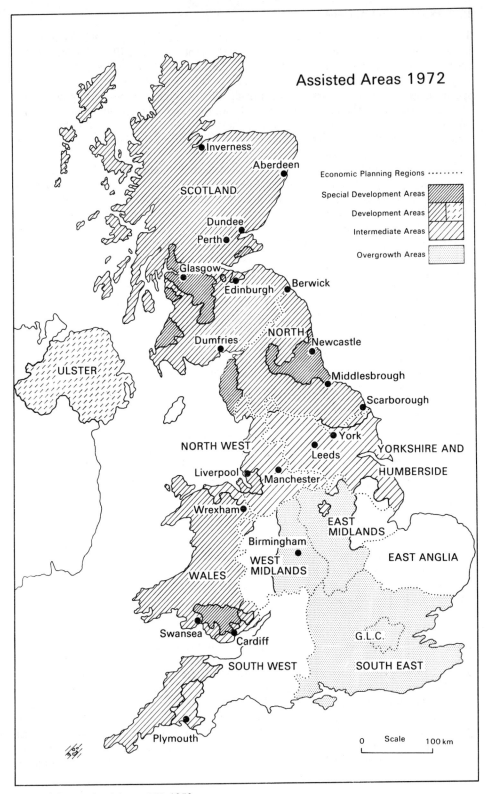

Figure 1.4   Assisted Areas, UK, 1972.

III.2 Pre-1939 and Wartime

The mounting depression and severe unemployment of the early 1930s led to government intervention in South Wales, North East England, Cumberland and Clydeside, designated special areas under the 1934 Act of that name. Though powers were few and the effects very limited, only 4 per cent of factories established in Great Britain 1934-8 going to the special areas, the pre-war years saw the introduction of trading estates, with powers to build and lease factories. Policy was directed towards relief of unemployment *in situ* but, uniquely for regional policy in the UK, there was some attempt at planned interregional transfer and resettlement; however only 30,000 families were moved in six years, at high cost, and the experiment was never repeated.

Rearmament and the upturn of the trade cycle achieved much more than the special areas policy, though unemployment relief has remained in the forefront among objectives ever since. In 1940 the Royal Commission on the Distribution of the Industrial Population (Barlow Commission)[25] drew attention to the marked disparity in economic growth trends, in favour of the South East and the Midlands (the axial zone) and at the expense of the North, Wales and Scotland. The report called for national action on distribution of industry and population, recommended decentralisation from congested urban areas, the redevelopment of older regions and the introduction of balance and diversification into their regional economies. Creation of garden cities and satellite towns was recommended, together with the expansion of rural towns. These far-reaching recommendations necessitated a new central organisation for planning and in 1943 the Ministry of Town and Country Planning was born. A further view by the Commission was that there should be strategic dispersal of industries, to avoid the risks inherent in major vulnerable concentrations. This objective was in fact considerably furthered during the war through the policies of the Board of Trade, creating large ordnance factories and influencing the location of much new engineering, aircraft and vehicle production towards the peripheral and less exposed industrial regions of the north and west. Some of the major ordnance factories were available for conversion to trading (industrial) estates after the war, as at Aycliffe and Spennymoor in the North East, or Hirwaun and Bridgend in South Wales. Furthermore a pool of skilled labour, especially women, had been created in the special areas, capable of retraining for post-war industry, management had had the experience of operating successfully in the areas and their general communications had been improved. By 1945 unemployment in the special areas had fallen to the record low level of 1.5 per cent.

III.3 Post-war to 1960

Almost equally formative in changes in the UK space during this period were the Distribution of Industry Act (1945) and the Town and Country Planning Act (1947). Though the former was responsible for industrial location controls and inducements, and was vigorously prosecuted in the early post-war years, whilst the latter was concerned with development control, monitoring and programming changes in land use, the two objectives overlapped. Until 1954 there was also government control of building through a system of licences.

The development areas designated under the 1945 Act were more extensive, covering a population of 6.5 millions (13.5 per cent of the nation), in comparison with the 4 million people in the pre-war special areas. In territorial terms they were extensions of the special areas, to include major towns which had previously been excluded. As the agent for location policy the Board of Trade had powers to build factories and buy land, make loans to trading estate companies, finance basic public services, make loans and grants to firms and to reclaim derelict land. In addition, under the 1947 Planning Act all applications to build factories or factory extensions of 5000 ft² (465m²) or more had to have an industrial development certificate (IDC) issued by the Board of Trade. In issuing such certificates the Board sought to ensure the 'proper' distribution of industry, a loose and flexible objective, but one which was used, with varying insistence, diminishing through the 1950s, to the advantage of the development areas (DAs). As far as a common objective can be established it seems to have been the need to diversify the industrial structure of the DAs by the introduction and stimulation of new growth elements. A geographical outcome of this policy was a threefold division of the UK into: 'overgrowth' areas, mainly in the Midlands and South East England, in which manufacturing growth was discouraged; the DAs; and the remainder of the UK, commonly referred to as 'grey' areas, in which neither encouragement nor discouragement was officially applied to those seeking industrial growth. Northern Ireland had similar legislation and effectively, though not in name, DA status. Further DAs were later added to the original four: Wigan and St Helens (1946); Merseyside, and parts of the Scottish Highlands (1949); North East Lancashire (1953).

In the years 1945-51 the DA policy showed dramatic results, no less than two-thirds of all recorded moves in manufacturing going to development areas. There was at that time plenty of mobile industry seeking new or additional factory space, the inducements in the DAs were substantial, not least in the availability of modern or converted wartime factories for rental, plus a skilled or semi-skilled labourforce on the spot. In the two years to June 1947 233 tenants occupied rented DA factories, employing 50,000, whilst 301 new or extended factories in the areas provided only 20,000 new jobs during the same period. The early momentum was soon lost, however, and between 1948 and 1952 only 1,096 IDCs were granted for factory space in DAs, compared with 1,069 in London and the South East, and 808 in Greater Birmingham. Priority for exporters, many of whom sought to expand existing operations or develop new capacity in the more affluent areas, coupled with declining unemployment in the DAs, led to the relaxation of regional policy on industrial location. As an indication of this no 'advance factories', the spearhead of economic aid to the dispersed, less attractive sites in DAs, were built in the entire period 1947-59. Additionally, during the 1950s, the New Towns created under the 1946 Act were beginning to develop as powerful magnets for some of the light industries which might otherwise have been persuaded to move to DA sites.

The nationalisation of the rail services, electricity generation and supply, the gas and coal industries, together with the alternating public and private control of the steel industry, permitted unusual coherence of central decisions, forward planning and rationalisation of these key sectors. Although the collective outcome of decisions in these and other infrastructural sectors such as roads and ports, might thus have reinforced the regional and spatial policy objectives on industrial location or use of the land, the opportunities were not fully taken and, indeed, rationalisation in the sense of taking high cost or less profitable production units as links out of the industrial or communications networks threatened to have a precisely contrary effect. It is of course possible to argue that such a coordinated overview of spatial decision-taking would have been foreign to any post-war political climate in the UK, a verdict somewhat confirmed in due course by the demise of the ill-fated National Plan of 1964. The lack of such interrelated policy-making in the 1950s, in part the result of the independence rather than interdependence in the formulation and prosecution of policies by individual Ministries, was undoubtedly costly and frustrating to any thoughts of coherent regional planning. Concurrently the development plans by the counties and boroughs under the 1947 Act were being conceived and implemented without proper national context or allocation of resources, somewhat independent even of adjacent areas, and there continued that bugbear of planning in the UK, the lack of adequate interrelationship between economic, social and land use aspects of planning policies concerned with space.

During the later 1950s, however, economic conditions deteriorated, unemployment rose again, became particularly severe in localised pockets and official thoughts turned once again to the need for a more effective spatial, if still not a regional policy. The DA policy had been largely allowed to lapse and was revived, somewhat in piecemeal form, in amended legislation in 1958 (Distribution of Industry, Industrial Finance Act), recognising the special needs of the pockets of more severe unemployment within the larger, but virtually defunct development areas. The decline in the fortunes of coal from 1957 onwards (see chapter 4) foreshadowed the emergence of many problem localities where pits closed on a rising crescendo during the following decade. The steel industry similarly felt a recession and the capital goods industries, whose post-war revival had so effectively buttressed the economies of the major development areas, showed disturbing tendencies to instability and downturn once more. In 1959 the Cotton Industry Act involved public funds in a major reorganisation and reequipment operation for one of Britain's traditional staple industries.

III.4 Since 1960

During the past decade public policies on the UK space have widened, become more coherent and interrelated, with emergence for the first time of regional economic planning. There has been recognition that although relief of unemployment and social justice remain the priority objectives for the least favoured areas, and that this may lead at times to inefficient public investments in 'lame ducks' or localities, there is a more fundamental need, on a continuing basis, to examine, plan, programme and monitor the economic and social change in the major regions of the UK. To do this effectively requires not only the appropriate planning mechanisms at national and regional level, but also implies that all major investment decisions, even by private entrepreneurs, need to be reviewed and approved since they are likely to have regional or local repercussions, multiplier or 'spin-off' effects. The point that the social costs of the development of firms or industry are borne by the community has been well taken, justifying close and prior review of the locational intentions of any leader firm or key industry. Similarly the role and significance of key decisions on major infrastructural improvements, such as roads, harbours, airports, housing or office space are now more fully understood and can be, though regrettably not always, taken into account in the context of regional development. In short, the regional development process is nowadays more comprehensively studied, its ingredients more fully appraised and the relationships between manufacturing and services, in particular, more effectively understood. Belatedly, but importantly, the necessity of bringing local government units and functions more into line with the requirements of the times has also been appreciated. Finally, the reducing of inequalities over the UK space is thought likely not only thereby to satisfy demands for fuller and more diverse employment, social justice, regionalist aspirations or the wish for improved living environments in less favoured areas, but also in its own right to make a significant contribution to overall national development. On the eve of UK entry into the European Common Market the future course of regional policy and the implications of incorporating the national space into the European land-sea space of the enlarged Six must for the time being remain somewhat speculative.

Policies on industrial location have varied over the past decade. Under the Local Employment Acts (1960 and 1963) the spatially-coherent development areas were abandoned in favour of more rapidly changing and highly localised development districts, identified initially by an unemployment level double the national average over a period of six months; in time 4·5 per cent became a general yardstick for this, and imminent unemployment was also accepted as a justification for the scheduling of districts. Some of the grant and loan powers of the Board of Trade were extended, Industrial Estates Corporations were established for England, Wales and Scotland (though some estates now fall outside the scheduled Districts) and the IDC system was widened to include conversion of non-industrial buildings. Yet the policy was negative: the scheduled districts were fragmented and transitory, being descheduled when the employment situation rose above the statutory unemployment threshold; and the districts variously included rural areas, localities of mining decline, or coastal holiday resorts with off-season unemployment, outmigration and lack of alternative work. In 1961 12·5 per cent of the national population was covered by Development Districts, in 1963 7·2 per cent, in 1966 16·8 per cent. Scheduling bore no relation to a District's potential for development, indeed often the converse was true, and competition between districts, as for example between Merseyside and Snowdonia, was very uneven. Industrialists lacked confidence in the continuity of scheduling, the growth potential and the adequacy and skills of any labour force available in or near these pockets of heavy unemployment. Nevertheless in the period 1960-8 no less than £269 million were spent under the Local Employment Acts and an estimated 428,000 jobs created.[26]

1963 was a very formative year in the emergence of regional planning, first with the production of White Papers on Central Scotland and North East England.[27] These recognised that economic first aid to a dispersed and changing set of limited locations would not solve even the basic problems of development districts, and might well be at the expense of the economic health of wider regions, that larger and more coherent regions would need to be designated and that within these the concentration of public investment at growth points or growth zones would be the most effective means of promoting regional development. Infrastructure was to have a high priority in regional programmes for the two areas, the living environment should be improved, but diversification of the industrial structure and relief of unemployment remained enduring priorities.

In quite different spheres 1963 also saw the creation of the government-sponsored Location of Offices Bureau, part of the policy of persuading office development to move out of Central London (1,156 firms and 84,254 jobs moved in 1963-72 but mostly to other locations within the South East),[28] the Beeching Report on the rail system[29] and the Water Resources Act of the same year. All contributed to the new thinking on how to achieve economic growth by fuller use of resources, balanced development for all economic regions and the recognition that such development might increasingly come from redistribution of services as much as from changes in location of new manufacturing. Nevertheless in several key decisions in the early 1960s the government showed itself alive to the need to influence location of new car assembly plants (at Linwood and Bathgate in Central Scotland, or three plants on Merseyside), aluminium smelters (Invergordon, Lynemouth in Northumberland and Anglesey) or major greenfield steel plants (Ravenscraig on Clydeside and Newport Llanwern in South Wales).

There followed quickly the creation under the short-lived Department of Economic Affairs of the eight economic planning regions of England (1965), each with its Council of lay members and its Board comprising senior representatives of the relevant Ministries at regional level.[30] The Councils and Boards have outlived their parent and, although consultative and advisory, have come to represent effectively the regional interest upwards to central government, downwards to their constituent local authorities. They have counterparts in the Welsh Office, the Scottish Development Department and until recently in the Economic Council for Northern Ireland. The greater part of section 1.IV is concerned with examining the economic and social problems faced at regional level, the strategies and courses of action recommended and the likely impacts of the first decade of even this rudimentary beginning of true regional planning. Outline or interim strategies have been published for all regions, but only the South East has reached the stage of a definitive strategy,[31] accepted by the government as the framework for future structure planning in that region under the 1968 Town and Country Planning Act.

Meanwhile control over the location of services as well as manufacturing continued to be the spearhead of policies for regional balance, relief of unemployment or social justice in less favoured areas. The introduction of Selective Employment Tax (1965) had a differential effect on the regions; in development areas, with an already lower ratio in service occupations the effect was less than in more affluent areas. In 1966 a new Industrial

Development Act abolished development districts and re-created coherent development areas, covering virtually all the Northern Region, large parts of South West England and virtually all Scotland and Wales; Northern Ireland had similar status, but under its own legislation. These were the largest and most coherent development areas hitherto, with 40 per cent of the UK space and 20 per cent of the UK population. There has since been some conflict of interest between those favouring an economic growth and investment concentration policy for these areas, and others who continued to stress the merits of discriminatory, at times dispersing policies of relief to unemployment in or as near as possible to the localities afflicted.

The 'teeth' of the location policies were strengthened, the threshold for IDC exemptions was raised with industrial development in the Midlands and South East more positively restricted, but financial inducements to industrialists to move to development areas were also increased: grants were made towards building costs, loans made available at low rates of interest and rent-free accommodation provided in some cases. Investment grants were provided in development areas at double the national rate, no longer limited in relation to jobs created, and in 1967 a Regional Employment Premium was introduced, helping to reduce labour costs there. In the same years localised special development areas (SDAS) were defined within development areas, largely in response to the severe local unemployment being created by coal-mining rundown. The SDAs enjoyed additional advantages of higher grants on new buildings, rent-free government factories for periods up to five years and assistance to cover operating costs. These measures led to a sharp rise in industrial moves to the development areas and in jobs created there: in 1966-7 over 30 per cent of industrial building approvals in Britain were for the scheduled areas compared with only 13 per cent in 1961-2.

In 1970-1 policies on industrial location were revised and investment grants were replaced by depreciation allowances on plant and machinery. In development areas a system of free depreciation was introduced and assistance under the Local Employment Act was strengthened. The general feeling in the areas was that the new measures would diminish the inflow of mobile industry, particularly the capital-intensive projects, and that it would be important to make the inducements to inmigrant firms equally available to established industry.

The very success of the 1966 measures led to marked reaction in the regions bordering the development areas, whose problems were neither so wide-ranging nor so severe, least of all in the fashionable indicator of unemployment levels, and yet whose economic growth rates were scarcely more favourable. This led to an investigation into the problems of the so-called 'grey' or 'intermediate areas'.[32] The main conclusion reached was that such areas were diverse in character, strongly represented in Yorkshire and Humberside, in the North West, in certain coalfields of the Midlands, on the borders of Wales, at Plymouth and at Edinburgh-Leith. There was some evidence that parts of these areas were suffering economically from being within the shadow of adjacent development areas and were receiving few benefits in return. Though the recommendations of the Hunt Committee for the scheduling of wide intermediate areas were not accepted by the government of the time (1969), and incidentally a proposal to de-schedule Merseyside as a development area was refused, an intermediate level of regional aid was granted to more restricted scheduled Intermediate areas. In the 1972 White Paper [33] (figure 1.4) a wider definition of intermediate areas was proposed embracing most of Yorkshire and Humberside, together with the North West (outside Merseyside), Wrexham, the south-east borders of Wales, the Plymouth hinterland and Edinburgh-Leith; to this list of scheduled areas parts of Derbyshire and Nottinghamshire have since been added. The UK thus now has no less than five gradations of economic and social aid to scheduled areas, on a descending scale of priorities and an ascending scale of interdictions, as follows: special development areas; development areas; intermediate areas; non-scheduled areas; overgrowth areas. Such sophisitication is ideal for allocation and channelling of growth when the national growth momentum is high and sustained. It is somewhat illusory in the slow, fitful growth situation more characteristic of national economic trends in the UK during the decade 1960-70.

In support of the policies on new or expanded manufacturing location the Location of Offices Bureau policy was strengthened during 1965 and had notable success in influencing intraregional dispersal within the South East or within the West Midlands. In spite of steady growth in modern office accommodation and lower rentals in the DAs, however, it was the planned dispersal of government rather than private offices which had the most marked effect on the inflow of such service jobs to the North, Scotland or Wales. Government-sponsored moves accounted for about 3,000 per annum in the 1960s, whilst for the early 1970s some 41 per cent of government jobs planned for dispersal were to go to the Development Areas.

In terms of infrastructure regional allocations in the later 1960s came to reflect more effectively the needs and priorities of regional development, though it is less clear that the motorway programme had this intended effect. The growth of widespread and mounting concern for conservation of both urban and rural environment also played its part in the eventual decisions on the third London airport and in discussions on the proposed London Motorway Box.

Feasibility studies, 1969-71, probed the possibilities of fast economic and population growth on Humberside, Tayside and Severnside for later in the century,[34] though specifically without intended detriment to the priorities for the development areas up to 1981. For the extensive agricultural and recreational components of the UK space the 1966 Agriculture Act and the 1968 Countryside Act were especially formative, whilst the 1968 Town and Country Planning Act instituted a more flexible planning system with better integration between economic and social planning at national level, reflected through the economic regional strategies, and physical or land use planning at the level of a new pattern of local government units. The regional strategies, once approved in definitive form by the government, are to provide the framework for the flexible structure plans of the constituent local authorities. It is to the proposed pattern of such new local authorities that attention is now turned.

III.5 New Patterns for Democracy

In a democratic society it is not surprising to find that local government units are diverse in size, character and resources, that many were established early and there has been persistent reluctance to accept change in either boundaries or in functions. For the more limited purposes for which they were designed the countries or boroughs served well enough and many have had a continued existence since early times. The Local Government Acts of 1888 and 1894 confirmed the existence of many such units but it is universally accepted that during the present century the pattern of units has proved increasingly unsatisfactory, not least because their functions have been increased, major changes in economy and society have taken place and the relationships between central and local government have become more complex. Nevertheless there remains even today a widespread feeling that in local government the least change is the best change, and it is equally clear that in defining and seeking acceptance of any new pattern of units or redistribution of functions the English penchant for compromise will certainly be called into play.[35] Compromise is needed in several respects: for example, on the balance of powers and the extent of devolution from the centre to the constituent nations, regions, cities, counties or districts; on the size of units for various kinds of function and the pattern and nesting of such units within a nation-wide administrative hierarchy, particularly having regard for the important relationships between town and hinterland. The 'viability of local democracy' has more than once been a priority principle in official reports on local government reform. The difficulty is to preserve this without doing violence to the economy, efficiency, convenience or choice which people have come to expect in an increasingly mobile and sophisticated urban society. With the grafting of a wide range of planning functions onto local government since the 1947 Act and the rise of regional planning in the 1960s the search for new patterns has become increasingly urgent.

Successive attempts at local government reform since the war have foundered less at the stage of principle than when new boundaries or new units have been proposed to take the place of counties, boroughs or districts, in whose 'iconography' so many have believed for so long.[36] Yet the need for reform has steadily become more pressing and the advantages to be derived more clearly seen in post-war years. This led finally to major investigations into the question, in the late 1960s, in all the national units of the United Kingdom,[37] enquiries made the more urgent by a rising tide of regionalism in England and a renewed sense of national identity, even of grievance in Scotland, Wales and Northern Ireland. During the same period the Royal Commission on the Constitution (Kilbrandon Commission) was set up and its findings are expected late in 1973, to provide an essential link in the problem of redistributing powers between centre, the nations and the regions, if indeed that seems desirable or possible.

The Commission on England (Redcliffe-Maud) was voluminous, innovating and controversial, surely the most substantively researched document ever likely to appear on local government reform. Even here there were two clearly conflicting schools of thought represented respectively in the Majority Report and in the Memorandum of Dissent by Senior, both limited by their terms of reference, to report 'within existing functions' of local government. The Majority Report proposed 61 new local government areas, each covering town and country; in 58 of them, termed unitary areas, none less in size than 250,000, none larger than 1,000,000 people, a single authority would group all personal and social services with no lower second tier, whilst in the other three, the metropolitan areas around Birmingham, Liverpool and Manchester, as already for London (1960), there was to be a second tier of metropolitan districts. Counties and boroughs were to disappear and the economic planning regions to be replaced by provinces, each with a provincial council of undefined powers. The Memorandum of Dissent declined to accept the unitary area principle, seeing in it a violation of both the facts of social geography and the principles of democracy, which required more local ties than the large unitary authorities might permit. A two-tier system was preferred by Senior, based on city-regions, with directly elected authorities, and a second order of town districts, below which there should be common councils at community level.

The proposals aroused discussion and controversy in academic [38] and political circles. There was general agreement among geographers on the importance of the provincial level in any new patterns for planning or democracy, but a division of opinion on the merits of the unitary as compared with the two-tier systems, and a good deal of criticism about the nature of specific units or boundaries. In the author's view the unitary principle had much to recommend it, in its cleaner break with the past, the designation of units large enough for effective planning, the coherence of functions intended and the possibility of capitalising upon the rising mobility and enlarging space perceptions of the population. Such a fresh system of units would require new concepts of community, but offer the prospect of abandoning the parochialisms, which for so long have bedevilled planning in the UK, even as high as the level of large towns or counties.

Though the substance of the Majority Report proposals were acceptable to the government of the day [39] they did not find the same favour with its successor.[40] The proposals forming the basis of the Local Government Act 1972 recognised two forms of operational authority, counties and districts, with a two-tier metropolitan-type structure for Merseyside, South East Lancashire-North East Cheshire (SELNEC), the West Midlands, West

Yorkshire, South Yorkshire and the Tyne-Wear area. These metropolitan authorities had boundaries which most commentators have regarded as too tightly-drawn, thus infringing the city-hinterland principle, and relying perforce for their effectiveness upon the right planning decisions being taken at the strategic regional level. The pattern of local government areas initially proposed is seen on figure 1.5, which brings out clearly the considerable disparity in size and rateable value per capita among the first-order units, and underlines the point that together with the problems arising from economic restructuring and unfavourable location the development areas must accept poorer, and at times larger, local government units for the most part. During the passage of the legislation through Parliament amendments to the units have been vigorously pressed, as on Teesside (Cleveland County), Herefordshire-Worcestershire and the north-eastern borders of Essex. Larger cities which become county districts under the new scheme have campaigned strongly for greater devolution of planning powers to the second tier authorities, but it seems that the units shown on figure 1.5 will for the most part come into operation in the Spring of 1974. The definition and longer-term revision of second tier units is the responsibility of the Local Government Boundary Commission for England,[41] but the districts are to correspond as far as possible with existing county districts, lie within or close to the preferred population range of 75,000 to 100,000 and be acceptable in large measure to the local authorities concerned.

The Wheatley Commission proposals for Scotland rejected the unitary principle as unworkable for Scotland, believing that a single-tier solution would result neither in efficient planning and administration of the major services, nor in satisfactory democratic representation.[2] On the other hand the regional level was already a reality in the regions of Scotland adopted for planning purposes and Scotland itself had a measure of economic and social powers devolved from Whitehall. The second tier in Scotland might best be represented by 37 'shires' and a third level, if required, could be made up of 'localities', typically a small town plus hinterland; of these there might be between 100 and 250 according to the criteria for definition. In the event the Commission settled for the 37 shires for local services and allocated personal services to the region; community councils were recommended for the localities. The 1971 White Paper accepted the Wheatley proposals in principle, but changed the pattern of units, first by abandoning attempts at uniformity throughout Scotland and, secondly, by increasing the number of the new authorities. The regions proposed were increased from seven to eight by separating the Borders from the Edinburgh city region, whilst the Northern Isles were detached from the Highland region and made into two all-purpose authorities, each with a population of about 17,000. The number of districts in the second tier was increased from 35 to 49, but the population of some of the new districts fell unacceptably below 10,000. The allocation of functions between the tiers in the Wheatley proposals has had to be modified in the new scheme, with the Northern Isles to become dependent on the mainland for certain services, and planning functions for the three rural regions (the Highlands, the Borders and the South West) to be exercised at the level of the region. Planning authorities will still number 41, but the strategic planning of Scotland will effectively be carried out through the five city regions based on Glasgow, Edinburgh, Falkirk-Stirling, Dundee and Aberdeen, together with the three rural regions previously mentioned (Figure 1.7).

The proposals for Wales (1971) regroup local government into 7 county councils, 5 of which are to bear historic Welsh names and 36 district councils, to replace the 13 counties, 4 county boroughs and 164 district councils, the larger units mostly dating from local government reform 80 years earlier. Most of the new county councils would have populations of more than 200,000, but Powys no more than 100,000 spread thinly over 1·3 million acres (0·5 million ha) of rural territory. On the other hand East Glamorgan, a unit whose creation has since been successfully contested by the local people, would have had over 900,000; the solution has been to insert a third subdivision into Glamorgan. The

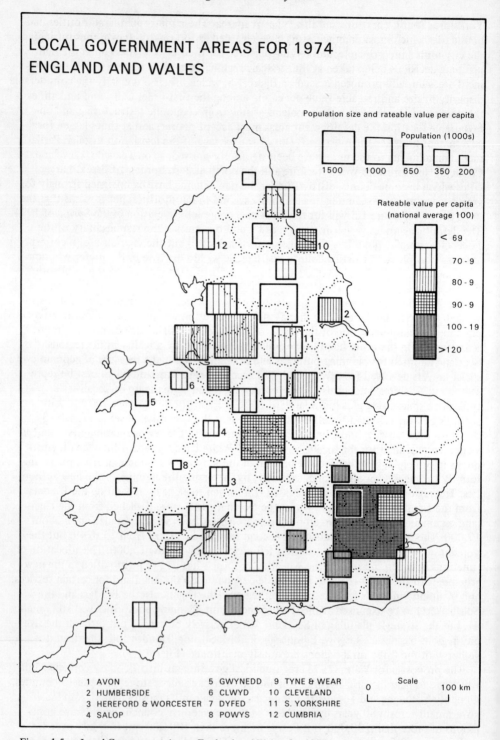

Figure 1.5   Local Government Areas, England and Wales, for 1974.

two-tier system is similar in division of functions to that intended for England, with the county councils responsible for highways and traffic, education and personal social services and district councils for housing, refuse collection, public cleansing, clean air and the prevention of nuisances. Town and country planning would be shared between county and district councils.

The lack of uniformity in size, by area or population, of the new local government units for both Scotland and Wales recognises that in remote rural or mountainous areas there is justification for special treatment. Furthermore the diversity reflects traditional community ties and loyalties and thus gives expression to the over-riding principle of 'preserving or fostering a viable local democracy'.

Northern Ireland is the first UK area to complete local government reorganisation. Since the creation of the Stormont parliament in 1922 local government had been carried on through 73 directly-elected units, 27 of them with populations of less than 10,000. These units had the characteristic two-tier structure of counties and county boroughs, with dependent urban or rural districts. The local government franchise has been restricted, generally throught to be biased against minority groups and there have been persisting complaints of the effects of gerrymandering at the time the boundaries were originally established. Reform proposals in 1969 favoured a reduction from 73 to 17 single-tier local government units, with strengthening of the powers of Stormont as a central upper tier of authority. The principle behind the definition of the new units was alleged to be town-hinterland relationships, or everyday circulation spaces; with exception of Fermanagh there was a clean break with previous territorial units.

The proposals encountered widespread opposition and in 1970 new proposals emerged from an independent review body. These confirmed that the local government functions of Stormont should be increased, to include all 'regional' services, whilst 'district' services should be devolved to 26 districts, each based on a town with its immediate hinterland; Londonderry and Belfast were to remain county boroughs but with transfer of some powers to Stormont. Johnson [43] believes that the increase of powers to an upper tier provincial authority might well be justified, in terms of the area, size of population, rateable value when the province is compared to larger English county or city authorities.

On 1 April 1973 the 26 District Councils, elected by Proportional Representation, were to become responsible for local environmental services. Regional services will come directly under the Ministry of Development, whilst Area Boards will administer locally education, public libraries, health and personal services. Belfast (291,239 people) and Londonderry (50,018) will be the largest districts, but will have no additional powers.

IV   ECONOMIC PLANNING REGIONS AND NATIONS

IV.1 Regional Strategies

The formulation of regional strategies was one of the principal tasks entrusted to the eight regional economic planning councils of England, together with the comparable bodies for Scotland, Wales and Ulster, at their inception in 1965. Strategy has been formulated in three stages and thus far only that for the South East (1970) [44] has been completed, and approved in principle by the Minister. The characteristic first stage is an assessment of the problems facing the region, followed by recommended courses of action, and priority targets for 1981. At this second stage preferred spatial allocations are specifically mentioned in some strategies, but by no means equally emphasised in all. The third and definitive stage is a tripartite exercise involving central government, economic planning council and board and the constituent local planning authorities, leading to a 'strategic plan'.

Presentation of regional strategies in the UK is thus far uneven in several respects: stage reached; emphasis on space allocations; degree of regional initiative; extent of cooperation and agreement between economic planning council and local authorities. In reality the process is a continuing one since councils are responsible for advising Ministers on the regional implications of national policies and, at the same time, are constantly pressing regional needs and priorities upon central government. Regional conditions and problems are never static and even after the final stage of an agreed strategic plan it is necessary to set up a monitoring and feedback system, to test and modify the plan as it is implemented. When approved by the Minister the regional strategic plan becomes the framework within which the structure plans of the local authorities must be fitted, as provided for in the Town and Country Planning Act of 1968.

In considering current regional strategy proposals in the UK it is convenient to group the regions as in table 1.4.

TABLE 1.4

Economic Planning Regions and Nations, UK, 1971

	Popn.1971 (million)	% growth 1961-71	Density 1971 (persons)		% in conur- bations	Employment 1965-9, % in fast growth	% in fast decline
			p.acre	p. ha			
Development							
Northern	3.29	1.0	0.69	0.28	24	42	18
Scotland	5.22	0.7	0.27	0.11	48	42	23
Wales	2.72	3.2	0.53	0.21	–	38	15
N. Ireland						40	14
Intermediate							
Yorks and Humberside	4.79	3.4	1.37	0.55	36	36	13
North West	6.72	2.6	3.40	1.37	54	45	8
Mixed trends							
South West	3.76	9.4	0.64	0.26	–	46	12
East Anglia	1.66	11.4	0.53	0.21	–	45	17
Growth							
E. Midland	3.38	8.7	1.12	0.45	–	36	14
W. Midlands	5.10	7.1	1.59	0.64	46	39	8
South East	17.13	4.8	2.52	1.02	43	48	8

Sources: Abstract of Regional Statistics (HMSO; Department of Employment data 1971)

For each region there is a review and evaluation of current problems, the policies proposed and the strategy put forward. Since this is a geographical interpretation there is particular regard for the spatial implications and intentions expressed in regional strategies. To illustrate some of the key trends of economic and social change, and the strategies proposed, there is a diagrammatic map for each region (figures 1.6 to 1.14 inclusive). These maps are not uniform, reflecting the diversity of the strategies themselves, and are not

intended to be comprehensive. Rather they attempt to guide the reader by indicating some
of the formative elements in the strategy for each region. A more comprehensive carto-
graphical overview is provided in the *Regional Planning Atlases* of the Department of the
Environment.

IV.2 The Development Regions

Of the four regions identified as 'development regions' three (Scotland, Wales and Northern
Ireland) have a national identity and enjoy a measure of political devolution. Only the
Northern region of England lacks this degree of independence in regional decision-taking.
All four are characterised by certain common problems, though their incidence and mix
vary, and there are differences too in the policies adopted and the extent of their success.
The problems include: higher and persistent unemployment rates; a narrow industrial base,
with a higher ratio of fast decline industries, not adequately compensated for by new post-
war growth elements; lower median incomes; persistent outmigration, particularly of the
young and more able; peripheral location in the UK space, and prospectively even more
marginal in an enlarged Common Market economy; and a less favourable living environment for the majority, especially in the cities. The development regions, on the other
hand, have been and continue to be the main beneficiaries of the regional and industrial
location policies by successive governments discussed in section 1.III.

Northern England (figure 1.6): In the nature, range and severity of its economic and social
problems the Northern region is a microcosm of all the development regions.[45] For this
reason, perhaps, it has consistently been used as a pilot-area for application of government
location policies, from the 1934 Special Areas Act to the present day. Much of the earlier
legislation was remedial in character, with relief of unemployment as a perennially high
priority. In the 1963 White Paper,[46] however, for the first time the emphasis was firmly
laid on economic growth by diversification, improvement of the infrastructure and the
living environment and, most significantly, on the concentration of future public investment into a designated 'growth zone'. These more comprehensive objectives were followed
up and codified in the first stage strategy document, entitled *Challenge of the Changing
North* (1965).[47] Three years later an *Outline Strategy for the North* was published,[48] one
of only a small number of second stage strategies to have as strong a spatial as a sector perspective in its recommendations. Perhaps for this reason the subregional proposals did not
find favour with the local planning authorities and the document was looked upon by the
optimists as falling short of legitimate regional aspirations. Others regarded the diagnosis
and recommendations as both realistic and practical, a view shared by the government of
the day. A third stage or definitive strategy starts in 1973. In the meantime the economic
planning council has kept under review the basic problems of the region, publishing reports
on key sectors, such as housing, education and ports.[49] The local authority-sponsored
North East Development Council has concurrently undertaken successfully the major
task of promoting the North East and aiding more official efforts to attract industry and
improve regional living conditions.
    It is fair to ask how far all these reports and all this activity has solved, or mitigated the
basic problems affecting the Northern region. The verdict must be more cautious than com-
mendatory. For all the fluctuations in unemployment levels in the UK since the war the
Northern region level has obstinately remained between one and a half and twice the
national figure; late in 1971 it stood at 1.6 times the national average, and it is difficult to
envisage secular, long-term improvement based on present policies (1972). Industrial restructuring has made significant progress: the growth-decline mix in employment has improved markedly (fast growth sector: 38 per cent of jobs 1947, 51 per cent in 1966; fast
decline sector: an improvement from 34 to 21 per cent over the same period). Diversif-

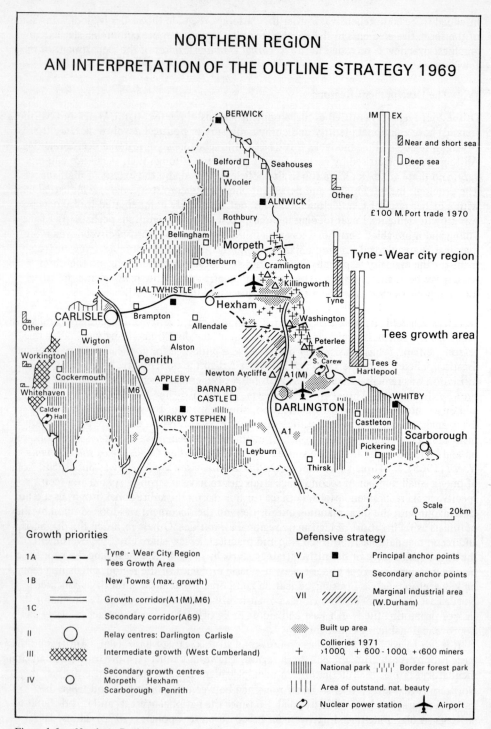

Figure 1.6   Northern Region.

ication and job choice have both increased, with a significant number of industrial moves into the region coming from the South East, followed by moves from Yorkshire and Humberside, the adjacent economic planning region and then the affluent West Midlands. The employment of 103,000 in some 400 firms on 90 'industrial estates' and sites financed by government (September 1971), together with the approval since 1960 of some 92 'advance factories' for the North indicates the scale of direct government aid. In support, IDC approvals were given, 1960-70 inclusive, for 40.5 million ft.^{2} (4.3 million m^2) of new factory space in the region. Outmigration, a persistent ebb-tide from the North, has been perceptibly slowed, but it is too early to ascribe this to the working of regional policies.[50]

On the debit side, however, high unemployment seems to be endemic. The problem has certainly been aggravated by the dramatic downturn in the region's basic industries during the 1960s. Overall between 1960 and 1970 some 138,000 jobs were lost, and they were mostly male jobs, in only five industries: coal-mining, agriculture, shipbuilding, steel and transport. In spite of the build-up of alternative employment, by 1970 there were 80,000 fewer male jobs than ten years earlier. Prospective further substantial male job loss during the 1970s, the result of continuing rundown in basic industries and also the mounting effects of automation, means that industrial restructuring will continue to be the most critical problem in the Northern Region. This necessitates the continuance of strong, even stronger regional policies and a growth-orientated, streamlined strategy for taking the region to the end of the century. Short-term indications, judged by IDC approvals 1968-71, are unfavourable since during that period the Northern region share of national approvals fell from 14.8 to 6.6 per cent, whilst that for the South East rose from 11.2 to 29.4 per cent.

Diversification is not solely a matter for manufacturing employment. The services economy in the North has traditionally been under-represented [51] and government incentives to its growth have been lacking. The limited extent to which offices have been persuaded to move from the London region or the West Midlands to the development areas has already been commented upon. 3,000 government clerical jobs have been created in the North since 1963 but the scale of such growth is clearly insufficient to aid economic restructuring in a significant way. The importance of research and development projects in building up the newer image of the North has constantly been stressed, and the need for government to decentralise major establishments to the development areas during the next decade.

If the Northern region was to be fully competitive it required also both improved communications of all types and a modernised living environment. The M6, A1(M) and the Durham motorway, the Inter-City and Freightliner rail services (with electrification being extended to Glasgow), the regional airports at Newcastle (Woolsington) and Teesside, and the port facilities, such as Teesport or the Tyne ore- and ferry-terminals, contributed to the transport network. The up-dating of the housing stock to a present state that is comparable with that of other regions, the improvement of educational facilities and achievements, the range of entertainment and recreation provision all helped towards the objectives of a better living environment.

The sector objectives were elaborated in the Outline Strategy (1969), but it also stressed the need for a spatially-defined and interrelated growth hierarchy of settlements and subregions. Appropriate defensive elements were proposed for areas likely to be adversely affected by general decline or by concentration elsewhere. Figure 1.6 tentatively completes the hierarchy which was put forward only in broad outline in the 1969 document. Furthermore it allocates priorities, stressing the cardinal importance of the two major areas of growth potential, the Tyne-Wear city region and the Teesside growth area. The Tyne-Wear conurbation has 40 per cent of the regional population, a manufacturing structure with overrepresentation of decline sectors (including the coalfield hinterland) and a concentration of service population. In the early post-war years a new and diversified industrial base was implanted, especially on the industrial estates, and this gives a better prospect of short-term growth to 1981 from established firms than on Teesside. Teesside has the twin pillars of industrial strength, iron and steel with associated fabricating industries and chemicals, with a strong and growing relationship to the local post-war oil refineries.With greater prosperity in its basic industries Teesside had less diversification through industrial estates. However during the 1960s there were forecasts of rationalisation of plants and further redundancies by technological change in the steel industry, whilst the chemical industry continued to increase its output substantially but without adding to its labour force. With the oil refineries also capital-intensive but with small contribution to new jobs, Teesside unemployment rose and remedial government action has followed. In contrast to the Tyne the estuarine lands of the Tees offer large tracts for industrial and port development. Hopefully among other prospects for the area is a major 'brownfield' steel development to grow alongside the new Redcar ore terminal.

A successful regional strategy for the North must get the sums and the spatial allocations right, as between Tyne-Wear and Tees. The Teesplan (1965) forecast possibility for accommodating +220,000 people by 1991 and +422,000 by A.D. 2001 and the current Tyne-Wear investigation is also likely to reveal sizeable capacity for future growth and concentration. Without being able to programme subregional allocation of growth, except in broad and indirect terms, it is important for planners in the North to see Tyne-Wear and Tees as interrelated cores for a regional industrial growth complex. Presently they are less interrelated economically than might be the case.

Both Tyne-Wear and Teesside conurbations are embedded within a major coalfield which has been undergoing dramatic rundown in employment since the late 1950s (1951, 156,000 mining jobs; 1961, 118,000; 1971 only 50,000). The impact at community level of the many pits which have closed has been severe, though many of the redundant men have been re-employed at other pits. The New Towns, at Peterlee, Newton Aycliffe, Washington together with the county council developments at Cramlington and Killingworth have implanted growth and a new living environment in the coalfield. The Special Development Area policy since 1967 has also helped in the provision of new jobs in or near the mining settlements. Yet as pits close it is accepted that districts may lose their *raison d'être* and both regrouping and decline by outmigration of people may be the logical answer, as it seems to be for West Durham.

As a small-scale microcosm of the problems of the Northern Region, West Cumberland faces continued restructuring with the prospective close-down of coal-mining and the cessation of steel-making at Workington. Redundancies have been offset by introduction of new jobs under government location policies, and by a remarkable community spirit of enterprise. However West Cumberland was designated for only an intermediate level of growth and it was felt in 1969 that Carlisle had the better long-term potential of land and location, to act as a 'relay' centre to build up employment and diffuse growth over a wide hinterland. Currently the prospects for growth in Carlisle and West Cumberland are being investigated in a subregional study.

Other novel elements in the Outline Strategy were the proposals for corridor growth at nodes along the main south-north motorways and rail links east and west of the Pennines. The corridor concept through Durham aroused memories of earlier thinking on a prospective Tyne-Tees linear city. For the vast rural hinterland it was accepted that growth at the most logical centres in conurbation or cities would increase gradients in living standards, to the disadvantage of the countryside, and lead to accelerated rural depopulation. To stabilise the rural areas and indeed to build up jobs in both industry and services, to support the primary agricultural population, rural 'anchor point' settlements were to be designated. Figure 1.6 shows a suggested pattern for these, with principal and secondary centres.

The Outline Strategy (1969) was indicative, a discussion basis, and was lacking in precision as to space allocations, timings or priorities. These were to be built-in at a later, subregional stage. In the event new proposals are likely to emerge from the definitive tri-partite strategy for the North, expected by 1975.

Scotland (figure 1.7): The basic regional development problems of Scotland have much in common with those of Northern England, but there are differences of significance, both in degree and in kind. The differences in degree arise from the greater territorial size and population of Scotland, a more marked degree of concentration of that population in the industrial Central Lowlands, with a vast thinly-peopled rural hinterland, and an even more peripheral location in respect of the major economic growth areas of the Midlands and South East England. Differences in kind arise from the degree of autonomy exercised by representatives of the Scottish nation, the distinctive problems posed by slow population growth, the need to decongest and distribute massive overspill from the Clydeside conurbation, the sharp contrast offered by major rural problem areas, and a particular sequence of stages in regional planning.

Perhaps the most important factor of all lies in the economic, social and political identity of Scotland, giving coherence and purpose to its planning and strengthening its independent voice in UK affairs. This identity was referred to by Cairncross in 1954,[52] speaking of the Border as 'not a barrier between two economic systems but a line between two segments of a single economy'. He further added 'yet the segment lying north of the Border is a distinct society with a unity and cohesion of its own', and he was in no doubt that the Scottish economy functioned as a unit and had an independent momentum. Later writers have confirmed this diagnosis,[53] which is indeed derived from the facts of geography, with the concentrated urban population of Central Scotland well away from the southern Borders and 100 miles (160 km) from the nearest industrial region of England, on Tyneside.

Already in the special areas years of the early 1930s Scotland had a Secretary of State, compared with only commissioners in other areas. This degree of continuing autonomy and independence in economic and social decision-taking or planning has been advantageous in two ways: clearer formulation of the problems, through the availability of Scottish statistics, and coherence in the design or application of policies. It is possible for Scotland, but not as yet for the regions of England, to measure national income and to calibrate and monitor economic change more effectively. This has proved particularly valuable during the 1960s when UK regional policies have shifted in emphasis from unemployment relief towards achievement of balanced economic growth.

McCrone [54] believes that gross domestic product (GDP), the sum of values added in all production pursuits in the economy, provides the most accurate indicator of Scotland's economic progress. Changes in the Scottish GDP since 1961 indicate that living standards in Scotland fell relative to those in the UK in the late 1950s and early 1960s, and although Scottish GDP per capita increased more rapidly than that of the UK in the 1960s, this was probably due in large part to a fall in the Scottish proportion of the UK population. Johnston , *et al.*[55] derive the gloomy prediction from post-war trends in Scotland that she is 'in some danger of reverting to the position of poor relation of England and Wales as existed for some time in the past'.

Scotland has faced the same industrial restructuring problems as other development regions in post-war years, but her legacy from past industrial revolutions had been more unfavourable than most. Moreover the resulting secular unemployment in declining industries such as coal-mining, mechanical engineering, or ship building was highly concentrated in and around Clydeside and in Lanarkshire, affecting the economic health of sizeable, congested populations. The nature and course of industrial restructuring in a Development Area has already been treated under Northern England and only specifically Scottish features need touching upon. Shipbuilding was uniquely hard hit (1959, 73,000 jobs; 1971, 44,000), culminating in the failure of Upper Clyde shipbuilders; the Dundee

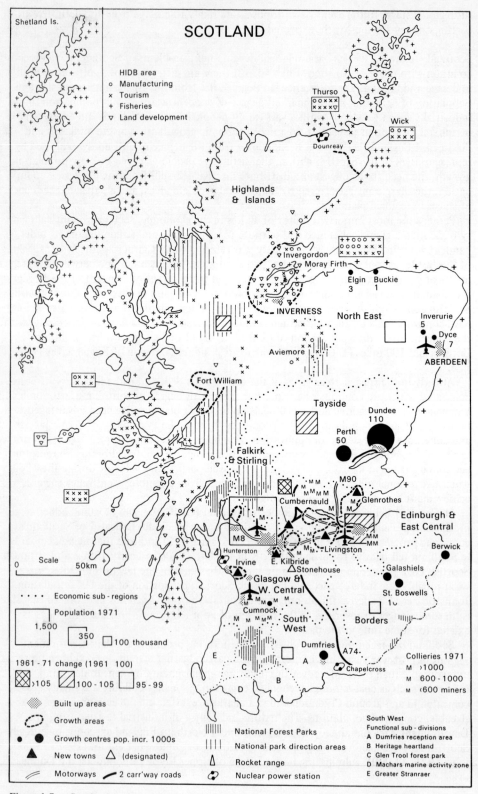

Figure 1.7   Scotland.

jute industry passed through particularly difficult times, whilst employment in the primary industries fell sharply (agriculture, forestry and fishing: 1959, 104,000 and 1971, 55,000; mining and quarrying: from 102,000 in 1959 to 40,000 in 1971). On the credit side the electronics industry had a sharp rise from 7,500 to 40,000 jobs in the period 1961-70 and United States investment in Scotland has been striking (89 manufacturing companies in 1969, employing 73,000). Yet the overall verdict must be similar to that for Northern England: the massive rundown in male jobs in basic industries has not been fully compensated for by the growth of new forms of employment and the situation would have looked even more dramatic had there not been a marked rise in jobs for women in manufacturing. Rates of growth in service employment have lagged behind UK levels and, as in Northern England, there is the same clamour for more Research and Development units, more head offices, and a more forceful decentralisation of central government establishments, to add to the Savings Bank already established in Glasgow.

Regional planning had an early start in Scotland and its effectiveness has proved a valuable aid both to economic development policies generally, and to the formulation of subregional proposals within an overall Scottish programme. The Clyde Valley Regional Plan (1946) appeared at a time when the government was particularly active in steering industry under the 1945 Distribution of Industry Act.[56] Though the result of undue concentration of such industrial moves into Clydeside helped to diversify industry there it was at the expense of balance in the Central Lowlands or indeed over Scotland as a whole. Scottish economists and planners were early alive to the need for balanced distribution of growth and equally emphatic in both the 1952 Cairncross Committee[57] and the 1961 Toothill Report[58] that this objective would not be realised by the 'worst-first' policy of priority for unemployment relief where it was most severe. Indeed Toothill spoke deliberately of the need to build-up industrial complexes and centres which offered the best prospect of becoming zones of growth. This found an echo in the White Paper of the following year,[59] which designated nine growth areas (figure 1.7). These included the then four New Towns of Central Scotland, together with Irvine (later designated a New Town) and the Grangemouth/Falkirk area, both the latter with considerable potential for both industrial and housing development. Other growth areas were older industrial tracts like North Lanarkshire, Central Fife, the Lothians around Livingston and the Vale of Leven, which had land and labour but where social capital was rundown.

Though the 1966 Industrial Development Act defined the greater part of Scotland as a development area and thus temporarily annulled the 'growth area' concept, the philosophy of concentrating growth at designated nucleii has proved remarkably persistent, cropping up in all the later subregional studies. Since Scotland was the proving ground it is interesting to note the comments of Cameron and Reid in 1966.[60] They concluded that from an industrial location point of view Central Scotland was too small and well-developed for small growth areas to have particular advantages in terms of external economies. Their view was that the growth areas were really the means of integrating various strands of economic and social policy, with an emphasis on potential for substantial population growth. From the White Paper, however, it is clear that the growth areas were to be the most ready and effective channel for attracting industrial investment and creating locally new living environments, the benefits of which would be diffused through their labour hinterlands and would indeed link up with the development proposed in the main centres of Glasgow and Edinburgh.

Equally innovating, the publication of a plan for expansion of the Scottish economy 1965-70[61] sought to speed up the evolution of a modern industrial structure in Scotland, make the fullest use of manpower and to cut the net outmigration rate from 40,000 per annum in the 1960s to only 10,000 per annum by 1980. It provided a planning framework both in sectoral terms and in respect of subregional patterns of growth and expansion. Between 1965 and 1971 initial strategies had been prepared for seven of the eight planning regions of Scotland [62] and two major transportation studies had been achieved, for Greater Glasgow and Perth. Physical planning, so active in English regions during the same period, lagged behind subregional plan formulation in Scotland. This puts Scotland in a better position to develop structure plans within a set of existing subregional strategies and within the overall context of a short-term Scottish Plan.

In the strategies the regional development problems of Scotland emerge as of three types: those of the peripheral rural regions, sizeable, diverse but overdependent on primary industries and with severe infrastructural deficiencies, notably in public transport; the decaying industrial tracts in need of diversification, rehabilitation and an improvement in living environment; and thirdly, the problems of an overdeveloped, congested conurbation on Clydeside. It is the latter, with an almost stagnant population of about two millions, which uniquely dominates the Scottish planning scene and has overshadowed all other subregions there since the war.

Decisions on the future shape, structure and size of Clydeside have been and remain the key to the prospects for dispersal of population and the dissemination of growth throughout Scotland. [63] With the preparation of the last of the regional strategies, the West Central Scotland Plan, [64] the dimensions and prospects for the Clydeside economy will become clearer. For the moment the short-term problems there are only too tragically apparent, and it seems uncertain if economic growth can be generated on the scale necessary to permit the massive redistribution of people and work which many think desirable. The dilemma may be posed thus: Clydeside is too congested and its industrial structure cannot adequately be transformed within its borders, yet the large-scale redistribution of overspill population has not been adequately matched by attraction of industry out of the Clydeside habitat. The overspill plan for Glasgow envisages a movement of no less than 200,000 more out of the city by 1980, the latest phase of a trend which had seen the population of the city fall by 183,000 between 1951 and 1970. No fewer than 54 local authorities have overspill agreements with Glasgow, plus the 5 New Towns, but planned overspill over long distances has been difficult to achieve. Most industrial firms to leave Clydeside have preferred sites within 30 miles (48 Km), whilst the 'growth areas' of Central Scotland had by 1965 attracted no less than 60 per cent of overspill families and three-quarters of industrial moves to overspill areas. The government expectation back in 1963 was that the growth areas would absorb 300,000 by 1981. In 1971 a New Town was designated at Stonehouse (Lanarkshire) with a target population of 35,000 to assist in this process of decentralisation.

The risk that the solution to Clydeside's problems would be at the expense of the rest of Central Scotland has been diminished by the possibility of creating a major fast-growth subregion based on Tayside, [65] the open-end of industrial Scotland, and also by the vigour of other subregional planning proposals. [66] The Tayside proposals established that an additional 300,000 could be settled in that subregion by the year 2001, two-thirds of them into the Dundee and Perth areas, though for the first ten years there would have to be a vigorous programme of rehabilitation allied with growth. With the prospective population of Scotland by the end of the century now estimated at +½ million, rather than the two millions early anticipated, the full potential of Tayside may not be required.

One of the most intriguing prospects for revitalisation of the role of Central Scotland is the Oceanspan proposal (1970) [67] for creating a land-bridge with rapid transit systems between the Atlantic and the North Sea. A first stage in the project is to be the creation around Hunterston, in North Ayrshire, of a major new deepwater port and industrial zone. During 1970 the case for the port and the zoning of land for an iron ore terminal, and for general industrial purposes, were accepted by the government; permission for an oil refinery was refused, as it had been for the Murco proposal for a refinery at Bishopton (near Glasgow

The problems of Scottish marginal regions bring out a contrast between the Highlands and Islands, with North East Scotland, on the one hand, and the Border and South West on the other. The case for the diversion of investment to the Highlands and Islands, in the face of overall Scottish priorities is not universally accepted, and indeed there are those who argue that even north of the Central Lowlands there is a better case for investing in the modernised agrarian structure, manufacturing base and growth prospects of North East Scotland.[68] Certainly the Gaskin Report [69] cautiously confirms the 'substantial assets for further development' in the North East, but sees an important ingredient in the solution of the problems of that region in the redistribution of overspill from the Aberdeen city region to two main growth zones: the lower Don valley and, on a smaller scale, the lowlands of Banffshire and Western Morayshire.

Redevelopment and growth in the Highlands and Islands is almost an 'act of faith' for many Scots[69] and it is impossible to ignore the substantial achievements of the Development Board created for that region in 1965. These have been equally impressive whether once considers the many disseminated improvements in fisheries, tourism, manufacturing or land development, or the larger-scale proposals to create growth areas: on the Moray Firth,[70] in the Wick-Thurso region or around Lochaber (Fort William).[71] Increasingly a policy of concentration and urbanisation seems called for [72] and the eastern littoral is likely to prove a powerful magnet for major new developments. Already the aluminium reduction works at Invergordon is in full production and the early stages of 'spin-off' from adjacent North Sea oil exploration are being felt. Two sites have been approved for the fabrication of off-shore platforms, an undersea pipe-line is to come ashore in Cruden Bay; housing, roads, water and other infrastructural improvements may be expected later.

By contrast the strategy proposals for the Central Borders [73] and the South West [74] must be interpreted, in the first place, as programmes for arresting decline and outmigration. By the careful promotion of a regional community as an interrelated and regrouped pattern of small towns, with St Boswells and Berwick as growth centres, the Borders plan seeks to exploit intermediate location of the area, whilst seeking new industries and developing Galashiels as a commercial centre. The strategy for the South West is couched more in sectoral terms with proposals for new job creation and relief of unemployment, attraction of industry and improvement of communications. The tourist plan [75] for Galloway touches on one of the most promising prospects, with detailed proposals for the subregions shown on figure 1.7.

Wales (figure 1.8): In comparison with Scotland, Wales is smaller, lacking in economic coherence and its three economic subregions are ever more interdependent with areas of the English economy. As a senior Welsh geographer put it,[76] 'we certainly cannot accept that what is now Wales in a political sense represents a unity of any kind', though he was quick to point out the cultural identity of a smaller Welsh heartland redoubt. Yet, paradoxically, there is a strong, mounting feeling for greater political devolution than even present institutions represent. The Secretary of State at the Welsh Office has direct responsibility over many economic, social and local government sectoral functions devolved from Whitehall, and acts jointly with other Ministers for agriculture, employment, trade, industry and transport. The Welsh Council (1968) is responsible for economic strategy proposals, and there are many institutions at national level to reinforce the Welsh cultural personality.[77] On the whole, however, Wales lacks the degree of self-sufficiency or economic independence [78] appropriate to Scotland and in reality the devolution of economic, social or political decision-taking has been more apparent than real. A realistic estimate is perhaps that UK policies have been tempered in Wales 'to suit the particular circumstances' as the Treasury has put it. At times this may have led to the reducing of economic growth rates or prospects to preserve Welshness and avoid damaging effects on society or community. The truth is that, like all development regions, Wales is a net recipient of funds from the rest of the UK.[79] In respect of central government finance in Wales in 1968 there was a deficit of 20 per cent, when comparing receipts with expenditure (total public government expenditure in Wales: 1963-4, £326 million; 1970-1, £921 million). Finally, Wales has been even more closely bound into

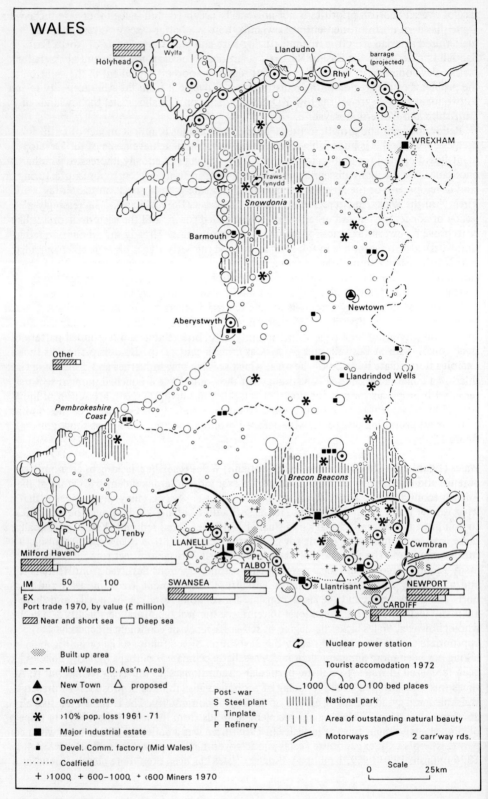

Figure 1.8   Wales

the English economy by the strategy of communications in post-war years, by ties of capital flows and by the establishment of branch plants of English companies in the principality.

Wales passed through the characteristic stages of the development region life-cycle from the early 1930s, but her geographical layout, particularly the constraints imposed by relief, and disposition of resources, conditioned a different degree of response. The extent of concentration in mining areas like the Rhondda was unparalleled and subsequent readjustment the more agonising. From over 215,000 coal-mining jobs in the valleys in 1921 the figure fell to 92,000 in 1958 and 52,000 in 1970; by 1980 the numbers will be appreciably smaller. Iron and steel, and tinplate manufactures grew rapidly in the nineteenth century but during the 1920s-30s suffered dramatic changes in location and in technology. The industrial specialisation was high, the industrial base narrow and, because it was smaller in scale, proved more difficult to diversify later. Wartime brought munitions factories, chemical, aluminium and vehicles plants, helped retrain labour and brought women into the factories, encouraged journey to work, and led to closer economic ties with England.

Post-war benefits under successive government policies were substantial. Outmigration from Wales was first slowed down and then reversed (1946-57, net loss of 17 per 10,000; 1961-70, +19 per 10,000). Comparable figures for Scotland over the same two periods were, -70 and -68 per 10,000; and for Northern Ireland, -67 and -47 per 10,000. Rates of industrial investment were high in the 1950s and early 1960s, partly the result of major capital-intensive projects in basic industries such as the Llanwern integrated steel-making plant. Diversification had played its part in the growth of new industrial and service jobs, but the limited size of the total labour force imposed constraints on the tempo of the process. Most of the new employment was located off the South Wales coalfield though nearly half the population continued to live there amidst industrial dereliction and an outworn social fabric. Between 1958 and 1968 employment in Welsh manufacturing grew 18.7 per cent, five times the UK rate, although Wales had a working population only one-tenth that of London. Moreover new manufacturing jobs replaced 91 per cent of the jobs lost in mining and quarrying (cf 18 per cent in Northern England, 26 per cent in Scotland). Though Scotland made the running in foreign investments in her industry in the 1950s Wales bids fair to lead in this respect in the 1970s.[80]

Yet regional planning had been disappointing [81] to the time of the 1967 White Paper [82] which defined spatial objectives only secondarily to those for economic and social sectors. Furthermore the proposals were as for three scarcely related economic subregions: South Wales, Mid-Wales and North Wales. This strong subregional level of strategic thinking has still to be incorporated effectively into a Welsh national context. Yet the basic problems are nation-wide: economic restructuring, especially jobs for men; improvement of external and internal accessibility, and the need for a coherent geographical overview.[83] The problems of South Wales [84] tend to overshadow the Welsh scene as did those of the Central Lowlands in Scotland. With some two-thirds of the Welsh population living within 35 miles (56 km) of Bridgend the economic restructuring, settlement regrouping and environmental rehabilitation are concentrated in this major industrial and urban area. The 1967 White Paper proposed to concentrate efforts to attract new industry along improved east-west communications linking up towns at the mouths of the mining valleys where these debouched onto the coastal plain. The valleys would then conserve their communities, journeys to work would develop down the valleys and the environment would be renewed; the Heads of the Valleys road would also attract some industries.

Several growth points were defined, including importantly the New Towns of Llantrisant, designated in 1972, and Cwmbran (1949). Llantrisant, already the site of part of the Royal Mint, is to help reduce outmigration and to attract industry. It is to grow from its present population of 25,000 to 70,000/75,000 by 1991 and by natural increase to 90,000 by the year 2001. Cwmbran is to regroup population from the Monmouthshire valleys (present population 45,000; target 55,000). Other growth centres are to be seen on figure 1.8, notably those at Bridgend, Kenfis (Port Talbot), Landore-Morriston (Swansea) and Fforestfach. As capital of the principality Cardiff is to reinforce its commercial, administrative and educational function.

There are however potential spatial growth presssures not taken adequately into account. Proposals to develop Severnside as a coherent subregion must stimulate growth in the Newport subregion. The M4 motorway will powerfully extend economic linkages of South Wales with Greater London, to match those along the M5 to the West Midlands. The delay in granting the Newport area 'intermediate' status (1969) meant a lack of growth momentum and the tendency to think of the south-east coastal tract as a perimeter area of Wales rather than an economic bridge seems endemic in planning circles. On the other hand current studies on Milford Haven (45,000 population in 1970), which is likely to be refining 30 per cent of UK throughput of crude oil in 1973, indicates a further and major hidden growth potential. But is there likely to be sufficient population in Wales to provide for all these developments?

The problems of Mid-Wales [85] are almost an exact antithesis to those of the South, as are those of the Highlands to those of Central Scotland. But, unlike the Highlands, Mid-Wales lacks a comprehensive development organisation, and Welsh social and economic problems, though smaller in scale, require more sensitive planning. Depopulation down to threshold levels is the key issue, with political as well as social and economic undertones, but the numbers leaving are few in total. Unemployment and underemployment are both endemic but the numbers in any one place are often not sufficient to attract an industrialist. The largest town is Aberystwyth (11,000) and the New Town commenced in Montgomeryshire in 1970 has an objective of raising the population from 5,500 to only 11,000/12,000 in 1981. Sceptics feel that the New Town proposal is rather to serve overspill needs of the English Midlands, but to achieve its target will necessitate a careful policy of attracting small firms. In any case repopulation of Mid-Wales is likely to be necessary if the area is to prosper in the longer-term.

The objectives of Welsh rural strategy are to establish a firmer economic base by restructuring agriculture in commercially viable units, whilst maintaining the family farm (though a Rural Development Board was declined), building up forestry, using water resources more to the advantage of Wales, conserving the landscape heritage, developing tourism and attracting industry to small country towns. Basic to all is the underpinning of Welsh rural society as a way of life. Figure 1.8 shows the sparse and fragmented tourist capacity in hotels in Mid-Wales, in striking contrast to the north coast. It also indicates the pattern of small rural growth points to which small firms are to be attracted. The work of the Industrial Development Association and the Development Commission has had notable successes (30 factories in 10 years, with 600,000 ft^2 (64,500 m^2) of new floor space). In 1970 it was estimated that return to the Exchequer had been 23 per cent on public capital invested. By these means a self-sustaining economic base may be created, but it will be a delicate task, and the developing of both internal and external communications will be a key factor.

North Wales is to have a similar concentration of growth at selected centres. Several of these are tourist centres, with a rising population including those coming for retirement. Introduction of industry to balance seasonal unemployment is proposed. Portmadoc is to serve as a centre for regrouping population in an area of high unemployment, whilst the Holyhead-Anglesey area with an aluminium smelter and nuclear power station has a unique growth potential. Finally, in north-east Wales there is a microcosm of South Wales problems in coal and steel. Now that the Dee Planning Study (1971) [86] has shown a crossing to be both feasible and viable the development potential of the Flintshire coast for water storage, recreation and industrial expansion has been greatly enhanced. It is estimated that the present Deeside population could be increased from 109,000 to 320,000 in the longer term.

Northern Ireland (figure 1.9): Until the prorogation of Stormont in 1972 Northern Ireland had on balance benefited from its degree of political and economic autonomy. Had the province been a self-financing unit, providing all its own services, locally generated revenue in 1967-8 would have been £110 million per annum below requirements (cf Scotland's calculated deficit in the same period £276 million, though with a population 3.5 times that of Ulster).[87] In 1972 the annual UK Exchequer contribution to Northern Ireland from the National Loans Fund was given as £200 million. The Stormont Parliament exercised powers over agricultural and industrial development and was also responsible for both physical and economic planning. On the other hand it is possible to argue that with direct ministerial control from Whitehall more substantial public investment might have been forthcoming, and the impact on the fundamental economic problems of the province that much greater.

In common with other development regions Northern Ireland has a problem mix compounded of economic structure and location, but there are distinctive features. The total population is scarcely more than one-third that of the Scottish Lowlands, no less than two-thirds being concentrated within 30 miles (48 km) of Belfast. This spatial imbalance which has resulted reflects sharp differences in living standards and economic potential within the province. The overall average annual income is only 75 per cent that of the UK, but in the rural areas it is even lower. Post-war unemployment in Northern Ireland has usually been the most severe for any of the economic planning regions; since 1963 it has never fallen below 5.9 per cent, and during 1972 stood at 9.1 per cent (11.5 per cent for males). At first sight the rural hinterland seems to have lower levels than in Belfast or Londonderry, towns in which the declining basic industries have been strongly represented. There is however much concealed rural underemployment, incomes are low and economic prospects have traditionally been poor. The flows of population within Ulster 1961-6 (figure 1.9) indicated the gravitational pull of Greater Belfast but, perhaps surprisingly, also the small scale of movement out of the least privileged rural areas. This may have been the result of strong rural community ties as much as the uncertain job prospects at that time in the larger towns.

The problems arising from economic structure and internal location within Northern Ireland were early seen to be interrelated and it was recognised that solutions might be the more difficult to achieve in view of the peripheral, and overseas position of Ulster within the UK space.[88] The Wilson Report (1965) [89] clearly formulated the need to promote economic expansion and to do so both by an orderly planning of physical development, involving major spatial redistribution of growth in the longer-term, and also by direct attacks on the problem of unemployment through effective restructuring of the economy. From a rather different standpoint, that of the planning problems facing Greater Belfast, the 1964 Regional Survey and Plan [90] reached similar conclusions, though the study area was too restricted to take into account the problems of outlying areas of the province. In order to check imbalance being further reinforced in Greater Belfast a major effort to reverse the process was to be initiated: growth in Belfast was to be limited, a New Town created at Craigavon (Portadown-Lurgan) and further population and industrial growth to be dispersed, as much as possible to fifteen designated centres. Just as the Wilson Report recognised the important arguments for spatial redistribution of growth and opportunity so did the Greater Belfast Plan accept also that to achieve such an objective a 50 per cent stepping up of the industrial growth rate 1956-61 would be required. The case in favour of limiting the growth of Belfast was not only that of economic and social justice to outlying towns and villages. It was also that unless the population within the Belfast stopline could be limited to 600,000, instead of the 800,000 it might reach by 1984 unless planning intervened, the redevelopment and economic growth of the city would be made unacceptably difficult.

In the 1970 Northern Ireland Development Programme [91] the sectoral and spatial objectives were consolidated within a coherent programme for investment and planned

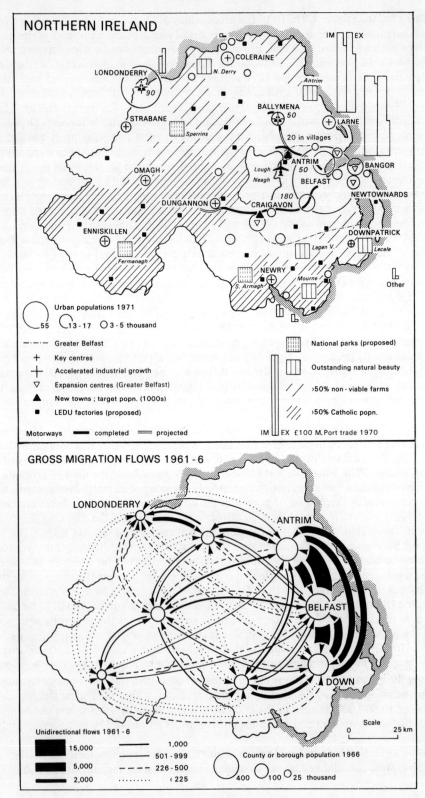

Figure 1.9   Northern Ireland; gross migration flows, 1961-6.

growth. Priority targets were to be the reduction of unemployment and the raising of living standards, both seen as relevant to eradicating the root causes of unrest within the Ulster community. It is appropriate to look briefly at the physical development strategy agreed upon and, secondly, at the stage reached in economic restructuring.

The concept of growth areas formulated in both the 1963 and 1965 studies is accepted as the basis for a regional and economic strategy, and there is to be a coordination of all public sectors to achieve such concentration at centres of accelerated industrial growth (Londonderry and Ballymena) and at eight key centres (figure 1.9). The New Town developments at Craigavon, Antrim-Ballymena and Londonderry are the spearhead of such disseminated growth. Within seven years of the Development Commission taking over at Craigavon the population had been built-up by 10,000; there were 33 factories with 4,500 jobs and a further 46 factories were under construction. Antrim-Ballymena, one of the most prosperous localities in the UK had attracted leader firms, in Michelin and British Enkalon, whilst Londonderry was programmed to rise from 70,000 to 90,000 people by the mid 1980s; the basis for such growth will come from jobs provided on the industrial estates recently established.[92]

The intention is that both industrial and services growth at the designated centres will diffuse benefits over a wider rural hinterland, in which the main problem is a declining labour force (Ulster 1948, 103,000; 1971, 52,000) with few alternative jobs.[93] To underpin this policy, having regard to the lower rate of car ownership and decay of public transport in rural areas, a micro-level programme for dispersal of small industrial plants is in progress under the Local Enterprise Development Unit (LEDU). The pattern of initial LEDU investment can be seen on figure 1.9a, with Advance factories (2,800 ft^2; 300 m^2) and nursery workshop combines (four units, each of 550 ft^2; 59 m^2) suited to a wide range of small industries. By the end of 1972 600 jobs had been provided in LEDU factories.

Greater Belfast poses a major urban redevelopment problem, with replacement of much of the housing stock and decongestion key issues. The expansion centres to which population is to be moved from the city are seen on figure 1.9. The strategy for Belfast thus rests upon improvement of its attractiveness for industry, the modernising of a substandard living environment and promotion of growth at the capital city of Ulster. The attractiveness of the outer Belfast commuting area is shown by a 73 per cent population increase 1951-69, in comparison with only 18 per cent in five other towns in Ulster in the same period.

Finally, a word on industrial restructuring. Wilson (1965) forecast the need for 30,000 new manufacturing jobs by 1970, if his proposals were to be effectively implemented. Although this target figure was reached by 1971, unfortunately there was an overall decrease of 10,000 jobs in manufacturing since decline in employment had continued in shipbuilding and linen textiles in particular. This was not compensated for, even by the impressive employment growth in man-made fibres (9,000 jobs, distributed over several centres) or in lighter engineering industries. Most recently (1972) the government-supported Harland and Wolff development programme is likely to provide a further 4,000 much-needed jobs in shipbuilding. There is indeed impressive industrial growth momentum at the present time in spite of disruption in the economic life of Ulster. From mid-1969 to mid-1972, 151 manufacturing firms had been disrupted by civil unrest, but only 10 closed, with the loss of 621 jobs.

IV.3 The Intermediate Regions

There is some generalisation involved in identifying as intermediate regions the whole of Yorkshire and Humberside, and the North West. Though both economic planning regions were scheduled in 1971 for Intermediate Area benefits, extending the previous fragmentary zoning after the decisions on the 1969 Hunt Report, the North West also includes the Merseyside development area (1949). Further, as figure 1.4 shows, there are intermediate areas elsewhere in the UK, notably in the South West, the eastern periphery of Wales and at Edinburgh-Leith.

Nevertheless the two trans-Pennine economic planning regions most fully represent the problems of the intermediate areas and have very substantial populations living in sizeable, well-established towns and cities. Employment is sluggish or falling, though unemployment since the war has rarely been high enough for development area status to be conferred; the only exceptions to this, apart from Merseyside, were the short-term scheduling of parts of South East (1946) and North East Lancashire (1953). Regional incomes have been rising more slowly, and the industrial structure has been weighted with slow growth or decline sectors. Outmigration has been a less severe problem than in the development areas, though it has been ever-present. Furthermore the intermediate regions had a major legacy from the Industrial Revolution in their townscapes and there was a serious problem of dereliction. To meet all these problems, in aggregate at times scarcely less severe than those of the development areas there was no special locational aid from successive governments. It was only in 1969 that lesser scale of aid became available and then only for strictly localised areas. The 1971 extension of intermediate status to virtually all of the Yorkshire and Humberside, and North West regions permits for the first time a coordinated thrust towards economic as well as social or physical objectives in their regional development.

Both regions are less than 200 miles (320 km) from London, linked by the direct motorway network and fast Inter-city rail services. They are thus subjected to greater locational pulls from the Midlands and South East than are the development areas; in return they may hope to offer less disadvantageous freight hauls to incoming industry, in respect of service to major national markets.

Yorkshire and Humberside (figure 1.10): Fawcett (1919) spoke of Yorkshire as a 'microcosm of England'. The same might be said for the regional development problem posed today for the entire economic planning region. It lacks homogeneity or coherence, and there have persisted clear differences of emphasis as between alternative strategies for growth and development. Broadly speaking the planning region may be differentiated into western, central and eastern zones, each with distinctive characteristics and problems. Within the Pennines and their fringe zone west of the A1(M) are concentrated 3½ millions, no less than 75 per cent of the regional population, This is an urban-industrial zone with major cities and smaller, specialised industrial towns, the home of the woollen and worsted industries, engineering and other sectors which have been stagnant or declining in employment since the war. It is also a zone with a relatively low population growth and serious environmental difficulties, notably so in the smaller, specialised woollen towns in the more remote Pennine valleys. In the south, around Sheffield-Rotherham, concentration on the steel industry and its specialised product range means too narrow an employment base and poses particular problems of economic vulnerability, with an even more pronounced counterpart around the integrated steel plants at Scunthorpe to the east. In the West Riding conurbation the problems are thus those of a massive slow growth to decline urban and industrial complex, without obvious means of achieving an industrial transformation.

The central zone includes the most productive localities of the Yorkshire coalfield, flanking the major north-south arteries of the A1(M) and the main east coast rail link and set within a rural hinterland. Since the late 1950s there has been a sharp rundown in mining jobs, even in this prosperous coalfield. The development problem is that of regrouping mining and agricultural populations and finding alternative work within daily travelling distance, to absorb those displaced by redundancies. In meeting this problem the nodal location on the national communications network should prove a major asset.

The problem in the third zone, Humberside, is of a different order. The north bank, around Hull, has had a limited port-based industrial structure and has suffered from relative isolation within the UK space. There are also physical planning problems, particularly those

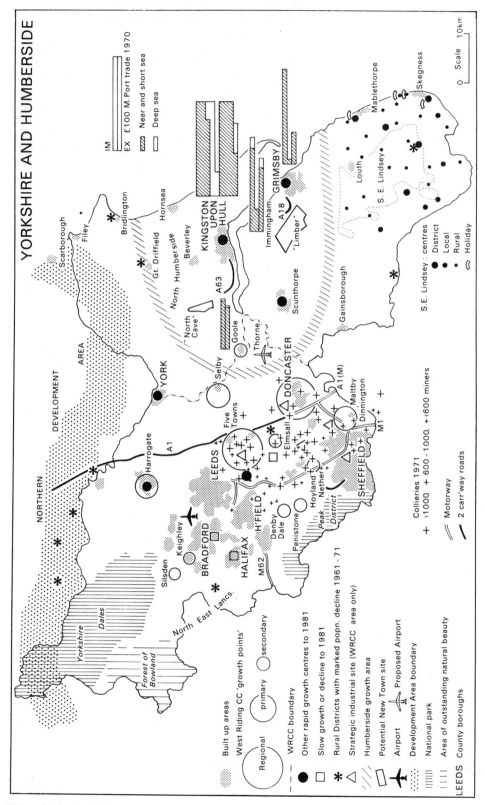

Figure 1.10 Yorkshire and Humberside.

of urban redevelopment and conservation of high grade agricultural land. On the south
bank industry has grown rapidly since the 1950s, but many plants have been capital-
intensive rather than providing great numbers of new jobs. There is, however, ample land
in the Humberside region to accommodate both population and industry. This potential
was clearly established in the Feasibility Study (1969),[34] to which reference is made later.
Though a final verdict on such a massive estuarial growth prospect has not yet been made
the consent to a Humber bridge, to be completed by 1976, is a vitally important first step.

The fundamental problem for Yorkshire and Humberside is then to decide on broad
spatial allocations and priorities for growth as between the major zones, for both the shorter-
term (to 1984) and to the end of the century. Strongly-held convictions in cities and Ridings
have not made the tasks of formulating and gaining acceptance of a coherent strategy any
easier. Nor is the task lightened by the difficulties of forecasting the tempo and nature of
economic growth which may be expected, whilst the region enjoys only Intermediate status.

The 1966 Review [94] emphasised the complexity and diversity of the region and underlined the varied needs and problems of each sub-region. The 'collective regional action and
new sense of coherence' then called for have since been slow to materialise. Basic to the
arguments of the review is the proposition that the problems of each subregion should be
mitigated largely *in situ* and there are no proposals for intraregional transfers of population,
or selective investment in areas where economic growth might be most readily induced. The
defence may well have been that mobile industry would be difficult to attract, without
greater government incentives, that existing industry had prospects for regeneration and
this would have to take place on existing sites, and that with the outlook for only very
modest additions to the labour force by the mid-1980s no dramatic intraregional transfers
were either practicable or desirable. The insistence that future development should be concentrated mainly on existing centres of population, that existing industries should power
such development, and that the need to improve the general urban environment in the
Pennines was paramount, has persisted to the present time in economic planning council
thinking. So too has the early emphasis on subregional analysis [95] and the lack of an adequately interrelated overall framework. For example in the Halifax and Calder valley study
the recommendation is made for growth at the mouths of the valleys and along the M62,
a micro-strategy similar to that for South Wales, but this subregional solution is not set
within any wider regional context.

In the Hunt Report on the intermediate areas [96] a clear difference of opinion arose on
prescription for the future development of Yorkshire and Humberside. The majority view
was that growth centres should be selected and a strategy of selective investment for them
pursued.[97] Industrial estates at strategic points, capable of drawing in labour from a
wider hinterland, would play the role they had already had in development areas. Concentration on growth centres should not be at the expense of other parts of the region
and, indeed, no inherent conflict of interests was envisaged. A.J. Brown [98] laid stress on the
scale of the large urban concentrations and the importance of channelling growth to these,
even after the needs of any growth centres had been met. He further saw the coalfield as
the one location in Yorkshire and Humberside where a growth centre might be justified.
To him the growth centre concept was appropriate only when the entire pattern of settlement was being changed, as in the regrouping of agricultural or mining populations, or
when substantial moves from congested cities were being made through overspill schemes.
Growth centres would contribute less to the problems of a massive slow-growth industrial
and urban complex.

The division of views on strategy surfaced again in the development plan review of the
West Riding County Council,[99] which admittedly did not have responsibility for the problems of its included county boroughs. The strategy proposals therein were for the longer-
term, to the year 2001, and were firmly based on the designation of growth points and,
indeed, an even greater emphasis upon such selective investment as the future population

for the region seemed likely to be lower than in earlier forecasts. The pattern of suggested growth points, at regional, primary and secondary levels is seen on figure 1.10; the selection of Doncaster confirmed the potential already identified in the EPC subregional study. The pattern of growth points was carefully chosen to exploit under-utilised resources of land or labour, capitalise in other cases upon favourable location, and on other occasions lead to environmental improvement. In addition, a series of strategic industrial sites, each of over 100 acres (40 ha), (figure 1.10) and major sites (not less than 20 acres – 8 ha) were proposed. All but one lay within what had since 1970 been scheduled as an intermediate area. Furthermore no less than 51 key villages were selected for expansion.

In 1970 the Yorkshire and Humberside *Regional Strategy* [100] was published by the EPC. This confirmed the basic recommendation of the 1966 Review and suggested that in view of the longer time-scale of the WRCC Development Plan (2001 rather than the year 1984) there was no fundamental conflict between the different perspectives on strategy. The Regional Strategy re-emphasised that growth should follow the broad pattern of existing settlement, that the larger towns had the better and more diversified growth prospects, particularly for attraction of service industries, but that growth should also be disseminated throughout the urban system at all levels. For Bradford, Huddersfield and Halifax the current adverse trends were to be stabilised, with some increase at Huddersfield, whilst in the longer-term Leeds was recommended as a major growth area for employment and population. Urgent provision of new jobs for men was prescribed for Greater Doncaster, Barnsley, the Five Towns (Castleford, Knottingley, Pontefract, Featherstone and Normanton) and Wakefield, with some decline in population in the central coalfield. For Sheffield and Rotherham the conomy was to be diversified and the possibility kept open for accommodating regional population growth in the longer-term. The strengthening of the economic base and improvement of the environment were priorities for Humberside, whilst conservation or modest development were envisaged for country areas and market towns.

Apart from the degree of emphasis upon growth in the industrial-urban complex of the Pennines as against the coalfield, through which passes the north-south communications corridor, there are two other fundamental uncertainties. Can the industrial structure be regenerated or transformed to serve the priorities of regional planning adequately, and what might be the effects of a government decision to press ahead with Humberside as a fast-growth estuarine industrial region? The economic planning council remains cautious and exploratory on the first issue.[101] Brown [102] had already drawn attention to the sharp structural changes in employment which had taken place prior to 1965. Though these had not been cumulative as in the development areas, nevertheless 1965 marked a threshold after which unemployment began to rise differentially and income per capita began a decline relative to other regions. The EPC recognised these problems and indeed reviewed the 1965-70 continuation of the trends. Among further declines in employment were listed: coalmining, -30,000 jobs; wool textiles, -31,000, though future decrease was thought likely to be small;[103] metal manufactures, -14,000; construction, -26,000; the distributive trades, -26,000. On the other hand, some service industries had shown a rapid increase, e.g. professional and scientific services, +41,000 jobs. Unfortunately declines were taking place in areas different from those with growth in employment and, moreover, there were skills and training of a different order required in any attempt to balance growth with decline. Projection of trends identified further declines, requiring up to 35,000 new jobs in the coalfield by 1975, a considerable problem arising from redundancies in the steel industry, to say nothing of the implications of further automation or Common Market entry. On the credit side the attraction of new industry had proved minimal, for the period 1945-65 only 24,500 male jobs from all manufacturing moves into the region. Moreover even under intermediate area stimulus the rate of new job provision was inadequate to replace losses. The conclusion must be drawn that in the short-term the inducements for industrialists have to be maximised within the region. This would seem to strengthen the case for designation and selective investment in an interrelated hierarchy of growth points as soon as practicable.

The problem posed by the future development of Humberside is longer-term and national in the first instance but its regional implications are profound. If shortly the government accepts the case for rapid estuarine growth on Humberside [104] between now and the end of the century a safeguard has already been built-in to protect the development areas up to 1981, but no such protection has been vouchsafed for adjacent areas of Yorkshire and Humberside. In national and local terms [105] the case for Humberside development is strong, potentially dramatic. The case for between an additional 320,000 or 720,000 people by the year 2001 is substantiated, with alternative growth and urban location strategies, including New Town development at Limber or North Cave (figure 1.10). It is anticipated that major growth will take place by spontaneous mass movements from the 1980s onwards, but that in the short-term industry and people might be attracted more from the Midlands and the South East, partly by planned overspill. The impact of such major developments, if acceptable to government, upon the massive slow-growth industrial and urban complex in the Pennines, to say nothing of general strategic balance within Yorkshire and Humberside, poses extraordinary problems, even within an enhanced European future.

The North West (figure 1.11): The problems of the North West[106] arise initially from the very size of the regional population (6.7 millions in 1971), its concentration between the Ribble and the Mersey (5.9 millions), a low population growth rate, and the scale of industrial transformation and rundown which have taken place in cotton, coal and engineering since the war. Though there has been some replacement of jobs in growth industries, especially so in services, the region is still characterised by a low level of autonomous economic growth. In common with Yorkshire and Humberside the urban-industrial problem is most serious in the traditional single-industry towns in the Pennines, but in the North West the decline of employment in cotton textiles has been more profound and its subregional effects more traumatic. Furthermore the presence of major conurbations on Merseyside (1.2 millions) and at Greater Manchester (2.3 millions) in lowland Lancashire, each hitherto controlled by independent planning authorities, has weighted the restructuring problem and coloured policies for development and change. Merseyside has been consistently scheduled as a Development Area since 1946, to its great advantage, and has acted as an engine of economic growth in the North West;[107] the only other DA has been Furness, on the borders of the Northern Region. Manchester, on the other hand, failed to attract the same scale of new industrial investment but has built-up service employment. Both conurbations need substantial and continuing overspill schemes to permit redevelopment and decrease congestion, and there is a major problem of priorities as between the subregions for the distribution of such population and employment. Nowhere in Britain is the range of possible regional development options greater: dissemination of growth and subregional balance; perimeter additions to one or both conurbations; major developments at the New Towns, including the Central Lancashire New Town (CLNT); balance between growth in the Ribble Belt (CLNT and North East Lancashire) and the Mersey Belt, particularly in the subregion between the conurbations; concentration of growth in areas most attractive to industry or remedial measures in problem subregions. Nowhere in Britain has there been such a slow-growth momentum, in population or employment, in relation to the scale of the problems to be faced and scarcely anywhere else has the fragmentation of planning authorities made coherent policies so difficult to achieve. On the other hand, the growth of the motorway network, the extension of main line electrification on the west coast route and developments in the ports are creating a new dimension in regional economic potential within the UK system.

The North West study (1965)[108] stressed the twin objectives of better living conditions and the need to stimulate economic growth. The problem of housing obsolescence was placed in the forefront, and has remained a major preoccupation. The forward projections

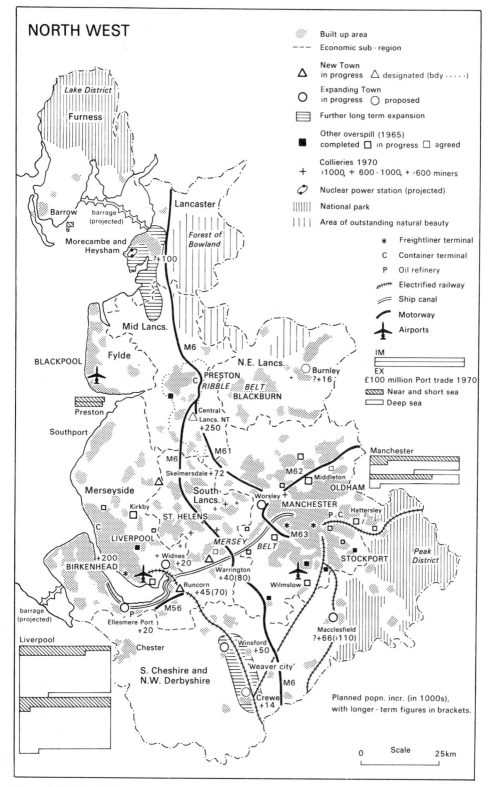

Figure 1.11 North West

for the regional population were then more sizeable (800,000 to 930,000 by 1981), even though outmigration was assumed to continue. Overspill schemes for intraregional redistribution (figure 1.11) were numerous but for the most part small and separately negotiated by the conurbation local authorities. The New Town designated at Skelmersdale, together with proposals for similar developments at Runcorn, Warrington and Leyland-Chorley were also to accommodate overspill, and it was not anticipated that other overspill schemes would be required, certainly not before the last decades of the century. The problem industrial areas within the Pennines were scarcely touched upon.

A counterpart study for Merseyside [109] noted the youthful population and a high natural increase rate. Though there had been a net migration loss of 72,000 nevertheless the population had risen by 117,000 between 1951 and 1964. The industrial economy was changing during the same period from narrowly port-based to a greater diversification linked to the hinterland of the North West. Yet industrial transformation had not been sufficient to offset job loss in port-based industries and still meet the needs of an increased labour force. Unemployment has persisted, particularly for young persons, and justified the scheduling of Merseyside as a Development Area as far back as 1949.

The 1966 Strategy [110] optimistically proposed to reduce net outmigration and contemplated a population increase of one million by 1981. Two growth areas were proposed: in North Lancashire and South Cheshire; but the Green Belts around the conurbations were to remain inviolate and there was to be no infilling in the intervening Mersey Belt. The industrial problem areas of Rossendale and the North East were considered in the context of the effects of the 1959 Cotton Industry Act, which had achieved massive rationalisation and reduction of both capacity and employment in that industry. Yet North East Lancashire had been descheduled under the 1960 Local Employment Act and the prospects of attracting sufficient new industrial growth correspondingly reduced.

The Strategy II (1968) [111] had less regard for allocations of population growth, whose target figure for 1981 had now fallen to +750,000, but much greater emphasis upon the need for industrial location efficiency, buttressed by effective action on transport, housing and schools. The environment was to be improved by urban renewal and attacks on the problems of derelict land [112] and pollution. Peripheral growth of the conurbations by inroads into green belt land was rejected in favour of continued growth at the New Towns and by town expansion schemes. Increased journeys to work were anticipated both to these new developments and to industrial sites within the marginal problem localities in Rossendale, the North East and the Pennine fringe. The early development of the CLNT was firmly supported and the urgency of local government reform seen as necessary if a coordinated strategy was to be achieved. Currently a strategic plan is in course of formulation by a tripartite team from central government, the economic planning council and board, and local planning authorities; its publication is expected in 1973-4.

In its proposal, not accepted by the government, to deschedule Merseyside as a development area, the Hunt Report (1969) [113] brought into the open one of the principal strategic issues, the role of the conurbations in regional economic growth, and particularly the extent of distortions in growth which development area scheduling may have introduced. It was argued that in the two years 1966-8 Merseyside had attracted 5,350 jobs by industrial moves from neighbouring areas (27 per cent of all new jobs created by moves), probably mostly from Manchester. In its perimeter industrial estates with their major housing developments, the greenfield industrial sites capable of taking motor vehicle plants, the nearby New Towns of Skelmersdale and Runcorn and the overspill town of Winsford Merseyside represented the major North West growth complex. It was for this reason that descheduling was proposed but opposed by Brown.[114] Brown argued that the high natural increase and immigration, leading to perhaps an additional 200,000 people within 20 years, required continued government support policies for creating new employment. If the area was to be descheduled it did not follow that the same industrial growth would be available for other sites in the North

West. In the event development area status was retained and North East Lancashire was designated an intermediate area in 1970, a status extended to the entire North West in 1972.

The Central Lancashire New Town,[115] intended to build-up to a population of no less than 500,000 by 1991, from the present 250,000 in the designated area, has clearly the potential to act as a counter-magnet to the two principal conurbations, and also as a major growth centre to underpin the industrial economy and help stabilise the population of the entire Ribble Belt. Indeed it is intended deliberately to relieve growth pressures in the Merseyside-Manchester axis, to act as a base for concentrating large immigrant growth industries, and to provide an attractive environment and modern living conditions. There must be some uncertainty about the prospects of attracting sufficient mobile large-scale industry in time, some doubt about the potential adverse effects upon North East Lancashire, and some regrets that the designated area did not extend further south, to help relieve unemployment problems in the area north of Wigan. To clarify the possible effects upon North East Lancashire an Impact Study (1968)[116] was commissioned, to be followed up by a project study for a fast road link to the North East. The Impact Study argued that the needs of the North East were for improved communications, south towards Manchester as well as along the Ribble valley, rehabilitation and urban renewal. It was felt that the effects of CLNT would on balance be favourable. Outmigration from the towns of North East Lancashire might rise by 10,000-15,000 over the twenty-year period 1971-91, but would probably rise to double that figure had the New Town not been introduced. The effects would increase after 1981 in a period of faster CLNT growth but there would be closer economic and social linkages with existing towns from Blackburn eastwards.

The options in the North West remain open. Much will depend on national economic growth rates, in an area lacking in sufficient indigenous momentum. If growth is fast and sustained the CLNT can be vigorously prosecuted and a Ribble Belt economy regenerated. At the same time the Mersey Belt can gain momentum, with maximum growth in towns and overspill centres. On the most favourable outlook for growth major developments may be required in the Lancaster area and South Cheshire (Weaver City) by the end of the century. The conurbations are likely to be restructured but not to grow on any hypothesis for the region. On a slow-growth hypothesis agonising choices between alternatives will be needed, not least for the many smaller or remote industrial towns, whose problems have been neglected in most policies to date.

IV.4 Regions of Mixed Trends

The South West and East Anglia economic planning regions do not fall into any clear category, though they share certain common features. Neither has coherence, least of all the South West, and indeed each has four distinctive subregions. As a result there are built-in conflicting economic and social trends, and a marked territoriality between urban and rural interests. Both are identified by the lowest population densities among UK economic planning regions, but nevertheless there are strong pressures for growth and development in parts of both the South West (Severnside, Swindon) and East Anglia (New Town and town expansion schemes). In both regions the influence of the metropolis is increasingly felt and is spreading; this too adds to the problems of developing a regional iconography.

The South West: The 1966 *Draft Strategy for the South West* [117] accepted from the outset that very different treatment would be required for each of its four component subregions. Indeed, in view of the distinctive economic and social problems of each, the strength of county-based loyalties, the lack of a clear capital for the region and the extent of outside, particularly metropolitan influences, it is not surprising that a coherent and universally agreed strategy has not yet emerged. Furthermore, each of the four subregions is further differentiated internally, which adds to the problems of the regional planner. The strategic issues facing Bristol and Severnside are those arising from strong population and economic growth pressures, with the need to define priorities for proper physical planning of future growth, to avoid congestion and loss of amenity and to balance development of manufacturing with that of services with least detriment to the environment. Linkages through the motorway and port network have set the region more firmly within a national context, as one of the most impressive prospects for fast growth during the latter part of this century. The influence of Greater London has spread along the M4, beyond the planned expansion centre of Swindon (+75,000 overspill population by 1981); the motorway has also linked Severnside more effectively with South Wales.

Even growth industries have their problems, however, and for example some of the 20,000 direct jobs on Concorde airframes and engines in the South West might be threatened unless sales for the aircraft improve markedly. The Concorde project has led to about £15 million per annum investment at Filton, Patchway, Fairford and at dispersed centres through the south-western counties. Similarly, though further port development at Bristol may prove to be an income generator it is less likely to provide many new jobs. Tertiary employment, particularly in the office sector, may offer better prospects. Though Bristol is only eighth in size among UK urban areas the city is already the fourth largest office centre outside London.

The central subregion lacks focus, is strongly rural in character and has limited growth potential in its market towns and at selected south coast resorts. It is subjected to strong growth influences from Bristol-Severnside to the north and, to a lesser extent, from the metropolis. These are indeed likely to increase with the extension of the M5 into Somerset in 1973, to Exeter by 1975 and to Plymouth by 1980. The Southern and Western subregions comprise Devon and Cornwall, with a fringe area of north-western Somerset (figure 1.12). The problems here are firstly those of establishing and maintaining viability for an economy with agriculture and the holiday trades as its basis, and thereafter of promoting growth by the introduction of a balance of industry. With remoteness and economic inaccessibility underlying weaknesses [118] the improvement of communications is a vital priority. Official recognition of the problems of Devon and Cornwall came with the scheduling of several localities under DATAC (Development Areas Treasury Advisory Committee) or Development District legislation between 1958 and 1966. In 1966 much of Cornwall became a Development Area and during 1969 Plymouth was granted Intermediate Area status.

Pressures for growth on Severnside, in either the short- or long-term, are unlikely to benefit Devon and Cornwall, and may indeed prejudice any kind of balanced development in the rural or outer areas of the South West. Present trends of growth on Severnside are among the most substantial in the UK and the verdict of the Severnside study (1971) [119] was that the potential for population growth by the end of the century was double that expected from projection of even the present buoyant trends. The industrial employment mix is diverse and contains powerful growth elements, [120] as in the aircraft and airspace, engineering, paper and printing industries of the Bristol area; the high level of mechanical and instrument engineering in North Gloucestershire; and the iron and steel industry in Monmouthshire-Ross.

There has been a steady net inmigration to Severnside since the war, the product of economic opportunity and attractive environment. Furthermore, the building of the Severn bridge and linkages along the M4 and M5 have strengthened the infrastructure for a coherent Severnside region, with close attachment to the South East, the Midlands and South Wales. Today, for example, Bristol (Parkway) is within 1hr 35mins of London by non-stop fast rail service. The feasibility study forecast continuing growth tendencies sufficient to attract a net inward flow of about 7,000 people a year, which if sustained, together with natural increase, would add 450,000 to the population by 1991 (650,000 by the year 2001). This might be stimulated to a maximum potential for an additional population of 600,000 by 1991 (one million by 2001). The allocation of such massive potential growth was distri-

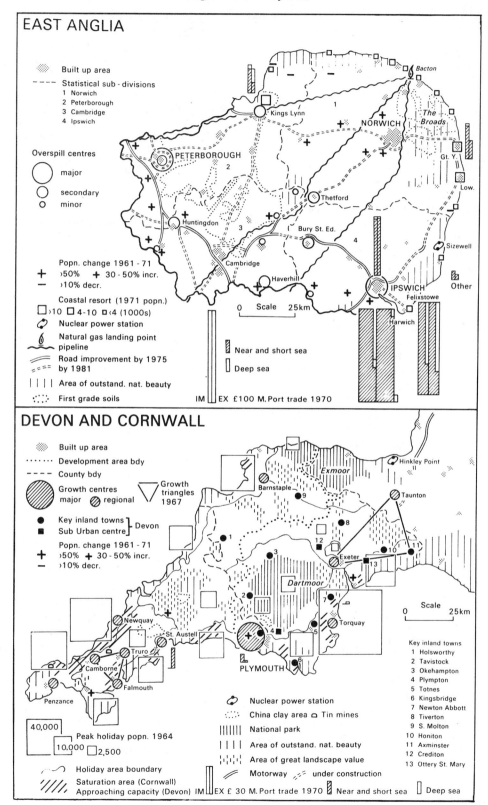

EAST ANGLIA

- ░░ Built up area
- - - - Statistical sub-divisions
  1 Norwich
  2 Peterborough
  3 Cambridge
  4 Ipswich

Overspill centres
- ◯ major
- ◯ secondary
- ○ minor

Popn. change 1961 - 71
- ✛ ›50%   ✚ 30 - 50% incr.
- — ›10% decr.

Coastal resort (1971 popn.)
- ☐ ›10 ☐ 4-10 ▫ ‹4 (1000s)
- ♻ Nuclear power station
- 🜂 Natural gas landing point
  ═ pipeline
- ═ Road improvement by 1975
  ═ by 1981
- | | | | Area of outstand. nat. beauty
- ░⋯ First grade soils

Kings Lynn
PETERBOROUGH
2
NORWICH
The Broads
Gt. Y.
1
Low.
Thetford
Huntingdon
3
Bury St. Ed.
Sizewell
Cambridge
4
Haverhill
IPSWICH
Felixstowe
Harwich
Bacton
Other

0   Scale   25km

IM ☐ EX £100 M. Port trade 1970
▨ Near and short sea
☐ Deep sea

DEVON AND CORNWALL

- ░░ Built up area
- ⋯⋯ Development area bdy
- - - - County bdy
- ◍ Growth centres
  major ◉ regional
- ▽ Growth triangles 1967
- ● Key inland towns ⎤ Devon
- ■ Sub Urban centre ⎦
- Popn. change 1961 - 71
- ✛ ›50% ✚ 30 - 50% incr.
- — ›10% decr.

- ☐ 40,000
- ☐ 10,000
- ☐ 2,500
  Peak holiday popn. 1964
- ⌒ Holiday area boundary
- ⁄⁄⁄⁄ Saturation area (Cornwall)
  ⁄⁄⁄⁄ Approaching capacity (Devon)

Exmoor
Hinkley Point
Barnstaple
Taunton
9
8
1
12
Exeter
10
11
13
3
Dartmoor
Newquay
St. Austell
2
7
Truro
Torquay
Camborne
4
5
Falmouth
6
Penzance
PLYMOUTH

Scale
0   25km

Key inland towns
1 Holsworthy
2 Tavistock
3 Okehampton
4 Plympton
5 Totnes
6 Kingsbridge
7 Newton Abbott
8 Tiverton
9 S. Molton
10 Honiton
11 Axminster
12 Crediton
13 Ottery St. Mary

- ♻ Nuclear power station
- ░⋯ China clay area ⌂ Tin mines
- |||||| National park
- | | | | Area of outstand. nat. beauty
- ¦¦¦¦¦ Area of great landscape value
- ▭ Motorway ⁇ under construction

IM ☐ EX £ 30 M. Port trade 1970 ▨ Near and short sea ☐ Deep sea

Figure 1.12   Devon and Cornwall; East Anglia

buted to several major sites: 200,000 to 300,000 to Bristol-Bath by 1991, if there can be major development at the Frampton Cotterell site; 150,000 to 250,000 in North Gloucestershire, possibly involving a New Town on the west bank; and 100,000 to 150,000 people in Monmouthshire-Ross, representing almost the maximum physical capacity of that area. The preferred strategy is thus for a major centre of industrial and population growth associated with existing urban development in each of three areas, posing a testing problem of harnessing and channelling growth, without suffering the dangers that could accompany excessive size.

The problems of the outer subregions of the South West could scarcely be more different: to promote rather than restrain growth, and to do so from a narrow agricultural-tourism base; to create better accessiblity rather than channel growth arising from an ultramodern communications net; to attract industry and reduce unemployment rather than avoid 'overheating' arising from rapid economic growth; to create many small centres of growth rather than major urban growth concentrations.

The 1966 Draft Strategy stressed the importance of strengthening agriculture and horticulture, whilst accepting that employment in these sectors would continue to fall, by amalgamation of holdings, increase in gross output per holding and more effective marketing. Tourism was seen as a major but vulnerable growth industry, which might be interrelated with other elements of the rural or coastal economy, but one whose prospects could not alone carry Devon and Cornwall to prosperity.[121] Farming and tourism would provide the base from which self-sustaining economic growth might be promoted by the introduction of manufacturing and its location at selected major, regional or local growth centres (figure 1.12). Plymouth was recommended as a major centre for growth and potential of the two growth triangles, Exeter-Honiton-Taunton, and Truro-Camborne-Falmouth specifically indicated. Indigenous population growth might be insufficient to provide sufficient labour at the growth centres and the prospects for self-supporting growth would be enhanced by planned overspill location of inmigrants from Greater London.

At present population growth comes disproportionately from the influx of retired persons whilst younger people continue to leave Devon and Cornwall in search of work. The multiplier effect of retired people on the local economy might be as much as the equivalent of one service job equivalent per retired household compared to £1,500 as the public cost of creating one new job in manufacturing, but the manufacturing job is likely to be the more stable long-term investment.

During the period 1966-70 Devon County Council [122] carried out feasibility studies for several growth centres, the Cornwall Council investigated the proposals for West Cornwall, [123] and the economic planning council published the Plymouth area study.[124] Neither county council accepted that the growth triangles should have precedence for investment, or indeed that population or employment should be channelled into such areas. Furthermore the proposal that Greater London overspill should contribute to the build-up was strongly resented locally and, indeed, in 1968 the GLC announced that no further town development schemes would be accepted for the time being. In Devon and Cornwall the strategy is rather for smaller scale and interrelated growth points, with redistribution of population from larger towns like Exeter or Plymouth into an immediate hinterland. As in Wales there is a strong sentiment for promoting development from indigenous resources and population.

Studies in industrial development at Plymouth and in Devon and Cornwall[125] have shown the difficulties of generating and maintaining sufficient momentum without government aid and, even with it, the problems of attracting new developments on the necessary scale and with adequate growth prospects. There is some expectation that EEC entry will help rather than damage the South West. Early favourable indications include: a roll on/ roll off service Plymouth-Roscoff (Brittany); a possible container outport at Falmouth; and a potential increase in tourism from Europe.

East Anglia (figure 1.12): Difficult to establish in the first place, the identity of this region risks being increasingly submerged by metropolitan influences expressed through the communications network and the pattern of New and overspill towns. The Outer Metropolitan Area bounds the region on the south and London lies only 120 miles (193 km) from the furthest point of the Norfolk coast. The location of East Anglia has traditionally been interpreted as oblique to the main axis of national economic life and its identity has been built-up as one of the foremost agricultural regions in the UK, somewhat isolated by poor communications, but with a degree of coherence from the interlinking of subregions based on Norwich, Peterborough, Cambridge and Ipswich. The economic planning council came into being later than others (1966) and it seems clear that in official circles East Anglia had hitherto been something of a statistical abstraction.

The East Anglia Study (1968) [126] recognised the problem of consolidating an identity for a region lacking homogeneity and subject to strong external influences from the south. The regional development problem is compounded of conflicting trends. On the one hand, the size of population (1.6 millions in 1971) is small and the overall density is low, whilst the traditional economic structure has been developed from an agrarian base. Manufacturing is poorly developed with many small firms in food and fish processing, and light engineering. Labour has a restricted range of skills and average incomes are lower than for any UK region other than Scotland; furthermore, there have been persistent but highly localised unemployment 'black spots' in coastal and rural Norfolk. Not only is the internal road system inadequate but rural transport, both road and rail, has declined markedly. Housing, education and health standards have been lower than those of the nation. Not surprisingly rural depopulation has proved to be a characteristic feature.

On the other hand the total population of East Anglia has shown the fastest regional growth rate since 1951 and this is likely to be sustained until 1981 at the least. This growth has been generated from the South East with the influx of sizeable London overspill population. In the study it was estimated that between 1966 and 1981 between 85,000 and 114,000 additional males would be seeking jobs, three-quarters of them at the New Town of Peterborough or in overspill areas. The distribution of overspill schemes is seen on figure 1.12. Under the 1952 Town Development Act (1952) ten local authorities made overspill agreements with what is now the GLC and it is estimated that a total capacity, 1966-81, for about 250,000 people might be made available in East Anglia. This would represent a maximum and no further overspill agreements have been entered into by the GLC since 1968.

The strategy problem facing the East Anglian council was to draw up a plan which would strengthen the regional economy and benefit from the London-inspired growth momentum, without at the same time becoming no more than a peripheral extension of the South East. Indigenous growth was likely to have been small and hard to realise since the region had never had development area status and only intermittently and in piecemeal fashion aid under the 1960 and 1963 Local Employment Acts. Additionally office development had been restricted, in principle, and firms could not be attracted, under overspill arrangements, from the adjacent Outer Metropolitan Area.

A strategy for concentration of development along radial growth corridors from the South East: to Peterborough (A1M), or to Ipswich (A12) and thence to Norwich was rejected as damaging to the coherence of East Anglia. Transverse growth corridors seemed unlikely to be realised, although a Haven Ports-Cambridge-Northampton axis was developing in the 1960s, and there would be a loss of subregional balance. Nor did a major New Town growth in Breckland seem in the interests of the region and the proposed scale of such a development, at Thetford, also threatened amenity.

The proposed strategy envisaged the build-up of the four city regions, each with a dispersed hinterland of about 15 miles (24 km) radius. Norwich, Peterborough, Cambridge and Ipswich were nodally located, though large parts of the hinterland of the first three lay outside the East Anglian planning region. Second-order urban regions were to be based on

King's Lynn, Great Yarmouth-Lowestoft and Bury St Edmunds and it was intended to
select smaller scale rural growth points. In commenting on the proposed strategy the government agreed that there was no reason to concentrate development in any one part of the
region, but rejected any notion of uniform subregional growth. Subregional studies were
to be undertaken to identify areas with the greatest growth potential. Office development
controls were lifted and firms from the OMA would be permitted to move to new or
expanding towns. The rural growth point strategy was acceptable and some IDC relaxation
might be expected.

The prospects for the four subregions are uneven and differential growth might disturb
or distort any coherent strategy for East Anglia. Norwich (160,000 in the city; 500,000 in
subregion) typifies the regional problem, in its diverse industrial structure (food processing,
shoes, engineering) with few growth elements, the less prosperous hinterland (including
small coastal resorts) and the least adequate intraregional and long-distance communications.
Peterborough, on the other hand, is a New Town with major expansion programmed.[127] The
1965 population of 78,000 might be built up to 172,000 by 1981, if a planned intake of
70,000 is achieved, but clearly such a growth rate implies problems in scale and timing of
job provision, even though there is growth potential in the local industries of mechanical
and electrical engineering.   The Fenland peat basin hinterland of Peterborough typifies
the agrarian problem of the vulnerability of high grade horticulture with its associated food-
processing industries. Within this hinterland King's Lynn is programmed to grow to 55,000
by 1981, with a strong influx of overspill population.

The Cambridge subregion poses the problem of conserving the special qualities of a university town under strong economic growth pressures. The 1952 Cambridgeshire Development Plan proposed to stabilise the town population at 100,000, with an encircling green
belt, and to distribute a further 25,000 people over the immediate hinterland. The 1968
Study recommended a greater build-up at the technological scientific complex of Cambridge, but the government wished to keep its options open. The government decided not
to go ahead with the Ipswich New Town proposal outlined in the 1967 South East Study
but the town has strong growth potential based on its relationship to Greater London and
the nearby Haven Ports-Colchester growth area.

IV.5 The Growth Regions

As far back as the Barlow Commission (1940) the growth potential of the Midlands-South
East axis had been recognised. Indeed during the inter-war period it was the reception area
for the so-called 'drift to the south', it had and still has the cardinal advantages of location
on the rail and motorway network, access to the major gateway ports, and has long had the
sites preferred for a wide range of twentieth-century growth industries. The living environment, for the most part, has escaped the worst of the Industrial Revolution heritage. With
all these assets, confirmed by agglomeration, the economies of scale, the creation of an ever
larger market in the rising population, it is entirely justifiable to speak of 'growth regions'.
Yet the term is not applicable in all parts of the regions and in the late 1960s there have
emerged ominous signs of unemployment locally above the national average. Within a coherent growth zone encompassing large parts of all three regions it is somewhat arbitrary to
treat each separately. In the present state of regional planning and the fomulation of
strategies, however, the intentions of each economic planning council must be taken into
account. They will be found to be different and, it may be thought, still insufficiently interrelated.

The East Midlands (figure 1.13): Both major reports by the East Midlands economic planning council [128] strike a confident note. It lies in the heartland of England, nodally located
astride four major national communications arteries: the M1 and A1(M), and the East

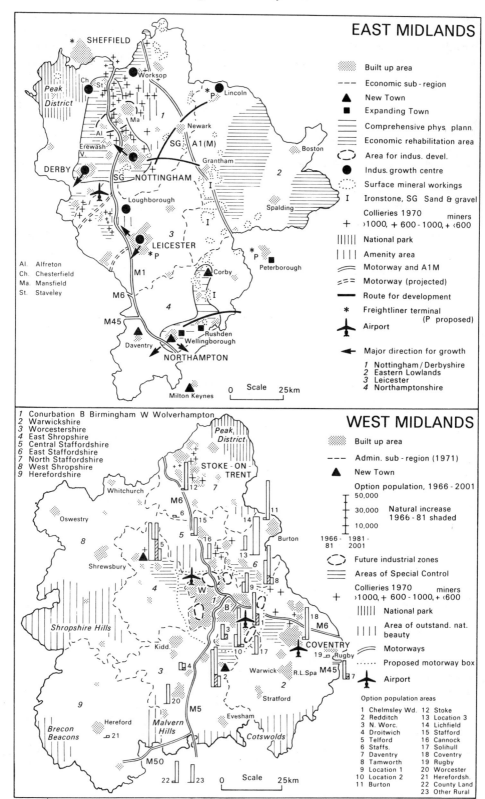

Figure 1.13 The Midlands

Coast and the electrified Euston-Manchester-(Glasgow) rail links. It is equally well-connected
to the national power systems, and has the most striking regional concentration of thermal
electricity generation. The industrial structure has strong representation of key national
growth industries, in engineering and electrical products, and its industrial cities are sufficiently close-knit to permit linkages and economies of scale to develop. The strong population growth trend is a stimulus to further economic development, and regional unemployment levels have been consistently below the national average. Unlike the West Midlands or
the South East, the East Midlands has no single massive and congested conurbation to dominate its development strategy. Not least among its many assets are reserves of space for
industrial and urban development, or redeployment of people and work. Provided its economy remains vigorous and well-balanced the region should make a growing contribution to
national prosperity and may well accommodate a significantly larger share of the UK population by the end of the century.

On the other hand the region is somewhat lacking in coherence, not only by virtue of
its internal diversity, but also because there are powerful and independent economic
influences just beyond its borders. The metropolitan influence is strongly felt in the Northampton subregion, only 60 miles (96 km) from London, and its growth potential has also
to be measured against that of nearby Milton Keynes or Peterborough. The influence of
Sheffield penetrates southwards to Chesterfield, whilst Greater Birmingham is a powerful
magnet to the south-west of the region. In many ways the divided state of Lincolnshire,
with Lincoln a border town of the East Midlands, is the most vexatious of all, not least
because of the prospects of major estuarine developments on Humberside to the north.
In the face of these many conflicting pulls around the perimeter the East Midlands has
sought a corporate identity with the creation of many regional bodies and the strengthening
of others. Nevertheless the city-based loyalties are strong and local government reform
is likely to prove a valuable precursor to more effective regional planning.

Diversity in the East Midlands economy has overall been a force for stability, but not
all parts of the region are prosperous or have equal prospects. There are declining coalfield
settlements in both the Erewash valley and in Leicestershire and a general subregional
employment restructuring problem in many parts of the East Midlands coalfield. The
decrease in agricultural jobs has led to unemployment and outmigration, particularly in the
Eastern Lowlands subregion, whilst job loss in traditional industries such as hosiery or footwear affects the fortunes of specialised towns outside the main Nottingham-Derby-Leicester
manufacturing belt. However the regional planners are confident that, with the intermediate
area status granted to the most seriously affected localities in 1969 and extended recently,
the East Midlands has sufficient growth momentum to take care of most of these problems
within its borders. There is, however, likely to be some difficulty in phasing employment
growth in newer industries, such as electrical goods or light engineering, with redundancies
in declining industries, and in creating the new jobs within daily travelling distance of the
old. In particular, there is the prospect of large redundancies in the Nottinghamshire coalfield but the area of most rapid employment growth is to be in the Northampton subregion.
Here there will be competition with the overspill population scheduled to come from the
Greater London area.

The population growth momentum of the East Midlands is due to accelerate. Already
between 1961 and 1970 some 6,000 net migrants were being added annually, and natural
increase rates in a population with a youthful age structure were high. On the most optimistic estimates net inmigration will rise to 15,000 per annum up to 1981, with no
allowance made for the likely effects of inmigration from overseas. The population capacities for growth by 1981 are high in all subregions: Northampton +200,000, with a strong
inmigration of overspill population; Leicester +115,000; Nottingham-Derby +355,000; and
the Eastern Lowlands, +60,000. There are likely to be two powerful constraints, however,
arising from the massive public investment which would be required to effect such dramatic

changes, and the uncertainty as to the volume and intentions of mobile industries in a period during which development areas have been assured of a continuing priority for government locational aid.

The prospects for growth in employment are the most impressive in engineering and the electrical industries, though a shadow has recently passed over the prospects for aero-engine manufacture. Engineering in particular is extremely diverse and there are many growth firms, both large and small. Such an industrial group is polygamous in its linkages but generally capable of being persuaded to locate in the interests of regional planning. Chemical manufactures are underrepresented, with only one firm making man-made fibres, and knitting also has good job prospects. It is however rather to the possibilities of fast growth in services that attention has been turning recently.[129] Hitherto the ration in service jobs has been below the national average (38.6 per cent, East Midlands; 49.7 per cent, national), but it has been estimated that by 1981 perhaps one quarter of the regional labour force may be in office employment. Rejuvenation of areas with declining industries, though, will still be dependent on attracting mobile manufacturing units, the base upon which service and office jobs can develop. The proposed pattern of physical development includes concentration of some of the growth originating in Derby or Nottingham into the Alfreton-Mansfield area, and part of that from Sheffield into the Chesterfield-Worksop area; the continued expansion of Leicester as a free-standing town and Loughborough as a technological centre; the creation of a new industrial subregion around Northampton; and a readiness to encourage small developments in Newark, Grantham and possibly other Lincolnshire towns as a base for later expansion.

The Northampton subregion is likely to show the most dramatic growth during the next decade[130] principally as the result of overspill schemes from the South East and West Midlands. At Northampton the target of the Development Corporation is for expansion from 124,000 to between 213,000 and 222,000 by 1981; at Corby New Town. from 43,000 to 87,000 by 1989 and 105,000 by 1998; at Wellingborough from 31,860 to 91,000 by 1981; and at Daventry from 6,690 to 36,600 during the same period. Growth is expressed in population terms rather than in rate of prospective job expansion. With the limited range of mobile industry nationally and the built-in problems of decline in the footwear industry, which employs 40 per cent of those in manufacturing and is dominant at Wellingborough and Kettering, there is also clearly going to be a difficult restructuring problem. The targets for Corby are the only figures to have firm Ministerial approval as yet, but there also is a need for diversification in an overspecialised steel town, with an inadequate range of jobs for both men and women.

The Leicester subregion may well contain one million by the end of the century. During the period 1951-66 employment rose sharply, in spite of contractions in agriculture, the hosiery and footwear industries and a stringent policy on the release of Industrial Development Certificates. Growth came mostly from the establishment of new industries such as light engineering, electronics and some of the distributive trades, the latter strongly influenced by the northward extension of the M1. The 1969 Subregional Plan [131] recommended concentration of expected growth in and around Greater Leicester, with greater emphasis on suburban locations. It also proposed the development of two growth corridors, a more substantial one to the north-west, linking up with and diffusing growth towards the declining coalfield, and a lesser corridor towards the south-west. Nottingham and Derby are the complementary industrial poles of their subregion, which includes half the population and many of the more serious problems of the East Midlands. Nottingham has the more diverse economy, with emphasis on lighter consumer goods, including textiles and tobacco; Derby is a centre for capital goods, with half its manufacturing employment in vehicles, 8 per cent in textiles and 7 per cent in engineering. Northwards there stretches a compact mining and industrial zone, linking in the north with the outskirts of Sheffield. Within this zone the western portion, in the Erewash and Rother valleys, has the more difficult problems of landscape and settlement renewal, restructuring of employment and stabilisation of communities in an area where coal mining and industrial decline have been endemic. Further east the collieries are larger but mining decline has spread and there is a need for balanced employment to be brought in for settlements which are scattered, shapeless and often deficient in basic amenities. Prospects for this area are strengthened by its location astride the M1 routeway and the London-Leeds rail line.

The Subregional study (1969)[132] ambitiously recommended a major growth zone for the Mansfield-Alfreton area, with new city forms and a population which might rise to at least 260,000 by 1986 and maybe 350,000 by the end of the century. The functions of Nottingham and Derby were to develop in complementary fashion, whilst other growth points were recommended for West Hallam, west of Ilkeston (for some growth from Derby or Nottingham), and between Staveley and Renishaw.

As in so many economic planning regions the Eastern Lowlands is a somewhat neglected rural counterpart to the urban-industrial complex in the west. The local economy is based on agriculture, particularly so along the eastern coastal area where the local market town economy has been undermined by reductions in manpower. The Subregional study (1971)[133] distinguishes this more rural zone as having sparse population, low density of small or dispersed settlements, low rateable values and small scale local finances. Depopulation has been continuing, but the Holland County Council has worked out an ingenious and inter-related pattern of rural growth points for stabilising the rural economy.[134] A transitional zone in the western half of the Lowlands comes under the influence of towns either on its periphery or outside the East Midlands. The economic planning council speaks cautiously of growth possibilities at Grantham, Newark and Retford along the main communications axis, but higher priorities are likely to be conferred elsewhere. The expansion of Peterborough and the prospective major estuarine growth on south Humberside also cast their shadows.

West Midlands (figure 1.13): In the general nature of their regional development problems the West Midlands have certain features in common with the South East. Both have traditionally been areas of faster and, until recently, stable economic growth, with lower than average unemployment and a persistent attraction for migrants from other areas of the UK, or from overseas. Each has at its heart a major conurbation, Birmingham-Black Country and Greater London respectively. With rather more than 40 per cent of the regional population in the statutory conurbation in each case (Birmingham-Black Country, 46 per cent; Greater London, 43 per cent, 1971) the problems of these great city clusters dominate those of the region, and tend to take precedence, some would say excessively so, in the formulation of regional strategies. Furthermore the West Midlands has shared with the South East a nodal location on the main axes of economic growth in the UK since the early 1930s. later confirmed by the development of the motorway network and the electrification of the main railway route northwest from Euston. In both cases the conurbations and their hinterlands are so bound into the national economy, and provide so much of its growth momentum and potential, that it is vital that the strategies for both regions should develop from a framework of national rather than regional growth priorities. Policies for each of these growth regions should seek to maximise their contribution to the solution of regional problems elsewhere in the UK, but without detriment to their own prospects and with adequate priority for meeting their own difficult internal problems of redistributing a growing volume of people and work. The complicated balancing act implied by what seem at first sight conflicting objectives can be interpreted through successive phases of post-war government location policies, but the overall interim verdict must be that the compromise achieved thus far has indeed benefited the development areas, but now begins to threaten the vital growth momentum in the Midlands and the South East and their potential for powering major intraregional shifts of economic growth between now and the end of the century.

There are, however, significant differences in scale, industrial and services structure, location and overseas role as between the West Midlands and the South East. The West Midlands with 5.1 million people (1971) has less than one-third the population of the South East, and the Birmingham-Black Country conurbation, 2.3 millions in 1971, is only one-third the size of Greater London. The West Midlands and the South East share an economic structure with diverse fast growth sectors but the composition is essentially different: West Midlands, 53 per cent in manufacturing, 44 per cent in services (1970); the South East, 32 per cent and 66 per cent respectively. The national and international role of Greater London needs no emphasising, but it contrasts with a greater dependence on manufacturing, and indeed on a narrower range of industries in the West Midlands. Not only has Greater London been the seat of national decision-taking, but it has also had an economic structure less vulnerable to the growth restriction on manufacturing industry which has been the fundament of government location policies for the two regions since the war.

Two issues are thus peculiarly important for effective regional planning in the West Midlands: the extent to which economic, and particularly industrial growth generated in the region can be used to regional rather than national advantage; and the growth pressures likely to be generated along the communications axes passing through the region. A correct assessment on both will determine the degree of success of both the sector and the spatial regional strategies published in 1971.[135] The north-west to south-east axis is dominant at present and confirmed by the M1-M6 line and the Euston-Manchester-Glasgow electrification scheme; any major growth on Deeside would weight this axis westwards. The north-east to south-west axis may in the longer-term have no less significant effects, if there are to be fast-growth estuarine developments on Humberside and/or on Severnside. The 1971 strategy also refers to a U-shaped axis from Merseyside through the West Midlands and northwards to Sheffield, encompassing urban centres with common problems and constraints, which might be relieved by a coherent policy for growth. The effect of nodal position in relation to these axes has been to generate growth and to channel it along corridors radiating from the conurbation, whilst reducing travel times and permitting greater mobility and flexibility in strategic proposals.

As always the problems and potential for growth are concerned with people and work. The West Midlands have long had a natural increase rate above the average, a youthful population with a strong representation of young adults, and an overall net inmigration balance. Between 1961 and 1970 the population rose by 5 per cent and there was an average net inmigration of 6,000 persons per annum; gross migration flows were considerably more, some 100,000 passing across the region's boundaries between 1961 and 1966 alone. Even with the reduced longer-term population targets for the end of the century the West Midlands are likely to have 6.4 millions, with 40 per cent of the growth coming before 1981. The scale and problem implied by such a growth rate is underlined by the fact that much of it will be generated within the conurbation, which already has major problems of congestion and continuing renewal. As in London a conurbation containment policy has been advocated since the early post-war years [136] but this has already resulted in a major overspill issue which will become more dramatic between now and the end of the century. Thus far relief by overspill redistribution has indeed been modest, only 25,000 being moved by planned overspill between 1945 and 1965. The estimated overspill population to be relocated between 1966 and the end of the century is no less than 867,000, some 154,000 being moves between subregions outside the conurbation. The sheer scale of such redistribution is staggering; the fine tuning needed to redistribute work, of the right variety, to the right place at the right time is no less problematical. It is indeed the relative immobility of workplaces allied with outward dispersal of Birmingham-Black Country residences, that explains the sharp rise in commuting to work, no less than 58 per cent of movements using the private car (1966, 83,500; 1981 estimated 190,000; 2001, estimated 330,000). The impracticability of accommodating such a massive journey to work is a determining imperative in any strategy formulation.

The economic prosperity of the West Midlands rests essentially upon four manufacturing sectors: engineering and electrical goods, £486 million net output 1968; vehicles, £426 million; metal goods, £309 million; and metal manufactures, £263 million. Together these provided 70 per cent of the net output in all manufacturing, and the region has long been distinctive for its pattern of close and proliferating industrial linkages. This has made manufacturers reluctant to develop new capacity outside the region, or indeed in many cases, even outside the conurbation. The extent of subregional specialisation by industry is well-known and introduces further rigidities: the conurbation, with metal-using industries, motor vehicle manufacture, electrical engineering, metal manufacture and small metal fabrication; the Coventry belt, with motor vehicles, electrical and mechanical engineering and aerospace industries; North Staffordshire, with pottery manufacture, engineering and electrical goods. Immobility tends to be underpinned by the localisation of skilled labour and, for all these reasons, industrial moves have been less than desirable to fulfil regional planning objectives. Between 1960 and 1965 only 1,000 per annum went to other sub-regions, though it is expected that 29,000 manufacturing and 37,000 service jobs might be moved out between 1967 and 1981. Restructuring of industry is continuing within the conurbation but newer kinds of employment tend to grow rather in areas where decline is reducing labour in traditional employment. The greatest pressures for growth are on the conurbation rim and it is there that the 1971 strategy envisages regrouped major industrial zones.

The 1971 strategy appeared in two separate studies, an economic appraisal from the regional economic planning council and a more general strategy from the local authorities planning consortium. The planning council study makes a strong case for greater regional powers to promote economic growth and greater autonomy for local industrialists to choose their locations. It also emphasises that the economic health of the conurbation is the most vital regional issue and that this should have at least parity in shared economic growth with other subregions, New Towns or expanded towns for the remainder of this century. The argument is that the advantages of agglomeration, the linkages and the growth prospects are greater in the conurbation and that industry cannot easily be made more mobile without unacceptable economic loss.

This thinking contrasts with that for Greater London or indeed even with that of the 1970 strategic plan for the South East, where decentralisation and the development of powerful counter-magnets on the perimeter of the region are a major strategic proposal. The limited decentralisation desirable from Birmingham and the Black Country is, however, a continuing theme in West Midlands regional planning since the war. Certainly the re-zoning of industry in the five 'comprehensive redevelopment areas' of central Birmingham, or the clearance of dereliction in the Black Country are both impressive achievements, and the preservation of a green belt around the conurbation is no less so. On the other hand, the limited success in building up the New Towns at Telford (1968 in its present form) and Redditch (1964) and the small-scale of overspill redistribution thus far make the 1971 plan seem remarkably ambitious.

The 1971 local authorities' study is exceptionally thoroughgoing. It defines an option population of 1,021,000 by the year 2001 which will need to be located in relation to the basic growth which is to be expected anyway. Figure 1.13 shows the proposed allocation of the option population to 23 localities, differentiating the growth allocated for 1966-81 and that for 1981-2001. No less than 87 per cent of the growth is allocated to the 'central urban complex', a zone larger than the present conurbation and bounded by Stafford-Worcester-Telford-conurbation-Coventry. The locational pulls of the north-west to south-east axis are admitted and the schemes already committed, e.g. at Chelmsley Wood, are reinforced by growth just outside the conurbation at locations 1 and 2. These developments will function as part of the conurbation in the early years due to limited employment mobility, but later will link with more distant sites. The Lichfield-Burton zone and growth in the Coventry belt are logical responses to economic development pressures, but there is no coordinated growth point policy for outer settlements or subregions. The study sees the urban fabric of the West Midlands as too closely-knit to permit islands of growth to develop independently.

The strategy is thus very conurbation-orientated, identifying there the nodal points for longer-term economic growth, even admitting the shorter-term and continuing problem of renewal, restructuring and elimination of pockets of serious deprivation. Around the central city activities there will be new industrial zones on the conurbation rim, flanked by service industry growth corridors from Solihull to Redditch on the south and Sutton Coldfield to Lichfield on the north.

Critique of the 1971 strategy documents has pointed out the absence of policies for the North Staffordshire subregion or for the rural economies of the western and southern subregions. The impression is that what is good for the conurbation must be good for the West Midlands, just as what is good for the West Midlands must surely be in the national interest.

The South East (figure 1.14): With almost one-third of the UK population (1971, 17.1 millions), the greatest concentration of fast growth services and manufacturing, and the most favoured nodal location at the hub of a radial communications network within the UK, facing Europe and overseas, it is not surprising that the South East is uniquely important in British regional planning. The basic issue is the extent to which Greater London is to be permitted to make its distinctive and vital contribution to the national economy, with least detriment and indeed maximum stimulus to policies of regional balance or social justice for other parts of the UK. Allied with this is the question of how, if at all, the growth pressures throughout the South East may or should be controlled or channelled, and how far the growth of Greater London should be restrained, not only in the interests of its citizens, but also those of the region and the nation.

There has been no unanimity of view on these matters. As far back as 1940 the Barlow Commission Report spoke of 'the continued drift of the industrial population to London and the Home Counties as a social, economic and strategic problem demanding attention'. Between 1921 and 1951 there had been a 30 per cent growth in employment in Greater London compared with only 19 per cent nationally. The role of London had grown steadily, nationally and internationally, and there was fast growth in a wide range of manufacturing and services. The arguments against longer-term continuing growth concerned physical and mental health, on both of which counts London came out well — overcrowding and poor housing — but slum clearance and urban renewal had greatly decreased this problem; air pollution and environmental hazards; the social costs of congestion, traffic and journey to work; strategic issues of the vulnerability of large population concentrations; and wider issues, such as the promotion of regional balance in the UK or the rising strength of provincial regionalism.[137] Many of these issues are town planning problems, though indissolubly inter-linked with wider regional questions.

The Abercrombie Greater London Plan [138] set London within its regional context and ambitiously sought: first, to plan for a stabilised population of ten millions in the plan area; secondly, to reduce urban sprawl by establishing a green belt; thirdly, to reduce net residential density in London by a massive overspill programme to relocate some 750,000 from the LCC area and a further 500,000 from areas outside, to a ring of New Towns and expanded towns beyond the green belt. The plan was approved in 1947, with raised population targets, but several basic assumptions proved to be false. Employment was not effectively controlled by restrictions on new industries in the London area; indeed no less than 52 per cent of all new employment growth in the UK, 1952-8, took place in the South East and 32 per cent in London. Much of the manufacturing growth was in the outer urban ring, whilst the inner ring lost jobs heavily; Central London attracted much of the growth in services, and there was a massive increase in commuting, especially to office

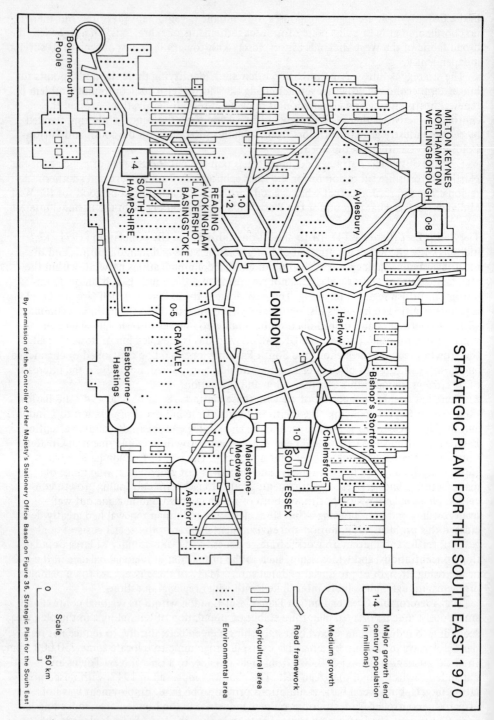

Figure 1.14   South East: Strategic Plan (1970)
               Source: Fig. 35, *Strategic Plan for the South East*
               (HMSO 1970).

employment. Secondly, the overspill movement fell short of expectations: in 1946-61 the New Towns took 235,000 but not all came from London and many who did so commuted back to work; the expanded towns took only 28,000 through overspill schemes in the same period. Thus the interdiction policy on growth in London and the South East largely failed. The government did not press restrictions for fear of damaging national economic growth or the export trade. Many central services could not effectively be decentralised and, overall, the growth pressures had been much greater than anticipated. In particular, there had been an unexpected surge in the national birth rate in the mid 1950s and a sharp influx of immigrants from overseas.

In the early 1960s a more rigorous restriction policy came through the Local Employ-ment Acts, but the growth in service jobs continued largely unchecked, since only new office space was controlled. Growth was especially fast in technological services, design and development, and in new manufactures, such as light engineering, vehicles or electro-nics. Indeed economic growth generally was more rapid and structural than the plan process could acommodate. Between 1948 and 1959 the LCC had licensed no less than 50 million ft^2 (5.3 million m^2) of new office space. There had been some movement out by manufacturing firms (-80,000 jobs, 1960-4) but these jobs were more than replaced by the growth in construction (+28,000) and services (+169,000) in the same period. The Outer Metropolitan Area (OMA), beyond the GLC boundaries but within 40 miles of London, increased in population by 40 per cent from 1951-66, the product of the first generation of New Towns, the strong inmigration from other parts of the UK and its own youthful age structure. The Outer South East (OSE) began to grow more rapidly during the 1960s and regional planning has since become increasingly concerned with allocations of growth, in population and employment, as between the concentric zones around Greater London.

The South East Study (1962)[139] proposed a second generation of New Towns and major town expansions in the region, proposals which envisaged some very large concen-trations of people and work between 50 and 100 miles (80 and 160 km) out from Central London. Such major growth might create cities in their own right and act as a series of counter-magnets to the continuing attractions of agglomeration around Greater London. From 1965 office development throughout the metropolitan region was brought under official control, whilst in the following year creation of the South East Economic Planning Council strengthened the regional voice against that of Greater London.

The South East Strategy (1967)[140] had similar policies, but added new priorities: the urban renewal of London; redesign of the transport system, with corridors and orbital roads; stimulus to the large new city regions, to act as counter-magnets to the metropolis; and protection of the countryside. If London was to be more efficient its growth should be restricted to not more than eight millions, whilst the remainder of the South East region should be able to absorb into employment not only its own natural increase, but also most of London's continuing overspill and, additionally, a much reduced immigration from other parts of the UK. Overspill movement by 1981 was estimated at about one million, to be accompanied by decentralisation of work. For the first time overspill was programmed outside the regional boundaries: 500,000 to East Anglia and the East Midlands; 200,000 to the OMA; and 300,000 to the OSE.

A more coherent spatial strategy was postulated by the proposals for radial growth along corridors linking Greater London with the counter-magnet cities. Within the corridors urban growth was to be concentrated in a few localities, and each corridor had parallel major and minor axes. Industrial investment was to be concentrated when possible into medium- and large-scale firms and commuting to London was to be reduced. Rural land was to be conserved, extending the concept underlying the green belt to all parts of the South East.

The 1967 Strategy thus sought to solve the problems inherent in prospective growth of population by 4 millions (A.D. 2001) by spatial allocation within the economic orbit, but not altogether within the boundaries of the South East. Such redeployment of growth was to improve the efficiency of the region, both nationally and internationally, but the effects upon the prospects for less-favoured regions were left uncertain. In short the strategy of 1967 recognised that growth pressures in the South East were too great to be effectively countermanded, and that economic growth had displaced welfare as the fundament of regional policy.

The strategic plan for the South East (1970),[141] with its reports of studies,[142] affords the first definitive tripartite regional planning study, the product of central government, regional planning council and board, and local authorities. The strategy (figure 1.14) is primarily concerned with the period after 1981, by which time the regional population is likely to be 18.6 million (+1.5 million), up to the year 2001 (estimated population 21.5 millions, +4.5 millions). By 1981 the Greater London population is likely to be 7.3 millions, that of the OMA 6.2 millions and the OSE 5.2 millions. In other words there will be a decline in Greater London, a slower growth in the OMA and faster growth in the OSE.

The planned redevelopment and rehabilitation of London remains the central planning issue.[143] Even in world terms this is an exceedingly complicated problem, at the heart of which lie the difficulties of sustaining an adequate but not excessive concentration of jobs, particularly service jobs in central London. There is currently a suggestion that decline in employment is going on there more rapidly than is desirable for economic health. Additionally there is the need to strengthen London's national and international role in finance, commerce, administration, tourism and culture, which necessarily implies a rising crescendo of investment in land and buildings. At the same time the needs of the less privileged who live in Inner London must be catered for.

A main feature of the 1971 strategy is confirmation of development at a limited number of major growth areas at varying distances from London, using existing or planned urban settlements as bases for growth. The far-sighted corridor concept has been abandoned in favour of a more flexible strategy, to allocate growth both within and outside the London metropolitan region, according to the changing needs of the times. With slow growth, the three designated areas: Reading-Wokingham-Aldershot-Basingstoke; South Essex; and the Crawley area are likely to absorb a higher proportion. If faster growth, then the South Hampshire[144] or Milton Keynes-Northampton-Wellingborough[145] schemes might be accelerated, so that these self-contained counter-magnet cities might begin to play their role earlier and more substantially.

Additional flexibility in the plan is to come from the expansion of a number of medium-sized employment centres, which might be used to relieve unacceptable pressures in the major growth areas or compensate for failure to achieve desired rates of growth. Such smaller centres would also assist in the restructuring of the metropolitan region. Greater London is to 'accommodate the maximum number of residents consistent with the achievement of improved housing conditions and improved environmental standards at reasonable cost'. It is further intended to ensure that commuting does not increase further and this means phasing the outward movement of jobs with that of population. Hitherto there has been optimism on this point, in contrast to the views for Birmingham and the Black Country. Tentative estimates are for 15,000-20,000 mobile jobs a year in manufacturing and a similar number in services needed to phase in with population growth in areas selected for substantial population growth. The consultants' advice was that all parts of the South East were acceptable to industrialists, provided labour was available and the environment reasonable. The strategy will succeed or fail on the ability to adjust job relocation with population redistribution. Its novelty lies in the flexible approach, even if the preferred development pattern is less imaginative and more permissive than the 1967 Strategy. Flexibility will certainly be at a premium if there are to be any further decisions such as that to create the third London airport at Foulness (Maplin).

IV.6 A Final Note

The review of regional strategies indicates the diversity of policy mixes, the different stages of preparation and indeed varied degrees of forcefulness in presentation and advocacy. None of the strategies published thus far has been fully costed, all lack adequate context of national priorities, and there is a conspicuous absence of sufficient liaison between adjacent economic planning boards and councils in the formulation of what at times appear to be mutually conflicting proposals. Furthermore it is only since 1969 that published strategies have quantified and weighed alternative options. The techniques have been lacking until recently and it must be said that, even today, when a preferred strategy is advanced it tends to bear the hallmarks of political compromise.

Yet the strategy documents illustrate the growing strength of corporate regionalism, a sense of economic, social or political identity at less than UK but more than local authority level. Just as governments in the future need to set a more adequate framework for spatial, economic and social affairs nationally, with more coherent regional priorities, so too these priorities will need increasingly to take account of the legitimate aspirations of the component nations and provinces of the UK space to a fuller, more prosperous life and a better living environment.

FURTHER READING

Aldcroft, D H and Fearon, P, *Economic Growth in Twentieth Century Britain,* (London 1969).

Beckerman, W, *et al. The British Economy in 1975,* National Institute of Social and Economic Research, 23 (1965).

Chisholm, M D I, (ed), *Resources for Britain's Future,* (Harmondsworth 1972)

London and Cambridge Economic Service, *The British Economy, Key Statistics, 1900-66.*

Prest, A R, *The UK Economy: A Manual of Applied Economics,* (London 1966)

Youngson, A J, *Britain's Economic Growth, 1920-66,* (London 1968).

REFERENCES

1   W Smith, *An Economic Geography of Great Britain* (London 1949).
      J Wreford Watson and J B Sissons (eds), *The British Isles, a Systematic Geography* (Edinburgh 1964).
      L D Stamp and S H Beaver, *The British Isles: a Geographic and Economic Survey* (London 1971).
      G.H Dury, *The British Isles, a Systematic and Regional Geography* (London 1968).
2   Department of the Environment, *Long Term Population Distribution in Great Britain* (HMSO 1971).
3   R H Best, *The Major Land Uses in Britain* (Wye College 1959).
      R H Best and J T Coppock, *The Changing Uses of Land in Britain* (London 1962).
      L D Stamp, *The Land of Britain: its Use and Misuse* (London 1962).
4   M D I Chisholm and G Manners (eds), *Spatial Policy Problems of the British Economy* (Cambridge 1971)
      J W House, 'Geographers, Decision-takers, and Policy Makers', in M Chisholm and B Rodgers (eds), *Essays in Human Geography* (London 1973), p. 272-305.
5   *Royal Commission on Local Government in England,* 1966-9 (Redcliffe-Maud Report) Cmnd 4040 (HMSO 1969).
6   J W House, 'Future Trends of Regionalism in Britain', *British Journal of Marketing,* 3 (1969), pp.176-82.
      D J Robertson, 'A Nation of Regions?', *Urban Studies,* 2.2 (1965), pp. 121-36.

7   M J Wise, 'The City Region', *Advancement of Science,* **22,** 104 (1966), pp. 571-88.
       R Grieve and D J Robertson, 'The City and the Region', *Univ of Glasgow, Social
       and Economic Studies,* Occasional Papers 2 (1966)

8   C B Fawcett, *Provinces of England* (1919), revised by W G East and S W Wooldridge
       (London 1960).
       E W Gilbert, 'Practical Regionalism in England and Wales', *Geographical Journal,*
       94 (1939) pp. 29-44.

9   G P Wibberley, 'Some Aspects of Problem Rural Areas in Britain', *Geographical
       Journal,* **120** (1954), pp. 43-61.

10   V H Woodward, 'Regional Social Accounts for the United Kingdom', *NIESR,
       Regional Report I* (Cambridge 1970).

11   A C Hobson, 'The Great Industrial Belt', *Economic Journal,* (1951), pp 562-76.
       J N L Baker and E W Gilbert, 'The Doctrine of an Axial Belt in England', *Geographi-
       cal Journal,* **103** (1944), pp. 49-71.

12   M D I Chisholm, 'Freight Costs, Industrial Location and Regional Development',
       Ch. 8 in M D I Chisholm and G Manners (eds), *Spatial Policy Problems of the
       British Economy* (Cambridge 1971), pp. 213-44.

13   G C Archibald, 'Regional Multiplier Effects in the UK', *Oxford Economic Papers* (196

14   A E Smailes, 'The Urban Hierarchy in England and Wales', *Geography,* **29,** (1944),
       pp. 41-51.
       A E Smailes, 'The Urban Mesh of England and Wales', *Institute of British Geographers*
       Publication 11 (1946), pp. 87-107.
       A E Smailes, 'The Analysis and Delimitation of Urban Fields', *Geography,* **32** (1947)
       pp. 151-61.
       F H W Green, 'Town and Country in Northern Ireland', *Geography,* **34** (1949),
       pp. 89-95.
       F H W Green, 'Urban Hinterlands in England and Wales. An Analysis of Bus Services',
       Geographical Journal, **116** (1950), pp. 64-88.

15   F H W Green, 'Bus Services as an Index to Changing Urban Hinterlands', *Town Plan-
       ning Review,* **22,** 4 (1952), pp. 345-56.

16   W I Carruthers, 'A Classification of Service Centres in England and Wales', *Geogra-
       phical Journal,* **123** (1957), pp. 371-85.
       W I Carruthers, 'Service Centres in Greater London', *Town Planning Review,* **33**
       (1962), pp. 5-31.

17   C A Moser and W Scott, *British Towns: A Statistical Study of Their Social and Eco-
       nomic Differences* (Edinburgh 1961).

18   P G Hall, 'Spatial Structure of Metropolitan England and Wales', Ch. 5 in M Chisholm
       and G Manners (eds), *Spatial Policy Problems of the British Economy* (Cambridge
       1971), pp. 96-125.

19   G McCrone, *Regional Policy in Britain* (London 1969).
       NIESR, 'The Regional Problem', *National Institute Economic Review,* **25** (1963),
       pp. 40-57.

20   J W House, 'Margins in Regional Geography: An Illustration from Northern England',
       in J W House (ed), *Northern Geographical Essays* (Newcastle-upon-Tyne 1966),
       pp. 139-56.

21   B E Coates and E M Rawstron, *Regional Variations in Britain* (London 1971).
       B E Coates and E M Rawstron, 'Regional Income and Planning, 1964-5', *Geography,*
       52 (1967), pp. 393-402.

22   P Self, 'North Versus South', *Town and Country Planning,* **33** (1965) pp. 330-6.

23   G McCrone, *Regional Policy in Britain* (London 1969).
       G McCrone, 'The Location of Economic Activity in the UK', *Urban Studies,* **9**
       (1972), pp. 369-75.

L Needleman, 'What are we to do about the Regional Problem?', *Lloyds Bank Review,* **75** (1965), pp. 45-58.

R K Wilkinson and G F Rainnie, 'Criteria for Regional Policy', *Town Planning Review,* **41** (1970), pp. 207-22.

T Wilson (ed), *Papers on Regional Development* (Oxford 1965).

T Wilson, 'Policies for Regional Development', *University of Glasgow Occasional Papers,* **3** (1964).

24   A A L Caesar, 'Planning and the Geography of Great Britain', *Advancement of Science,* **21** (1964), pp. 1-11.

25   *Royal Commission on the Distribution of the Industrial Population,* Report, Cmnd 6153 (HMSO 1940).

26   *Local Employment Acts 1960 to 1966. Eighth Annual Report by the Board of Trade* (HMSO 1968), p.8.

27   *Central Scotland. A Programme for Development and Growth,* Cmnd 2188 (HMSO 1963).

The North East: A Programme for Regional Development and Growth, Cmnd 2206 (HMSO 1963).

28   *Location of Offices Bureau, Annual Report 1971-72,* 1972, p.8.

J Rhodes and A Khan, 'Office Dispersal and Regional Policy', *University of Cambridge, Department of Applied Economics, Occasional Papers,* **30** (1971).

29   *The Reshaping of British Railways* (HMSO 1963).

30   P Turnbull, 'Regional Economic Planning Councils and Boards', *Journal of the Town Planning Institute,* **53** (1967), pp. 41-9.

31   South East Joint Planning Team, *Strategic Plan for the South East* (HMSO 1970).

32   *The Intermediate Areas* Cmnd 3998 (HMSO 1969).

33   *Industrial and Regional Development* Cmnd 4942 (HMSO 1972).

34   A C Campbell and W D C Lyddon, *Tayside: Potential for Development* (HMSO 1970).

Central Unit for Environmental Planning, *Humberside: A Feasibility Study* (HMSO 1969).

Central Unit for Environmental Planning, *Severnside: A Feasibility Study* (HMSO 1971).

T W Freeman, *Geography and Regional Administration* (London 1968).

35   B C Smith, *Regionalism in England* 3 vols. (Acton Society Trust 1964-5).

36   E W Gilbert, 'Boundaries of Local Government Areas', *Geographical Journal,* **111** (1948), pp. 172-206.

E W Gilbert, 'Practical Regionalism in England and Wales', *Geographical Journal,* **94** (1939), pp. 29-44.

J G Thomas, 'Local Government Areas in Wales', *Geography,* **37** (1952), pp. 9-19.

J P Mackintosh, *The Devolution of Power* (Harmondsworth 1968).

37   *Royal Commission on Local Government in England 1966-9* (Redcliffe-Maud Report) Cmnd 4040 (HMSO 1969).

Royal Commission on Local Government in Greater London (HMSO 1960).

Report of the Royal Commission on Local Government in Scotland (Wheatley Commission), Cmnd 4150 (HMSO 1969).

Welsh Office, *The Reform of Local Government in Wales. Consultative Document* (Cardiff HMSO 1970).

Government of Northern Ireland, *The Reshaping of Local Government: Statement of Aims* Cmnd 517 (Belfast HMSO 1967).

Government of Northern Ireland, *The Reshaping of Local Government: further proposals* Cmnd 530 (Belfast HMSO 1969).

Report of the Review Body on Local Government in Northern Ireland, Cmnd 546 (Belfast HMSO 1970).

38   J R James, J W House and P G Hall, 'Local Government Reform in England', *Geographical Journal,* **136** (1970), pp. 1-23.

D. Thomas *et al*, 'The Redcliffe-Maud Report: Royal Commission on Local Government in England 1966-9', *Area, Institute of British Geographers*, **4** (1969) pp. 1-20

39   *Reform of Local Government in England* Cmnd 4276 (HMSO 1970).

40   *Local Government in England, Government Proposals for Reorganisation* Cmnd 4584 (HMSO 1971).

41   Local Government Boundary Commission for England - Designate, *Memorandum on Draft Proposals for New Districts in the English Non-Metropolitan Counties Proposed in the Local Government Bill* (HMSO 1972).

42   Scottish Office, *Reform of Local Government in Scotland* Cmnd 4583 (HMSO 1971)

43   J H Johnson, 'Reorganisation of Local Government in Northern Ireland', *Area, Institute of British Geographers*, **4** (1970), pp. 17-21.

44   South East Joint Planning Team, *Strategic Plan for the South East* (HMSO 1970).

Northern Region

45   J W House, *The North East* (Newton Abbot 1969).
      P J Bowden, 'Regional Problems and Policies in the North East of England', in
          T Wilson (ed), *Papers on Regional Development* (Oxford 1965), pp. 20-39.

46   Secretary of State for Trade, Industry and Regional Development, *The North East: A Programme for Regional Development and Growth* Cmnd 2206 (HMSO 1963).

47   Northern Economic Planning Council, *Challenge of the Changing North* (HMSO 1966).

48   Northern Economic Planning Council, *An Outline Strategy for the North* (NEPC 1969).

49   Northern Economic Planning Council, *Report on Housing Needs for the Northern Region* (NEPC 1971).
      Northern Economic Planning Council, *Regional Ports Survey* (NEPC 1969).
      Northern Economic Planning Council, *Report on Education* Part I (NEPC 1970).

50   J W House (ed), *Papers on Migration and Mobility in Northern England*, 1-11 (University of Newcastle upon Tyne, Department of Geography, 1964-72).

51   B Fullerton, 'The Pattern of Service Industries in North-East England', University of Newcastle upon Tyne, Department of Geography, *Research Series* **3**, (1960).
      B Fullerton, 'Geographical Inertia in the Service Industries: an Example from Northern England', in J W House (ed), *Northern Geographical Essays* (Newcastle upon Tyne 1966), pp. 157-77.

Scotland

52   A K Cairncross (ed), *The Scottish Economy* (Cambridge 1954), p. 1.

53   T L Johnston, N K Buxton and D Mair, *Structure and Growth of the Scottish Economy* (London 1971).
      G McCrone, 'Scotland's Economic Progress, 1951-60: a Study in Regional Accounting', University of Glasgow, *Social and Economic Studies*, **4** (1965).

54   McCrone, *Regional Policy in Britain* Ch. 2, pp. 20-30.

55   Johnston, Buxton and Mair, *Structure and Growth of the Scottish Economy*, p. 69.

56   P Abercrombie and R H Matthews, *Clyde Valley Regional Plan* (HMSO 1949).

57   A Cairncross, *Local Development in Scotland* (Scottish Council 1952).

58   J N Toothill, *Inquiry into the Scottish Economy* (Scottish Council 1961).

59   Scottish Development Department, *A Programme for Development and Growth* Cmnd 2188 (HMSO 1963).

60   G C Cameron and G L Reid, 'Scottish Economic Planning and the Attraction of Industry', University of Glasgow, *Social and Economic Studies,* Occasional Papers **6** (1966).

61   Scottish Office, *The Scottish Economy, 1965 to 1970. A Plan for Expansion* Cmnd
      2864 (HMSO 1966).
      R E Nicoll, 'The Physical Implications of the White Paper on the Scottish Economy,
      1965-70', *Journal of the Town Planning Institute* 52 (1966), pp. 314-8.
62   J H McGuiness, 'Regional Economic Development, Progress in Scotland', *Journal of
      the Town Planning Institute,* 54 (1968), pp. 103-11.
      P Self *et al,* 'Scotland: Planning and Economic Development', *Town and Country
      Planning,* 35 (1967), pp. 265-325.
63   C L W Minay, 'Town Development and Regional Planning in Scotland', *Journal
      Town Planning Institute,* 51(1965), pp. 13-19.
64   Study Team, *West Central Scotland Plan,* Stage A, Draft Report (HMSO 1971).
65   A D Campbell and W D C Lyddon, *Tayside. Potential for Development* (HMSO
      1970).
66   D J Robertson and P E A Johnson-Marshall, *Grangemouth/Falkirk Regional Survey
      and Plan* (Scottish Development Department 1968).
      D J Robertson and P E A Johnson-Marshall, *Lothians. Regional Survey and Plan,*
      2 vols. (Scottish Development Department 1966).
67   Scottish Council, *Oceanspan I: A Maritime-based Development Strategy for a
      European Scotland, 1970-2000* (1970).
68   D I McKay and N K Buxton, 'The North of Scotland Economy: a Case for Rede-
      velopment', *Scottish Journal of Political Economy,* 13 (1965), pp. 23-49.
      M Gaskin, *Survey of the Economy and Development Potential of North East
      Scotland* (Edinburgh HMSO 1968), p. 27.
69   D C Thomson and I Grimble, *The Future of the Highlands* (London 1968).
70   Highlands and Islands Development Board, *Moray Firth. A Plan for Growth in a
      Subregion of the Scottish Highlands* (Jack Holmes Group, Glasgow 1968).
71   Scottish Council, *Lochaber Study* (1968).
72   D Turnock, *Patterns of Highland Development* (London 1970), p. 212.
73   Scottish Development Department, *The Central Borders. A Plan for Expansion,* 2
      vols (HMSO 1968).
74   Scottish Development Department, *A Strategy for South-West Scotland* (HMSO
      1970).
75   Scottish Tourist Board, *Galloway Project* (Strathclyde University 1968).

Wales

76   E G Bowen (ed), *Wales: A Physical, Historical and Regional Geography* (London
      1957), p. 267.
77   M G Lloyd and G F Thomason, *Welsh Society in Transition* (Council for Social
      Service for Wales and Monmouthshire 1963).
78   E Nevin, A R Roe and J I Round, 'The Structure of the Welsh Economy', *Welsh
      Economic Studies,* 4 (University of Wales 1966).
79   C R Tomkins, *Income and Expenditure Accounts for Wales, 1965-68* (Welsh
      Council 1971).
80   Brinley Thomas, 'Economic and Social Planning in Wales', *Journal of the Town
      Planning Institute,* 56 (1970), pp. 262-3.
81   D F Hagger and H W E Davies, 'Regional Planning in South Wales', *Advancement of
      Science,* 18 (1961), pp. 65-73.
82   *Wales. The Way Ahead* Cmnd 3334 (HMSO 1867).
83   G Manners, 'Wales. The Way Ahead', *Journal of the Town Planning Institute,* 54
      (1968), pp. 67-9.
84   G Humphrys, *Industrial Britain: South Wales* (Newton Abbot 1972).
85   *A Strategy for Rural Wales* (HMSO 1971).

Welsh Office, *Depopulation in Mid Wales* (HMSO 1964).

Development Commission, *Mid Wales. An Assessment of the Impact of the Development Commission Factory Programme* (HMSO 1972).

E Houston and R Jenkins, *The Heartland. A Plan for Mid Wales* (London 1965).

Northern Ireland

86   Ministry of Housing and Local Government, *Dee Crossing Study, Phase I* (HMSO 1967).

87   J V Simpson, 'Regional Analysis: the Northern Ireland Experience', *Irish Economic and Social Review* (1971), p. 528.

88   K S Isles and N Cuthbert, *An Economic Survey of Northern Ireland* (Belfast HMSO 1957).

89   *Economic Development in Northern Ireland* Cmnd 479 (Belfast HMSO 1965).

90   R H Matthew, *Belfast Regional Survey and Plan,* 2 vols. (Belfast HMSO 1964).

91   *Northern Ireland Development Programme 1970-5* (Belfast HMSO 1970).

Government of Northern Ireland, *Northern Ireland Development Programme 1970-5, Government Statement* Cmnd 547 (HMSO 1970).

92   J Munce Partnership, *Londonderry Area Plan* (1968).

93   Northern Ireland Ministry of Agriculture, *The Changing Structure of Agriculture* (HMSO 1970).

Yorkshire and Humberside

94   Yorkshire and Humberside Economic Planning Council, *A Review of Yorkshire and Humberside* (HMSO 1966).

95   Yorkshire and Humberside Economic Planning Council and Board, *Doncaster: An Area Study* (HMSO 1969).

Yorkshire and Humberside Economic Planning Council and Board, *Halifax and Calder Valley* (HMSO 1968).

Yorkshire and Humberside Economic Planning Council, *Huddersfield and Colne Valley* (HMSO 1969).

96   *The Intermediate Areas* Cmnd 3998 (HMSO 1969).

97   *The Intermediate Areas* para 443, p. 132.

98   *The Intermediate Areas* A Note of Dissent by Professor A J Brown, pp. 155-65.

99   County Council of the West Riding of Yorkshire, *The County Strategy* (WRCC 1969)

County Council of the West Riding of Yorkshire, *The County Strategy for Development* (WRCC 1971).

100 Yorkshire and Humberside Economic Planning Council, *Yorkshire and Humberside Regional Strategy* (HMSO 1970).

101 Yorkshire and Humberside Economic Planning Council, *Growth Industries in the Region* (YEPC 1972).

102 M B Brown, 'The Concept of Employment Opportunity with Special Reference to Yorkshire and Humberside', *Yorkshire Bulletin of Economic and Social Research,* 22, 2 (1970), pp.65-100.

103 W S Atkins and Partners, *The Strategic Future of the Wool Textile Industry,* Economic Development Committee for the Wool Industry (HMSO 1969).

104 Central Unit for Environmental Planning, *Humberside, A Feasibility Study* (HMSO 1969).

105 P Lewis and P N Jones, *Industrial Britain. The Humberside Region* (Newton Abbot 1970).

J Craig, E W Evans and B Showler, 'Humberside: Employment and Migration', *Yorkshire Bulletin of Economic and Social Research,* 22, 2 (1970), pp. 123-42.

The North West

106   D M Smith, *Industrial Britain. The North West,* (Newton Abbot 1969).
     T Nuttall and M F Batty, 'The North West —Problem Area for Regional Planning',
       Town Planning Review, **41** (1970), pp. 372-82.
107   *Merseyside Social and Economic Survey* (Liverpool University 1968).
108   Department of Economic Affairs, *The North West. A Regional Study* (HMSO 1965).
     North West Economic Planning Council, *Housing in the North West Region*
       (NWEPC 1970).
109   Department of Economic Affairs, *The Problems of Merseyside* (HMSO 1965).
110   North West Economic Planning Council, *An Economic Planning Strategy for the*
      North West Region, Strategy I (HMSO 1966).
111   North West Economic Planning Council, *The North West in the Seventies,* Strategy
      II (NWEPC 1968).
112   North West Economic Planning Council, *Derelict Land in the North West* (NWEPC
      1971).
113   *The Intermediate Areas* Cmnd 3998 (HMSO 1969), p. 151.
114   *The Intermediate Areas,* p.159.
115   Ministry of Housing and Local Government, *Central Lancashire. Study for a City*
      (HMSO 1967).
116   R H Matthew *et al, Central Lancashire New Town Proposal. Impact on North East*
      Lancashire (HMSO 1968).

The South West

117   South West Economic Planning Council, *A Region with a Future. A Draft Strategy*
     for the South West (HMSO 1967).
118   A A L Caesar, 'Devon and Cornwall', in G H J Daysh (ed), *Studies in Regional*
      Planning (London 1964), pp. 197-223.
119   Central Unit for Environmental Planning, *Severnside. A Feasibility Study* (HMSO
      1971).
     F Walker, 'Economic Growth on Severnside', *Transactions, Institute of British Geo-*
      graphers, **37** (1965), pp. 1-13.
120   J N H Britton, *Regional Analysis and Economic Geography. A Case Study of Manu-*
      facturing in the Bristol Region (London 1967).
121   Ministry of Housing and Local Government, *The Holiday Industry of Devon and*
      Cornwall (HMSO 1970).
122   Devon County Council, *Feasibility Studies,* Barnstaple, Exeter and District, Honiton,
      South Brent and Ivybridge, Tiverton-Sampford Peverell (1966-70).
123   Cornwall County Council, *West Cornwall Study* (Truro 1970).
124   South West Economic Planning Council, *Plymouth Area Study* (SWEPC 1969).
125   J L Braithwaite, 'The Post-War Industrial Development of Plymouth: an Example of
      National Industrial Location Policy', *Transactions, Institute of British Geo-*
      graphers, **45** (1968), pp. 34-50.
     D J Spooner, 'Industrial Movement and the Rural Periphery: the Case of Devon and
      Cornwall', *Regional Studies,* **6**, 2. (1972), pp. 197-215.

East Anglia

126   East Anglia Economic Planning Council, *East Anglia. A Study* (HMSO 1968).
     East Anglia Consultative Committee, *East Anglia. A Regional Appraisal* (EACC 1969).
127   Ministry of Housing and Local Government, *Expansion of Peterborough* (HMSO
      1966).

East Midlands

128 East Midlands Economic Planning Council, *The East Midlands Study* (HMSO 1966).
East Midlands Economic Planning Council, *Opportunity in the East Midlands* (HMSO 1969).

129 M Burrows and S Town, *Office Services in the East Midlands. An Economic and Sociological Study,* 2 vols. (EMPC 1971).
M Gibson and M Pullen, *Retail Trade Patterns in the East Midlands, 1961-81* (EMP 1971).

130 Ministry of Housing and Local Government, *Northampton, Bedford, North Bucks. Study* (HMSO 1966).
Ministry of Housing and Local Government, *Expansion of Northampton* (HMSO 1966).

131 Leicester City Council and Leicestershire County Council, *Leicester and Leicestershire Subregional Planning Study* (Leicester 1969).

132 Nottinghamshire-Derbyshire Subregional Planning Unit, *Nottinghamshire and Derbyshire Sub-regional Study* (1969).

133 K R Fennell, *The Eastern Lowlands Subregional Study,* (Kesteven County Planning Department 1971).

134 Holland County Council, *Rural Policy Structure* (1970).

West Midlands

135 West Midlands Economic Planning Council, *The West Midlands. An Economic Appraisal* (HMSO 1971).
West Midlands Regional Study, *A Developing Strategy for the West Midlands* (WMRS 1971).

136 M J Wise, 'The Birmingham-Black Country Conurbation in its Regional Setting', *Geography,* **57.** 2 (1972), pp. 89-104.
Department of Economic Affairs, *The West Midlands. A Regional Study* (HMSO 1965).
West Midlands Economic Planning Council, *The West Midlands. Patterns of Growth* (HMSO 1967).
Coventry City Council *et al, Coventry-Solihull-Warwickshire. A Strategy for the Subregion* (1971).

South East

137 P G Hall, *London 2000* (London 1963).
138 P Abercrombie, *Greater London Plan* (HMSO 1945).
139 Ministry of Housing and Local Government, *The South East Study, 1961-81* (HMSO 1964).
140 South East Economic Planning Council, *A Strategy for the South East* (HMSO 1967)
141 South East Joint Planning Team, *Strategic Plan for the South East* (HMSO 1970).
142 Department of the Environment, South East Joint Planning Studies, vol.I: *Population and Employment;* vol.II: *Social and Economic Aspects;* vol.V: *Report of Economic Consultants Ltd.*(HMSO 1971).
143 Greater London Council, *Greater London Development Plan* (1969).
144 Colin Buchanan and Partners, *South Hampshire Study,* 3 vols. (HMSO 1966).
145 *The Plan for Milton Keynes,* 2 vols. (1970).

2

People and Work

I INTRODUCTION

I.1 General Context

In a mature industrial society and long-settled land such as the UK, the population map mirrors environmental, economic and social contrasts and changes in these over both time and space. The population distribution map (fig. 2.1) therefore reveals much of earlier origin as well as more recent trends and forces. Many consequences are still with us from nineteenth-century industrial and urban growth, when population was concentrated by a coal-based, steam-powered and railway-linked economy, and from eighteenth- and nineteenth-century agrarian reform, which resulted in much increased output per unit of land and of manpower, and led to a declining agricultural labour force. Thus, powerful and long-established economic and social forces underlie long-standing population trends: losses from the countryside; a continuing move to urban areas; a progressive focusing on London and the major provincial cities. These pose some of the greatest problems in population and regional planning for the present and the immediate future as they have done for the past century. To these long-established forces have been added variants of specifically twentieth-century origin. More mobile, technologically-based and assembly-line industries which demand access to labour and markets rather than to power or raw materials have broken the dominance of the nineteenth-century industrial regions and drawn population south-eastwards to Greater London and the Midlands. The growing significance of services and commercial activities in the economy have focused a large and increasing section of employment on the conurbations. Increasingly, mass transit systems and greatly augmented car ownership have markedly increased mobility, permitting increasing separation of home and workplace and accentuating the growth of city regions, within which dispersal of housing areas and concentration of jobs are pulling in different directions. Thus, while in the true countryside population has continued to decline, in a growing rural-urban fringe around *all* large cities population has increased rapidly, both through private house-building and, especially since the Second World War, through local authority estates and overspill agreements.

Such trends reflect not only the process of urbanisation, which has been such a prominent feature of the UK since early Victorian times, but also the recent and present inter- and intraregional mobility which is reshaping its real social regions. Population change, in turn, is basic to many aspects of present and future economic, social, political and administrative organisation.

A population of over 55 millions living on only 59·5 million acres (24·0 million ha) much of which is unsuitable for cultivation or settlement, especially in highland Britain, creates densities of population second only in Europe to the Netherlands and among the highest in the world. The position is more severe in England and Wales, as Best has shown.[1] At the beginning of this century only 5 per cent of the land surface was in urban land use but during the inter-war sprawl of towns loss of farmland reached levels of some 62,000 acres (over 25,000 ha) per year. Better planning controls since the war have seen this loss reduced to an average 39,000 acres (15,800 ha) per year. Even so, the

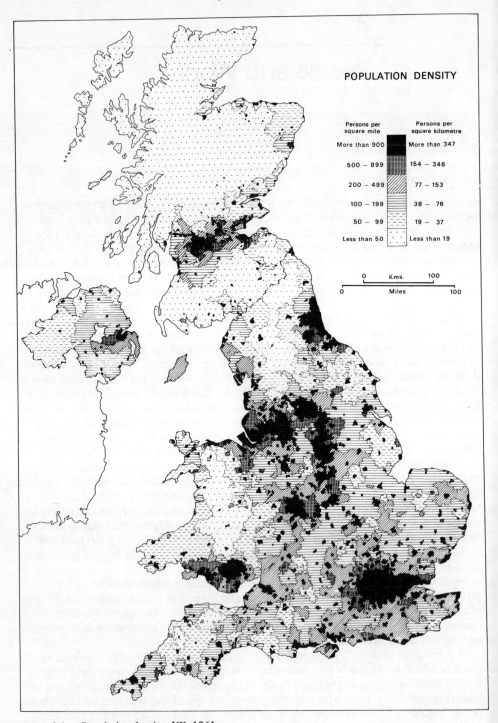

Figure 2.1   Population density, UK, 1961

built-up area of England and Wales had increased from 5 per cent of the total area in 1900 to 10 per cent in 1950 (UK, 1950: 7·3 per cent) and, despite the reduced rate of consumption of land, to over 11 per cent at present (UK, 1965 : 8·5 per cent). At current rates of conversion the proportion of land in urban use in England and Wales could rise to some 15-16 per cent by the end of the century, though for the UK as a whole (11·3 per cent in 2000 AD) the long-term prospect is somewhat less daunting (table 1.3).[2] Moreover, it has been pointed out by Best and Champion that during the 1960s urban growth was greatest around the midland and northern conurbations and, in general, did not correspond closely with the pattern of population change.[3] New house building for existing population has been the dominant force in urban growth since 1951.

Improvements in housing and urban amenities in substandard regions have contributed very considerably to urban demands for land; land for communications, water supplies and recreation, already considerable, will increase, together with demands for industrial sites. It is now increasingly urged that we should not add to the pressures arising from existing population by further population increases, even though in many parts of the UK there is room for more population growth.

In economic terms, however, it may be argued that population is the greatest single asset of the UK, both now and in the future. Among problems in post-war economic growth shortage of labour due to a relative decline of population in the productive age groups led to acute pressure of demand, for both skilled and unskilled workers, and contributed to the considerable influx of immigrants in the late 1950s and early 1960s (see section II.6). While this was in part a product of the age structure of the population, in itself a legacy of demographic trends from the early twentieth century onwards, it undoubtedly contributed to the general feeling in the immediate post-war period that population growth was no bad thing.

I.2   Recent Demographic Trends: Some Basic Factors

Following upon the toll of the First World War on the young men of Britain and its consequent effect on marriage-rates, the economic depression of the early 1930s contributed to the continuing fall in fertility. The crude birth-rate in the UK, which had reached a peak of 35 per 1,000 in the early 1870s, declined gradually to the First World War and fell rapidly in the inter-war years. The idea of the smaller family spread through all sections of society and fertility fell below replacement level in the 1930s. Although population continued to increase slowly, supported by a net gain by migration, the long-term prospects for population growth were poor. A continuing decline in death-rate contributed to a slowly growing, but ageing, population (table 2.1). Hence, the population predictions of the 1930s, almost without exception, were of future decline. The most optimistic forecast of the 1949 Report of the Royal Commission on Population for GB was of a population of 52 million by the end of the century; the least optimistic assumption placed it as low as 41 million.

Three sets of forces have rendered these predictions invalid in the post-1945 period. First, birth-rates increased markedly in the baby boom of the immediate post-war years when crude birth-rates reached an average of 18 per 1000 in 1946-50. Despite considerable fluctuations in birth-rate, involving a fall in the early 1950s, birth-rates have generally remained well above those of the inter-war years (fig. 2.2; table 2.1). General fertility has also increased due to earlier and more universal marriage. In England and Wales the average age of first marriage for women, at 25·5 years in the 1920s and 1930s, fell to less than 25·0 after 1945, and continued to fall in the 1960s to its present level of 22·5 years. Moreover the proportion of women aged 15-49 with experience of marriage increased in England and Wales from 529 per 1000 in 1931 to 700 in 1961, and was 698 in 1969; the equivalent figures for Scotland are 483,677 and 697.

People and Work

TABLE 2.1 Birth, Death and Marriage Rates UK, 1901-71

	1901	1911	1921	1931	1951	1961	1966	1967	1968	1969	1970	1971
Births per 1,000	28·6	24·6	23·1	16·3	15·8	17·8	17·9	17·5	17·1	16·6	16·2	16·2
Fertility rates per 1,000 women 15-44	114·9	99·1	91·5	66·5	73·0	90·1	91·1	88·4	89·8	85·9	84·4	84·4
Percentage illegitimate births	4·2	4·7	4·9	4·8	4·9	5·8	7·7	8·2	8·4	8·4	8·3	8·4
Deaths per 1,000	17·3	14·1	12·7	12·2	12·6	12·0	11·8	11·2	11·9	11·9	11·8	11·6
Male deaths/1,000	18	15	14	13	13	13	12	12	12	13	12	12
Female deaths/1,000	16	13	12	12	12	11	11	11	11	11	11	11
Average age of first marriage												
male	27·2	27·3	27·6	27·4	26·8	25·6	24·9	24·8	24·7	24·7	24·4	24·6
female	25·6	25·6	25·5	25·5	24·6	23·3	22·7	22·7	22·7	22·5	22·5	22·6
Percentage women ever married: 20-24	-	24·0	27·0	25·5	47·3	57·4	58·2	58·2	57·1	57·1	-	-
25-29	-	55·8	58·2	58·4	77·5	84·3	85·5	85·5	85·7	85·7	-	-
40-44	-	81·6	81·6	81·4	85·3	90·1	91·3	91·3	91·5	91·7	-	-

Source: Social Trends 1, (1970), 'Population and Environment' Tables 11 and 13 (to 1969) and on *Registrars' General Quarterly Returns* 1970 and 1971 birth and death rates calculated on the basis of the revised mid-year estimates for 1971

United Kingdom

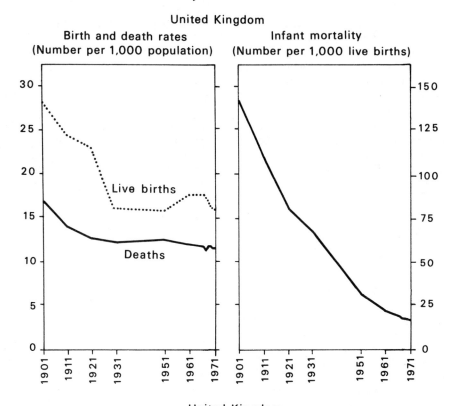

United Kingdom

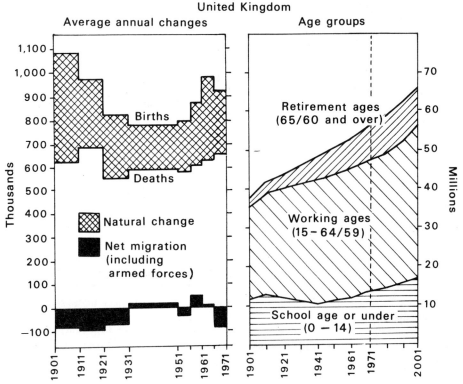

Figure 2.2   UK, Vital trends, components of population growth (1961-71), and age structure (1901-2001).

All these factors are reflected in the growth of the average number of children per marriage in Britain from the low level of 2·05 for marriages in 1936, to 2·23 for 1951, to an estimated 2·50 for 1961, but falling for those married in the late 1960s to, perhaps, some 2·45. These slight increases have been enough to create the situation of post-war growth and of projected growth in the future. Yet, if the 1960s level of about 5 children born to every two families were to be reduced slightly to 9 children for every 4 families the population in the year 2000 would be 2 to 3 million less than the 1969 estimate, whilst a reduction in births of 1 child in 3 families would eventually stabilise population numbers. It is, as yet, too early to judge the longer-term impact of the recent decline in birth-rate from the second post-war peak of 1964 (table 2.1). But the completed families born to the generation of the post-war baby boom, many of whom are now parents, may well be smaller than the relatively high fertility-rates of the mid-1960s led us to believe.

While increased fertility has greatly increased the numbers and proportion of young dependants, continuing improvements in health and standards of living have been reflected in a slow lowering of mortality. Although due in part to an ageing population structure, crude death-rates have fallen but slowly, from 12·7 per 1000 in 1921, to between 11 and 12 in the 1960s (Fig. 2.2). Expectation of life has increased steadily, especially for women, and is reflected in the increased proportion of retired people in the population (table 2.5). A second factor in continuing population growth, this is also one reason for the increased dependency ratios which have been a feature of the post-war years.

A third factor in population growth since the 1930s has been the general gains, on balance, from overseas migration. In contrast to the losses from migration sustained during the nineteenth and early-twentieth centuries, during the 1930s and 1940s a slowing down of emigration and increased immigration, much of it of refugees from Europe, combined to reverse the UK's long-standing net loss from migration. Moreover from the mid-1950s a new wave of immigration from the New Commonwealth countries has contributed to a considerable continuing inward movement which produced a net gain due to migration of 20,000 in the civilian population 1951-61 and of 113,000 in 1961-6 (table 2.2). This was slowed down by the 1962 Commonwealth Immigrants Act and nearly arrested by the 1968 Act, though the influx of dependants of previous migrants has continued to generate considerable immigration. Nevertheless, increasing control of immigration and deteriorating economic conditions, especially in terms of labour surpluses, have resulted in a considerable recent loss by migration (see table 2.2). The effects of this distinctive, if short-lived, process on the composition of the population have been considerable. In certain areas overseas immigrants have become dominant in social and demographic structure, though it is difficult at this stage to judge their longer-term effects upon population trends.

I.3   General Population Trends, Rural and Urban

Since 1945 the dominant trends have been those characteristic of the last 50 years: the drift to the South East from the older industrial regions; movement from rural to urban areas; the counterflow from city centre to suburb (fig. 2.3). Especially since 1961, however, some significant variations on these themes have become apparent (fig.2.4). In particular, the large cities and conurbations of the North have all experienced marked losses, while other conurbations throughout the UK have experienced losses similar to those of adjacent areas (tables 2.3 and 2.4).

The rural areas of the UK had been characterised by population losses throughout the Victorian period. After the mid-nineteenth century all types of farming areas experienced population decline as outward migration exceeded natural increase. Despite

TABLE 2.2   Natural and Migrational Components of Population Change, UK, 1901-71

(1,000s)	Census enumerated								Mid-year estimates							
	1901-11		1911-21		1921-31		1931-51		1951-6		1956-61		1961-6		1966-71	
Population at start of period	38,237		42,082		44,027		46,038		50,290		51,184		52,816		54,654	
Average annual change	Total	%	Total	%	Total	%	Total	%	Total	%	Total	%	Total	%	Total	%
Births	1,091	2·85	975	2·32	824	1·87	785	1·71	797	1·58	880	1·72	988	1·87	938	1·72
Deaths	624	1·63	689	1·64	555	1·26	598	1·30	583	1·16	603	1·18	633	1·20	645	1·18
Net natural change	467	1·22	286	0·68	268	0·61	188	0·41	214	0·43	277	0·54	355	0·67	293	0·54
Net Migration Civilian	−82	−0·21	−92	−0·22	−67	−0·15	+22	+0·05	−48 } −0·07		+30 } +0·10		+12 } +0·02		−18	−0·03
Armed Forces									+13 }		+20 }		+1 }			
Total average annual change	385	1·01	195	0·46	201	0·46	213	0·47	179	0·36	327	0·64	368	0·69	275	0·50

Source: Social Trends 1 (1970), 'Population and Environment' Table 10 (p.53) and *Registrar General's Estimates* (for 1969-71). *Social Trends* 3 (1972) estimates net migration for 1961-7 as −33,000 (Civil) and −15,000 (Armed Forces). The figures of change 1966-71 are based on pre-census estimates and are subject to revision in the light of the final figures from the 1971 censuses.

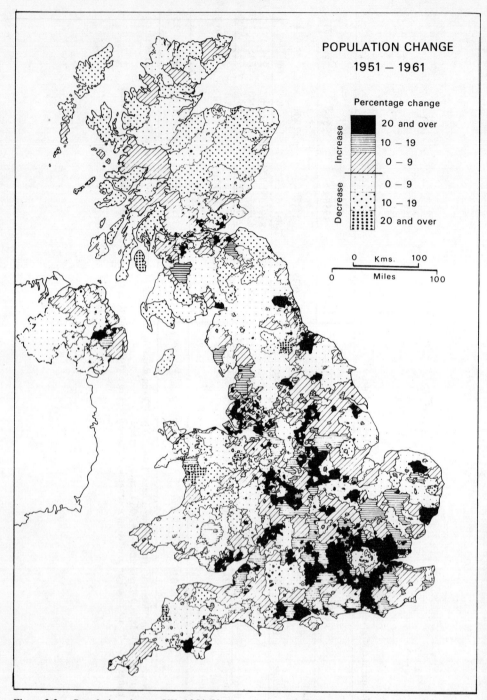

Figure 2.3   Population change, UK, 1951-61

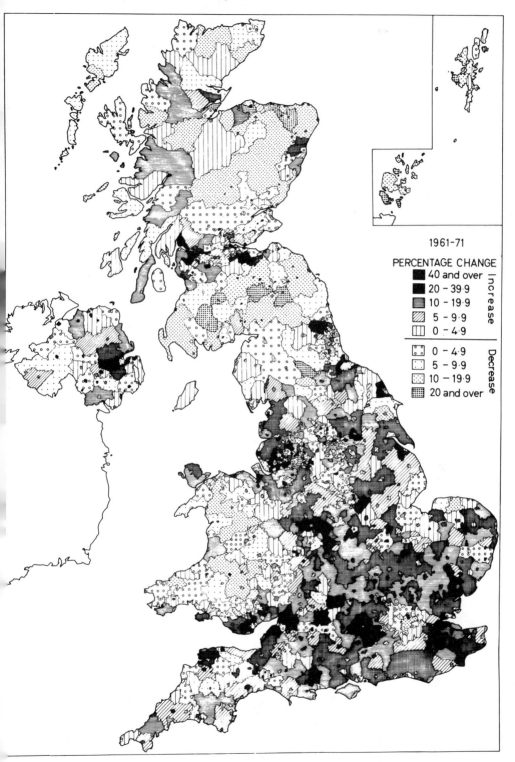

Figure 2.4   Population change, UK, 1961-71

TABLE 2.3 Population Changes in Urban and Rural Areas, UK, 1951-71

	Total population (1,000s)		Percentage change	Total	Percentage change
	1951	1961	1951-61	1971	1961-71
England and Wales	43,758·9	46,104·5	5·2	48,593·7	5·3
Conurbations	16,794·4	16,741·9	− 3·4	15,928·0	− 4·8
Urban areas					
over 100,000	6,279·2	6,640·4	5·8	6,754·1	1·7
50-100,000	4,423·1	5,008·7	13·2	5,382·2	7·5
under 50,000	8,067·7	8,759·7	8·5	9,961·2	13·7
Rural districts	8,193·4	8,953·9	9·3	10,568·3	18·0
Scotland	5,096·7	5,179·3	1·6	5,227·7	0·9
Conurbation	1,763·7	1,807·8	2·7	1,731·0	− 4·2
Other cities and large burghs	1,315·6	1,441·9	9·6	1,491·8	3·5
Small burghs	793·4	866·6	9·2	994·8	14·8
Districts of County	1,223·7	1,065·4	−11·9	1,018·4	− 4·4
Northern Ireland	1,370·9	1,425·0	3·9	1,527·6	6·8
County boroughs	493·8	469·6	− 4·9	412·0	−12·3
Other urban areas	256·4	300·4	17·2	429·9	43·2
Rural districts	620·7	655·0	5·5	685·7	4·7
UK	50,255·2	52,708·9	4·9	55,346·6	5·0
Conurbations	18,558·1	18,549·7	− 0·5	17,659·0	− 4·8
Large urban areas	8,092·6	8,551·9	5·7	8,657·9	1·4
Other urban areas	13,540·6	14,935·4	10·3	16,768·1	12·3
Rural districts	10,037·8	10,674·3	6·3	12,272·4	15·0

Source: Census of 1951, 1961 and 1971

Because of the different basis of classification in Scotland, figures for urban and rural areas have had to be adjusted and do not exactly equal the total.

the slowing down of such excessive draining of population from the countryside in the early-twentieth century, rural depopulation, as measured by net outmigration, continued during the inter-war years, especially from the more remote areas. In the post-Second World War period, despite the reversal of aggregate losses from the rural areas in England and Wales and in Northern Ireland, and their slowing down in Scotland, depopulation of the remoter rural areas continued. Most of the rural districts which have increased their population have done so by overspill into administrative rural districts from adjacent towns. The balance of gain in rural districts must chiefly be seen as a response to suburban dispersal and the increase of commuting or of movement by people on retirement. In Scotland, where such changes are mainly limited to Central Scotland or a few small growth points such as those near Fort William, Inverness and the Moray Firth, rural depopulation continues (table 2.3).

In contrast to the inter-war situation, large cities and especially the conurbations have experienced marked and increasing losses of population since 1945. In the more closely-settled areas of the UK many large urban authorities are losing population to suburbs in adjacent local authority areas, often to rural districts. Accompanied by loss of rateable value and, often, by increasing social segregation of centre and periphery in essentially interdependent urban regions, this process is reflected in the growth of population in the smaller urban areas, many of which are suburban satellites of the large cities. In all parts of the UK small towns are in the fastest-growing group of settlements.

Cumulatively, the result has been to shift the balance of regional growth within the UK. During the nineteenth century the most rapidly growing regions included northern England and the industrial areas of Central Scotland and South Wales. But since the First World War, the Northern, Yorkshire and Humberside, and North West regions of England, together with Wales and Scotland have suffered a relative fall in population, while the Midlands and South East have increased their relative share of population and are expected to continue to do so up to the end of the century.

I.4   Effects on Population Structure

These changing distributions reflect changing economic forces, but the demographic results of changes in natural and migrational components of population trends also carry considerable economic and social implications at both national and regional levels. The declining birth-rate and falling mortality of the early twentieth century caused a consider-able increase in the elderly (over 60 years), both numerically and as a proportion of the total population (table 2.5). In 1911 the 60+ age-group formed 9·2 per cent of the total population, but by 1941 it was estimated at 13·9 and, in 1971, 18·6 per cent. The increase in older dependants was offset, between the wars, by falling birth-rates; the proportion of those under 15 years fell from 30·8 per cent in 1911 to 21 per cent in 1941. Hence, the dependency ratio (conventionally measured by the proportion of those aged 0-14 years and of retirement age, here reckoned as 60 years and above, as related to the 15-59 age group) which was 61·5 in 1911 had dropped to 53·9 in 1941. Today, however, because of generally higher birth-rates since 1945 and increased expectation of life among older people, the dependency ratio is 70·8. While from 1941 to 1971 the under-15s increased by 34 per cent and the over-60s by 53 per cent, the main workforce increased by a meagre 2 per cent. Hence, in the 1950s and 1960s we have experienced a relative decline in the workforce, though the actual numbers of the population of working age have increased slightly.

This stagnation in the potential workforce has been somewhat offset by drawing more women into gainful employment, a trend accelerated by two World Wars and by changing attitudes to the role of women in society and their potential role in professional, commercial and industrial life. These changes are reflected in the increase in the proportion

TABLE 2.4   Components of Population Change, UK Regions, 1951-69

(1,000s) Region	1951	1951-61 average annual change		1961	1961-6 average annual change		1966
		natural	migration		natural	migration	
Northern	3,127	19·3	−8·0	3,246	20·7	−7·1	3,314
Yorkshire & Humberside	4,509	19·5	−9·6	4,631	28·1	−1·0	4,767
North West	6,417	23·5	−12·4	6,545	38·0	−5·7	6,713
East Midlands	2,896	15·8	+3·9	3,108	23·4	+8·7	3,266
West Midlands	4,426	27·6	+4·7	4,761	41·1	+7·1	4,999
South East	15,216	66·4	+43·8	16,346	110·2	+20·8	17,006
Greater London	8,206	33·3	−61·1	7,977	52·3	−82·7	7,832
Outer Metropolitan	3,509	24·2	+77·5	4,521	43·5	+54·8	5,013
Outer South East	3,502	8·9	+27·3	3,848	14·5	+48·7	4,161
East Anglia	1,388	6·5	+2·7	1,489	8·7	+11·9	1,582
South West	3,247	10·5	+9·9	3,436	16·9	+24·8	3,635
Wales	2,589	8·4	−4·9	2,635	11·5	+1·9	2,704
Scotland	5,103	33·9	−28·2	5,184	38·7	−38·8	5,191
Northern Ireland	1,373	14·6	··8·9	1,427	17·4	−6·9	1,478
UK	50,291	246·0	−7·0	52,807	354·6	+15·7	54,654

Source: Eversley (1971); *Abstract of Regional Statistics* (1971); and *Long-term Population Distribution in G.B.: A Study* (1971)

Figures are derived *Registrar General's mid-year Estimates;* those for 1971 are estimates revised in the light of the provisional figures of the 1971 censuses

of women in employment, especially during and since the Second World War, though there are considerable regional variations in female activity rates (fig. 2.15).

One of the factors in 'full employment' since 1945 has been the coincidence of labour shortage, due to changing population structure, with a generally expanding economy. These were also basic factors attracting immigrant labour to the UK in the 1950s and early 1960s. A relatively stagnant economy coupled with increasing economy in the use of labour in the face of rapidly rising labour costs has now changed this situation and is reflected in increases in unemployment, a fall in activity rates and a decline in the immigration of workers though not yet of dependants.

Sex structure   From the 1920s to the 1940s the catastrophic casualties of the First World War, reflected in the relatively high ratios of women to men (table 2.6), were a factor contributing to reduced fertility between the wars. Since the Second World War much improved ante- and post-natal care has resulted in a marked increase in the surplus of male births. (There is a tendency in all mammals for a greater conception of males and a higher proportion of males, at birth, but this has been offset in the UK by higher male mortality at all ages). Despite higher male mortality at all ages, especially in later life, the imbalance of the sexes in the inter-war years in the UK is now much reduced. Current estimates show that men outnumber women in all age-groups up to 44 years in England and Wales and up to 19 years in Scotland and Northern Ireland where the lower age of male deficits is due largely to differential migration.

A very notable feature of changing age and sex structure is the increasing dominance of women in later age-groups. Among the over-60s the ratio of men to women is about 1:1·5 but among the over-70s it is 1:1·8 and 1:2·4 for the over-80s. As Thompson states: 'The problem of caring for the increasing number of very elderly people is very

BLE 2.4 (cont.)

| 1966-9 | | | 1951-69 | | | | | | revised estimate | |
| erage annual change | | 1969 | Total | | Natural | | Net Migration (+) | | 1971 Total | 1951-71 |
tural	migration		No.	%	No.	%	No.	%		% change
5·7	−5·8	3,346	219	7·0	344	11·0	−133	−4·3	3,301	5·6
6·5	−13·5	4,811	302	6·7	415	9·2	−141	−3·1	4,809	6·7
2·6	−15·1	6,770	353	5·5	523	8·2	−198	−3·1	6,738	5·0
2·4	+4·5	3,349	453	15·6	342	11·8	+96	+3·3	3,391	17·1
0·7	+6·7	5,145	719	16·2	604	13·6	+103	+2·3	5,119	15·7
8·5	−8·8	17,195	2,079	13·7	1,510	9·9	+515	+3·4	17,259	13·4
3·2	−88·7	7,703	−503	−6·1	725	8·9	−1,290	−15·7	7,418	−9·6
1·6	+36·8	5,253	1,744	49·7	584	16·6	+1,160	+33·1	5,344	52·4
3·6	+43·1	4,338	836	23·9	202	5·8	+646	+18·4	4,497	28·4
8·5	+16·1	1,657	269	19·4	134	9·7	+135	+9·7	1,681	21·1
4·7	+16·6	3,730	483	14·9	234	7·2	+269	+8·3	3,792	16·8
9·0	−3·0	2,725	136	5·3	169	6·5	−48	−1·9	2,725	5·3
3·4	−34·3	5,195	92	1·8	633	12·4	−579	−11·3	5,324	4·3
7·7	−6·3	1,513	140	10·2	286	−20·8	−143	−10·4	1,529	11·4
9·6	−42·9	55,535	5,244	10·4	5,192	10·3	−121	−0·2	55,668	10·7

(+) excludes Armed Forces

much that of caring for an increasing proportion of elderly women'.[4]

I.5   Population Composition and the Workforce

In a Select Committee report for 1970-1 it was noted that, after a post-war phase of increased dependency-rates perpetuated by the proposal to raise the school-leaving age to 16 in 1973, the working population would increase from 1974.[5] Compared with the period 1941-69, when the population of working age increased by a mere 4 per cent, and with an estimated decrease of some 1 per cent 1969-73 there is likely to be an increase of 20 per cent (1·62 million) in the population of working age by the end of the century.

    This will be both an opportunity and a challenge. Any increased labour force may contribute to increased output, quite apart from increases in productivity per unit of manpower. Thus the changing demographic structure is of considerable potential economic significance. Similarly the changing employment situation in the 1950s and 1960s is partly related to a changing manpower situation. The present labour surpluses, though far from general, are a product of increased supply, especially in the younger age-groups, at a time of economic recession and increasing economy in the use of man-power in a high-wage economy. There should be no parallel bottleneck of labour shortage in the 1970s to that which hampered the economy in the 1950s and 1960s and generated a demand for immigrants to fill the gap in home labour supplies. Nevertheless varying regional demands for labour and changing skills and demands for these will no doubt involve continuing labour mobility leading to further population migration.

I.6   Population Trends and Social Provision

Provided that increased manpower can be put to work, some of the burden of dependency which has fallen upon a relatively static working-age population during recent times may

TABLE 2.5 Age Distribution, UK, 1911-2001

Age group	Total population (millions)					Per cent of total population					Percentage changes		
	Census enumeration			Projections*		Census			Projections		1911-41	1941-71	1971-2001
	1911	1941	1971	1981	2001	1911	1941	1971	1981	2001			
0-14	13·0	10·1	13·5	(14·1)	(16·5)	30·8	21·0	24·1	(23·9)	(24·8)	− 22·3	+ 33·7	(+ 22·2)
15-59	25·7	31·4	32·1	33·6	39·1	61·1	65·1	57·2	57·3	58·8	+22·2	+ 2·2	+ 21·8
60 and over	3·4	6·8	10·4	11·1	10·9	8·2	13·9	18·6	18·9	16·4	+100·0	+ 53·0	+ 4·8
All ages	42·1	48·3	56·0	58·9	66·5	100·1	100·0	99·9	100·0	100·1	+ 14·8	+ 15·9	+ 18·8

Source: Social Trends, 1, (1970), Tables V and VI and *Census 1971, Preliminary Reports* (HMSO)

* The projections are those of 1968: bracketed figures are estimates of those as yet unborn

be eased. Post-war increases in children and old people have placed heavy pressures upon the whole range of social services, such as education, health, social and family benefits, and also upon housing. For example, the boom in births of 1945-7 led to a 30 per cent increase in school intake in 1950-2 which reached the universities and colleges in the Robbins boom period of 1963-5. Similarly the upward trend of births of the period 1955-64, which produced a second post-war increase of 29 per cent in school entries, has exerted a more gradual, but increasing, pressure on educational facilities, youth services, etc. which has yet to work its way through.

Meanwhile, increased longevity is requiring the provision of more special services for the elderly. These fall unequally on the community both in regional terms (fig. 2.11), as between urban and rural areas, or between older-established and more recently formed communities. The general tendency to an ageing population since the First World War has not been off-set by increased births since 1945. Taking 1969 as base year, the index of rates of change in the older age-groups has shown a marked upward trend which is expected to continue, especially among the aged, calling for much greater provision of special homes, hospitals and other services than is yet available (table 2.7).

TABLE 2.7   Older Age-Groups, UK, 1941-2001

		Actual				Estimated		
		1941	1951	1961	1969	1981	1991	2001
All retirement ages	Total	65	78	89	100	111	113	109
	M	71	84	89	100	118	122	120
	F	65	78	89	100	108	108	104
85 and over	Total	35	53	81	100	118	146	160
	M	32	50	77	100	102	134	145
	F	35	53	81	100	124	150	166

Source: Social Trends, 1, (1970), Table VIII, p.29

II   POPULATION DISTRIBUTION AND TRENDS

II.1   Intraregional Contrasts

With an average of 0·92 persons per acre (2·27 persons per ha) the UK is one of the most densely populate d areas of the world. Moreover there are very wide variations, ranging from the extremely crowded inner residential areas of the large towns, with densities of over 10 per acre (24 per ha) rising to over 50 per acre (123 per ha), to thinly populated rural areas of under 0·1 per acre (0·25 per ha) and extensive, uninhabited moorlands which cover much of upland Britain (fig. 2.1). The key to the intensity of occupation lies in an unusually high degree of urbanisation. In 1911, after over a century of rapid urban growth, 78 per cent of the population of England and Wales lived in urban districts and perhaps as many as nine-tenths were 'urbanised'. Similarly in Scotland population numbers were dominated by the large towns and industrial districts of Central Scotland. Even in Northern Ireland, where Belfast is the only large industrial city, about one-half of the population were urban-dwellers.

The proportion of urban-dwellers, narrowly defined as those who live under urban administrations, is still at about the level of 50 years ago according to the 1971 census: 77·7 per cent in the UK; 78·3 per cent in England and Wales; 81·5 per cent in Scotland and 55·1 per cent in Northern Ireland. Many large towns, Greater London included, reached their peak population before the First World War, however, and have since maintained growth by outward movement to suburban satellites. Even where land has been available within the city boundaries for new housing, slum clearance and lower-

People and Work

TABLE 2.6   Female:Male Ratios, UK, 1911-2001   Census of population

Total in millions	1911			1921			1931		
	Total		F per 100M	Total		F per 100M	Total		F per 100M
	M	F		M	F		M	F	
England and Wales	17·45	18·62	106·8	18·01	19·81	109·6	19·13	20·82	108·8
Scotland	2·31	2·45	106·2	2·35	2·53	108·0	2·33	2·52	108·3
Northern Ireland	0·60	0·65	105·9	0·61	0·65	106·2	0·60	0·64	106·7
UK	20·36	21·72	106·7	20·97	22·99	109·5	22·06	23·98	108·7

Source: Censuses; Registrar General's Estimates (1969 base)

density house-building has led to large net losses of population by migration and, since the Second World War, a fall in total numbers of people in the majority of the large cities of the UK.

Although some 33 per cent of the population of England and Wales today lives in the 6 conurbations officially designated in the 1951 Census[6] this proportion has fallen from the 38 per cent of 1951. There has been a similar reduction from 35 to 33 per cent in the population of Scotland who live in the central Clydeside conurbation, due to a fall in the total since 1961.

This relative loss of population from the conurbations is paralleled in most large towns. Yet in terms of the urban regions the loss is illusory. Reduced densities in the inner areas are the result of clearance either for commercial and other redevelopment, or for housing renewal at much lower densities, even where high rise apartments have been built. However, compared with the very high intensity of occupation in nineteenth-century housing areas and due to enhanced standards of space for amenities such as schools and open spaces, even such intensive redevelopment does not usually absorb more than half the pre-existing population. The people displaced do not usually 'leave' the city but are rehoused on the periphery often in adjacent local authority areas, many of which are still designated as 'rural districts'. Thus the moderately high-density areas have extended their bounds around the cities and there has been some evening-out of the population gradient between city centre and periphery. While less marked than in the inter-war years, the physical expansion of towns continues.

Fears have been expressed of megalopolitan tendencies in the corridor from Greater London to North-West England and West Yorkshire, which contains about 51 per cent of the population of England and Wales, though Best argues that this danger lies some distance into the future.[1] Moreover this is only one aspect of a general problem of concentration. Another 11 urban tracts in the UK, each with over one-quarter of a million people, together with the conurbations, add up to some 60 per cent of the UK population.[7] Of the rest, only some 2 million, less than 5 per cent of the population, in England and Wales live over 10 miles (16 km) from a major city. Hence the activities of a large part of the workforce focus upon the major urbanised areas.

Population densities within purely rural areas continue to decline, despite more than a century and a half of outward migration from the countryside (figs. 2.3 and 2.4). Indeed within the remoter areas of highland Britain a mere one per cent of the country's population lives on over one-third of its land area. In such thinly-peopled areas, there is a progressively ageing structure, many places experience excess of deaths over births, and, slowly but surely, such places are dying in demographic as well as in economic and

TABLE 2.6 (cont.)   Census of population

| 1951 | | | 1971 | | | 1981 | | | Estimated in 2001 | | |
| Total | | F per 100M | Total | | F per 100M | | | F per 100M | | | F per 100M |
M	F		M	F		M	F		M	F	
21·02	22·74	108·2	24·05	25·28	105·8	25·40	26·48	104·3	28·94	29·65	102·5
2·43	2·66	109·2	2·50	2·70	107·1	2·60	2·77	106·5	2·90	3·02	104·2
0·67	0·70	105·3	0·75	0·78	103·8	0·81	0·84	103·8	1·00	1·01	101·0
24·12	26·10	108·3	27·30	28·76	105·5	28·81	30·09	104·4	32·84	33·68	102·5

social terms. Lack of basic amenities, including transport, difficulty of access to schools and other services, suggests that in much of central Wales and the Scottish Highlands and Islands further depopulation is likely except in more accessible recreational areas. Even where farming prospers and supports a range of active professional and service functions in local market towns, population decline or stagnation often continues. Increased food output has been achieved by greater productivity, much of it by increased mechanisation. The farm labour-force has declined to less than half its 1945 total, while amalgamations continue to reduce the number of farms. Indeed, the UK now has only 3 per cent of its working population engaged in agriculture, though the area of tillage and stock numbers alike are considerably above inter-war levels.[8]

Although, at first glance, the fall in aggregate rural population has abated and even been reversed in many parts of England and Wales, in central and eastern Scotland, and in Northern Ireland, such a trend is frequently illusory. Increasing population and higher densities in the rural areas of the UK are mostly the result of dispersal of town-dwellers beyond urban administrative limits or, in certain favoured seaside and country districts, are due to the inward movement of population to live in retirement. Dispersal into adjacent rural areas is no longer confined to the private housing sector. Increasingly, from the 1950s, local authority housing estates and overspill agreements have moved outside urban boundaries into rural districts, enlarging commuter hinterlands and extending the real city regions. In this sense the urbanised areas within England and Wales have tended to coalesce (fig. 2.1) and the same process is going on in Scotland and in Northern Ireland, principally around Belfast.

II.2   Regional Components of Population Change

Within the basic pattern of population distribution and change, there are considerable contrasts in regional trends. Moreover, despite the persistence of trends characteristic of the last 50 years — rural decline, urban overspill and the drift south-east — there have been recent shifts in the scale and intensity of population movements which presage future change. During the first half of the twentieth century the major population growth was concentrated into three standard regions (as at present defined): the South East, and the West and East Midlands. The redistribution of the late-eighteenth and nineteenth centuries had been partially reversed. The South East region increased its share rapidly and the Midlands regions more gradually. In the older industrial areas higher birth rates were offset by massive outmigration. During the depression years of the 1930s unemployment rates in the Midlands and South East were often only half the national averages while in the depressed industrial areas of South Wales, Scotland and Northern England they were well

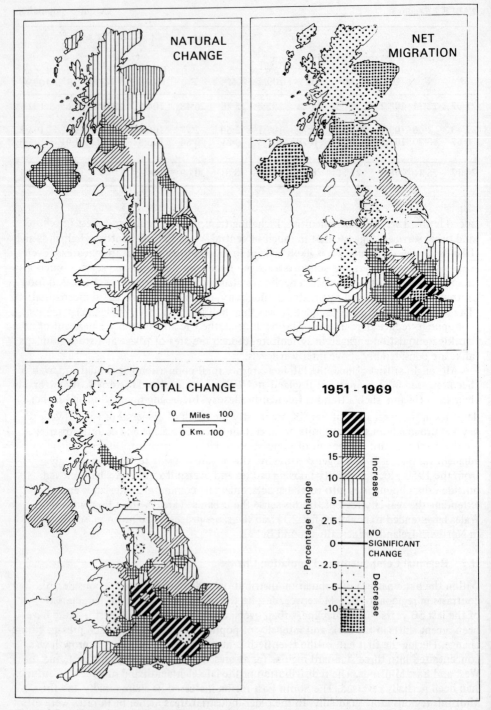

Figure 2.5   Natural, migration and total population change, UK Economic Planning subregions,
              1951-69

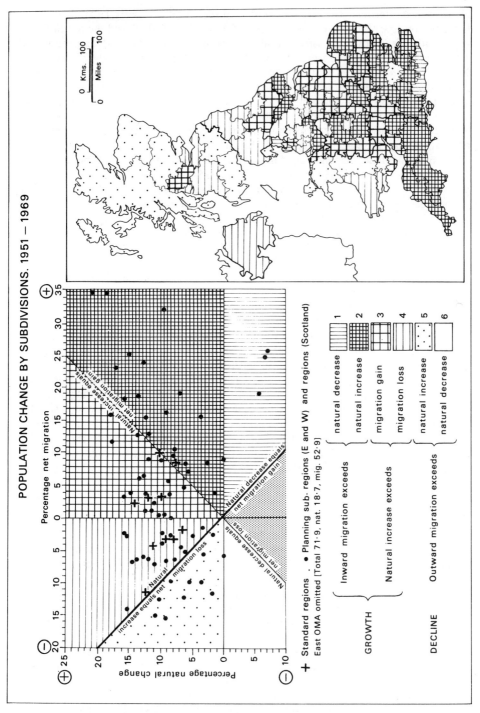

Figure 2.6   Components of population change, UK Economic Planning subregions, 1951-69
Source: *Long Term Population Distribution in GB: A Study* (1971), Fig. 9
OMA = Outer Metropolitan Area

above average. Between 1921-51 the South East region gained nearly 1·2 million people by migration, the Midlands region over 300,000 between 1931-51 and the South West region rather fewer over the same period. In contrast, between 1921-51, the net migration losses of Northern England were 912,000, Wales 434,000, and Scotland 675,000. Northern Ireland's losses, a continuance of nineteenth-century rural-urban movement to Britain, were somewhat abated in the stagnant UK industrial economy of the inter-war period; against an increase of 23,000 in population from 1926-37 must be offset an estimated net migration loss of 70,000 during the same period.

One of the aims of post-war planning has been to diminish the continuing drain of population from the so-called depressed areas of the inter-war period. The extent to which planning policy has succeeded in this may be judged, in part, from population trends, not least rates of net migration. Between 1951 and 1961 the South East's population increased by 1·13 million with a net migration gain of 438,000; the adjoining regions, East Anglia and the South West, which received overspill from and growth associated with the South East had increases of 111,000 and 189,000, respectively (table 2.4). The other regions of population growth, the West and East Midlands, which increased by 335,000 and 212,000 respectively, also had considerable migration gains. All other areas of the UK experienced losses by migration between 1951 and 1961, which were substantial in some cases, as for example from Scotland and the North West.

Despite vigorous attempts in the 1960s to attract industry to the development areas and to control the supply of new jobs in the growth regions (chapters 1 and 4) these population trends have persisted. Thus, since 1966, the South East region has lost population by migration, but largely to the adjacent regions of East Anglia and the South West. In the Midlands, however, there has recently been a significant slowing down in the growth rate of the East Midlands. This last case apart, however, the ratio of regional to national population trends reflects the same essential features as those of the 1950s, though relative recovery of population growth, and corresponding reduction of outward movement, in Northern Ireland, Scotland, Wales and Yorkshire and Humberside is interesting. On balance, we must agree with the recent verdict of Eversley that, although regional policies have not succeeded in arresting population losses from areas of long-standing decline, 'Without government policies the situation would be far worse'[9] and it may well be that some levelling out of regional rates of change may be expected in the future.

II.3 Subregional Patterns of Change

While regional trends pick out the main features of population change since the war, they are on too broad a scale to permit accurate assessment of the relationship between components of population change involving considerable intraregional contrasts, such as between urban and rural areas or between urban core and periphery; furthermore, both natural and migrational components must be considered. Areas of high natural growth, such as the coalfields of North East England and South Wales, or the Merseyside subregion, have traditionally exported surpluses arising from high birth-rates. Many rural areas still have a higher natural growth than they can support. Thus a certain level of migration must always be expected at both regional and subregional level as a regulator of population growth; but when such migration seriously affects population and social structure, especially by continuously draining away the younger and more talented sections of the population, it may create serious problems.

From the Registrar General's mid-year population estimates and census tabulations for 63 planning sub-regions in England and Wales and 22 in Scotland it is possible to analyse components of population change in fair detail, though at the time of writing only a limited range of data is available for the Scottish subregion (figs 2.5 and 2.6).[10]

Total change: The pattern of total population change at subregional level between 1951-69 (fig. 2.5) underlines those features already analysed, drawing particular attention to the contrasts between decrease in the remote rural areas, the stagnation or decline in such old industrial regions as the South Wales coalfield, and the West Yorkshire and East Lancashire textile districts. The fall in Greater London's total population is typical of the inner areas of conurbations and has also occurred in all other conurban subregions, except the West Midlands, since 1966.

Natural change: Some of the features of total change are quite closely related to natural change, i.e. the balance between births and deaths. High growth areas in South East England and the Midlands are marked by above-average natural increase, except in inner urban areas. But many areas of slow overall growth or even of decline have relatively high rates of natural increase: such are the Glasgow region and industrial North East England, while in Northern Ireland the moderate total increase since 1951 is considerably below the rate of natural growth. Much of rural Scotland has a moderate level of natural increase, but overall population stagnation or decline. In contrast, the south coast of England, an area of generally high total increase of population has little or no natural increase or may actually show a natural decrease, as in the Sussex coast subregion. While certain of these contrasts are due to differences in age structure, they also imply considerable variations in migration.

Net Migration: Even at subregional level net migration conceals a good deal of inter- and intraregional mobility which can only be fully analysed from information on changes of residence first collected in the 1961 census.[11] Net migration figures reflect the resultants of more complex patterns of inward and outward movements and are often regarded as a good indicator of the relative power of 'push' and 'pull' forces acting upon population at a regional level. The pattern in fig. 2.5 is a remarkably concise commentary on the continuing pull of population to the more prosperous economy and attractive social image of the south-eastern quadrant of Britain. Apart from migration losses from the Greater London and West Midlands conurbation subregions, much of which has been due to outward movement to adjacent areas in a process of intraregional overspill of housing and population, with corresponding increases in commuting, this quadrant is one wholly of migration gain. This growth now extends into the South West and Bristol-Severn areas, and into East Anglia, both of which have had higher migration gains in the 1960s than the inner metropolitan subregions (table 2.4). In part such increases have been due to retirement migration to rural or seaside areas, especially in the South West and along the south coast.

Components of Population change: These often complex interrelationships can be conveniently summarised by combining in a single diagram the natural component of change (on the vertical axis) and the migrational component (horizontal axis) (fig. 2.6). Of the resultant eight possible type-areas of population change only six are represented in the 1951-69 period. In most areas there was growth in total population (types 1-4). In a very few cases, confined to the retirement areas of the Fylde, Morecambe-Lancaster, the Sussex and North Wales coasts, natural losses were more than compensated for by net migration gain, leading to population increase (type 1). In contrast, areas where natural increase exceeded migration loss (type 4) include most of the conurbations and older industrial areas, together with less remote rural areas of South West Wales, Northern England and Southern Scotland which, either by retaining sufficient of their

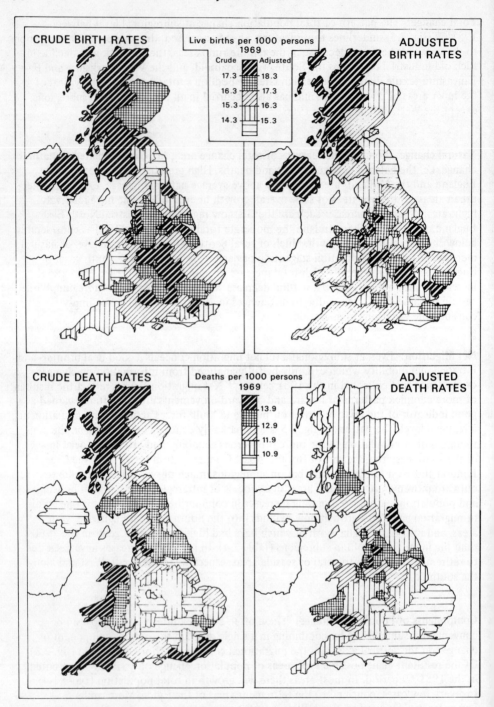

Figure 2.7   Birth- and death-rates, UK Economic Planning Subregions, 1969

natural increase or by attracting migrants from adjacent areas, have increased in population over the post-war period.

Fastest growth occurs generally in areas of both natural and migrational increase (types 2 and 3). Natural increase predominates over migrational gain (type 3) in much of the East Midlands, peripheral areas of the West Midlands and the north-western parts of the Outer Metropolitan Area. Apart from the growth area of Bristol, the Severn estuary and the Welsh border, influenced by overspill from the West Midlands, such growth patterns are virtually absent from the rest of the UK. However, rural North Yorkshire and the Falkirk-Stirling area, both of which have been affected by outward movement from adjacent urban regions, show this type of trend. The latter has received much of the overspill from the central Clydeside conurbation and east-central Scotland.

The major areas of attraction for population are picked out by retention of natural increase together with a larger element of growth due to net migration (type 2). This type of growth accounts for very large increases in population in most of the inner and outer metropolitan areas. Much of southern and the whole of south-western England now shares these characteristics, due to considerable recent gains by migration, a trait shared with much of East Anglia, where a good deal of recent in-movement is associated with the effects of overspill agreements with Greater London (fig. 2.23). Similar features have occurred in the outer subregions of the West Midlands but, apart from the suburban commuter belts of north Cheshire (with links to Manchester and Merseyside) and of mid-Yorkshire (with links to Leeds-Bradford and Hull), this 'healthy' type of population trend is absent from the rest of the UK.

The remaining areas fall into two categories of population loss. In one area, North East Lancashire, a long-continuing net outward migration is combined with a slight natural decrease (type 6), due largely to the region's ageing population structure, the only example of natural losses outside the 'retirement' areas. Yet there are a number of areas where net outmigration exceeds natural gain to produce a fall in total population (type 5). These occur in two distinct types of area. The first includes Greater London where, as in all central city areas, population is moving out. In two nineteenth-century industrial areas, Furness and the north-eastern parts of the South Wales coalfield, both long-standing industrial decline and an ageing population contribute to population losses. The second type of area of population loss is confined to the remote rural areas including most of Southern and Highland Scotland, and Mid and North Wales. Here long-standing out-movement has created an aged population with a low rate of natural growth and stagnating or slowly declining populations.

II.4   Vital Trends

The broad components of population change reviewed in section II.3 are resultants of three basic factors in population dynamics: births, deaths and migration. Variations in the fertility, mortality and morbidity of the population reflect economic and social conditions; they are also the outcome of present population structures and are determinants of future population trends and structure. Thus, vital and migrational differences are basic elements in explaining and planning for economic and social problems at both national and regional levels.

Birth-rates: The rapid decline of birth-rate in all social classes and all regions of the UK was one of the most remarkable demographic features of the early twentieth century and the inter-war years. While the reduction in family size was general, significant variations in fertility and family size remain between social classes and are found between the various parts of the UK. Glass and Grebenik showed, in 1954, that higher fertility persisted among wives of manual workers, despite the general decrease in family size.[12] The tendency to a somewhat larger average family since 1945 has been more marked

among professional and managerial classes, changing slightly the progression of high
social class/small family to low social class/large family which was characteristic up
to the Second World War.

The 1961 census revealed that between couples of equivalent age of marriage, e.g.
those married between ages 20-4, the average size for *all* durations of marriage among
manual workers was higher than among non-manual workers. Even among those married
for less than 5 years in 1962, these differentials were found (table 2.8).

TABLE 2.8   Variations in Family Size, England and Wales, 1961

Children per marriage	manual workers			non-manual workers		
	unskilled	semi-skilled	skilled	professional	employers and managers	intermediate
All durations of marriage	2·55	2·16	1·92	2·10	1·82	1·64
Married for up to 5 years	1·74	1·47	1·36	1·69	1·34	1·29

Source: Census (1961)

However the differential fertility between social classes has narrowed. According to
Glass: 'The ratio of fertility of manual to non-manual groups, which has been around
1·4:1·0 for the marriages of the 1920s and early 1930s, fell to less than 1·2:1·0 for the
marriages of the 1940s.'[13]

However, while fertility among semi- and unskilled workers has tended to stabilise
at relatively low levels, that for employers and professional workers has tended to rise
since 1945. The Population Investigation Committee's national survey of Britain of
1967-8 observed little difference between social classes in the proportion of recently
married couples adopting birth control methods and noted that the gap between manual
and non-manual groups had narrowed considerably over the previous 20 years.

Geographical patterns of birth-rates substantiate the social differences between
fertility within all cities. For example, on Merseyside, traditionally an area of relatively
high fertility, the fertility-rates are clearly zoned from high rates, 75 per cent above
national rates, in the central and inner residential areas of Liverpool and Bootle CBs,
through moderate levels 50-75 per cent above national average in intermediate areas,
including much inter-war corporation and some private residential areas, to low values
20-25 per cent above national average, in outer areas of recent corporation and private
housing estates.[14]

Despite the general evening-out of birth-rates during the 1960s, crude regional birth-
rates ranged from 12·1 to 23·6 per thousand in 1969 (fig. 2.7), as compared with 16·3
per 1000 for England and Wales, 17·4 for Scotland and 21·4 for Northern Ireland. Two
major types of area of high crude birth-rate stand out: first, the rural areas of Northern
Ireland and Scotland where, despite heavy and long-continued out-movement of young
adults and quite high proportions of older people, relatively high levels of fertility persist;
secondly, industrial regions in Central Scotland and the axial belt from London to South
Lancashire and West Yorkshire where manual worker groups and younger population
structures both seem to be elements in explanation. In contrast, lower crude birth-rates
are associated with the rural regions of Wales and Northern and South West England, and,
not surprisingly, with many of the retirement areas of North Wales, Southern and South
West England. Thus, while in the past higher birth-rates prevailed in the north and west
of Britain (especially Scotland and Northern England), by the mid-1960s this differential
had to some extent been ironed out. Indeed, the fall in birth-rate since 1964 seems to have
affected the North relatively more than the Midlands and South.

However, crude birth-rates are affected by the age structure of the population and the

Registrar General's adjusted rates allowing for this show the regional position more clearly. High rates still characterise Northern Ireland and the Highlands and Islands of Scotland. The highest adjusted birth rates in England and Wales and Southern Scotland tend to occur in the suburban and peripheral areas of the large cities and industrial areas, though this is less marked in South East England. Adjusted rates narrow the overall range of birth-rates and certain rural areas, for example in North Wales, South West England and North Yorkshire, achieve moderate or above-average birth-rates when age structure and the small number of total births are taken into account.

Death-rates: The patterns of mortality in the UK, though offering many parallels, are in certain respects more clear-cut than those of fertility. General mortality-rates and those from many specific diseases are well above average in large urban authority areas and much below average in rural districts. There is also a general regional gradient from relatively high death-rates in north-western Britain to relatively low rates in south-eastern Britain in areas of equivalent character, whether urban or rural.

   Some of the highest death-rates in the UK are found in association with poor environ-ments and higher-than-average incidence of social and economic problems. Many such conditions occur in the large nineteenth-century industrial towns and, in turn, within all urban areas there is still a marked gradient between unhealthy inner areas and the suburbs, partly due to environmental conditions, partly to social and demographic characteristics. The average risk of death in Salford, one of the highest mortality areas, was 33 per cent higher than in Bournemouth, one of the lowest, in 1969, according to adjusted death-rates. Similarly wide contrasts occur between inner urban areas and the outer suburbs as witness the Merseyside comparison between a 1969 adjusted death-rate of 16·19 per thousand for Bootle and the much lower rates for the middle class suburban areas, e.g. 10·71 in Wirral UD or 7·16 for Formby UD.

   Many contrasts are, however, generic rather than regional in character. Clearly, different social classes have very different mortality experience (table 2.9).

TABLE 2.9   Standard Mortality Rates, Socio-economic Classes, UK, 1921-51

| | Socio-economic classes | | | | |
	I	II	III	IV	V
1921	82	94	95	101	125
1931	90	94	97	102	111
1951	97	86	102	104	118

Source: Kelsall (1967)[15]
National rates = 100

   Despite the narrowing of the mortality differentials between social classes, due doubtless to the progressively better health, dietary and housing conditions of the lower classes, a considerable range remains, involving many factors, social, environmental and, perhaps, genetic. Among indices of class differentials in mortality experience, infant mortality, regarded as a sensitive measure, is 2 to 2·5 times higher among children of socio-economic class V parents than of class I (table 2.10). Factors quoted include the higher incidence of premature births, linked to the earlier age of child-bearing among working-class mothers, more closely spaced pregnancies, poorer ante- and post-natal care, and greater risk and poorer treatment of infection in children such as bronchitis and gastro-enteritis, all of which are often coupled with poor and overcrowded housing conditions.

   The pattern of crude death-rates by planning subregions (fig. 2.7) is misleading in that areas with a high proportion of old people are bound to have a higher relative number of deaths than those with a more youthful population. This is reflected to some extent in

TABLE 2.10   Infant mortality, England and Wales, 1964-5

Infant deaths per 1,000 live births	Socio-economic classes		
	I and II	III	IV and V
Neonatal	9·2	11·8	13·2
Post-natal	3·5	5·4	7·6

Source: Kelsall (1967), p. 49

the high rates for North West Scotland, North and South West Wales, South West and Southern England; when adjusted for age-structure, these relatively high rates are modified in most cases.

Above-average adjusted death-rates pick out Central Scotland, especially the Glasgow region, the industrial North East of England, a belt from South Lancashire through West Yorkshire to Humberside, and the South Wales coalfield. The West Midlands have generally modest rates, though mortality is higher in the Potteries and the West Midlands conurbation. In general, the rural Midlands and the Welsh border, East Anglia, South East and South West England have low or moderate rates, though the higher figures for Greater London underline the less healthy and poorer social conditions of inner urban areas.

The regional patterns of general mortality and of morbidity of particular diseases have been fully mapped and analysed by Howe,[16] whose maps, using standardised mortality-rates, support the more general picture given in fig. 2.7. He observes that, in the 320 administrative units mapped, 53 areas had very high male mortality ratios of which only four were in the London area, the rest being in northern and western Britain with the Glasgow and South Lancashire areas having the greatest concentration of high rates. While the pattern of female mortality differs in detail, it is similar to that for men, though there is a rather less marked concentration of high rates in Greater London, North East England, South Lancashire and South Wales.

Infant Mortality: One of the most telling demographic indicators of social and environmental conditions and, indeed, of overall living standards, is the rate of infant mortality. Not only are there marked class differences in its national incidence (table 2.10), but there are pronounced regional differences.[17] In the majority of local authority areas in South East, Eastern, Southern, South West and Midland England infant mortality rates are relatively low. The greatest incidence of high infant mortality occurs in Wales, North West and Northern England and Yorkshire, and in particular in Central Scotland and Northern Ireland. Despite the fall in infant mortality in the UK since 1945, in continuance of a marked downward trend since the mid-Victorian period (fig. 2.2), which has reduced rates from around 31 per 1000 in 1917 to about 19 per 1000 in 1969 in England and Wales (21 per 1000 in Scotland and 24 per 1000 in Northern Ireland), significant regional variations persist. For example, whereas the infant mortality rates in the central Clydeside conurbation in 1969 were 24·2 per 1000 they ranged from 19·8 to 14·0 in the Scottish New Towns; similarly, there was considerable variation at subregional level in England and Wales, the highest (24 per 1000) being experienced in the South East Lancashire and North East Cheshire (SELNEC) and Merseyside conurbations and in the central and eastern South Wales valleys while in the Essex subregion the rate was only 13 per 1000.

Ironically, those areas with the poorest mortality and health records are frequently those with the poorest medical and health services. Despite the overall improvement in provision under the National Health Acts of 1946-8, the National Health and Social Services have not yet succeeded in levelling out substantial regional inequalities. Thus

TABLE 2.11   Regional Mobility, GB, 1965-6

Regions	Migrants, 1965-6 (1,000s)			Migrants, 1961-6 (1,000s)		
	(1)	(2)		(4)	(5)	
	Total from region	local	$\frac{2}{1}\%$	Total from region	local	$\frac{5}{4}\%$
Northern	308·1	260·0	84	1,069·6	906·9	85
Yorkshire and Humberside	464·6	398·6	86	1,499·6	1,294·9	86
North West	609·7	536·8	88	2,011·9	1,787·6	89
East Midlands	294·1	238·5	81	928·8	773·4	83
West Midlands	479·2	408·6	85	1,496·6	1,283·7	86
East Anglia	152·4	116·3	76	440·8	352·0	80
South East	1,799·9	1,605·2	89	5,364·8	4,816·3	90
South West	378·0	305·4	81	1,098·9	901·2	82
Wales	229·0	193·0	84	730·2	620·6	85
Scotland	52·7	480·7		165·1	1,520·2	

Source: Sample Census 1966

'local' refers to the numbers of migrants not moving outside the region in which they are enumerated

The figures under columns 1 and 4 for Scotland are not comparable with those from the much less extensive English regions

the average number of patients on general practitioners' lists tend to be higher in industrial towns in the North than in towns of the Midlands and South, and the lists bigger in poor inner-city residential areas than in the middle class suburbs.[18]

II.5   Migration

After a flurry of movement in the early war years involving 19 per cent of the population of England in non-local moves in 1940 (7·5 million) this mobility had dropped to 7·4 per cent by 1950 (3·2 million moves).[11] According to the figures of residential mobility, gathered by the sample census of 1966 the percentage of movers respectively over 1 and 5 years had fallen to 4·7 and 4·8; moreover, only 29 per cent of the non-local moves involved distances of over 40 miles (64 km). Thus, though the total volume of migration is likely to increase, there will be much greater growth of short-distance movement, strengthening the ties between cities and their hinterlands and leading to a much greater volume of daily journeys to work, to school, to shop and to share in all city services.

Interregional Migration: Though of considerable importance to regional variations in population growth, net migration conceals both the volume and patterns of movement which are difficult to study from British census sources before 1961, when information concerning changes in residence were first collected. Contrasts in migration between town and country or between inner and outer zones of urban regions are part of a mobility continuum which involves not only inter- and intraregional residential migration but also considerable personal mobility in all sections of the community. Up to 1961 the only census source of information on migration flows was derived from birthplace statistics which do not permit direct study of movement over specific time periods. In its 10 per cent sample the 1961 census enquired about change of address over the year prior to the enumeration. The 1966 sample census extended the question to

TABLE 2.12   Interregional migration, GB, 1960-1 and 1965-6

Planning region	All ages above one year (1,000s)						Net balance of working age 15-59		
	1960-1			1965-6			1965-6		
	in	out	net	in	out	net	male	female	total
Northern	35·9	45·6	−9·7	45·3	48·1	−2·8	−0·8	−1·2	−2·0
Yorks and Humberside	53·4	60·8	−7·4	66·4	66·0	+0·4	+1·0	−0·8	+0·2
North West	61·9	68·9	−7·0	70·5	72·9	−2·4	−0·4	−2·2	−2·6
East Midlands	55·9	48·6	+7·3	67·4	55·6	+11·7	+4·3	+3·3	+7·6
West Midlands	63·5	61·4	+2·0	66·0	70·5	−4·5	−0·3	−3·0	−3·3
South East	173·3	153·2	+20·2	174·6	194·8	−20·1	−3·8	−0·7	−4·5
Greater London	61·7	59·7	+2·1	60·7	78·7	−18·0	−3·1	−1·9	−5·0
Outer Metropolitan Area	111·6	93·5	+18·1	52·0	60·1	−8·1	−1·9	−1·8	−3·7
Rest				61·9	55·9	+5·9	+1·2	+3·1	+4·3
East Anglia	35·0	30·8	+4·2	48·1	36·1	+12·0	+3·0	+3·9	+6·9
South West	87·0	67·7	+19·3	93·2	72·6	+20·7	+4·1	+6·3	+10·3
Wales	33·9	38·7	−4·8	36·7	36·0	+0·7	−0·5	−0·3	−0·8
Scotland	27·4	51·6	−24·2	37·0	52·7	−15·7	−6·6	−5·3	−11·9
GB	627·1	627·1	−	705·2	705·2	−	−	−	−

Source: Long Term Population Distribution, GB: A Study (HMSO, 1971), Appendix 2, Tables 1a and 1e

include change of residence over a 5-year, as well as a 1-year, period prior to the census (table 2.11). These data permit analysis of in-, out- and gross migration in varying regional detail down to local authority areas and may be cross-tabulated by age, sex, occupational group, etc.

Net interregional mobility: The relatively small net balance of migration in all regions in both 1960-1 and 1965-6 concealed considerable in- and out-movements; indeed gross migration usually exceeded net by over 10 to 1 and for many regions was a good deal higher (table 2.12). It is not easy to summarise interregional movements, even at the very general level of the UK economic planning regions, since it is difficult to link these various components to the population at risk. The scale, direction and balance of the migration streams are much what one would expect from general population trends. Net balances are small, mostly under 5 per 1,000 of the resident population, but gross migration indices for population aged 1 year and over exceed 40 per 1,000 in some areas (table 2.12). The greatest mobility rates in 1960-1 occurred in East Anglia and the South West region, followed by the East and West Midlands. Though by far the greatest numbers moved into and from the South East region, its gross migration rates were relatively small, especially in Greater London. Many regions had very similar degrees of movement and very small differences between inward and outward rates of migration as shown by modest net balances; such features well exemplify the dictum that every migration flow produces a counter-flow. Hence, the differentials in migration rates between such regions as the North West, Yorkshire and Humberside, and Wales differ little from 'healthy' growth areas of the West Midlands or even the South East.

In 1965-6 migration rates confirmed the attraction of East Anglia, the South West and the East Midlands. The most sluggish were those for the North West and Scotland and,

Planning region	Migration rates of resident population (per 1,000)							
	1960-1				1965-6			
	in	out	gross	net	in	out	gross	net
Northern	11·0	14·0	25·0	−3·0	13·6	14·5	28·1	−0·9
Yorks and Humberside	11·5	13·1	24·6	−1·6	13·9	13·8	27·7	+0·1
North West	9·4	10·5	19·9	−1·1	10·5	10·9	21·4	−0·4
East Midlands	18·0	15·7	33·7	+2·4	20·6	17·0	37·7	+3·6
West Midlands	13·4	12·9	26·3	+0·4	13·2	14·1	27·3	−0·9
South East	10·7	9·4	20·1	+1·2	10·3	11·4	21·7	−1·2
Greater London	7·6	9·9	17·5	−2·3	7·8	10·1	17·9	−2·3
Outer Metropolitan Area	11·5	13·3	24·8	−1·8	10·4	12·0	22·4	−1·6
Rest	16·1	14·5	30·6	+1·5	14·9	13·4	28·3	+1·5
East Anglia	23·8	20·9	44·7	+2·9	30·4	22·8	53·3	+7·6
South West	25·5	19·8	45·4	+5·7	25·6	20·0	45·6	+5·7
Wales	12·8	14·6	27·5	−1·8	13·6	13·3	26·9	+0·3
Scotland	5·3	10·0	15·3	−4·7	7·1	10·1	17·2	−3·0
GB	−	−	−	−	−	−	−	−

in terms of migration rates, Greater London, despite the latter's large volume of both in- and out-movement. The migration rates to the development areas were generally higher than in 1960-1; in particular, the inward balance of movement to Wales suggests that development area policies in the 1960s were beginning to make an impact on population trends. Scotland's very low rate of inward migration and considerable net loss remained, however.

It is not possible to show the complexity of interregional movements on a single map, but the balance of migration of population aged over 1 year for the period 1961-6 gives a graphic picture of both the essential mechanism and the resultants of such movements (fig. 2.8). The inset map of net migration rates and the actual net flows are a clear commentary upon the drift south-east. Interregional movement is seen to be not so much a direct transfer from areas of loss to areas of gain but rather a 'shunting' movement culminating in the transfer of considerable numbers of people to only four major regions: East Anglia, the East Midlands, the South West and the Outer South East. The latter is involved in a second major determinant of post-war migration, the movement from inner London which is now spreading from Greater London to the Outer Metropolitan Area (OMA) and which involves rehousing of people from these areas of the South East in a second generation of New Towns and overspill schemes mainly located in the three adjacent planning regions.

Those regions which gained population by residential migration in the 1960s all reflect the same basic features. The South West gained from all other regions over the period 1961-6, not only from gains by outward movement from the metropolitan area but also to its own attractions in the Bristol-Severnside growth area and in the rural and coastal retirement areas of Devon and Cornwall, a fact reflected in the age structure of the migration (table 2.13). However by 1965-6 over 90 per cent of the region's gains were from the South East, West Midlands and North West. East Anglia gained from all other regions except the South West and, perhaps surprisingly, Wales, though this interaction was on a very small scale. The East Midlands similarly gained from all regions, except East Anglia and the South West to both of which there were small net losses. The South East epitomises many of the features of both intra- and interregional movement. While there were large net losses from the Greater London subregion to the Outer South East and adjacent regions, it attracted large numbers in the 15-24 age-group, a feature also found in the Outer Metropolitan Area. Residential dispersal from the centre to the periphery is seen in the gain in all age-groups of the Outer South East subregion which is comparable in this respect to East Anglia and the South West.

All other regions suffered a net loss of population by migration, though this did not occur in every age-group. The West Midlands' losses were mainly to adjacent regions, the North West and East Midlands, and to the 'gain' areas of East Anglia and the South West; but it gained from all other regions. The North West gained from other regions of the north of England, from Scotland and the West Midlands, but lost to all other regions, while Wales gained from the North West, and the North, Scotland and East Anglia. Those with the weakest attraction in this phase were Yorkshire and Humberside, which lost to all regions except the North and Scotland; the North, which lost to all save Scotland, and Scotland, which lost population to every other region and in every age-group.

Age-selective migration: Population migration is highly age-selective. All recent studies of migration in the UK confirm the tendency of young Britons to be more migratory than the population as a whole. There is a strong movement of school-leavers and people in their late 'teens and early twenties from both rural areas and stagnating industrial regions of limited employment opportunities. In areas of residential development accessible to large towns, rural out-migration is offset by inmigration of young families. But the inner residential areas of the cities, especially London, are generally a zone of population loss, offset in certain cases by an influx of overseas immigrants and of single young people, including many students. Cumulatively, such differences contribute to striking contrasts between the age structure of migrants and that of the population as a whole (table 2.13). The 15-24 age-group is by far the most mobile with migration-rates in 1965-6 75 per cent above that of the next most mobile group, 25-44 years. On the limited evidence of the 1960-1 and 1965-6 data, migration-rates seem to be rising more quickly in the 15-24 age-group than in any other. Inasmuch as there has been a considerable increase in the number of people in full-time higher education, a proportion of this may be ascribed to temporary migration but there is much evidence to support the belief that such migration leads to permanent movement away from home, especially in the case of those moving from rural areas or depressed industrial regions.

Such age-selective migration is reflected both in the structure of the migration itself and in the age structure of both sender and receiver areas. The clear-cut losses of 1960-1 in virtually all age-groups from the three northern regions of England and from Scotland and Wales, had been ameliorated by 1965-6 (fig. 2.9). Scotland alone shows a net migration loss in every age-group throughout the period and this was quite severe for the young and mature age-groups of 15-44 years, representing a substantial draining of

TABLE 2.13   Age Structure of Interregional Migrants and Total Population, GB, 1961 and 1966

| | Per cent of age-group | | | | All ages |
	1-14	15-24	25-44	45+	1+
Population, 1961	22	13	27	38	100
Migrants, 1960-1	23	23	35	19	100
Population, 1966	22	15	25	17	100
Migrants, 1965-6	24	26	33	38	100

Source: Census 1961; Sample Census 1966

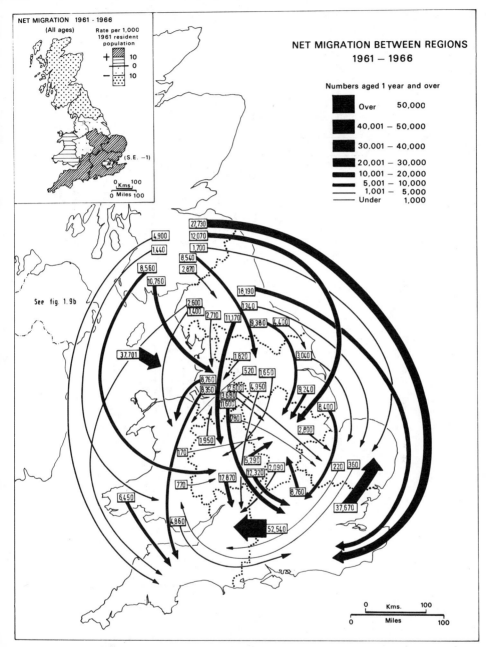

Figure 2.8   Net Interregional migration, UK, 1961-6
              Source: *Long Term Population Distribution in GB: A Study* (1971), *Census, N. Ireland*
              (1966).

vigorous, working-age population of both sexes from the region. This loss of the active,
youthful population persisted in the North West and for Wales, despite a general slowing
down of the migration flow; indeed in the North West there was an increase of one-third
in the net loss from the 15-24 group between 1960-1 and 1965-6. The population
situation of Yorkshire and Humberside has become more encouraging in that losses in
all three younger age-groups (0-44 years) have been arrested. But in the West Midlands

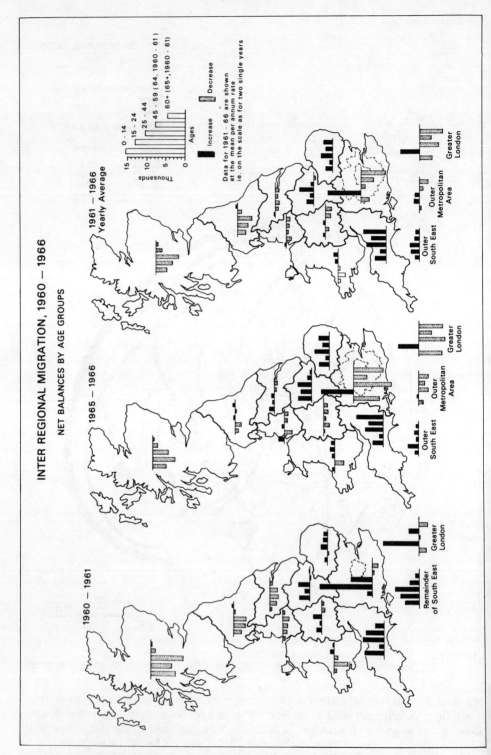

Figure 2.9   Interregional migration by age-groups, GB Economic Planning Regions, 1960-6
Source: *Long Term Population Distribution in GB: A Study* (1971), fig. 20

there has been a reversal of the modest gains in the younger age-groups, though the losses in the 15-24 groups were mainly female.

In contrast, the regions of gain not only added considerable numbers of population but, apart from the South West, had their greatest gains among the under-45s. It is clear that East Anglia and the South West in particular, and the East Midlands to an extent, were closely linked with the South East in an age-selective redistribution of population. In the South West the growing dominance of migration by the age-groups over 45 is reflected in the fact that by 1965-6 over one-third of the net migration gain was in the over-60 'retirement' groups which came mainly from the South East, West Midlands and North West. East Anglia is mainly a recipient of family migration from Greater London, reflected in the large net gains in the 25-44 and 0-14 groups and the smaller gains of 15-24 year olds.

The key to much selective redistribution lies in the South East region. Despite a striking reversal of migration balance between 1961 and 1966, there was still a considerable gain in the 15-24 age-group, the migrants coming from all regions of the UK and from overseas. However, by 1965-6 major out-movement had developed in all other age-groups with a considerable overspill movement of young families to East Anglia (the 0-44 year group). That to the South West was dominated by the over 45s, and the over 60s were very important, especially women.

Within the South East gross movements in 1965-6 were almost as large as the gross movements with all other regions (304,000 as compared with 370,000). Moreover a massive dispersal of families from the centre of Greater London and the Outer Metropolitan Area to the periphery (the Outer South East) involved two distinct types of mover: first, a residential migration of ages 1-14 and 25+; secondly, retirement migration of the over 60s to the south coast in particular, reflected in the fact that one-third of the flow from Greater London to the Outer South East in 1965-6 was of those over 60 years.

The effects on population structure may be derived from the relationship between the regional net migration balance and the gross movements in each age-group (table 2.14).

Two aspects of migration have shaped trends in the distribution and structure of population since 1945. First, fluctuations in net overseas migration have had considerable impact at both national and local level. Secondly, differential interregional movement, the net resultants of which explain much of the regional variations in population growth, is of considerable importance in its effects on regional structure and future population trends. Though in demographic terms both have much in common, their social impact is very different: thus each will be discussed in turn.

II.6 Immigration from Overseas

General review: Despite its importance, precise information on the scale and regional impact of immigration is limited. Immigration statistics leave many gaps, while census data on immigration are defective in a number of ways. British census tables of birthplace before 1971 show nothing of the date of movement and give nationality but not ethnic origins. Moreover, the census probably under-enumerated the overseas-born in both 1961 and, especially, in the 10 per cent sample census of 1966. Furthermore, it is difficult to distinguish persons born overseas of British parents. Not until the publication of information derived from the questions in the 1971 census concerning place of birth, nationality and place of birth of parents and year of first entry into Britain of overseas-born will it be possible to give a fuller and more accurate picture of immigration from census sources.

There have been three phases in post-war immigration to the UK. Between 1945-55 renewed emigration to the Dominions led to slight net migration losses, despite a

TABLE 2.14   Regional Migration Gain or Loss, by Major Age-groups, GB, 1965-6

	Percentage gain or loss as percent of gross flow					All ages
	1-14	15-24	25-44	45-54	60+	1+
Losses						
Scotland	−15·4	−27·8	−13·7	−17·1	− 2·2	−17·5
Northern England	− 4·9	− 8·4	+ 0·6	− 2·5	+ 6·9	− 2·9
North West	+ 0·7	+ 2·0	+ 1·6	− 8·0	− 9·2	− 1·7
West Midlands	+ 6·3	− 1·8	− 1·5	− 8·4	−11·5	− 3·3
South East	− 8·9	+ 9·3	− 8·1	−10·9	−25·6	− 2·8
Greater London	−28·2	+12·8	−15·9	−31·6	−51·6	−12·9
Outer Metropolitan	− 5·6	+ 1·6	− 7·6	−11·2	−31·9	− 7·2
Gains						
Wales	+ 3·7	−13·9	+ 3·1	+15·9	+12·5	+ 1·0
Yorkshire and Humberside	+ 3·3	0	+ 1·8	− 5·7	− 8·8	+ 0·3
East Midlands	+17·7	+ 9·8	+ 8·6	+ 8·2	+ 5·1	+ 9·5
East Anglia	+10·6	+ 5·5	+14·1	+26·4	+38·2	+14·3
South West	+ 7·7	+ 2·9	+ 9·8	+24·4	+39·9	+12·5
Outer South East	+ 2·8	+16·7	+ 0·8	+10·4	+ 6·7	+ 5·0

Source: Long Term Population Distribution in GB: a Study, (1971), Appendix 2, Table F, p.127

considerable gain of European refugees, especially those of Polish origin. Nevertheless, during this period England and Wales gained by migration, not least because of continuing immigration from Eire (table 2.2). After 1955, immigration from the New Commonwealth increased considerably, leading to a relatively large net inward movement of 479,000 1958-62. Rising labour demands, especially in the early 1960s, had much to do with this influx which produced net gains of 45,000 in 1958 rising to 172,000 in the peak year of 1961, which led to restriction of movement under the Commonwealth Immigrants Act of 1962. This Act created a graded system of employment vouchers which immigrants were required to hold to obtain entry: 'A' vouchers were issued to those who had jobs to come to, 'B' vouchers were for those with particular needed skills or qualifications (such as nurses or doctors), and 'C' vouchers were issued to unskilled workers. Preference was given from the outset to A and B categories. C vouchers were officially discontinued from 1965, and the policy of selective recruitment of high-qualified persons was confirmed by new regulations in 1968.

The 1962 Act allowed dependants of immigrants already in the country freedom of entry, though this was tightened up under the 1968 Commonwealth Immigrants Act. Since 1962, therefore, the emphasis has shifted from the immigration of workers to their families and dependants: thus, in 1969 of 36,557 Commonwealth immigrants 29,459 were dependants.[19] A further group of coloured Commonwealth immigrants are the holders of British passports, mainly East Africans of Asian origin, the estimates of whom vary considerably: for example, estimates of the potential numbers involved in recent expulsions from Uganda vary from 23,000 to over 50,000 against the estimated 27,000 who had arrived in Britain at the expiry of the expulsion deadline in November 197

In relation to the total population of the UK, the increase of immigrants, more particularly of coloured Commonwealth immigrants, is not large (table 2.15); but it has led to considerable changes in the characteristics of the overseas-born population of the UK since 1945 and, in some localities, has had very marked social and demographic consequences. As compared with about 1 per cent overseas born in 1931 (perhaps 1·5 per cent allowing for those whose birthplace was not stated), the increase in GB to 1,053,200 (2·1 per cent) in 1951, 1,507,600 (2·9 per cent) by 1961, to 1,876,300 (3·5 per cent) by 1966 and to 3,100,000 (5·8 per cent) by 1971 represents a considerable change. In 1966 less than half the 1·88 million people of overseas birth in Britain were

People and Work

TABLE 2.15   Estimated Population of Major Immigrant Groups, England and Wales, 1966-86

Area of origin	Born overseas	1966 born in UK	Total	1971	1981	Low 1986 fertility estimate	High fertility estimate
India	180·4	43·2	223·6	377	579	768	890
Pakistan	109·6	10·1	119·7	211	306	408	485
Ceylon	12·9	3·2	16·1	NA	NA	NA	NA
Jamaica	188·1	85·7	273·8	343	411	474	529
Other Carribbean	129·8	50·5	180·3	229	293	341	375
British West Africa	43·1	7·6	50·7	68	80	83	94
Far East	47·0	13·0	60·0	NA	NA	NA	NA
Total	710·9	213·3	924·2	1,228	1,669	2,074	2,373

Source: Rose *et al.* 1969, tables 10.2 and 30.1

NA = Not available

The estimates exclude Indians and Pakistanis of British origin.
For 1971 and 1981 the estimates are based on low fertility assumptions.

coloured (852,750) a figure which is estimated to be 1,030,000 by 1971; it is around these figures that most of the debate on immigration has focused. It is difficult to estimate precisely the numbers of coloured population, since this also involves children born to immigrants in the UK. It has been suggested that 500,000 children should be added to the 1 million people from the New Commonwealth recorded in the 1971 census. Such figures indicate a total of about 1·5 million New Commonwealth immigrants in the UK in 1971.[20]

Distribution: The problem is not primarily one of overall numbers of immigrants, but rather of their proportionate distribution. Like most immigrant communities, past and present, coloured immigrants tend to concentrate in relatively few areas. In 1951 the greater part of the overseas-born population of the UK lived in London and South East England, though at that time these were chiefly European-born. Since that time the overseas-born have increased much more rapidly than the population as a whole and have become even more concentrated in distribution. While the South East planning region (including Greater London) was by far the main focus of coloured immigrants, consider-able increases had taken place in the West Midlands and, especially of Indians and Pakistanis, in the North West, Yorkshire and Humberside, and the East Midlands (table 2.16). By 1971 these proportions remained much the same. While the percentage of New Commonwealth immigrants in the conurbations had fallen slightly, it had done so at about the same rate as the total population.

By far the greater proportion and the highest densities of coloured immigrants are to be found in the inner areas of the major cities, particularly of the metropolitan boroughs and the West Midlands conurbation. Every local authority with over 5 per cent coloured population in 1966 was in Greater London.[21] The highest rates of increase between 1961 and 1966 were found in a few areas of Greater London and the preliminary evidence from the 1971 census indicates that this has continued. The degree of concen-tration is even more marked at the local level. In 1966, 16,770 (5·6 per cent) of the population of Ealing was from New Commonwealth countries, but in Northcote Ward 31 per cent of the population was coloured.[22] Even with such a high proportion of immi-grants and the widespread belief that this was a predominantly Indian area, half the households surveyed were European. It is this sort of evidence which has led Glass to argue that these concentrations do not yet constitute ghettos.[23]

Nevertheless, the considerable concentration of coloured immigrants into a few parts of the inner-city and the developing segregation among such groups of working-class population, especially of West Indians, *is* a matter for serious concern. Studies of Birming-

TABLE 2.16　Main New Commonwealth Immigrant Groups, England and Wales, 1966 and 1971

	(1) India*		(2) Pakistan		(3) West Indies		Total of 1-3		Total population	
	1966	1971	1966	1971	1966	1971	1966	1971	1966	1971
Total (1,000s) in England and Wales	163·8	313·4	73·1	135·7	267·9	301·4	504·9	750·5	47,135·5	48,602·9
Percentage in										
Conurbations										
Tyneside	0·9	0·6	0·8	0·6	0·1	0·1	0·5	0·4	1·8	1·7
West Yorks.	5·6	5·1	17·3	16·1	3·1	3·4	6·0	6·4	3·6	3·6
SELNEC	3·7	4·0	7·0	9·1	4·0	3·5	4·3	4·7	5·1	4·9
Merseyside	0·9	0·7	0·6	0·3	0·6	0·5	0·7	0·5	2·8	2·6
West Midlands	14·9	14·3	19·3	17·0	13·4	13·1	14·7	14·3	5·0	4·9
Greater London	33·9	34·2	22·0	22·1	56·7	55·4	44·3	40·5	16·3	15·2
Total	60·0	58·9	67·0	65·2	77·9	76·0	70·5	66·8	34·6	32·9
Rest of England and Wales	40·0	41·1	32·9	34·8	22·1	24·0	29·5	33·2	65·4	67·1

Source: Sample Census 1966 and Census 1971, Advance Analysis
* excluding White Indians

ham show that over half the enumeration districts of the CB had no West Indians, while 30 per cent of this group was concentrated into wards in which they formed over 15 per cent of the total population.[24] At such a stage of assimilation this is, perhaps, to be expected; historical parallels may be seen in the segregation of Irish immigrants in the mid-nineteenth century and of Jewish immigrants from Eastern Europe in the late-nineteenth century. But difficulties arising from colour and custom, aggravated by housing shortages and problems of education, are unlikely to lead to rapid acceptance by or assimilation into the community at large.

Structure and trends in immigrant populations: Immigration is highly age-selective, particularly in the early stages when it is dominated by young persons, especially men. Dependants usually follow to give a more normal age and sex structure to the immigrant community. In the case of the Commonwealth immigration of the late 1950s and 1960s this process is still in train, with consequent effects on the demographic and social structure and fertility patterns.

A large-scale survey of Irish, and Old and New Commonwealth immigrants in 1961 showed that 75 per cent were men, 62 per cent were between 18 and 34 and 83 per cent under 45, as compared with 62 per cent in the population at large; only half the men were married as compared with 73 per cent of the population over 19 years in England and Wales.[25] These characteristics are still apparent, especially in the remarkably low proportions of over-45s and the predominance of mature adults of 25-44 (table 2.17). The female:male ratios are universally low, especially among Pakistani (39:100 in 1971) and, to a lesser extent, Indian and West African groups, but the trend towards normality may be seen in lower sex ratios among the 1961-6 arrivals, while the considerable number of dependants among post-1965 arrivals is leading to a further balancing of the population structure. Moreover, the large number of women among West Indian immigrants to London was a notable feature of the 1960s.

The impact of a mainly young immigrant population can be seen in the above-average 0-14 age-group and in a high rate of natural increase. It is difficult to compare the fertility of immigrants with British rates, since most immigrant families are still in the process of formation. 1961 Census data suggest that for marriages of comparable duration immigrant fertility is, at present, higher than among native-born English; but the highest rates were among Irish women (40 per cent above the English rates) while those for coloured immigrant women were 20 per cent above native-born.[26] There is some evidence that the differential is lower among completed immigrant families and not significantly different from British-born people of comparable social class. Much has been made of a survey in 1969 by the Ministry of Health and Social Security showing that 11·8 per cent of all births in England and Wales were to foreign-born mothers but, of the 11·8 per cent, 3·2 per cent were to Irish mothers and 2·8 per cent to other white immigrants, leaving 5·8 per cent of births to coloured immigrants. True, in areas of high concentration of immigrants much higher figures obtained; e.g. in Lambeth and Brent, 1 in 3 births were to mothers from the New Commonwealth; in some parts of the Midlands similarly high proportions were found, e.g 1 in 4·5 in Wolverhampton and 1 in 6 in Birmingham and Leicester, while in Huddersfield the figure was 1 in 5.

With many immigrant women in the younger, child-bearing ages, such crude statistics can be very misleading. What limited calculations were made of fertility rates among immigrant families suggest that they 'are larger by about one-third than those of the English population'.[27] On the basis of such evidence it is difficult to justify some of the wild forecasts of future coloured population. Even using 'high fertility' assumptions the numbers in England and Wales are unlikely to exceed 2·37 million by 1986 (4·5 per cent of the estimated total), perhaps 3·5 million (6 per cent) by the end of the century, far below the 4·5-7·0 million quoted in some quarters. A 'low fertility' estimate is likely

People and Work

TABLE 2.17   Age and Sex Structure among Selected Groups of Commonwealth Immigrants, GB, 1966

Age		India	Pakistan	Jamaica	Rest of Caribbean	British W. Africa	Cyprus	Total population
		1966	1966	1966	1966	1966	1966	1966
0-14		33	24	40	39	23	35	23
15-24		16	15	11	12	16	18	14
25-44		40	51	41	41	59	34	25
45+		11	10	8	8	2	13	38
Males per								
1,000	1966	1,479	4,231	1,066	1,026	1,614	1,191	940
females	1971	1,193	1,568		1,004*	1,205†	1,165	944
M:F (1961-6 arrivals)		1,373	3,541	733	809	1,452	1,016	

Source: Rose *(et al.) Colour and Citizenship* (1969) and *Census 1971*, Advance Analysis

* West Indies as a whole

† Africa as a whole

to give some 2·5-3·0 million by the end of the century and finds some support in the downward trend in fertility with length of stay in Britain found among West Indian immigrants, but high fertility estimates give figures of 2·4 million by 1986 (Table 2.15).

II.7   Differential Interregional Movement

Two further aspects of population migration in the UK deserve special mention: rural-urban movements and differential migration according to socio-economic groups. Though the massive flood-tide of rural migration of the nineteenth century has since abated, there are still considerable losses from many rural areas. The aggregate population of rural districts is actually increasing (table 2.3) due to urban overspill from areas of maximum population concentration whilst areas peripheral to these and in commuting distance of town jobs are enabled to retain natural increase. In contrast to these more accessible areas, the remoter country districts, especially the hard core areas of depopulation in upland Britain, continue to lose population on a considerable scale.[28]

Rural population loss is markedly greater among the youthful than among the mature age-groups.[29] Limited opportunities for jobs and higher education in rural areas force young people to leave home. Though facilities for primary and secondary education are generally good in the countryside, in some remote areas of Wales and, especially of Scotland, closure of schools is one factor in continuing family migration. Higher education or instruction for the professional or skilled trades requires a move to town. Hence, country districts tend to be 'denuded of people of superior abilities'.[30] Once gone, they seldom return. Jones has shown for Central Wales that 'over half the distant migrants were taking their first job after leaving school or college'[31] many of them in large cities such as Liverpool or Birmingham, with the main flow to London and the South East. An official enquiry of 1964 noted that such selective out-migration '. . . must influence adversely the quality of the community'.[32]

A similarly long-established draining of population from rural Scotland, especially from the remoter parts of the Highlands and Islands, continues and indeed is the cause of actual or threatened depopulation.[33] The extent of such migration from Scotland 'increases with education attainment': the rate of migration of highly qualified persons is some two and a half times that of the population of Scotland in the same age group.[34]

Detailed studies of Northern England have indicated that while all young people in rural areas are mobile, school-leavers were especially so.[35] Though they went mainly to adjacent towns, the next most important flow was a long-distance movement to London and the South East. In some cases family migration resulted from the wish to give children a better chance of a career without them having to leave home.

These examples may be multiplied from other parts of the UK as population in remoter rural areas contracts, educational opportunities there tend to narrow and the gap in opportunity between urban and rural areas is likely to continue to widen, thereby increasing the flow of able young people from the countryside. The less skilled remain, though the girls tend to be more mobile. Farm families also tend to be less migratory, in contrast to the nineteenth-century situation when many farm labourers left the countryside.

Varying social and economic opportunities are also key factors in the pattern and scale of both interregional and intra-urban migration. The growing concentration of higher services upon a relatively few major cities has increased socio-economic differentials between regions in the post-war period, leading to increased differential mobility of highly qualified manpower. Few investigations have been made of this aspect of migration, but the general relationship between levels of education and interregional movement have been observed in the context of manpower and employment.[36] Friedlander and Roshier have observed that '. . . in general, the higher occupational (and education) groups were found to be more mobile and this differential increased with distance moved'.[37] Recently, a detailed study of professional and managerial manpower showed that the greater opportunities for upward social mobility have led to a pronounced movement of these groups to the major cities, especially to Greater London.[38] Conversely, the progressive decrease in the proportion of high status jobs in both rural and declining industrial regions highlights the contrasts in this type of interregional migration. The migratory élite, as they have been described, are more mobile both in terms of distance moved and as a proportion of their age-group.

Much presentday migration in the UK is local or intraregional. Short-distance movements, often primarily changes of residence mainly for social reasons, account for 80 per cent of the moves, nine-tenths of which are under 10 miles.[39] Movements of this kind are mainly within urban regions and take two forms: first, the displacement of working-class families from rented accommodation in the residential areas affected by slum clearance, who move to peripheral local authority housing or, more recently, farther afield to New Towns or overspill areas; secondly, a large outward migration to private residential areas, often in adjacent rural districts, of managerial and professional classes and certain types of skilled workers. Such people rise professionally and socially through a series of higher positions, moving residence within the community in which they live. This 'spiralist society, as it has been called' thus produces 'a characteristic combination of social and spatial mobility'.[40]

This process of peripheral migration from the inner areas of large cities is exemplified in a study of migration on Merseyside.[41] Internal migration between and within local authorities on Merseyside has increased with the rapid sprawl of the conurbation in the twentieth century. Movement within the region has increased considerably since 1950, a fact underlined since 1966 by the development of the New Towns of Skelmersdale and Runcorn. Indeed between 1961 and 1971 the population of Liverpool CB fell by 138,916, a decrease of 19·9 per cent, almost the same percentage loss as experienced by Manchester and paralleled by some of the inner London boroughs. While the pattern of migration between the Merseyside local authorities is fairly complex the general picture revealed by a study of migration fields in 1965-6 is one of outward movement to the outer conurbation and periphery including the adjacent areas of south-central Lancashire and North Wales (fig. 2.10).

Most of the residential migration to the peripheral areas up to 1966 was of professional and managerial groups. For example, population of the rapidly growing suburb of Formby UD leapt from the 12 per cent increase of 1951-6 to a staggering 100 per cent in 1961-71.

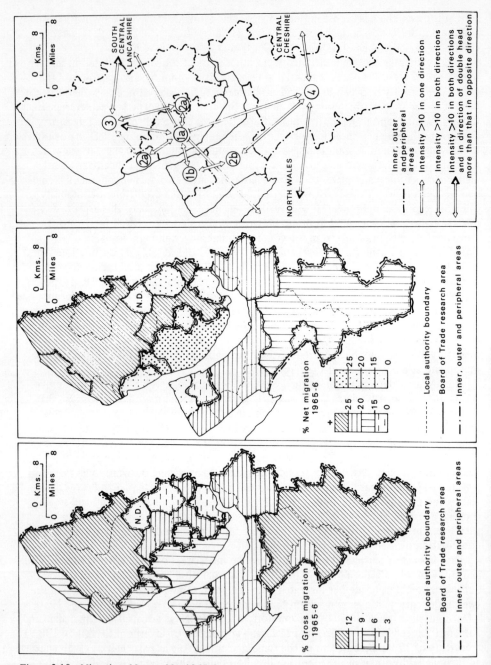

Figure 2.10   Migration, Merseyside, 1965-6
Source: K.G. Pickett, *Merseyside: Social and Economic Studies,* figs. 15 and 16

Already in 1966 the population structure was mainly young: 31 per cent were between
25-44 years as compared with Liverpool's 24 per cent, and 28 per cent under 15 years
(Liverpool, 25 per cent). Formby is a predominantly middle-class area with 39 per cent
in the social classes 1 and 2 (Liverpool 10 per cent). One-quarter of the population had

changed address in 1965-6 and of a sample social survey conducted in 1968[42] nearly one-half of the movers had come from the Merseyside conurbation, over one-quarter from Liverpool itself. This is endorsed by the survey finding that 49·5 per cent of the whole sample but 58·9 per cent of the migrant heads of households travelled to work in the inner areas of the conurbation. These findings are supported in a wider context by a research study on migration between major centres and their surrounding areas carried out by the Maud Commission[43], which showed a strong positive correlation between migration loss from county boroughs and low indices of men over 15 in professional and managerial classes and of males 25-44 as a proportion of all males of 15 and over. Taking England outside Greater London as = 100, the indices were:

TABLE 2.18   Mobility of Professional and Managerial Workers, England, 1961-6

	Per cent net migration	Proportion managerial and professional		Proportion of males 25-44 to males 15+	
	1961-6	1961	1966	1961	1966
All CBs	−3·19	79	78	100	97
CBs with migration losses (61 out of 78)	−4·10	74	73	101	98

Source: Redcliffe-Maud Commission (1969), vol. III, appendix 3, table 1, pp. 48-9

In a more detailed study of fourteen towns it was shown that the migration loss of men aged 25-44 in the professional and managerial classes was roughly twice that of losses among all males over 15 years[44] (table 2.18).

While there is some compensatory inmigration to the city centres, as observed for Greater London, this does little if anything to offset the loss of the more prosperous and vigorous sections of the population. Indeed many of the vacated residences are occupied by poor people including, in many areas, a large proportion of overseas immigrants. Thus the four county boroughs of inner Merseyside included 23,820 (2·3 per cent) Irish-born and 14,330 (1·3 per cent) from overseas. In Liverpool most of the New Commonwealth immigrants were concentrated into three central wards and in the 1960s this influx has increasingly focused in one, Granby Ward, which also has high indices of virtually all criteria of social decay.

III   POPULATION STRUCTURE

Contrasts and changes in natural and migrational trends result from and influence population structure. In the UK differential migration as between different age groups and between men and women is an important factor in regional differences in population structure and future population trends alike.

III.1 Sex Ratios

Due to the better survival rates of male children and the diminishing importance of the 'lost generation' of men killed during the First World War, the pronounced imbalance between the sexes of the 1921-51 period has been progressively modified since the war (table 2.6). There are, however, considerable regional variations from the present UK figure of 105·5 females per 100 males. In broad regional terms (fig. 2.11) this average is exceeded only in rural Wales, Southern and much of Eastern Scotland, South West England, Greater London and the Outer Metropolitan Area, and North West England. At the higher level of definition of administrative county and county borough (fig. 2.12),

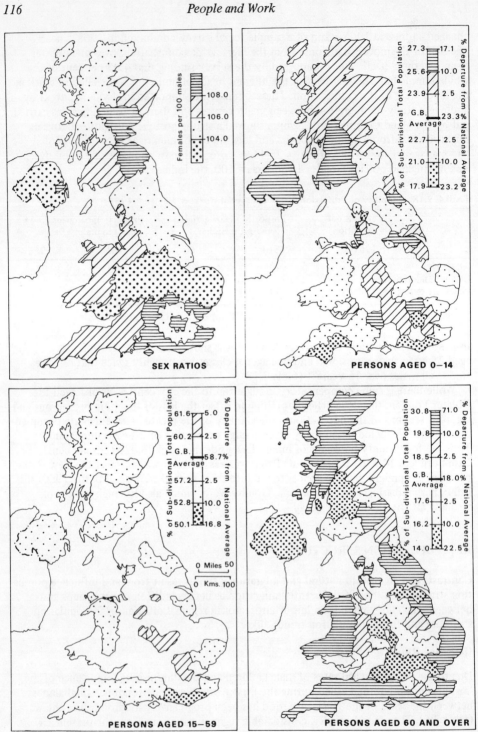

Figure 2.11   Age and sex structure, UK Regions, 1966

the main factors involved in these differences become more apparent.

In 1971 the majority of rural areas had a below-average ratio of women to men. The long-standing tendency for women to be more migratory than men and the more restricted job opportunities for women in rural areas both contribute to this situation. The lowest female:male ratios are found in parts of Northern Ireland and the Scottish Highlands, but most of the rural areas from the Welsh border to the Fenland counties also have relatively low ratios. Women dominate the population structure of retirement areas, in which resorts and spas have notably high ratios: due to their greater longevity, there are very large proportions of elderly women in such areas. This accounts for such ratios as 122 in Peebles and Pitlochry, 126 in Torbay, 128 in Bournemouth, 133 in Eastbourne and 123 in Southport.

In addition, above-average female:male ratios are found first in Greater London and, secondly, in textile districts such as the North West and the Scottish Border country. A recent detailed study of the Scottish Border counties has shown that differential migration and occupational structure account for considerable variations in sex ratios at local as well as at regional level, in which a sharp upswing in the proportion of women in the population in the later-nineteenth century was due to female employment in the textile industry.[45] Though much less pronounced than in the past, due to the absolute and relative decline of jobs in the cotton mills, some of East Lancashire textile towns, for example Blackburn and Burnley (108), have above-average ratios, though the Lowry-like image of shawled and beclogged women clattering over cobblestones to work in the spinning mills is now a picture from the past, as the below-average ratios for many South East Lancashire mill towns show. In a very different context, the majority of Greater London boroughs have high proportions of women, though the highest ratios tend to be found in West London. This tendency for higher proportions of women is indeed typical of the inner residential areas of many large towns.

Apart from the male-dominant rural areas, districts with below average sex ratios, and hence relatively more men than average, tend to be associated with heavy industrial areas. Some of the lower ratios are found in coalfield areas of south-east Wales (e g 104·8 in Glamorgan AC) and North East England (e g Durham AC, 102·6). The lowest tend to be in the heavy industrial districts such as the West Midlands, where Wolverhampton, Walsall and West Bromwich all have ratios of around 101, or South Yorkshire, where the Barnsley and Rotherham ratios are 102.

III.2 Age Structure

The general increase in numbers in both young and older age-groups since 1945 has already been shown to underlie continuing population growth in the UK (table 2.5). An increased birth-rate has brought the proportion of under-15s to 24·3 per cent in 1971, comparable with the 24·1 per cent of 1931. Meanwhile, population of retirement age has greatly increased to an estimated 16·0 per cent for 1971 as compared with 9·6 per cent in 1931. However, very considerable spatial variations in age structure exist and were analysed in some detail for local authority areas in 1961 by Dewdney.[46] In his study of four age-groups 0-14, 15-44, 45-64 and 65+, Dewdney stressed two aspects: first, the distribution of different age-groups; secondly, the age-structure within the various local authorities or regions in which, he observes, the various age-groups are complementary, so that: 'Quite different mechanisms of population growth and movement may give rise to similar results as far as the age composition of a particular area is concerned.'[47]

The essential features of Dewdney's detailed analysis are reflected at the more general of UK economic planning subregions for 1966 (fig. 2.11). Above-average proportions of young people (0-14 years) may result from a variety of causes. High birth-rates explain the relatively large proportion of young people in much of rural Scotland and Northern

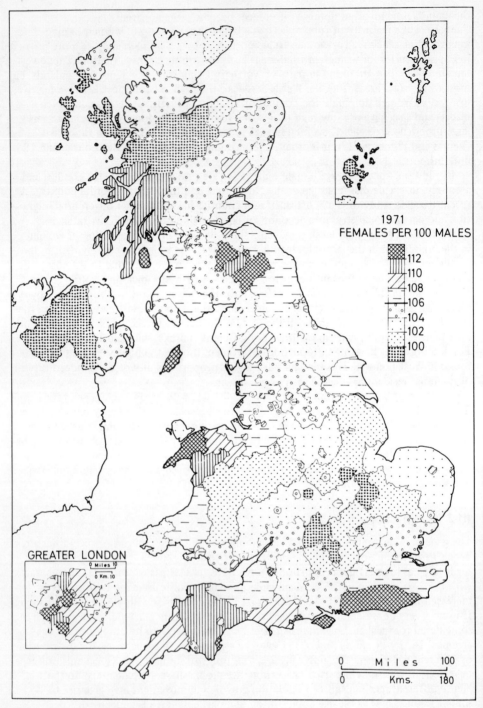

Figure 2.12   Şex ratios, UK, 1971

Ireland. In both areas birth-rates remain high, despite long-standing outmigration, and a continuing migrational loss of young adults increases the relative importance of other age-groups. High birth-rates also explain the high proportions of under-15s in certain industrial regions, including Central Scotland, North East and North West England, and Yorkshire and Humberside. A growing tendency to outward migration of young families from inner residential areas to the periphery of the large towns tends progressively to increase the proportion of children in the population of many parts of the major city regions, notably in the outer metropolitan areas.

The 15-59 group is a rather large one which tends to conceal differences between the more mobile 15-44 and more stable 45-59 year age-groups. Dewdney's analysis showed that relatively high proportions of the younger adult population were found in areas of economic growth and inmigration, and tended to be prominent in the conurbations and large industrial areas, though residential overspill has reduced the proportion of this group in the inner metropolitan areas as may be seen in the 1966 map. In contrast, the 45-59 group has many different tendencies. The inner areas of large cities have considerable numbers of small households made up of parents over-45 whose families are grown up and have left home. Elsewhere, in declining industrial areas of long-standing outmigration, the older mature population has above-average representation, but the broad ' 15-59 age-group conceals the deficiency of younger adults in the population.

In rural areas of Wales, Scotland and Eastern England, along the south coast of England and in the South West, there is a considerable representation of over-60s, arising from two frequently interrelated factors. Prolonged outmigration of young adults often leads eventually to a deficiency of births, thus creating a predominantly elderly population, as in much of rural Wales and the Scottish Highlands. Indeed this situation is sometimes found in industrial areas, notably in the small industrial towns of North East Lancashire. In the resort areas, of the south coast of England and North Wales for example, the reasons for very large proportions of over-60s are more positive and, as has been shown previously, involve a considerable inmigration of people of retirement age.

Without a very carefully integrated analysis of age-sex structure, area by area, it is difficult to summarise the regional interrelationships of these various age-group patterns. However, certain broad groupings emerge. In Northern Ireland, high birth-rates are reflected in the large proportion of under-15s but the deficiencies in the other age-groups reflect long-standing outmigration. Much of rural Scotland shares the characteristic of relatively high proportions of children but in areas of marked depopulation in the Highlands and Southern Scotland this is associated with large proportions in the over-60 group and a deficiency in the 15-59s, especially due to large outmigration of younger adults. The Central Valley of Scotland, in contrast, like many English industrial regions has a high proportion of both children and young adults; above-average proportions of over-60s in the Scottish industrial subregions are found only in the Fife coalfield.

In England and Wales there is a generally clear distinction between the rural areas, with below-average under-15 and 15-44 age-groups and above-average shares of the elderly, which become very pronounced in retirement areas, and the urban and industrial areas. The urban regions are more complex with many contrasting structural features which are not apparent at subregional level. Intraregional migration tends to produce a series of zones within the city region. The central areas have relatively few young and old, and are often dominated locally by young adults, as in parts of central London. The older residential areas of the inner city are frequently dominated by mature adults and elderly people, with younger families and children depleted by outward movement to the suburbs. The peripheral areas complement the inner city and are dominated by families at an active stage of formation, with above-average proportions of children and young adults, though in the outer areas the 45-59 age-groups are dominant, as for example in the outer metropolitan region.

All these situations are dynamic, and age structures reflect economic and social change, especially in the progressive extension of urban-based population into rural areas. Thus the implications of present and projected age structures are of considerable significance to both physical and social planning on a regional basis.

III.3 Social Structure

Experience of fertility, mortality and migration varies regionally to produce differences in age and sex structure. Many of these demographic contrasts are due, in part, to differing social structure. Hence, an analysis of population trends must take account of differing social structures at both regional and local level. Moreover, social contrasts are themselves often a resultant of aspects of population dynamics; thus selective migration varies not only with age and sex but also with education, skills and job mobility.

Socio-economic indices: The analysis of social structure is hampered by the lack of any one generally agreed or readily measured criterion. British population censuses have collected information on occupations in some detail since 1841. In association with the fertility analysis of the 1911 census the Registrar General adopted a system of social groups and classes based on occupation which has led to the present socio-economic classification.[48] Such classifications are very valuable, especially in cross-tabulations with other population data, but they raise a number of problems of comparison, especially as between 'middle-ranking' manual and non-manual occupations.

Hence they are often used in association with other socio-economic information. Since housing is one of the biggest investments made by a family, it may be expected that the quality and spaciousness of dwellings will reflect household income and may, therefore, be a useful surrogate of living standards and social class. A number of housing variables concerning type of tenure, intensity of occupation and amenities have been used with considerable effectiveness by social geographers and sociologists in defining the social areas of towns.[49] Moreover, the characteristics of housing and the relationship of residential trends to employment are of direct interest in relation to many aspects of daily mobility, and of the structure and development of urban regions.

Educational qualifications have become increasingly important in the modern UK for professional, business and technical skills; hence educational achievement is increasingly valuable as a measure of social class. From 1951 there has been increasing information on educational achievement in British censuses which now provide data on the terminal age of education, scientific and technological qualifications (1961 census), higher educational qualifications (1966 census) and, in the 1971 census, school-leaving qualifications. In addition the Department of Education and Science issues annually the six-volume *Statistics of Education* which includes much information on the educational provision by local authorities, the proportions of various age groups in full-time education, qualifications of school leavers and the like.[50]

Personal income is one of the best indices of social class but is not available in any detail for the UK[51]. Some aggregate data on personal incomes are published by the Inland Revenue, tabulated for counties.[52] Since 1965 these have been used as the basis of figures published in the annual *Regional Abstract of Statistics.* From these data it is possible to analyse, in broad terms, the distribution and trends in personal incomes.[53]

While each individually is of value in social analysis, such criteria may be combined with demographic variables through the use of multi-variate statistical techniques, such as principal components analysis, to delineate spatial variations in social structure more fully. Work of this kind has been pioneered for British towns by Moser and Scott.[54] Such studies are of particular value in distinguishing the differing character of social areas within cities, in which demographic, social and economic conditions are often closely interrelated and in which an understanding of population distribution and trends is inseparable from social geography.

III.4 Housing and Households

Of the UK's 19·3 million dwellings, nearly 8 million have been built since 1945 but some 6 million are pre-1920 in date. Half the dwellings are owner-occupied, about one-third rented from local authorities or public corporations and the rest mainly rented from private landlords[55] (table 2.19). Although the number of dwellings now roughly equals the number of households there are still housing shortages in the conurbations and industrial areas, especially in inner city areas.

The large inter-war building and slum clearance programme added nearly 4 million dwellings to the housing stock of England and Wales, about 30 per cent of which were built by local authorities. Yet this very large increase only slightly exceeded the rate of growth of households; indeed 1901-39 the number of dwellings built lagged slightly behind the increase in families. Hence, if essential slum clearance is taken into account, there was an estimated deficit of housing in 1939 of over half-a-million homes in England and Wales alone.[56]

Moreover, at that time conditions of overcrowding were still widespread, though the yardstick of 1½ persons per room was generous by nineteenth-century standards. The virtual cessation of building during the Second World War and the damage to and loss of property by bombing, which affected one in three of all dwellings in England and Wales, both contributed to a general post-war housing shortage in the UK, which was particularly acute in the large cities. Despite the building of nearly three-quarters of a million homes in Britain between 1946 and 1950,[57] there was a shortage of over one million dwellings at the time of the 1951 census, when the ratio of households to dwellings was 1·056 for GB (table 2.20).

Since 1951, the situation has improved considerably, though the continuing high rate of formation of new households, due to high marriage rates and a falling average age of marriage, together with immigration and interregional migration to certain areas of rapid population growth, has caused regional shortages of housing to persist. Estimates of formation of new households due to marriage *less* losses due to deaths, together with a falling demand from immigrant households suggest that there may be some reduction of demand for new homes from about 145,000 per year at present to some 120,000 per year in the mid-1970s rising to 130,000 per year around 1981.[58]

A further considerable post-war demand for additional housing has come from slum clearance. Some 992,000 houses were 'demolished or closed' in England and Wales from 1955-71 and 250,000 in Scotland, and 2·25 million people have been rehoused since the mid-1950s, but 2·1 million unfit dwellings remain.[59] In addition to clearance an average of 80,000 houses per year were improved in England and Wales, between 1965-71, under various sections of the Housing Acts (of 1957, 1961 and 1969) and the Public Health Acts. In an attempt to upgrade the 4·5 million dwellings in England and Wales and 200,000 in Scotland which lack amenities or are in poor repair, though structurally sound,[60] an average of 125,000 improvement grants per year were made in Great Britain and this had increased to 100,000 in the first half of 1971 alone.[61]

Although the number of slums in England and Wales was reduced from the 1·8 million dwellings estimated as unfit at the time of the House Condition Survey of 1967 to around 1·35 million by 1970, a considerable number of pre-1919 houses remain in all regions of Britain (table 2.19). To cater for the estimated net increase in households of some 145,000 per year at present, and perhaps 120,000-130,000 per year in the 1970s, *and* to clear existing slums at a current rate of about 100,000 per year, perhaps rising to 150,000 in the late 1970s, would require 250,000-300,000 new houses per year. If, in addition, a

TABLE 2.19   Estimated Housing Stock, GB Regions, December 1969

Region	Number of dwellings (1,000s)		Tenure (percentages)				Age of dwellings (percentages)			Percentage households without fixed bath
	1969	1971	Owner-occupied	local authority or New Towns	private owner	Other tenures	Pre-1919	1919-44	Post-1944	
				Rented from						
ENGLAND	15,773	(16,076)	51	28	16	5	37	25	38	14·6
Northern	1,144	(1,161)	41	37	15	7	38	22	40	16·1
Yorks and Humberside	1,719	(1,736)	48	30	17	5	39	25	36	17·5
North West	2,325	(2,358)	54	26	17	3	40	26	34	17·6
East Midlands	1,173	(1,197)	50	27	17	6	36	25	39	16·1
West Midlands	1,698	(1,730)	49	34	12	5	31	27	42	15·0
East Anglia	597	(614)	51	26	14	9	39	19	42	19·8
South East	5,803	(5,931)	52	25	18	5	35	28	37	11·9
Greater London	2,499	(2,537)	46	26	25	3	-	-	-	14·8
Outer Metropolitan	1,744	(1,792)	57	27	11	5	-	-	-	8·4
Outer South East	1,560	(1,602)	57	20	16	7	-	-	-	10·4
South West	1,314	(1,349)	57	24	12	7	39	20	41	12·5
WALES	943	(96)	54	28	13	5	49	16	35	20·9
SCOTLAND	1,772	(1,802)	30	50	13	7	38	20	42	20·0
GREAT BRITAIN	18,488	(18,839)	49	30	16	5	37	25	38	15·4
NORTHERN IRELAND		(450)	43	31	25	1	55 (Pre-1919 & 1919-44)		45	-
UK		(19,290)	50	31	14	5	59 (Pre-1919 & 1919-44)		41	-

Source: Social Trends, 1 (1970) *and Housing Statistics, GB,* 23 (Nov. 1971); *Social Trends* 3 (1972)

TABLE 2.20   Permanent Dwellings Completed, UK, 1945-70

	England	Wales	Scotland	N. Ireland	GB	UK
	Average annual completion of permanent dwellings (1,000s)					
1945-50	115	7	15	3·6	137	141
1951-5	237	13	33	7·3	284	291
1956-60	248	12	30	6·0	290	297
1961-5	284	16	31	8·5	331	340
1966-70	325	18	41	11·4	384	395
1971*	213	11·4	28·1	10·9	252	263
*Total 1945-71	6,375	347	798	199	7,519	7,718
†Annual av. 1945-71	239	13	30	7·4	282	289

Source: Housing Statistics GB, **23** (1971).
* to 30 Sept. 1971
† adjusted pro rata for 1971.

reserve of at least 3·5 per cent is to be created to allow for vacancies required by movements of households, the need for new dwellings in the UK is likely to be between
355,000-400,000 per year up to 1976 and 345,000-390,000 per year up to 1981; of these
perhaps 55-65 per cent will be owner-occupied and 32-40 per cent provided by local
authorities.[62] Such a rate of house-building (345,000-370,000 per year, as compared with
320,000 completions in Britain in 1970) is well below the maximum annual completions
in Britain of 414,000 dwellings reached in 1968 (426,000 in the UK). It would give
Britain a housing stock of 21·1 million dwellings in 1981 as compared with an estimated
19·7 million households, a much healthier position than at present (table 2.19).

Interregional housing contrasts: There are considerable regional differences in the relative
supply of housing in relation to households and population, in the degree of overcrowding,
in the characteristics of housing tenure and in the amenity of housing. These partly reflect
population trends over a considerable period, partly relate to pressures of recent population movements, and partly reflect broad social and economic contrasts between regions.
Most of these features also reflect two distinctive and sometimes pronounced intraregional
contrasts between rural and urban areas and, secondly, more marked contrasts between
inner and outer residential areas of large cities.

Tenure: One of the characteristics of housing in the UK since 1920 has been the
increasing importance of local authority housing (table 2.19). Inter-war corporation
housing estates became a distinctive element in the British townscape and gave birth
to almost exclusively working-class residential suburbs which were marked by many
problems of social adjustment to the new environment. During the 1920s and 1930s
much early-Victorian housing, mainly privately rented, was being cleared from city
centre slums. While most of the surplus population from these grossly over-crowded
areas was decanted to the new local authority estates, a considerable amount of housing
renewal, mostly through blocks of flats, was also leading to social and visual changes
in the inner city.

Since 1945 these trends towards replacement of slums by local authority housing
have continued, leading to a shortage of rented property in the private sector, in great
contrast to the nineteenth century or even the inter-war situation. Since 1950 the total
housing stock has increased at an average annual rate of 1·57 per cent per year. New
building in the private sector (mainly for purchase) increased by 1·2 per cent per year
and in the public sector at 1·0 per cent per year. While owner-occupied dwellings have
grown at the rate of 1·8 per cent per year and local authority and New Town property
at 1·1 per cent per year, the privately rented housing stock has *decreased* continuously

at an average of 1·2 per cent per year. Thus, the proportion of owner-occupied dwellings has increased from 20 per cent in 1950 to 42 per cent in 1960 and 49 per cent in 1970; property rented from local authorities and New Town corporations has grown over the same period from 18 per cent to 27 per cent and now to 30 per cent; privately-owned property has fallen from 45 to 26 and now to 16 per cent (table 2.19). This betokens a social revolution of considerable proportions.

While the proportions of housing in different tenures varies regionally, owner-occupied houses provide the majority of the stock in all regions except Scotland and, to a lesser extent, Northern England and Greater London. A high level of owner occupation is the hallmark of rural and many suburban areas, though the further extension of peripheral local authority housing estates is changing this situation. Many areas of the inner city and of the older industrial regions have lower proportions of owner-occupation. In very broad regional terms this situation is reflected in the above-average proportion of owner-occupied property in the south-eastern quadrant of Britain from the Midlands to the south and east coasts (Greater London excepted) and in Wales, and in the below-average proportion in the industrial north and in central Scotland. In detail, as Storrie has shown,[63] there are contrasts; for example the high percentage of owner-occupied houses in the textile towns of East Lancashire.

Privately-rented dwellings dominated the housing stock up to the mid-1950s, especially in the large cities and industrial towns. Slum clearance and the gradual decline of the small-scale property owner,[64] who was most affected by rent control, have led to a rapid reduction in this sector of the housing market; between the Rent Acts of 1957 and 1965 there was a fall of one million in such properties (one-quarter of their total). Rural areas have been less affected by this so that the proportion of privately rented dwellings is above-average in many rural areas, especially of Northern and South-West England, of Wales and of Northern Ireland.

As privately rented property has declined, so local authority rentings have increased, especially in the urban areas. The proportion of such property is most marked in those regions of greatest housing need, especially in those areas where local administrations, often Labour-controlled councils, have invested heavily in housing as one of the most vital social services. Hence, Central Scotland, industrial North East England, South Yorkshire, the Black Country and much of the South Wales coalfield stand out on a detailed map of local authority tenure.[65] More recently, local authority overspill to peripheral areas such as New Towns and overspill areas (figs. 2.22 and 2.23) have led to rapid increases in such tenures around all city regions. Thus, the major contrasts are intra- rather than interregional, apart from the considerably above-average values for Scotland, Northern England and the West Midlands (table 2.19). As may be expected in predominantly owner-occupied areas, such as the Outer South East (OSE), South West England and East Anglia, the proportion of local authority houses is relatively low.

Amenities: Housing quality provides a useful variable diagnostic of general social characteristics of the population. Amenity is a complex notion involving a wide range of factors influencing property valuations, such as: state of repair; freedom from damp; adequate lighting, heating and ventilation; water supplies; cooking facilities; sanitary arrangements; and food storage.[66] The most easily comparable data are those collected in censuses concerning water supply, bathroom and sanitary facilities. In the 1966 and 1971 censuses the exclusive use of a hot-water supply and fixed bath and WC were regarded as evidence of adequate amenities from this viewpoint. The lack of sewerage in rural areas tends to dramatise relatively poor levels of amenity in the countryside. At the regional level there is a perceptible gradient between the low level of amenities in most inner city areas rising to very high levels in all suburbs (private and local authority), and falling to lower levels in the rural hinterlands.[67] Growing affluence, slum clearance and increasing standards in all housing sectors are rapidly ironing-out regional differences in housing quality as judged by such limited criteria, though relatively high proportions of housing without those basic amenities, especially that of a fixed bath, persist in the older industrial regions of Scotland, Wales and Northern England, and in many rural areas (table 2.21).

Overcrowding: Many studies of conditions in cities have shown that one of the more useful criteria of social structure is some measure of overcrowding. Though appropriate standards vary over time and between social classes, the number of persons per room is generally regarded as an acceptable measure of overcrowding.[68] The currently accepted index of overcrowding in the UK is the proportion of households at any occupancy rate of over 1·5 persons per room, though in the Britain of the 1970s 1 per room might be a better yardstick. The highest proportions of overcrowding are in Northern Ireland and Scotland, where smaller dwellings and the larger average size of household, together with poor economic and social conditions, are responsible. Similar, though less extreme, conditions are reflected in the higher rates of overcrowding in parts of the industrial North and Midlands, especially in the conurbations, and in Greater London. The major contrasts, however, are intraregional, with a general emphasis on the greater amounts of overcrowding in rural areas, especially of western and northern Britain and Northern Ireland, and in the inner-city areas. The city slums still have considerable levels of over-crowding, especially among immigrant communities, where subdivision of housing and 'Rachmanite' exploitation of tenants by private landlords have been a reproach to both national and local administrations in post-war Britain.

Studies of immigrants' housing in the Greater London and West Midlands conurbations have shown very high densities of occupation, high proportions of sharing of dwellings, very low proportions of local authority housing and very high proportions of rented furnished accommodation among all immigrant groups (table 2.22). Moreover, there has been little overall improvement in the situation since the early 1960s, though more enlightened policy concerning local authority accommodation in some areas is beginning to make an impact. Nevertheless the view that 1961-6 '. . . has been one of improvement for English residents of these boroughs' (of inner London) while '. . . the coloured immigrants were being left even further behind as the general level of housing amenity has risen'[69] is unfortunately largely true today.

In general, better control of rented housing, slum clearance and local authority building have led to the reduction in the proportion of homeless and overcrowded families in the 1960s, though many black spots exist and the UK is still some way from solving its shortage of housing. Above all, while a situation persists in which over one-third of Britain's housing stock is pre-1919 in age, a situation which is general throughout all regions (table 2.19), we are clearly far from a situation of satisfactory housing standards for all. Thus, despite half-a-million demolitions 1955-65, the remaining number of houses classed as unfit was almost as great as at the beginning. In the less fortunate areas the proportion of substandard property was very much higher: as compared with 12 per cent unfit houses in England and Wales in 1967, the South East's proportion was only 6 per cent, while the North, Yorkshire and Humberside and North West Regions had 15 per cent.[70] Such regional inequalities point to fundamental contrasts in the social geography of modern Britain, and it is in such deprived areas where environmental and social needs are greatest that the house improvement schemes of the late 1960s may be expected to make the greatest impact.

Households: During the twentieth century separate households have tended to increase at a faster rate than population in the UK. In part due to decreasing family size, in part to increased mobility of population leading to break-up of two-generation adult house-holds, it also reflects a considerable social revolution, that of a separate home for each individual family unit of parents and children. In England and Wales, for example, the

TABLE 2.21   Regional indices of housing and households, UK, 1966

Regions and Conurbations	Total (1,000s)				Percentage of households		
	Persons	House-holds Hh	Dwellings Dw	Ratio Hh : Dw	In multi-dwelling buildings	At > 1½ persons per room	Without all 3 amenities
NORTHERN	3,264	1,062	1,079	0·984	12	1·4	27·9
Tyneside Con.	832	278	279	0·996	33	1·9	29·5
Remainder	2,432	784	800	0·980	4	1·2	27·4
YORKS + HUMBERSIDE	4,669	1,580	1,606	0·984	5	1·1	28·0
West Yorks Con.	1,708	596	607	0·982	7	1·3	26·1
Remainder	2,961	983	1,000	0·983	4	0·9	29·2
NORTH WEST	6,615	2,195	2,203	0·996	7	1·1	29·8
Selnec Con.	2,404	821	827	0·993	7	1·1	32·4
Merseyside Con.	1,338	411	399	1·030	12	1·9	30·3
Remainder	2,874	963	977	0·986	5	0·7	27·3
EAST MIDLANDS	3,262	1,084	1,096	0·989	3	0·8	29·7
WEST MIDLANDS	4,909	1,568	1,571	0·998	8	1·5	26·6
West Mids. Con.	2,374	758	746	1·016	9	2·0	28·2
Remainder	2,535	810	824	0·983	6	0·9	25·2
EAST ANGLIA	1,540	519	534	0·972	5	0·5	30·2
SOUTH EAST	16,652	5,649	5,309	1·064	18	1·5	26·2
Greater London	7,671	2,689	2,347	1·146	27	2·4	34·4
Outer Metropolitan	4,906	1,558	1,565	0·996	8	0·8	16·1
Remainder	4,074	1,402	1,397	1·004	11	0·7	21·5
SOUTH WEST	3,560	1,182	1,183	0·999	7	0·7	23·1
WALES	2,663	855	869	0·984	4	0·8	33·7
I (South East)	1,906	603	604	0·998	5	0·8	35·9
II (Remainder)	758	253	265	0·955	4	0·8	28·4
SCOTLAND	5,168	1,654	1,691	0·978	52	5·4	21·9
Central Clydes. Con.	1,766	555	567	0·979	72	9·0	26·0
Remainder	3,403	1,098	1,123	0·978	41	3·6	19·7
GB	52,304	17,348	17,140	1·012	14	1·6	27·1

Source: Sample Census 1966

rate of household formation in the inter-war period was three times that of the increase in population.[71] Post-war increases in marriage-rates and the reduction in the average age of marriage, together with increasing expectation of life, have accentuated these tendencies since we must now cater for separate homes for three generations: elderly people; mature married couples with children; and young married couples or single persons. Each requires a home of a different type and location, a fact underlying the considerable level of intraregional residential migration which reflects changing needs during the family cycle. Thus since 1951 households have continued to grow at two to three times the rate of the growth of population throughout the UK (table 2.23).

The regional structure of household size reflects both demographic and social trends. Intraregional contrasts are often of greater significance than interregional differences. The average household remains much bigger in Northern Ireland than elsewhere in the UK, due to higher fertility, while Scotland's is somewhat higher than that for England and Wales (table 2.23). The lowest figures of average size of household are generally found in areas where there are high proportions of young adults (especially in single-person households) or of elderly people. Thus central residential areas of cities frequently have small households, as for example in Greater London, mainly because of the large

| Regions and Conurbations | Tenure (% households) | | | Percentage households | | |
	Owner-occupied	Rented from L.A. or New Town	Privately rented	1- or 2- person (hd) with person(s) of pension-age	Car-owning 1 car	2 + cars
NORTHERN	37·4	35·4	20·3	23·8	33·2	4·0
Tyneside Con.	30·3	37·3	30·1	24·7	27·8	2·8
Remainder	39·9	34·7	16·9	23·4	35·1	4·4
YORKS + HUMBERSIDE	44·9	28·2	21·7	25·1	34·0	4·4
West Yorks Con.	49·6	26·8	21·1	27·1	31·7	3·6
Remainder	42·1	29·0	22·0	30·1	35·0	6·1
NORTH WEST	50·0	24·5	22·7	24·9	34·1	4·5
Selnec Con.	48·3	25·3	24·2	24·9	32·3	4·1
Merseyside Con.	36·2	28·9	32·8	22·2	29·9	3·8
Remainder	57·3	21·9	17·1	25·9	37·4	5·1
EAST MIDLANDS	46·0	27·1	20·6	23·5	40·1	6·0
WEST MIDLANDS	46·3	31·7	17·1	21·0	41·6	7·4
West Mids. Con.	41·6	38·2	17·6	21·1	38·8	6·3
Remainder	50·8	25·5	16·7	21·0	44·4	8·4
EAST ANGLIA	46·2	25·5	18·7	25·8	44·9	8·3
SOUTH EAST	46·2	22·1	27·1	24·1	40·0	7·5
Greater London	38·5	21·6	37·1	23·2	36·1	5·8
Outer Metropolitan	53·5	25·7	15·3	20·6	48·8	10·3
Remainder	52·7	19·1	21·2	29·8	42·2	7·4
SOUTH WEST	52·1	23·1	17·4	26·3	45·3	8·0
WALES	50·7	26·0	18·1	23·6	40·0	6·3
I (South East)	51·4	26·9	17·7	22·0	38·5	5·3
II (Remainder)	49·0	24·0	19·2	27·6	43·6	8·8
SCOTLAND	28·3	46·8	17·9	22·9	31·7	3·9
Central Clydes. Con.	23·6	50·8	23·6	21·4	25·4	2·5
Remainder	30·8	44·8	15·0	23·8	35·0	4·7
GB	46·2	27·5	20·7	24·0	38·5	6·2

Source: Sample Census 1966

numbers of young people living in flats. At the other end of the scale retirement areas, such as the South West, or areas of long-standing outmigration, both rural (e g rural Wales — Wales II) and industrial (e g West Yorkshire and much of Lancashire), have above-average numbers of one- or two-person households of pensionable age.

The relationship of such indices, which may be elaborated by other aspects of household size and composition, are best illustrated from a specific case, that of Merseyside.[72] Post-1945 clearing of housing in the inner areas has led to growth of both large-scale corporation housing estates and private residential developments in the intermediate and, more recently, peripheral areas of the conurbation. Moreover, the character of the larger terraced and villa housing of former middle-class areas of the later-nineteenth century has changed with subdivision into flats. In general, though the proportions of overcrowding as measured by the number of persons per room has considerably declined, it is still relatively high by national standards (table 2.24).

In a principal components analysis for census enumeration districts of the 1961 census, Gittus showed that components related to intensity of occupation, household amenities, shared dwellings and multi-dwelling buildings (type III dwellings) accounted for 68 per cent of the variation between the variables analysed.[73] Figures related specifi-

TABLE 2.22 Housing Tenure of Coloured Immigrants and English: Greater London and West Midlands Conurbations, 1966

Area	Owner-occupiers		From local authority		Renting			
					Private unfurnished		Private furnished	
	Coloured immigrants	English	Coloured immigrants	English	Coloured immigrants	English	Coloured immigrants	English
Greater London	32·6	38·9	4·2	22·3	18·1	29·0	43·6	7·3
West Midlands conurbation	59·4	41·1	7·7	39·1	9·4	14·6	21·2	2·6

Source: Rose (*et al.*), *Colour and Citizenship,* p. 133

TABLE 2.23 Population, Dwellings and Households, UK, 1951-66 (in 1,000s)

	Total population	per cent change	Total households	per cent change	Total dwellings	per cent change	Persons per household	Households per dwelling	Per cent >1½ persons per room
England and Wales									
1951	43,758		13,118		12,389		3·53	1·056	8·8
1961	46,072	5·3	14,890	13·5	14,646	18·2	3·09	1·017	5·3
1966	47,136	2·3	15,694	5·5	15,449	5·5	3·05	1·016	1·2
Scotland									
1951	5,096		1,436		1,424		3·54	1·008	35·2
1961	5,179	4·8	1,609	12·0	1,627	14·2	3·22	0·989	22·4
1966	5,168	-0·2	1,654	2·8	1,691	3·9	3·12	0·978	5·4
Northern Ireland									
1951	1,371		338		343		4·05	0·985	25·5
1961	1,425	3·9	373	10·3	387	12·8	3·82	0·964	

Source: Censuses of England and Wales, of Scotland (1951, 1961, 1966) *and of Northern Ireland* (1951, 1961)

The totals are for all households (present or not) and all dwellings (occupied and vacant)

TABLE 2.24   Housing Indices, Merseyside, 1951-66

(Totals in 1,000s)		Central			Intermediate			Peripheral			Merseyside		
		1951	1961	1966	1951	1961	1966	1951	1961	1966	1951	1961	1966
Persons per household (present on census night)		3·58	3·41	3·26	3·63	3·49	3·42	3·51	3·19	3·02	3·58	3·34	3·15
Households in shared dwellings	Total	64·1	30·7	27·2	2·2	0·6	1·3	11·6	6·0	6·9	77·9	37·3	35·4
	%	16·6	7·6	6·6	4·1	0·8	1·2	12·1	5·5	6·1	14·6	6·3	5·6
% Households at: >1½ per room		8	5	2	4	3	1	7	2	1	8	4	2
at >1 person per room		21	15	9	14	13	7	20	10	5	20	13	8

Source: K.G. Pickett *Merseyside: Social and Economic Studies* (1970) pp. 86-8

Central, Intermediate and Peripheral areas are as shown on figure 2.10

cally to single criteria diagnostic of those components are mapped for wards from the 1966 census, together with a simple grouping of all four indices in what is, in effect, a map of social areas derived from housing criteria (fig. 2.13). Of the 16 possible groupings in a 4 × 4 matrix, using a simple positive or negative deviation from the Merseyside average, 7 are dominant and the few cases in the other 9 types can be linked to these. The inner area is dominated by working-class districts (types 1-3). Type 1 has low standards of amenity and moderately high proportions of shared dwellings, though because of a high proportion of small households (many of pensionable age) some areas (type 3) are distinctive in being less overcrowded. The classic combination, for poor social areas, of high intensity of occupation, below-average amenities and a good deal of sharing is, in the redevelopment areas of the centre, now found together with high proportions of multi-dwellings in high-rise flats (type 2). In certain sectors of formerly high-class villa and large terrace property (the middle-class merchants suburbs of mid-Victorian Merseyside) high proportions of shared buildings and multi-dwellings pick out the young middle-class family areas of the inner conurbation.

Groups 5-7 are the post-1920 suburbs of which type 7, low on measures of congestion and high in amenity, largely occupy the middle-class commuter belts of the Wirral and along the rail routes to Southport and Ormskirk, and much of south Liverpool, though they are less dominant here than formerly. Types 5 and 6 are more complex, with high

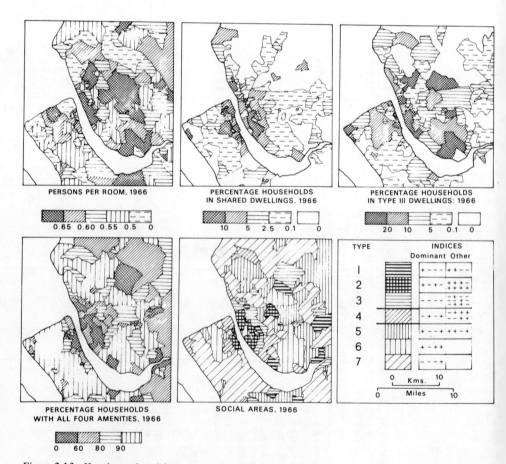

Figure 2.13   Housing and social characteristics, Merseyside, 1966

persons-per-room indices indicating large families on corporation overspill estates, with considerable numbers of high rise flats, found in parts of south Liverpool, and in Huyton and Kirkby.

III.5 Educational Achievement and Personal Incomes

Indices of housing and the like are closely related to other social criteria, such as those based on educational achievement and income, which are often more directly indicative of social status and of social and economic health or deprivation (fig. 1.3). The better educated and qualified part of the population are more mobile, both geographically and socially, and the patterns of their mobility reflect regional and intraregional opportunities.

Public expenditure on *education* has increased from 2·2 per cent of GNP after the Second World War to 4·0 per cent at present; meanwhile the size of the 5-14 age-group has greatly increased, from 7·0 million in 1951 to 8·8 in 1971, while the numbers in full-time higher education have leapt from only 100,000 in 1951-2 to 457,000 in 1970-1. Of the estimated 10·6 million of school-age in the mid-1980s almost certainly a higher proportion will stay on into the sixth-form and go on to higher education.

However, there has been no general levelling-up of opportunities in education, even in the public sector. The varying investment in education by local authorities as well as by individual families, points to the diversity in regional opportunities, which in turn reflect levels of prosperity as well as differing choices in the allocation of resources. One important criterion of educational opportunity is the proportion of those who stay on to 16 (the O-level group) or to 18 years (the A-level group). The proportions of pupils staying on after the compulsory age are above average only in the South East and in Wales (table 2.25). 18+ leavers show less striking variations, but the Welsh tradition of higher education stands out, while the South East and Yorkshire and Humberside are also above average. Some of the industrial regions, for example the Northern Region and the West Midlands, are below average. Whilst many rural districts have below-average numbers of 18+ leavers East Anglia is the only economic planning region among the mainly rural areas which is below average. However, post-war censuses show that while the proportion of both girls and boys in full-time education up to the age of 17 was above average in rural areas, it fell sharply for boys in the 18+ group and was well below average for the 20-4 year group, though the proportion of girls in those age-groups in full-time education was above average.

Although no full-scale analysis of these inequalities has yet been made the general implications are known. *The Report of the Committee on Higher Education* of 1963 (the Robbins Report) underlined the varying opportunities for high-school education, especially as between different social groups: in areas of generous provision and high social status 14·5 per cent of 17 year-olds were in school in 1960; in low status, low-provision areas, only 6·4 per cent had full-time schooling at that age. In regional terms, Southern and South East England had low proportions of people with a terminal age of education at 15 and under and much higher-than-average proportions of 15-19 and, especially, of those with a 20+ terminal age of education. In Scotland, the proportion of 15 year-old leavers was fairly high especially in the industrial regions, but the proportion continuing in full-time education at 20+ is similar to that for England and Wales; in the crofting counties high proportions in this group echo the traditional Welsh emphasis on higher education.

These differences reflect both affluence and social class differentials but also involve the diversity in emphasis given to education by local authorities. In detail there are many puzzling differences in local authority provision for education, especially as between the county boroughs. Coates and Rawstron[74] have shown that not only does provision of private schooling directly reflect regional character and extent of affluence, but many

TABLE 2.25   School-Leavers and Pupils at School beyond the Statutory Age, UK, 1967-71

REGION	School-leavers Percentage leaving school at						University		Going to Colleges of Education or other full-time education		Employment		% Pupils remaining at school beyond 15 (State maintained schools only)			
	15		15-17		18+								1964 at age		1968 * at age	
	1967	1970	1967	1970	1967	1970	1967	1971	1967	1971	1967	1971	16	18	16	18
North	52	33	37	50	11	17	4	5	12	14	84	81	20	5	27	6
Yorkshire and Humberside	49	31	38	48	13	20	6	6	14	15	81	80	22	6	30	6
North West	47	30	40	51	13	19	6	6	13	13	81	81	23	5	28	5
East Midlands	53	33	35	49	13	18	5	6	12	14	83	81	21	5	28	5
West Midlands	49	30	39	52	12	18	5	5	13	14	82	81	23	4	30	5
South East																
Greater London	31	20	52	54	17	26	7	7	10	12	83	81	33	6	40	8
Rest	35	22	48	54	16	24	7	7	16	18	78	76	-	-	-	-
East Anglia	47	30	42	52	12	18	4	5	16	18	79	77	21	4	27	5
South West	38	23	47	54	16	23	7	7	17	19	76	74	27	5	33	5
Wales	42	29	41	46	17	24	7	7	18	18	75	75	30	9	36	9
Scotland	30	33	61	60	9	7	12	13	5	5	83	81	23	3	31	3
Northern Ireland													14	5	21	6

Source: *Statistics of Education* (1967 and 1971)

* 18 year-old pupils as compared to the 13 year-old group 5 years earlier

For non-maintained (private) schools the respective percentages were 71 and 14 in 1964, and 75 and 15 in 1968

similarities appear in the provision of sixth-form education. Private school places are well above average in all the counties of England south of a line from Suffolk to Gloucester, except Essex, Wiltshire, Somerset and Cornwall, and are important around Edinburgh. There is above-average sixth-form provision for Greater London, the South East and in Wales. Whilst there was some levelling-up in opportunities during the 1960s, in general there is still poorer provision in the county boroughs than in the administrative counties of England; the level of provision of sixth-form places is especially poor, especially for girls, in such industrial areas as Durham county, parts of the West and East Midlands and in some of the more rural areas, notably in East Anglia.

These features undoubtedly reflect considerable regional disparities in *personal incomes.* Though data available for study of incomes are limited, a number of studies by Coates and Rawstron have drawn attention to salient features of the distribution of personal incomes in the UK.[75] Their analysis shows that in respect of tax on all types of income — schedule E (basic salaries and wages), schedule D (on fees) or on investment income — the South East quadrant of Britain is a favoured area. Levels of income are highest in Greater London and the South East, shading away west and north through average levels of income over most of the industrial quadrilateral of the Midlands to reach the lowest levels in the Scottish Highlands and Islands and in Northern Ireland. Moreover, during the 1960s the greatest improvement in incomes was largely within the South East, but outside Greater London; no doubt out-movement of higher income groups from the centre explains this. The lowest increases and the greatest relative declines in incomes were experienced in Scotland, much of Northern England and in Northern Ireland. By the mid-1960s the disparities in personal incomes ranged from an index of 72 in counties Londonderry and Tyrone to 108 in Hertfordshire (UK = 100). Significantly, between 1949-65 generally above-average indices were found only in Leicester and Rutland, Bedfordshire, Essex, Hertfordshire, Greater London, Surrey, Buckinghamshire, Oxford, Staffordshire (not in the mid-60s), Warwickshire, Worcestershire and Monmouthshire. The best Scottish counties were all in Central Scotland, but the highest index of 96 was reached only in West and Mid-Lothian; in Ireland the best county, Antrim, had an average index of only 90.

It is not unrealistic to speak of continuing poverty within the UK, not only in the poorer social classes but in poorer areas. While real wages have increased considerably since 1951, during which time the average weekly earnings of manual workers have increased more than three-fold, many poorly-paid workers still depend on various supplementary payments for support. One of those measured by Coates and Rawstron, free school meals, shows that a similar gradient to that of incomes exists in England and Wales, with low levels of claim in the South East quadrant increasing westwards and northwards to reach peaks in Northern England and Mid-and North West Wales.

Once more, however, greater contrasts exist within urban areas. While most of the county boroughs of Northern and North West England, Yorkshire and South Wales have high proportions on free school meals, the proportions are greatest in the inner city. Here they join forces with the various indices of social deprivation which were used to identify the priority areas designated under the Plowden Report.[76] The primary schools selected for special assistance are almost wholly concentrated into central city areas of low incomes, poor housing, high levels of social malaise and general over-crowding; in Liverpool, for example, of 25 priority schools, 17 were located in 9 central wards, out of the city's 40 wards. These were all areas with high proportions of poor housing and other census measures of low socio-economic status, which lay within the inner zones defined in the 1951 census: zones 1 (the inner core), 2a (the inner bye-law residential area) and 2b (in 1951 regarded as better class pre-1914 housing, but much deteriorated by the late 1960s). These wards also had the highest incidence of various criteria of social malaise, according to a City Planning Department survey of 1969, and the highest cumulative indices of social deprivation which were matched only in two other wards, both in peripheral areas of predominantly local authority housing.

IV   THE WORKFORCE-DISTRIBUTION AND DAILY MOBILITY

While on a broad regional scale incomes reflect many of the demographic and social contrasts within the UK, they are also closely related to considerable regional contrasts in employment and unemployment (table 2.26).

TABLE 2.26   Working Population, UK, 1951-81 (in thousands)

	Actual		Projected	
GREAT BRITAIN	1951	1961	1971	1981
Total working population	23,239	24,773	25,600	26,388
male	15,798	16,366	16,605	16,956
female	7,441	8,407	8,995	9,432
married female	4,227	3,958	3,507	3,238
Activity rates				
male	87·2	86·8	83·1	81·9
female	37·1	40·6	41·7	42·6
married female	26·1	34·0	39·2	41·9
NORTHERN IRELAND				
Total working	466·0	539	595	
male	295·0	365	394	
female	171·0	174	201	
Activity rates				NA
male	62·3	63·2	64·2	
female	35·8	33·6	35·2	

Source: Social Trends, I, (1970), and *Abstract of Regional Statistics*

The data for Northern Ireland are not directly comparable with those for GB

NA = Not available

IV.1 Size and Structure of the UK Workforce

Demographic structure determines the size of the potential workforce now and for the future. The rapid increases in both under-15s and retirement age groups in the last 30 years will not be repeated over the next 30 when the greatest increases will probably occur in the working age-groups, especially in the 15-44 year olds (table 2.5). Though present dependency-rates (656 per 1,000 of working age in 1970) will rise to an estimated 677 by 1981, they will probably fall thereafter to 642 per 1,000 by 2001. It is not easy to relate such age-structure trends to the available workforce, since this involves knowledge of factors influencing activity rates in the various sections of the population. The proportion of married women and elderly people at work varies with labour demand; the proportion of school-leavers going on to higher education, which has risen continuously and relatively rapidly in the 1960s, may continue to do so, but less rapidly. However, assuming a continuing increase of demand from labour and taking account of the raising of the school-leaving age to 16 in 1973, which will lead to a sharp apparent drop in the workforce for that year, the available workforce is expected to increase between 1974-85 by an estimated 6·4 per cent (4·7 for men and 9·2 per cent for women) (figure 2.14). This presents both a challenge and an opportunity in the context of a Common Market area in which in the past there have been some regional shortages of labour. It also assumes a somewhat larger proportion of married women in the workforce than at present, which is in turn very much larger than in 1951 (table 2.26).

IV.2 Factors Influencing Regional Trends in Employment

The capacity to absorb these increased numbers will depend on the state of the economy; at regional level this will be related to varying trends in employment (see chapter 1) and population. Hence, if migration to the South East is to be contained, greater provision of employment will have to be made in the less prosperous regions of high unemployment and slow economic growth (chapter 1. IV.1). Measures taken since the war have been partly successful in slowing down population losses from the poorer areas, but have been followed with varying rigour (chapter 1. IV.2). Of a total of 870,000 jobs resulting from movements of manufacturing industry between 1945 and 1961, 427,000 were from Greater London, 98,000 from the rest of the South East and 62,000 from the Midlands, in all 687,000 (79 per cent of the total) from the prosperous regions.[77] Of these jobs only 231,000 (34 per cent) went to the less prosperous regions, 119,000 between 1945-51, a mere 28,000 from 1952-9 and 84,000 in 1960-5.

Moreover, for nearly twenty years after the war no attempt was made to influence the distribution of employment in services, the fastest-growing sector of employment since 1945 and that in which the South East is dominant, especially in administrative and managerial (Standard Industrial Classification − SIC − Group 25) and professional and technical (SIC group 26) workers (figure 1.2). Voluntary movement of offices from London was first encouraged by the Location of Offices Bureau, set up with government assistance in 1963, though initially few firms moved far from Greater London and the main beneficiaries were places like Croydon, whose new office complex led to a remarkable increase in jobs in the borough in the mid-1960s, and the New Towns. Some government departments moved to development areas, eg the Post Office Savings Bank to Glasgow and the National GIRO to Bootle. Even after the Control of Offices and Industrial Development Act of 1965 brought office development under controls similar to those for manufacturing industry and restricted new office building within 40 miles of Central London, the policy had to be relaxed in the face of shortage of office accommodation in the South East. Moreover, only 1 per cent of office employers were willing to move to a development area in the period 1963-9,[78] even to Merseyside where there was a surplus of good office accommodation.

According to the Hunt Report, the greater part of the 4 per cent growth in employment between 1961 and 1966 was due to a 6 per cent increase in the prosperous regions: in most of the development areas, Merseyside and the South West apart, there were small increases in total employment and a fall in industrial employment.[79] Most indices of economic development in the less prosperous areas continue to compare unfavourably with national trends (table 2.27). In the 1960s the development areas fared badly in terms of unemployment, changes in employment, female activity rates and average male earnings and very badly in some of the sub-regions.[80] Not surprisingly these facts were reflected in the total net migration figures for the regions (table 2.12), though the presence of other than economic factors influencing migration is apparent in the high levels of net inmigration to the South West, an area of generally low earnings and some pockets of considerable unemployment, but of great environmental attraction, especially to older people. The general 1965-6 pattern of interregional mobility of working-age population shows the position very clearly (table 2.28). Considerable losses by Scotland and the North and a

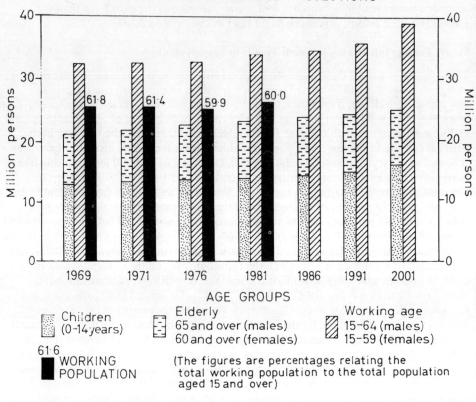

GREAT BRITAIN
WORKING AND DEPENDENT POPULATION
DERIVED FROM 1969-BASED PROJECTIONS

Children
(0-14 years)

Elderly
65 and over (males)
60 and over (females)

Working age
15-64 (males)
15-59 (females)

WORKING
POPULATION

(The figures are percentages relating the
total working population to the total population
aged 15 and over)

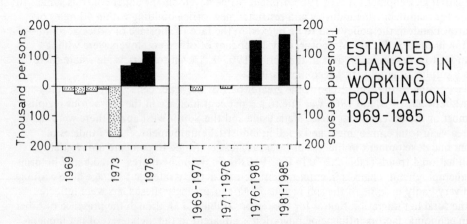

ESTIMATED
CHANGES IN
WORKING
POPULATION
1969-1985

Figure 2.14   Working and dependent population, GB, 1969-2001
Source: *Long Term Population Distribution in GB: A Study* (1971), figs. 11a and b

TABLE 2.27   Some Regional Indices of Employment, Unemployment, Earnings and Net Migration, GB, 1960s

| | Sub-regional range (regional value in parentheses) | | | | | | | 1965-6 | 1961-6 | |
| | Unemployment (%) | | | Employment change 1961-6 (%) | | Women at work | | Index of male earnings | Net inter-regional migration | |
	1961-6*	1968	1971	Total	Male	% 1966	Changes in in % 1961-6		total (1000s)	%
Regions mainly in Development Areas										
Scotland	1/10 (3·4)	1/10 (3·7)	3/9 (5·6)	+1/−5 (+1)	−1/−7(−2)	28/44 (40)	0/+3 (+2)	90·6	−79	−1·5
Wales	1/5 (2·7)	2/10 (3·9)	3/9 (4·5)	0/+13(+3)	−5/+12(−1)	22/38 (30)	+1/+4 (+3)	93·9	0	0
Northern England	2/4 (3·1)	3/5 (4·5)	3/9 (5·5)	+1/+6 (+2)	−4/+3(−1)	25/37 (35)	+1/+3 (+2)	92·2	−48	−1·5
Regions partly coinciding with Development Areas										
North West	1/4 (2·0)	1/5 (2·4)	3/17 (3·7)	−5/+5 (+1)	−4/+4 (0)	33/47 (43)	−4/+1 (0)	97·0	−18	−0·3
South West	1/4 (1·7)	1/5 (2·5)	1/5 (3·4)	+3/+10 (+6)	+1/+7 (+4)	27/37 (33)	+1/+3 (+2)	92·7	+101	+3·0
Regions with no Development Areas										
Yorks. and Humberside	0/3 (1·1)	1/4 (2·5)	2/9 (3·7)	0/+9 (+3)	−3/+5 (+2)	25/44 (40)	−1/+4 (+1)	94·5	−17	−0·4
E. Anglia	0/3 (1·4)	1/3 (1·9)	2/3 (3·0)	+13/+15(+13)	+11/+12(+11)	31/35 (34)	+1/+4 (+2)	91·5	+50	+3·4
E. Midlands	0/2 (1·0)	1/3 (1·8)	1/5 (2·8)	+4/+7 (+6)	0/+5 (+4)	36/47 (40)	+1/+2 (+2)	95·7	+44	+1·4
W. Midlands	0/2 (1·1)	1/3 (1·9)	2/7 (2·9)	+4/+10 (+6)	+3/+9 (+5)	33/50 (44)	+1/+4 (+1)	103·0	−16	−0·3
South East	0/3 (0·9)	1/4 (1·6)	1/4 (1·9)	0/+11 (+5)	−1/+17 (+4)	28/55 (44)	0/+4 (+2)	109·5	−17	−0·4
GREAT BRITAIN	1–2	2–3	3–4	+4	+2	40	+2	100	0	0

Source: *The Intermediate Areas* (1969), Appendices C and D; and *Department of Employment Gazette*, 53, 7 (July 1972)

* Regional averages for 1966 for South East, East Anglia, East Midlands, Yorks. and Humberside.

TABLE 2.28   Net Interregional Flows of Working-age Migrants (15-59), GB, 1965-6 (100s)

Net gain from (+) or loss (−) to

		North		Midlands		South		Wales		Scotland		Total	
		M	F	M	F	M	F	M	F	M	F	M	F
North	M			− 9·1		− 5·0		− 9·7		+22·1		− 1·7	
	F				− 9·5		−38·1		− 9·8		+15·6		−41·8
Midlands	M	+ 9·1				+ 6·9		+ 6·3		+17.8		+40·1	
	F		+ 9·5				−22·9		+ 1·6		+14·8		+ 3·0
South	M	+ 5·0		− 6·9				+ 7·0		+27·1		+32·2	
	F		+38·1		+22·9				+ 9·9		+24·3		+95·2
Wales	M	+ 9·7		− 6·3		− 7·0				− 1·0		− 4·6	
	F		+ 9·8		− 1·6		− 9·9				− 1·3		− 3·0
Scotland	M	−22·1		−17·8		−27·1		+ 1·0				−66·0	
	F		−15·6		−14·8		−24·3		+ 1·3				−53·4

Source: Long Term Population Distribution in GB. A Study (HMSO 1971) Generalised from Appendix 2, Table 6

'North'   includes the Northern, Yorks and Humberside and North West planning regions;
'Midlands'   includes the East and West Midlands;
'South'   includes the South East, East Anglia and the South West.

small out-movement from Wales were transferred, though not directly, to the Midlands, where the main gains were of male workers, and the South, which had considerable gains of both men and, especially, of women. Much of this movement was of highly-qualified professional and managerial workers. Waugh has shown that between 1961 and 1966 the North and West lost both population and 'a disproportionate share of talent and expertise'.[81] This no longer went directly to the South East and West Midlands, and indeed the South West and East Anglia benefited most in the early 1960s. Yet the South East, which had in 1961 the greatest concentration of high-status socio-economic groups (groups 1-4), made the greatest gains in these groups 1961-6, Greater London apart, both in managerial and professional groups. Conversely, most rural counties showed a decline in such groups and in many of the depressed industrial areas, notably the coalfields of North East England and South Wales, the proportions of high status population were low despite an increase in commuter residents in the 1960s. Thus, regional contrasts in socio-economic status have continued to increase, with upward social mobility reinforcing the already strong position of the more prosperous regions, though the precise details of distribution are being reshaped with intraregional changes in residence and workplace.

IV.3 Economically Active Population

Two aspects of employment are relevant to the analysis of social and economic health of the regions of the UK: the numbers and proportion of those in employment and of those out of work. Though complementary in many respects, they illustrate different facets of labour demand and supply, and of population structure as related to the actual and potential workforce.

Employed population: The employed population is partly a function of age structure, partly of socio-economic factors, especially the proportions in full-time education beyond the compulsory age, and partly also of demand for labour. For example, opportunities of well-paid jobs for school-leavers may partly account for relatively low proportions of boys staying on at school in the West Midlands (table 2.25). The relatively high proportions of employed population in East Lancashire result from a long-standing tradition of women mill-workers; the much smaller percentage working population of coal-mining areas is, by contrast, due to low proportions of women in the workforce, a response to a tradition of women staying in the home in an area of shift workers, as well as of lack of job-opportunities for girls. In many areas the reserve of labour among married women not at work offers one of the best ways of expanding the labour force in the short-term, often using part-time labour. Yet when demand for labour falls such women are often the first to be laid off; since they often are not in benefit and do not register as unemployed they may well in times of high unemployment represent a considerable measure of concealed unemployment. Workers of pensionable age, also often employed part-time, perform a similar role in the labour force.

Activity rates: Thus, the proportion of persons in employment, as a percentage of the population over 15, as in table 2.26 and figure 2.15, is a significant index of the varying intensity of economic activity and labour utilisation. Figures derived from the *1971 Census Advance Analysis* for the administrative counties and county boroughs show clearly the higher proportions of the economically-active, both men and women, in industrial and urban areas than in rural, though this is more pronounced for the male population. In part this is due to the more elderly population structure of rural areas but it also reflects the narrower range of job opportunities as well as economic activities. Where this is wider, as in the textile areas of the Scottish Border counties, activity rates are much higher.

The highest regional proportions of active male population are in Greater London and parts of the inner Metropolitan area and in the West Midlands (figure 2.15). There is a general gradient towards decreasing activity rates southwards and westwards, though there are exceptions as, for example, in the western parts of the Fenland counties, while the industrial areas of the North and West tend to have higher rates than the regional average (for example, South Wales), though the rates for Central Scotland are low.

Female activity rates vary considerably at the regional level (table 2.27) and there are also considerable variations within regions, or even counties, as between employment exchange areas. The highest levels of female activity in 1966 were in the South East and West Midlands, also the regions with the highest local figures, though the North West was above the national average and the East Midlands, Yorkshire and Humberside and, perhaps surprisingly, Scotland were at the national rate. There were, however, very considerable variations at subregional level.[82] Moreover, although rates of increase in female activity rates between 1961 and 1966 were at or above the national rate in some of these low-activity areas, these were insufficient to close the gap.

In 1971, the highest female activity rates were clearly in the boroughs of the axial belt but, Lancashire apart, were mainly concentrated into Greater London and its surrounding metropolitan area and in the West and East Midlands (figure 2.15). The highest Scottish rates were mainly in Glasgow, Edinburgh and other major towns and, apart from these, rates were low except in the Border textile districts. Wales, the South West, Northern and North-eastern England tended to have low or very low female activity rates. This is a pattern which fits closely the differing intensity and patterns of labour demand in the prosperous and less prosperous regions, a pattern which a number of studies have shown to exist also at intraregional level.[83] Moreover the trends in activity rates fit closely the regional rates of change in employment which between 1966 and 1970 declined more sharply in the less prosperous regions, especially so far as male employment was concerned, and where, apart from the North West, female activity rates are low[84] (table 2.27).

The variations in female activity rates have been related to unemployment, degree of urbanisation, and unfavourable industrial structure. Hence they suggest a considerable labour reserve locally and in certain regions, notably in 1966 in the North, Yorkshire and Humberside, Wales and the North West, but also in the South East. Assuming a 'norm' for female activity rates as some 8 per cent above the national average, estimates

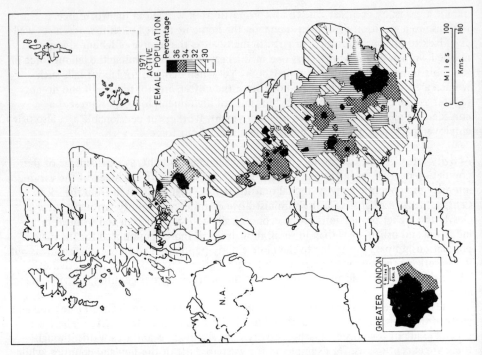

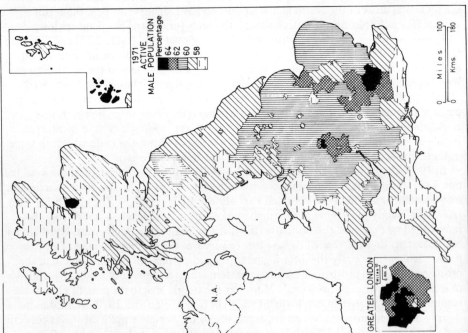

Figure 2.15   Economically active population, GB, 1971

for 1961 suggested a female labour reserve of about 800,000 for the UK. This was a cautious estimate but one should remember that any such 'reserve' would include a high proportion of part-time workers. Taking account of the increasing proportions of women entering employment (table 2.26) this figure might now be greater, though at the time of the 1966 census a gross female labour reserve of only 300,000 was calculated by Gordon.[85]

IV.4 Unemployment

Many regional indices of social inequality and of demographic, notably migrational, experience are related to varying regional rates of unemployment. Since the Second World War neither national nor regional rates of unemployment have reached the extremes of the inter-war period, but there remains a wide gap between rates in the more prosperous and less prosperous regions. Despite many efforts to diminish the uneven distribution of job opportunities, unemployment rates are above-average in the development areas which in the period 1961-8 had one-fifth of the working population, but over one-third of the unemployed,[86] and which experienced unemployment at up to 2½ times the national rate. Moreover, the North, South West, Wales, Northern Ireland, together with most of Scotland and the North West, have higher-than-average proportions of long-term unemployed, of unskilled workers and of out-of-work in the 18-44 age-group. Furthermore, these regions have tended to suffer bigger swings in cyclical unemployment. In such areas there is a great need for retraining of labour to attract new types of industry, for the level of provision of industrial re-training is generally much too low.

Unemployment rates (excluding school-leavers) in Great Britain have ranged between 1 per cent in the mid-1950s to 3·5 per cent (July 1972), while regional figures have ranged from as little as 0·4 per cent (West Midlands) and 2·2 per cent (Scotland) in 1955 to the present 2·0 (South East) to 6·2 per cent (Scotland) (figure 2.16). Throughout, Northern Ireland's unemployment rate has been far above that for the UK as a whole. Intraregional rates have an even wider range. The Hunt Report showed that in 1961-6, a period of relatively low unemployment, rates reached 10 per cent in parts of the Scottish Highlands and Islands and in most regions of Britain there were local pockets of unemployment of two to three times the regional rate. Thus, though present regional rates are below 5 per cent except in the North, Scotland and Northern Ireland, the unemployment rate in the development areas as a whole is 6·1 per cent and is 3·8 per cent (above the average for Great Britain) in the intermediate areas. At the level of employment exchange areas or groups of areas unemployment rates range up to 17·4 per cent in Furness and 16·1 in Newry while, on the other hand, in the South East there are many areas with less than 2 per cent unemployed.

On the basis of data for 'development areas, intermediate areas and certain local areas'[87] an impression may be gained of the incidence of local unemployment (figure 2.17). High unemployment is found in many parts of Northern England, South Wales, Scotland and Northern Ireland, and in parts of the South West. Moreover, areas little affected by unemployment until recently now have above-average unemployment, especially of male workers. Thus Coventry and Birmingham now have over 4 per cent unemployed, including skilled workers in engineering and allied industries. The fall of jobs in manufacturing industry since 1970, the growing hard-core of unemployed among older men and the difficulties of both school-leavers and graduates in finding jobs underline the generality of the problem and emphasise the need for some regulation of regional distribution of employment in the servicing and commercial sector.

Unemployment statistics alone do not show the full situation, since not all those who are out of work register as unemployed, especially women. The data on active

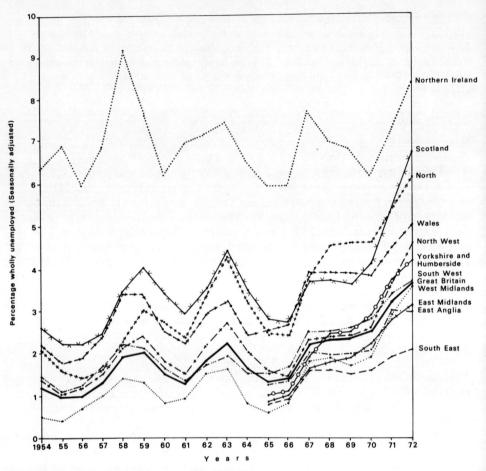

Figure 2.16   Regional unemployment, UK, 1954-72

population who were recorded in the 1971 census as 'not working' forms a useful basis of analysis at county and county borough level (figure 2.18). The same marked regional differences appear, if anything more strongly, with high proportions of both men and women not in work in Scotland, Northern England and Wales and relatively low proportions in the Midlands and South East. The relatively high proportions of women not working in the Midlands, East Anglia and South East suggest that there may well be much concealed unemployment or underemployment of women, though in certain areas seasonal unemployment may be involved, as for example in the resort areas of the Fylde, the Isle of Wight and South West England. In rural areas the relatively higher proportions of active females not working suggests a reservoir of labour. Within all regions the 1971 census data suggest higher levels of unemployment in central city areas, especially in Greater London and the conurbations where there are higher proportions of both men and women out of work in the central boroughs than in the surrounding areas. This reflects the higher levels of unemployment among the semi- and unskilled groups among whom New Commonwealth immigrants are particularly adversely affected. Many of these people came to Britain in the late 1950s and 1960s to make up regional shortages of unskilled labour, but now find it difficult to get jobs in an economy which finds it increasingly difficult to absorb unskilled labour. From 1961 and 1966 census data Davison showed that unemployment among New Commonwealth immigrants was

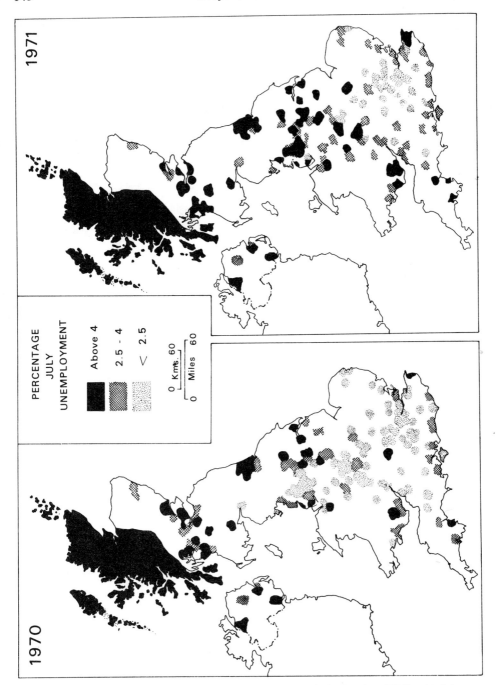

Figure 2.17   Some unemployment Black Spots, UK, 1970 and 1971. Based on DE Gazette data.

above the 3·2 per cent average for English people, especially for Jamaicans (7·4 per cent), other West Indians (6·0 per cent), Pakistanis (5·4 per cent) and, to a lesser extent, Indians (4·4 per cent).[88] These rates, for example for West Indians, correlate inversely with the low proportions in higher socio-economic groups and directly with

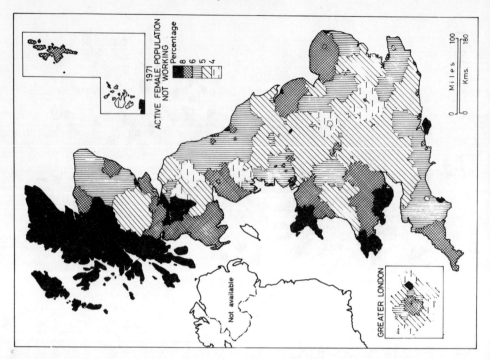

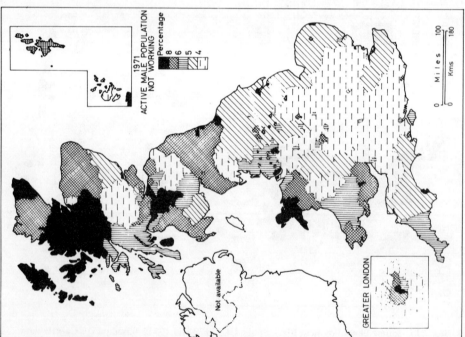

Figure 2.18   Active population not working, GB, 1971

high proportions in manual and unskilled groups. The *1971 Census, Advance Analysis*
shows that a higher proportion of New Commonwealth-born are out of employment as
a percentage of all in this group than are in employment or in the total population
(table 2.29). Moreover, all the main coloured-immigrant groups have higher proportions
out of employment than their total numbers would suggest and this is especially so in
the case of West Indians.

TABLE 2.29   Commonwealth Immigrants Employed and Out of Employment, UK, 1971

Born in	Total (1,000s)	% of GB	Employed	Out of employment	Student and others inactive
	Population enumerated (1971)				
			Per cent of total		
UK	50,514	92·85	92·77	91·34	95·18
Irish Republic	721	1·34	1·87	2·83	0·82
Old Commonwealth	145	0·23	0·29	0·29	0·25
New Commonwealth	1,157	2·15	2·57	3·38	1·72
Foreign and not stated	1,077	2·00	2·28	2·01	1·68
Totals	53,826		23,560	1,355	28,469
India	323	0·60	0·75	0·87	0·46
Pakistan	139	0·26	0·32	0·38	0·20
West Indies	303	0·56	0·81	1·30	0·31
Cyprus	73	0·14	0·15	0·19	0·12
Africa	176	0·33	0·30	0·39	0·34

Source: Census 1971, Advance Analysis

It has been argued that these people find it hard to break out of this situation and to
gain the educational and occupational skills which will permit them to rise in socio-
economic status.[89] Discrimination in employment and isolation within poor residential
areas will only compound the problem. That this *is* now a problem can be seen in the
statistics gathered since 1969 on unemployed coloured workers. In May 1972 coloured
workers formed 2·7 per cent of all unemployed in Great Britain as compared with a total
of 2·15 per cent New Commonwealth immigrants living in Britain at the time of the
1971 census, with rates of unemployment particularly high among West Indians and, to a
lesser extent, among Pakistanis.

IV.5 Workplace and Residence

General features: One of the distinctive characteristics of population distribution in the
modern UK is the increasing separation of workplace and residence. Successive censuses
from 1921 have revealed a growing volume and intensity of daily travel to work. By 1961,
36 per cent of the economically-active population in England and Wales and 25 per cent
in Scotland worked outside the local authority area in which they lived. Between 1921
and 1961 the numbers who travelled to work outside their area of residence in England
and Wales increased by 115 per cent from 2·6 to 5·6 million as compared with a 29 per
cent increase of the working population. The Redcliffe-Maud report estimated that,
excluding Greater London, daily travel to work was 70 per cent higher in 1966 than in
1921, and showed that in all regions this increase had been much greater than for the
population as a whole.[90] Taking 1921 values as 100, the 1966 index of daily out-movement

ranged from 144 in the South East, already a considerable commuter area in 1921, to 250 in East Anglia.

The rapid growth in both numbers and range of commuter journeys has been especially marked since 1945. Two sets of forces are involved: first, concentration of jobs, with an increasing range of labour recruitment from surrounding residential areas; secondly, residential dispersal from the inner city to commuter suburbs,[91] a feature of post-war population mobility reflected in intra-urban migration and commuting alike, and permitted by improvements in both public and private transport. The causes have been conceptualised by Warnes as the result of structural changes in industry and the economy, principally increases in real incomes, decreasing hours of work, increasing size and concentration of manufacturing units and a growth in employment in the tertiary sector; the latter is mainly located in central city areas.[92] These lead to concentration of employment in fewer units, focused in fewer locations, particularly in the urban areas. High incomes, however, leave more money for increased travel costs which, combined with a widening search for land for housing outside the city centres, has led to dispersal of both private and local authority housing. Even where, as in the case of London's New Towns and overspill agreements, the intention is to disperse both homes and jobs, the outcome is usually an increase rather than a decrease of both volume and distance of journey to work.

One of the features of recent changes in population has been a growth of adventitious population resident in rural areas but working in the towns. The growing extent of the dependence upon urban employment is seen in the considerable increase in the proportion of people commuting from rural districts. Between 1921 and 1966 daily out-movement of resident working population from rural districts in England increased from 22 to 47 per cent as against 21 to 34 per cent in all types of area (excluding Greater London) and rural commuter flow to urban areas increased from 387,000 (14·2 per cent of the occupied resident population) in 1921 to nearly 1·5 million (37·4 per cent) in 1966. In over one-third of rural districts in 1966, over 40 per cent of the active population travelled to work in urban areas as against 3·5 per cent at this level in 1921; conversely, in only 22 per cent of rural districts of England in 1966 was there less than 20 per cent daily out-movement as compared with 78 per cent in 1921.[93]

Working, residential and commuter population, 1951-66: The basic changes in journey to work may be focused upon two aspects: first, on relative growth of the residential and working population of the major cities of the UK; second, on changes in daily movement to and from these major centres. In this analysis, attention has been focused upon 24 metropolitan centres with a working population of about 100,000 and over in 1966; two others, West Ham (now part of the London Borough of Newham) and Wolverhampton, have been excluded because boundary changes preclude comparison (table 2.30). Between 1921-66 the residential population of the majority of these cities fell, by as much as one-fifth in some cases, though three (Coventry, Croydon and Southampton) increased (figure 2.19). Moreover, in all but three cases (Croydon, Plymouth and Aberdeen) the rate of increase of working population exceeded that of residential population, or declined at a lesser rate. The fact that residential populations are smaller than working populations indicates that populations are spreading into the suburbs, while jobs remain focused on a few areas, especially in the centre. This is reflected in job ratios, an index of working population: resident active population x 100. Ratios of over 100 indicate a surplus of jobs and of under 100 show job deficit (table 2.30). Not only did all the cities studied have a job surplus in 1966 but job ratios were higher than in 1951; except in four cases, Bradford, Bristol, Southampton and Stoke, job ratios had also increased between 1961 and 1966.

The various exceptions to the concentration of jobs are readily explained. Plymouth

TABLE 2.30 Aspects of the Journey to Work, Major UK Cities, 1951-66

(Thousands)	Total Population				Daily in-movement			Daily out-movement			Job ratio		
	Resident occupied		Working									Change	
	Total 1966	% Ch. 1951-66	Total 1966	% Ch. 1951-66	Total 1966	% Change 1951-66	1961-6	Total 1966	% Change 1951-66	1961-6	1966	1951-66	1961-6
City of London (CL)	3·7	4·2	357·9	5·7	360·6	−7·0	7·4	1·0	31·6	29·9	9852·5	−2055	526·1
Birmingham (B)	538·8	−4·5	625·9	−1·0	150·1	54·4	6·7	43·2	43·3	4·8	120·8	8·8	2·9
Bradford (Bd)	142·4	−4·7	152·9	1·9	31·7	30·6	3·0	16·8	38·9	25·5	110·8	2·7	−0·9
Bristol (Br)	201·6	1·2	208·3	3·8	44·8	93·9	15·8	27·1	20·1	6·9	109·3	9·0	−10·6
Cardiff (Ca)	112·0	4·5	135·7	19·6	37·8	58·9	15·7	8·0	19·8	−11·2	128·1	12·1	6·7
Coventry (Co)	162·1	27·1	186·0	24·3	40·6	22·1	8·9	12·5	11·9	−25·1	117·8	0·4	4·1
Croydon (Cr)	155·4	34·0	125·1	39·1	42·8	76·5	20·8	64·3	27·8	15·7	85·3	7·8	0·7
Derby (De)	60·3	−13·1	99·5	−1·6	46·9	28·1	1·9	5·8	57·0	24·7	170·5	22·1	4·8
Hull (H)	129·9	0·9	137·7	1·1	23·5	49·2	16·2	11·1	35·1	4·6	110·0	4·1	3·1
Leeds (Le)	242·7	−4·2	258·9	−3·8	49·9	49·0	18·6	22·0	27·9	15·6	112·1	5·6	2·8
Leicester (Lr)	143·5	−2·9	174·5	3·8	49·6	74·3	3·5	12·5	61·2	21·7	126·8	12·8	1·0
Liverpool (Li)	307·8	−15·4	372·1	−9·8	122·4	39·1	8·3	45·1	14·5	9·6	126·2	12·8	5·0
Manchester (M)	287·9	−20·0	380·2	−7·8	168·8	22·8	−0·5	63·9	0·9	1·4	138·1	17·5	5·1
Newcastle (Ne)	109·4	−18·9	167·7	−16·0	85·8	32·4	5·8	22·3	10·2	−0·1	160·7	12·7	12·0
Nottingham (No)	149·7	−2·5	174·2	0·4	56·6	31·3	5·0	25·6	10·5	3·9	121·6	8·6	2·7
Plymouth (Pl)	88·7	−1·4	84·1	−14·7	14·5	22·1	6·4	4·8	50·8	23·9	113·8	4·2	1·2
Portsmouth (Po)	95·1	−5·4	109·6	3·0	28·4	115·0	22·3	9·0	6·7	19·2	121·5	16·8	2·5
Sheffield (Sh)	234·4	−5·1	262·0	5·9	52·5	99·3	19·2	15·1	18·9	2·2	116·7	11·2	4·7
Southampton (So)	95·8	23·9	101·9	24·3	24·6	64·7	10·6	13·3	28·5	25·9	112·5	6·6	−0·3
Stoke (St)	135·2	−5·8	147·6	−6·5	34·6	24·3	−1·3	16·9	26·4	14·9	113·7	3·6	−1·4
Aberdeen (A)	80·6	4·1	80·7	1·2	8·8	40·6	16·6	5·8	44·8	0·7	103·9	1·0	0·9
Dundee (D)	87·5	4·4	91·4	5·0	7·8	40·7	17·3	2·4	3·7	11·8	106·3	2·6	1·5
Edinburgh (E)	215·1	2·5	229·8	4·4	34·2	89·0	25·8	10·9	37·4	27·9	111·3	6·5	3·9
Glasgow (Gl)	430·1	−12·2	457·6	−10·9	105·5	26·9	5·4	62·5	6·0	−0·1	110·4	5·5	4·9
Belfast (Be)	161·6		209·8		66·9			18·6			130·0		

Source: Census, 1951 and 1961; Sample Census, 1966

The initials in brackets are those used in figs. 2.19 and 2.20.

The job ratio, a measure of job concentration, is the ratio of working population: resident occupied population X 100

Changes in job ratio are the differences in the ratio over the period indicated

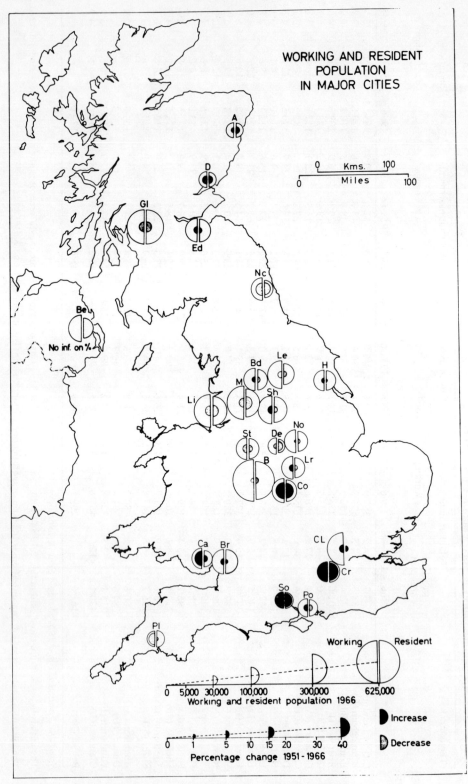

Figure 2.19   Working and resident populations, major cities, UK, 1951-66

had lost jobs in the centre with the decline of its naval dockyards and much of its new industry is on sites outside the borough boundary; the changes in Aberdeen are small, but the low growth of the working population of the city is due to location of many new jobs on peripheral industrial estates. By contrast, Croydon, which until the 1950s was predominantly a commuter suburb of Greater London with a low job ratio, has greatly increased its job potential with the injection of 10,000 new office jobs in the mid-1960s alone, an acquisition of 79 per cent of offices and nearly 60 per cent of office jobs decentralised from London between 1963 and 1968.[94]

Analysis of trends in daily in- and out-movement (figure 2.20) show that in only one case, the City of London, did in-movement between 1951-66 decline, mainly due to the office decentralisation already mentioned. In every other large city not only were there large increases in daily in-movement (34 per cent in aggregate) but these generally greatly exceeded out-movement (21 per cent aggregate increase) and, except in the case of Coventry, far exceeded the changes in resident population. Only in the City of London, Bradford, Derby, Plymouth, Stoke and Aberdeen did the rate of increase in out-movement exceed that of in-movement, though the levels of in-movement in 1966 were still considerably higher than in 1951. This was usually due to recent development of peripheral industrial estates, a fact which is adding to the volume and complexity of cross-currents of commuting around most metropolitan centres.

Two forces are at work in job location, leading to greatly increased daily travel. In the tertiary sector of the economy, the sector of most rapid growth in employment, until recently most jobs were created in the central areas of cities, though some decentralisation has taken place since the mid-1960s, mostly in London. On the other hand, many new industrial sites, and a greater proportion of jobs in industry, have moved to the periphery of towns, seeking space, cheaper land and easier transport access and thus leading to a reverse flow of commuting of workers from the city, together with an enlargement of the commuter hinterland into surrounding suburban and rural areas. This peripheral journey to work, as it is often described, is of increasing importance in all advanced industrial economies.

Such trends in journey to work may be epitomised from the example of Merseyside. The largest concentration of jobs is found in the conurbation centre of Merseyside to which, in 1961, 157,000 workers travelled daily. By 1966 there has been a fall in this movement to 136,000, due largely, one suspects, to dispersal of warehousing. Office and service workers are drawn mainly from the suburbs of south Liverpool, Wirral and the commuter areas along the electrified railways to Southport and Ormskirk. Dockside employment in both shipping and industry still attracts a considerable movement along the waterfront, much of it from the suburbs following widespread slum clearance in the dockside residential areas, but jobs have declined in this sector. Most of the newer labour-intensive industries drawn to Merseyside by development area policy since 1949 have gone to peripheral industrial estates and many 'port industries', such as oil-refining and petro-chemicals, have developed up-estuary and along the Manchester Ship Canal, especially at Ellesmere Port. However, residential dispersal and industrial dispersal are not in harmony. Kirkby, for example, a post-war overspill town for Liverpool, has many new industries on its extensive industrial estates and a job ratio of 121·7 in 1966. But it drew 58 per cent of its workers from other parts of Merseyside, while 48 per cent of its resident active population travelled to work outside the town, mainly to Liverpool. Similarly, in the early stages of the development of Skelmersdale, Merseyside's first New Town, industry typically lagged behind residential development, as reflected in the 1966 job ratio of 82·3, but 56 per cent of residents worked outside the New Town and 46 per cent of workers were drawn from outside.

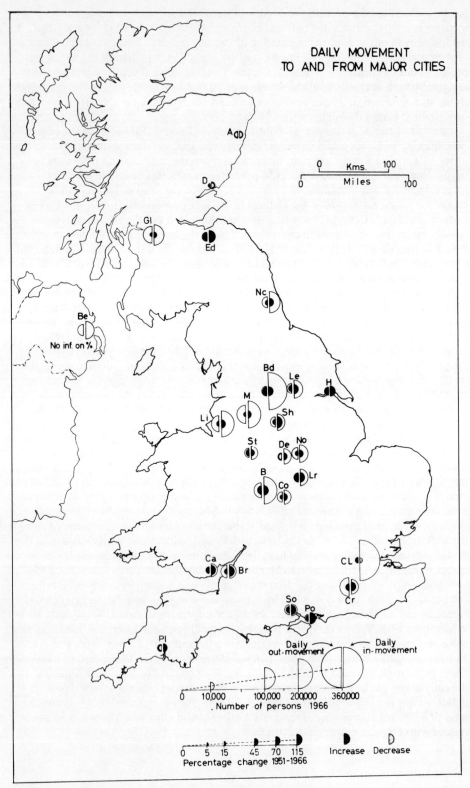

Figure 2.20   Daily in- and out-movement, major cities, UK, 1951-66

Commuter hinterlands: The loss of population from central city areas has not been matched by a corresponding redistribution of jobs. Even where industry has been decentralised, it draws labour from wider hinterlands. Over the past 50 years in the North West, according to Warnes, journey to work distances have increased by an average of 0·8 km in 1921-51, 1 km in 1951-61 and 1·2 km in 1961-6, resulting in an overall increase of 50 per cent in the mean journey to work from 2·35 to 3·54 kms between 1921 and 1966.[95] These increases were greatest and the commuting range most extensive in the outer suburban areas of the Merseyside and SELNEC conurbations and in the rural hinterlands of such towns as Lancaster and Barrow-in-Furness.

The general increase of commuter hinterlands can be seen in any simple analysis of the volume and pattern of daily movement between towns and their surrounding territories in urbanised and rural areas alike.[96] The major foci, both in terms of their commuter demand and the range over which daily movement is drawn, are the large boroughs. The hinterlands of 52 such cities, together with the City of London, are defined in terms of those local authorities which supplied over 100 commuters in 1961 (figure 2.21). These cover the most populous regions of the UK, and also correspond broadly with the areas from which the greatest proportions of daily out-movement (over 40 per cent of the resident population) are recorded. The extent of these areas of high job-dependance has grown considerably in the last twenty years. In the North West Warnes suggests that, by the end of the century, the distance travelled to work could increase by as much as 50 per cent on the evidence of recent trends.[97] From a number of recent studies it seems that longer-distance commuting is increasing most rapidly, a process aided by the wider availability of private transport. The major metropolitan centres increasingly dominate the social and economic life of all regions of the UK and are of fundamental significance to the interdependence of town and country as the various local government studies, including the Maud Report, showed in the 1960s. The Report's Research Appendices showed that commuting and intra-regional migration are interdependent. In a detailed study of 14 towns of varying size and character it was shown that all had lost population in the 15-44 age-group, especially among professional and managerial classes, but that the return daily flow among these groups was stronger than in the journey-to-work pattern as a whole.[98] Intraregional migrants who move to the rural fringes of large towns thus continue to be linked to them through the journey to work as well as for shopping and other services.

Such interdependence is not, however, confined to the hinterlands of large towns or industrial regions but may be found also in rural areas at much lower levels in the urban hierarchy. True, apart from rural Wales, parts of Northern and South West England, and Southern and Highland Scotland, there are few areas of the UK beyond commuting reach of the employment opportunities in large towns. Yet even in such areas a small town may exert a considerable influence on its region, attracting considerable numbers of workers from an extensive hinterland. For example, Aberystwyth, with important commercial, servicing and cultural functions, in which the University College of Wales plays an important part, had a job ratio of 141·3 in 1966. There are many other similar cases, notably in county towns, though quite small market centres may provide surrounding rural districts with a focus of jobs absorbing 20-40 per cent of their resident occupied population. In most 'rural' counties of England and Wales, therefore, the mean job ratio of municipal boroughs and urban districts is relatively high, while only Merioneth of the rural Welsh counties has a collective urban job ratio of under 100. Somerset's combined urban job ratio in 1966 was 116·2, with very high values in towns like Taunton (136·2) and Yeovil (157·2). Similar examples could be quoted from Cumberland, Hereford, Lincolnshire, and West Suffolk, to mention only a few counties.

A particularly significant aspect of commuting is that associated with the conurbations. All have job ratios of over 100 and massively large daily movements of population

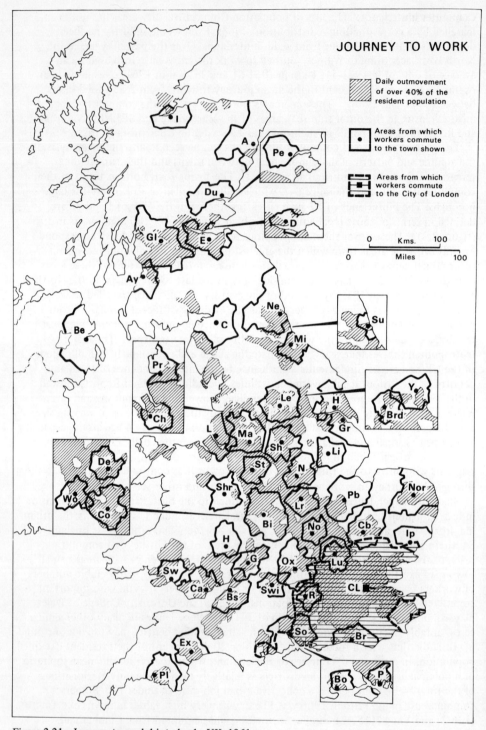

Figure 2.21   Journey-to-work hinterlands, UK, 1961

into their industrial and service areas. In the period 1951-66 the numbers travelling to work in the five English provincial conurbations increased by 87·5 per cent. Out-movement also increased substantially, largely due to travel to peripheral industrial estates. Even from a simple analysis of areas contributing over 100 workers per day, the conurbation hinterlands appear very large, extending up to 20 miles (32 km) from the centre in the provincial conurbations and in the case of Greater London forming a vast region containing many complex cross-currents of daily movement of some 50 miles in diameter. In all these regions, the level of commuting has greatly increased in the 1950s and 1960s and the greatest increases, for example in the North West's conurbations and in Greater London, have been recorded from the outer areas, a response to the greater dispersal of homes than of jobs.

IV.6 New Towns and Overspill

An important aspect of population policy and distribution since 1945, and one of particular significance for the conurbations, has been the attempt to relieve congestion and to provide new homes and jobs through the building of New Towns and development of overspill arrangements with existing towns. Such planned decentralisation is not unique, but the first post-war New Towns set up under the 1946 Act were a pioneer venture aimed at providing 'balanced communities of a manageable size, with improved living conditions, employment opportunities of sufficient range to ensure economic stability, besides full social services, including physical and cultural amenities'.[99]

   The 28 New Towns established in Britain and two in Northern Ireland to date (figure 2.22), are at very varying stages of development. The British New Towns have already provided 175,000 new dwellings and absorbed a population of over 600,000. The first wave of New Towns were largely provided for Greater London, some 25-30 miles (40-48 km) out, beyond the green belt. Initially mainly concerned with providing housing, they have increasingly developed their employment base, though many are still over-dependent on one or two large firms. Collectively, the 'first wave' London New Towns had a population of 461,000 at the end of 1969, of which some 372,000 was overspill, as compared with their planned capacity of 629,000 (table 2.31).

   Relatively small in size and close to London, the largest is planned to reach 134,000, the counter-attraction of the conurbation and the relatively restricted number and range of job opportunities within the individual towns have necessitated a considerable degree of commuting, including a sizeable element of travel to work from the New Towns to Central London. In 1961 only Bracknell, Stevenage and Welwyn had job ratios of over 100 and the levels of out-commuting ranged from 14-40 per cent, while 6·8 per cent of men and 3·7 per cent of women still travelled to work in the County of London. In 1966, 26 per cent of the active population worked outside the eight London New Towns and 29 per cent of their working populations were drawn from outside. Clearly the number and range of jobs was healthier in the 1960s, including more in the service and commercial sector but it would seem that even where the objectives include that of a balanced community' a considerable level of commuting is unavoidable in an economy in which more than one member of a household is in work and transport is relatively easy, in terms of cost and accessibility.

   Similar problems have been encountered in the New Towns of other regions, though often in a more marked form. The second wave of New Towns of the 1960s, in the South East and elsewhere, have generally been focused on existing towns, farther from the major city and often with a considerable initial population of their own (table 2.31 and figure 2.22). Their target populations are much larger and this presents a greater opportunity to develop a wider range of jobs and facilities and, since they are farther from the metropolis, they may succeed in becoming more independent than the first

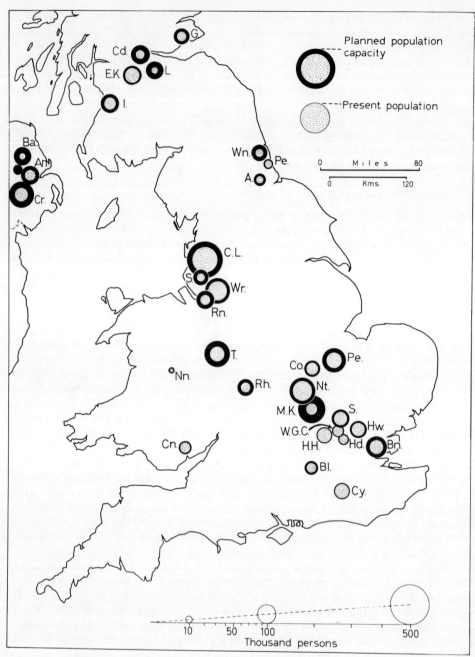

Figure 2.22   New towns: present and target populations, UK, 1971
Source: *Long Term Population Distribution in GB* (1971)

wave of New Towns. The target populations are much greater, up to 430,000 in the
case of Central Lancashire, and represent an addition of up to 200,000 population as
at Milton Keynes, perhaps the most ambitious New Town in the UK to date.

   While London has progressed much farther in its programme of New Town building,
the case is paralleled in Central Scotland where pressing problems of urban renewal, job

provision and population overspill, especially from Central Clydeside, have led to the designation of four New Towns with a present population of 150,000. Glenrothes, the fifth Scottish New Town, was developed in a depressed mining area of Fife and has much in common with Peterlee and Washington in North East England. During 1972 Stonehouse was designated a further Scottish New Town. The dual motives of overspill housing and job provision are present also in the New Town programme for the West Midlands and the North West, where, in both cases, the later developments are of greater size than the earlier. Wales so far has only one New Town at Cwmbran in south east Wales, specifically for the problem area of the eastern coalfield. The recent development at Newtown is modest and designed to attract some industrial growth to Mid-Wales, perhaps from the West Midlands, rather than to take large-scale overspill. In Northern Ireland, Belfast and Londonderry, which alike present enormous problems of slums and unemployment, have led to the designation of New Towns at Craigavon, Antrim-Ballymena, and Londonderry itself (figure 1.9).

Despite the relative success of New Towns in terms of absorbing population and attracting new jobs, the scale of development has been inadequate and additional overspill arrangements have been sought by many large cities to relieve pressing problems of housing and population. A variety of arrangements have been made in England under the Town Development Act of 1952 and in Scotland under the Housing and Town Development Act of 1957. Under these Acts an 'exporting' authority will negotiate with a 'receiving' authority for transfer of population, often bearing the cost of housing. Not all such housing is available for overspill, for firms moving to these towns often need accommodation for their labour force, but the schemes have been of material assistance to large towns in relieving pressure on their housing lists.[100]

Of the 9 British cities which have made overspill arrangements under these Acts, by far the biggest scheduled developments are for Greater London (a target of 89,453 dwellings), Glasgow (23,261 dwellings), Birmingham (21,600 dwellings) and Liverpool (18,526 dwellings). No less than 65 schemes involving 60 'receiver' towns exist in England and Wales, and Glasgow has 66 schemes scattered throughout virtually the whole of Scotland and ranging from a mere 8 houses at Innerleithen to 4,725 in Renfrew county (figure 2.23).

Altogether 50 schemes are presently active, some of which are considerable developments of substantial benefit to the towns involved, since they frequently bring new economic activity. As with New Towns, the success of overspill schemes varies with the local and regional economic situation. Thus, Liverpool's overspill agreement with Ellesmere Port has made rather slow progress because of the considerable local demand for housing in a rapidly expanding economy. In the Worsley overspill scheme for Salford CB, completed in 1966, the success in providing homes was not matched with success in overspill families obtaining work locally, so that many commuted to work in Salford and Manchester. In 1966 Worsley had a job ratio of 81 and 58 per cent of its active residents worked elsewhere while 49 per cent of its workforce was drawn from outside the town, a situation not dissimilar from that in the earlier stages of the scheme.[101] Another overspill scheme for Liverpool, at Winsford, Cheshire, has been successful both in terms of rehousing Liverpool's population and gaining jobs for the local authority's industrial estate.

There is little doubt that overspill schemes will cumulatively make a considerable impact in relieving housing and social problems in many British cities. But to date progress has been limited and often slow, while many aspects of their economic potential and its relationship to the regional labour market need careful thought.[102]

TABLE 2.31 New Towns and Overspill Schemes, UK, 1946-71

REGION (and New Towns) (with date of designation)	NEW TOWNS POPULATION (1,000s)			Towns	OVERSPILL AGREEMENTS Dwellings (1000s)			Overspill population 1968-81 (1,000s)
	Original	Planned	1971		No. of Schemes	To be Built	Completed	
LONDON and SOUTH EAST: TOTAL	356·4	1,366·4	709·5	Greater London	31	89·5	41·4	181
First Wave: Stevenage (1946); Crawley, Harlow, Hemel Hempstead (1947); Hatfield, Welwyn Garden City (1948); Basildon, Bracknell (1949).	98·4	668·5	441·9					
Second Wave: Milton Keynes, Peterborough (1967); Northampton (1968)	258·0	697·6	267·6					
MIDLANDS and SOUTH WEST: TOTAL	117·7	423·0	158·9	TOTAL	23	28·4	14·5	
First Wave: Corby (1950)	15·7	83·0	47·7	Birmingham	15	21·6	7·9	48+
Second Wave: Redditch (1964); Telford (1968).	102·0	340·0	111·2	Wolverhampton	4	4·5	4·3	–
				Bristol	4	2·3	2·3	–
NORTH WEST: TOTAL	413·2	809·0	416·6	TOTAL	9	31·5	10·9	66
Second Wave: Skelmersdale (1961); Runcorn (1964); Warrington (1968); Central Lancs. (1970).	413·2	809·0	416·6	Liverpool	4	18·5	5·0	41
				Manchester	4	8·5	1·4	25
				Salford	1	4·5	4·5	–

NORTH EAST: TOTAL	20·3	155·0	67·3				
First Wave: Aycliffe (1947); Peterlee (1948).	0·3	75·0	42·0				
Newcastle				2	10·5	1·5	21
Second Wave: Washington (1964).	20·0	80·0	25·3				
WALES: TOTAL	17·5	68·0	46·6				
First Wave: Cwmbran (1949)	12·0	55·0	41·0				
Second Wave: Newtown (1967)	5·5	13·0	5·6				
SCOTLAND: TOTAL	47·2	495·0	179·0				
First Wave: East Kilbride (1947); Glenrothes (1948). Cumbernauld (1955).	6·5	275·0	123·0				
Glasgow				66	23·3	9·6	-
Second Wave: Livingston (1962); Irvine (1966).	40·7	220·0	56·0				
TOTAL GB	972·3	3,316·4	1,577·9				
TOTAL GB				131	183·2	77·9	-
NORTHERN IRELAND		390·0	179·8				
Second Wave: Craigavon (1965)	-	180·0	61·8				
Antrim-Ballymena (1966)	-	120·0	48·0				
Londonderry (1969)	-	90·0	70·0				

Sources: Long Term Population Distribution in GB: A Study (1971), tables 6.2 and 6.3; Manners, *Regional Development in Britain*, tables 5A, B and C; *Census 1971*

Data on overspill population targets are incomplete

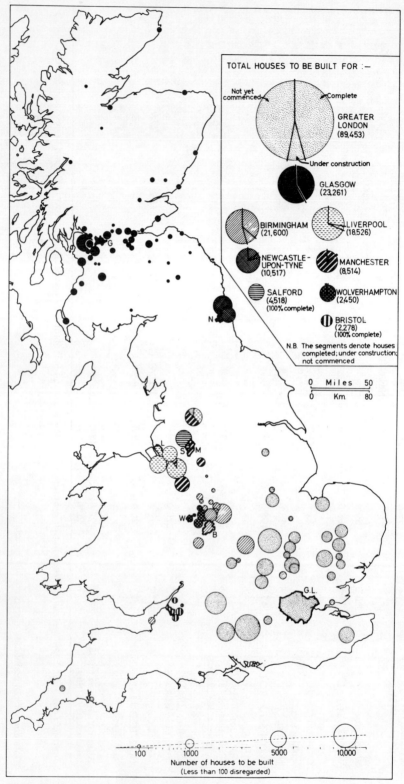

Figure 2.23. Overspill schemes, UK, 1971
Source: *Long Term Population Distribution in GB* (1971).

REFERENCES

1. R H Best, 'March of the Concrete Jungle: Urban Hazards in Britain' *Geographical Magazine,* **45,** 1 (1972), pp. 47-51.
2. *Long Term Population Distribution in Great Britain: a Study* (HMSO 1971).
3. R H Best and A G Champion, 'Regional Conversions of Agricultural Land to Urban Use in England and Wales, 1945-67', *Transactions, Institute of British Geographers,* **49** (1970), pp. 15-32.
4. Jean Thompson 'The Growth of Population to the End of the Century', in Muriel Nissel (ed.), *Social Trends* **1** (HMSO for the Central Statistical Office, London 1970), p. 27.
5. *Population of the United Kingdom,* First Report of the Select Committee on Science and Technology, Session 1970-1 (HMSO 1971).
6. These were Greater London, Merseyside, South-East Lancashire (now South-East Lancashire and North-east Cheshire, or SELNEC), Tyneside, West Yorkshire and the West Midlands.
7. A E Smailes, 'The Urbanisation of Britain', *Problems of Applied Geography: Polish Academy of Sciences Geographical Studies,* **25** (1961), pp. 131-40.
8. J T Coppock, 'Farming for an Urban Nation', in M Chisholm (ed.), *Resources for Britain's Future* (Harmondsworth 1972), p. 36.
9. D E C Eversley, 'Population Changes and Regional Policies since the War', *Regional Studies,* **5** (1971), pp. 221-28
10. A considerable range of tabulations and maps for 1951-69 are available for sub-regions of England and Wales and regions of Scotland in *Long Term Population Distribution in Great Britain.* Recently some data have been tabulated for Scottish planning subregions in *The Size and Distribution of Scotland's Population: Projections for Planning Purposes,* (HMSO for Scottish Development Department, Edinburgh 1972).
11. Unlike many European countries (notably in Scandinavia, the Netherlands, West Germany, and most of Eastern Europe) the UK has no system of registration recording personal or residential mobility. The only information of this kind was the wartime National Register; a study of mobility based on this is M P Newton and J R Jeffrey, *Internal Migration: Studies in Medical and Population Subjects* **5,** (HMSO 1951).
12. D V Glass and E Grebenik, *The Trend and Pattern of Fertility in Great Britain* (London 1954).
13. *Population of the United Kingdom,* p. 189, para. 8.
14. For a detailed analysis see K G Pickett, 'Merseyside's Population and Social Structure' in R. Lawton and C M Cunningham (eds.), *Merseyside: Social and Economic Studies,* (London 1970), especially pp. 92-7. Fertility rates are the number of children under 1 year per 1,000 women aged 15-44.
15. R K Kelsall, *The Social Structure of Modern Britain: Population* (London 1967), pp. 50-2.
16. G M Howe, *National Atlas of Disease Mortality in the United Kingdom,* 2nd ed. (London 1970).
17. See for a general discussion of variation in levels of living, B E Coates and E M Rawstron, *Regional Variations in Britain* (London 1971); they discuss infant mortality on pp. 227-35.
18. Coates and Rawstron, *Regional Variations in Britain,* table 7.5, p. 188.
19. In 1968, 250,000 dependants were estimated to be eligible for entry into the UK, mostly from India and Pakistan, though there is no guarantee that all of these will come. D E C Eversley and F Sukdeo, *The Dependants of the Coloured Common-*

wealth Population of England and Wales, Institute of Race Relations Special Series (London 1969).

20. E J B Rose *et al., Colour and Citizenship,* Institute of Race Relations (London 1969). *Social Trends* 3 (HMSO 1972), p. 27, estimates those of New Commonwealth origin at 1½ million (2·7 per cent of GB population).

21. For a full discussion and a series of distribution maps showing actual numbers and relative importance of various groups of overseas born, see Coates and Rawstron, *Regional Variations in Britain,* ch. 6, pp. 122-73.

22. Report of a survey of the ward (*Children in Southall*) carried out in 1969 by the Southall Indian Workers Association, discussed by N Deakin *et al. Colour, Citizenship and British Society,* based on the Institute of Race Relations Report (London 1970).

23. Ruth Glass, *Newcomers: West Indians in London* (London 1960), p. 41.

24. P N Jones, 'The Segregation of Immigrant Communities in the City of Birmingham, 1961', *University of Hull, Occasional Papers in Geography,* 7 (1967).

25. E Krausz, *Ethnic Minorities in Britain* (London 1971), pp. 45, 146, quoting the Economist Intelligence Unit, *Studies on Immigration from the Commonwealth. The Immigrant Communities,* 2 (London 1961).

26. J.Thompson, 'Differential Fertility among Immigrants to England and Wales and Some Implications for Population Projections' *Journal of Biosocial Science,* Supplement 1 (July 1969).

27. Krausz, *Ethnic Minorities in Britain,* p. 49, quoting E J B Rose *et al. Report on Race Relations. Social Trends* 3 (HMSO 1972) suggests that recent age specific fertility rates for New Commonwealth mothers are just 50 per cent above general fertility rates, (p. 27).

28. G P Wibberley, 'Some Aspects of Problem Rural Areas in Britain', *Geographical Journal,* **120** (1954), pp. 43-61.

29. For a fuller breakdown of interregional migration by age group see *Long Term Population Distribution in GB: a Study* (1971), Appendix 2, pp. 89-131.

30. F Musgrove, *The Migratory Elite* (London 1963), p. 3.

31. H R Jones, 'Rural Migration in Central Wales', *Transactions, Institute of British Geographers,* **37** (1965), p. 35.

32. *Report of the Committee on Rural Depopulation in Mid-Wales* (HMSO 1964), p. 4.

33. See, for example, D Turnock, 'Regional Development in the Crofting Counties' *Transactions, Institute of British Geographers,* **48** (1969), pp. 189-204, and J B Caird 'Population Problem of the Islands of Scotland with Special Reference to the Uists', unpublished paper presented to a symposium on Scottish Population Problems, *Institute of British Geographers* (Aberdeen meeting, 1972).

34. D I Mackay, *Geographical Mobility and the Brain Drain: a Case Study of Aberdeen University Graduates 1860-1960* (1969), p. 209.

35. J W House, A D Thomas and K G Willis, 'Where did the School-leavers go? ', University of Newcastle upon Tyne, Department of Geography, *Papers on Migration and Mobility,* 7 (1968).

36. B C Roberts and J H Smith (eds.), *Manpower Policy and Employment Trends* (London 1960).

37. D Friedlander and R J Roshier, 'A Study of Internal Migration in England and Wales', *Population Studies,* **20** (1966), pp. 45-59, (quotation from p. 57).

38. M Waugh 'The Changing Distribution of Professional and Managerial manpower in England and Wales, 1961-6', *Regional Studies,* **3** (1969), pp. 157-69.

39. A I Harris (assisted by R Clausen), *Labour Mobility in Great Britain 1953-63,* Social Survey Report SS 333, Ministry of Labour and National Service (HMSO 1966).

40. W Watson 'Social Mobility and Social Class in Industrial Communities', in *Closed Systems and Open Minds* (1964).

41. 'Migration in the Merseyside area', ch 5 of R Lawton and C M Cunningham (eds.), *Merseyside: Social and Economic Studies,* (London 1970).
42. Pickett, *Merseyside: Social and Economic Studies,* p. 133.
43. *Royal Commission on Local Government in England 1966-9,* Cmnd 4040 (HMSO 1969), vol. III, appendix 3, pp. 39-56.
44. *Royal Commission on Local Government in England,* vol. III, pp. 43-5.
45. E M Soulsby, 'Changing Sex Ratios in the Scottish Border Counties', *Scottish Geographic Magazine,* **88** (1972), pp. 5-18.
46. J C Dewdney, 'Age Structure Maps of the British Isles', *Transactions, Institute of British Geographers,* **43** (1968), pp. 9-18.
47. Dewdney, *TIBG* (1968), p. 9.
48. The first major comparative classification of occupational groups, was that of Charles Booth, 'Occupations of the People of the UK', *Journal of the Royal Statistical Society,* XLIX (1886), pp. 314-435. In the 1951 Census, 13 socio-economic groups and 5 socio-economic classes were derived from occupations and these were replaced by 17 groups and 5 classes in 1961.
    For a review of the changing social structure of England see D C Marsh *The Changing Social Structure of England and Wales, 1871-1951,* 2nd ed. (London 1965).
49. The major study of C A Moser and W Scott, *British Towns* (London, 1961) used a principal components analysis and included a considerable number of indices of housing among the variables. Similar studies of individual cities or regions have found that housing indices form significant components in defining social areas; see, for example, E Gittus, 'An Experiment in the Definition of Urban Sub-areas' *Transactions of the Bartlett Society* (University College London 1964) and B T Robson, *Urban Analysis* (Cambridge 1969).
50. Vol. 1 deals with Schools, vol. 2 with School-leavers, vol. 3 with Further Education, vol. 4 with Teachers, vol. 5 with Finance and Awards and vol. 6 with Universities (UK) (DES, *Statistics of Education* (HMSO), annually.
    Education Statistics for the United Kingdom is prepared by the Department of Education and Science in collaboration with the Scottish Education Department, the Northern Ireland Ministry of Education and the University Grants Committee (HMSO), annually.
51. A question on personal income in a pilot census survey was unsuccessful and it was omitted from the schedule for the 1971 census.
52. *Annual Reports of the Commissioners of H M Inland Revenue* (HMSO).
53. See, for example, Coates and Rawstron, *Regional Variations in Britain,* ch. 2.
54. For a recent classification also involving a range of socio-economic variables relating to population and activity, and environmental and locational factors (132 variables in all) see G Armen, 'A Classification of Cities and City Regions in England and Wales, 1966', *Regional Studies,* **6** (1972), pp. 149-82.
55. *Housing in Britain,* Central Office of Information Reference Pamphlet 41 (HMSO, 1970), p. 1.
56. J.B Cullingworth, *Housing Needs and Planning Policy* (London 1960).
57. A E Holmans 'A Forecast of Effective Demand for Housing in Great Britain in the 1970s', *Social Trends* No. 1 (1970), pp. 33-42.
58. *Housing in Britain,* pp. 8-9.
59. *Housing Statistics, Great Britain* No. 23, Nov. 1971 (HMSO 1972), tables 38 and 39, p. 48.
60. *Our Older Homes – A Call for Action* (the Denington Report), (HMSO 1966). *The Older Houses in Scotland – A Plan for Action,* Cmnd 3598, (Edinburgh HMSO 1968).

61. *Housing Statistics,* No. 23 (1971), table 34, p. 46.
62. Holmans, *Social Trends,* pp. 33-42.
63. M C Storrie, 'Household Tenure' in A J Hunt (ed.), 'Population maps of the British Isles, 1961', *Transactions, Institute British Geographers,* **43** (1968), pp.25-30.
64. J B Cullingworth, *Housing in Transition* (London 1963).
65. Storrie, 'Household Tenure', fig. 10.
66. *Our Older Homes. A Call for Action.* Report of the Sub-Committee on Standards of Housing Fitness, (HMSO 1966).
67. G Humphrys 'Housing Quality', in A J Hunt (ed.), *'Population Maps of the British Isles',* pp. 31-6.
68. J I Clarke 'Persons per Room: an Index of Population Density', *Tijdschrift voor Economische en Sociale Geografie,* **51** (1960), pp. 257-60.
69. N Deakin, *Colour, Citizenship and British Society* (London 1970), p. 72.
70. *The Intermediate Areas,* Cmnd 3998 (HMSO 1969), p. 29.
71. R Lawton, 'Recent Trends in Population and Housing in England and Wales', *Sociological Review,* **11** (1963), pp. 303-21.
72. R Lawton, 'Housing and Social Structure' in J A Patmore and A G Hodgkiss (eds.), *Merseyside in Maps,* (London 1970), pp. 33-4.
73. E Gittus 'An Experiment in the Definition of Urban sub-areas' *Transactions of the Bartlett Society* (University College London, 1964).
74. Coates and Rawstron, Regional Variations in Britain, ch. 10.
75. For a summary see Coates and Rawstron, *Regional Variations in Britain,* ch. 2.
76. *Children and their Primary Schools,* Central Advisory Council for Education (England) (HMSO 1967).
77. R S Howard, *The Movement of Manufacturing Industry in the UK,* (HMSO 1968).
78. G Manners *et al., Regional Development in Britain* (London 1972), p. 21.
79. *The Intermediate Areas,* Cmnd 3998 (HMSO 1969), paras. 38-43, pp. 14-15.
80. For an analysis of these indices at subregional level see *The Intermediate Areas,* appendix C.
81. M Waugh, 'The Changing Distribution of Professional and Managerial Manpower in England and Wales between 1961 and 1966', *Regional Studies,* **3** (1969), pp. 157-69.
82. P. 25, *The Intermediate Areas* (1969) noted that the proportion of women over 15 at work in GB was 40 per cent in 1966 but that regional percentages varied between 22 and 45.
83. For example, I R Gordon, 'Activity Rates: Regional and Sub-Regional Differentials', *Regional Studies,* **4** (1970), pp. 411-24, and B E Coates and E M Rawstron, *Regional Variations in Britain,* (1971), ch. 5.
84. See also G Manners *et al., Regional Development in Britain* (London, 1972), table 6, pp. 40-2 and A R Prest (ed.), *The UK Economy. A Manual of Applied Economics,* 3rd ed., (London 1970), ch. 5, table 5.10.
85. Gordon, 'Activity Rates: Regional and Subregional Differentials'. For a case study of local labour reserves see J Taylor 'Hidden Female Labour Reserves', *Regional Studies,* **2** *(1968), pp.231-31.*
86. *The Intermediate Areas* (1969), p. 20, para. 53.
87. 'Area Statistics of Unemployment', *Department of Employment Gazette* (HMSO London).
88. R B Davison, *The Black British* (Oxford 1966), table 3, p. 89.
89. E Krausz, *Ethnic Minorities in Britain* (London 1971), ch. 4, especially pp. 111-22, and N Deakin, *Colour, Citizenship and British Society* (London 1970), pp. 72-82.
90. *Royal Commission on Local Government in England, 1966-9,* vol. III Research Appendices (HMSO London 1969), especially pp. 25-8 and 87-94.

91. R Lawton, 'The Journey to Work in Britain: Some Trends and Problems', *Regional Studies,* **2** (1967), pp. 27-40.
92. A M Warnes, 'Estimates of Journey to Work Distances from Census Statistics', *Regional Studies* **6** (1972), pp. 315-26.
93. *Royal Commission on Local Government,* vol. III, appendix 2, table 6 and map 12.
94. P W Daniels, 'Office Decentralization from London – Policy and Practice', *Regional Studies,* **3** (1969), pp. 171-8.
95. A M Warnes, *Regional Studies,* **6** p. 325 and table 1.
96. See, for example, R. Lawton 'The Journey to Work in England and Wales: Forty Years of Change', *Tijdschrift voor Economische en Sociale Geografie,* **34** (1963), pp. 61-9, and *Royal Commission on Local Government,* vol. III, pp. 25-6 and map 12.
97. A M Warnes, *Regional Studies,* **6.**
98. *Royal Commission on Local Government,* vol. III, appendix 3, pp. 39-47: the towns analysed, ranging in population from 427,800-32,800, were Bristol, Coventry, Nottingham, Leicester, Luton, Northampton, Norwich, York, Exeter, Doncaster, Colchester, Shrewsbury, Taunton and Canterbury.
99. K C Edwards, 'The New Towns of Britain', *Geography,* **49** (1964), p. 279.
100. D I Scargill, 'The Expanded Town in England and Wales', in R P Beckinsale and J M Houston (eds.), *Urbanization and its Problems. Essays presented to E.W Gilbert* (Oxford, 1968), pp. 119-42.
101. H B Rodgers, 'Employment and the Journey to Work in an Overspill Community', *Sociological Review,* **7** (1959), pp. 213-29.
102. G. Manners, *Regional Development in Britain,* pp. 33-4.

3

Environment and Land Use

I   LAND USE

I.1   Land Utilisation Surveys

The first land utilisation survey of Britain, directed by Stamp from 1930-47, was designed as a national inventory which could be used as a basis for land use planning. To achieve national coverage in an acceptable length of time (the field survey was completed between 1931 and 1934) detail was not possible and the classification had to be simple enough to allow accurate mapping by volunteers, many of them school children. Seven forms of land use, subdivided, were mapped at the six-inch scale and subsequently plotted on one-inch maps. Between 1936 and 1948 one-inch sheets and county reports were published as they were completed. A summary of the work done in the survey and an analysis of the findings was published by Stamp.[1] The Geographical Association of Northern Ireland became interested in the survey in 1936 and by 1939 had completed a survey of Northern Ireland, using the same classification. Due to different farming methods and the amount of land of a marginal character in Northern Ireland some modifications were adopted; for example, all grassland whether rotation or permanent was grouped in one class. One-inch sheets were published by the Government of Northern Ireland between 1945 and 1951. A memoir was written for the Belfast sheet,[2] but a description and analysis for the whole of Northern Ireland was not published until 1963,[3] which allowed the work of the original survey to be extended by considering trends up to 1953.

Stamp's land utilisation survey proved invaluable in post-war planning, but rapid changes in agriculture and urban growth soon rendered it obsolete. A second survey was inaugurated in 1960[4] and, in it, an attempt to map more detail. Factories were mapped according to industrial group and crops identified. The 12 types of vegetation proved too difficult for volunteer surveyors and this aspect of the mapping was undertaken by the Nature Conservancy, to be published on 1:100,000 maps in *A Wildscape Atlas for England and Wales.* This scale will permit mapping communities of at least 5 acres (2 ha) in extent. The land use maps have been produced at the scale of 1:25,000 showing 64 categories grouped to give 2 levels of intensity: first, the Old World divisions of the World Land Use Survey, but with transport, open spaces, derelict and unvegetated land added; second, subdivisions were made by variations in tone and the overlay of symbols. For example, grassland was indicated in green with symbols and letters to show ley, infestation by rushes, scrub and bracken, etc. By 1968 all England and part of Wales had been completed in manuscript and by 1972 just over 100 sheets had been printed. Many of these are scattered widely, but there is a useful cover in the London area, South Wales, the Vale of York and in North East England. The survey of Scotland is incomplete, but 2 sheets have been published.

I.2   Land Classification

On the assumption that land utilisation in the pre-war years 1931-9 was a consequence of the nature of the land, Stamp produced a classification which was used in many planning reports.[5] Although criticised by soil scientists because of its basis in use rather than soil,[6]

the Soil Survey could not meet the urgent need for a complete mapping cover. With
rapidly expanding urban population, good agricultural land needed delimitation if the
country were to avoid serious losses of good land. The Land Utilisation Survey divided
England, Wales and Scotland into 10 categories: 1 - 4 were of high agricultural value, 7 - 10
land of low agricultural value, and types 5 - 6 of intermediate quality (fig. 3.1). First class
arable land was considered to be as valuable as first class grassland, but would require
different physical conditions. In Northern Ireland land classification began in 1954 but
was made difficult because of lack of information apart from the land use maps and only
a few soil survey maps. While the same principles of classification were applied, a scheme
emerged which was similar to that of the Department of Agriculture of Scotland. However,
the field by field analysis carried out in Scotland could not be attempted in Northern
Ireland because of the smaller fields and the great number of small farms which produced
a greater variation in management. The first class land in Northern Ireland was that considered suitable for all crops which the climate permitted and some of this would not have
been graded first class land in Scotland. All these classifications attempted an assessment
of short-term potential assuming reasonable drainage, fertilisation, etc. However, it is
important to realize that herbicides and fertilisers have since led to greater intensification
of use and many of the lands classified as poor or very poor have proved productive under
forest.

     In 1962 the Agricultural Land Service Research Group attempted to improve on these
classifications by finding a classification[7] which would have relevance at the scale of the
individual farm and yet be consistent in its grading throughout Britain. Following the
principle adopted by earlier surveys,[8] physical characteristics of the land were considered
most important, largely because of their permanence and the difficulty in altering them.
The difficulty, clearly recognised by the survey, is that it is impossible to evaluate the
land without considering the uses to which the land might be put. Moreover, it was
difficult to be objective in the absence of a comprehensive soil survey, and data on local
climates. The interrelations between physical factors and land productivity being
imperfectly known made the choice of parameters often purely arbitrary. 5 grades were
chosen according to the limitations imposed by physical factors and mapped at the one-
inch to one mile (1:63,360) scale (Fig. 3.2). At the same time productivity, assuming
standard management, was estimated as a check for each area mapped. The great number
of holdings within any one physical group makes this a difficult exercise without considering farm structure, equipment and location. Grade I is land with very minor or no
physical limitation to agricultural use, which because of climate, soil and slope conditions
occurs most readily on the lowlands of South and South East England. Limitations
associated with the soil will produce grade II, while more serious limitations of soil such as
the poor drainage of the Lias, Oxford and London Clays as well as the glacial drifts, and
slope and climate produce grade III classifications. Grade IV has severe limitations of soil,
either wetness or low water-holding capacity, shallowness or stoniness. The steepness,
high rainfall and short growing season of the upland margins also will put these areas into
this grade. Grade V is of little agricultural value because the limitations of soil, slope and
climate are very severe. Thus flood plains of rivers, as well as much of the uplands above
1,000 ft (304 m), are grouped in this class together with areas seriously affected by
pollution either from the atmosphere or due to waste disposal. Insufficient information on
the range of output per unit area for each of these 5 grades and the differences in type of
farming within any one grade makes interpretation difficult. The survey gives merely an
indication of the range of productivity for the dominant type of farming likely to occur
within the physical class. It serves no more than to test the accordance between physical
and economic gradings.

     At the same time the Soil Survey of England and Wales and of Scotland produced a
Land Use *Capability Classification* with the aim of assisting planners and other land users.

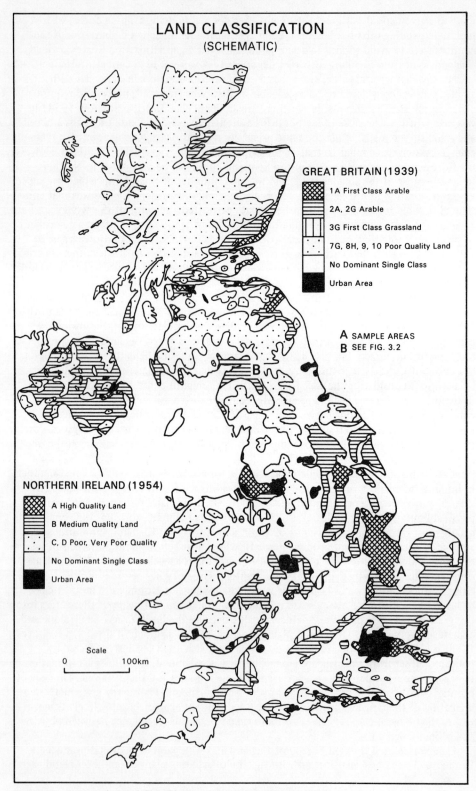

LAND CLASSIFICATION
(SCHEMATIC)

GREAT BRITAIN (1939)

▨	1A First Class Arable
▤	2A, 2G Arable
▥	3G First Class Grassland
⋯	7G, 8H, 9, 10 Poor Quality Land
☐	No Dominant Single Class
■	Urban Area

A SAMPLE AREAS
B SEE FIG. 3.2

NORTHERN IRELAND (1954)

▨	A High Quality Land
▤	B Medium Quality Land
⋯	C, D Poor, Very Poor Quality
☐	No Dominant Single Class
■	Urban Area

Scale
0   100km

Figure 3.1   Schematic Land Classification, GB 1939; N. Ireland 1954.

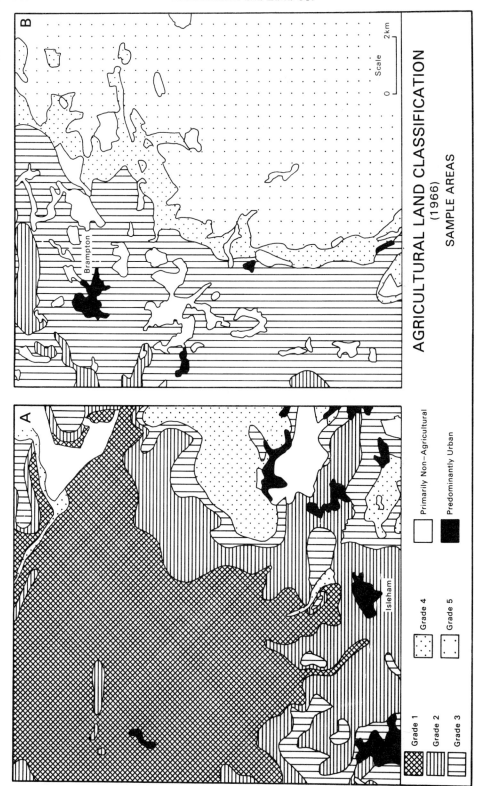

Figure 3.2   Agricultural land classification, sample areas, UK, 1966

This is a cooperative effort between the Agricultural Development and Advisory Service, the Soil Survey of England and Wales, the Meteorological Office and the Agricultural Land Service. Experimental mapping on the 2½ in to 1 mile (1:25,000) scale has been done for the Tideswell area of Derbyshire and the Melton Mowbray sheet and will be published in the *Soil Survey Memoirs* (in press); a further 4 sheets are in preparation. The classification[9] was modified from that developed by the Soil Conservation Service of the United States Department of Agriculture. The major modification is the omission of class 5 which relates to flat wet land. Thus seven classes range from land with minor or no limitations (I) to that with extremely severe limitations that cannot be rectified (V). These are sub-divided by the physical limitations which put them in this class. The system is firmly based on purely physical limitations and economic considerations are completely ignored. It does, however, attempt a more careful evaluation of the physical properties of the soil and draws upon the basic soil maps of this survey. Interpretation of the soil data depends on the more detailed studies of selected soils, which have been termed 'benchmark' soils. These studies cover 4 years and consider potential yields under normal rotation conditions in commercial farming. One of these studies in the Vale of Belvoir, Nottinghamshire and Leicestershire was commenced in 1968 and involved 6 soil series. Soil profile analyses, together with meteorological observations, were related to problems of soil preparation, fertiliser application and crop yields. An attempt was also made to assess susceptibility to disease and physiological limitations at each site. This would have been an impossible task if applied universally, but the aim was to concentrate on key agricultural areas and apply the results to similar soils elsewhere. Information on crop responses exists and is accumulating in results of field experimental studies of crop response to nutrients, effect of crop variety, technique and management on crop yields, together with weed, pest and disease effects, as well as data provided for advisory work and a great body of farming experience. This classification involves both analysis, that is the individual components of the soil system, and synthesis, where the data is interpreted according to the classification. Thus the final classification is an appraisal of soil characteristics, crop-yields and management and it is only the quantitative evaluation of the individual components which reduces its subjectivity. The proposal to use computers for future analysis and mapping will not improve the classification but of course will greatly facilitate its application.

II   ENVIRONMENTAL FACTORS AND AGRICULTURAL LAND USE

II.1   Introduction

Land classifications have been largely concerned with agricultural land use and indeed most had the original aim of preserving the best agricultural land from urban use. The various classifications differ in their relative emphasis on physical characteristics and land use, but they all share the uncertain relationships which exist between land use and environment. Elements in the environment are measurable, though imperfectly, but the real problems lie in identifying those which limit productivity and the weighting given to each in the complex interrelationships. This section deals with the measurement of these factors in the UK, the parameters derived from them and their relevance to land use and productivity. The opportunities for improving productivity by controlling the environment are also discussed, as well as the consequences of agricultural land use polluting the environment.

II.2   Measurement of the Climatic Environment

Precipitation: Precipitation comes mainly in the form of rain and an extensive network of about 6,500 rain-gauges is in operation.[10] Since the last century these gauges have been standard, that is 5 in (12·7 cm) diameter with the rims 1 ft (0·3 m) above the ground. The accuracy of the readings varies from site to site. At Wallingford differences of up to 15 per cent in winter months were found between standard and ground level gauges, though this was reduced to less than 5 per cent in June and July. Greatest errors occur with high winds and small raindrop size, when turbulence diverts most of the rain away from the funnel of a standard gauge.[11] It is obvious that rainfall in the wetter areas of the west and upland areas is underestimated. The Institute of Hydrology has developed a grid to be used with ground level gauges which largely removes the effect of turbulence. Recording rainfall in isolated mountain regions has proved difficult in the past, but auto-mation is likely to overcome this. Experiments by the North of Scotland Electricity Board, using a rotating collecting funnel and 32 bottles, have reduced recording to monthly visits. Also at Glen Kingie a radio rain-gauge transmits information powered by solar cell batteries while at Achnasheen a telephonic gauge allows remote reading in units, tens or hundreds, depending on the frequency of the signals. Less progress has been made in measuring snow which is a significant proportion of precipitation in highland regions in winter. The interpolation of rainfall is made difficult by the fact that the effect of altitude varies with the synoptic situation and seasonally. In Scotland it has been shown that no satisfactory regression is possible for short periods.[12] Point sampling by gauges has limited value when spatial variations in rainfall are required, and even if the rainfall for a crop or forest is required, gauging must be at the site. Radar readings related to gauge recordings may provide clearer patterns for these purposes.

Evaporation: Evaporation, or the transfer of water from the earth's surface, includes the loss from water surfaces, the soil and that transpired by plants; however, loss from a vegetated surface is termed evapotranspiration. The measurement of evaporation by pans or tanks is made difficult by the effects of advection, so that under dry conditions the evaporation rate is much higher than over a large open water surface where advection effects are limited to the edges. Nevertheless at least 20 stations in the UK have tank data, 16 of these recording data since 1956. This data is from standard evaporation tanks which are sunk in the ground, but the more recent class 'A' pan which is placed above ground level has been installed at many stations as well. The accuracy with which the water level in a tank will indicate evaporation losses depends to a large extent on the gauging of rainfall. Also in winter many pans and tanks cannot be used to record evaporation. It is usual, therefore, to use the summer half-year, April to September, which accounts for about 80 per cent of the annual total, to estimate the 12 month total and by assuming a symmetrical curve in evaporation from January to December, redistribute the evaporation between the months to give a 'norm'. Calculations based on this method are published in *British Rainfall.* Using rainfall data and measured runoff it is possible by subtraction to estimate the amount evaporated or transferred from the surface. This has been calculated by the Meteorological Office for the period 1937-62 for 14 catchment areas in England and Wales. Both tank data and catchment data indicate evaporation in excess of 20 in (51 cm) in southern England and less than 17 in (43 cm) in the north. However it is impossible to construct an accurate map when each site may not be regionally representa-tive as regards exposure.

Estimates of evapotranspiration using lysimeters have only recently been made in this country. By weighing a tank of soil and vegetation, irrigated lysimeters allow a measure of the loss by evaporation. Since irrigation ensures a constant supply of water to the plants the loss can be considered the potential. The Nature Conservancy has 22 stations with lysimeters but with only a short run of recordings.[13] However, they generally show a ratio of lysimeter potential evapotranspiration (PE) to tank evaporation of between 1 and 1·25.

Calculations by the Penman method[14] avoids the error caused by condensation which results in higher tank evaporation readings in winter. However, for summer months which are most critical for land use problems, Penman estimates of potential evapotranspiration accord fairly closely with the tank and lysimeter data.[15] The application of the Penman formula depends on the measurement of meteorological elements, temperature, humidity, radiation, wind and sunshine. The importance of potential evapotranspiration in irrigation, as well as in other problems, prompted the Ministry of Agriculture to publish a detailed description of the Penman method and tables of values for the British Isles.[16] Averages for the period 1950-64 were calculated or estimated for over 100 stations. Interpolation beyond these stations depended on distance from the coast, where higher radiation increases the potential evaporation rate, and on altitude.

Height increases wind and relative humidity but decreases temperature and sunshine in a complex relationship. Observations have allowed an empirical correction during summer of 0·2 in per 100 ft (16 mm per 100 m) in England and Wales and 0·25 in per 100 ft (20 mm per 100 m) in Scotland and Northern Ireland. In winter these corrections become 0·15 and 0·1 respectively. These corrections have been used to derive values for: the coastal strip 5 - 10 miles (8 - 16 km) wide; for each county at the mean height; and at 1,200 feet (365 m) where appropriate. As these values are averages it is important to account for year by year deviations of the meteorological controls, of which the dominant in summer is radiation and in winter the saturation deficit. Since the weighting of these factors varies from place to place and month to month they have been published for each station. Thus for a summer month, deviation from average potential transpiration is x times the deviation from the average sunshine. The x factor varies between 0·14 and 0·38, the higher values occurring in June. The factors are generally lower in spring and autumn in the North than in the South but in mid-summer higher factors are needed for northern locations. These tables were prepared for use at any location in the British Isles,[17] but isoline maps would be unsatisfactory at a small scale although they have been constructed from this data by others. Fig. 3.3 shows the pattern of potential evapotranspiration based on average county data. It is useful to reflect that potential evapotranspiration is a theoretical concept and refers to a green crop, completely covering the ground with an adequate supply of soil water at its roots. Variation in plant height and colour of the crop will influence the potential evapotranspiration. Also the supply of water to the roots will depend on the soil type and the rooting habit of the crop. Thus the application of these tables to agriculture and, in particular, irrigation control requires careful appraisal of the specific problem and location. Errors which exist in the Penman results, notably in summer, are often compensated by under-estimation of rainfall though it has been suggested that they could still lead to over-irrigation.[18] However, since potential evapotranspiration rates change very slowly from place to place and changes from year to year are very small compared with rainfall, most irrigation planning can be based upon the averages for the area as derived from these tables. It is on this assumption that water balances have been calculated for long-term planning of irrigation and these are discussed in the next section.

Temperature: Temperature is given particular importance because of its obvious control over growth and in particular the length of the growing season. Maps of temperature have been based upon readings from the standard exposure of a Stevenson screen. Accumulated temperature is an attempt to integrate the excess or deficiency of these temperatures to a fixed datum. 42°F (6°C) is used as a base because of its significance for the commencement and maintenance of growth. Maps of accumulated temperature above 42°F (6°C) by Gregory[19] were based upon mean monthly temperatures. More detailed calculations were made by Shellard[20] for 49 stations in the UK, and he also calculated accumulated temperature below 70°F (21°C), 60°F (15°C) and 50°F (10°C) because of the importance in heating engineering. More important, however, is his use of the standard deviation of temperature to allow for departures from the means which is a vital consideration when the mean temperature is at or near the base level. An attempt to produce a larger-scale

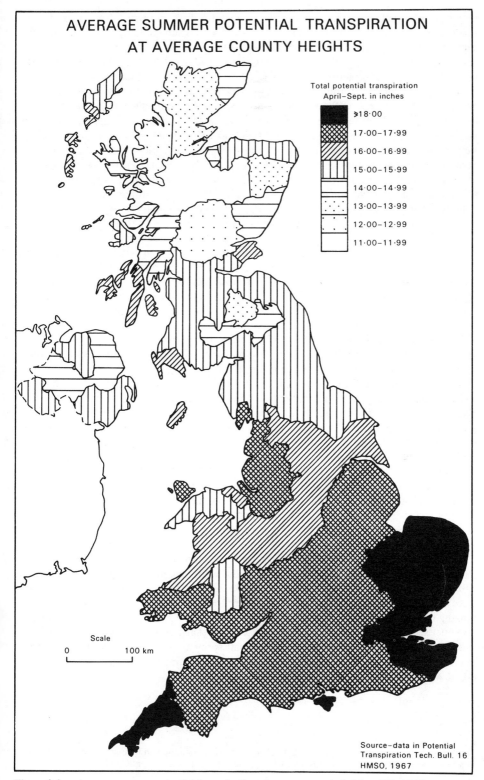

Figure 3.3   Average summer potential transpiration at average county heights, UK, 1967

map of more practical use has been made recently by Birse and Dry[21] for Scotland. For this map the base was 42°F (5·6°C) but the method was similar to that of Shellard. For each station the accumulated temperature was calculated at intervals of 328 ft (100 m) assuming a lapse rate of 1°F per 300 ft (0·6°C per 100 m). Thus contour lines could be used in drawing the isopleths, at intervals of 495 day degrees F (275 day degrees C), differentiating zones according to length of growing season. Using the same procedure accumulated deficiency in temperature below 32°F (0°C) provided a measure of frost severity. This work on temperature was combined with calculations of moisture conditions and exposure on 2 maps at the scale of 1:625,000 giving the climate of sites to help in field surveys of soil and vegetation. It is of obvious value in agriculture, particularly in Scotland where relief imposes rapid changes in local climates. Local climates or meso-climates* which take into account the special circumstances of relief, exposure, aspect, soil and vegetation cover are clearly of more value in agro-climatology than the macro-climates[22] suggested by the long-term means from standard meteorological exposures.

There is the assumption in all descriptive maps that conditions will remain unchanged. Lamb[23] has shown the nature of changes in the past and while there is insufficient evidence to be able to forecast climatic trends, the purpose of the study should determine the choice of the period of records. Elsewhere Lamb has cast doubts on the validity of the 30-year norm for agro-climatic work. It is also difficult to relate screen temperatures to the conditions under which plants are growing. Soil temperatures have been recorded by agrometeorological stations since the 1920s. The nature of the surface, its colour and vegetation cover is therefore of importance. Most of the readings for depths less than 12 in (30 cm) are taken only once per day and are therefore of limited value. Gloyne[24] has attempted to map the 46°F (8°C) average annual mean daily earth temperature because of its significance in the processes of soil formation.

Records of hours of bright sunshine and net radiation are available for many stations and both have been used in estimating potential evaporation by the Penman method. The relevance of these to agriculture depends very much on the aspect, exposure and slope of the particular site. The theoretical energy which would result from optimal insolation[25] together with the study of the effects on air temperature or soil temperature[26] is of importance particularly in relation to earliness of crops.

Wind speed is measured at the standard height of 33 ft (10 m) in open level country. Friction affects wind speed as high as 1,000 ft (305 m) and land-forms can obstruct or create their own circulations. Gloyne has suggested that wind will follow the surface if windward slopes are less than 40° and leeward slopes less than 11° which has obvious implications for shelter effects. The effect of wind speed is to reduce temperature extremes but wind speeds in excess of 25 mph (40 kmph) can dessicate plants. The map of exposure by Birse and Dry (1970) is the only attempt to consider topography in mapping wind speed. The 34 stations in Scotland were inadequate for mapping purposes and were supplemented by an assessment of the visible effect of exposure on broad-leaved trees and on common heather, *Calluna vulgaris*. The map shows 5 categories of exposure ranging from sheltered, 8·5 ft per sec (2·6 m per sec) wind speed, to extremely-exposed, 26 ft per sec (8·0 m per sec). The authors point out that the limits define exposure satisfactorily so long as other factors such as salt spray are not also having an effect on plant life. This shows one of the major problems of equating a single parameter with an effect when relationships are not fully understood.

---

*Mesoclimates can refer to areas less than 10 sq miles (25 km^2) and can be mapped at 1:25,000 scale, whereas macroclimates refer to areas over 100 sq miles (258 km^2) and are mapped at 1:250,000 scale.

II.3 Influence of Climate on Agricultural Land Use and Productivity

As with other developed countries assessment of land potential is important for decisions on the conflicting claims on the land, and displacement of agricultural enterprises by urban growth has called for reappraisal of other areas to which the farmers could move with hopes of success. Hogg[27] quotes a survey of potential sites for horticulture in England which was prompted by the needs of displaced growers in the Lea Valley. To some extent the measurement of the climate described above has been prompted by a practical need so that the parameters have relevance to land-use problems. However, it is the derived values such as day degrees or evapotranspiration which are used. The relationships between climate and the crops which can be grown and their yields are complex. Even if these relationships are understood it is often impossible to apply these results beyond the limits of the experimental plots because of lack of data. In general agricultural surveys the climate can usually be expressed in macroclimatic terms and uncertainties only exist in marginal areas. Fruit growing has been a rewarding field of study, for growth of buds, leaf growth, fruit set and maturity can be correlated with micro-climate. Attempts have been made at Long Ashton, Bristol to relate fruit tree microclimates to screen or standard exposures. Practical applications follow from detailed experimental work only if the knowledge can be applied to broader areas. The present network of stations is not nearly close enough and the validity of the principles used to apply the data from them needs verification. The Meteorological Office provides a frost-warning service and irrigation advice to farmers. This is mainly for high-value horticultural enterprises which can afford the cost of protection. The initial improvement in productivity due to irrigation or frost protection is undoubtedly large enough to pay for the exercise. It is, however, difficult to justify further improvements in relation to the cash returns. The methods used in frost prediction have had some value in planning the expansion of horticulture, particularly soft fruit growing. Microclimatic readings over a short period are related to screen temperatures. The long-term screen records are used to predict the occurrence of the frost detected in the micro-study. Requests for irrigation advice based upon generalised water balance calculations are now largely met by the *Atlas of Long-term Irrigation Needs for England and Wales.*[28] Practical agrometeorologists are forced to adopt subjective methods because of the lack of data and knowledge. However, the high-value horticulture is invariably in more favoured areas and the hazards can be estimated with some degree of certainty. A more recent area of study of relevance to land use has been the study of workdays, the climatic requirements depending very much on the type of work, whether it be sowing, weeding, harvesting, etc. So far most of this work has been done in grass farming where the distinction between dry days, when work is possible, and wet days, when it is not, is clear cut.

Farming activities are not equally sensitive to environmental conditions and in many cases changes in management can bring about more significant improvements. Also climate has more influence on crops than on livestock. There is little point in investigating the actual limits of growth for a particular crop, because economically it becomes impracticable long before this is reached and this depends on fluctuating prices as the changing margins of moorland in our uplands indicate. Thus present land use cannot help in identifying the degree of control imposed by environmental factors.

Water: With the exception of their woody parts actively growing plants have 75 - 90 per cent water. Together with the fact that vast amounts of water must pass through the plant and evaporate from the leaf surface, this accounts for the importance of water in growth. Alfalfa requires over 950 lb (431 kg) of water to produce 1 lb (0·45 kg) dry matter. Drought affects agriculture in the UK to some extent and the degree depends very much on location. A broad view can be obtained from a simple subtraction of average potential transpiration from average rainfall, to give mean potential soil moisture deficit. This relates to crop distribution, the ratio of grass to crops and grass decreases at a constant rate from a mean potential soil moisture deficit of -6 in to +4 in (-150 mm to +100 mm); above this the proportion of grassland decreases more rapidly.[29] However, this is of limited value to agricultural planning as excess rainfall in winter could cancel out high deficits during the crop-growing season. There is a limit to the amount of water which can be held in storage in the soil and a great deal of the winter excess runs off the land in streams and is lost to plants. Detailed water balances can be made which will take these factors into account. Day to day balances will be most accurate though, for most purposes, 5 or 10 day or monthly periods will suffice. The water balance as developed by Thornthwaite[30] must include some basic assumptions. Apart from the problem of estimating potential evapotranspiration which has been outlined above, the accuracy of the balance depends mainly on the limits of our knowledge of soil - plant - water relationships and inevitably any agroclimatic model using water balance data must be simplified for practical application. As a general principle crop water use is related to atmospheric conditions. A factor, is frequently used to reduce Penman E_0 to potential evapotranspiration, in the UK about 0·6 in winter and 0·8 in summer months. For annual crops this factor should increase from a small fraction when the plant emerges, to the maximum when leaf area achieves full ground cover. However, wide spacing can reduce this maximum level. Actual evapotranspiration depends on the presence of water in this root zone. When the soil is fully charged with water it is said to be at field capacity. As the soil begins to dry the tension rises until it reaches permanent wilting point (16 atmospheres) when roots can no longer extract water. The water held between these extremes is termed available soil water (AW). Soil textures can alter the limits; field capacity can range from ·5 in per ft (4 cm per m) in sand to 2 - 2·5 in per ft (17 - 21 cm per m) clay loam. Permanent wilting point is more difficult to define and is probably a function of plant type as well as soil. Clarke[31] quotes figures of available water in inches per foot according to texture, sand and loamy sands ·25 to ·5, sandy loams 1, fine sandy loams 1·5 to 1·75, loams 2, clay loams 3 and clay 3·5 (metric equivalents are 2 to 4, 8, 12·5 to 14·5, 16·6, 25 and 29 cm per m respectively). However rooting depth is probably of more importance than texture. The depth of root penetration depends on the plant, but generally it will be shallow when the water-table is high. Since roots do not extend into unaerated soil the plant is depending entirely on water from precipitation. If the water-table is kept constant by controlling drainage a significant part of the water used by plants can come from the ground-water; however for most farmland in the UK the water-table rises in wet periods causing roots to die back, and falls in dry weather permitting root extension.

Thornthwaite assumed that potential evapotranspiration (PE) only occurs at field capacity and the rate of actual evapotranspiration becomes a progressively smaller fraction of PE as the soil dries. Another school suggests that water is equally available until permanent wilting point is reached. Denmead and Shaw[32] have shown that the critical level of soil water above which evapotranspiration occurs at this potential rate depends on atmospheric conditions. For example if the potential evapotranspiration is low (E_0 = 1 mm/d) the critical value is near permanent wilting point, so that plants will transpire at the potential rate until all other available water is removed. On the other hand, under high potential evaporation conditions (E_0 = 7 mm/d) the rate of evapotranspiration will decrease as soon as soil water falls below field capacity. Penman[33] has suggested that water is equally available if we consider the root range only. Plants however do extract beyond this and movement of water to the root system would slow down transpiration rates and if potential evapotranspiration is high the actual rate could be a small fraction of this.

The concepts of field capacity and permanent wilting-point are an over-simplification of the complex soil hydrological horizons. In the process of drying, water is removed from the surface horizons first and progressively each horizon follows a strict succession of phases ranging from total saturation to below permanent wilting-point or physical dessication.[34] The process of soil wetting is usually from above and the water content of each horizon is suddenly increased to the maximum.

For the *Atlas of Long-term Irrigation Needs for England and Wales* (1967)[28] water balances were calculated for a 20-year sample, 1930 - 49, for 79 stations in England and Wales. These balances consider only growth periods between April and September and in calculations assume soil water to be at field capacity at the beginning of each period. Certainly in most areas of the UK the soil has its maximum water content at the end of the winter, but for periods beginning in June, July or August it is unlikely that conditions of field capacity will always occur. A half-monthly balance was considered frequent enough to show the effect of dry spells, though it was probably chosen to correspond with the maximum frequency with which irrigation can be satisfactorily applied. However in South East England heavy rain from summer thunderstorms can balance the total water needs of the 15-day period, and in many cases, obscure serious deficits. Since these balances include the application of irrigation water, when required, transpiration was considered to continue at the potential rate. Balances were calculated allowing maximum soil moisture deficit of 1 in (25 mm), 2 in (50 mm), 3 in (76 mm) and 5 in (127 mm) at any time. Since water from rainfall or irrigation enters the soil profile from the surface and percolates downwards, each of these calculations refers to soil water deficits within a surface layer whose available water capacity equals this. Thus the total need with a planned 5 in (127 mm) deficit would apply to deep-rooting plants; in sandy loams this could be 5 ft (1·5 m) and in clay loams 1·5 ft (0·6 m). Shallow rooting plants where the planned deficit must be smaller, say, 1 in (25 mm), require more frequent irrigation. Crops will undoubtedly respond to a situation where soil moisture deficits are kept at a minimum. However, it has been shown[35] that the practice of restoring the soil to field capacity by irrigation whenever it reaches a certain deficit may not be economically sound. Because of the costs of irrigation, higher profits per acre can be obtained only by limited irrigation. Watering to achieve only 90 per cent maximum yield would appear to be the most efficient programme for grain crops, but for crops whose vegetative growth is harvested, irrigation for maximum yield would be the most efficient use of water.[36]

Grass may require irrigation anytime between April and September. However, other crops have much shorter growth periods and irrigation may be required only for a short period of the growth cycle. Thus combinations of successive periods of 2, 3, 4, 5 and 6 months have been calculated. For the 1 in (2·5 cm) soil moisture deficit plan (SMD) all lowland England would require irrigation 17 years in 20, but a 5 in (12·7 cm) SMD plan would require irrigation 8 years in 20 in the North East and over 14 in 20 in the South East. Using the 1 in (2·5 cm) SMD plan the driest year in 20 would require 8 in (20 cm) in the North East and 13 in (33 cm) in the South East. The atlas is a good example of the application of a simplified water balance calculation to a practical problem. More detailed balances are possible for specific sites where more assumptions can be made appropriate to the crop and soil. For example, a crop of grass can be assumed to transpire at this potential rate as long as water is available in the top layers of soil, the first 2 in (5 cm) AW. The second 2 in (5 cm) AW will be used at one-half of the potential and the final 1 in (2·5 cm) AW will be used at one-quarter of the potential. Water balances calculated in this way for growing seasons have agreed with actual field conditions.[37] This method has the advantage that soil moisture conditions are estimated for each horizon in the soil rather than integrated in a single soil moisture deficit for the whole profile.

It has been shown that grass growth is sensitive to the first 3 inches AW and when this is removed growth practically ceases even though deeper roots may allow continued transpiration.[38] Nutrition is obviously a complicating factor and as this is concentrated within surface layers of soil, the presence of available water in these horizons is vital for growth. This is further supported by high correlations between hay yields and the actual transpiration during periods when deficits were less than 2 in (50 mm).[39] Hurst calculated daily water balances for 50 stations in East Anglia in 1961 and counted the grass growing days, that is days when the moisture deficit was 2 in (50 mm) or less. Using empirical relationships with monthly water balances he mapped grass growing days in England and Wales, and showed how these rough estimates correlated with milk production.

Most studies of the effects of water on growth have been concerned with the increased production brought about by irrigation. Fischer and Hagan[40] review research on the effects of water stress on a variety of crops and distinguish them according to their economic yield: vegetative, eg in the case of grass; a carbohydrate storage organ, eg in sugar beet or potatoes; or a reproductive organ, eg grain crops and fruit. Correlations between actual evapotranspiration and yields have been shown for crops of *Lucerne*[41] in Wales. However, such studies can only be of practical value if they can be used to forecast harvests, or on the basis of accurate seasonal forecasts of water stress permit an economic assessment of the yield improvement in relation to expenditure on irrigation. Outside the UK investments in weather protection have been assessed using simplified models of operating costs. Certainly where water for irrigation is limited its efficiency becomes important.

In the drier areas of South East England the effects of irrigation are likely to be most important. Vegetative production, as in the case of grass, is particularly sensitive to water supply. But Goode[42] has shown that the cumulative effect of irrigation on fruit production can also be significant. This is because fruit production depends very much on plant vigour and, in the case of soft fruit, new growth becomes fruit-bearing in the following season. Over a period of 5 years irrigated bushes had 100 per cent more fruit than unwatered bushes. The cumulative effect of irrigation over 10 years produced a 50 per cent increase in apple yields. Undoubtedly this is due to the prevention of a growth check when the soil dries out, but as well as this the absence of large soil water deficits reduces the need for an extensive root system, which would deplete the assimilates available for shoot growth and fruit production.

The growing season: The studies of grass growth and fruit production in relation to water availability, described above, refer to the summer half-year, April to September, when temperature does not prevent growth. However, the influence of temperature and radiation on the beginning of the growing season and its length is obvious and their variation within the UK considerable. For early production the months January to April are most important. The South West of England has more than 250 degree days above 42°F (139 day degrees C above 6°C) in January and February (fig. 3.4). Radiation and sunshine in these months are noticeably higher in south coastal areas, while positive temperature anomaly associated with the Atlantic and the south-west winds favours the western coasts. In particular, maximum temperatures are raised in coastal areas of the South West, which is important for early growth. The beginning of the growing season has been taken as the average date on which mean screen temperature rises above 42°F (6°C).[43] Soil temperature which will allow germination differ as between crops. Hogg assumed growth will commence when the 4 in (10 cm) soil temperature at 0900 GMT remains above 42°F (6°C). However, soil type is a major factor controlling this parameter as has been demonstrated by the difference in 'earliness' between sand and peat areas in south-west Lancashire.[44]

The effects of altitude on the growing season are most obvious in the highland areas of the West and North. In Scotland there is an average of 2,475 day degrees F (1,375 day degrees C) on the lowlands of the Moray Firth, Fife and Angus while the Highlands above 1,800 ft (549 m) have less than 1,485 day degrees F (825 day degrees C). However, light is as important as temperature in the growth of hill pastures.[45] Western areas benefit from the maritime influences, but in day degrees the differences between east and west coasts

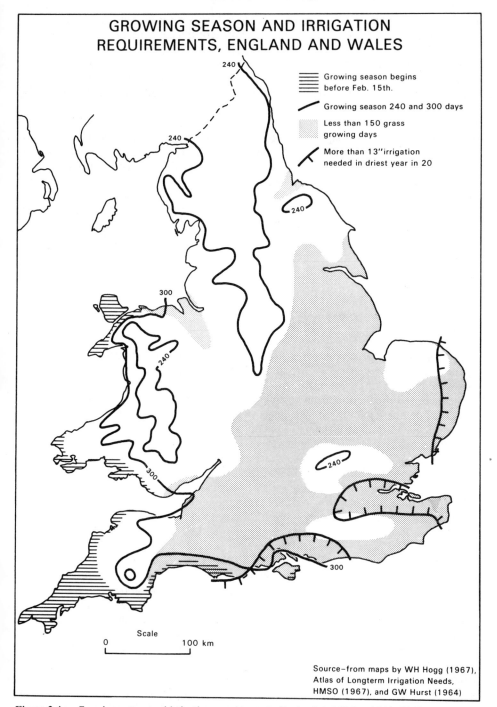

GROWING SEASON AND IRRIGATION REQUIREMENTS, ENGLAND AND WALES

Growing season begins before Feb. 15th.

Growing season 240 and 300 days

Less than 150 grass growing days

More than 13″ irrigation needed in driest year in 20

Scale

0   100 km

Source—from maps by WH Hogg (1967), Atlas of Longterm Irrigation Needs, HMSO (1967), and GW Hurst (1964)

Figure 3.4   Growing season and irrigation requirements, England and Wales, 1964, 1967

are not significant and inland from the east coast, higher summer temperatures tend to raise the accumulated temperature figure. In Northern Ireland equivalent day degree isotherms are believed to occur at generally higher elevations than in Great Britain, although this is based on a very limited number of observations.[46] The advantages of a westerly position are most apparent in the monthly accumulated temperatures of southern England where the effect extends from January to March; in March, Plymouth has 135 day degrees F above 42°F (75 day degrees C above 6°C) while Dungeness has only 83 (46). The growing season decreases by 10 days for every 260 ft (79 m) of altitude in the north of England, although such estimates can only be a general guide. Calculations of accumulated temperature at Chopwell Wood (820 ft, 250 m) in Durham suggest a growing season 15 days shorter than at Tynemouth (100 ft, 30 m, ASL). Higher altitudes can have the compensating effect of increased moisture but grass yields can be diminished by 2 per cent per 100 ft (30 m) altitude.[47]

The date of the start of the growing season can be greatly influenced by micro-climatic influences, particularly aspect and shelter. Within any region of the UK favoured areas may have an advantage in local markets with early crops of potatoes and vegetables. This is true of the coasts of County Down in Northern Ireland and in Wigtown in south-west Scotland. However, mapping of the average date of the start of the growing season (figure 3.4) shows the considerable advantage enjoyed by the early growing areas of Angelsey, south-west Wales, Cornwall, Devon, south Hampshire and the Isle of Wight. Even here, however, southerly aspect can increase radiation in the short days of January by as much as 50 per cent on a 10° slope, though the effect is reduced to only 15 per cent in April.[48]

Frost is a hazard to early growing and is an important factor in location. Frost surveys by the Meteorological Office in horticultural areas, mainly in the South West, have been successful in delimiting areas of risk and expressing the probability of satisfactory crops or the increased production made possible by protecting from frost by sprinkling. Hogg[49] describes how the feasibility of installing a frost prevention scheme on a Somerset farm can be calculated from an estimate of the probable duration of night frosts in April. In areas of light soils, irrigation equipment is often already installed to overcome summer deficits and can be used for frost protection in Spring as well. Soil is usually kept moist when there is a frost risk, estimated by a grass minimum temperature below 28°F (-2·2°C). Damage to a crop of early potatoes by a single night's frost, grass minimum of 25°F (-3·9°C), at the end of May was averted by sprinkling. The unretarded crop was able to fetch high prices and the protection probably saved the farmer about £3,000.[50] With reliable frost warning it is possible to plant earlier without undue risk of failure. Frost is very much a local problem, for cold air drainage at night causes greater frequency of frost in hollows and valley floors. Differences of 5 - 6°F (2·7 - 3·3°C) in daily minimum temperatures have been reported within a few hundred acres in fruit growing areas of Southern England. On the assumption that downflow will cease on slight slopes, ie less than 2°, areas of frost liability in Somerset have been estimated from 1:25,000 topographical maps.[51] This approach together with air photographs, taken where shallow radiation fogs occur, could augment the few scattered meteorological stations to provide maps of local climate with more immediate application than the macro-climatic maps already discussed.

Exposure: Work on the effects of shelter have suggested that yields of crops are significantly improved if protected even from relatively light winds. Increases of 27 per cent in the yield of lettuces due to lath shelter have been reported.[52] Sheltered valley sites can have wind speeds 20 per cent below more exposed neighbouring sites. This has an important effect on crop growing since the power to damage is proportional to the cube of the velocity. The frictional effect of trees, hedgerows or artificial windbreaks are more important in that they can be modified. Artificial windbreaks have the advantage of being immediately effective, whereas trees are slow to establish themselves and compete with the crops for moisture and nutrition. The shelter given by a windbreak depends on the width/height ratio as well as the degree of permeability. If too wide, the wind on crossing the barrier descends rapidly and the eddy zone to the lee is greatly reduced. If the break has an edge inclined to the windward the wind is deflected upwards and little penetrates. However for agriculture it is important to prevent stagnation of air which would increase frost risk and for this reason permeability is favoured. Systems of narrow parallel windbreaks can shelter wide areas if the distance between each belt is 26 times the height of the windbreak.[53] Studies by Hogg suggest that wind and evaporation are more affected by shelter in autumn and winter, while temperature shows its greatest effects in summer. In this connection it is worth mentioning that with increase in field size, hedgerows have been removed and the effect is to increase exposure. The upslope valley winds induced by sun and aspect are not so important in this climate, though near industrial areas they have the damaging effect of carrying pollutants to agricultural areas.

Disease: Since disease and pests have strong associations with weather and climate they have a place in the complex crop - weather interaction. Penman has thus described them as second order effects.[54] If the onset of the disease can be anticipated, timely action, eg spraying against potato blight, can be done effectively. When the potato plant is receptive to blight, ie when carbohydrate reserves are high, it will occur only with suitable local weather conditions. Since the spores will only grow on wet surfaces, attempts have been made to anticipate condensation on leaves. This can be done by moisture meters or estimated from minimum temperature and relative humidity readings.[55] Work on black stem rust in wheat[56] illustrates how the origin of the spores can be traced to countries in Europe. A close connection was found between deposition of spores in South West England and upper air trajectories from the south or south-east during spring and early summer. However, epidemics only developed if humidities were high in June and July, and temperatures high in July and August. Not enough is yet known about most diseases, their vectors and their relationships with the weather to be able to provide effective early warning systems.

The flexibility of land use: Green[57] has discussed this question in relation to the water balance and suggests that the potential land use is rarely achieved because of social and economic considerations. Areas of excess water are less flexible than the deficient areas which can respond to irrigation under conditions of high radiation. Varieties of farm crops and farming systems are used because of their adaptability to the fluctuating seasonal conditions. Reliable long-term forecasts could allow greater flexibility, though the necessary information on the relationships between weather and the performance of different varieties will take some years to accumulate.

II.4   The Amelioration of Climate by Man

Some of the ways in which climate can be improved locally to benefit crop production have been touched upon in the preceding section. Apart from changing the plants' immediate environment by irrigation or shelter, completely artificial climates are created by glasshouses. It has already been suggested that improvements in production are possible if the prevailing conditions can be accurately anticipated, but it is also important to recognise that great improvement is possible by controlling growth to suit sub-optimal conditions.

Drought: Generalised irrigation needs have been discussed in the previous section. Of the total acreage quoted by Prickett[58] 50 per cent was in the east and in south-east England (table 3.1). Heavy concentration of irrigation occurred in the early horticultural areas of

TABLE 3.1   Acreages of Crops Irrigated during Droughts, England and Wales, 1967

Grass	82,339
Second early and main crop potatoes	43,483
First early potatoes	21,019
Vegetables	41,892
Sugar beet	31,514
Orchard fruit	9,839
Cereals	6,964
Small fruit	6,430
Hops	2,977
Other crops	11,142
Total	257,599

Source: C N Prickett (1970)

South West England and Pembrokeshire, but even in the North considerable acreages had irrigation; for example over 8,000 acres (3,238 ha) in Yorkshire and 1,000 acres (400 ha) in Northumberland. Irrigation is characteristically on land with good natural or artificial drainage, but there would be problems if drainage were poor or the soil unstable. Suitable water, for example not saline, is not equally available for irrigation. The cost of water and the need to provide storage to take advantage of low winter charges is reducing the practice of irrigation for low-value crops.[59] Horticulture, particularly small fruit, is becoming a more important water-user. Glasshouses in particular are heavy users of irrigation is equivalent to the needs of a herd of 70 to 100 dairy cattle. Crops such as grass and potatoes require sufficient irrigation to maintain water at near field capacity, which ought not to be practised in successive years for it prevents the beneficial effects of cracking during drying out of heavy soils.

Emulsions sprayed on the soil surface can reduce evapotranspiration for up to 2 months. Soil water storage is improved if the surface soil is rough, encouraging the retention of water. Yields have been increased by arresting excessive drainage in sandy soils using asphalt barriers below the root zone. These devices developed largely for arid climates may have applications in high value crops and in soils hitherto unproductive.

Soil wetness: For most of the UK wetness is more of a problem than drought. The large scale drainage schemes in the Fenlands date back to the seventeenth century and illustrate the way in which the water-table in level alluvial areas can be controlled by engineering. They provide over 800,000 acres (324,000 ha) of the richest farmland in Great Britain. Elsewhere drainage can be considered a major soil factor, since moderate drainage can increase yields by as much as 20 per cent.[60] It has been suggested that the failure of modern varieties of crops to reach full potential yield is due to defects in soil structure and drainage.[61] Cereals are particularly susceptible to soil conditions which affect root development. Waterlogging excludes air and the anaerobic conditions cause roots to die back, leaving the crop more susceptible to drought later, but it has the effect also of limiting operations with machinery. If a soil is at field capacity or wetter, it usually has insufficient strength to hold machinery or livestock and is too plastic for ploughing or cultivation. Soil texture and structure is important but the smearing effect of ploughing wheels and treading can reduce porosity and cause surface ponding. The early work of Thornthwaite on the water balance was partly concerned with the ability of soil to bear weight. The date of the return to field capacity has been calculated from meteorological records[62] for sites throughout England and Wales. These demonstrate the early return to field capacity in the western areas, but also show the advantage of light freely-drained soils and the considerable variation between wet and dry years at all sites. However, estimates based upon meteorological data can only be approximate, for no universal relationship exists between soil water tension and estimated soil water deficits. It is suggested that a more useful correlation may be found between interpolated soil shear strength and accumulated moisture deficit.[63]

Extensive areas of farmland were underdrained prior to 1939, though many no longer function effectively and need replacement or improvement. Collapse or silting of old drains is common but more intensive use of this land can lead to puddling of surface soil which prevents water percolating to the under drains. Removal of the old ditches associated with the small fields of Wales to create the large units of arable farming frequently necessitates new systems of drainage, though cultivation is in any case less flexible than grass in its soil water requirements. In the wetter areas of the west higher stocking rates increase the need for more drainage or subsoiling. Since 1966 there has been an annual increase of 10 per cent expenditure on drainage in the South West. Without improved drainage overstocking can lead to poaching of pastures and this is a feature of the intensive dairying area of Cheshire. Wetter than normal summers extend the dangers of poaching throughout the season, particularly in the low evaporation areas of the Pennine foothills. For cultivation in the wetter areas, drainage is usually the only way of ensuring enough work days. Even in the drier areas of the east, heavy soils are manageable only within a very narrow moisture range and only regular subsoiling and mole drainage can keep them in production. Among these difficult soils are the keuper marls, coal measure soils and boulder clays of the East Midlands, Oxford clay, London clay and the clays of the low Weald. However, drainage in many of these areas is not practicable because of their flatness and low elevations. Improvements in arterial drainage can make the draining of low-lying areas feasible. For example, in Northern Ireland, since the 1947 Drainage Act, 900 miles (1,449 Km) of main water courses have been altered in drainage schemes giving flood relief to 65,000 acres (24,000 ha) and, ultimately, affecting drainage of about one-quarter of the province. The danger of continual ploughing is to create subsurface pans which seriously restrict the depth of rooting, and yields are greatly reduced. Intensive arable can cause serious structural changes. Continual culviation of early potatoes in Pembrokeshire has led to clod formation in the soil which may limit future use.

Drainage of any kind brings improvements and the problem is usually the degree of water control required, which is often decided on the lines of cost. Since 1939 grants have increased areas under drainage by 200,000 acres (80,000 ha) in Yorkshire and Lancashire, 100,000 (40,000 ha) in the North, 140,000 (57,000 ha) in the West Midlands and 90,000 (36,000 ha) in Wales. However, it has been estimated that over 7 million acres (2·8 million ha) or 26 per cent of the total farmland could be improved still further.[64] Because of soil and relief and its intensive land use, eastern England has a very large area, 1,600,000 acres (650,000 ha), which could be usefully drained and this is being improved at the rate of about 47,000 acres (19,000 ha) per annum.

Temperature and radiation: Modifications of temperature are possible by using windbreaks or spraying to prevent frost, but major changes are possible by using glass and artificial heating. Hogg[65] quotes heating periods for some horticultural crops which range from approximately 4 months for chrysanthemums to 10 months for cucumbers. Heating requirements in terms of fuel have been estimated using accumulated temperatures below $60°F$ ($15°C$)[66] and Hogg has calculated this for the heating periods of each crop (table 3.2). Assuming 10 degree days requires 1 ton of coal per acre of glass he has estimated that 40 - 45 tons more coal is needed at Cheltenham for one acre of glasshouse tomatoes than at Weymouth, and there is a similar difference between Weymouth and Penzance.

TABLE 3.2   Heating Requirements for Cultivated Plants, Selected UK Stations, 1966

		Average number of day degrees below 60°F (15°C)		
Crop	Heating period	Penzance	Weymouth	Cheltenham
Tomatoes	4 Nov - 28 May	2,470	2,870	3,290
Cucumbers	4 Oct - 4 July	2,780	3,180	3,700
Lettuce	11 Nov - 27 Apr	2,190	2,585	2,975
Carnations	4 Nov - 27 Apr	2,260	2,665	3,080
Chrysanthemums	27 Nov - 28 Mar	1,710	2,015	2,325

Source: W H Hogg (1966)

II.5   Harmful Accidental Effects of Agricultural Activity

Farming activity can lead to damaging effects and this is more likely if there is a change in the type of farming or its intensity. The more obvious are effects on soil water conditions but equally serious are the structural changes which can reduce productivity and in many cases lead to soil erosion. Exposed flat lowlands of eastern England suffer from soil erosion by wind and the sandy soils and those with more than 35 per cent organic matter, such as Fenland soils, are particularly susceptible. High wind speed, in excess of 50 mph (80 kmph) is the main cause, and it is also related to soil moisture content. The methods of preparing seed beds for vegetables and the application of herbicides have recently aggravated the situation.[67] Large-scale sugar beet growing which began in the 1930s is considered an important factor in the peat fens. The removal of hedges is thought to have contributed to the severe blowing of soil in the Vale of York in 1967,[68] but the decrease of hedgerows in areas of stable soils is not having any serious effect.[69] Studies of sediment yields from catchments have not provided any conclusive evidence that there has been any general change in the rate of soil erosion and suggest that it is only serious locally. For control it is necessary to reduce windspeed, stabilise the soil and trap blowing soil. Windbreaks have a limited effect, especially if strong winds come from several directions. Strip cropping and inter-row cropping can also reduce wind velocity and soil moisture can be retained better by reducing cultivations, creating rough soil surfaces or mulching. Only high-value cash crops warrant such expensive control measures.

The practice of growing grass leys and green manuring are declining in farming and the soil structure deteriorates due to reduced organic content. Inorganic fertilisers are preferred as the balance of nutrients can be easily controlled. There has been an increase of about 150 per cent in nitrogen application since 1957. However, organic fertilisers are important in the livestock areas of the UK. In 1969 farmyard manure was used on 23 per cent of the arable land of Northern England and Wales; the percentage was less elsewhere, but 36 per cent of the permanent pasture of Yorkshire and Lancashire was so treated. Inorganic fertilisers do confer benefits in that they encourage better root growth and thus improve soil structure and they give better vegetative growth which can be ploughed into the soil. Nitrogenous fertilisers have the effect of reducing the calcium in soil and thus increase its acidity. Damage to soil organisms by pesticides is less in soils with a high organic content. The most serious are the organochlorides which harm beneficial insects and persist in food chains, to appear ultimately in milk and meat.[70] Use of organochloride insecticides in England and Wales fell from 460 tons in 1963 to 300 tons in 1967. It has been suggested that these ecological effects are much less than those in lakes and seas. In the UK the contribution of agricultural chemicals to pollution of streams and rivers is very small. Less than 9 per cent of the nitrogen in rivers can be attributed to run-off from agricultural land and sewage contributes a significant proportion of the phosphates in rivers.

III   WATER SUPPLY

III.1 Hydrology of Water Resources

Considering the demands by evaporation, the amount of rainfall and its seasonal distribution appears adequate, but the problem is really one of annual and monthly departures from the mean. The severe drought of the summer of 1959 emphasised the inadequacy of the existing water supply and prompted the government action which led to the Water Resources Act 1963. Three important trends have aggravated the situation, the rise in population, increasing individual requirements due to rising living standards and the growing industrial needs, calling for action to plan water resources for the future.

It is difficult to define hydrological zones in the UK, because of the lack of coincidence between the physiographic and climatic factors which control the hydrology. Slope is important to runoff, but its effectiveness depends on whether the rock is pervious or not. Potential evaporation is only closely related to runoff if the rainfall is always high enough to meet the atmospheric demand. In South East England actual evaporation often falls below the potential during periods of drought in summer. Granite uplands have a similar effect due to rapid drainage, which limits the amount of water which can be held in the soil and made available for evaporation. Because of the dependence of actual evaporation upon water storage, variability of rainfall is usually adopted as a guide to runoff characteristics. In eastern areas the summer months have more than 50 per cent of the annual total, while elsewhere summers are drier and in the South West summers have 38 per cent of annual total rainfall. High mountains have the highest runoff, exceeding 78 in (2,000 mm) pa in the wettest areas, but in South East England the average annual runoff is 5 in (125 mm) and in dry years it can fall to 1 in (25 mm). The coefficient of variation of rainfall in the South East is more than 16 per cent, so that rainfall would be less than 80 per cent of the average, once in 10 years. The River Greta in Cumberland reflects the runoff regime from a wet mountain area (figure 3.5) with a minimum flow in May and June when rainfall is at its lowest. The River Great Ouse, on the other hand, represents the drier South East and the minimum in September corresponds to the time of greatest soil water deficit. The mountains of the north and west have average rainfalls of over

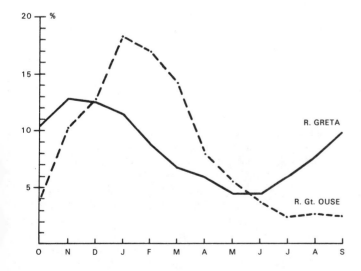

Figure 3.5   Monthly average as percentage annual average runoff,
rivers Greta and Great Ouse

98 in (2,500 mm) and these are areas of lowest evaporation; south-eastwards rainfall
decreases to less than 20 in (500 mm) in South East England and evaporation increases.
Thus hydrometric areas can be roughly arranged in order of wetness: the Islands and
Western Highlands of Scotland; the rest of Scotland, excepting the East Central area,
Northern Ireland, North West England and Wales; the South West peninsula; East Central
Scotland and North East England; Severn and Humber; and South East England,
including the Wash. The minimum river flow becomes progressively later in the year as
one moves from the wetter areas to the dry South East. The absence of any surplus in the
South East has created a water-supply problem. However, extensive aquifers, especially in
chalk, absorb some winter surplus and help to augment summer flows. Winter storage in
the form of snow is significant only in the Cairngorms area. Flooding is a feature of the
wet mountains of the north and west, but the area most prone is the South West peninsula
where falls of 0·9 in (23 mm) have been recorded on four occasions. Since the rainfall in
these mountain areas is orographic the heavy falls tend to be widespread. On the drier
lowlands the heavy falls are associated with thunderstorms and the North Sea coast is the
most prone; however, individual falls rarely exceed 5 in (125 mm). Land use is as important as rainfall and slope in influencing runoff and flooding. Flooding is not a major
problem in the lower parts of UK rivers except on the lowlying east coast, where sinking
of the North Sea basin has caused a rise in normal tides of about 2·54 ± 0·38 ft
(77 ± 10 cm) per century. Deep depressions over the North Atlantic can cause gales in the
North Sea and when associated with abnormally high tides can cause serious flooding, as
in 1953. Since 60 sq miles (155 km^2) of the Thames floodplain are increasingly at flood
risk a barrage is being designed for protection.[71]

The basic problem is one of storage to provide for times of deficit and to transfer water
from areas of plenty to areas where it is scarce. The total requirements exceed the residual
rainfall, which is the rainfall less the demands of evaporation and evapotranspiration. At
the same time it is necessary to provide for the exceptional drought which may occur only
once in a period of 100 years.

Upland catchments have been the main suppliers of water for the urban areas of the UK
because of their high rainfall and impervious rock, and also because of the short growing
season and isolation which have restricted settlement. Until fairly recently there has been
little organised resistance to the building of reservoirs.[72] Water supply can be considered
as another way in which urban demands for space are threatening agricultural land,
although the use of land for water storage is only a small fraction (about one-half per
cent) of the 150,000 acres (60,705 ha) currently lost annually to urban expansion. The
benefits of increased water supply and increasing production by irrigation, could outweigh
the acreage lost to agriculture. The South East has an annual residual rainfall of only 5 in
(127 mm) and every acre of urban settlement could demand as much as 27 in (700 mm).[73]
Sites for storage in this area would have to be on productive farmland and because of the
nature of the topography wide shallow valleys would have to be drowned. The alternative
is to impound upper streams and, without affecting existing settlement, 4 times the present
storage could be obtained at costs little different from that of existing reservoirs. Only
one-third of this would be required this century. The water from these reservoirs could
regulate the flow of rivers and ensure a steady supply for abstraction downstream.

Storage in impounded estuaries or maritime basins is another possibility. Estuary
storage has been considered for the Dee, Severn, Morecambe, Solway and the Wash, as
well as many smaller schemes in Wales and South East England (figure 3.6). For most the
cost is likely to be a major drawback, especially if they are separated from demand areas
by high mountains. The cost of including the Dee barrage in any development scheme for
the Midlands would be £6 - 8 million in excess of the alternatives. The Solway barrage was
suggested as a source of water for the Tyne, while the Morecambe Bay would serve
Lancashire and, across the Pennines, the West Riding conurbation. The Wash would serve

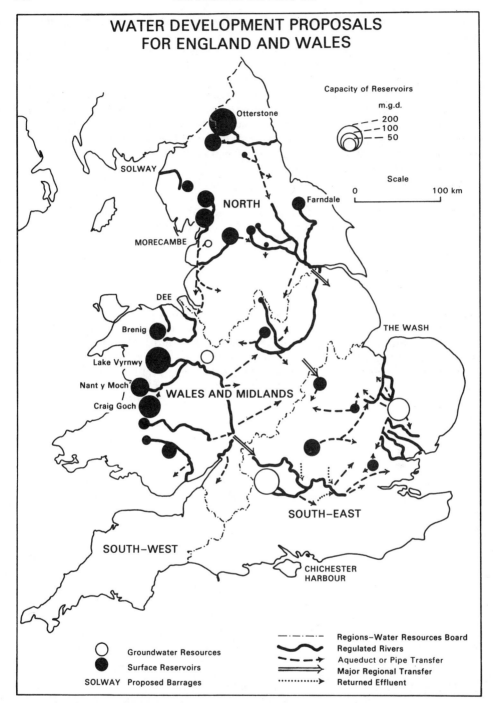

**WATER DEVELOPMENT PROPOSALS
FOR ENGLAND AND WALES**

Capacity of Reservoirs

m.g.d.

— 200
— 100
— 50

Scale

0   100 km

Otterstone

SOLWAY

NORTH   Farndale

MORECAMBE

DEE

Brenig   THE WASH

Lake Vyrnwy

Nant y Moch

Craig Goch   WALES AND MIDLANDS

SOUTH–EAST

SOUTH–WEST   CHICHESTER
HARBOUR

○ Groundwater Resources   — · — · — Regions–Water Resources Board

● Surface Reservoirs   ∿∿ Regulated Rivers
                               - - - ➤ Aqueduct or Pipe Transfer

SOLWAY Proposed Barrages   ⟹ Major Regional Transfer
                               · · · · · ➤ Returned Effluent

Figure 3.6   Water development proposals, England and Wales, 1966–71

the water-scarce areas of South East England. Together Solway, Dee, Morecambe and Wash barrages could hold 400,000 Mgal (1,818 Mm³) and meet all demands this century. Barrage schemes are difficult to evaluate because of the possible effects on silting and

fisheries. There is also the problem of water quality and some of these schemes might
require desalination.

In Jersey and Guernsey, where the peak summer demands could not be met by surface
reservoirs, desalination has been developed for water supply. A desalination study in connection with the Wash suggested that it might be competitive by the end of the century in
coastal areas of the South East and an experimental plant is to be established at Ipswich.
For inland areas, where rivers can be regulated, desalination is likely to be too costly an
alternative unless it proves too difficult or expensive to clean up the grossly polluted
rivers like the Trent for abstraction. Apart from the cost of desalination, which must
include rapid deterioration due to corrosion, objections to the building of the plants at the
coast are very likely on amenity grounds.

Another alternative is to use underground aquifers for storage. In winter ground-water
can give a high yield in the form of flow from springs but in summer pumping is necessary
and in this way it has been estimated that the chalk of the Thames and Great Ouse basins
could store about 150,000 Mgal (681 Mm^3). Since the outcrops of these aquifers could
receive only a limited amount of rainfall artificial recharge would be essential. The Thames
Conservancy has undertaken a pilot scheme. If the water for recharging contains effluent
then treatment is necessary.

In North Lincolnshire up to 95 per cent of winter percolation could be abstracted in the
following summer without causing encroachment of sea-water. However, overdevelopment
of boreholes in the London Basin has already caused a serious decline in ground-water and
any further development must be accompanied by recharging. The other major aquifer is
in the Bunter sandstone, mainly in the Midlands and on both flanks of the Pennines. The
major difficulty with the Triassic rocks and coal measures is that much of the ground-water
is mineralised. The most important area of potential development in the Trias is in
Shropshire. At present 40 per cent of the water in England and Wales is from ground-water
sources, but in Scotland and Northern Ireland it accounts for less than 10 per cent of the
total supply.

III.2 Water Supply and Demand

Rapid urban growth during the industrial revolution led to the development of nearby
uplands as sources of water supply, and as demand increased more distant uplands in the
North of England and Wales served the industrial belts of the Midlands, Yorkshire and
Lancashire. The catchments of the reservoirs were controlled to preserve water quality.
All major storage works built in the past 120 years were designed for a particular town or
city, the main consideration being cost. As potential sites diminished the larger urban
authorities had an advantage.[74] Amalgamation of smaller boards was encouraged in the
1950s: in 1945 there were 1,100 water undertakings in England and Wales, but by 1966
these had been reduced to 286. In addition to statutory undertakings there are water
companies operating under individual Acts of Parliament or Orders by the Minister. All
undertakings in Scotland are by local authorities which were reorganised into 13 regional
water boards by the 1967 Water (Scotland) Act. In Northern Ireland distribution of
water is mainly in the hands of local authorities but grants towards water schemes are
made under the Water Supplies and Sewage Act (NI) 1945.

The Metropolitan Water Board is the largest water undertaking in the UK, supplying
368 Mgal (1·67Mm^3) per day to 6·25 million people. The effects of population concentration were first felt in the industrial areas. Grossly-polluted rivers were no problem
as long as new sources of water could be found in the uplands, which had been the case up
to the Second World War. Subsequent population growth led to water demands which
approached the limit of available supplies. Together with an increasing awareness of the
recreational value of the uplands, this led to a new concept of water supply. Reservoirs

were to be regulators for the rivers, maintaining the volume needed for abstraction in the lower reaches. However, the purity of the river needs to be assured and this is part of the cost. The Thames receives 180 Mgal (0·81 Mm^3) of sewage effluent per day and 40 Mgal (0·18 Mm^3) per day from industry, yet two-thirds of London's water, 300 Mgal (1·36 Mm^3) per day, is abstracted from the river. Manchester and Liverpool have so dominated the water resources development of the Lake District and North Wales, respectively, that any further move for developing river resources is vigorously resisted. Yet Manchester maintains that industry demands high quality water supplies. The use of rivers as transporters provides the opportunity to economise, but also permits twice the yield obtainable if reservoirs were used for direct piped supply. It also has the advantage of permitting flood control and maintaining dry weather flow. To be most efficiently used regulating reservoirs require management on a wider scale than hitherto possible and the Water Resources Act (1963) was the first move towards this end; this Act applies only to England and Wales. So far, in Scotland and Northern Ireland pressures on water resources have not called for this kind of administrative machinery. In Northern Ireland management of water resources is under review, in anticipation of further industrial development.

Under the Act, 29 River Authorities were created and the government appointed the Water Resources Board as an advisory body to plan and coordinate their efforts, by overseeing their proposals for meeting demand at 7-yearly intervals. Amenity and recreation are considered as well as water supply. The Water Resources Board has undertaken 3 major studies of future demand and has formulated the strategies which are outlined below.

It is more economical to meet the needs for several years ahead with one major scheme, rather than by a programme involving a succession of small schemes. By increasing a dam from 60 to 110 feet (18 m to 33 m) in height the capacity per unit cost is increased 3 times.[75] The amount of land flooded would be 4½ times greater, but since land costs are only 2·7 per cent of the total this is not likely to be relevant except for social and amenity considerations. There is a limit to the size as the larger the storage capacity the longer it takes to refill after a drought. The rate of refill is also dependent on the locality. In North West England an impounded estuary would be drawn down 2 ft (61 cm) for 6-month periods only twice in 32 years, while a pumped storage reservoir in South East England would have a similar draw down on 6 occasions, 2 of which would remain at this level for 2 years at a time.[76]

The aggregate residual rainfall in the UK (15 Mgal, 0·068 Mm^3 per annum or 850 gal, 3,864 l per person per day in England and Wales) is much greater than is likely to be required by the community. The maximum possible yield in England and Wales is 40,800 Mgal (185 Mm^3) per day;[77] current abstractions are about 14,000 Mgal, (64 Mm^3) per day. 12,850 Mgal (584 Mm^3) per day were abstracted in 1969 in England and Wales, 347 Mgal (1·57 Mm^3) per day in Scotland and 100 Mgal (0·45 Mm^3) per day in Northern Ireland in 1955. Northern Ireland is already fully-served by well-distributed uplands and the centrally-placed Lough Neagh, so that any supply problems are local and can be solved by normal development. Scotland is equally well-placed and the problem is one of distribution to the Central Lowlands. The Loch Lomond and Loch Bradan Schemes will provide for all industrial and urban growth except in Fife. Apart from the administrative problems, the Southern Uplands effectively separate Scotland from England and no water resources of Scotland have been developed for transfer to England.

Demands for water have been increasing at the rate of 2·4 per cent per annum; in England and Wales demands from the public water supply increased from 1,957 Mgal (8·9 Mm^3) per day in 1955 to 2,900 Mgal (13·2 Mm^3) per day in 1969. This trend will probably continue and by the end of the century water needs could be doubled. but the net requirement may be much less if the siting of new industry and the treatment of effluent is advanced enough to allow increasing re-use of water. Table 3.3 is taken

TABLE 3.3   Estimated Regional Water Supply, UK, 1990

	Estimated demand Mgal/d	Average net water available Mgal/d	Surplus resources gal/head popn. in 1990
N. Ireland	100	4,800	2,600
Scotland	640	50,000	7,270
N. England	950	13,100	810
Wales and Midlands	560	12,700	1,275
SW. England	200	5,200	1,575
SE. England	1,900	9,800	235
UK total	4,350	95,600	–

Source: Pugh (1963)

from estimates by Pugh.[78] Estimates of deficiencies have been made in the reports of the Water Resources Board which are summarised in table 3.4. If these estimates prove to be right then the area with the greatest future problem is the South East.

TABLE 3.4   Estimates of Regional Water Deficiencies, Selected UK Regions, 1981 and 2001

	Public water supply Mgal/d		Direct industrial and agriculture Mgal/d		Total Mgal/d	
	1981	2001	1981	2001	1981	2001
Wales and Midlands	150	759	58	179	208	938
North	265	860	45	105	310	965
South East	310	860	100	225	410	1,085

Source: Water Resources Board (1966, 1970 and 1971)

Additional supplies will be needed for: domestic purposes; industrial processes; and in agriculture, for cleaning as well as irrigation. Apart from these uses water is needed for: navigation, mainly in the Trent, Severn and Thames; amenity and recreation. However, if the rivers are to be used as a source for abstraction, regulating reservoirs will be needed to maintain flow in the upper courses and returned effluent will ensure sufficient volume in the lower reaches. Quality of the water is likely to affect fish before other forms of life.

Domestic demand: Domestic use in England and Wales amounts to 37 gal (153 l) per head per day. While in 1951 over one-third of houses in the UK had no fixed bath, today the figure is less than 10 per cent. Houses are being built at a rate of 350,000 to 450,000 per annum and all have modern facilities, yet 11 million pre-1939 houses require modernisation or replacement. Washing machines, dishwashers, car washing, etc. are increasing and make demands upon the public supply. It is estimated that needs may rise to 60 gal (270 l) per head per day by the end of the century.[78]

Industrial demand: At present industry uses about 23 per cent of the water abstracted (table 3.5), whilst the CEGB uses a further 51 per cent for cooling. The quantity which industry consumes is small compared with the amount circulated within industry. However, this assumes that the returned effluent is fit for re-use. Water abstracted for power generation is returned altered in temperature, but a great volume is needed for circulation. This is called a direct cooling system, which for 2,000 MW output will circulate 50 Mgal (0.27 Mm^3) per hour. A smaller volume is needed if cooling towers are used, since the same water can be constantly recycled, though some is lost by evaporation. Also water is needed to flush the system to prevent salt concentration and thus in total up to 50 per cent of the water abstracted would be dissipated to the river. A 2,000 MW station at full output requires 30 Mgal (0·06 Mm^3) per day of which 14 Mgal (0·13 Mm^3) could be lost. The desirability of siting power stations near the areas of demand has become vital in the South East. Coalfield sites are not as favoured because of possible changes in sources of fuel, as well as distance from the demand areas, whilst coastal sites may be unacceptable for amenity reasons. New stations will be sited near the major water transfer networks or major sewage outfalls.[79]

The extent to which returned industrial effluent can be re-used depends on the quality requirements. Sewage and saline water can be used for cooling but food industries require high standards. Effluents from food industries are usually of reasonable quality but those from engineering and chemical industries are often highly toxic and may even inhibit the biological processes used by sewage works. Re-use is essential to save substantial construction in meeting the industrial needs of the future. In estimates of needs up to the year 2000, the Water Resources Board in its report on the North[80] has assumed repeated re-use of river water so that the increase in industrial effluents will offset the 300 Mgal/d (1·36 Mm^3/d) of new demands from industry. This makes the estimating of future industrial needs more difficult than that for domestic needs, which relate to population numbers. In 1959 the Central Advisory Water Committee estimated a 2·5 per cent per annum increase in demand. This was based on 10-year projections by a few sample industries, but a later report changed the figure to 5·2 per cent. Currently, 1,350 Mgal/d (6·14 Mm^3/d) are abstracted from private sources, 919 Mgal (4·18 Mm^3/d) from the public supplies and it is thought this could double in 30 years. The cost of water may encourage the economy of re-using water and the treatment of effluent, so that Rees[81] estimated 0·79 per cent increase per annum for the future, but this figure could be altered by a change in the cost of water.

TABLE 3.5   Authorised Abstractions of Water by Industry (excluding CEGB) and Agriculture, Selected UK Regions, 1969

| | Industry | | | | Agriculture | |
	Licences	Mgal/d	(1,000 m^3/d)	Licences	Mgal/d	(1,000 m^3/d)
North	2,857	2,255	(10,250)	4,883	37	(170)
Wales and Midlands	2,307	1,508	(6,855)	10,108	37	(170)
South East	2,480	843	(3,835)	11,007	107	(485)

Source: Water Resources Board (1971)

Agricultural demand: The growth in demand is closely related to the extension of mains supplies to rural areas. Rural Water Supply and Sewerage Acts have made grants available for this purpose and areas of low population have been able to get water at lower prices than if it were developed privately. 350,000 farms in England and Wales now have mains supply, though water required for cleaning and animals is a small proportion of the total demand. In recent years spray irrigation, especially for potatoes, vegetables and fruit has increased and could be doubled by the end of the century, demanding 120 Mgal/d (0·54 Mm^3/d). In South East England alone, the peak seasonal demand for spray irrigation in 1965 was 17,000 Mgal (77 Mm^3) and is expected to reach 35,000 Mgal (159 Mm^3) by the end of the century. Unlike water used by industry most of this is transpired and is therefore lost to the rivers. There is a need for storage on the farm to meet these and future demands and this might be a serious disincentive for low-value crops.

In 1963 there was enough equipment to irrigate 130,000 acres (52,611 ha) and this is increasing at about 15,000 acres (6,070 ha) per annum. Most of this is in the south and east, particularly in East Anglia. It pays to irrigate high-value crops in small areas in Pembrokeshire, Cornwall and in the lower Tees valley. However, it is unlikely to be economic in areas with rainfall in excess of 35 in (890 mm). Future development is possible for large acreages of low-value crops where large quantities of water are available cheaply. Because they require less water small areas of high-value crops can more easily find a source and because of high profits earned can pay for it.[82] About 1½ million acres (607,000 ha) in all could benefit from irrigation, which would need 3,000 Mgal (13 Mm^3) per day.

The most common source of water for irrigation is from surface streams, but this is difficult in the South East where many dry up in summer. Improvements in land drainage have aggravated the situation by increasing the efficiency of catchment drainage. Apart from irrigation, water is also needed for spraying, as a protection against frost, for stock, milk cooling and cleaning.

III.3 Strategies

At the time of writing the Water Resources Board has produced 3 regional reports, assessing the probable demand for water up to the end of the century and possible programmes of development to meet these needs. The reports stress the importance of flexibility in long-term planning and the need for regular revision which could, in the future, be the responsibility of the 10 Regional Water Authorities. The North, Wales, the Midlands and the South East have special problems which emerge clearly from these detailed regional surveys, but the Board intends to publish a survey of England and Wales integrating the 3 reports. All three reports already show that developable resources exist in the UK to meet all foreseeable demands, but the problem is finding the optimal programme of development.

In the South East the basic problem is lack of internal resources to meet future demands and development of surface storage would encroach upon valuable farmland. The report on the South East is most concerned with providing water for the very large deficiency zone within the South East requiring an additional 650 Mgal/d (2·95 Mm^3/d) by the year 2000. A combination of surface and underground storage including schemes like the Chichester barrage, if acceptable, could provide more than the estimated needs at the end of the century. However, it is probably more realistic to assume that long-term schemes must include bulk imports from the west and north. For climatic reasons river regulation can be met only by ground water. Using ground water to augment summer flows and artificially recharging the aquifers in winter could yield as much as 125 Mgal/d (0·56 Mm^3/d) in the Ely - Ouse, equal to the internal needs of the Great Ouse area by 2001. The Thames could also be regulated using ground-water from the chalk to meet all needs this century provided it is possible to recharge the aquifer which is in places already over-pumped and threatened by salt water intrusions. Many of the rivers in the South East are only indirectly polluted and, if regulated and further deterioration prevented, can continue to be used for abstraction. Re-use of water in the South East is a significant aspect of the water-supply pattern. In the Wales and Midlands regions, the Severn is used for abstraction, even though it receives some effluent, but the Trent and many of the larger northern rivers are so grossly polluted as to preclude them as sources for public water supply. There are, of course, in Wales and the North, many clean rivers like the Wye whose obvious amenity and recreational value is likely to safeguard their purity and they will be used increasingly to transport water and for abstraction in the future.

Industries sited on the rivers of the Midlands and North use and re-use the river water. This is particularly so of the Trent which provides the most substantial service to industry of any river in the UK. Further industrial demand can be partly met from recycling the increased effluent from the industries themselves. However, the industrial effluents may need treatment and because of the nature of the industries this is a greater problem than in the South East. Industry in the North requires more water than elsewhere in England

and Wales and this explains the higher per capita consumption, 61 gal (278 l) per day compared to 56 gal (254 l) per day in South East England. However, the North requires less for agriculture since the greater part of the agricultural use is for spray irrigation.

Additional storage needed to regulate rivers for the Wales and Midlands regions can be found in the Welsh Valleys and Peak district. Public supply in Wales and the Midlands still finds 80 per cent of its water directly from upland reservoirs. Aqueducts carry 77 Mgal (0·35 Mm^3) per day from the Elan reservoir on the Wye to Birmingham, 44 Mgal (0·20 Mm^3) per day from the Vyrnwy, a tributary of the Severn, to Liverpool. Direct supplies from the Derwent, a tributary of the Trent, serve Sheffield, Derby, Nottingham and Leicester. But the Severn, which is regulated by the Clywedog reservoir, is a source for abstraction as far downstream as Gloucester. The dry weather flow of the Trent is almost entirely effluent so that it cannot be used for direct supply. A study is in progress to assess the feasibility of it becoming a potable source by the mid 1980s.

To avoid shortages in the next few years the urgent requirement of the Wales and Midland regions is to find a regulator for the Severn and a further supply for the North Midlands. The Water Resources Board has proposed an enlargement of the Craig Goch, or alternatively completely new developments at Dulas, Marton Pool or Afon Gam. A new reservoir is suggested at Henmore or Brund to regulate the Trent.

In the North there is no shortage of resources as the region includes the Lake District, with the heaviest rainfall in England and Wales. The development of regulating reservoirs for the northern rivers could provide an additional 2,250 Mgal (10·2 Mm^3) per day and more than satisfy the region's long-term needs, estimated to be 840 Mgal (3·82 Mm^3) per day in 2001. The problem lies in the siting of storage reservoirs and the systems for transporting the water. The cheapest solution suggested by the Water Resources Board would involve 17 regulating reservoirs, 10 of which would be in National Parks. Whilst it is possible to cost the loss of productivity of agricultural or forestry land, it is more difficult to estimate the value of amenity or to judge the demands from the environment of the often conflicting urban and rural users. The use of surface reservoirs for direct supply would require 41 reservoirs, of which 25 would be in National Parks and, moreover, they would require 3,514 sq miles (9,100 km^2) of land compared with 23 sq miles (59 km^2) if regulating reservoirs are to be used. Unlike the Midlands, the North has no very large rivers, but a number of small rivers polluted to varying degrees. Any regional strategy must involve transfers by pipeline between unpolluted rivers. The South Tyne is suggested as a major transporter eastwards and the Swale southwards. The most flexible development for the Northumberland River Authority is the Kielder reservoir, although an alternative scheme could involve 3 smaller reservoirs on the Irthing, at Middleton and at Witton-le-Wear. Eventually this water would be transferred south to the Yorkshire Ouse and thus help to alleviate the supply problems posed by the probable development of a Humberside conurbation in an area where reservoir sites are difficult. To the west of the Pennines there is at present a major transfer south from the Lake District. The amount of further surface water abstraction in the Lake District and the West Pennines depends on whether estuary storage in Solway and Morecambe Bay is feasible and acceptable to government. However this development would not preclude the need for an additional supply from inland sources, equivalent to the yield from the proposed Kielder scheme and that of Brenig in North Wales.

III.4 Conservation

Water conservation has been defined as the 'preservation, control and development of water resources whether by storage, including natural ground storage, prevention of pollution, or other means, so as to ensure that adequate and reliable supplies of water are made available for all purposes in the most suitable and economical way whilst safeguarding legitimate interests'.[83] The White Paper was followed by the Water Resources Act 1963.

In the UK the problem of water conservation lies in the last clause of the official definition, for the reconciliation of conflicting interests becomes more difficult with increasing population pressure.

In England and Wales[84] there are 2 main categories: the water undertakings who supply water, and the River Authorities who are concerned with the wider problems of water conservation and management of river basins. At central government level these two categories are supervised by the Water Resources Board. The 1963 Water Resources Act did not, however, overcome the problem of the divided responsibilities for water supply, river management, water conservation, pollution control, sewerage and sewage disposal. The division of responsibility for industrial effluents between the sewerage and river authorities, in particular, has been a major problem. Further proposals were made by the Central Advisory Water Committee[85] which, subject to government legislation, will introduce a new structure in 1974. The functions of the present river authorities, together with water supply and sewage disposal at present in the hands of some local authorities, would become the responsibility of 10 Regional Water Authorities. They are envisaged as multi-purpose authorities who might take over canals as well. The proposals include a National Water Authority taking over from the Water Resources Board, but while the latter had a vital role in coordinating the efforts of 29 river authorities, the 10 Regional Water Authorities would be more self-sufficient. The proposals suggest that each authority should revise from time to time the strategies outlined by the Water Resources Board. In Scotland and Northern Ireland conservation problems have not yet warranted major reorganisation, though Regional Supply Boards and a central body are being considered.

Pressure on the land has led to more opposition to water storage proposals, and brought to the fore attempts to make better use of present resources by waste prevention, re-use by industry, dual systems for potable and non-potable supplies. Industry frequently uses water of high quality when lower quality would serve equally well. Also economies could be encouraged by metering, off-peak tariffs or rationing. Useful as these may be the additional 100 Mgal/d (0·45 Mm/d) required each year can only be met by surface reservoirs, estuary barrages, aqueduct systems, and increasingly by desalination, recirculation and complementary use of ground- and surface-water. The great deficiency in the Water Resources Act is the inability of the River Authorities to make a comprehensive management plan. The lack of a policy on the quality of river water seriously limits the effectiveness of any of the strategies outlined by the Water Resources Board. The proposed Regional Water Authorities would have the advantage of control of industrial effluents, however, which was denied to the River Authorities. Water supply to industry and to the public must be safeguarded by control over effluent discharges. The building of a new sewage works to raise the quality of river water to permit abstraction may be the alternative to a new reservoir and has the added attraction of improving amenities. The cost of cleaning rivers like the Trent must be considered along with the amount of water made available for abstraction. However, to allow abstraction, the quality must be higher than the Royal Commission Standard and the costs can only be met by a levy on all the users. There is little incentive for a local authority to implement sewage treatment which can only benefit users downstream. The proposed reorganisation of water and sewage services in a small number of Regional Water Authorities could do much to improve quality of river water.

Costs of conservation: Alternative schemes usually include combinations of upland storage, barrages and ground-water development. Evaluation must go beyond the costs of construction; it must also consider the treatment. For example, desalination is part of the cost of a marine barrage storage scheme. There are many other considerations, such as National Parks, salmon fishing and flood control. In considering a scheme a decision must be made on whether or not the extra cost of the more expensive alternative is a fair price to pay for the preservation of an environmental factor. The Water Resources Board has approached this problem in terms of cost effectiveness, but unless a scheme is multi- purpose it is extremely difficult to weigh the desirable and undesirable effects of develop- ment. At present the primary concern is for water, recreation is secondary and flood control is only important if schemes are otherwise equal. These are only part of the analyses and are frequently based on inadequate information. The Nature Conservancy is now concerned with the construction of models to guide land use decisions in the uplands.

The Water Resources Board has been urging regional control because of the effect that water is likely to have on future industrial location. Surplus can either be exported or used to attract industry, and river authorities can already exercise some control by issuing or refusing licences and by charging for private abstraction. In South East England some industrial concentrations are attracted to waterways or are located on aquifers. Rees[86] has shown that availability of potable water is a major location factor for food, drink and some chemical industries. Plastics and chemicals also need a great volume of water for disposing of noxious effluent. As suitable sites for water abstraction become scarce, water may exercise greater control over distributions of industry.

IV   FORESTS

IV.1   Afforestation

The Forestry Act of 1919 established the Forestry Commission with the task of replanting areas which had lost timber through decades of uncontrolled exploitation and so replenish a seriously depleted resource. In 1971 the Commission had a total estate of 2·9 million acres (1·2 Mha), of which 1·8 million (0·7 Mha) were planted in trees, and this is expanding at the rate of 45,000 acres (18,200 ha) per annum. Cheap land was inevitably land of poor agricultural value and for this reason the dominant land type for afforestation has been upland heaths and moors, accounting for 70 per cent of the total area in 1963.[87] Deciduous hardwoods, mainly in private forests, occur on the more productive soils of the lowlands, but the poorer soil and harsher climate of the uplands is better suited to the introduction of conifers which account for 90 per cent of all Forestry Commission wood- land. The conifers have proved that they can be highly productive even on poor site con- ditions. The average growth rate of Sitka spruce and Douglas fir is more than three times that of oak and twice the growth rate of beech.[88] Much of the planting has been in the more favoured parts of the uplands, though recent techniques have allowed the planting of peat bogs. There are still vast areas suitable for forestry so that the difficult areas, such as the exposed west coast of Scotland may not be developed for extensive forests for some time. In 1950 the Forestry Commission's activity in Scotland came under the Secretary of State for Scotland, but its role has remained unchanged and much of the recent planting has been in the Highlands. Forestry in Northern Ireland has been the concern of the Ministry of Agriculture of the Northern Ireland Government set up in 1922. By 1970 Northern Ireland had 99,000 acres (40,000 ha) planted in trees.

The establishment of vast forests of conifers in what seemed to be the less productive uplands has raised one of the most difficult problems of land use management. The profitability of forests depends to a very large extent on the nature of the site, the soil drainage and exposure in particular. Agriculture and especially sheep or cattle farming would not be so sensitive to environmental qualities and it would be difficult to decide on an optimum land use pattern based on productivity alone. In any case this would entail a fragmentation of forest blocks which would be uneconomic and may not be compatible, for example, with the practice of the spring burning of grazing areas, which is a hazard to forests. Comparisons of productivity may be meaningless at another time when new

techniques of either forest or agricultural management may be developed. A land survey
has been carried out jointly by the Departments of Agriculture and Forestry in Northern
Scotland, in which land suitable for forests is identified and, on the basis of its agricultural
potential, is either earmarked for purchase by the Forestry Commission or retained for
agriculture.[89] Assessment of changes resulting from different agriculture and forestry
policies have not been attempted in the United Kingdom.[90]

Much afforestation by the Commission in the 1920s was on grazing lands, especially
in the Highlands of Scotland. Whilst the presence of forest had the value of providing
shelter for stock, the forests were largely planted on the lower slopes and effectively
isolated the high grazings from the valley floors, thus reducing their value for stock farming. Technology has made it possible to plant over a wider range of conditions so that this
serious conflict need not occur with new plantings.

Forestry Commission planting has been in large units, of which 55 per cent are over
1,000 acres (400 ha) in extent and the landscape effect is less pleasing than the fragmented
pattern of small private woods and farmlands typical of the lowlands. However, attempts
to landscape their estates and provide a valuable resource for recreation led the Forestry
Commission to establish four large forest parks in Scotland, Snowdonia forest park in
Wales, the Forest of Dean and Wye and the Border Forest park in England. In Northern
Ireland five forest parks were established, in the Mourne mountain and Sperrin mountain
areas (figure 3.7).

IV.2   Environmental Factors in the Productivity of Commercial Forests

The large-scale commercial forests established by the Forestry Commission since 1919
have been developed on low-value land, most of which was marginal for agriculture. In the
1950s forests were expanding at the rate of 40,000 acres (16,000 ha) per annum and most
of this was on the rough grazing land of the uplands. Although similar to agriculture in
that trees are planted like a crop and harvested at the optimum stage of growth, forestry
was forced to develop in areas of difficult conditions of climate and soil. Productivity has
been improved through increasing knowledge of the relationships between growth and
environment, and the development of technology to take advantage of this knowledge.
The scale is also very different from agriculture, which makes the control of temperature
and moisture in nurseries a more difficult task. The softwoods have predominated largely
because of their rapid growth and their ability to survive in a wide range of conditions.
Although Scots pine is the only native conifer, spruce is preferred for the upland plantations and, in the wetter areas of the west, Sitka spruce predominates.

The Sitka spruce, a native of the wet Pacific coast of North America, grows well on the
wet western mountains, but under dry conditions the tree becomes susceptible to attack
by aphids. For this reason the low rainfall and the dry sandy soils of the Breckland in East
Anglia and the Culbin Sands, Morayshire, have suited Scots and Corsican pine rather than
spruce. In the Border forests, pine is also grown in the poorest deep peats, while the mid
and upper slopes are exclusively in spruce.[91] Larch is usually planted on the areas of better
soils, for example the bracken sites of the uplands, and was successfully planted on large
private estates in Scotland in the late-nineteenth century.

Despite the generally poor conditions in the forested areas, elevation, topography and
position influence the local climate and soil. Growth is dependent on length of season,
temperature and moisture. Since the growth rate in trees depends on the leaf area available,
soil water deficits in winter can retard the new season's growth; girth and volume are
increased from April onwards. The conditions for survival in the early years, such as freedom from dried-out surface soil, attacks by rabbits, grouse and deer and late frosts are not
needed once the trees are established, but they do succeed in eliminating forests from
many areas unless they can be remedied, as by high fencing in the Highlands of Scotland,

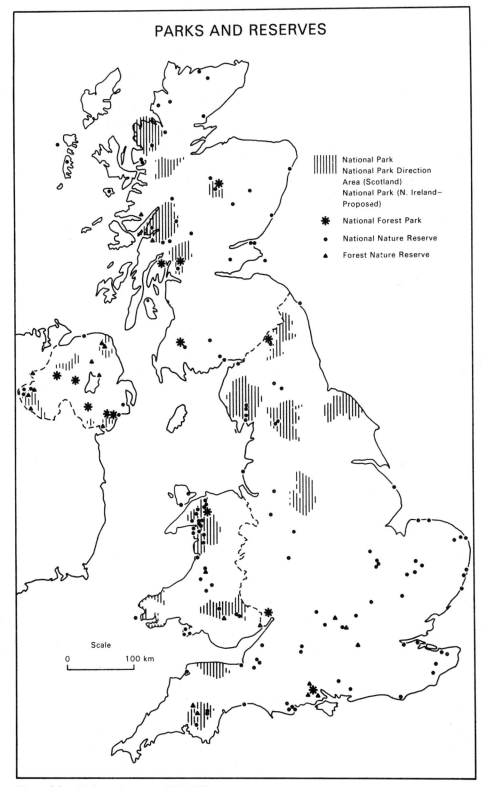

PARKS AND RESERVES

|||||| National Park
National Park Direction
Area (Scotland)
National Park (N. Ireland—
Proposed)

✳ National Forest Park

• National Nature Reserve

▲ Forest Nature Reserve

Scale

0   100 km

Figure 3.7   Parks and reserves, UK, 1972

to protect seedlings from deer. The effects of environmental conditions on the growth of
mature trees can be considerable. The average annual growth increment of 280 ft^3 per
acre (19 m^3 per ha) for Corsican pine in East Anglia was reduced by 30 per cent in a dry
year.[92] However, multivariate analysis suggests that winter temperature, sunshine, content
of clay and stones in the soil, depth of the water table, soil depth, humus type, soil pH
and phosphorus content are significant components in the growth of the species.[93] Once
trees are established the environmental conditions can change, such as the improved soil
water capacity due to the growth of root systems which can be substantial, even for
shallow-rooting trees in peats.[94]

Interception of precipitation in forests is appreciable. Together with the direct evaporation from the soil, which may be as much as 10 per cent of the total, it forms an important
part of the water balance. Conifers differ from deciduous trees in that they transpire and
intercept precipitation throughout the year. In wetter areas the evaporation of inter-
cepted water can be as much as that transpired by the trees. The deep-rooting habits of
trees, which under conditions of free drainage are commonly 6·5 ft (2 m), increase the
available water capacity to 12 - 20 in (300 - 500 mm) depending on soil type, which permits a long period of unrestricted evapotranspiration after the onset of drought. For this
reason forests transpire more than grassland under the same conditions of potential
evapotranspiration and the difference is greatest in South East England. Thinning
reduces evapotranspiration; in one case, streamflow from a forest increased by 1·8 in
(4·5 mm) after clearing 10 per cent of the trees. This is only temporary as the branches of
the remaining trees rapidly grow to fill up the spaces and the roots extend to occupy all
of the soil volume.[95]

Temperature is also important to growth, so that altitude and latitude are of significance. In the uplands, records of temperature are sparse and assumptions must be made on
crude lapse rates which need not be constant from time to time nor apply without variation over a very wide area. The present tree line in the UK is not entirely determined by
nature, but the upper level of potential growth must be based on physical conditions,
which in upland areas are complex. In the Cairngorms it is probably about 2,250 ft
(690 m) on sheltered slopes, but about 2,000 ft (600 m) on exposed sites.[96] While the
physical limit can be defined broadly as a mean summer temperature of 50°F (10°C), the
effects of temperature conditions on growth rates are more difficult to isolate.

Studies in Hampshire have shown that Douglas fir starts growth when the mean weekly
average rises to 45°F (7°C) and continues as long as this mean rises, but growth is checked
with even a slight fall in this mean.[97] However, the mechanism is not understood and in
any case is not likely to apply to all species.

Wind effectively excludes trees from the exposed western coasts, where the salt content accentuates its effects, whilst at high altitudes wind speed and temperature are interrelated. However, the dessicating effect of high wind velocity is more general. Areas in
Scotland which have poor tree growth correspond with mean wind velocities of 14 - 20 ft
per sec (10 - 14 mph) — 4·4 - 6·2 m per sec (16 - 23 kmph) — though other factors com-
plicate this general relationship in coastal areas and at high altitudes.[98] On sites with mean
wind velocities of about 17 mph (27 kmph) young seedlings of Sitka spruce grew better
than Lodgepole pine but larch failed completely.[99] The effect of strong winds on large
plantations is to prevent the emergence of dominant trees and in the Border forests
growth is generally restricted by exposure to the south-west and in more exposed sites the
result may be rapidly tapering stems which would have limited commercial value.[100] Wind
is reduced by 10 per cent in a 3 - 4° hollow, by as much as 40 per cent at the base of a
7 - 12° lee slope, whilst a reduction of 75 per cent has been noted on a lee slope of 14°.[101]

At one time forests were planted with little or no preparation of the soil, but recent
work in Inverness has shown that cultivation before planting can double the height of six
year-old Scots pine and Lodgepole pine. The problem is often mechanical and is especially

difficult on wet peat and soils with iron pans. Rapid growth on ploughed ridges, thought to be due to increased mineralisation of nitrogen under thicker peat, may not be sustained, for the larger trees eventually feel the mineral deficiencies while smaller, less demanding trees will continue to grow.

Pollution, particularly of the air, may present problems, notably on urban and industrial sites which are to be planted in the rehabilitation of derelict land. Sulphur dioxide has caused discoloration of leaves and premature leaf fall in forests near Port Talbot.[102] Together with dust, which limits photosynthesis, this is thought to contribute to poor growth in Sitka spruce, though some genetic variations have a degree of tolerance.

As knowledge of the nature of environmental problems in forestry grows, it is possible to control the natural hazards and improve soil conditions by nutrients and drainage. Wind throw is a problem in exposed areas. The problem has become increasingly important as trees grow to heights of over 35 ft (10 m), when they become more susceptible. Between 1961 and 1967, 2,400 acres (970 ha) suffered wind throw, half of this Sitka spruce, mainly 30 to 40 year-old timber which had reached between 30 and 60 ft (9 - 18 m) in height. In years of strong winds, as in 1961 and 1962, great damage was done. Damage tends to occur during single severe storms. In January 1968, 30 million ft^3 (850,000 m^3) of timber was lost in Central Scotland due to wind throw, during a 40 knot (75 kmph) westerly wind which persisted for six hours.[103] Wind is reduced in passing over an extensive forest, and wind speeds in the tree tops of the Border forests are only 10 per cent of the speeds in open country. However, gaps for roads and firebreaks create higher speeds, due to turbulence, and the highest incidence of wind throw is around small clearings. The eddy effect is also obvious near the base of lee slopes. Wind throw can be reduced at forest margins by high pruning which increases permeability but the damage by wind throw in the UK does not justify extensive treatment of all forest margins. Improvements in rooting can be brought about by drainage, particularly in clay soils. It has been estimated that about 90 per cent of the Border area needs improvement, though deep rooting in peaty podsols requires breaking of the iron pan, which can only be done at planting.[104] Drainage and cultivation can increase the critical height for winds of 40 knots (75 kmph) from 50 to 70 ft (15 - 20 m). While shelter belts can effectively reduce wind speeds by 40 per cent for distances 10 times the shelter height, this can only be of use in young forests. Established forests can benefit most from a margin inclined to the windward as this reduces the risk of turbulence.[105] Losses due to wind blow are mainly the lost potential growth but the difficulty of recovering the fallen timber incurs additional expenditure. Felling before the timber reaches full height reduces the risk of windfall but the crop has not then realised its full potential. Forest management in the Border forests where wind blow is a serious hazard has made use of simulated effects to decide on the optimum time for felling.[106]

Fire is less of a problem in the UK but its high incidence in spring is related to the dryness of the forest and surrounding vegetation. Rouse[107] has devised an empirically-derived scale of fire risk which depends on the number of days after rain, over 0·25 in (6 mm) in 24 hours; temperatures above 60°F (15°C), wind speed and relative humidity. Fire risk can be reduced during these critical periods by forest management.

V   URBAN AND INDUSTRIAL LAND USE

V.1   Introduction

While the location of certain types of industry can be considered the product of economic history, the development of industry in the nineteenth century was to a large extent influenced by the coalfields. With the exception of Belfast heavy industry is concentrated on or near the coalfields. Twentieth-century growth of light industry has not favoured the northern coalfields, but rather lowland England. Since the 1950s the growth of urban land has been greatest in an axial zone from Lancashire through the Midlands to London, and the total demand for additional development may be of the order of 1·7 million acres (700,000 ha) by the year 2000 (table 1.3). An estimated 1 per cent per annum of land in this area was lost to agricultural use from 1955 - 60 and the percentage of land in urban use in the South East is likely to reach 36 per cent by the end of the century. The area in urban and industrial use, estimated by Best at no more than 15 to 16 per cent of the land surface of England and Wales, will still be small compared with that in rural use.[108] The effects of industrial activity range from the sprawling New Towns and industrial estates in the South East to the dereliction of the declining heavy industries and old mines in South Wales, the North East, Central Scotland and on the flanks of the Pennines. While coal-mining and heavy industry have left vast areas of derelict spoil heaps which present major problems of rehabilitation, surface mining and, in particular, gravel extraction has also made increasing demands upon the land. The annual consumption for these latter purposes was about 3,950 acres (1,600 ha) in 1967 which could increase to 8,000 acres (3,200 ha) by about 1980.[109] Modern power stations make heavy demands on land and because of the need for vast supplies of cooling water are sited on major rivers like the Trent or, in the case of nuclear-powered stations, at the coast. Petrochemical industries needing deep-water sites have formed vast complexes on the major estuaries. Through its effects on the atmosphere, the land surface, the rivers and the surrounding seas, industrial and urban land use has influenced the environment far beyond the area of land which it occupies. The most serious effect is that of pollution.

V.2   Pollution

Pollution occurs when man's activity adds substances to the environment which because of their properties or quantity constitute a danger to health and well-being. It is perhaps more useful to broaden the influence to systems in the environment rather than to man alone. It is difficult to define pollution scientifically since many of the substances causing pollution occur naturally. Carbon dioxide, for example, is essential to life, yet in high concentrations it contributes to chronic respiratory disease. Phosphates are also essential to the growth of vegetation yet the great increase in the use of detergents in this country has contributed possibly as much as 50 per cent of the phosphate content of streams and rivers causing enrichment or eutrophication. Some natural substances, such as lead and mercury, may be more damaging since they can accumulate in organisms and disturb biochemical processes and through food chains present a hazard to man very much greater than if the substances were diluted in the environment. Increasingly man-made substances such as the chlorinated hydrocarbons used in pesticides have been adding to the pollution problem. As industry increases in sophistication, the emission of effluents whose effects are not yet known will increase.

When an effect of pollution is suspected there are usually moves to control it. The inversion of temperature in London in the winter of 1952 - 3 had the disastrous effect of unusual accumulations of smoke and carbon dioxide.[110] The deaths caused by the smog, some 3,000 to 4,000 in excess of a normal winter, led to the Clean Air Acts. In the same year, air pollution in East Lancashire caused lost production estimated at £2,600,000.[111] Toxic pollutants from some individual industries have led to action. For example, fumes from brickworks in the Midlands causing fluoride poisoning in cattle, lead smelting causing deaths of stock, fluorine in effluent from the aluminium smelters at Fort William contaminating pastures on the leeward side have all led to the offending industries being required to clean their effluent. The effect of the pollutant depends very much on the toxicity, persistence, mobility and ease of control. These are all-important, for a highly toxic pollutant which breaks down quickly is less serious than a less toxic but more persistent pollutant. For this reason organophosphorous pesticides are preferred to organochlorides though they are equally toxic.

The stability of the environment is important[111] but cannot be seen as a UK problem in isolation. Nicholson[112] estimates that artificial ecosystems, which constitute most of the UK surface, account for only 10 per cent of the globe, the rest being natural or biologically-exploited natural ecosystems. All our pollutants finally reach the sea, carried by rivers, dumped by man or washed by rain from the air. The sea appears to be able to breakdown and recycle waste and so far the harmful effects seem to be localised. However, there may be no grounds for complacency in UK waters, as we share the North Sea with other highly populated countries which use it as a sink. Equally, the almost enclosed waters of the Irish Sea may be particularly vulnerable in the future. The global atmosphere has shown an increase in carbon dioxide of 0·2 per cent per annum since 1958, largely as a result of fuel combustion. Stratosphere traffic, which must increase in the future, will continue to add water vapour and carbon dioxide. The possible climatic effect of this, together with the impact of sulphur dioxide which finds its way to the stratosphere where its life is prolonged, has not yet been assessed, but in air corridors with dense traffic a 60 per cent increase in water vapour is suspected, leading to more stratospheric cloud.[113] Shipping and offshore drilling for oil in the North Sea add to the pollution of the seas. Indeed it has been estimated that approximately 2 million tons of oil enters the oceans annually.

V.3 Air pollution

Atmospheric pollution is mainly the result of combustion of fossil fuel so that the main sources are the built-up areas. The UK climate has required fires in winter and the problem of pollution was recognised centuries ago in Edinburgh and London. The high concentration of pollutants in the cities was largely due to the back-to-back housing, narrow streets and an absence of open spaces which characterised the early growth of industrial cities. While industry was controlled to some extent from 1863 onwards the emission of household smoke, which constitutes some 85 per cent of total smoke emitted, remained unabated until the Clean Air Acts of 1956 and 1968. Sulphates and carbon monoxide are added to the atmosphere from the sea and the bacterial decomposition of organic debris adds ammonia and hydrogen to the atmosphere. Combustion can occur naturally as forest fires, whilst soil erosion from farmland in eastern England during dry springs adds dust to the air. There is no question of eliminating these natural pollutants but rather of finding the acceptable level; simple models have been devised to reduce ground level pollution to acceptable levels.[114] With exotic pollutants concentrations must not be allowed to exceed the toxic levels, at threshold limits of 7 - 8 hours a day.[115] However, less is known about the effects on plants and it is likely that vigour may be adversely affected at lower concentrations than those actually causing damage. It is difficult to measure pollution at low concentrations and therefore most of the evidence is of a crude nature and confined to the most obvious: sulphur, carbon dioxide, carbon monoxide, nitric oxide and particulate matter. The latter includes both larger particles of dust and grit with diameters exceeding 10 μm, which quickly settles, and the finer particles which may remain in suspension forming mist clouds and haze and thus obstructing radiation. The problems of measurement were reviewed by Ball who suggested the use of laser and low temperature infra-red spectroscopy for future work.[116]

The effect of air pollution on climate is measurable. Dust in suspension obstructs solar radiation. Average monthly hours of bright sunshine in the winter months in Central London (Kingsway) between 1958 and 1967 showed a 50 per cent increase over the 30-year normal[117] when little or no change was recorded in the suburbs. This increase took place during a period when global solar radiation levels were generally low. This trend has continued with increasing smoke control; at present 83 per cent of homes within London control areas have been converted to smokeless fuel practices. Because of its well known 'greenhouse' effect of permitting incoming short-wave radiation while obstructing outgoing long-wave radiation, carbon dioxide influences temperature. This is more important on a global scale than within the UK, where the local effects of carbon dioxide concentration are probably counteracted by the reduced insolation caused by smoke and dust. For this reason neither temperature nor radiation change can be reliable indicators.

Effects on life forms have been explored as possible indicators. Sulphur dioxide concentrations in Tyneside inhibit the epiphytic flora of ash trees.[118] Fallout on hillsides near Port Talbot is thought to be the reason for the local lichen desert and is considered a contributory factor in the poor growth of Sitka spruce in the nearby Margam forest.[119] The sensitivity of lichens to sulphur dioxide has also been used to map zones of air pollution levels.[120] Since they are based on frequency of species each locality must have a different scale; however, they provide a rapid qualitative assessment.

A national survey of smoke and sulphur dioxide began in 1961 and there are now over 1,200 sites where sulphur dioxide levels are recorded, and smoke dust and grit are measured either by filtering of air or rain water. Sulphur dioxide is produced mainly by the burning of coal. When this was the dominant fuel in the UK, sulphur dioxide was a reliable guide to all gaseous pollution, but today there are other sources, such as high temperature furnaces, road traffic exhaust and jet exhaust at airports, all of which are increasing. Pollution at airports is difficult to assess, because of the inadequacy of measuring techniques, but it is assumed to be comparable to that of an industrial estate. In winter Heathrow receives as much pollution from West London as it generates and in summer the difference between the airport and its surrounds is slight.[121] Road traffic is a more serious problem. Average monthly measurements of carbon monoxide concentrations in busy streets in England and Wales show that for Manchester and Glasgow a total of 60 hours had more than 10 parts per million (ppm) but levels over 50 ppm averaged less than 1 minute in a monthly period, except for Cardiff with a total of 10 minutes at this level.[122] Concentrations of 50 ppm is considered the threshold for continuous exposure for 8 hours day after day. Industrial furnaces contribute nitric oxide to the atmosphere, though as much as 50 per cent of the total concentration may be due to traffic. Nitric oxide has shown concentrations as high as $29 \cdot 5 \mu g$ per m^3 at Islington,[123] but it changes chemically and can be washed from the air by rain. Lead, largely from petrol exhaust, showed a mean concentration of $3 \cdot 2 \mu g$ per m^3 in Fleet Street for the year 1962 - 3. Although these concentrations appear small, lead can accumulate in the body and continuous exposure over long periods could be harmful. Only a few yards from the busy thoroughfares these concentrations fall rapidly and become negligible at 50 yd (45 m). Measurable levels of photochemically-produced ozone occurred in southern England in July 1971 during anticyclonic conditions and at the same time oxidised sulphur dioxide in the form of sulphuric acid and sulphates were much higher than during windy or cloudy weather.[124] However, because of the topography and climate in the UK the serious photochemically-produced fogs in Los Angeles are not likely to occur.

The regional distribution of smoke and sulphur dioxide in 1968 - 9 shown in table 3.6, shows higher concentrations of smoke in the north of England, about $100 \mu g$ per m^3 (microgrammes per cubic metre), and much less in the south where the lowest was $33 \mu g$ per m^3 in the South West. However, sulphur dioxide concentration is just higher in Greater London than in the North West and North. The table reflects the balance between the industrial built-up areas, which are the major sources of pollution, and the open country and at the same time the degree of pollution control that has been achieved in the urban areas.

The concentrations of smoke and sulphur dioxide depend very much on the degree of dispersion, which varies with wind and the vertical temperature gradient. Temperature inversions prevent vertical mixing and lead to the heaviest concentrations. Certain areas may be more prone to inversion because of their topography, for example the valleys on

TABLE 3.6   Average Concentrations of Smoke and Sulphur Dioxide, UK Regions, 1968 - 9

Region	Smoke $\mu g/m^3$	Sulphur dioxide $\mu g/m^3$
North West	109	147
North	108	97
Yorkshire and Humberside	97	140
Scotland	88	87
Northern Ireland	79	96
East Midlands	77	102
West Midlands	63	119
East Anglia	51	87
Greater London	46	151
South East	39	78
Wales	39	62
South West	33	68

Source: Craxford and Weatherley (1971)

either side of the Pennines.[125] Siting of new factories in such areas ought to be avoided, for landscaping can only hope to control shallow radiation fogs by encouraging cold air drainage. It is difficult to devise generalised models since each pollution source may be affected in a different way by architecture, topography and atmospheric dispersal. Sophisticated models allowing for these variables could only be applied if a much clearer picture of micro and local meteorology becomes possible. The building of high stacks[126] can control ground level concentration even from large installations to an upper limit of 460 μg per m^3. Ground level concentrations are inversely proportional to wind speed and the square of the effective height of emission. Low chimneys below 300 ft (91 m) have effluents of low buoyancy while the high stacks which may be over 800 ft (244 m) in height send plumes rising to 1,800 ft (550 m), though even this may not be high enough to penetrate high stratus cloud cover. High stacks relieve the pollution of the immediate surrounds but transport the effluent far beyond the region. Although UK emissions have been held responsible for increasing soil acidity in upland Sweden it has been argued that they have not the capacity to carry the necessary amount of sulphur and there is no evidence of the same effect in our own uplands. Transfers within the UK have been proved. The pollution in country around Leicester can be attributed to more distant urban areas, while in Yorkshire downwind drifting has been shown to carry 31 to 37 miles (50 to 60 km) from the source.[127] Light winds favour drifting for the turbulence and mixing associated with strong winds leads to dispersal. There is a limit to the distance that pollutants can be carried in high concentrations, and coastal sites, for example in Norfolk, record low annual figures. Few records exist for open country and they are usually at sites where a pollution source exists or is suspected. The sites listed in table 3.7 all had some sources of pollution. Scottish sites remote from industrial centres and Western coasts show low levels but country sites near urban conurbations can receive considerable smoke concentrations, due to drifting which has been known to raise daily values to 200 μg per m^3 at open sites 12 miles (20 km) east of industrial South Yorkshire. Lytham St Annes had 12 daily concentrations exceeding 500 μg/cu m in the winter of 1962 - 3 (figure 3.8).

The effect of smoke control under the 1956 Clean Air Act is difficult to assess because there has been a change in fuel since its inception, but a general reduction in pollution has occurred and the most dramatic fall has been in urban areas. Industrial sources were so effectively controlled that by 1968, 85 per cent of the total emission was from domestic fires. The introduction of more smoke control areas will further improve the situation. In 1970 smoke control orders were made for 43 per cent of the dwellings in areas of Scotland liable to heavy pollution and 54 per cent of those in England. The mean daily concentration recorded at sites classified as high density residential areas within built-up areas was 210 μg per m^3 for smoke and 207 μg per m^3 for sulphur dioxide for the year

TABLE 3.7   Atmospheric Pollution, Selected UK Rural Sites, 1962 - 71

	Smoke concentrations in $\mu g/m^3$ per day			
	Monthly average		Highest daily	
	1962 - 3	1970 - 1	1962 - 3	1970 - 1
Lerwick, Shetland	3	1	38	17
Pembroke	NR	4	NR	27
Stornoway, Lewis	5	3	93	58
Amroth, Pembrokeshire	NR	3	NR	11
Eskdalemuir, Dumfries	14	6	115	32
Fakenham, Norfolk	28	NR	187	NR
Cardiff	33	18	205	109
Sheffield	75	28	277	286
Lytham St Annes	104	40	860	639
Norton, Runcorn	NR	30	NR	256

NR = No record

Source: Warren Spring Laboratory (1963 and 1971)

1963. In 1971, after subsequent smoke control the mean concentration at similar sites was 90 μg per m^3 smoke and 118 μg per m^3 sulphur dioxide. Some of the areas in the 72 UK cities used to calculate the mean figure became controlled after 1963, and these were omitted in the 1971 calculations whilst some new stations were included, to give a total of 63 cities in the 1971 calculation. The standard deviation of the 72 stations in 1963 was 87 μg m^3 smoke and 89 μg per m^3 sulphur dioxide, and of the 63 stations in 1971, 47 μg per m^3 smoke and 39 μg per m^3 sulphur dioxide.

The effects of smoke control are more dramatic at some individual sites. For example, at one site at Salford the winter mean daily concentration of smoke fell from 558 μg per m^3 in 1963 to 414 μg per m^3 in 1971 and sulphur dioxide from 621 μg per m^3 in 1963 to 261 μg per m^3 in 1971. The maximum daily concentrations of 1,871 μg per m^3 smoke and 3,081 μg per m^3 sulphur dioxide in 1963 were reduced to 1,227 μg per m^3 smoke and 898 μg per m^3 sulphur dioxide in 1971. For the same period the number of days recording more than 500 μg were reduced from 103 to 53 for smoke and 91 to 9 for sulphur dioxide. These changes were achieved without any control within the area, although other areas of Salford had become smoke control zones. The direct effect can be seen in table 3.8, referring to areas which became controlled between 1963 and 1971 and show a drop of more than 60 per cent in smoke, with the exception of Glasgow. The measures to control smoke do not effect sulphur dioxide, which reflects the sulphur content of fuels. In the case of Barnes there has, indeed, been a rise of 4 per cent. The introduction of natural gas and nuclear energy has gone a long way to reduce sulphur dioxide, and with changes in domestic heating has brought about an estimated national reduction of about 30 per cent since 1960.

Attempts have been made to remove sulphur dioxide from emissions but the processes developed are only viable for large installations like Battersea power station. Even here the expenditure would not relieve South East England of pollution unless similar measures were taken in neighbouring European countries. Much more success has been achieved with smoke control. Fuels have been developed to reduce smoke and their improved efficiency partly compensates for the higher cost; furthermore, grit- and dust-arresting devices are in operation. There are no technical problems in removing pollutants such as oxides of nitrogen and sulphur but the process often has noxious effluent and the cost is often prohibitive. Washing of gases lowers their temperature, which reduces their buoyancy. High concentrations of washed gas can be as undesirable as the untreated smoke. Thus despite the cost of approximately £1m per 650 ft (200 m) of chimney, high stacks are still a better way of reducing ground level pollution.

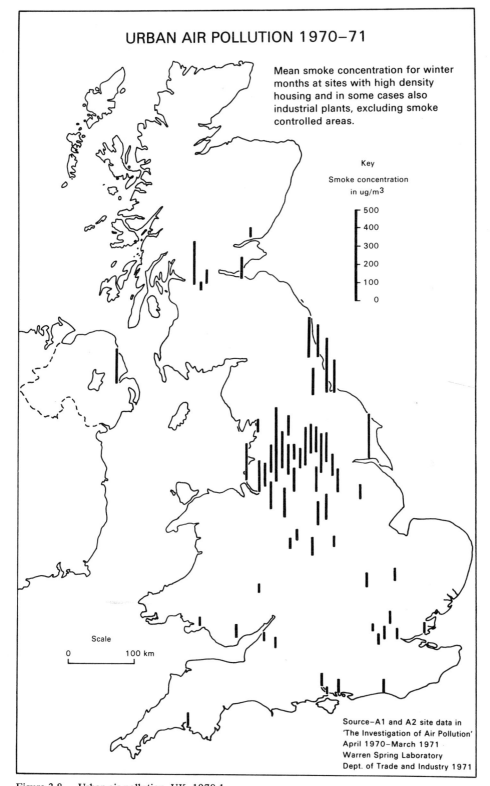

URBAN AIR POLLUTION 1970–71

Mean smoke concentration for winter months at sites with high density housing and in some cases also industrial plants, excluding smoke controlled areas.

Key

Smoke concentration in ug/m3

500
400
300
200
100
0

Scale

0   100 km

Source–A1 and A2 site data in 'The Investigation of Air Pollution' April 1970–March 1971 Warren Spring Laboratory Dept. of Trade and Industry 1971

Figure 3.8   Urban air pollution, UK, 1970-1

TABLE 3.8   Change in Mean Daily Concentrations of Smoke and Sulphur Dioxide, After Smoke
            Control, Selected UK Sites, 1963 and 1971

| | Smoke (μg/m^3) | | | Sulphur dioxide (μg/m^3) | | |
	1963	1971	% change	1963	1971	% change
Barnes	82	32	-61	121	126	+ 4
Burnley	178	71	-60	254	147	-42
Enfield	126	47	-63	195	138	-29
Glasgow	290	164	-43	181	108	-40
Hornsley	134	39	-71	193	117	-39
Norwich	108	10	-91	78	29	-63
Sheffield	250	64	-74	241	167	-31

Source: Warren Spring Laboratory (1972)

V.4   Pollution of the Land Surface

The effects of agriculture on the land have been discussed earlier. Pesticides, herbicides and fertilisers form an important part, though less than in North America, of the total pollution of the land surface. In the UK, industrial and urban activity has created more tangible effects on the landscape. The effects of early lead and fluorspar workings have persisted in the carboniferous limestone areas. When soil is polluted from the air or by surface water it can be controlled by statutory regulations, but only recently, in 1972, has any attempt been made to check the indiscriminate dumping of toxic materials. Dumping can have an immediate danger to individuals or can represent a more widespread hazard by contaminating streams or ground water. Pollution by nuclear waste from industry is much smaller than fall out from nuclear explosions, but nevertheless important since the danger period before the complete decay may be thousands of years. For these reasons it is not surprising that the permissible levels for emissions into the Irish Sea are low. However, the disposal of the residue, which is 99·9 per cent of the total waste produced and is highly radioactive, presents a major pollution problem. This residue is stored in steel tanks, encased in 8 ft (2·4 m) walls of concrete, with stringent safety precautions. In fact radiation is more carefully monitored than any other pollutant and in 1970 - 1, 28 per cent of all research expenditure was on problems of radioactivity. Pollution by other forms of industrial waste creates problems due more to volume than to toxicity. About 50 per cent of the volume of raw material used by industry is waste and its disposal has been treated with much more apathy than if it were more highly toxic. The increase in the amount of waste will continue and, with highly sophisticated industrial techniques, more of it will be toxic. The problem is to find suitable ways of disposing of this increasing volume of urban and industrial waste. One alternative, most frequently used up to the present, is the land surface; another is the sea, with effects described in the next section.

   In a recent estimate[128] of the annual 20 million tons of waste disposed of by local authorities 72 per cent was domestic and trade refuse. However, many industrial concerns dispose of waste in other ways and no comprehensive estimate of industrial waste is possible. It is thought that about 11 million tons of toxic waste, including 4 million tons of solids, are produced annually by industry,[129] but over 80 per cent of this toxic material is relatively inert. Local authorities dispose of 90 per cent of the refuse by direct tipping on the land, 71 per cent of this being controlled, usually because of a need for material for reclamation (figure 3.9). Large areas have been reclaimed in this way for port facilities, for example at Southend, Liverpool and Portsmouth. At Belfast mudflats have been reclaimed in this way for the expansion of aircraft works and runways. Tipping on the land requires planning permission and the Coast Protection Act controls tipping below the high water mark, though the harbour schemes already completed or in progress have not caused any serious pollution of tidal waters. Tipping is cheaper than the other alternatives,

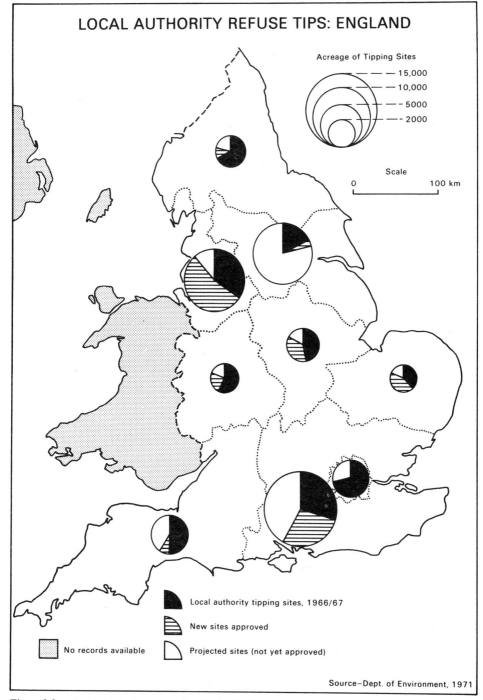

Figure 3.9   Local Authority refuse tips, England, 1966-7

pulverisation, incineration or composting. Pulverisation has grown in importance since 1960, but still handles little over 1 per cent of the refuse and the existing plants can serve only small populations of less than 50,000. Composting is not likely to be encouraged by demand from agriculture, largely because of its low nutrient content and the possibility of toxic elements. Its potential use is probably limited to improving marginal land.

Refuse is increasing in weight annually, though the annual increase rate of 0·7 per cent per person in the ten years, 1955 - 65, has since decreased, largely due to the rapid reduction in consumption of solid fuel. Since 1957 dust and cinder content has fallen by two-thirds. Paper, plastics, packaging and non-returnable bottles have increased rapidly and are likely to increase 5 times in the next 10 years, so that the volume of refuse is increasing, though it is of lower density than in the past.

It has been estimated that less than one-fifth of the excavations made by mineral extractors annually could accommodate all the house refuse produced. Opencast mineral workings are increasing at about 5,000 acres (2,023 ha) pa, half of this by sand and gravel excavators. Land made derelict by industry could be improved using refuse as infill and reclamation of tidal mud flats is another possibility. Tipping can create derelict land unless treated. In the past 20 years, 20,000 acres (8,000 ha) have been reclaimed for other uses but 7,260 acres (2,900 ha) still remain derelict and within the next 8 years there will be added a further 11,500 acres (4,600 ha) when tipping on existing sites is completed unless the rate of restoration is increased. Currently 2,000 acres (810 ha) of land is reclaimed annually, and this includes industrial land.

One of the problems of choosing sites is the pollution hazard to ground water resources. Compacted refuse covered with soil can absorb rainfall and give a low rate of percolation. For the first year percolating water is heavily polluted but it rapidly declines to reach low levels within 3 years. Sand or gravel can act as a natural filter protecting ground-water. Bacteria will die off within a few feet of the surface, but chlorides and nitrates will persist in solution. Where the underlying rock is fissured, percolation can be very rapid, but sealing with puddled clay can protect ground-water if drains are led to filter beds or a sewer. Alternatives are to line the base of the tip with 2 - 3 ft (60 - 90 mm) of aerated gravel or to prevent any percolation by sealing the surface and this causes rapid surface run-off. Tipping directly into water is more of a hazard than dry tipping since de-oxygenation can occur rapidly, allowing bacteria to produce hydrogen sulphide. Wet gravel pits require the added expense of chlorination in hot weather; clay pits on the other hand can be pumped dry before tipping.

Streams emanating from tips can become de-oxygenated or, more commonly, fouled by sewage fungus. River Authorities have been responsible for all discharges but have no powers to control dumping on the land surface. However, because of the risks to water pollution, they have invariably been consulted.

Tipping is likely to continue as the most common method of waste disposal, but in the future if space becomes scarce, other methods may be developed, eg pyrolysis where high temperatures are used to reduce all waste, including plastics to carbon, oil, tar and gas. The water content is reduced to one-tenth in this process. Scrap motor cars increase in numbers annually. In 1969, 13 million cars were in use and 1 million became obsolete. After compression and separation of non-ferrous material some can be sold as scrap for steel mills. A few large hammer mills do the separation of ferrous metal magnetically. To use pulverisers economically they must be working continuously, which is only possible in large conurbations. 400,000 vehicles are processed annually at a London plant, 200,000 vehicles at one in Hertfordshire and the same number at a plant in Lancashire. If used to capacity these 3 could convert 80 per cent of all waste vehicles into separated steel scrap, but the problem is the transporting of vehicles from other areas. Rubber tyres are discarded at the rate of 12 million per annum and, except for Merseyside which has a factory for reclaiming rubber, there is no easy method of disposal. Many London authorities, for example, will not accept them.

A recent survey of more than 1,000 firms showed that about 1·8 per cent of all industrial solid and semi-solid waste is toxic. Only 0·8 per cent is dealt with by local authorities, the rest being disposed of by individual contractors. About 75 per cent of this toxic waste is dumped on surface tips, where it creates a serious hazard to ground-water. The effect of the toxic material may be to destroy normal biological activity on the surface and if it is soluble no filtering is possible in its percolation through permeable strata. More often the tips are on impermeable strata and so the percolate drains to surface streams. There are more cases of river pollution than ground-water pollution. Ground-water under a gravel pit used for chemical waste had an oxygen demand of 4,000 mg/l and the chemicals inhibited biological oxidation. Tips have been known to pollute ground-water for 80 years after all tipping ceased. In 1963 an industrial tip polluted surface water in a neighbouring farm and caused animals to die. These are extreme cases but it is common to have some phenol contamination in water supplies. Large ground-water reserves are less vulnerable because of dilution, and because of their size the authority can exercise more control over surface tipping. The greatest hazard comes from unauthorised tipping which is difficult to solve as tighter restrictions can lead to greater dangers from illegal jettisoning of material. If land sites are to be used for toxic waste, it can be kept dry, compacted and the surface sealed to prevent all percolation; another alternative is dumping at sea. Unused mines are only satisfactory if they are deep and not linked to exploitable aquifers. A large mine in the Midlands is being used in this way but attempts to use old mines elsewhere have been opposed.

V.5 Water Pollution

Much of the pollution of the land and air reaches surface streams and therefore the land use of the catchment has an important effect on the state of the river. Runoff carries fertiliser and pesticides from agricultural land and industry discharges effluents which demand oxygen. Some water pollutants are nutrients, such as nitrates and phosphates, which cause enrichment or eutrophication and the excessive growth of fresh-water plants. These can block dams, whilst some algae produce toxic products and on dying oxygen is removed from the water. This has the same effect as excessive organic wastes from sewage which led to a lifeless Thames in the mid-nineteenth century. In England and Wales only 5 to 9 per cent of the nitrogen in rivers comes from agriculture. Despite the fact that consumption of nitrogenous fertilisers has doubled in 10 years the level in UK rivers has not increased. By 1968 - 9 organochlorate pesticides replaced DDT but despite the persistence of organochlorides less than 0·05 mg/l occurred in UK rivers in 1966, well below the 1 mg/l threshold for trout. Between 1953 and 1966 the phosphate concentration doubled but this was due to sewage and effluent rather than to fertilisers. Damage to fish population may not be judged by concentrations below a lethal threshold, for lower levels may destroy food and changes in water softness could increase the toxicity of some pollutants. Salmon and trout are the most sensitive to pollution and for this reason often used to indicate levels of toxicity.

Pollution is measured in terms of biochemical oxygen demand (BOD). The Royal Commissions on Sewage Disposal, 1898 - 1915, produced the standard 30 mg/l suspended solids and 20 mg/l BOD which are still accepted. However, these levels required dilution by 8 parts of water to 1 of effluent which may not be possible during dry periods in UK rivers. The Irwell, Tame, Rother, Mersey, Don and Avon (Severn) have as much as half their dry season flow in the form of treated sewage effluent. Slight pollution is made harmless by dilution; increased pollution and decreased dilution can have the same effect.

In 1958, 73 per cent of rivers in England and Wales were unpolluted, that is with less than 3 mg/l BOD, but 6 per cent were grossly polluted with over 12 mg/l BOD and so deoxygenated and without fish. In 1972, 77 per cent were unpolluted and 9·4 per cent grossly polluted.[130] Improvements have been achieved only on short rivers, such as the Lea, while the rivers draining the main industrial regions, the Trent, Mersey, Ouse and its tributaries, the Tyne and Tees remain polluted. Cleaning of these rivers is possible, and a tributary of the Trent, the Derwent, once grossly polluted by the industrial effluents of Derby, is now clean enough for fish. While rivers can carry away waste and at the same time provide water for industry, it is doubtful if the standards as measured by BOD are satisfactory when the water is extracted for human consumption, for industrial effluents can contain toxic as well as oxygen-demanding elements. Further industrial development is limited by the availability of water and facilities for discharge. Effluent may be accepted by a local authority for sewage treatment if it is within the authority's capacity of the industry may discharge into rivers with the consent of the River Authority. Industries pay the local authority for treatment either directly or through rates, but some firms may treat effluent, which if sophisticated may require high capital and running costs. The Confederation of British Industry estimates that industries are spending 2 to 15 per cent of their total capital investment on treatment. The expenditure will rise further with demands for higher quality effluent from river authorities wishing to abstract public supplies from the river, but could be a serious handicap to many industries competing with European countries where the quality of effluent is less carefully controlled.

Sewage is mainly water and therefore forms a significant part of the flow of many rivers. About 3,100 Mgal (14,000 Ml) are discharged into sewers, about one-half from industry and the other from domestic sources. The Greater London Council sewage works discharges 550 Mgal/d (2,500 Ml/d) into the Thames and its successful treatment allows the extraction of about one-third of South East England's water needs from the river.

Many sewers built during the last century no longer have the capacity to deal with modern developments. In Coventry, for example, it has been necessary to reconstruct the main sewage system. The problem is aggravated at times of heavy rain since surface run-off can augment the sewers and cause overflow, polluting streams with untreated waste. Storm water balancing tanks are used to rectify this. Oxygen-demanding water can be readily treated. Sewage works can remove as much as 95 per cent of the oxygen-demanding and sludge-forming constituents by settlement and biological processes. In the past, sewage farms did this by spreading, but the enormous demands that this would make on land to-day have led to the use of biological filters and a process of activated sludge which accelerates the anaerobic process. At present about four-fifths of the population of the UK is served by such biological plants. Ammonia is oxidised to nitrates, the effluent is clear and can be discharged without seriously affecting the river, and in some cases as at Luton, the effluent is below 10 mg/l solids and 10 mg/l BOD and the river Lea can supply London with water. These high standards of treatment must be maintained both by sewage works and industry since in the upper Lea their effluents form as much as 50 per cent of the normal daily flow. However, not all sewage works are so efficient for in 1964 - 5, 60 per cent had effluents with averages in excess of the Royal Commission standard, which was designed for disease prevention rather than public re-use. If effluents are to be improved more extensive treatment must be carried out. For example pathogens are not removed, but would be destroyed naturally by bacteria. Chlorination is undesirable because the effluent contains the toxic by-products of the chemical process and the necessary bacteria would be destroyed. Conventional biological treatment only removes 37 to 46 per cent of phosphates. These together with nitrates can lead to eutrophication and some UK rivers have shown this effect in years of high sunshine. It is not a problem likely to develop in running water and no large inland water bodies receive enough effluent for the effect to be felt. However, the Irish Sea receives effluent from Lancashire as well as from Dublin and it has been suggested that eutrophic conditions will spread outwards leading to a slow deterioration, similar to what is now happening in the Baltic.[131] While 42 per cent of the nitrogen reaching the sea has its origin in agricultural land, as much as 80 per cent of the phosphates comes from domestic and industrial effluents, including 30 to 50 per cent from detergents. The appearance of synthetic detergents on the market in 1949 created a major treatment problem which led to their replacement by biologically degradable constituents in the 1960s. Organochlorides in UK rivers have reached levels in excess of concentrations reported from the USA. Most of these come from industry where they are used in mothproofing, etc. Although pesticides have generally low levels in UK water the danger is through accumulation in algae.

The disposal of sludge creates a greater problem than the liquid discharged. After a process of anaerobic digestion which largely destroys pathogens about one-fifth of the sludge is dumped in the sea beyond the 3 mile (4·8 km) limit. Manchester and London use this method, and London has a special fleet of ships. It has the advantage of economy but the effects on the sea are not certain. The dilution and purification processes in the sea may not be very effective in disposing of organic material when it is dumped in deep water. Below 3,300 ft (1,000 m) microbial activity is greatly reduced and dilution may put the pollutant beyond microbial attack. Two-fifths of the treated sludge is used as fertiliser, but it will not replace balanced artificial fertiliser as the total output of sludge could only supply 4·5 per cent of the nitrogen and phosphate required and it is very deficient in potash. The presence of toxic metals limits its use and in any case it can only be economically distributed within a 10 mile (16 km) radius of sewage works. It has been assumed that tidal estuaries have unlimited capacity to receive pollution and the practice of discharging untreated sewage and industrial effluent has continued almost unabated. The large volume of water in estuaries dilutes the effluent, and mixing by tidal movements promotes natural purification, but recently the levels of pollution have reached heights which threaten shell fisheries. In 1958 only 41 per cent of all tidal estuaries were considered clean and 12 per cent were grossly polluted. Many have become the focus of industry and dense urban concentrations. The Tyne, for example, receives 37 Mgal/d (168 Ml/d) of sewage and 10 Mgal/d (45 Ml/d) of trade waste from its banks while the Severn receives waste from a population of over 1 million. At times of reduced flow the Ouse and Trent discharge water with 200 ton per day of effective oxygen demand which would use up oxygen from about 5,000 Mgal (22,730 Ml) of sea-water in the Humber. In these circumstances bacterial pollution extending far out to sea has been reported, as for example up to a distance of 5 miles (8 km) beyond the Tyne. The badly polluted estuaries are being cleaned up by sewage improvements costing: on Tyneside, £40 million; Teesside, £20 million; and for the GLC £100 million. However, many estuaries like the Solent could become as heavily polluted if they continue to receive untreated effluents.

The problem of discharge to the sea is not confined to estuaries, for many sewage authorities dispose of untreated sewage by discharge into the sea. A Cooperative Research Report in 1967, however, came to the conclusion that the coastal waters of the UK showed little pollution and this was localised near outfalls from coastal industries.[132] Yet few existing discharge pipes extend far enough out to sea to prevent beach pollution, though with modern techniques it is now economically feasible to lay pipes 2 to 3 miles (3 to 5 km) out to sea. Bacterial contamination has its effect on marine life, especially shell fish, but industrial effluents have been known to kill off marine life around the outfall, the most toxic being organochlorat pesticides and polychlorinated biphenyls. Toxic materials in effluents discharged offshore come outside the scope of the Clean Rivers (Estuaries and Tidal Waters) Act of 1960 and can only be controlled through the powers of the Sea Fisheries Committee, which only applies to England and Wales.

Beyond the 3 mile (4·8 km) limit there is no effective control over dumping at sea. Disposal of highly toxic materials at sea is usually in very deep water, exceeding 2,000 fathoms (3,650 m) beyond the continental shelf, where slow diffusion of pollutants from their containers is diluted so much that there is no danger of surface contamination. The total effect is difficult to measure, much of the research being directed towards the influence of heavy metals on ecosystems. More is known about the pollution of the Irish Sea because of the concern over effluents from the Windscale reactors though it is said that present levels of nuclear waste reaching the sea are unlikely to have any observable effect on the natural environment. Natural runoff from mineral rich areas like North Wales or Devon contributes to the presence of metals in coastal waters but high concentrations, for example 47·6 µg/l zinc in Liverpool Bay which is ten times the level in the open sea and the 4·2 µg/l cadmium level in the Bristol Channel which is 30 to 40 times that at sea[133] can be attributed to industry. Also the North Sea has shown high cadmium levels offshore from industrial sites, such as North East England. However, these are all localised peaks and concentration falls away rapidly from the coast. The levels have not increased in the past 10 years and in fact cadmium has decreased except for the local concentration off Barry in South Wales. However, the detrimental effects of heavy metal concentrations could become serious in the long term if they accumulate in offshore sediments.[134] Evidence of biological changes is difficult to interpret. In the 1930s nutrient salts and zooplankton declined in the English Channel seriously, reducing the regular winter herring fishing indus-try but recovered again in 1965 probably due to climatic fluctuations which cause north and southward shifts of marine populations.[135]

The waste disposal problems of agriculture have changed in character in recent years and become more serious with the growth in intensive animal farming. Since 1946 pigs have trebled and poultry doubled. Large units find it difficult to dispose of manure cheaply. Despite the obvious nutrient value for arable farming there are problems of trans-port and difficulties of application compared with artificial fertilisers. Access to fields is not always possible if soils are heavy and the high water content of slurries could lead to waterlogging if soil water is at or near field capacity. The bacteria present in slurry presents a health hazard especially if used to fertilise grass on dairy farms and manures from animals fed with chemicals or antibiotics could be harmful to plant growth. Poultry manure which has the highest concentration of NPK (nitrogen, phosphates, potash) of all farm animals has been dried for fertiliser as well as for animal feeding but this disposes of only a small proportion. Some are treated by storage in ditches while oxidation takes place and then discharged to streams. Sewage works have not the capacity to deal with agricul-tural refuse.

Unlike radioactivity we have no clear idea of the safe level of oil pollution. So far the effects have been limited to the destruction of some marine communities like shellfish and seabirds. Oil persists for 14 months on beaches and because of some toxic and persistent constituents may enter food chains and have far-reaching effects. Since dilution of these toxins reduces landwards, the coast, which may include spawning grounds, is the most vulnerable. The Torrey Canyon disaster in 1967 was the most damaging incident in UK waters, but the immediate destruction of eggs and young fish in the South West of England by oil and oil removers has not had long-term effects and fishing recovered the following season. North Sea fisheries have shown increased landings over the past 50 years which suggests no detrimental effects of oil pollution but exploitation of the North Sea oil field adds a further hazard to marine life.

Thermal pollution of water can occur through the return of water from cooling systems, particularly in power stations and will increase as they reach peak capacity. The Trent has power stations generating 12,000 MW in a distance of 100 miles (160 km).[136] Temperatures of discharged water are often 50°F (10°C) above river water temperature, but studies in the USA[137] suggest that this becomes undetectable 2 miles (3 km) from the outfall. Tower cooling at power stations also increases the oxygen content of the water. Studies of the effect of discharging sea water heated 50°F (10°C) above ambient tempera-ture at 20 Mgal per hr (91,000 m³ per hr) have been made at Hunterston, Ayrshire. These suggest that the effect on marine life is to prolong the breeding season in the immediate vicinity of the effluent,[138] but the overall effect in a temperate climate is very small.

VI CONSERVATION

VI.1 Nature Conservation

The conservation movement in North America was stimulated by the disastrous effects of reckless agricultural exploitation, whilst in the UK the need for conservation has become obvious due to the rapid expansion of urban and industrial life which has depleted the natural landscapes and through its demands changed the rural agricultural scene. For this reason much of the conservation movement in the UK has been directed towards the preservation of natural habitats,[139] but these measures may in many cases only artificially prolong the life of some rare species in danger of extinction. Although man-made, the common lands are open spaces and their preservation desirable on aesthetic grounds. True natural habitats are more difficult to preserve in the UK except in the large areas set aside by the Nature Conservancy in Scotland, the North of England and Wales. The Conservancy established in 1949 and, since 1965, under the wing of the Natural Environment Research Council, is more concerned with management of these reserves by ecological methods than with isolating them. Most of these areas are in uplands, but none can be considered wilderness for the present condition is largely the result of man's activity.[140] The upland moors are largely the result of degeneration while natural fires occurred before man's occupation, their incidence being greatly increased with the use of the uplands for grazing. Burning does not seriously deplete nutrients by removing them in volatile form, but severe burning can destroy the seeds on the ground and thus slow down the rate of recolonisation which is in any case a slow process on high exposed sites. Thus many areas of upland Scotland have suffered soil erosion, the degree depending on physical conditions and land use both at the site and in other areas within the same catchment.[141]

In the lowlands direct changes in habitats have been brought about by agricultural developments. Hedges have been removed in the cereal-growing area of South East and Eastern England; in places as much as 70 per cent of the hedges have disappeared. While intensification of grassland has led to similar changes in the pastoral areas the amount of hedgerow removal is much less serious and in any case the small farms of the West, including Northern Ireland, have a high density of hedges. The removal of some hedges has the effect of reducing species of birds as well as insects, though if the remaining hedges are well cared for the loss could be greatly reduced. The relationship between the wild life and changes in crops is being investigated. Chemicals used on crops or as herbicides on field and road margins can have deleterious effects on wild flowers with harmful effects to useful insects such as bees which are vital in the pollination of fruit trees. Pesticides used on or near waterways can destroy fish. Intensive rearing units for livestock have the special problem of disposal of waste, but until adequately monitored the degree of pollution can not be assessed. The drainage of the wetter lowlands and marshes, whilst creating new agricultural lands, can have a serious effect on water resources and wild life. Dredging and straightening of rivers greatly reduce the cover for birds and animals as well as fish, apart from the often permanent destruction of water plants. Forestry has also changed natural habitats on hillsides and peat bogs, while many old established woodlands have been replanted with conifers. Pure stands of spruce, when mature, have a very limited fauna except on the margins and along breaks. However, the problem is great only with the very large forest units, since small forests provide much more cover for wild life than the open moorlands and farmland they replaced. The policy of planting a variety of trees, including deciduous species, has improved the habitat of many forests though it is difficult to create variety without increasing the risks of windthrow. The planting of windbreaks for both forests and farmland is an opportunity to improve habitats.

VI.2 Land Use Conflicts

Scarcity of agricultural land in the UK has aggravated land use conflicts, for although there is a need for space to be used economically, the land is also a natural resource which will be depleted if not used properly. There is a need for effective control of future development, which has proved possible for nature reserves, but where there is economic exploitation principles of ecology are more difficult to apply. There is no overall authority responsible for resource conservation. The uplands can be used productively both for forests and for annual grazing. Planting of coniferous trees is acceptable on the acid soils but the production of acid *mor humus* by these trees can lead to degradation of soils by accelerated leaching, while deciduous trees, particularly birch, can bring nutrient salts to the surface. The application of fertilisers to make up deficiencies has had the effect of accelerating erosion of peats,[142] but the development of drainage and planting techniques for the wet moorlands has helped to check the accumulation of peat. Grazing is not without its problems for trampling can destroy soil structure and grazing by sheep has led to the spread of *Nardus stricta* previously controlled by cattle. Undesirable effects of sheep grazing can only be remedied by management of the grassland using fertilisers and re-seeding. Since returns for these investments depend on soil, areas of the Scottish Highlands, cultivated before the rapid shrinking of arable in the nineteenth century, are being reseeded. Immediate returns must not be the only consideration as soil improvement gives a longer term return on capital.

The uplands provide facilities for recreation which is almost impossible to evaluate in the same terms as productivity of pasture or forest. Even more than agriculture, forest lends itself to multiple use. The setting-up of forest parks is an example of multiple use and it has been suggested that in future forests should be zoned according to the relative importance they have for timber production, pulp production, or sport and recreation.[143] The Nature Conservancy is attempting to solve the problem of multiple use in the uplands by constructing models to guide future decisions. However, classification of land needs to be further advanced to provide the necessary data.

VI.3 Industrial and Urban Derelict Land

In the lowlands the most serious problem has been the dereliction left by industry. The disposal of waste, destruction of the surface by extensive opencast working, slag heaps and tips have devastated an area estimated at about 250,000 acres (101,000 ha). Despite reclamation this area is growing annually at about 3,500 acres (1,400 ha),[144] and urgently needs rehabilitation. Unlike the development of the uplands, dereliction which frequently occurs in areas of urban blight, should present a unique opportunity at least to improve the existing landscape; the question of optimum use need not arise. Although large acreages of conifers have been planted with the help of the Forestry Commission, the nature of the derelict land greatly reduces its potential for timber. Purely rural areas are also affected, such as china clay tips in Cornwall, and within National Parks and areas of outstanding natural beauty there are 4,500 acres (1,800 ha) of derelict land.[145] Reclamation in the urban areas has been largely for housing development or industral re-zoning and only a small proportion has been developed as open space or for recreation areas.

From a purely physical standpoint the problem of reclamation depends on the type of derelict land. Oxenham usefully differentiates between the mounds and spoilheaps, including those from collieries, quarries, a variety of industries and the opencast workings, and the pits and excavations created in the aftermath of mining. All of these have problems related to their size, shape and the composition of the waste. The number of disciplines involved in the Swansea Valley Project[146] demonstrates the extent of the physical problem of attempting to develop a large area devastated by the spoilheaps from heavy iron and steel industries. It has been suggested earlier that instead of creating new tips on fresh pieces of land the hollows left by the extractive industries could be simultaneously reclaimed. This would not always be possible, but at least some knowledge of the future of the area devastated by tipping could allow effective control over the nature of the tipping. This still does not solve the problem of the great area of existing derelict land. After infilling or levelling the composition may make landscaping difficult. For example in the Swansea project neither the zinc nor the copper waste tips had much vegetation, though steel slag could support growth and there is little knowledge of the degree of tolerance by plant species. Very often the problem is one of excessive drainage which could lead to wilting during rainless periods, rather than toxicity. Some minerals present in waste, while not preventing grass growth, could accumulate and become a hazard to grazing animals. The surface can be made acceptable by topsoiling, applying fertiliser or organic matter and pioneer vegetation, most commonly grass, can be established. Many spoilheaps in the West Riding have been successfully planted in grass. Difficult sites have been planted using soil conditioners which create the necessary crumb structure and improve germination. Steep spoilheaps have been rapidly covered, using sets of creeping bent. Derelict land developed for playing fields requires much more careful landscaping and preparation than these efforts to reduce the ugliness of the landscape. Trees have been planted extensively in County Durham and large schemes in Lancashire have been very successful. Rapid results, though expensive, are obtained by transplanting mature trees using machinery. The total cost of reclaiming the 59,000 acres (24,000 ha) of what has been called 'hard core' derelict land has been estimated at £3½ million over a 10-year period[147] and this still leaves the task of improving the landscape of a further 190,000 acres (77,000 ha).

REFERENCES

1. L D Stamp, *The Land of Britain: Use and Misuse* (London 1947).
2. D A Hill, *The Land of Ulster 1. The Belfast Region* (Belfast HMSO 1947).
3. L J Symons (ed), *Land Use in Northern Ireland,* (London 1963).
4. A Coleman, 'The Second Land Use Survey', *Geographical Journal,* **127**, 2 (1961), pp. 168-80.
5. *The Greater London Plan* (HMSO 1944).
   A Plan for Plymouth (HMSO 1944).
   A Plan for Merseyside (HMSO 1944).
6. Stamp, *The Land of Britain,* p. 353.
7. Agricultural Land Service, *Agricultural Land Classification,* Technical Report 11 (MAFF 1966).
8. North East Development Association, *A Physical Land Classification of Northumberland and Durham and Part of the North Riding of Yorkshire* (Newcastle upon Tyne 1950).
9. J S Bibby and D. Mackney, *Land Use Capability Classification,* Technical Monograph 1 (Soil Survey 1969).
10. A Bleasdale, 'Improvement of Raingauge Networks', *Meteorological Magazine,* **94** (1965), pp. 137-42.
11. J C Rodda, 'Definite Rainfall Measurements and their Significance for Agriculture', in J A Taylor (ed), *The Role of Water in Agriculture,* **12**, (Aberystwyth 1970), pp. 1-10.
12. P A Smithson, 'Effects of Altitude on Rainfall in Scotland', *Weather,* **24**. 9 (1969), pp. 370-6.

13. F H W Green, 'Some Isopleth Maps based on Lysimeter Observations in the British Isles in 1965, 1966 and 1967', *Journal of Hydrology,* **10** (1970), pp. 127-40.

14. H L Penman, 'Natural Evaporation from Open Water, Bare Soil, and Grass', *Proceedings of the Royal Society,* Series A, **193** (1948), pp. 120-45.

15. H L Penman, 'Evaporation over the British Isles', *Quarterly Journal Royal Meteorological Society,* **76** (1950), pp. 372-83.

16. Ministry of Agriculture, *Potential Transpiration,* Technical Bulletin, **16** (HMSO 1967).

17. Ministry of Agriculture, *Potential Transpiration.*

18. K A Edwards, 'Sources of Error in Agricultural Water Budgets' in J A Taylor (ed), *The Role of Water in Agriculture,* **12** (Aberystwyth 1970), pp. 11-23.

19. S Gregory, 'Accumulated Temperature Maps of the British Isles', *Transactions, Institute of British Geographers,* **20** (1954), pp. 59-73.

20. H C Shellard, *Averages of Accumulated Temperatures and Standard Deviation of Monthly Mean Temperature over Britain* (HMSO 1959), pp. 121-50.

21. E L Birse and F T Dry, *Assessment of Climatic Conditions in Scotland,* Macaulay Institute (Aberdeen 1970).

22. For definition of terms see W H Hogg, 'The Analysis of Data with Particular Reference to Frost Surveys', *World Meteorological Organisation, Proceedings of the Regional Training Seminar in Agrometeorology* (Wageningen 1968) pp. 343-50.

23. H H Lamb, 'Britain's Changing Climate', in C C Johnston and L P Smith (eds), *The Biological Significance of Climatic Changes in Britain* (London 1965), pp. 3-31.

24. R W Gloyne, 'A Note on the Average Annual Mean of Daily Earth Temperature in the UK', *Meteorological Magazine,* **100** (1971), pp. 1-6.

25. K Knoch, 'Die Landesklima Aufnahme, Wesen und Methodik', *Berichte des Deutschen Wetterdiensts,* **85**.12 (1963), pp. 1-64.

26. J A Taylor, 'Economic and Ecological Productivity under British Conditions', in J A Taylor (ed), *Climatic Factors and Agricultural Productivity,* **6** (Aberystwyth 1964), pp. 1-5.

27. W H Hogg, *Climate and Surveys of Agricultural Land Use,* UNESCO Natural Resources Research 7, Agroclimatological Methods, (Reading 1966), pp. 281-9.

28. W H Hogg, *The Atlas of Long-term Irrigation Needs for England and Wales* (MAFF 1967).

29. W H Hogg, 'Climatic Factors and Choice of Site, with Special Reference to Horticulture' in C G Johnston and L P Smith (eds), *The Biological Significance of Climatic Changes in Britain* (London 1965), pp. 141-55.

30. C W Thornthwaite and J R Mather, 'The Water Balance', *Drexel Institute of Technology, Laboratories of Climatology,* **8**.1 (1955), pp. 22-67.

31. G R Clarke, *The Study of Soil in the Field* (Cambridge 1971).

32. O T Denmead and R H Shaw, 'Availability of Soil Water to Plants as affected by Soil Moisture Content and Meteorological Conditions', *Journal of Agronomy,* **45** (1962), pp. 385-90.

33. H L Penman, 'Available and Accessible Water', *Proceedings of the Ninth International Congress of Soil Science* (Adelaide 1968), pp. 29-37.

34. A A Rode, 'Hydrological Profile', *Proceedings of the Ninth International Congress of Soil Science* (Adelaide 1968), pp. 165-72.

35. E J Winter, P J Salter and R F Cox, 'Limited Irrigation in Crop Production', in J A Taylor (ed), *The Role of Water in Agriculture,* **12** (Aberystwyth 1970) pp. 147-60.

36. R A Fisher and R M Hagan, 'Plant Water Relations, Irrigation Management and Crop Yield', *Experimental Agriculture,* **1** (1965) pp. 161-77.

37. Ministry of Agriculture, *Potential Transpiration,* p. 17.

38. W Stiles and E A Garwood, 'Drought, Soil Water and Grass Growth', in J A Taylor (ed), *Climatic Factors and Agricultural Productivity,* **6** (Aberystwyth 1964) pp. 19-24.

39. C A Hurst, 'Grass Growing Days' in J A Taylor (ed), *Climatic Factors and Agricultural Productivity,* **6** (Aberystwyth 1964) pp. 25-9.

40. Fisher and Hagan, 'Plant Water Relations, Irrigation Management and Crop Yield', pp. 161-77.

41. W E Davies and B F Tyler, 'The Effect of Weather Conditions on the Growth of Lucerne', in J A Taylor (ed), *Climatic Factors and Agricultural Productivity,* **6** (Aberystwyth 1964) pp. 12-18.

42. J E Goode, 'The Cumulative Effects of Irrigation on Fruit Crops' in J A Taylor (ed), *The Role of Water in Agriculture,* **12** (Aberystwyth 1970) pp. 161-70.

43. W H Hogg, 'Meteorological Factors in Early Crop Production', *Weather,* **22**. 3 (1967), pp. 84-118.

44. Taylor, *Climatic Factors and Agricultural Productivity,* p. 3.

45. S A Grant, 'Temperature and Light Factors in the Growth of Hill Pasture Species', *Hill Land Productivity,* **4**, (British Grassland Society 1969) pp. 30-4.

46. Symons, *Land Use in Northern Ireland,* p. 86.

47. R F Hunter and S A Grant, 'The Effect of Altitude on Grass Growth in Eastern Scotland', *Journal of Applied Ecology,* **8**. 1 (1971), pp. 1-19.

48. Hogg, 'Meteorological Factors in Early Crop Production', p. 90.

49. W H Hogg, 'Basic Frost Irrigation and Degree Day Data for Planning Purposes', in J A Taylor (ed), *Weather Economics,* **11** (Aberystwyth 1970), pp. 27-43.

50. Hogg, 'Meteorological Factors in Early Crop Production', p. 117.

51. W H Hogg, 'Measurements of the Shelter Effects of Landforms and Other Topographical Features', *Scientific Horticulture,* **17** (1965), pp. 20-30.

52. Hogg, 'Climatic features and Choice of Site with Special Reference to Horticulture', pp. 141-55.

53. J M Caborn, 'Shelter Belts and Microclimate', *Forestry Commission Bulletin,* **29** (HMSO 1957).

54. H L Penman, 'Weather and Crops', *Quarterly Journal Royal Meteorological Society,* **88** (1962), pp. 209-19.

55. J Grainger, 'Meteorology and Plant Physiology in Potato Blight Forecasting', in J A Taylor (ed), *Weather and Agriculture* (1967), pp. 105-113.

56. W H Hogg, 'The Use of Upper Air Data in Relation to Plant Disease', in J A Taylor (ed), *Weather and Agriculture* (1967), pp. 115-27.

57. F H W Green, 'The Flexibility of Land Use in Relation to the Water Balance', in J A Taylor (ed), *The Role of Water in Agriculture,* **12** (Aberystwyth 1970), pp. 185-194.

58. C N Prickett, 'Current Trends in the Use of Water', in J A Taylor (ed), *The Role of Water in Agriculture,* **12** (Aberystwyth 1970), pp. 101-19.

59. T O'Riordan, 'Spray Irrigation and the Water Resources Act 1963, *Transactions, Institute of British Geographers,* **49** (1970), pp. 33-46.

60. J T Coppock, *An Agricultural Geography of Great Britain* (London 1971), p. 45.

61. Agricultural Advisory Unit, *Modern Farming and the Soil* (HMSO 1970).

62. AAU, *Modern Farming and the Soil* pp. 60, 67, 74, 81, 86, 91, 97.

63. Military Engineering Experimental Establishment, *The Prediction of Soil Water Tension from Weather Data,* MEXE Report, 1025 (1969).

64. AAU, *Modern Farming and the Soil,* p. 33.

65. W H Hogg, 'Climate and Surveys of Agricultural Land Use,' *UNESCO Natural Resources Research,* **7**, *Agroclimatological Methods* (Reading 1966), pp. 281-9.

66. H C Shellard, *Averages of Accumulated Temperatures and Standard Deviation of Monthly Mean Temperature over Britain, 1921-50,* Meteorological Office (HMSO 1959).

67. E Pollard and A Miller, 'Wind Erosion in the East Anglian Fens', *Weather,* **23.** 10 (1968), pp. 415-17.

68. I Douglas, 'Sediment Yields from Forested and Agricultural Lands', in J A Taylor (ed.), *The Role of Water in Agriculture,* **12,** (Aberystwyth 1970) pp. 57-88.

69. AAU, *Modern Farming and the Soil,* p. 50.

70. *Royal Commission on Environmental Pollution,* First Report, Cmnd 4585 (HMSO 1971).

71. R W Horner, 'The Thames Barrier Scheme', *Journal of the Royal Society of Arts,* **5178,** 119 (1971), pp. 369-80.

72. S Gregory, 'Some Aspects of Water Resource Development in Relation to Lancashire', *Problems of Applied Geography* (Warsaw 1964) p. 270.

73. H Speight, 'Upland Catchment Management: a Water Resources Board View', *Upland Catchment Management Conference* (1968), pp. 3-18.

74. S Gregory, 'Water Resource Exploitation, Policies and Problems' *Geography,* **49** (1964) pp. 310-14.

75. Speight, 'Upland Catchment Management: a Water Resources Board View', p. 12.

76. B Rydz, 'Water Conservation', *Water Resources Committee. Association of River Authorities Year Book* (1969), pp. 195-214.

77. *Central Advisory Committee on the Growing Demand for Water,* First Report of the Sub-Committee (1959).

78. N J Pugh, 'Water Supply', *Symposium on the Conservation of Water Resources in in the UK,* Institute of Civil Engineers (1963), pp. 8-14.

79. *Water Resources of the South East,* Water Resources Board (HMSO 1966).

80. *Water Resources in the North,* Water Resources Board (HMSO 1970).

81. J A Rees, Industrial Demand for Water: a Study of South East England, *LSE Research Monograph,* **3,** (1969) p. 150.

82. Prickett, 'Current Trends in the Use of Water', p. 117.

83. *Water Resources of the South East,* WRB, (HMSO 1966). *Water Resources in the North,* WRB (HMSO 1970). *Water Resources in Wales and the Midlands,* WRB (HMSO 1971).

84. *Water Conservation: England and Wales,* Cmnd 1693 (HMSO 1962).

85. *The Future Management of Water in England and Wales,* DOE (HMSO 1971).

86. Rees, 'Industrial Demand for Water: a study of South East England'.

87. P A Wardle, 'Land Use Policy: The Claims of Forestry on Resources and its Contributions', *Timber Grower,* **19** (1966), pp. 18-25.

88. A J Grayson, 'Forestry in Britain', in J. Ashton and S J Rodgers (eds.), *Economic Change and Agriculture,* (Newcastle upon Tyne, 1967) pp. 168-89.

89. D N McVean and J D Lockie, *Ecology and Land Use in Upland Scotland* (Edinburgh 1969).

90. Grayson, 'Forestry in Britain'.

91. D G Pyatt, 'Soil Problems in Border Forestry', *Proceedings of the North of England Soils Discussion Group,* **2** (1966), pp. 43-5.

92. G P Rouse, 'Some Effects of Rainfall on Tree Growth and Forest Fires', *Weather,* **16.** 9 (1961), pp. 304-11.

93. Forestry Commission, *Forest Research* (HMSO 1968), p. 55.

94. P J O'Hare, 'A Comparison of the Effect of Young Forest and Grassland on the Water Table in Blanket Peat', in J A Taylor (ed.), *Research Papers in Forest Meteorology* (Aberystwyth 1972), pp. 126-33.

95. A J Rutter, 'Evaporation from Forests' in J A Taylor (ed.), *Research Papers in Forest Meteorology* (Aberystwyth 1972), pp. 75-90. J W Holmes and J S Colville, 'On the Water Balance of Grassland', *International Congress of Soil Science*, **9**, 1 (Sydney 1968), pp. 39-46.

96. N V Pears, 'Interpretation Problems in the Study of Tree Line Fluctuations', in J A Taylor (ed.), *Research Papers in Forest Meteorology* (Aberystwyth 1972), pp. 31-45.

97. Rouse, 'Some Effects of Rainfall on Tree Growth and Forest Fires', p. 306.

98. E L Birse and L Robertson, *Assessment of Climatic Conditions in Scotland*, **2** (Soil Survey of Scotland 1970).

99. Forestry Commission, *Forest Research*, p. 38.

100. A I Fraser, 'The Effect of Climatic Factors on the Development of Plantation Structure', in J A Taylor (ed.), *Research Papers in Forest Meteorology* (Aberystwyth 1972), pp. 59-74.

101. D G Roberts, 'The Modification of Geomorphic Shelter by Shelter Belts', in J A Taylor (ed.), *Research Papers in Forest Meteorology*, (Aberystwyth 1972), pp. 134-46.

102. G E Jones, 'An Investigation into the Possible Causes of Poor Growth in Sitka Spruce', in J A Taylor (ed.), *Research Papers in Forest Meteorology*, (Aberystwyth 1972), pp. 147-55.

103. Pyatt, 'Soil Problems in Border Forestry', p. 41.

104. P A Wardle, 'Weather and Risk in Forestry', in J A Taylor (ed.), *Weather Economics* (Aberystwyth 1970), pp. 67-82.

105. Coburn, 'Shelter Belts and Microclimate'.

106. Wardle, 'Weather and Risk in Forestry', p. 78.

107. Rouse, 'Some Effects of Rainfall on Tree Growth and Forest Fires', p. 309.

108. R H Best, 'Land Use and Resources', *Institute of British Geographers*, Special Publication 1 (1968), pp. 89-100.

109. S H Beaver, 'Changes in Industrial Land Use, 1930-67', *Institute of British Geographers*, Special Publication 1 (1968), pp. 101-9.

110. J K A Bleasdale, 'The Effects of Air Pollution on Plant Growth', in W B Yapp (ed.) *The Effects of Air Pollution on Living Material*, Institute of Biology Symposium 8 (London 1959), pp. 111-30.

111. *Royal Commission on Environmental Pollution*, First Report, Cmnd 4585 (HMSO 1971); Second Report, Cmnd 4894, Third Report, Cmnd 5054 (HMSO 1972).

112. M Nicholson, *The Environmental Revolution* (London 1970).

113. C L Wilson (Director), *Man's Impact on the Global Environment* (MIT 1970).

114. Ministry of Housing and Local Government, *Chimney Heights*, 1956 Clean Air Act Memorandum (HMSO 1967).

115. *Dust and Fumes in Factory Atmospheres* (HMSO 1968).

116. D F Ball, 'The Identification and Measurement of Gaseous Pollutants', *International Journal of Environmental Studies*, **14** (1971), pp. 267-74.

117. E N Lawrence, 'Recent Trends in Solar Radiation, Maximum Black-bulb and Air Temperatures in Britain', *Weather*, **26**. 4 (1971), pp. 164-72.

118. O L Gilbert, 'Some Indirect Effects of Air Pollution on Bark Living Invertebrates', *Journal of Applied Ecology*, **8**. 1 (1971), pp. 77-84.

119. Jones, 'An Investigation into the Possible Causes of Poor Growth in Sitka Spruce', p. 154.

120. D L Hawksworth, 'Lichens as Litmus for Air Pollution', *International Journal of Environmental Studies*, **14** (1971), pp. 281-96.

121. A J Robinson, 'Air Pollution', *Journal of the Royal Society of Arts*, **5180**, CXIX (1971), pp. 505-16.

122. L E Reed and P E Trott, Continuous Measurement of Carbon Monoxide in Streets, 1967-9, in press, quoted by A J Robinson (1971) p. 514.

123. Ministry of Technology, *The Investigation of Atmospheric Pollution, 1958-63* (HMSO 1965).

124. D H F Atkins, R A Cox, and A E J Eggleton, 'Photochemical Ozone and Sulphuric Acid Aerosol Formation in the Atmosphere over Southern England', *Nature* **235** (1972), pp. 372-6.

125. A Garnett, 'Weather Inversions and Air Pollution', *Clean Air* (1971) pp. 16-21.

126. Ministry of Housing and Local Government, *Chimney Heights,* 1956 Clean Air Act Memorandum, 2nd ed. (HMSO 1967).

127. B D Gooriah, *Distribution of Pollution at Some Country Sites* (Warren Spring Laboratory 1968).

128. Department of the Environment, *Refuse Disposal* (HMSO 1971).

129. *Report of the Technical Committee on the Disposal of Toxic Solid Wastes* (HMSO 1970).

130. Department of the Environment, *River Pollution Survey of England and Wales.* Updated 1972 (HMSO 1972).

131. A J O'Sullivan, 'Ecological Effects of Sewage Discharge in the Marine Environment', *Proceedings of the Royal Society,* Series B, **177** (1971), pp. 331-51.

132. D S Woodhead, 'The Biological Effect of Radioactive Waste', *Proceedings of the Royal Society,* Series B, **177** (1971), pp. 423-37.

133. M I Abdullah *et al.,* 'Heavy Metal Concentration in Coastal Waters' *Nature,* **235** (1972), pp. 158-60.

134. G Bryan, 'The Effects of Heavy Metals on Marine and Estuarine Organisms', *Proceedings of the Royal Society,* Series B, **177** (1971), pp. 389-410.

135. F S Russell *et al.,* 'Changes in the Biological Conditions in the English Channel', *Nature,* **234** (1971), pp. 468-70.

136. F B Hawes, 'Thermal Problems "Old Hat" in Britain', *CEGB Newsletter,* **83,** (1970).

137. D Merriman, 'The Calefaction of a River', *Scientific American,* **222** (1970), pp.42-52.

138. P R O Barnett, 'Some Changes in Intertidal Sand Communities due to Thermal Pollution', *Proceedings of the Royal Society,* Series B, **177** (1971), pp. 353-64.

139. L D Stamp, *Nature Conservation in Britain* (London 1969).

140. W M Pearsall, *Mountains and Moorlands* (London 1950).

141. D N McVean and J D Lockie, *Ecology and Land Use in Upland Scotland* (Edinburgh 1969).

142. R E Parker, 'Factors Limiting Tree Growth on Peat Soils', *Irish Forestry,* **19.** 1 (1962), pp. 60-81.

143. McVean and Lockie, 'Ecology and Land Use in Upland Scotland', p. 105.

144. J.Barr, *Derelict Britain* (London 1969), p. 15.

145. J R Oxenham, *Reclaiming Derelict Land* (London 1966).

146. K J Hilton (ed.), *The Lower Swansea Valley Project* (London 1967).

147. G Christian, *Tomorrow's Countryside: the Road to the Seventies* (London 1966).

4

Power and the
Industrial Structure

I   THE POWER INDUSTRIES

I.1   Significance and Structure

The fuel and power industries play a vital role in the economic, social and political life
of the modern UK. The dependence of manufacturing on energy supplies, the large
numbers of people they employ and the long debates in Parliament over various aspects
of energy policy, serve to indicate their all-pervasive importance. It is hardly surprising
therefore that the geography of these industries has always been of practical relevance and
concern. Recently their geography has undergone a phase of rapid change; change so far-
reaching that for some of the industries the geographical patterns of the late 1950s were
barely recognisable by the early 1970s. Such transformation has considerable planning
implications, and it is the purpose here not just to describe what has happened, but also
to indicate the main forces generating change and shaping the results. This task is somewhat complicated by the variety of industries forming the fuel and power group, and
the recent changes in their relative importance and in some cases their individual character.

In the past there was a distinction between the primary energy industries of coal and
petroleum which could provide direct energy, and the secondary energy industries of
electricity and gas which used the primary energy sources for their production. The use
of natural gas and of nuclear power in electricity stations has complicated this simple
distinction. Natural gas is now a primary fuel not derived from conversion, and nuclear
power is a primary input but usable in electrical form. A distinction also exists between
the older industries of coal and gas, with their much more influential inherited structures,
and the newer petroleum and electricity industries which are products of a much later
stage in the industrialisation process.[1] Despite these complexities it is possible to identify
certain major factors explaining the spatial patterns that can be observed. In terms of
classical location theory these are transport economies, markets, political factors including
ownership, technology and physical geography. The importance of all these is brought out
in each of the power industries in turn.

The major primary sources of power in the UK in 1970 were coal, oil, natural gas and
nuclear energy. Water power also made a minor contribution but with little potential
for expansion. Each of these primary sources can be used directly, but one-third of the
energy consumed in the UK in 1970 was in the secondary form of either electricity or
manufactured gas. All the primary sources were used for electricity generation, and coal
and oil were used as sources of gas to supplement the supplies of natural gas available.
Table 4.1 shows the consumption of each of these sources of energy in the UK in 1970.

The most striking feature of the table 4.2 is the continuing dependence upon coal,
which still provided nearly half the nation's energy requirements. But twenty years earlier
coal was providing 90 per cent of the energy consumed, and even in 1960 it accounted

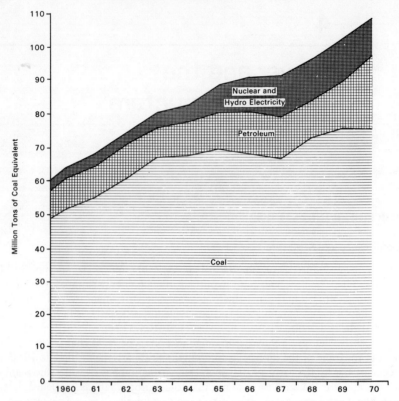

Figure 4.1a   Primary energy consumption in the fuel conversion industries, UK, 1960-70

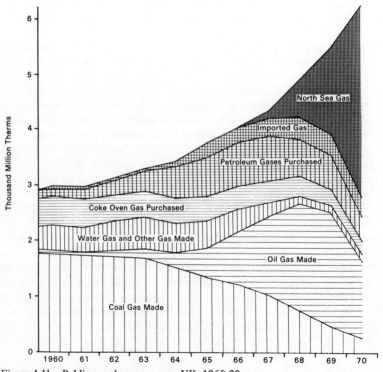

Figure 4.1b   Public supply gas sources, UK, 1960-70

TABLE 4.1   Energy Consumption, UK, 1970

	Million tons of coal or coal equivalent			
	Amount	%	Used by electricity industry	Used by gas industry
Coal	154·5	47·1	76·0	4·2
Petroleum	145·6	44·4	21·1	7·6
Natural gas	16·0	4·9	0·2	10·4
Nuclear electricity	9·4	2·8	9·4	-
Hydroelectricity	2·6	0·8	2·3	-
Total	328·1	100·0	109·0	22·2

Source: Digest of Energy Statistics HMSO (1971)

for 75 per cent. The decline of coal was part of the shift which occurred in the UK energy budget as alternative energy sources were developed. Until 1960 the UK was essentially a two-fuel economy dependent upon coal and oil. Prior to 1956 coal had had difficulty in meeting the growing fuel demands of the nation, and petroleum consumption rose to fill the energy gap. Although declining in *relative* importance, however, coal *production* was actually increasing, reaching a peak post-war output of 217 million tons in 1956. Subsequently coal consumption declined and petroleum output underwent massive expansion. In the 1960s the use of nuclear power and natural gas became significant, and by 1970 they contributed 3 per cent and 5 per cent respectively of the national energy consumed. The UK had by then changed from a two-fuel to a four-fuel economy.

Within the total picture there were significant shifts in the use of coal, and in the gas industry. For coal the major change was from direct consumption to indirect consumption as sales to the electricity generating industry rose from less than 20 per cent of the total in 1950 to nearly 50 per cent in 1970 (table 4.2). For gas, the major shift was the replacement of coal as the primary source of fuel input during the 1960s, first by petroleum and then by natural gas (figure 4.1). The effect of these changes on the geography of production and distribution of gas was dramatic, and the implications of the availability of cheap natural gas were beginning to affect all the fuel industries in 1970.

TABLE 4.2   Coal Consumption, UK, 1950-70 (million tons)

		1950	1960	1970
	Electricity power stations	33·0	51·9	76·0
Indirect	Gas Works	26·2	22·6	4·2
consumption	Coke ovens	22·6	28·8	24·9
	Other fuel conversion	3·0*	2·3	4·1
Total Indirect Consumption		84·8	105·6	109·2
	Agriculture	0·8	0·3	0·2
	Collieries	10·7	5·0	1·9
Direct	Industry	44·6	34·9	19·3
Consumption	Rail and water transport	15·4	9·3	0·2
	Domestic	37·5	35·5	19·9
	Public services ⎫ Miscellaneous ⎭	5·7	4·0	2·9
Total Direct Consumption		114·7	91·1	45·2
GRAND TOTAL		199·5	196·7	154·4

Source: Digests of Energy Statistics (HMSO)

*   Estimated

I.2   Coal

Coal-mining is almost the archetype primary industry. It experiences high weight loss in use since the energy it produces has little or no weight and the residue after the energy is extracted is waste. Coal production is tied to fixed locations, since the raw materials are available only at the coalfields. It has a high weight output per employee, and its location pattern has been considerably affected by increased economies of scale and by mechanisation. More than any other fuel industry it has suffered from government policies, having had to balance direct economic profit against maximum public good in the national economy. It has also been much more affected by technological change than the other fuel industries, because being much older it had a much greater inheritance of obsolescence. Unlike the others it has suffered continuing decline of output since 1960 and so had the unenviable task of coping with massive innovational change at a time of contraction. Being older, it had acquired a whole set of social and economic responsibilities in the coal-mining regions which coloured government decisions about its development.

In examining the main features of the geography of the industry attention is focused on the National Coal Board (NCB) deep-mining operations. Private coal-mining and open-cast mining operations are included in a final section.

Coal resources: Estimates of the amount of coal available in the UK vary according to the criteria which are used. For the present we may take it that, at current production rates around 140 million tons a year, there is sufficient to last for at least two more centuries. How much of this will ever actually be extracted depends not so much upon the quantity available as upon the circumstances which prevail in the future when mining decisions are made.

Traditionally the distribution of coal-mining has been shown on a map by the geological boundaries of the coalfields. By 1970 these were somewhat misleading, since deep-mining is now confined to only parts of the geological coalfields. For understanding the pattern of mining it is much more relevant to have a knowledge of the types of coal being mined in each area and of the structural features which affect mining operations. The types of coal being mined in 1970 are shown in fig. 4.2. The lower the number of a coal, the higher its quality. Certain coals are required for specific purposes: anthracite is best suited to space heating and smokeless zone use, coking coal for steel-making, steam and general coals for electricity generation. Figure 4.2. shows that in general the higher quality specific coals commanding higher prices form a higher proportion of output in North East England, Scotland and Wales, and the lower quality general coals dominate output in the interior English coalfields.

Structural conditions vary significantly over the coalfields. The Scottish and Welsh coalfields suffer most from variation of geological conditions. Not only is there much more faulting and folding on a major and minor scale, but variations in seam thickness are much more frequent. In general the more regular the coal seams the more amenable they are to mechanised working and automation. Clearly production control and planning is easier and more successful under uniform conditions, all factors contributing to lower mining costs.

Added to these features is the importance of the past history of mining. Those areas with coal occurring at or close to the surface, especially near the coast, were the earliest to experience mining on an industrial scale. Such areas have the most depleted reserves, but more than that they have older and generally smaller collieries. In contrast, where the coal lay deepest or concealed beneath later rocks, coal-mining developed much later. The collieries in these areas were initially larger and laid out on more recent lines to tap seams previously unworked. In the first group are the peripheral coalfields of Scotland,

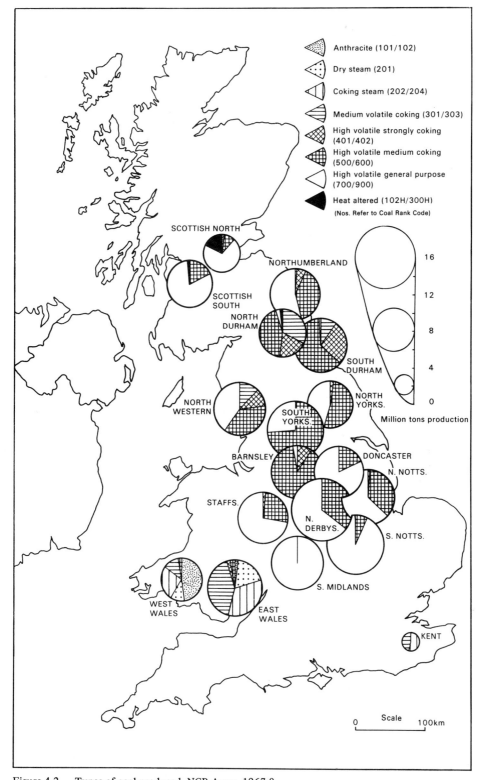

Figure 4.2   Types of coal produced, NCB Areas, 1967-8

Wales, the North West and the North East of England. The newer areas where deeper coal is being worked are East Durham and the eastern areas of the Yorkshire, Derbyshire and Nottinghamshire coalfields and the Kent coalfield.

Nationalisation to 1970: In 1947 the NCB inherited an industry both obsolete and run-down. Profits in the inter-war period had been inadequate to allow sufficient invest-ment to keep the industry up-to-date. The position had been aggravated by the subsequent six years of war, during which time capital, men and equipment were all in short supply and the industry was operated with only the minimum amount of maintenance to maintain output. The first task of the NCB was to right these inherited wrongs, and bring the industry to an acceptable modern state. Large sums of money needed to be invested but this could be justified only where sufficient reserves were thought to be available to give an economic return. Until 1956 the industry was unable to meet all the domestic demand for coal, the inability of the coal industry to raise output caused serious concern,[2] and all plans laid up to that date were based upon a continuing need to increase output. There was no serious competition from alternative fuels.

Between 1956 and 1960 demand for coal slackened, for three main reasons. The first was a period of industrial recession which reduced the overall demand for energy; the second was the changing structure of the UK economy. The expanding sectors were those dependent upon oil and electricity, whilst the heavy coal-using industries were slow-growing or in decline. The third cause was the increasingly efficient use of coal by the heavy coal consumers such as the steel and electricity industries, and the conversion of other traditional coal consumers to new fuels such as occurred in the dieselisation of the railways. After 1960 coal also began to suffer severe competition for its markets from other fuels. At the beginning of the decade the main competitor was fuel oil, but by 1970 the availability of cheap natural gas in large quantities offered a further threat. During this decade the coal industry switched emphasis to minimising costs, in place of maximising output which had been the aim in the 1950s. Planned output targets which had been maintained at over 200 million tons per annum up to 1960 were progressively reduced, until in 1970 the target of 140 million tons a year looked rather high.

TABLE 4.3   NCB Productivity and Production Costs by Regions, 1950 and 1960

	Productivity output per man shift		Production costs per ton saleable	
	1950	1960	1950	1960
	cwt	cwt	s/d	s/d
Scottish	22·8	22·4	46/9	101/6
Northern	22·9	27·3	48/11	87/9
Durham	20·0	22·3	51/7	97/2
N. Western	21·3	26·0	50/0	93/1
W. Midlands	26·3	28·6	42/7	87/0
S. Western	18·6	20·6	54/7	107/3
Yorkshire	26·3	31·0	42/5	76/3
E. Midlands	34·5	42·1	36/6	63/5
Kent	24·8	23·3	49/4	106/7
Total	24·2	28·0	45/5	84/5

Source: NCB

Geographical impact of the changes: Overall there was a decline in deep-mined coal output of 35 per cent between 1950 and 1970. Table 4.4 shows that there were consider-able differences from coalfield to coalfield. All the northern and western coalfields experienced a halving of their tonnage output. Output in the West Midlands fell by a

TABLE 4.4   NCB Deep-mined Coal Production by Regions, 1950-70

	Output (million tons saleable coal)			%		
	1950	1960	1970*	1950	1960	1970
Scottish	23·0	17·7	11·4	11	10	8
Northumberland	13·2	12·0	6·9	7	6	5
Durham	26·3	22·8	13·6	13	12	10
Yorkshire	42·4	40·4	35·9	21	22	25
N. Western	14·2	12·9	7·0	7	7	5
E. Midlands	39·9	43·7	42·8	20	24	30
W. Midlands	17·3	13·8	8·6	8	8	6
S. Western	24·1	19·1	12·8	12	10	9
S. Eastern	1·7	1·5	1·1	1	1	1
UK	202·4	183·9	140·0	100	100	100

Sources: Digests of Energy Statistics (HMSO), and NCB

* Distribution between regions is estimated because of changes in regional boundaries between 1960 and 1970

similar percentage, whilst production in the Kent coalfield remained virtually unchanged. The lowland coalfields which stretch from the Aire Valley in Yorkshire along the eastern flanks of the Pennines as far as Leicestershire, were much less affected by the decline. Production in Yorkshire fell by only 15 per cent over the two decades, and in the East Midlands output actually increased. The major geographical effect was for coal output to be increasingly concentrated in the Yorkshire and East Midlands fields, which were responsible for producing nearly 60 per cent of the nation's coal by 1970, compared with only 41 per cent in 1950.

There are several reasons for this regional shift. Of the factors listed earlier as being of major importance, technology linked with physical conditions has played the greatest role. This was especially true after 1960 when minimisation of production costs assumed priority. The much more regular geological conditions of the East Midlands and South Yorkshire coalfields were more suited to the increased use of machines and made forward planning more reliable; in addition, it is the deeper coal seams and those concealed beneath younger rocks which are being worked. Under these conditions both higher productivity rates and greater economies of scale have been easier to achieve, and production costs are lower as shown by tables 4.3. and 4.5.

What is less obvious from the figures is why coal-mining has been continued to such an extent in the high-cost coalfield areas. It is here that the market, transport economies and political factors play an important part.

The market has influenced the pattern in several ways. Not all coal is alike and certain markets require specific types of coal. As a general rule the highest quality coals form a much higher proportion in the peripheral coalfields than in the east central coalfields. High quality and high costs have in the past thus been spatially correlated. Good examples are the anthracite coals of western South Wales, and the coking coals of West Durham. As long as the markets exist for these coals, output will be maintained. The high price charged for these coals also partly compensates for their higher production costs.

Markets also help to explain continuing production in another way. Of all the sources of energy, coal is probably the most expensive to transport. In 1967 the cost of transporting coal added an average £1 per ton or 20 per cent to the cost of production.[3] Distance to a certain extent thus protects the local markets of the high-cost coalfield coal from competition from coal brought in from other places.[4] This has certainly been the case in Scotland and parts of Wales, which are the remotest areas from the low-cost East Midlands and South Yorkshire coalfields. Similarly output in North East England

TABLE 4.5   NCB. Deep-mined Coal Operations, 1963-4 and 1970-1

	Saleable output		Productivity OMS overall		Costs per ton saleable†	Number of collieries in production at end of year	
	Million tons		Cwt		£ p		
	1963/4	1970/1	1963/4	1970/1	1970/1	1963/4	1970/1
Scottish North	7·5	5·3	28·5	40·1	6·74	47	10
Scottish South	9·0	6·0	27·7	36·1	6·70	40	22
Northumberland	11·0	6·3	32·8	41·3	5·88	35	16
North Durham	9·4	5·1	25·2	34·1	7·13	52	19
South Durham	12·1	7·6	26·9	35·1	6·73	35	15
North Yorkshire	10·4	9·5	38·2	42·0	4·90	30	21
Doncaster	9·8	8·0	37·2	47·8	5·73	14	10
Barnsley	11·7	7·8	36·3	43·2	5·86	36	22
South Yorkshire	11·2	9·5	34·3	45·1	5·60	22	19
North Western	12·8	6·1	30·0	33·8	7·48	42	16
North Derbyshire	14·6	9·8	41·9	60·9	4·52	34	14
North Notts.	11·1	12·1	49·3	60·8	4·38	12	15
South Notts.	14·0	10·6	52·9	57·3	4·73	19	12
South Midlands	11·1	8·9	43·7	58·8	4·97	17	15
Staffordshire	10·9	8·3	36·1	51·2	5·48	35	13
E. Wales	11·9	6·9	25·2	28·3	7·63	51	30
W. Wales	7·6	4·8	22·1	31·0	8·23	51	21
Kent	1·6	1·0	28·2	27·4	8·49	4	3
UK	187·6*	133·4*	33·4	44·2	5·80	576	293

Source: NCB

*   Columns do not add up to total because of rounding

†   Figures for 1963/4 not available.

was higher than it would otherwise have been because of the low cost of sending coal by ship to its traditional market area of South East England.

Transport costs contributed to the increased dominance of the East Midlands and South Yorkshire coalfields. With coal production costs cheaper there, they attracted large proportions of the coal-fired electricity generating stations built since 1950. It is cheaper to send base load electricity to markets than to send the coal and generate the electricity there. Consumption of coal for electricity generation has risen markedly between 1950 and 1970, maintaining and strengthening the position of the East Midlands and South Yorkshire coalfields. Geographically the low-cost coalfields also lie closer to the major coal consumption areas of the West Midlands and South East England. They thus benefit from lower land transport costs to these markets.

Political factors are important in explaining the maintenance of so much deep-mined output in the high-cost areas. The government has always taken account of the fact that coal is an indigenous fuel, whereas until 1970 most of the alternatives had to be imported at the cost of foreign exchange. In addition, in many parts of the coalfields, coal-mining has long been the mainstay of local communities. Reduction of output has regional social and economic repercussions of considerable significance. With these in mind, successive governments have taken measures to limit the rate of coal-mining decline since 1960 and to ameliorate the local impact of colliery closures. Although this benefits all the coalfields, it is the high-cost areas that have most of the marginal units, which would have gone out of production without such protection. On the national front, the government imposed a special tax on fuel oil to limit its effectiveness in competition with coal. This gave an effective price advantage to coal of 130p per ton. In addition, permission for the import of coal was granted only under special circumstances and the conversion of coal-fired power stations to other fuels was restricted. The 1967 Coal Industry Act went further and arranged for additional consumption of coal at power stations by means of subsidies. The extra coal used in this way amounted to some 6·5 million tons in 1968-9.[5] Government financial support was also given to keep collieries open when closure would have caused local social hardship.

These changes in the coal industry affected the regional distribution of coal production, and the local patterns of collieries within each coalfield. Two main features are worthy of comment. In all the coalfields there has been a tendency for mining to cease along the long-worked outcrops, and to concentrate on working the deeper and concealed areas. The other feature has been the reduction in the number of collieries to a greater extent than the decline in output might lead one to expect. This occurred primarily because of the increases both in productivity and in the average size of individual collieries. The effect was to replace a pattern of a large number of small collieries, by one which was a much smaller number of larger collieries; furthermore the distance between collieries thus tended to increase. These two changes mean that larger areas within the geological limits of all the coalfields no longer have any collieries, and are not deep coal-mining areas.

With the political involvement must be coupled ownership, since the coal industry has been nationalised since 1947. The geographical effect of planning and operating the industry as a whole since then has been considerable. It is this that has made rationalisation and centralisation possible in a way inconceivable had the coal mines remained in the hands of a large number of privately-owned companies.

Open cast and private mining: The deep mines of the NCB are not the only producers of coal in the UK. Private mines still operate under licence from the Coal Board, but in the 1960s their output never exceeded 2 million tons a year so that their contribution is insignificant in a national context. Most of the output comes from South Wales, where it helps supplement production of high quality steam and anthracite coals from pockets too small to make exploitation by the Coal Board worthwhile.[6] Opencast mining is much more important: output in 1970 was 7·8 million tons. The mines are the responsibility of the Opencast Executive of the NCB who contract the actual extraction out to private firms. Most of the firms involved are well-known national construction companies such as Wimpey and MacAlpine who have the expertise and the equipment available for the heavy earthmoving tasks involved. Opencast sites exploit mainly shallow seams though they do extend to depths of 500 ft (152m) or more at times, and are thus normally located on the exposed coalfields mainly along the outcrops. Any one site is temporary, with an average working life of around five years, seldom more than ten years. Opencast mining has always been very profitable for the NCB and although up to 1970 production never exceeded 15 million tons a year, it could easily be increased substantially. With lower costs, opencast production would make coal much more competitive as a fuel than it is at present. The reason for restricted output is the agreement with the unions that opencast coal-mining be limited to that necessary to supplement the deep-mined output where the latter fails to meet the demand. Thus a large proportion of the anthracite consumed in the UK comes from opencast sites in western South Wales. Achievement of profitable deep-mined output there has always been difficult and opencast mining has expanded in supplementation. If controls on opencast mining were to be relaxed there is little doubt that output by this means would expand dramatically and the geography of coal-mining in the UK would undergo a further change.

Coal distribution: In 1958 a Report of Enquiry into coal distribution costs in Great Britain was able to state that, 'In spite of great changes which have taken place since the

1930s in the conditions in which the trade is carried on, the general methods of distribution and the structure of the trade do not appear to have undergone much change'.[7]
Until then, with coal in short supply and government control of the allocation of supplies,
the lack of change was not all that important. But coal distribution costs at that time
were equivalent to 25 per cent of the pit price of the coal. It was clear that under the
conditions of increased competition during the 1960s this was an area for considerable
improvement. A programme to modernise and rationalise coal distribution to cut costs
was begun in the early 1960s, and was nearing completion by 1970.[8] It was accelerated
by the reorganisation and rationalisation of the railways, in which the concentration of
services was taking place at the same time and much more realistic charges for the small
unit load movements were beginning to be made.

Deliveries of coal to power stations were the easiest to improve and were important
since they represented nearly half the inland market. Economies of scale here were
achieved by the introduction of 'merry-go-round' trains. These were trains used
exclusively between collieries and power stations, and were made up of wagons which
were never uncoupled. At the power-station end mechanical unloading and coal-handling
facilities made the process even cheaper. By 1970 a start had also been made in introducing
rapid loading techniques at the collieries as well. This kind of organisation, although still
using discontinuous transport media, gets closest to movement by pipeline, and has cut
delivered coal cost substantially. The other way in which economies of scale have been
achieved is through centralisation of the retail distribution depots; in 1958 there were
still some 5,800 in the UK. The average annual tonnage handled per trader using these
depots was 1,740 and there were 16,778 traders. Of this total, only 7,533 traders handled
over 1,000 tons of coal a year, and on this basis could be said to be fully employed in
the retail trade.[9] With so many depots involved, individual deliveries of coal were small
and few depots justified mechanical handling facilities for unloading, storing and bagging.
The trade was essentially labour-intensive. This was further encouraged at the consumer
level. There was little or no encouragement of domestic consumers, especially, to provide
larger storage space so that deliveries could be made in bulk. In the 1960s all this was
changed. Coal distribution depots were centralised, so that by 1971 only 519 remained.
Each of these was designed to deal with much larger quantities of coal, with adequate
ground storage to ensure continuity of supplies and with a modern efficient layout.
Supplies could be delivered by the trainload, and installation of automatic handling
equipment was justified by the larger quantities of coal handled. These depots were
located in those centres accessible to the largest number of customers in the shortest
distance. This reduced the transport element in the delivered cost of coal. The problem
of the small storage capacity of the domestic consumer remained. Colliery production
capacity is relatively inflexible in the short term, so that coal must be stored in sufficient
quantity to meet peak demands. This is best done by the consumer, since any other
solution involves strain on the transport facilities for delivery at times when bad weather
makes this strain difficult to bear. A differential price was introduced to encourage this,
making coal cheaper in summer and dearer in winter. This had some effect, but there
are still too many retail consumers who take delivery weekly or in one or two hundred-
weight bags and who invariably suffer in bad winters because supplies cannot be made
available immediately when demand takes a sudden and massive upsurge.

The basic pattern of distribution then has been one of concentration and rationalisation
to take advantage of economies of scale. This has changed the location of depots, concentrating them into the largest central places and increasing the scale of individual
depots. Ownership has been important in this. With one single supplier in the NCB the
improvements have been much more easily achieved than if the industry had remained
split between a large number of private companies.

I.3   Oil-refining

Prior to 1945, oil was a minor source of energy in Britain, and oil-refining was even
less important. As late as 1950 oil supplied less than 10 per cent of the British fuel market.
Total imports at that time amounted to less than 20 million tons, only half of which was
crude oil for domestic processing. From that limited base consumption rose rapidly, and
domestic oil-refining capacity underwent massive expansion. By 1960 total imports were
running at nearly 60 million tons a year, with British refineries processing 45 million tons
of crude oil; by 1970 consumption had further doubled to 90 million tons. Domestic
refineries were now capable of processing 112 million tons of crude oil a year, a tenfold
increase in capacity in less than twenty years. Part of the increase was of course attributable to the expansion of captive markets for oil in the transport and petrochemical fields.
Neither of these is considered in detail here, and attention is concentrated on power for
industrial and heating purposes. By 1980 the estimated UK refinery capacity is 181
million tons.

A number of factors contributed to the spectacular expansion of oil consumption in
the 1950s. Consumption of all forms of energy grew rapidly as the economy expanded.
Within this national growth, up to 1956 oil had relatively little competition. Coal could
not meet all the demand, and oil contributed to making-up the deficit. It did little more
than that, because it was still relatively expensive to import crude oil, but a number of
trends were already favouring increased oil consumption. The fastest-growing industries
were those using electricity or oil as their main source of energy and a number of traditional
major coal users were converting to oil, notably the railways. During the mild economic
recession of the late 1950s the oil-consuming industries suffered less from the downturn
in business. After 1960 oil consumption recovered with the economy and resumed its
previous rapid growth. Fuel oil now became more cost-competitive, had the advantage
over coal of being easier to handle and could be much more closely controlled quantita-
tively and qualitatively in its use. By 1970 even the electricity generation industry,
which took half the coal consumed in the UK, was taking 14 million tons of coal equivalent in oil, and was kept from taking more only by government intervention. It was only
in the late 1960s that a challenge to oil began to appear in significant quantities in the
British fuel market in the form of North Sea natural gas. By 1970 the availability of
this third primary fuel in the UK had had little effect on oil consumption, but there is
no doubt that use of gas will increase and that it will achieve at least some of its expansion at the expense of markets which would otherwise have gone to oil.

Geographical impact: The more than tenfold increase in British oil-refining capacity,
1950-70, brought about several spatial changes of geographical significance, as seen in
Table 4.6. The most striking feature was the spread of oil-refining into three new regions
in the 1960s; these had acquired 20 per cent of the British capacity by 1970. Most of
this change was at the expense of the North West, which failed to grow at a sufficient
rate to maintain its position, and of Scotland, both of which became relatively less
important. Despite these changes, over 40 per cent of the oil-refining capacity remained
concentrated in the South East of England (figure 4.3).

The other feature of geographical interest was the increase in average size of refineries.
In 1950 the largest could process only 2·6 million tons of crude oil a year. By 1970 there
were four with capacities of over ten million tons a year, i.e. individually greater than
the national refining capacity twenty years earlier, and ten others were larger than the
largest in 1950 (table 4.7). Nearly 90 per cent of the refinery capacity was concentrated
in these giant units. Clearly the pattern and landscape impact of these was much different
to that which would have resulted if refineries had remained individually small.

Market attraction played a dominant role in the location of oil-refining in the UK.

TABLE 4.6   Regional Distribution of Crude Oil Distillation Capacity, UK, 1950-70

	Million tons per annum at end of year		
	1950	1960	1970
South East	3·0	30·4	43·6
West Midlands			
North West	3·3	7·5	13·1
Scotland	0·8	3·6	9·3
North			10·3
Yorkshire and Humberside			10·9
East Midlands			
East Anglia			
South West			
Wales	2·6	7·7	23·9
Northern Ireland			1·5
Total	9·7	49·2	112·6

Source: Digests of Energy Statistics (HMSO)

With little weight loss in processing there is no heavy penalty incurred through carrying the raw material to market for refining. Moreover, with virtually all the crude oil imported, there is no attraction to a raw material site within Britain. Most refinery capacity is therefore located at an import point as close as possible to the market. Other locations have been chosen only where special factors operate. The largest market for refinery products has always been South East England, with Greater London having the largest single concentration of demand. It is hardly surprising therefore that the Thames Estuary has attracted the largest concentration of oil-refining, or that together with Fawley on Southampton Water, this south-east corner of the UK in 1970 had over 40 per cent of

TABLE 4.7   Distillation Capacity of Oil Refineries, UK, 1970

	Million tons per annum
Coryton	6·7
Eastham	0·5
Fawley	16·2
Isle of Grain	10·0
Kingsnorth	0·3
Shellhaven	10·0
Barton	0·2
Ellesmere Port	0·3
Heysham	2·0
Stanlow	10·5
Weaste	0·2
Ardrossan	0·2
Dundee	0·1
Grangemouth	9·0
N. Tees	5·0
Teesport	5·3
Killingholme	4·0
South Killingholme	6·9
Llandarcy	8·0
Milford Haven (Esso)	6·0
Milford Haven (Gulf)	4·0
Pembroke (Texaco)	5·9
Belfast	1·5
Total	112·6

Source: Digest of Energy Statistics (HMSO)

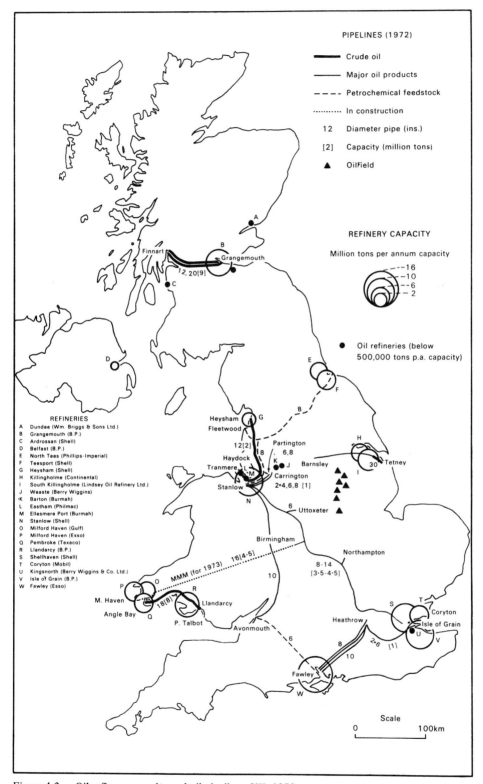

Figure 4.3   Oil-refinery capacity and oil pipelines, UK, 1970

UK oil-refinery capacity. These refineries were well-situated to serve in addition not only the inland markets of the Midlands, but also the smaller regional markets accessible by coastal vessels serving depots along the North Sea shores. The opposite end of the axial belt of industry and population in Britain reaches the sea in the North West region, which in 1970 had a further 13 per cent of the national refining capacity. With over 50 per cent of oil-refining taking place in these two areas, the other regional outputs are much smaller. Nevertheless the industrial regions of Central Scotland and South Wales both acquired the first British crude oil refineries in the early 1920s. Grangemouth in Scotland was chosen because of an earlier historical base in the extraction and refining of oil from the local oil shales of West Lothian; the Pumpherston refinery on the shale field was closed in 1964. Llandarcy, near Swansea, serves its local industrial area plus the Severn estuary and accessible areas of the south-west Midlands as well. Two regions which might have been expected to acquire crude oil refining earlier than the 1960s, were Humberside to serve the markets of the West Riding industrial complex, and the North East. But it was not until after 1960 that local demand in these areas was sufficiently large to justify local oil-refining to compete with refinery products brought from else-where, or that other inducements to develop locally were sufficiently strong. The same is true on a lesser scale of Northern Ireland. Relatively isolated, the small refinery completed there in 1962 is able to sell virtually all its products within the local markets, mostly in close proximity to Belfast.

While market attractions have dominated the oil-refinery distribution pattern, government inducements and transport economies have also played their part. Government influence showed up particularly strongly in the 1960s, when most of the expansion of oil-refining capacity in the UK took place in the Development Areas. This was because the grants and tax incentives available gave the Development Areas a considerable advantage over other parts of Britain for projects such as oil refineries, in which very large capital investment is involved. The government used its controls over industrial location through Industrial Development Certificates (IDCs) to the same end. The strength of this government influence is indicated by the fact that five new refineries and 65 per cent of the new refinery capacity completed in the 1960s were located in the development areas. There is some evidence that political considerations had influenced location decisions earlier than this. Llandarcy oil refinery in South Wales was located on what was thought to be a strategically safe site in the 1920s. Similarly, the only refinery built during the Second World War was sited at Heysham in North Lancashire with strategic considerations uppermost.

Transport economies have exercised a locational influence in several ways. All the crude oil refineries in the UK were located at least initially on sites easily accessible from oil tanker berths. Coastal locations not only minimise the transport cost of the crude oil, but also allow the distribution of refined products by coastal vessel wherever possible. The location of oil refineries within the UK has been considerably influenced by the increasing size of the tankers used to transport the oil to Britain. These have allowed a continuing reduction in shipping costs and therefore in the delivered price of the crude oil. In 1951 most of the ships in use were less than 20,000 deadweight tons and the largest was only 50,000. By 1961 the largest ships were over 100,000 dwt, and a decade later a 250,000 dwt tanker had discharged its cargo at Milford Haven in South Wales. In 1970 the total daily costs of a 200,000 dwt tanker per thousand tons were only 80 per cent of those of a 90,000 dwt tanker and less than 50 per cent of those of a 25,000 dwt tanker.[10] But in the UK the larger the tanker, the smaller the number of deep-water anchorages capable of accommodating such ships. To take advantage of supertanker economies, refineries either have to locate at these deep-water sites, or be linked to these terminals by pipelines. Both developments have occurred in the UK. The two terminals capable of taking supertankers of over 100,000 dwt in 1970 were at Finnart on Loch

Long, western Scotland, and Milford Haven in South Wales. The former was built in 1951 to serve the long established Grangemouth refinery by pipeline, whilst, Milford Haven acts in both capacities. The availability of the deep water there attracted three oil refineries to locate on the shores of the Haven by 1970; a fourth (AMOCO) is scheduled to be operational by the end of 1973. In addition a pipeline was built to Llandarcy near Swansea where direct imports to the refinery via the nearby Swansea docks had been limited to the use of 20,000 dwt ships. The North West region overcame the shortcomings of its limited depth anchorages by establishing terminals progressively further away, linked to the refineries by pipeline. Thus in 1954 a special oil dock was completed at Bromborough capable of taking 32,000 dwt ships, requiring a 7 mile pipeline link to the Stanlow site. This also soon proved inadequate, and a jetty was built at Tranmere Port which could take 65,000 dwt ships. By 1970 this too was proving to be inadequate and negotiations were put in hand to try to establish a deep-water terminal in Anglesey for serving the North West. These changes in transport were in effect attracting developments to the west coast with its deep water and shorter haulages, counteracting to some extent the market attractions concentrated in the east as discussed earlier. The proposal for an oil refinery at the proposed port complex at Hunterston on the Clyde remains controversial (1972).

Improved technology and technical considerations have also played a part in the changing picture. Until the 1940s the main consumer demand was for the light products produced from crude oil, principally for road vehicle consumption. When these were extracted large quantities of heavier products remained which were difficult to sell. In this situation there were advantages in refining the crude oil near to the oil wells. This problem was eased by the development of the cracking process by which some of the heavier oil was broken down to provide a bigger yield of the light products that were in demand, but there is a limit on how much of this can be done and it is expensive. The real solution came with the development of markets for the heavier products as well. Fuel oil in particular became much more competitive with coal in the UK after 1956, and in the 1960s the growing British petrochemical industries came to use more and more of the heavy residual materials produced. As a result of these developments saleable products now normally amount to some 95 per cent of the crude oil received at a refinery, with half of the rest being consumed by the refinery for its operation. This reduction in weight loss has made the market location much more attractive, so that whereas in 1950 domestic refinery capacity was only 50 per cent of refined product needs, by 1970 domestic refinery capacity exceeded demand.

The basic pattern of oil refinery location in the UK then can be understood in these terms. After 1960 government influence favoured the location of new developments in the west and north, with transport economies and physical geography adding their advantages. Market attractions favoured locations in the South East in particular, and favoured the location of smaller refineries near the major regional concentrations of industry and population.

Distribution and refinery products: Deliveries of petroleum products for inland consumption in the UK in 1970 totalled over 95 million tons, having more than doubled since 1960. Fuel oil consumption in 1969 constituted 40 per cent of the total, motor spirits 15 per cent and gas/diesel oil a further 17 per cent. Fuel oil consumption amounted to nearly 44 million tons distributed as shown in table 4.8. Regional deliveries of fuel oil, excluding that used by refineries and for gas-making and electricity generation, are shown in table 4.9. This shows over 20 per cent of consumption concentrated into the South East. The West Midlands and North West England took a further 15 per cent between them.

For distribution, oil products move in increasingly smaller quantities until the final consumers are reached. Because of economies of scale, and especially the large proportion

TABLE 4.8   Fuel-oil Consumption, UK, 1970 (thousand tons)

Steel industry	4,999
Chemical industry, including petrochemicals	2,370
Other manufacturing industries	11,913
Gas-making	183
Electricity generation	11,717
Other public utilities	147
Non-manufacturing industries	2,033
Non-industrial central heating	4,113
Petroleum industry (mainly refinery consumption)	6,431
Total	43,906

Source: Digest of Energy Statistics (HMSO 1971)

of total costs that are taken up by terminal costs of loading and unloading, the aim is to retain cheaper bulk movement as far as possible. The cheapest means of movement are by water and by pipeline, and both are used in Britain in addition to road and rail. Deliveries are usually made direct to customers located within about 60 miles (96 km) of a refinery. For bulk consumers with rail facilities, these deliveries are made by the trainload. Where justified by large continuous demand, oil pipelines are used.[11] For example, pipelines carry refined products from Stanlow to the Manchester area, from Fawley to Staines and Heathrow airport and from Llandarcy to the giant Port Talbot steelworks. The oil pipeline network in Britain has grown as individual markets have expanded sufficiently to consume continuous flows of oil products. In 1969 a 24 mile (394 km) pipeline was opened, feeding refined products to north London and the Midlands from refineries and installations on the Thames and Mersey, and another was planned, for completion in 1973, from Milford Haven to the Midlands and Manchester. These were in addition to the various specialised pipelines carrying petrochemical feedstock from some refineries to petrochemical complexes. In 1969 the tonnage of refined petroleum products transferred by pipeline in the UK began to exceed that going by rail. For other consumers delivery is normally by road, but since road transport is the most expensive per ton-mile, bulk oil depots are established to serve customers beyond the refinery supply area. Here physical geography plays a part. The UK has a long coastline compared with area, and all but a very few of the oil refineries are on

TABLE 4.9   Inland Deliveries of Fuel-oil, UK Regions, 1970
(Excluding deliveries for refinery fuel, gas-making and electricity generation) in thousand tons

South East	5,691
West Midlands	2,118
North West	4,103
Scotland	2,834
North	2,432
Yorkshire and Humberside	2,598
East Midlands	1,035
East Anglia	359
South West	1,331
Wales	2,884
Northern Ireland	690
Total	26,075

Source: Digest of Energy Statistics (HMSO 1971)

coastal sites. In addition, few industrial markets in Britain are more than 60 miles (96 km) from navigable water. Depots can thus be sited close to markets, yet be supplied by cheap water transport. As a result coastwise traffic in refined products in 1970 amounted to nearly 32 million tons, with a further 9 million tons transferred by inland waterway.[12] In the past oil was competitive at coastal locations, but as inland markets have grown and as more pipelines become economic, the cost of oil at inland sites will be reduced, making it more competitive with other fuels.

I.4   Gas

Public supply of gas in the UK dates from 1807, but until 1920 it was used mainly for lighting. After that electricity rapidly captured the lighting market and by 1945 gas was being used principally for heating. Between 1945 and 1970 the gas industry was radically transformed by two developments, with most of the changes occurring after 1960. By 1970 the industry had little in common with what can only be described as its technological predecessor of 1945.

The first major transformation followed the nationalisation of the industry in 1949. At that time there were 991 undertakings supplying gas in Great Britain, one-third of them belonging to local authorities. Under the 1948 Act the undertakings were grouped into 12 Area Gas Boards, and a major programme of rationalisation was undertaken to improve the quality and efficiency of the service; at the same time production and distribution facilities were modernised. Gas was being produced from 1,050 separate gas works with over 97 per cent of the raw material being coal or coke. By 1963 the number of works had been reduced to only 307, though production capacity was 30 per cent more than in 1949. In addition to the gas being made in its own works, the Gas Board bought 20 per cent of its gas supplies from outside sources, mainly coke ovens and the steel industry, and from oil refineries.

The second transformation was brought about by the change in source of gas used (table 4.10; figure 4.1). As late as 1960 over 90 per cent of the gas available was produced from coal or coke. By 1965 coal was supplying only 70 per cent of the gas, with petroleum and petroleum refinery gas supplying 25 per cent. But 1964 had seen the first commercial bulk deliveries of natural gas from the Sahara to the UK, and in 1965 the first productive natural gas well was discovered in the North Sea. By the end of 1970 gas from these two sources accounted for nearly 50 per cent of all the gas available in the UK. Gas from oil provided 37 per cent and gas from coal only 9 per cent. The largest supply of gas now came from primary sources, and the British gas industry had become essentially a wholesaler rather than a manufacturer as before. The implications of this revolution were still being worked out in the early 1970s (table 4.11).

In the early period after nationalisation gas sales rose much more slowly than sales of electricity. A major reason for this was the faster rise in the price of gas coal, than in the price of the general coals upon which the electricity supply industry depended.

TABLE 4.10   Primary Fuel Input used in the Gas Industry, UK, 1960 and 1970

	Million tons of coal or coal equivalent	
	1960	1970
Coal	22·6	4·2
Petroleum	1·4	6·1
Petroleum gases	0·5	1·5
Natural gas	0	10·4
Total	24·5	22·2

Source: Digests of Energy Statistics (HMSO)

TABLE 4.11   Production and Availability of Gas, GB, 1960 and 1970

	million therms	
	1960-1	1969-70
Gas made at gas works	2,212	2,220
Gas purchased		
Coke oven gas	509	330
Petroleum gases	156	499
Natural gas	13	2,693
Total gas available	2,890	5,742

Source: Digests of Energy Statistics (HMSO)

Although offering the advantages over coal of control of temperature to a fine degree and of not needing to be stored, gas did suffer some disadvantages compared with electricity. For industry it was essentially a supplier of energy in bulk, and did not compete with electricity for the small power market for machinery or lighting. In the domestic market electricity had the major advantage that virtually every house in the UK already used it for lighting purposes. Gas supply had to be provided specially as a separate additional service, and was essentially competing for the space-heating market. But it was not until the early 1960s that domestic central heating became a commonplace in new housing in the UK, or that the move away from coal as a general industrial fuel gave gas a better chance to compete for industrial space-heating. It was for these reasons that by 1960 gas sales were very little more than they had been in 1950. The 1960s saw a much more rapid expansion, mainly through aggressive and successful sales campaigns in the domestic heating market. Central heating systems were rapidly replacing open coal fires, and the flexibility of control, cleanliness, constant supply on tap without storage and relative cheapness made gas a strong competitor as the alternative fuel. Its use in industry also grew, and in the late 1960s sales to all markets benefited from the increasing availability of cheaper natural gas. By 1970 gas sales measured in millions of therms had more than doubled from what they had been just ten years earlier, with all the increase supplied by natural gas (table 4.12).

TABLE 4.12   Sales of Gas by Gas Boards, UK, 1960 and 1970

	million therms	
	1960	1970
Domestic	1,279	3,563
Industrial	858	1,462
Commerical	405	677
Public administration	42	68
Public lighting	24	3
Total supplied	2,608	5,773

Source: Digests of Energy Statistics (HMSO)

The geographical impact: In the first decade after nationalisation there were two important changes in the geography of the gas industry. The first was in the actual production facilities, the second in the development of regional gas grids, both inter-related. The pattern of production changed in the first decade through the closure of two-thirds of the plants inherited at nationalisation. Production was concentrated wherever possible on larger, more modern units and by 1960 71 of these were producing 71 per cent of the nation's gas.[13] As a rule it was the smaller local works that were closed, so that production was increasingly centralised in the larger population centres in each Gas Board area. The closures were hastened by the purchase of increasing quantities of gas from producers external to the industry. Up to 1960 the main external source was coke oven gas from the steel industry in particular, though oil refinery 'tail gases' had also begun to be used.

These developments were facilitated by changes in the distribution system. Prior to nationalisation each gas works supplied its own area through a discrete distribution system. Integration or even interconnection of these local networks was virtually absent except around Greater London. Upon formation in 1949, the new Gas Boards immediately set about developing regional gas grids for their own areas. Between 1949 and 1957 the mileage of mains in use rose from 74,400 (119,735 km) to 90,350 (145,404 km), most of which were developed for the integration of works and formerly separate discrete distribution systems rather than the result of extending the urban areas served.[14] This allowed concentration of production on the larger more efficient works, and made possible the more widespread use of gas from coke ovens and oil refineries. Not everywhere was able to benefit from these advantages at that time. It was not economic to extend the gas grids to replace small gas works serving isolated markets. This was especially true in Wales and Scotland where small gas works maintained a higher proportion of output.

In the early 1960s it was anticipated that supplies of gas made from coal, whether in gas works or from coke ovens, would in future form a decreasing proportion of supply. The main alternative possibilities then being actively pursued were the making of gas from oil, and the importation of natural gas from North Africa. At the same time a methane gas grid was developed to distribute imported natural gas from the import point at Canvey Island, east of London. This was in effect the beginning of a national gas grid which had been proposed by the Gas Council in 1958[15] and which was the next logical step in the evolution of the industry. The discovery of large quantities of North Sea gas in the mid-1960s necessitated a re-appraisal. Plans for increasing gas-making capacity were shelved, and the implementation of a national gas grid for the distribution of the new supplies was given priority. By 1970 the number of gas works in production was down to 158, distributed as shown on figure 4.4 which also shows the new natural gas transmission system developed in the late 1960s. In late 1972 natural gas accounted, directly or indirectly, for 90 per cent of UK gas output, with a peak output so far of 3,500 Mft^3 (99 Mm^3) from the North Sea.

Changes in the sources of gas have clearly played an important part in the changing spatial patterns that have been described. The form of the changes and the resulting pattern, however, owe much to the four factors of markets, technology, political control and ownership, and transport economies.

Rationalisation achieved by concentration of production capacity in larger, more efficient units, could be achieved only where an integrated distribution system was available to distribute their products; both required central ownership and control for implementation. Nationalisation is not the only way this might have been achieved, though in retrospect it is unlikely that any alternative centralisation of control would have occurred. In the first period, up to 1960, the regional Gas Boards developed in isolation. As late as 1964 movement of gas between Boards was virtually non-existent, and the national gas grid was still to be implemented (figure 4.6). The geography of production and distribution at this time could be understood only if it is recognised that each region was isolated, operating almost as a self-sufficient island. This was the next stage on from the pattern of local isolation which had prevailed in 1949 (figure 4.5). This regional heritage of the early 1960s was still obvious in 1970. But by then central authority was beginning to assert itself more strongly, aided by the appearance of North Sea gas and the development of the associated national gas network for its transmission. These had already begun to lead to a more rational pattern in the gas

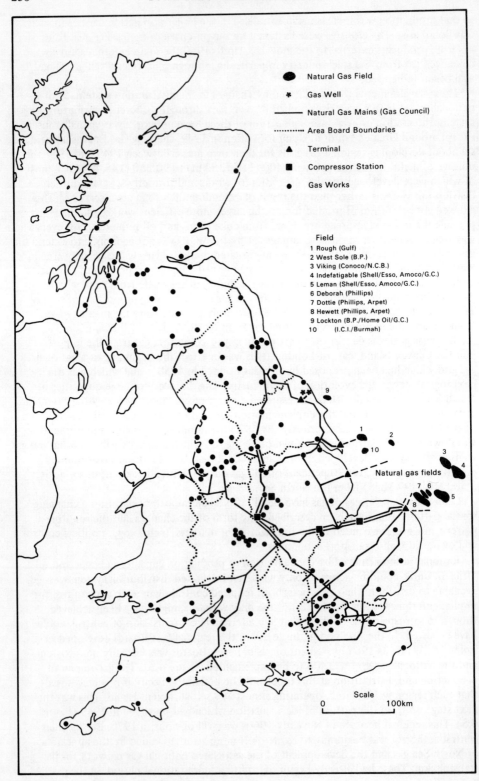

Figure 4.4   Gas fields, gas works and the gas grid, UK, 1970

industry related now not to regional but to national conditions. This latest process of pattern change was once again facilitated by the central ownership and control was further strengthened.in 1972 with the setting up of a new Gas Council with much stronger central authority.

The part played by transport economies will be increasingly important in the future as the industry becomes fully adjusted to the loss of its manufacturing operations and to its new function as simply a distributor. But they did also contribute to the changes in the past. In the post-war period gas transport costs rose much more slowly than transport costs for other forms of energy. As a result it became cheaper to transport gas by pipe than to transport coal overground. This contributed to the closure of small works and to the development of large gas works able to take advantage of economies of scale in getting coal supplies to them. These transport economies also help to explain the way rationalisation of the industry led, wherever possible, to a concentration of gas-making capacity at or near sources of raw materials, that is to say on the coalfields and near major oil refineries.

Pipelines, however, are competitive only with a high load factor. This is because 75 to 80 per cent of the cost of pipeline transport is capital cost which has to be borne regardless of the quantity of material being moved. In addition there are considerable economies of scale in using larger diameter pipes.[16] These economic aspects of transport have become even more important with the coming of natural gas. This has more than double the calorific value of manufactured gas, and so effectively doubles the fuel value capacity of pipes which hitherto carried manufactured gas. There is thus little to be surprised at in the alacrity with which Gas Board in the UK took to natural gas or in the speed with which the natural gas transmission grid has been established. There are further implications of this, though, stemming from the need for the natural gas transmission grid to be operated at a high load factor to be efficient. Unfortunately gas demands fluctuate seasonally, and if pipelines capable of meeting peak demands are laid, they would operate well below capacity for much of the time. The obvious solution is to have storage facilities near the markets to meet peak demands, with the pipelines capable of meeting base and middle load demands. A supplementary technique is to have an interruptible supply contract with large industrial consumers for which they receive special rates. Both methods are being used in Britain, and storage facilities are already being provided.

The location patterns of the gas industry have always been strongly influenced by the pattern of demand. Until 1949 the whole industry was essentially market-oriented. By then, wherever demand was sufficient gas works had been established, each with a discrete local distribution network, unconnected with its neighbours. In this situation obviously each local area had to have its own gas-making works. Locational choice was limited. Nationalisation however, brought with it rationalisation, and more especially the development of regional gas grids, with the result that within each region, production capacity could be concentrated near the major markets. Only where an area was too isolated, and had too small a market to justify the cost of extending the regional grid to it, were alternatives tried. Thus tanker or bottle gas is distributed in parts of Wales, and where coal based production is very expensive butane/air installations have been tried. It has been suggested, however, that in such areas it is a waste of financial resources for the two industries of gas and electricity to compete, and that the market in such areas should simply be left to electricity, which has to penetrate such areas anyway to provide lighting.[17] It is not difficult to see that the next logical development would have been the concentration of production at the best national sites, with a national gas transmission grid to ensure adequate distribution to all regions. But the need for such a development was overtaken by the discovery and rapid switch to North Sea gas, requiring a natural gas transmission grid. This too was influenced in its pattern by the geography

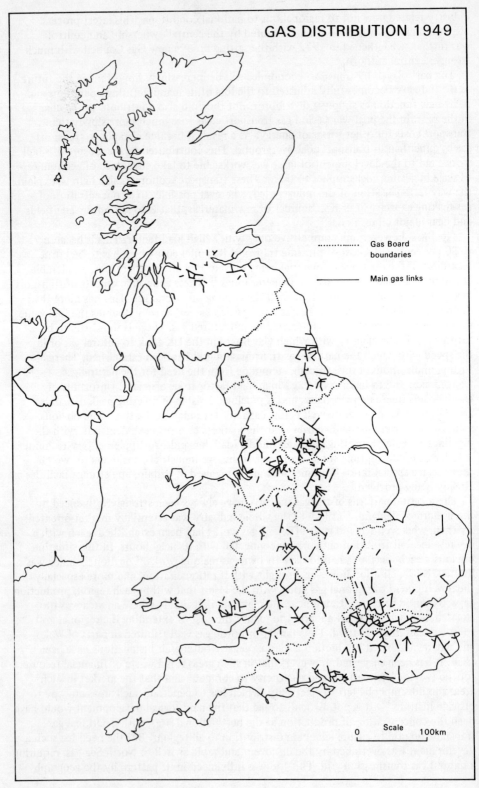

Figure 4.5   Gas distribution, UK, 1949

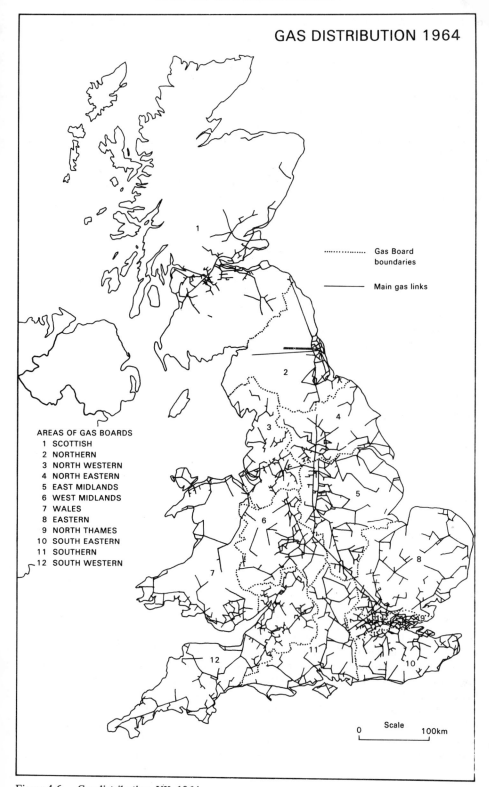

GAS DISTRIBUTION 1964

···················· Gas Board
boundaries

———— Main gas links

AREAS OF GAS BOARDS
1 SCOTTISH
2 NORTHERN
3 NORTH WESTERN
4 NORTH EASTERN
5 EAST MIDLANDS
6 WEST MIDLANDS
7 WALES
8 EASTERN
9 NORTH THAMES
10 SOUTH EASTERN
11 SOUTHERN
12 SOUTH WESTERN

Scale
0 ⊢——————⊣ 100km

Figure 4.6   Gas distribution, UK, 1964

. Allowing for the sources of supply being off the east coast of Britain, the grid coincides closely with other national network patterns of motorways, , and the electricity supergrid, and for the same reasons. They all conform of maximum demand. Burns pointed out in 1958 that over 70 per cent of the gas sales in Britain were made in a belt 35 miles (56 km) wide each side of a straight line joining London and Manchester.[18] In 1970 well over half the gas sales were made in the North Thames, South Eastern, West Midlands, and North Western Gas Board areas.

Technology played only a relatively minor role in the geography of the gas industry in 1970, though it had its effects earlier. Shortages and the cost of coking coal in the 1950s led the industry to seek alternative sources of gas. The cheaper Lurgi coal gasification process needed a coalfield location and plants were built in Scotland and the West Midlands. A gas-from-oil process, developed in the late 1950s, proved very attractive commercially and plants were built near oil refineries as at Shellhaven and Llandarcy. In addition, pipeline transport costs were also reduced through technological improvements, which made the development of regional and national gas grids more attractive. Techniques for underground storage of gas have also helped in the use of natural gas, though without specific geographical effects.

The most important single fact in understanding the geography of the contemporary gas industry then, is the changeover since 1965 from its being a producer of secondary energy, to being a distribution industry of a primary fuel. Even in the 1970s however the existing pattern could be explained only in the context of ownership, market location, transport economies and technological change in the twenty-year period prior to 1965.

I.5   Electricity

The first public supply of electricity in the UK dates from 1881. From its earliest days the industry has been subject to some degree of public control. In 1926 the government set up the Central Electricity Board to construct and operate a national grid interconnecting individual power stations. In the succeeding twenty years this resulted in generation and transmission being increasingly coordinated. In 1948 all municipal and private undertakings other than those in Northern Ireland were nationalised. The generation of electricity in England and Wales was put in the hands of the Central Electricity Generating Board who were made responsible for transmitting the electricity they produced in bulk to the twelve separate Area Electricity Boards. The area boards were made responsible for the distribution and selling of the electricity to consumers in their own areas. In Scotland the North of Scotland Hydro Electric Board and the South of Scotland Electricity Board both generate and distribute electricity. In Northern Ireland a joint electricity authority was set up in 1967 to coordinate electricity generation. The electricity is sold in bulk to the Belfast Corporation, the Londonderry Corporation and the Electricity Board for Northern Ireland, who distribute it to consumers in their own areas.

In the period between 1945 and 1970 the electricity industry experienced two important changes. The first was the change to centralised control and ownership on nationalisation in 1948. This had its main impact on the organisation of distribution, since electricity generation had been publicly coordinated since 1926. The second change was the increasing use of fuels other than coal for electricity generation (table 4.13). In 1950, except for hydroelectricity generation in northern Scotland, virtually the only source of electricity was coal-fired power stations. But by 1960 oil had come to supply nearly 20 per cent of the primary fuel used for electricity generation, and small quantities of electricity were becoming available from nuclear power stations. In the 1960s oil maintained its share, but nuclear power grew in importance, and by the end of the decade was supplying nearly 10 per cent of the electricity used. At the beginning of the 1970s natural gas also

TABLE 4.13   Fuel Input in the Electricity Industry, UK, 1950-70

	Million tons of coal or coal equivalent		
	1950*	1960	1970
Coal, coke and breeze	32·6	52·7	76·0
Oil	1·5	9·2	21·1
Natural gas	-	-	0·2
Nuclear power	-	0·9	9·4
Hydro electricity	0·8	1·7	2·3
Net imports of electricity	-	-	0·3
Total all fuels	34·9	64·5	109·3

Source: Digest of Energy Statistics (HMSO)

* Figures are approximate

began to be used to fire power stations, and was expected to increase its contribution. Despite this increasing use of new fuels, coal continued to hold pride of place. It became *proportionately* less important, but increasing *tonnages* of coal were used, as growth in demand for electricity absorbed more than the output contributed by other fuels.

Electricity consumption in Britain grew at a rapid rate in the post-war period. At nationalisation output capacity was 11·8 thousand megawatts and sales amounted to 38,821 million kilowatt hours (kWh). Subsequent growth is shown in table 4.14 where it can be seen that output capacity and sales more than doubled between 1950 and 1960, and nearly doubled again between 1960 and 1970. In achieving this success, electricity had several basic advantages over other power sources. The first was its virtual universal availability, since its use for lighting meant that nearly all potential consumers were already linked into the distribution system. The availability of electricity at the turn of a switch meant it was much more convenient than coal or oil where supplies have to be ordered and stocks maintained, and where often appliances have to be serviced more frequently. As a continuously available supply, storage provision of electricity is neither necessary nor normally economically possible.

TABLE 4.14   Output, Capacity and Sales of Electricity, UK, 1950-70

	1950	1960	1970
Number of generating stations at end of year	338	319	289
Plant capacity at end of year (GW)	15·1	31·9	60·5
Total sales to consumers (GWh)	45,912	102,363	193,907

Source: Digest of Energy Statistics (HMSO)

The geographical impact: There were two ways in which the location patterns of the electricity industry changed after nationalisation. The first was in the location of production facilities, and the second in the development of transmission grids for movement of electricity in bulk. At nationalisation regional and national organisation of production had proceeded much further than in the case of the gas industry. But there was a need for improvement both in the existing organisation and to meet the rapid growth in demand. The subsequent changes in the regional pattern of electricity generation are shown on table 4.15. In 1950 30 per cent of the generating capacity was concentrated in that corner of South East England lying south of a line from the Wash to Southampton Water. With a further 28 per cent in the West Midlands and

TABLE 4.15   Electricity Supply and Consumption by Generating Regions, GB, 1950-68

Division	1950 TWh sent out	TWh received	1960 TWh sent out	TWh received	Division	1968* TWh sent out	TWh received
London	9·1	5·2	11·7	8·8			13·4
S. Eastern	2·2	2·6	5·4	6·5	SE	42·0	10·6
Eastern	2·6	4·3	6·6	10·1			17·6
							41·6
S. Western	1·9	1·6	4·1	3·9			7·6
Southern	1·5	2·8	5·4	8·5	SW	25·7	15·1
S. Wales	2·8	2·8	6·7	6·0			8·8
							31·5
Midlands	5·8	5·2	9·2	11·0	Midlands		17·8
E. Midlands	3·5	3·9	14·3	8·4		43·4	14·4
							32·2
N. Western	8·7	8·3	14·9	15·5	NW		25·6
N. Wales	0·1	0·6	1·2	1·7		19·1	3·1
							28·7
Yorkshire	6·1	5·1	15·0	11·0	NE		18·2
N. Eastern	2·9	3·2	8·6	6·1		38·6	9·8
							28·0
S. Scotland	3·4	3·8	6·4	6·4		13·4	14·7
N. Scotland	1·3	0·7	2·4	2·3		3·7	3·4
Great Britain	51·9	50·1	111·9	106·2		185·9	180·0

Source: Digest of Energy Statistics (HMSO)

TWh = terawatt hours (thousand million kWh)

*   Minor boundary changes mean the figures for 1968 are not strictly comparable with earlier years

North West, the axial belt of England linking Thameside and Merseyside accounted
for nearly 60 per cent of British electricity production. Power stations were in fact
concentrated in and around the major urban consuming centres. The greater majority
of them were under 25 megawatts (MW) in size, but the 87 which had 50 MW of
installed capacity or more, actually contributed over 90 per cent of output. At that
time coal accounted for over 95 per cent of the fuel used, with hydroelectric plants
supplying most of the rest. By 1960 this pattern had begun to change. National output
had more than doubled but although every region experienced increases some expanded
their capacity more than others. As a result the axial belt regions declined in importance
and were providing only 47·5 per cent of output by 1960. The regions which had taken
a much increased share were the East Midlands and Yorkshire, which now contributed
26 per cent of output. The North East had also increased its share. Oil and water power
now contributed nearly 20 per cent of the primary fuel used to make the electricity,
and nuclear energy was also beginning to be used, though only in very small quantities.
Despite the doubling of output between 1950 and 1960, the number of generating
stations had declined, indicating a massive increase in their individual average size.
Now only 43 were less than 25 MW in size and in England and Wales just 50 stations
were responsible for 72 per cent of the total electricity generated in 1962.

   The next decade saw these changes extended (figure 4.7). By 1970 the Midlands
had become by far the largest capacity region with nearly 30 per cent of output. The
Midlands and the North Eastern region combined contributed over 50 per cent of the

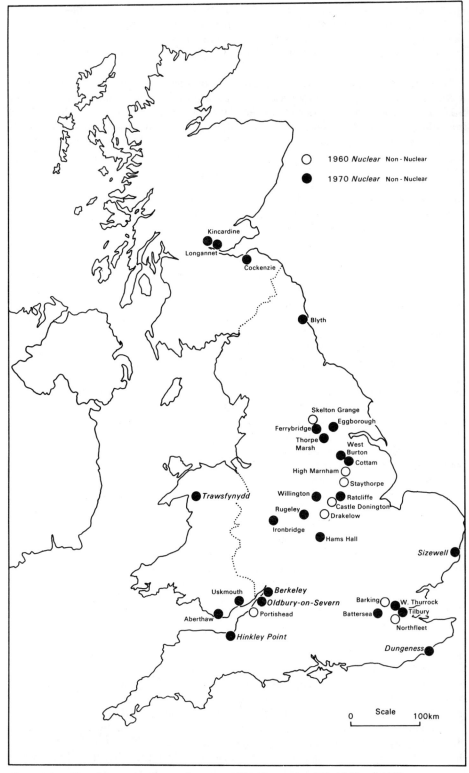

Figure 4.7   Electricity generating stations over 500 MW capacity, UK, 1960 and 1970
NB Berkeley 350 MW.

output in England and Wales. Since over 50 per cent of consumption took place in the South East region, there was a clear tendency for a shift in output location away from market. There had been a further shift in fuel sources too with nuclear power now responsible for nearly 9 per cent of the electricity generated and oil for a further 20 per cent.

The number of stations operating continued to decline despite the almost doubling of capacity, indicating further increases in the capacity of individual stations in the 1960s. In 1950 the largest stations had had less than 200 MW capacity. In 1963 the first 550 MW generating unit was installed near Doncaster; almost at the same time a 1,000 MW plant was opened at High Marnham, Nottinghamshire, and by 1970 there were 19 stations of this size or larger. By 1968 the first 2,000 MW stations were brought into operation at West Burton and Ferrybridge. Also by the beginning of 1970 twenty-two 500 MW generating sets had been installed, and by the end of that year there were ten stations with over 2,000 MW capacity in England and Wales. At Drax in Yorkshire 6 larger generating units each of 660 MW capacity were installed in the early 1970s indicating the potential for furtherance of these trends.

Distribution: These production changes required considerable adaptation in the electricity distribution system. When the industry was nationalised the distribution systems *within* the individual regions were already fairly well integrated. In addition, a 132 kV grid was available for transfer of limited amounts of electricity between regions. This grid was not designed to carry current in bulk over any great distances, however, and its inadequacy had become apparent with the heavy demands made on it during the Second World War. It was decided therefore to install a 275 kV grid to provide greater transmission capacity and allow freer choice in the best location for new power stations. By 1960, 650 miles (1,046 km) of this new supergrid had been completed. In the early 1960s it was decided to increase the capacity for transfers, and to minimise the number of environment-intruding transmission lines by developing a 400 kV grid. Most of this was created by upgrading the 275 kV grid, starting in 1965. By 1970, 5,512 miles (8,870 km) of 400 kV grid, and 2,174 miles (3,499 km) of 275 kV grid were in operation, none of which had existed twenty years earlier (figure 4.8). These developments made the UK system the largest integrated power network in the world.[19]

Although the explanation of the location of electricity generation is more complex than in the case of the other fuel and power industries, it is possible to recognise the more important factors involved. Transport economies have played a very important part in explaining the changes since 1945. At the time of nationalisation, electricity generation was essentially market-oriented. At first sight this is surprising since transmission of base load electricity was then competitive with all other forms of land transport of energy over distances of about 50 miles (80 km). It was more efficient therefore to locate base load power stations at the fuel supply and transmit the electricity to markets, than to put power stations at the market and carry coal supplies to them. In practice this had not occurred before 1948 because generating plant became obsolete so quickly. Technical improvements to make new plant more efficient took effect very rapidly as new plant was continually being built to meet the growth of demand. As a result any one generator did not contribute to base load electricity supply for more than a few years. For the rest of its useful life it was used to meet middle and peak load demand. But it was not economic to transmit middle and peak load electricity over any distance. In this situation even base load stations were located near to markets, in the certain knowledge that the short-term loss of having them there would be offset by the gains in the longer term when they would be suppliers of middle and peak load electricity only.[20] Nationalisation changed this. In the late 1940s it was thought unlikely that any further substantial gains would be made in the efficiency of generating

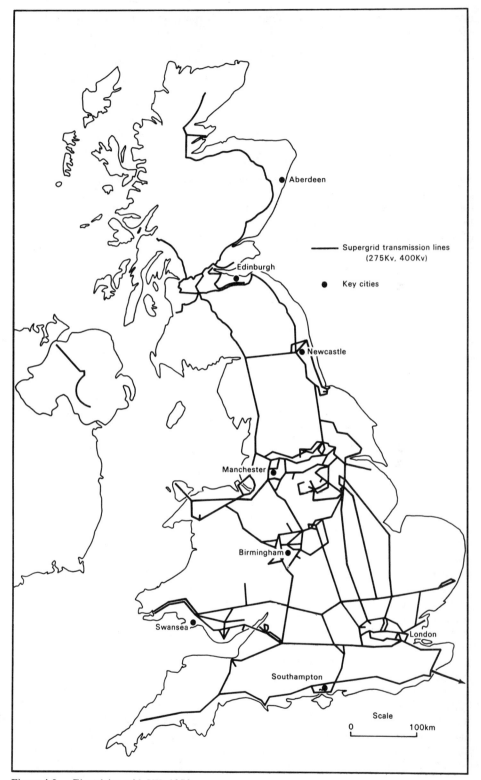

Figure 4.8   Electricity grid, UK, 1972

plants. The industry now turned to minimisation of transport costs to achieve further
economies and it was decided to build large new stations to meet base load demands
nearer to the fuel sources, which at this time meant the coalfields. The most attractive
coalfields for this purpose were those of South Yorkshire and the East Midlands. They
produced the cheapest coal in Britain and were closest to the south of England and
South Lancashire where electricity demand was growing fast and already exceeded local
generating capacity. These inland coalfields also had cooling water for power stations
readily available nearby in the valleys of the Aire, Calder and Trent Rivers. It was for
this reason that the South Yorkshire and East Midlands areas acquired such a large
proportion of the new electricity generation capacity built in the 1950s. At the same
time, however, coal-fired power stations were also being built at some market locations.
These were where the market lay close to a coalfield that could supply the fuel, or
where coal could be supplied cheaply by water transport. Middle and peak load stations
using coal were also built close to markets. In those cases it was cheaper to take coal to
them than to provide and maintain the extra transmission capacity necessary if they
were to be located elsewhere.

    These trends in coal-fired power station location were continued in the 1960s, but
by then the use of oil and nuclear energy was also becoming significant. Most of the
new oil-fired stations were built in areas where transport costs made coal more expensive.
Within these areas they have been built either near the major oil refineries, as at Milford
Haven, or on sites easily served by cheap water transport, as at Plymouth. Transport
costs are much less important in the location of nuclear power stations, since they are
used almost exclusively to supply base load electricity and their fuel transport costs are a
minor element in their operation. For them other factors are more important.

    From what has been said already it is clear that market attractions play an important
part in the pattern of power station distribution in Britain. If table 4.15 is examined it
can be seen that most market areas supply 90 per cent or more of their electricity
requirements themselves, irrespective of whether or not they have their own fuel
supplies of oil or coal. The areas with a surplus of these fuels take advantage of their
location on the coalfields or in proximity to oil refineries to a much lesser extent than
is sometimes assumed. In 1948 the industry was even more strongly market-oriented,
both at the regional and at the national level. Subsequently, although base load stations
were increasingly located closer to their fuel sources, installed capacity also increased
at the market. For coal-fired stations this was mainly, but not exclusively, to meet peak
load demand, as in the London region. The new oil-powered stations were fortunate
in that they could usually obtain their fuel oil from refineries located close to where the
electricity was to be sold. They therefore show much greater market orientation than
other forms of generation. For nuclear power, until the late 1960s the stations were
all located in areas deficient in coal, i.e. that were importing electricity from surplus
areas. They were attracted to areas where transport costs made coal-fired electricity
generation more expensive. In the late 1960s however, proposals were made to locate
some new nuclear stations in South Wales and the North East. As these were areas
with high coal production costs, this indicated a new trend in nuclear station location.
Intraregionally, urban areas still prefer not to have nuclear power stations too close,
and so siting factors have pushed them away from optimum locations *vis-a-vis* the
regional market.

    Technological development has influenced the patterns in several ways. It was men-
tioned earlier that in 1947 it was thought the peak of efficiency of stations was very near
and this was reflected in a pull to the coalfields. In fact this was not borne out in practice.[21]
Further improvements occurred which tended to reduce the attractions of the coalfield
sites in the longer-term, as explained earlier. Offsetting this to a certain extent were the
economies of scale being achieved, from less than 200 MW capacity in 1950 to 2,000 MW

capacity twenty years later. The 2,000 MW stations generated base load and were made possible by the availability of the grid by which their product could be distributed to wherever it was needed, since local demand could not consume all their output. Such developments reflect back on transport economies, since the larger the blocks of energy transmitted the cheaper the transport per unit becomes, and the larger the station the more efficiently it should operate in terms of thermal efficiency. It is technological developments that have also made nuclear power usable for electricity generation. The effect of this has been to locate more capacity nearer to markets than might otherwise have happened if coal and oil had remained the sole fuel sources. Nuclear power has heavy capital costs, making it much more suitable for base load supplies. This strengthens the attractions of locations away from cheap coal areas which were originally also base load oriented. The first nuclear power stations to supply electricity commercially to the supergrid were Bradwell in Essex and Berkeley on the Severn estuary in 1962. The first is located in the heavy electricity importing areas of the Eastern Region, the second close, in grid terms, to the heavy demands of the West and South West Midlands. Hinkley Point and Oldbury in the lower Severn estuary reinforced this pattern in the mid-1960s, and Trawsfynydd and Wylfa (1971) on Anglesey helped supply the Merseyside area. In Scotland Hunterston in Ayrshire is suitably placed to supply the Clydeside conurbation, which has been a deficit area for electricity since the 1950s.

Finally, government involvement has played a role in location throughout the development of the electricity industry. To the control provided in the setting up of the Central Electricity Board in 1926 was added public ownership in 1948. The centralisation of ownership gave freedom for the national organisation of the industry not fully possible under the mixed ownership which existed previously. From 1948 planning was able to take advantage of national rather than just intraregional locational advantages. It was this central planning of the industry on a national scale which allowed concentration of production on the cheap coalfields and of nuclear and oil-fired power stations at the nationally advantageous places. Apart from centralising ownership, the government also indirectly influenced location through its fuel policy. Sensitive to the social and economic problems associated with the coal industry, in 1961 a fuel-oil tax was imposed, aimed at limiting the competition of oil with coal. The effect was to encourage dependence on coal, and to attract power station capacity to where coal was available at an acceptable price. The government also influenced the pattern by financing the basic research necessary to make nuclear electricity generation a commercial possibility. Fierce arguments rage over the true cost of the electricity produced.[22] It can be made to look dearer or cheaper than that from coal-fired stations, depending upon whether the government financed research and development costs are included or excluded in the calculation. Either way it seems unlikely that nuclear power would have been supplying 9 per cent of the electricity used in the UK in 1970 if government sponsorship of the development had not been on such a massive scale. This 9 per cent would have had to come from other sources, and stations located differently to the nuclear power stations in 1970.

Distribution: The development of the fully integrated distribution grid in the UK reflects all the factors mentioned. Central control was essential for the full development of a national grid and this was contributed by the nationalisation of the industry. Transport economies determined the grid pattern since, as was pointed out earlier, high voltage lines are justifiable only where bulk movements are to be handled. They became necessary with the central decision to concentrate production in certain areas, from which large surpluses would have to be transferred. Markets also played their part in the grid pattern as can be seen from figure 4.8. The high density areas of the grid are to be found within the largest consumption areas in the axial belt of Britain, and lining it with surplus production centres like the East Midlands. Technology has not really influenced the location pattern of the grid except in so far as development of higher voltage lines has minimised the number of transmission lines that would otherwise have been necessary.

II   INDUSTRIAL STRUCTURE

II.1   Introduction and Method

The distribution of manufacturing and services in the UK is never constant. The patterns are continuously changing to meet new needs and circumstances, but in the longer term the *rate* of change fluctuates. Periods of slow growth or even stagnation are succeeded by periods when rapid development takes place. The quarter century from 1945 to 1970 belongs in the latter category. The major patterns inherited in 1945 were surprisingly similar to those in existence around the turn of the century 50 years before. The economic uncertainties of the 1920s and 1930s, in particular, had inhibited development, while from 1939 to 1945 all efforts had been directed to meeting the requirements of total war. The geographical distributions of 1945 were thus little adapted to the prevailing conditions of the mid-twentieth century. During the subsequent quarter century this situation changed as new patterns emerged to adapt to the new conditions. But even in this period the rates of change varied. The first decade after 1945 was essentially a time when the necessary foundations for subsequent development were being laid down. It was only from the late 1950s that economic growth and capital investment combined to re-order the geographical patterns in a striking way. The emergence of these patterns of manufacturing and service activities underpins most other aspects of the changing human geography of the UK, from population and settlement to land use. Understanding of the changes and trends is thus fundamental to any planning undertaken for the future.

In examining the changes this chapter works from the whole to the parts. The first section sets the overall scene by showing how the structural changes, which have occurred within and between the manufacturing and service sectors, have geographical implications. The second and third sections look separately at manufacturing and services respectively, to show what factors have been responsible for the spatial changes which can be observed in each.

Employment figures are used throughout the discussion to measure the distribution of economic activity because of their suitability for most geographic purposes. The spatial association between changes in economic activity, as indicated by employment, and the effects of those changes, is normally very strong. This is because most people in the UK live within the region in which they work. When other measures are used such as output, productive capacity or investment, the spatial association between the change and its effects is much less strong. For example, increase in output at a particular factory without an increase in employment or wages might have no effect whatsoever on the locality in which the factory is situated. Any increase in profits might accrue to share-holders living in a different region or even nation, and any increased demand for such things as transport or equipment might be met by firms based elsewhere. An increase in employment at that same factory, however, could be expected to be reflected through increased demands both economic and social in the local area where the workers would live. Employment figures have additional advantages in being more readily available over the period being studied, both for the nation as a whole and for the various regions, without the problems of inflation which bedevil monetary measures, or of comparability if measures of quantitative output are used for manufacturing and services. This is not to say that employment statistics have no faults; they have. Methods of collection have varied over time, changes in definition have occurred, and labour varies in quality and

composition, if only because male and female, adults and youths are all included under
the one heading. But for the present purpose employment figures are the best available.
In Britain employment is classified according to economic activity into 27 industry
orders using the Standard Industrial Classification (SIC).[23] Employment in manufacturing
industry is classified into orders III to XIX inclusive, and that in services into orders XX
to XXVII inclusive; orders I and II cover the primary activities of mining and agriculture.
(figure 1.2).

II.2   Structural Change

Chapter 2 described the relatively slow growth of the labour force in the UK in the
period between 1945 and 1970. Despite this slow growth the employment structure
of the labour force has changed substantially. In keeping with a trend common to all
the advanced nations of the world, there has been a continuing increase in the proportion employed in the service sector, with corresponding decreases in the proportion
employed in primary industries, and to a lesser extent in manufacturing. These trends
are plotted in figure 4.9 which shows their persistence throughout the two decades
after 1950. By 1970, services had grown to employ over 57 per cent of the nation's
employees, having expanded most rapidly in the 1950s. Manufacturing employment
also grew over the whole period, though much more slowly, and the number of
employees actually underwent a decline in the late 1960s. Even these figures under-
estimate the shift towards service activity that was taking place in the employment
structure of the UK at this time. This is because in most manufacturing industries
fewer and fewer people were engaged in actual production, and an increasing proportion were in white collar jobs. Statistics related to the actual job done, as opposed to
the industry within which a person is employed, are published in occupation tables
in the decennial census reports.[24]   These show that over the period 1950-70 *all* the
manufacturing industries had an increase in the proportion of their employees engaged
in clerical and allied occupations, irrespective of whether the total employment in an

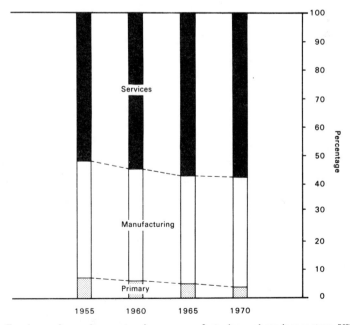

Figure 4.9   Employees in employment: primary, manufacturing and services sectors, UK, 1955-70

industry increased or declined.

These are the sectoral structural changes which occurred, but within each sector it is possible to recognise shifts in the same direction which confirm a general pattern and which, it will be shown later, have considerable geographical importance. These trends are best understood by recognising that the order of the SIC can be arranged along a continuum, starting with heavy industry at one end and ranging through light industry to central services, and finishing with consumer contact service. The heavy industries are those making capital goods or producer goods such as iron and steel or ships. Light industry extends from the making of components out of some of the products of heavy industry, to the manufacture or assembly of final consumer goods. Such industries include both durable consumer products such as television sets, and perishables such as fresh food products or newspapers. Central services are those such as bank or insurance company head-quarters, while consumer contact services are those where face-to-face exchanges are usual, such as retail shopping and medical care.

Traditionally British geographers have concentrated their attention upon the heavy industries, with consumer goods production receiving much less study and service industries neglected. Historically there were good reasons for this. In the past when geography was confined to the study of man's relationship with his environment, especially with his physical environment, it was in the heavy industries that such relationships seemed most obvious. These were also the dominant industries in the UK economy in terms of both employment and tonnage output. Pragmatically it was, and is, easier to study heavy industry. Statistics were and are more readily available in a more suitable form, and the number of production units involved is generally smaller and/or more areally restricted in distribution. The textile and tinplate industries afford good examples. But this emphasis by geographers on the heavy industries has outlasted the conditions which gave rise to it. Geography has expanded to become much more concerned with understanding the spatial structure of society, than just with man-land relationships. At the same time the heavy industries have lost their dominance, declining in manpower and relative importance as other industries have grown. Among the goods-producing industries, light manufacturing is now far more important in terms of net output and employment. But the production industries as a group have been overtaken anyway by the service industries, which have for long employed more people than manufacturing in the UK, as shown in figure 4.9. By 1970 there were over 12 million people employed in the service sector, compared with only 8 million in manufacturing and less than 2 million in primary production. The significance of these trends is that the light industry, which has been expanding rapidly, has different locational requirements from the heavy industries which are experiencing relative, and in some cases absolute decline. Particularly important for the location of light manufacturing is accessibility to markets. But markets are normally associated with people, and most people are now employed in services rather than in production industries. The location pattern of services is thus of major importance in understanding the economic geography of the UK. It is the geographical implications of these trends, and the factors influencing the changing patterns that are discussed in the following two sections, dealing first with manufacturing and then with services.

Manufacturing

III.1 Regional Change

Changes in the distribution of manufacturing in Britain occurred both between regions and within regions between 1945 and 1970. At the regional level there were the shifts described in chapter 2, while within individual industries there have been adjustments in location which have often been intraregional.

Much of the change in the regional distribution of manufacturing in the UK occurred because of the structural differences in employment between the various regions. Regions with a high proportion of growing industries and few industries in decline acquired an increasing proportion of the nation's total manufacturing labour force between 1945 and 1970, while regions with an opposite structure ended up with a smaller proportion. Studies of the growth industries of the 1950s showed that there were marked disparities in their regional distribution.[25] It was further shown that the national growth industries which were identified had different growth rates in each of the Standard Regions then in use. The pattern is shown on figure 4.10. There it can be seen that over 50 per cent of jobs in the three industries with the fastest employment growth, was to be found in just three regions: London and the South East, the Midlands and the North West. The peripheral regions of Scotland, Wales and Northern England, which had high percentages of declining industries, did not have more than 15 per cent of the employment in each of the growth industries to share between them. Even this understated the effect of structural differences. This is indicated in the second row of maps where the growth rates of the three industries in each region are mapped. These show that there were wide variations about the national rate in each case, and that in some regions the national growth industries actually underwent decline. The bottom row of maps shows the absolute increases in employment in the three industries. The striking feature here is that in two of the growth industries the London and South East region had about double the amount of the next largest regional increase shown. In the other industry, vehicles, the three peripheral regions of Scotland, Wales and Northern England had declining employment in what was a national growth industry.

The effect of these differences in growth on the location of manufacturing in the UK in the 1950s was being reinforced by the pattern of industries experiencing decline or only slow growth. The heaviest declines were taking place in textiles, shipbuilding and marine engineering, and the clothing and footwear group, while slow growth was occurring in the metal industries. Most of these were heavily concentrated in regions other than those shown earlier to have concentrations of growth. Further corroboration of these structural effects on the pattern of manufacturing growth come from studies in greater detail, using subdivisions of the industry orders. These showed, for example, that the greater part of the difference between manufacturing change in the UK and that in Scotland was accounted for by the structural factor, and that for South East England structural factors accounted for over two-thirds of that region's above average growth performance. The below average growth in Wales and Northern England was also shown to be largely accounted for by structural differences.[26]

Similar analysis of changes which occurred in the 1960s is hampered by the changes which occurred first in the methods of compilation of the statistics in 1963, then in the definition of the standard regions in 1964, and finally in the Standard Industrial Classification in 1968. The only period for which compatible figures are available for study is 1965-9. Even here interpretation is complicated because the late 1960s was a time of employment decline in the UK. The number of employees in employment fell from a peak of 23·7 million in 1966 to only 22·9 million in 1970. It was also a period of vigorous application of the Distribution of Industry policy, which encouraged the location of manufacturing growth in the development areas. Despite these shortcomings some comment can be made on the changes in the three manufacturing industry groups with the largest percentage increase in employment in the UK between 1965 and 1969. These were other manufacturing (order XVI), engineering and electrical goods (order VI) and paper, printing and publishing (order XVI), and the patterns are shown in figure 4.11. In each growth industry the South East and the East and West Midlands together had over 50 per cent

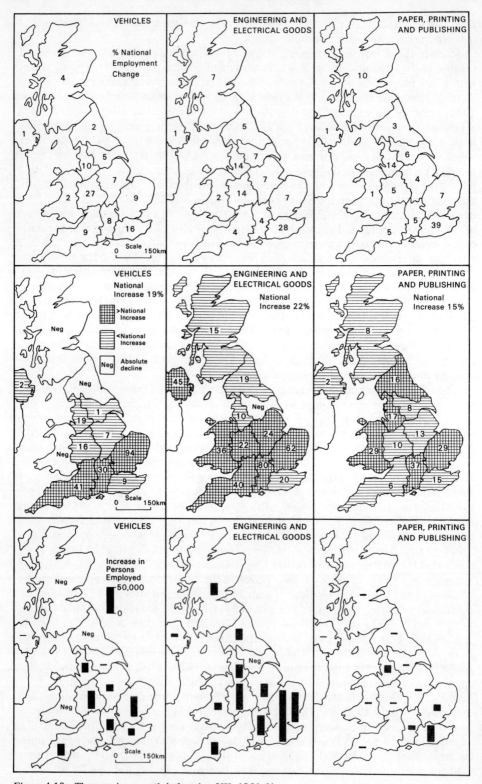

Figure 4.10　Three major growth industries, UK, 1951-61

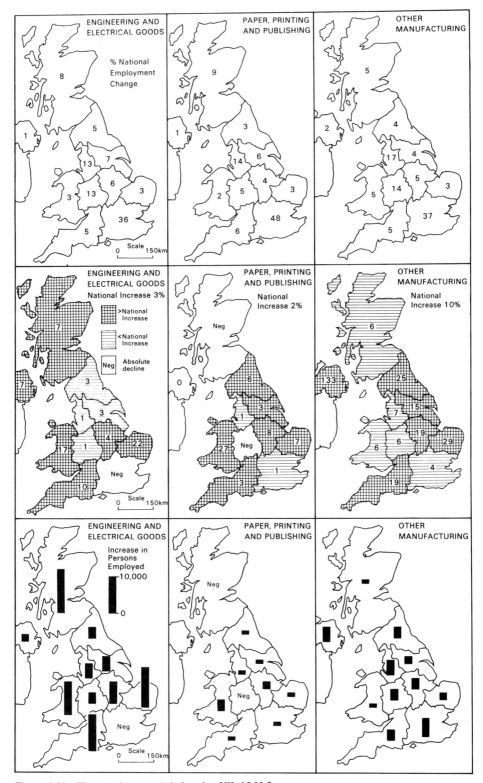

Figure 4.11   Three major growth industries, UK, 1965-9

of the national employment in 1970. With this in mind the figures indicate how government measures to aid the development areas helped Wales in particular to attract an
unequal share of the new employment in the growth industries, and restricted the rate
of growth in the West Midlands and the South East. But it is striking how East Anglia
appears among the three regions with the fastest growth in each case, and the South
West in two out of three of these growth industries. Both are adjacent to the South East
region, and undoubtedly benefited from firms moving as short a distance as possible
from areas of restricted development in the Midlands and the South East. When figures
for absolute growth are examined, it can be seen that 40 per cent of the new jobs in
the engineering group and in other manufacturing, and half the new jobs in the paper,
printing and publishing group were located in those regions south-east of a line drawn
from the Humber to the Severn. The pattern of concentration of manufacturing growth
in the southern regions of Britain during the 1950s was thus no more than modified by
the strong government action to influence the distribution of industry in the 1960s
(figures 4.12a and b).

III.2 Productivity

Structural differences between regions further contributed to spatial change by variation
in the impact of manpower productivity improvements. In the UK as a whole the largest
increase in actual numbers employed after 1945 occurred in the newer lighter industries,
while some of the older heavier industries had much smaller increases or in some cases
actually underwent decline. Some of the largest increases in employment took place in
industries where only modest increases of output occurred, while some of the industries
with little or no employment growth achieved considerable output expansion. The
explanation for this lies in productivity differences between various industries, and the
improvements in productivity over the period 1945-70. Smith pointed out in 1949 that
the farther along the production chain an industry lay the more labour intensive it could
be expected to be and the less important were raw materials in determining its location.
He illustrated his point by showing that in 1935 the weight of materials used per opera-
tive per year was 1,735 tons in blast furnaces, 155 tons in steelworks and rolling mills,
and only 9 tons in mechanical engineering shops.[27] This holds true for most manufacturing, with fewer people needed to manufacture a ton of flour from wheat compared with
the number needed to make a ton of bread from flour, or per ton of nylon fibre compared
with a ton of nylon shirts. Although the *Census of Production* no longer provides tonnage
figures for various industries, some indication of the extent of these differences between
heavy and light manufacturing can be gained by using instead the figures showing the
value of gross output per employee (table 4.16). These show that growth in demand for
consumer goods generates more employment per unit of output at the finishing end of
industry than in the primary manufacturing stages. The geographical relevance of this
is that the major concentrations of primary manufacturing industries in the UK were
established in the early industrial revolution, and their location changed little between
1900 and 1945. These palaeotechnic industries were mostly heavy weight-loss or bulk-
reduction industries, and so were initially strongly attracted to those places which had
available adequate supplies of their raw materials and fuel and water. Thus primary iron
and steel production was concentrated on the western and northern coalfields, textile-
making located along the eastern and western flanks of the Pennines and in Scotland,
brickmaking on the coalfields, and heavy chemicals were produced in the North East
and Cheshire and in connection with the coke and gas works on the coalfields. Most
of these areas had previously been only sparsely inhabited and the new industries
dominated the local economies.[28] Moreover, each region tended to specialise. While
these developments were taking place there was little alteration in the distribution
pattern of lighter manufacturing. This remained concentrated in central and southern

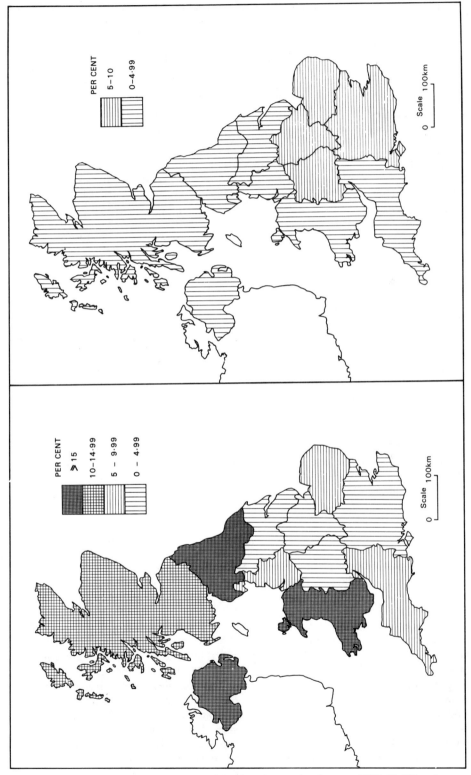

Figure 4.12a Manufacturing employment deriving from interregional moves, 1963-66, UK regions

Figure 4.12b Manufacturing employment in moves from a region 1953-66, as per cent manufacturing
employment in each UK Region, 1966

TABLE 4.16   Gross Output per Employee in Selected Industries, UK, 1963

	Gross output	Total employment	Gross output per employee	Region where this industry was largest % of manufacturing employment
	£ million	£ thousand	£ thousand	
Iron and steel (general)	1,316·5	268·9	4·9	Wales
Miscellaneous (non-electrical) machinery	773·4	289·1	2·7	East Anglia
General Mechanical engineering	467·6	211·9	2·2	South East
Grain milling	338·5	31·6	10·7	N. Ireland
Bread and flour confectionery	381·3	160·2	2·4	N. Ireland
Sugar (mainly refining)	230·2	15·9	14·5	*
Cocoa, chocolate and sugar confectionery	265·4	91·8	2·9	Yorkshire and Humberside
Production of man-made fibres	210·7	37·6	5·6	*
Spinning and doubling of cotton and man-made fibres	246·7	104·3	2·4	*
Overalls and men's shirts, underwear etc.	83·0	48·9	1·7	N. Ireland
Paper and board	383·3	88·2	4·3	Scotland
Cardboard boxes, cartons and fibreboard packing cases	178·9	63·4	2·8	South West
Synthetic resins and plastics materials	198·0	32·4	6·1	North
Plastics moulding and fabricating	175·9	72·6	2·4	South East

Source: Census of Production (HMSO 1963)

* Not available

lowland Britain, where it had been located previously, and where the largest concentrations of the population and hence of consumer demand remained. The only other manufacturing that was attracted to the heavy industrial areas was usually either directly dependent, such as textile machinery manufacture in Lancashire and wagon works in Wales and Scotland, or served the local markets, making such things as confectionery or milk products. The survival of these patterns until 1945 influenced subsequent development. Productivity differences meant that increases in output generated most employment in the central and southern parts of the economy where the light manufacturing was concentrated. Much less employment generation accompanied increases in output in the peripheral regions because of the dominance there of heavy industries with their higher gross output per man.

This was not the only way productivity made a contribution to the changing geography of manufacturing. Over the period 1945-70 the continuing improvements in manpower productivity affected employment in the older heavy industries in particular. They suffered not only from having been developed much earlier, but also from the inadequate investment in modernisation in the 1920s and 1930s. Thus in 1945 they had inherited per capita output rates well below what had been shown to be possible in other parts of the world. Newer industries were less affected since they had already incorporated much more advanced technology in their initial development, and so already had higher rates of output per man. All the heavy industries, however, both old and new, had higher manpower productivity figures than most light manufacturing. This meant that small percentage improvements in productivity in the heavy industries could cope with much larger increases in demand without increased employment than was the case in the rest of manufacturing. For most light manufacturing rapid growth in demand aided growth in jobs. The effect of percentage productivity improvements on employment were thus much greater in areas of heavy industry concentration than in areas with concentrations of light manufacturing. In fact in some of the heavy industries the manpower productivity increases outstripped the rate of increase of demand for their products, so that they had to reduce employment even as production went up. Classic examples occurred in the South Wales steel industry. At Port Talbot, for example, steelmaking capacity was increased from 3·0 to 3·4 million ingot tons a year between 1968 and 1972 while the labour force was reduced by over 30 per cent from 18,000 to 12,500. Even in the newer heavy chemical industry ICI doubled the value of its output at Billingham between 1946 and 1959, while reducing its labour force from 15,000 to 14,800. A further effect of productivity differences was that where new primary processing industries were developed, their high productivities and capital-intensive nature meant that they required fewer employees. Though spectacular in terms of output or capital cost, such industrial developments generated fewer direct jobs in the peripheral regions where they were often located, than processing their output generated in industries further along the production line towards the final consumer.

Finally, productivity differences between various industries were contributing to the different rates of manufacturing employment growth of the various regions through the process of structural change. This was particularly true in the peripheral regions, where the decline in jobs was in such labour-intensive industries as shipbuilding, cotton and linen textiles. The new growth that did take place in these regions was frequently of capital intensive industries which were the growth industries of the mid-twentieth century: steel strip mills and petrol refineries in Wales and Scotland, synthetic textiles and petrochemicals in Wales, electronics in Scotland, motor vehicle industries in Wales and Scotland. As a result there were insufficient new jobs available to employ all the available labour. In Wales for example textile manufacture, mainly man-made fibres, which was expanding had a net output per employee of £2,132, while railway carriages and wagon and tram manufacture, which was contracting, had a net output per employee of only £1,380. Substantiating these comments are those statistics which indicate that the peripheral regions of the UK had employment growth which was further behind the national average than their rate of growth of output. This showed that these regions were achieving a more rapid improvement of productivity than the country as a whole. Wales and Northern Ireland had above average rates of productivity growth in the 1950s and 1960s; Scotland achieved improvements roughly equal to the UK average in the 1950s, but in the 1960s her annual growth of productivity was 3·6 per cent compared with 3·1 per cent for the nation as a whole.[29] In this situation these regions needed a higher rate of growth of *output* than the national average to achieve a rate of *employment* growth equal to the national average.

III.3 Market Influences

The last section indicated that the slow growth and declining industries were concentrated where they were mainly for historic reasons. But this does not explain *why* the industries with more rapid employment growth were so unevenly distributed. The major factor in this was, undoubtedly, the distribution of the market in the UK. It has been suggested that under contemporary economic conditions a market location is now the 'norm' for modern industry. Locations other than at the market need to be explained by factors which prevent market location, or by lower costs elsewhere which outweigh the market attractions. Clark has produced a map showing the geography of the market in Britain.[30] (figure 4.13). It is based on his concept of economic potential, which he defines as the sum of incomes in areas adjacent to a particular geographical point divided by their

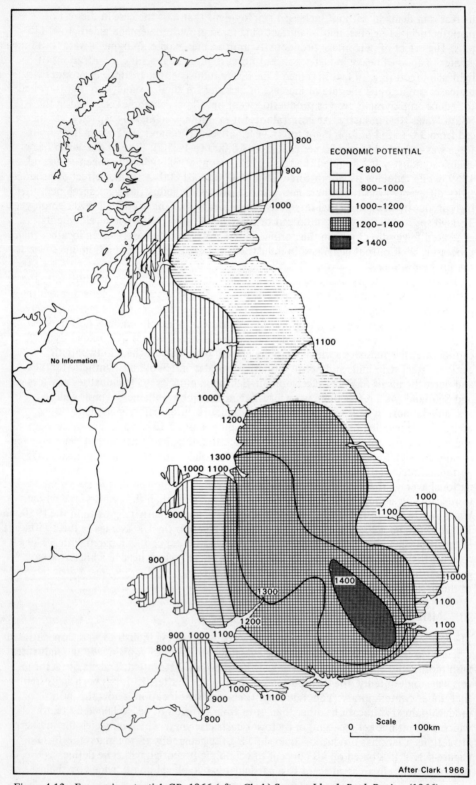

Figure 4.13   Economic potential, GB, 1966 (after Clark) Source: *Lloyds Bank Review* (1966)

distances from that point. The higher the economic potential the greater the power to attract economic activity. Figure 4.13 can be seen to correspond fairly closely to the pattern of regional economic growth in the UK discussed earlier. The reasons for this are not difficult to find. A number of manufacturing industries are essentially consumer-oriented, either because of the perishability of their product, for example the making of fresh bread and the manufacture of local or regional newspapers, or because of the need for personal consumer contact as in custom tailoring, or because of bulk gains or low value of the product as in the example of soft drinks manufacture or made-up boxes. Such industries are distributed roughly according to population, with the largest numbers employed where there are the largest population concentrations and/or market potential. These industries will grow fastest where population growth is strongest. In the UK the largest markets and the greatest increases in population were coincident between 1945 and 1970. They were found in the area reaching from London through the Midlands to the Lancashire industrial region. Other regions with smaller populations, and with much slower growing populations (figure 2.7), clearly will not have benefited to the same extent from development of these industries. A further stimulus in the central areas of the economy was the faster growth of service employments described later. With the service sector expanding more rapidly than manufacturing, this helped to stimulate consumer demand still further in the large population centres, adding to their attractions for the consumer-oriented industries. In this sense service industry development can be thought of as stimulating manufacturing expansion. Beyond these factors of sheer size and growth, it is also recognised that large and growing markets more readily generate new industries, and attract new industries that started elsewhere to them, and in both cases are more likely to nurture them successfully.[31] Various factors help explain this apart from sheer size. Labour in sufficient quantity and of appropriate quality is likely to be more readily available in the larger centres of economic activity than elsewhere. Factory buildings, especially small units, are usually available for rent or purchase in larger numbers. External economies are also more likely to be obtained from such things as greater ease of contact with consumers and with other industries supplying components or services, from the familiarity with initiative by local industry, from discussion with like-minded entrepreneurs, and from the greater pool of existing experience.

In the case of London, Hall also argued that these factors were no different in the twentieth century than they had been in the nineteenth. The difference was that in the nineteenth century the major heavy industries found even greater advantages in locating close to their raw material sources and especially close to their fuel supplies, than by locating in previously developed manufacturing centres. This situation explained the spectacular growth of the coalfield economies in particular. In the twentieth century raw material attractions became less important, and a greater range of industries have developed where the attractions of large markets, real or merely perceived, have been able to exert their influence much more strongly. It is these newer industries that were attracted to, and grew more strongly in, close proximity to the major markets in Britain. By 1945 London was the major focus of attraction with the largest concentration not only of people, but of manufacturing and of market potential as well. Further centres were the West Midlands focused on Birmingham, and the Merseyside-Manchester-West Riding areas further north.

The peripheral regions suffered relative disadvantage in having much lower market potential because of their smaller populations and their lower incomes.[32] Most of them suffered two other important disadvantages in addition. The first was a net outward migration of population, stemming largely from the fact that they had major industries which were contracting. Their market potential was thus declining, either absolutely or relatively, or was thought to be undergoing such decline. Secondly, the heavy industries that they possessed were themselves experiencing a change in the kinds of manufactured goods they needed. This kind of change was often one where in addition to, or instead of, using products of local industries that grew up to serve them, they turned to the products of the newer industries. An extreme example is the coal-mining industry. After nationalisation, two results of the capital investment and modernisation programme were the changeover of all collieries from steamdriven winding engines to electric winding, and the replacement of trams for underground haulage by conveyor belt systems where-ever possible. The old components had often been made in or near the mining areas. The new components were more likely to be produced elsewhere in Britain. Thus the older heavy industrial areas not only did not have the characteristics which encouraged growth of the light industries, but the heavy industries themselves stimulated the output of newer industries often located in other regions.

Discussion of market influences has so far been mainly concerned with the market for finished products. The market for manufactured goods, however, is not only or even mainly with the final consumer. In the production process many manufacturers never sell anything direct to the final consumer. They make parts or assemble components which are then sent on to another manufacturer who carries the process one stage further, and so on until the final product is put together. The most familiar example of this is the motorcar, which is assembled from the products of a wide range of manufacturers. Many of the components seen in the finished car carry names other than that of the company making the final assembly, e.g. Lucas, Dunlop, Triplex. The metal-based industries indulge in particularly heavy inter-trading of this kind, which contributes to spatial association of these industries within certain areas of preference. It is because of this factor that industry aiming to produce semi-manufactures for other industries generally prefers to locate close to where the market is largest and most varied. In Britain this is within or close to the polygon bounded by a line joining London-Southampton-Bristol-Birmingham-Liverpool-Sheffield-Leicester-London.

Apart from the national impact of these factors influencing the distribution of manufacturing between regions, they also had an intraregional impact. Those newer industries developed to serve mainly the markets of the region in which they were located, also tended to follow the national pattern at the lower scale. Within regions they congre-gated in the larger central places where the regional market was concentrated, or from which it was most accessible.

Given the pattern of economic potential and the attractions of the major growing market regions, it might seem surprising that there was as much expansion of manufac-turing employment, especially light manufacturing employment, in the other regions. Two main factors account for this growth. The first was the development of manufacturing serving mainly or exclusively local and regional demands, and the second was the effect of government policy. Industry serving regional or local markets was stimulated by the growing affluence which affected all parts of the UK. This was offset to a certain extent, in some of the regions, by the decline of working population and higher unemployment rates in some of the regions, as for instance in parts of Scotland and Northern Ireland. In the late 1960s the effects of economies of scale, discussed later, in some of these industries also eroded part of this growth, by shifting location to areas with higher economic potential. Over the 25 years since 1945, however, these locally-oriented industries did contribute to the expansion of consumer goods industries even in areas with relatively low economic potential. Good examples include some food industries such as brewing and soft drinks, stationery printing, packaging materials, and the mak-ing of building industry components such as doors and window frames, building blocks and concrete mixing. All these were noticeably at the consumer goods end of the continuum. A prominent feature of the location of these industries was their tendency to congregate in the larger central places within the smaller regions. They were exhibiting the characteristics of the national pattern within their regions by locating in the areas with the highest *regional* economic potential. Edinburgh in Scotland, Cardiff and Swansea in Wales, Belfast in Northern Ireland, Tyneside in the Northern region, and Bristol and Plymouth in the South West, all provide examples of this trend.

Government policy had a different effect. Ever since 1934 a major aim in regional planning had been the deliberate encouragement of manufacturing expansion in the regions of slow growth or decline, and the movement of manufacturing out of the regions of overgrowth especially in the South East and the West Midlands. This policy had a major impact in stimulating new manufacturing growth in the development areas of the UK. For many manufacturing industries certain conditions in the areas of high economic potential were conducive or even essential to their *initial* development. But once established there were no good economic reasons why many of them could not then be transferred, or have their expansion transferred, to other regions and flourish successfully.[33] Luttrell found in fact that the majority of British industry could operate successfully in any of the major industrial centres of Britain.[34] According to most location theories a main disadvantage such industries would have in moving in this way would arise from added transport costs. In practice such costs have been shown to be a relatively unimportant part of total costs in many British Industries. The Toothill Committee found the effect of transport costs on firms which chose to locate in Scotland for example, to be less than two per cent,[35] a figure they considered to be insignificant. Chisholm argued that such transport effects as did exist were diminishing quite rapidly. He further pointed out that uniform delivered prices are quoted for any location in Britain for many components or part manufactures used in production, and that in fact uniform delivered prices are more usual than unusual. Evidence to support this contention was drawn from a whole range of industries including car electric equipment, semi-manufactured copper and copper-based alloys, chemical fertilisers and pneumatic tyres.[36] Apart from transport costs, other detailed studies have indicated that in the clothing and radio industries, firms which have opened branch factories in development areas have not suffered substantial transport cost disadvantages compared with the branch they might have opened in London instead. In fact, overall, the advantage was slightly with the provincial plant.[37] Empirical evidence of the flourishing of so many new manu-facturing industries in the development areas would seem to bear out these findings. A word of caution is necessary, merely to point out that there are industries where these conditions do not apply. Notably the consumer contact industries mentioned earlier, and some of the heavy industries where raw material costs loom large or the product has low value per unit bulk, on which transport costs bear especially heavily.

III.4 Government Policy

By 1970 government policies to influence the geography of manufacturing industry in Britain had been applied for nearly 40 years. The effects had been substantial, though just how substantial is difficult to establish with any precision. This is partly because it is difficult to disentangle the effects of government policy from changes which would have occurred without it. It is relatively easy, however, to distinguish certain periods when the policies had maximum impact from those when there was little positive result (see section 1.III).

In the period between the passing of the earliest legislation, the Special Areas (Development and Improvement) Act of 1934, and the beginning of the Second World War, the policy had little impact on the geography of manufacturing. The special areas acquired only 4 per cent of the factories established in Britain between 1934 and 1939, though they contained over 8 per cent of the national population. By contrast Greater London acquired a 40 per cent share of the new factories. By 1939 the resulting employment in

the special areas amounted only to some 12,000 jobs altogether. In South Wales alone
there were 57,000 unemployed in that year, whereas the new factories built in the
previous 5 years employed only 3,000. During the succeeding period of the Second
World War the government exercised virtually complete control over industrial developments as part of the war effort. The results of this control on the geography of industry
during this period and even more so in the years immediately following 1945 were very
considerable, though this is seldom fully appreciated and no proper assessment of it has
yet been made. Most of the new industry which appeared at this time was geared to the
war effort. For strategic reasons much of it was located in the peripheral regions of previous high unemployment in the west and north, e.g. the huge munitions factories at
Aycliffe and Spennymoor in the North East and at Bridgend in South Wales. These and
other strategic industries created fixed capital in buildings and services, they created a pool
of labour with skills suitable for light manufacturing, and they demonstrated the capability
of the depressed areas for new industrial development. These proved invaluable assets in
the succeeding period up to 1950.

The creation of these assets would have had less effect in the succeeding years
without the implementation of a strong distribution of industry policy by the government. In 1945 a Distribution of Industry Act was passed which provided grants and
loans to help manufacturers establish in designated development areas, and allowed
the Board of Trade to assist further through the building of factories and improvement
of local infrastructure. In 1947 operation of the policy was strengthened through the
1947 Town and County Planning Act, for under the Act planning applications for
factory building involving 5,000 ft^2 (464 m^2) or more of factory space had to be
accompanied by an Industrial Development Certificate (IDC), issued by the Board of
Trade. This allowed the Board to control industrial building in overgrowth areas and
encourage it in the development areas. The combined effect of the new policy and
the wartime contribution was considerable, with the latter being especially important
up to 1948. By June 1947 the conversion of nine major ordnance factories and over
100 other wartime factories to peace-time use had attracted 233 tenants with nearly
50,000 employees to the development areas. By contrast the 301 *new* factories and
extensions in these areas were providing only 20,000 jobs. Since the development
areas had acquired over 50 per cent of the industrial space built in Britain between
1945 and 1947, the contribution of the wartime factories to the changing location of
manufacturing at this time was clearly substantial. The distribution of industry policy
was less effective at the end of the 1940s but, despite this, *two-thirds* of all recorded
moves by manufacturing firms in Britain between 1945 and 1951 were into the
development areas (table 4.17).

TABLE 4.17   Industrial Building in the Development Areas (DAs), GB, 1945-54

Annual average	Sq ft of Industrial building approved in DAs	DAs as a % of all GB industrial building	Insured population of of DAs as % GB
1945-7	15·7	51·1	19·9
1948-50	7·5	17·2	18·3
1951-3	8·1	21·7	18·2

*Source: Second Report of the Select Committee on Estimates Session 1955/6 The Development
          Areas* (HMSO)

In the 1950s much less new industry went to the development areas, and after 1951
a newly elected government relaxed all forms of control over the economy. For Greater
London, 1952-8, Powell suggested that very little of the increase could have been
moved elsewhere.[38] When rising unemployment caused reimposition of the distribution

of industry policy after 1957 it had limited effect because there was so little manufacturing expansion whose location the measures available could influence. By 1960 however, the government were landlords for 45 million ft^2 (4·1 million m^2) of factory space in development areas, with 1,095 firms and 201,000 employees in them[39].

In the 1960s recognition that the under-utilised labour resources of the development areas were a major asset for any potential national economic growth, resulted in renewed application and further strengthening of the distribution of industry policies. The effects were strongly felt in the late 1960s following the election of a new government in 1964 committed to regional planning and the proper location of industry to achieve national economic aims. The number of factories completed and the total expenditure in 1966-7 was more than double that of 1961-2. The amount of assistance provided for the development areas or districts for the four years 1960-4 amounted to £121 million, whereas in the period 1966-70 it amounted to over £250 million.

In implementing the policy the government by 1970 had effectively divided Britain into five types of area for the purpose of influencing the geographical distribution of industry (figure 1.4). There were the development areas with a range of incentives for manufacturers together with ready availability of IDCs. Within these there were special development areas where incentives were even more favourable for manufacturing growth. These had been set up mainly in response to higher unemployment resulting from closure of coal mines in certain areas after 1967. Outside the development areas were certain 'intermediate' or 'grey' areas which had only some of the inducements of the development areas. These were designated following the investigations of the Hunt Committee which reported in 1969, and have since been extended. Parts of the UK however were regarded essentially as overgrowth areas, best identified as those areas where office development was subject to control. Here attempts were made to limit and control employment expansion. Finally, in the remaining parts of Britain growth was neither positively encouraged nor positively discouraged. Outside these areas in Britain, with its own provincial government, there was Northern Ireland. In effect this had the same inducements to manufacturers as the development areas, though in most cases on a more generous scale.

What emerges from this is that government policy was *a* major factor, if not *the* major factor in the changes in the *regional* pattern of manufacturing between 1945 and 1970. Its contribution had greatest effect in stimulating manufacturing development in the peripheral regions which had the smallest manufacturing employment. For the South East, East Anglia, and West Midlands regions, the moves originating in them in fact represented less than 8 per cent of their 1966 manufacturing employment, and so did help constrain their growth but only to a limited extent.

III.5   Economies of Scale: Internal

Economies of scale played a particularly important part in the changing location of manufacturing in the 1960s. This was mainly through changing the inherited pattern *within* regions rather than between regions. The pattern of production inherited in 1945 was essentially one of small-scale units. Even in iron- and steel-making, no works had a capacity of more than one million ingot tons a year. Textile manufacture was in a large number of small mills; although there were some large car works, most motor car manufacture was in small factories, with output measured in hundreds rather than thousands of cars a year. In food production, small family bakers still dominated bread output, for example, and the few large breweries produced a small proportion of total output. One of the geographical implications of this state of affairs was that much more locational dispersion was possible. For a given output there were a large number of works and these could be, and usually were, widely dispersed. Being small they could be located in small places which had sufficient labour to meet their needs. Where such small factories employed several hundred people they dominated the economy of the small places in which they were located.

Well before 1945 it had been recognised that there were economic advantages to be gained from large-scale operations in many industries. But achievement of these economies was usually by replacement of men by machines to obtain higher productivity, and usually also meant larger premises to cope with expanded output. Both required the investment of capital which had been in short supply for much of the previous 25 years. There were other inhibiting factors like fragmented ownership, discussed below, which also contributed. As a result, by 1945 all too few industries had begun to take advantage of the economies of scale which were thought to be available. Some increases in size of unit began to appear by the early 1950s, but it was not until after 1955 that substantial changes occurred. This is brought out in table 4.18 where employment per

TABLE 4.18   Manufacturing Employment by Establishment Size, UK, 1947-68: Percentage Distribution of Employees in Manufacturing Industries in Establishments Employing more than Ten Persons

Size group of establishment	% total employees			
	1947	1955	1963	1968
11-24	4·0	3·4	4·8	4·4
25-49	6·9	6·6	4·5	} 11·3
50-99	10·5	9·7	8·2	
11-99	21·4	19·7	17·5	15·7
100-249	18·7	17·3	20·2*	} 37·0
250-499	15·6	15·0	11·4†	
500-999	13·9	14·6	14·0	14·0
100-999	48·2	46·9	45·6	51·0
1000-1999	12·3	12·8	13·7	NA
2000-4999	11·4	12·3	13·2	NA
5000 and over	6·7	8·3	10·0	NA
1000 and over	30·4	33·4	36·0	33·3
	100·0	100·0		

Source: *Annual Abstracts of Statistics and Census of Production* (HMSO)

*† Estimated, *Census of Production, 1963*

establishment is plotted. In some cases growth was achieved by expanding output on existing sites, in other cases by building new greenfield factories. Some industries had both. As the economy was growing these changes could be achieved by the large new units meeting the increased demand, while old factories continued in operation. In many cases, however, centralisation occurred with many smaller older units being closed down as output was concentrated in a few new larger factories. Classic examples occurred in the iron and steel and tinplate industries in South Wales (figure 4.14a and b).[40] Some industries which were virtually new could start off operating at the scale suited to contemporary conditions. This was particularly true of consumer durable manufacture, such as the production of washing machines or television sets, and of such new industries as plastics and artificial fibre manufacture in textiles. The geographical effect of these changes was to reduce the total number of works needed for a given output. Where an old-established industry was involved this usually caused local changes only, though in some cases an entire industry was lost from a region. Output was concentrated into fewer but larger-scale production units. The effect of implementing changes to achieve these

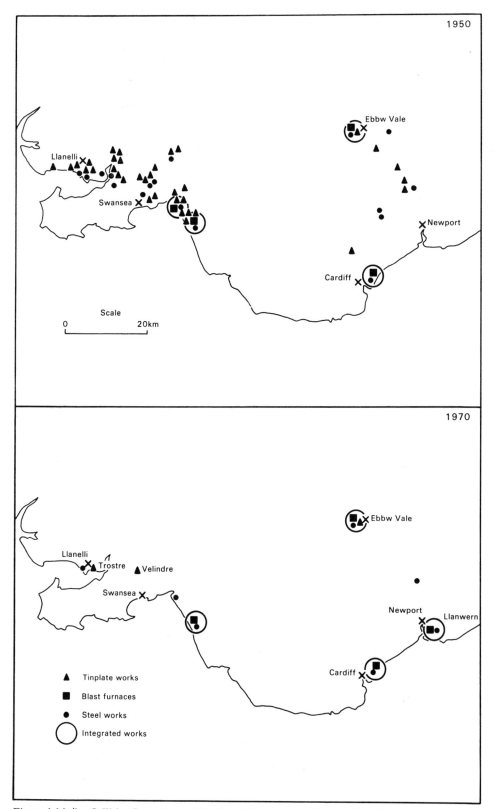

Figure 4.14a/b   S. Wales. Iron, steel and tinplate industry, rationalisation 1950-70

economies of scale normally meant increases in labour productivity, so that employment might be reduced even though output had increased. Good examples of these trends come from the flour-milling industry. Where it is an old geographical pattern that has been modified certain trends can be identified. Usually the larger newer works are located in a major urban centre, with the closures taking place in the smaller towns where the smaller, older works were located. Centralisation has meant *geographical centralisation* of production as well as *economic* centralisation. Because of increasing scale of operations the larger works or factories require better facilities for movement of materials and goods in bulk. They also need a large labour supply. This means locating in a large urban centre or at a point with a large enough journey to work hinterland to generate the quantity and quality of labour required. In spatial terms the location requirements are now more specific and limiting. There are a smaller number of locations likely to be able to meet them; indeed many of the smaller, older centres did not meet these requirements. On the other hand, extension of the journey to work, by use of the private motor car, has meant that the former production centres could often be within travelling distance of the location of the large new works or factory where production has been centralised. A further implication of the increased economies of scale is that of local diversification. With the average size of works increasing, a local economy is much more likely to be dominated by an industry than previously. Factories employing more than 4,000-5,000 are now fairly commonplace. Even in 1963 nearly 10 per cent of the employees in manufacturing were employed in establishments of over 5,000 employees. Two such factories could employ all the manufacturing workers in a town of 40,000 people, since the labourforce of such a town would be around 20,000 of whom roughly half could be expected to be in services.

III.6 Economies of Scale: External

The above discussion has been confined to internal economies of scale and the effects of increasing the scale of production in a single unit. There are also advantages to be gained from external economies of scale in manufacturing industry. These too have played a part in the creation of new patterns of industry in the UK. For small factories there are external economies of scale to be obtained by clustering. In this way some of the services needed can be jointly financed, while others can be more easily provided. As important has been the fact that the development of clustered factories on estates makes industry more manageable for planners. Such estates are also cheaper to develop, an important consideration where publicly financed or privately financed estates are set up in advance of occupance. Industrial estates became a familiar feature of the British industrial landscape between 1945 and 1970, whereas previously they had been an exception. Here again it was the *large* industrial estates which could benefit most, and these had to be located near large centres, or at accessible journey to work points for large numbers of people.[41]

The basic importance of economies of scale, then, has been the alteration of inherited patterns, the smaller urban places losing manufacturing jobs which have been centralised into large units located in the larger towns. New manufacturing industry has taken advantage of economies of scale by setting up large establishments initially. Smaller factories have been involved by being clustered together on industrial estates, whereas they would have been dispersed under previously prevailing conditions.

III.7 Ownership and Control

A contributory factor allowing the centralisation to achieve economies of scale to take place were the changes in ownership and control in the 25 years after 1945. Hamilton has pointed out how locational decisions are affected by ownership, with individual ownership, and corporate ownership differing in their location decisions from each other and from state organisations.[42] In particular, the private entrepreneur works within the context of satisfying his needs from usually a single establishment. The corporation is generally aiming to optimise economic returns from a number of establishments. State operations often have to operate within the constraint of contributing to national or regional economic needs as well as, or instead of, maximising economic returns from that particular operation. In 1945 the individual entrepreneur was common in manufacturing industry and many companies owned just one or two factories. Any one industry had a large number of controlling interests. This made agreement on rationalisation and centralisation of operations much more difficult. Individual entrepreneurs were frequently more concerned with protecting their interests as they saw them, and the interests of their factory and workmen, than in any potential increase in economic returns. After 1945 this situation was substantially changed. Until 1955 the changes were relatively small and mainly of two kinds. The first was state involvement, directly through nationalisation, as in the steel industry, and indirectly by various means such as allocation of defence contracts or state aid as in aircraft and shipbuilding. The second change was that much of the manufacturing growth was in new industries with strong corporate management. International companies became much more familiar in the UK and decisions were being taken on a larger scale. Initially there was little geographical change as a result of these ownership and control developments. For the large new industries this was a time of expansion anyway, which limited the need for centralisation. In the 1960s, however, the pattern began to change. A spate of company mergers and amalgamations, and of large companies buying small companies occurred. In other cases small companies simply went out of business in face of strong opposition. As a result, many industries ended up with control centred in a small number of hands (table 4.19). In many cases there were obvious gains to be had by rationalisation and concentration of production at a smaller number of larger factories. The need for such developments to make industry more efficient and competitive was recognised by the British Government in the late 1960s when they set up the Industrial Reorganisation Corporation. This body gave financial aid to industries where centralisation and rationalisation was to take place. The result of these changes was the reduction of operating units and the concentration of production at a smaller number of factories. The point here is that centralisation of ownership was a necessary prerequisite. The changes in geography would have occurred without such ownership and control changes, though they would have taken a lot longer, or some of the industries would have died before the necessary changes were achieved.

IV SERVICES

IV.1 Significance

Since at least as early as 1950 the service sector (orders XVII-XVIV 1958 SIC; XX-XXVII 1968 SIC) in Britain has employed more people than primary production and manufacturing combined. In the two decades up to 1970 this dominance was further strengthened as employment in services grew much faster than that in manufacturing, and employment in the primary sector declined (figure 4.9). Since employment in large part determines the location of the population, and most employment in Britain is in services, it follows that the pattern of service employment is today of fundamental importance in the human geography and the planning of the country. This is most obvious in those areas where service employment is growing, since such growth is normally accompanied by or caused by population expansion. This in turn stimulates spatially associated economic, social and physical demands for such things as shops, schools and housing. Beyond this the distribution of the service jobs has considerable

TABLE 4.19   Concentration of Sales of Selected Products by Larger Firms, GB, 1958 and 1963

Standard industrial classification, minimum list heading	Product or group of products	Number of enterprises	% total sales		Number of enterprises in 1958 with same concentration ratio as 1963
			1958	1963	
211 (part of)	White flour for bread-making	5	71·5	79·2	over 10
212	Bread sold in loaves or in rolls	5	31·5	71·4	over 10
	Flour con-fectionery	5	26·7	51·0	over 10
277 (1)	Polishes	5	67·1	79·6	9
352	Watches and clocks and parts thereof	5	72·7	80·8	9
364 (part of)	Television re-ceiving sets complete	5	52·7	81·6	over 10
383 (Part of)	Aircraft com-plete, new and reconditioned and air frames	5	86·6	98·0	over 10
384	Locomotives, complete	5	80·9	93·0	10
411	Man-made fibres	7	not available	100	not available
450 (Part of)	Men's, youths' and boys' footwear	5	22·2	30·3	9

Source: Census of Production (HMSO 1963)

significance for manufacturing. It was argued earlier that an important influence on the distribution of manufacturing, especially of light manufacturing, was the location of the market. When discussed in general terms the market means purchasing power, which in turn goes with jobs. Since most people in Britain work in services, it follows that they are an important element in determining where the consumer market is, thus influencing the location of manufacturing. Here a precautionary note must be introduced since this is one of the situations where differences within the employment figures are significant. The majority of the workers in services are women, and much of the expansion that has taken place has occurred by an increase in female participation in the labourforce (table 4.20). The relevance of this is that wage rates in services in general are lower than in manufacturing or primary industries, and wage rates for females have tended to be lower than for males in Britain in the past.[43]

IV.2 Flexibility of Location

Studies by economic geographers to explain these patterns of service location have been very limited in the past. One of the reasons for this was the false assumption, made not only by geographers but also by others such as economists and planners, that the location of services will coincide with the location of primary and secondary (industrial) growth which directly and indirectly controls the demand for them. While there is some validity in this assumption at the national level, at the regional, and more particularly at the intraregional level, there are too many exceptions involving a large number of employees for it to be even a working rule. In elaborating this it is necessary to distinguish clearly between ubiquitous and flexible services, a distinction which is fundamental to any understanding of the changes and trends in the geography of services in Britain.

Ubiquitous services are those which depend upon direct consumer contact, and are, therefore, located within the immediate vicinity of the populations they serve. Good examples of ubiquitous services are general practitioners, hairdressers, opticians and laundrettes. Other things being equal it can be expected that the distribution of these services will be closely correlated with the distribution of population. Flexible services on the other hand are those which do not need direct consumer contact, so that they are much more flexible in their choice of location. Examples of such services include head offices of building societies, national libraries, or electricity board headquarters. For these the choice of location is spatially circumscribed only by national or regional boundaries. The ubiquitous and flexible services thus described are, of course, the extremes of what in fact is a continuum grading from extreme ubiquity to extreme flexibility. This continuum is best illustrated by reference to the education service in the UK. It is generally accepted that primary schools need to be located as close as possible to the homes of the children attending them. To minimise the movement of pupils such schools are normally provided within the neighbourhood unit which they serve. At the next higher stage in education, junior comprehensive schools are fewer in number than the primary schools. They have larger enrolments and on average are further from pupils' homes, but still normally within the local community they serve. The senior comprehensive schools are fewer in number again, and so on average are still further away from pupils' homes, serving perhaps several communities. At the next level a further education college will usually have a much wider catchment area, and a college for the training of teachers will draw on a wider catchment still. Finally, a university or medical school can be built almost anywhere in the UK and will still attract students. In this context the university would seem to have complete flexibility in its choice of location. The example of the education service illustrates the whole range of location types in the services, from those governed by the need for close consumer contact, to those facing problems of having their location choice governed not so much by proximity to consumers as by other factors.

In practice this range of locational type is comparable with that found in manufacturing. Those manufacturing industries requiring close customer contact, such as jobbing printers, or which involve high bulk gain or whose products have high perishability, such as soft drink manufacture or bread baking, have a ubiquitous distribution. At the other end of the range those industries involving high weight loss or which use a high proportion of low-value raw materials, tend to locate at their raw material sources, or where the raw materials are imported, and are not governed by customer locations to the same degree, e.g. oil-refining, flour-milling or steel-making. It follows from this that far from the distribution of many services being controlled by the distribution of the population, they are much more akin to manufacturing in being influenced by other locational requirements.

In looking at the distribution of service employment in the UK after 1945, the distinction between ubiquitous and flexible services is important for two reasons. The first is that the flexible services tend to have grown more rapidly, and secondly, the degree of flexibility of most services has been increasing. The more rapid growth of the flexible services has been less significant in absolute numbers but nonetheless the trend was an important one.

IV.3 Changing Location

With considerable freedom from locating close to consumers much of the growth of the most flexible services in fact took place in the south-eastern corner of Britain, especially in and around London.[44] By 1964, for example, of the 76 main government research

TABLE 4.20   Increase in the Number of Employees, UK, 1950-70* (in thousands)

	Men	1950 Women	Total
Primary industries	1,626	135	1,761
Manufacturing industries	5,677	2,872	8,549
Service industries	6,694	4,116	10,810
Grand total	13,997	7,123	21,120

Source: Department of Employment and Productivity Publications

* Because of changes in definition and methods of compilation, the figures for each sector are not strictly comparable over time and are given to indicate the main trends only.

establishments 59 were in South East England.[45] In those cases where there were constraints to locate within particular regions, then the locations chosen were similar to the national pattern, that is, there was a marked preference to be in or near the regional capital.[46] Thus half the 1961 office rateable value in England and Wales, outside the South East, was located in a handful of regional cities: Manchester, Birmingham, Liverpool, Leeds, Newcastle, Bristol and Cardiff.[47] In the case of Scotland, Wales and Northern Ireland the similarity to the national pattern was even greater, in that the capitals in each case happen to be in the south-east of their territories. Although reasons can be suggested for this uneven distribution, such as availability of better communications or supporting services, or that this allows central government offices to be close together in the provincial capitals, none of these in the last resort is conclusive. There is little evidence to suggest, for example, that the Aluminium Research Association laboratories could not function just as successfully closer to major aluminium working centres in Scotland or Wales rather than in Oxford.[48] Similarly the development of three university-level institutions in Cardiff, the University College of South Wales and Monmouthshire, the University of Wales Institute of Science and Technology and the University of Wales School of Medicine, was a matter of inertia and historical accident rather than positive locational forces determining the choice.[49]

While the increasing concentration of the *growth* of *flexible* services, in the capital cities in particular, was bringing about changes in the distribution pattern, there were other changes of equal importance, in that they were making possible the *rearrangement* of *existing* service provision. For many services there was an observable trend towards increased flexibility in location. This had repercussions mostly at the intraregional level rather than the interregional level, but it was nonetheless important because of that. The main contributory factors to increasing flexibility were the changes in organisation which were taking place, the increasing opportunities to take advantage of economies of scale and the increasing mobility of the service consumers.

IV.4 Organisation and Control

Prior to 1945 many of the service industries were under the control of local government, or, in the commercial sector, were in the hands of a multitude of small companies, or of individuals who had limited means at their disposal and limited aims. Good examples of these conditions could be found in the environmental services of gas, electricity and water, in personal services such as medicine and education and in commercial services such as cinemas, retail distribution and dry-cleaning. The effect of this kind of control was that services were very dispersed. In the public sector, local authorities usually operated as if their areas were islands. For example, each local authority that provided a gas supply service in its area would normally have a gas-making plant and a full range

| | 1960 | | | 1970 | |
Men	Women	Total	Men	Women	Total
1,308	117	1,424	744	92	836
6,013	2,933	8,947	6,274	2,802	9,075
7,354	4,977	12,331	7,586	5,948	13,535
14,675	8,027	22,702	14,604	8,842	23,446

of necessary administrative and maintenance staff.[50] Similarly in the private sector many grocers owned and operated just one shop, and would adapt and accept reduced profits to stay in business at that place when commercial principles might indicate that the location had outlived its usefulness. Many of the services then had an organisation and a location pattern that had grown up in a previous period and suited to earlier conditions.

IV.5 Public Sector Developments

The inhibiting influence of small-scale organisation on change was drastically reduced after 1945. Major changes came about in several of the services through nationalisation. In some cases the effect of this was to transfer a service from the private to the public sector as happened with the railways. In other cases such as gas and electricity distribution, where both local authorities and private companies were involved, nationalisation imposed uniform public sector control. The effect in either case was to replace diverse and variously organised systems of small-scale operations by large-scale integrated organisation. The resulting centralisation of control created the necessary conditions for rationalisation to take place. The immediate spatial impact was in fact relatively limited. The lack of capital in a country still recovering from six years of war, and the need to gain operating experience, delayed change. The full effects did not really make themselves felt until after 1955, and it was only in the 1960s that the new patterns began to dominate. The basic change was that the newly nationalised services were no longer constrained by area or regional boundaries, imposed from outside, in their decisions on location of their activities. At the same time any duplication resulting from the previous multiplicity of ownership could be eliminated. Thus the gas and electricity boards were able to create their own patterns. (figure 4.16a). They established their own regions, within each of which there was a central headquarters with a hierarchy of district and area offices below that. These replaced the mixture of local authority and private undertaking offices which had existed previously in so many parts of Britain. The result of this rationalisation process, however, was to reduce employment and to centralise activities in the most suitable locations, reducing the number of places from which services operated. In the health services the changes in the pattern of hospital provision were detailed in the Hospital Plan of 1961.[51] There the same trend was observable (figure 4.15b). The aim of the plan was to achieve uniformly adequate hospital provision over the whole of the UK, in place of the considerable variation in hospital bed availability which had arisen prior to nationalisation. The location of the new and replacement hospitals could now be determined, not on the basis of availability of local funds or adequacy of local organisation as previously, but on the basis of proper distribution.

In the 25 years after 1945, partly as a result of nationalisation and the extension of public ownership, and partly by expansion and extension of previously existing government

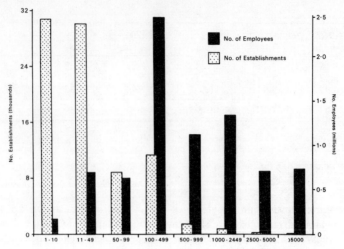

Figure 4.15a Employees and establishments, by establishment size, UK, 1963

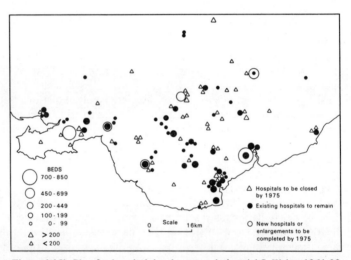

Figure 4.15b Plan for hospital development, industrial S. Wales, 1961-80

services, public control of the service sector grew to substantial proportions. By 1970 of the total employment in services of 13·6 million people, 5·6 million were working in such public sector services as gas, electricity and water supply, road and rail transport, health, education and government. Beyond this direct employment, indirect control was especially strong in the construction industry which in 1970 had a workforce of 1·9 million. 45 per cent of the construction industry output was for public authorities and government decisions on such things as availability of housing improvement grants considerably influenced the demand for the services of small local building firms. The implication of such extensive government ownership and influence in the service sector is that by 1970 the government had considerable control over employment in services, and especially over its location if it decided to exercise it. As a corollary, government, both local and national, had assumed considerable responsibility for ensuring a proper distribution pattern of service jobs and for the results of any changes initiated by policy decisions.

IV.6 Private Ownership and Control

In the private sector similar trends are readily identifiable, though with greater multiplicity of ownership and considerable inertia the effects have generally been more limited.
Most people are familiar with the changes which have occurred in the retail trade, especially in the ownership and organisation of food and clothing shops.[52] In most British
town centres, locally-owned foodshops have given way to those owned by large grocery
chains, and a similar process has taken place in men's tailors, women's clothing and shoe
provision. In 1961 nearly one-half of all speciality shoe shops in Britain were multiples,
with even higher proportions in men's outwear retailing and radio and television shops.
Furniture, electrical appliances and stationers are other examples. The geographical
effect of this is that the controlling companies maintain operations only where an
adequate return is earned on the capital invested. If sales or earnings drop below what is
considered acceptable, then a store is closed. This is in contrast with the small individual
shop owner, who would often accept a lower income or make other adjustments to
maintain his shop, since it is the only one he has.[53] With larger organisations there is
better chance too of locational investigation before a new store is opened, to ensure
as far as possible that the right choice has been made.[54] This again contrasts with the
private shop owner, who is more likely to be influenced by personal rather than commercial considerations. Again the greater financial resources and better management make
the larger organisations very competitive, so that they can often capture sales from small
shop owners if they are in competition for a limited market. Finally, rationalisation
occurs not only as a result of the above trends but also through mergers and takeovers
with one large organisation combining with another. Where both have outlets close
together in a shopping centre, there is a likelihood that only one will survive. Many of
these developments in the private sector took place in the 1960s on a significant scale,
but by 1970 not enough time had elapsed for the full effects to be worked out. What
was important however was that they made rationalisation and centralisation much more
possible, and it is likely that this will be taken advantage of to an increasing extent in
the 1970s.

The service least affected by these tendencies was order XX, construction. About 40
per cent of the employees in this order are engaged in building maintenance, which offers
little chance for rationalisation and is ubiquitous in distribution. Moreover, nearly one
quarter of the 75,000 firms in this activity are one-man businesses. Roughly 20 per cent
of the 1·5 million operatives are engaged by local authorities, which again limits
rationalisation. There are the beginnings of rationalisation observable here, however, in
two ways. The first is the reduction of on-site work in new construction. This is especially
noticeable in housebuilding, where increasingly such items as doors, windows and even
roof structures, plumbing items, and concrete, are delivered to the site having been
manufactured and assembled elsewhere. While prefabrication of complete dwelling
units has not yet become popular in the UK, prefabrication of many components for
assembly and installation by construction workers on site was a commonplace by 1970.
The second trend was the development of major companies operating nationally or
internationally. By 1970 there were over 220 firms, each with over 600 employees.[55]
Many of these had developed permanent central offices where much of the preparation
work such as design and administration could be centralised.

IV.7 Increased Mobility

A factor affecting the location of services at the intraregional level was the change in
the field of transport. Public road transport in many areas was improved by the provision
of faster and more comfortable services, while the cost of travel became much less of a
burden as average income per employee increased. Greater affluence over this same

period also resulted in many more people having their own private means of transport, in the form of a private car. This reduced the problems of overcoming distance quite considerably. Technical improvements both in vehicles and in road quality contributed to the same end. Empirical evidence for this, not surprisingly, suggests that households with cars tend to rely less on local centres, travel greater distances and to a wider variety of centres than households without cars.[56]

The resulting greater mobility has received most attention because of the greater distances people were prepared to travel to work, but there was an equally important impact on the journey to services. Because it became financially less of a burden and physically less of a strain, people not only could, but did, travel greater distances to obtain the services they required. This in turn relieved the services of the need to be within such close proximity of the population they aimed to serve, and allowed them much greater latitude in their choice of location. In this way many services have become more flexible in their location choice.

IV.8 Economies of Scale

The changes in organisation and transport discussed so far were important because they altered the basis on which locational decisions were made. Their greatest impact was probably achieved because they allowed advantage to be taken of the increasing economies of scale available in the service sector. When the distances people are prepared to travel are relatively short, then it is necessary to have a large number of service points close to the population being served. This was the position in the UK in the period before 1950. It was encouraged by the form of ownership and control, which favoured the retention of a wide distribution of service points in both the public and the private service sectors. But a wide distribution also meant small individual units, whether offices or shops. Changes in the constraints described above, however, made it possible to alter the pattern so that any one place served a much wider area. The advantage of this was that each operational unit could be larger, and through economies of scale, more economically efficient. Technological advance made such developments even more desirable. For example, the financial cost of providing expensive office or medical equipment can only be justified where there is sufficient demand to keep such equipment economically occupied. The greater the turnover of the office or hospital, the greater the demand is likely to be, while offices or hospitals with small turnovers might be below the threshold size at which investment in the facilities is considered justifiable. The effects of taking advantage of such economies of scale became increasingly apparent in the UK in the 1960s, although the process had begun much earlier. In the public services it could be seen in the 1961 Hospital Plan, where the underlying principle was one of closure of small hospitals and their replacement by fewer but larger hospitals at suitable central locations (figure 4.15b). Similarly in the gas and electricity services administrative work was concentrated into fewer centres. In the case of these utilities the process proceeded by stages with the effects of the initial rationalisation being relatively slight, but subsequent change was achieved by progressive increases in the size of the administrative areas and consequent reduction in their number, and in the number of area offices and of such things as stores and maintenance service depots.

The same trends were evident in the transport services, and even in railways which was one of the services to suffer major decline between 1945 and 1970. The rationalisation of the railways which took place after 1963 was based on the proposals in the Beeching Plan.[57] This had shown how resources were being misused in the railway services. 50 per cent of the stations provided only 1 per cent of the passenger receipts, and there were many places where lines were duplicated so that one set of income had to be used to maintain two lines. The proposed solution to the problem was the concentration of activities on the most-used facilities which could be shown to be paying their

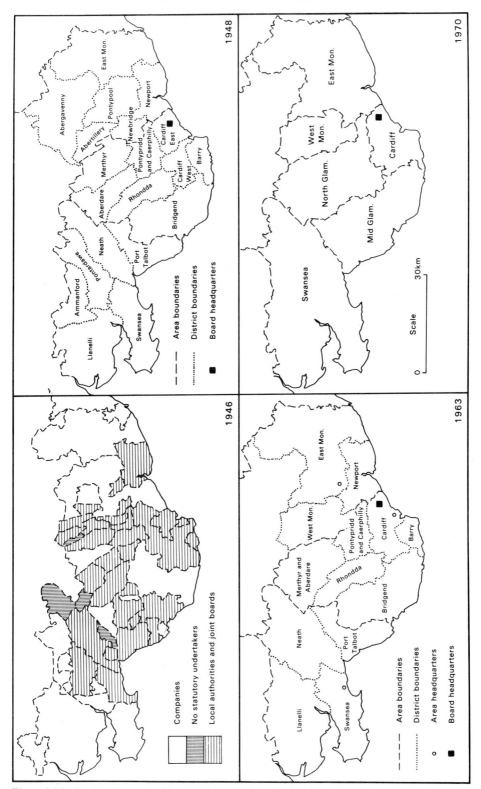

Figure 4.16   S. Wales Electricity Board. Rationalisation of Administrative Areas, industrial S. Wales, 1946-70

way. The effect of implementing this proposal was the withdrawal of services from areas which generated the lowest traffic income, generally areas with small dispersed populations, and improvement of services where traffic was greatest, usually between areas of dense population. Here again, even in decline, economies of scale played a major part in reforming the geographical pattern. Servicing, maintenance and goods depots were concentrated to achieve greater efficiency, and the number of passenger stations reduced, with consequent increasing intensity of use of those that remained.

In the private sector the largest employment group is distribution, including both retail and wholesale. The retail trade employs over half of all the employees in the service sector, and one in ten of the total insured labourforce. Scott commented, 'the main lesson the writing of it [the book] has taught me, a lesson learnt more sharply by many an independent retailer, is that there are pronounced diseconomies of small scale.'[58] This was substantiated in the UK in the 1960s by the rapid increase in the number of large stores for shopping and especially by the proliferation of supermarkets. Statistics show that in the grocery trade the number of self service shops operated by multiples with ten or more branches rose from 771 in 1957 to 2,569 in 1961. The number having 2,000 ft^2 (186 m^2) or more of selling space rose from 52 in 1957 to 524 in 1961.[59] Similarly all the major categories of shops in the clothing and footwear trades in the UK have experienced decline in the number of separate establishments since 1950, largely owing to the growth of multiple ownership and the increasing sales size of stores.[60] In the grocery trade again, turnover expanded by 15·3 per cent between 1957 and 1961 and went up again by 23·7 per cent between 1961 and 1966.[61] Under previous conditions this expansion would have resulted in a proliferation of small shops with a dispersed pattern. What actually happened was that the number of establishments in the grocery trade fell by 3·3 per cent 1957-61, and by 15·9 per cent 1961-6. Turnover per establishment was rising rapidly during this time, going up from £13,528 in 1957 to £16,016 in 1961, and to £23,566 in 1966.

The geographical impact of these trends has been quite marked, though in some areas of the UK, the effects in some services have been masked by the effects of the considerable local economic growth that has occurred. But basically there was a tendency for scale of operations to increase in all services. This happened either by increasing the average size of individual establishments, by closing small units and opening larger new ones as in the case of hospitals and schools, or by increasing the size of existing individual establishments as happened with the universities, or by the maintenance of the smaller old establishments while all the growth was accommodated in new establishments built much larger for the purpose, as happened in many instances in the retail trade. Most of these changes involve geographical change, either through the centralisation of a scattered distribution of establishments into a smaller number of places, or by a certain limited number of places growing relatively faster than others so that the relative strength changed. Whatever the method by which the changes occurred a definite geographical trend can be identified. In general it is that the higher order centres in any particular area or region tended to gain, while the losses were concentrated in the smaller centres which stagnated or declined.

This conforms with the hierarchy arrangement put forward in Christaller's Central Place Theory.[62] The theory shows how, under idealised conditions, services in greatest day-to-day demand are located in the smallest service centres, which serve very limited surrounding market areas. Since everyone living in the theoretical landscape would need to be served by a centre, every part of the landscape would be in a market area. In an idealised landscape these market areas would be hexagon-shaped for maximum efficiency. The smallest service centres and their associated market areas or hinterlands would lie within the hinterland of a larger service centre, which would provide those services less frequently demanded: a specialised delicatessen shop rather than a general grocers, the area headquarters of a bank rather than a branch bank. Each higher order centre would thus serve a wider area than the lower order centres in its hinterland. These higher order centres and their hinterlands would in turn lie within the hinterland of a still higher order centre providing services even less frequently demanded, or which control a number of lower order services. This is where the wholesale grocer or the regional headquarters of the bank would be located. There is therefore, a hierarchy of service centres, with the next higher order service centre having all the functions of the lower order centres below it, but with additional superior functions which they do not have.[63] The relevance of this theory for the changing pattern of service employment in Britain, is that the trends described have all tended to make the higher order centres more attractive relative to the lower order centres. Greater mobility and willingness to travel further has meant that services can locate further away from their customers. Changes in organisation and control described earlier have allowed advantage to be taken of this much more readily, a trend encouraged by the economies of scale available when services are concentrated in fewer larger units. The underlying geographical trend has been a shift of service activity away from the smallest, lowest order centres, to the smaller number of next higher order service centres. The latter have in this way grown at the expense of the former. These geographical shifts are most obvious in the public sector services, where central control is stronger and rationalisation more readily achieved. Thus the replacement of smaller hospitals by larger fewer units, or the development of giant comprehensive schools in place of the much smaller secondary schools are good examples. In the private sector, the reduction in the number of small independent grocers, or of bread and confectionery shops, and their replacement by supermarkets, shows the same process at work. The effects of these trends are offset in some areas because growth of population or purchasing power may allow a service centre to maintain itself. The corollary is that the effects are best seen in areas where the population is in decline or static. In such areas the population declines are accelerated in the smaller places by the removal of service employment which may be in small numbers in absolute terms but which made a significant contribution to the local economy.

IV.9 Flexible Services Location

Having explained the geographical shifts which have been important in the period 1945-70, it is also important to point out that for many of the more flexible services there seem to be no good economic or commercial reasons to justify the concentration of many of the jobs involved into the highest order centres. Gottman[64] has suggested some factors which might explain the need for *some* services to cluster, but Rhodes and Khan[65] found among executives who were responsible for location decisions 'an obsession with psychological and environmental factors' at the expense of financial consideration. From the present state of knowledge in this field, there appear to be no good reasons why much of the routine clerical work involved with the accounting side of the electricity and gas boards, for example, could not be located elsewhere within the administrative boundaries of the areas they serve than the largest city, which is where they are usually centred today. The location of the routine administration of county councils, or national government departments could similarly be shifted. At the national level, recognition that this *could* be done, and *needed* to be done, arose mainly from the development of office space and employment in London. 80 per cent of the office space in England and Wales for which planning permission was given between 1945 and 1962 was located in London.[66] Moreover in the central areas of London, where more than half the employment increase in the conurbation had been concentrated between 1945 and 1963, two-thirds of the increase had been in office jobs, and these trends continued in the 1960s. Between 1964 and 1967 there was a net increase of 19·5 million ft^2 (1·8 million m^2) of office floorspace in the South East planning region alone. This represented 56 per cent of the total growth of office floorspace in England and Wales during that period.[67] Hall pointed out that projections for employment growth in the London region over the period 1961-81 showed that two-thirds, or about 750,000 jobs, would be in office employment. He further concluded that, 'The real answer to the question of London's future, then, hinges on the economics of office location.'[68] Even in 1966 the South East region had 49 per cent of the 4 million office workers in England and Wales, as against only 36 per cent of the economically-active population. This expansion was a major cause of the overgrowth of London and the South East region in the period up to 1970. It was clear that some of this office employment could be located elsewhere and still be economically viable, and so efforts were made to distribute this growth away from central London. In the early 1960s a Location of Offices Bureau was established to persuade offices to move out, and office development permits were introduced by the government to control office building. The government went even further and set an example by locating employment-generating office developments of their own in other regions.[69] Thus the reorganised government business statistics office was developed at Newport in Monmouthshire and the premium bonds office was situated in Lytham St Anne's, Lancashire. After 1960 there were signs too, that at the intraregional level the possibilities of locating flexible service employment were being explored, and that the significance of such employment for planning was being recognised. With this growing awareness it seemed likely that, in the 1970s, the proper planning of the location of economic activity in the UK, would result in more of the flexible service activities being developed in scattered locations, in the same way as the location of 'footloose' industry was influenced after 1934.

REFERENCES

1. G Manners, *The Geography of Energy*, 2nd ed. (London 1971), p. 138.
2. *Programme for Nuclear Power*, Cmnd 9389 (HMSO 1955), p. 10.
3. *Fuel Policy*, Cmnd 3438 (HMSO 1967), p. 34.
4. G Manners, 'Some Economic and Spatial Characteristics of the British Energy Market', in *Spatial Policy Problems of the British Economy*, M D I Chisholm and G Manners (eds.) (Cambridge 1971), p. 165.
5. Central Electricity Generating Board, *Annual Report and Accounts 1968-9*, (HMSO 1969), p. 3.
6. M J Marnell and G Humphrys, 'Private Coal Mining in South Wales', *Geographical Review*, **55** (1965), p. 328.
7. *Report of the Committee of Inquiry into Coal Distribution Costs in Great Britain*, Cmnd 446 (HMSO London 1958), p. 2.
8. National Coal Board, *Annual Report and Accounts 1970-1*, vol. 1, (HMSO 1971), p. 20.
9. *Committee of Inquiry into Coal Distribution Costs*, p. 50.
10. G Hallett and P Randall, *Maritime Industry and Port Development in South Wales* (Cardiff 1970), p. 29.
11. E S Simpson, *Coal and the Power Industries in Post-War Britain* (London 1966), p. 127.
12. Ministry of Technology, *Digest of Energy Statistics 1970* (HMSO 1971), p. 82.
13. Gas Council, *Annual Report and Accounts 1959-60* (HMSO 1960), p. 62.
14. G Manners, 'Recent Changes in the British Gas Industry', *Transactions, Institute of British Geographers*, **26** (1959), p. 156.
15. Gas Council, *Annual Report and Accounts 1957-8*, (HMSO 1958), p. 7.
16. G Manners, *Geography of Energy* (1971), p. 119.

17. G Manners, 'The 1970s Power Game', *Geographical Magazine,* **42** (1970), p. 442-9.
18. J Burns, Publication 521, *Institution of Gas Engineers,* (London 1958), p. 11.
19. Central Office of Information, *Britain 1971* (London 1971), p. 265.
20. G Manners, *Geography of Energy* (1971), p. 161-2.
21. G Manners, *Geography of Energy* (1971), p. 166.
22. K D George, 'Economies of Nuclear and Conventional Coal-fired Stations in the United Kingdom, *Oxford Economic Papers,* **12** (1964), p. 294.
23. Central Statistical Office, *Standard Industrial Classification,* 3rd ed. (HMSO 1968).
24. Ministry of Labour, *Occupational changes 1951-61,* Manpower Studies No. 6 (HMSO 1961).
25. G Humphrys, 'Growth Industries and the Regional Economies of Britain', *District Bank Review,* **144** (1962) pp. 35-56.
     D M Smith, 'Recent Change in the Regional Pattern of British Industry', *Tijdschrift Voor Economische en Sociale Geografie,* **56** (1965), pp. 133-45.
26. G McCrone, *Regional Policy in Britain* (London 1969), pp. 173-4.
27. W. Smith, *An Economic Geography of Great Britain* (London 1949), p. 374.
28. E M Rawstron, 'Industry', in J W Watson and J B Sissons (eds.) *The British Isles: A Systematic Geography* (London 1964), pp. 307-12.
29. McCrone, *Regional Policy in Britain,* p. 160.
30. C Clark, 'Industrial Location and Economic Potential', *Lloyds Bank Review,* **82** (1966), pp. 1-17.
31. P G Hall, *The Industries of London since 1861* (London 1962), p. 168.
     Rawstron in *The British Isles,* p. 310.
     McCrone, *Regional Policy in Britain,* p. 57.
32. B E Coates and E M Rawstron, *Regional Variations in Britain* (London 1971), pp. 17-21.
33. E M Rawstron, in *The British Isles,* p. 315.
34. W F Luttrell, *Factory Location and Industrial Movement,* 2 vols (London 1962) pp. 347-8.
35. Scottish Council, *Report of the Committee of Enquiry on the Scottish Economy* (Edinburgh 1961), pp. 72-5.
36. M Chisholm, *Geography and Economics* (London 1966), pp. 182-93.
37. Hall, *The Industries of London since 1861,* p. 169.
38. A G Powell, 'The Recent Development of Greater London', *Advancement of Science,* **17** (1960-1), pp. 76-86.
39. R S Howard, *The Movement of Manufacturing Industry in the United Kingdom 1945-65* (HMSO 1968).
40. G Humphrys, *Industrial Britain: South Wales* (Newton Abbot 1972), pp. 117-27.
41. P S Florence, *Post-War Investment, Location and Size of Plant* (Cambridge 1962).
42. F E I Hamilton, 'Models of Industrial Location', in R J Chorley and P Haggett (eds.) *Models in Geography* (London 1967), p. 364.
43. Central Office of Information, *Britain 1971* (HMSO 1971), p. 239.
44. G Manners, 'Service Industries and Regional Economic Growth', *Town Planning Review,* **33** (1963), pp. 293-303.
45. E Hammond, 'Dispersal of Government Offices', *Urban Studies,* **4** (1967), p. 258-75.
46. Humphrys, *Industrial Britain: South Wales,* pp. 138-50.
47. R J Buswell and E W Lewis, 'The Geographical Distribution of Industrial Research Activity in the United Kingdom', *Regional Studies,* **4** (1970), pp. 297-306.
48. M Wright, 'Provincial Office Development', *Urban Studies,* **4** (1967) p.218.
49. See the comment in B E Coates and E M Rawstron, *Regional Variations in Britain* (London 1971) p. 180.
50. Ordnance Survey Map, *Great Britain; Gas and Coke 1949,* 2 sheets, Scale 1:625,000, (1951).

51. National Health Service, *A Hospital Plan for England and Wales*, (London 1962).
52. M Hall, J Knapp, and C Winsten, *Distribution in Great Britain and North America* (Oxford 1961).
     D Thorpe, 'The Main Shopping Centres of Great Britain in 1961. Their Location and Structural Characteristics', *Urban Studies*, 5 (1968), pp. 165-206.
53. P Scott, *Geography and Retailing*, (London 1970), p. 26.
54. Scott, *Geography and Retailing*, p. 42.
55. Central Office of Information, *Britain 1971*, p. 272.
56. Scott, *Geography and Retailing*, p. 61.
57. British Railways Board, *The Reshaping of British Railways* (London 1963).
58. Scott, *Geography and Retailing*, p. 9.
59. Board of Trade, *Census of Retail Distribution and Other Services, 1961 Supplement* (London 1971), p. S. 105.
60. Scott, *Geography and retailing*, p. 79.
61. Board of Trade, *Census of Retail Distribution and Other Services 1966* (London 1971), I, p. 20.
62. B J L Berry, *Geography of Market Centres and Retail Distribution* (Englewood Cliffs 1967), pp. 59-73.
63. Scott, *Geography and Retailing*, p. 16.
64. J Gottman, 'Urban Centrality and the Interweaving of Quarternary Activity', *Ekistics*, 29 (1970), pp. 322-31.
65. J Rhodes and A Khan, *Office Dispersal and Regional Policy* (Cambridge 1971), p. 27.
66. M Wright, 'Provincial Office Development', p. 221.
67. P W Daniels, 'Office Decentralisation from London: Policy and Practice', *Regional Studies*, 3 (1969), pp. 171-8.
68. P G Hall, *World Cities*, (London 1966), pp. 55 and 58.
69. E Hammond, 'Dispersal of Government Offices', pp. 258-75.

5

Transport

I INTRODUCTION: SOME THEORETICAL AND EMPIRICAL BACKGROUND

I.1 Transport Systems

Transport is a quantifiable means of interaction, potentially a measure of the 'differences between different areas' and it is important to an understanding of most economic, social and political distributions. Even today, however, traffic-flow statistics for the UK are inadequate and moving back in time any precision in measurement is very soon lost. Nonetheless it is important to appreciate the influence at any stage of contemporary modes of transport upon the patterns of economic activity and to acknowledge the legacy of this in the present landscape. The present transport system is the result of a long evolution continually modified by changing demands and developing technology. It was an evolution with overlapping phases of dominance; of coastal shipping and inland waterways in the eighteenth century, of the railway throughout much of the nineteenth and of road transport in the third-quarter of the twentieth century. The accumulation of modes and networks with few attempts at conscious integration has been well documented.[1] No consideration of present day transport in the UK begins with a *tabula rasa.* Thus in road transport, for example, it is a tribute to its adaptability that it could begin its modern rise to dominance without major initial investment, but it must face the major problems caused by high density operation on a road network still largely attuned to a horse-and-carriage age.[2]

The development of transport networks has been continuously influenced by considerations of physical environment, notably by relief.[3] More important, however, have been the influences of *dimensions* and *insularity,* reflected primarily in the limitation of the distances over which the systems could develop and work out a *modus vivendi.* These characteristics impart to UK transport a measure of distinctiveness, especially by comparison with Continental European systems. The critical influence in all transport development is need. Capital investment and operational viability rest ultimately on demand, usually an economic demand but potentially a strategic or social demand. Regrettably it is a demand often viewed in isolation and with an imperfect appraisal of the economic and technical characteristics of the available media and of their suitability to meet the needs in question.

The matching of the demand for transport with the available facilities has usually been made in terms of costs but this has been modified in some degree. For a growing majority of UK industries, for example, transport costs are now of limited importance.[4] It has been estimated that the share of transport in the total costs of producing and distributing is 9 per cent although there are very considerable variations according to the type of industry.[5] It is broadly true that as the pace and level of economic development increase then transport costs become less important and concern for the quality of the service increases.[6] Certainly it is becoming more common to consider goods transport as the *logistic* or *physical distribution* aspect of an industrial activity rather than as a discrete element of the tertiary sector, and transport costs will be subsumed within some form of the total cost concept. All these issues are reflected in the developing transport system of the UK and not least in the fact that it is clear that the larger portion of transport costs now relate to the movement of people and not of goods.[7]

There has been a gradual change in emphasis in the forces moulding the transport system. Increasingly technological achievement has made it possible to overcome any physical environmental problems but to do so at a cost. Thus in transport developments, as in so much of economic development, the point at issue is not whether it is technically possible but whether it is economically feasible. Moreover at the level of capital provision commonly required for transport development, economic feasibility tends to be interpreted largely in terms of whether the development is considered to be politically desirable. The same may be true of the maintenance, by subsidy, of existing facilities. The transport system thus tends to reflect the volume and nature of demand assessed in terms of the economic and technical characteristics of the available transport media, but viewed in the light of the existing socio-political order. An explanation of the development of the transport system must consider in particular technological change 'and public policy.

I.2   Transport Development 1950-70

Marshall wrote in 1890 of the development of transport as 'the dominant economic fact of our own age'.[8] He wrote in what was in very many respects a different age and the growth and elaboration of transport has continued unabated. His statement might be considered equally apt in the third-quarter of the twentieth century. Notwithstanding the important achievements of earlier times it is probable that the transport developments of the last twenty years will ensure that this period emerges as one of major and accelerated change. It is an important aspect of contemporary change that several transport media are involved and are increasingly integrated by these changes. Although incomplete, there has been a growing measure of coordination between media, at first in theory and then in practice. It is a further general characteristic of recent change that it has tended to an increased measure of concentration of activity within each media, that is, to the more intensive use of some parts of the system. Also changed is the relative importance of the various media within the total system. This change is related firstly to technological advances and, secondly, to changing demand for transport.

Technological advances are concerned primarily with an increase in load capacity in several sections of the total system. Some developments relate to the *vehicles* in use, for example the increased size and specialisation of merchant vessels (see section 5 VI.1) and the increased capacity of aircraft highlighted by the first commercial flight of the Jumbo Jet in January 1970. Load capacity is also a function of speed and efficiency. Commercial aircraft speed has increased greatly over this period and the railway, even in decline, saw important changes in traction with some mainline electrification but notably the spread of diesel and the end of an era with the final withdrawal of steam in August 1968. There were also notable increases in the *number* of carriers, for example, of merchant vessels, especially of tankers and outstandingly a five-fold increase in private motor cars. Developments in networks and in terminals were often no less important to advances in transport. In this the extension and elaboration of seaport and airport layouts and facilities have been important. There can be no doubt, however, that the most striking and novel achievement of the period since the Second World War has been the slow and as yet limited construction of a motorway system following the first short section (the Preston by-pass) in December 1958 and the initial 55 mile (88.5 km) section of the M1 in November 1959 (table 5.1). One important aspect of technological change, belonging mainly to the 1960s, and indeed mainly post-1965, has been the development of unit-load goods traffic which has transgressed the divisions between the media more effectively than ever before and assuredly to more lasting effect (see section 5 VI.1).

The change in demand for transport was engendered by the continuation of the inter-war trends resulting from the secular decline of heavy industry and the rise of consumer goods and service industries within a more prosperous and mobile society. Increased car

TABLE 5.1

Roads and Vehicles, UK, 1951-71

	1951	1961	1971	
Motorway Mileage	–	136	843	
Total trunk mileage	8,595	8,841	9,495	
Trunk road expenditure (£'000)	8,524	52,778	306,973	
Vehicles in use:				
Cars ('000)	2,433	6,114	12,358	
Goods vehicles ('000)	955	1,491	1,660	
New registrations: (GB only)				
Cars ('000)	136	743	1,302	
Goods vehicles ('000)	85	220	234	

Source: Basic Road Statistics, British Road Federation (1972)

ownership, in particular, placed sections of the system under severe strain, as for example the urban road network and the public transport services in both urban and rural areas. Indeed the increasing dominance of road transport is the most striking characteristic of the inland transport scene in the period since 1950. As noted earlier both vehicle numbers and improvements to the road system contributed to this and it became clear that the inter-city motorway programme was likely to be one of the more influential forces shaping the economic geography of the UK in the next decade.[9] Such road developments placed the rail system under severe competitive pressure as also, to a much more limited extent, did the increased volume of domestic air traffic, notably for passenger traffic on Anglo-Scottish services. The railways did not succumb without rearguard actions. Like the canals at an earlier time (the canal network of approx. 4,053 miles (6,485 km) at a maximum[10] is now reduced to 340 miles (544 km) of commercially-used route) the railways drastically reduced their network. The UK rail network in 1970 was reduced by over 8,000 miles (12,800 km) compared with 1951 and a further 2,700 miles (4,320 km) was available for goods services only, leaving less than half of the route mileage of 1951 still available for passenger working (table 5.2). Moreover British Rail attempted to concentrate its efforts upon the traffic and length of haul which were judged to be its most effective operations.

Table 5.3 summarises the changing volume of traffic and the changing relative importance of the media between 1953 and 1970. Within this period the total ton-mileage of goods traffic increased by 62 per cent but that on the roads increased by 250 per cent. The

TABLE 5.2

Rail Network, UK, 1938-70

Route open to traffic (miles)	1938	1951	1955	1961	1965	1967	1970
GB	20,007	19,357	19,061	18,369	14,920	13,172	11,799
N. Ireland	530	478	382	297	203	203	203
UK	20,537	19,835	19,443	18,666	15,123	13,375	12,002

Source: Annual Abstract of Statistics, CSO; *Committee of Inquiry into Internal Transport,* (Irish Stationery Office 1957)

TABLE 5.3

Goods and Estimated Passenger Traffic, GB, 1953-70

Goods traffic	Thousand million ton-miles				Per cent			
	1953	1960	1965	1970	1953	1960	1965	1970
Total	51.8	61.1	73.7	83.3	100	100	100	100
Road	19.7	30.1	42.1	50.8	38.0	51.3	57.2	60.9
Rail	22.8	18.7	15.4	16.4	44.0	31.9	20.9	19.9
Coastal shipping	9.0	11.9	15.3	14.2	17.4	16.2	20.7	17.0
Inland waterways	0.2	0.2	0.1	0.1	0.4	0.3	0.1	0.1
Pipelines	0.1	0.2	0.8	1.8	0.2	0.3	1.1	2.1

Passenger traffic	Thousand million passenger-miles				Per cent			
	1953	1960	1965	1970	1953	1960	1965	1970
Total	117,1	158.6	206.7	253.7	100	100	100	100
Road								
Private Transport	42.1	89.4	144.7	196.2	35.9	56.2	69.9	77.2
Public Service Vehicle	50.7	43.9	39.2	34.1	43.3	27.7	18.9	13.4
Rail	24.1	24.8	21.8	22.2	20.6	15.7	10.5	8.7
Air	0.2	0.5	1.0	1.2	0.2	0.3	0.5	0.5

Source: Annual Abstracts of Statistics, CSO

NB   Excludes traffic in Northern Ireland except (i) Petroleum moved by sea; (ii) air passenger traffic to and from GB

total passenger mileage increased by 115 per cent but there was almost a five-fold increase in private road transport. By 1971, 61 per cent of goods traffic and 91 per cent of passenger traffic was on the roads. Rail ton-mileage declined until 1967 (13,600 million tons) and has since risen slowly. Coastwise ton-mileage, a traditional British characteristic, reached a post-war maximum in 1966 (15,500 million tons) and from 1966-8 carried more ton-mileage than did the railways. Inland waterways, pipeline and domestic air transport make relatively small contributions to UK traffic totals although the absolute increases, for example, from 2 million tons in 1953 to 47 million tons in 1970 by pipeline and 200 million air passenger miles (1953) to 1,200 million (1970) are impressive. The increased volume and changing composition of UK traffic has posed particular problems of coordination and rationalisation, some of which are discussed in section 5 VI.

I.3   Transport Policies

Transport is so all pervading and the influences of transport are so widespread that 'almost every transport decision is a public issue'.[11] Moreover 'transport gives the government powers of positive planning unrivalled in any other field'.[12] It is perhaps then surprising that while there is a long history of government involvement it can rarely be accurately described as a widespread or positive influence upon UK transport. Historically the role of government was more that of a regulator than an initiator.[13] In the nineteenth century local authorities' responsibilities for the roads were widened and local public corporations assumed responsibility for most ports and for urban passenger transport. The private

development of the inland waterways and notably of the railways was curbed only by
regulations relating to safety, to the possible abuse of monopoly and to the protection of
the financial interests of the traders.[14] Government policies have been directed most frequently towards the attempted solution of some specific transport problem rather than
demonstrating any firm attachment to principle or to a national perspective. The Ministry
of Transport established in 1919 heralded much fuller and direct government concern.
The ensuing years have produced a large volume of legislation mainly aimed, as Gwilliam
points out, at tackling conflicts between rail and road, conflicts between private and
public carriers, and doctrinaire conflicts over ownership.[15]

For the most part government policy did not provide a context for the development of
an effective national network in any media and least of all for any coordination in an
integrated plan. Coordination was considered by the Royal Commission on Transport in
1930 but was not implemented except to a limited extent in the London Passenger Transport Board 1933 and, indirectly, in the obvious concern of the legislation to influence the
competitive relationships of rail and road. After 1930 this was largely a matter of restricting the capacity of the developing road transport by the Road Traffic Act 1930 (licensing
public service coaches) and the Road and Rail Act 1933 (licensing road goods vehicles).
On the other hand the Trunk Roads Act 1936, making a basic network eligible for Treasury support, could only improve the roads' attraction. In any event, in a sharply changing
transport demand situation, no moves towards a supposedly *fair basis* for competition
could significantly affect the declining status of the railway. However unrealistically, the
railways did tend to attribute their plight to the continuing influence of policies which
left their common carrier obligations unchanged and their distinctive rate structure.

It remained true that charges were not comparable on rail and road and the failure to
ensure the choice of the cheapest medium was a main reason for the limited achievements
of the Transport Act 1947, which was the first explicit attempt at a comprehensive view
of the national system. The newly created British Transport Commission (BTC) acquired
all railways, inland waterways and road haulage undertakings except those operating within 25 miles (40 km) of their base. The required provision of an *adequate* service seemingly
envisaged the support of some unremunerative services by a process of cross-subsidisation.[16]
An important continuing aspect introduced by the 1947 Act was the ability of transport
undertakings to negotiate Treasury grants via the Minister of Transport although the level
of this support has varied with government attitudes and reflected the advances and recessions of the economy. The Transport Act of 1953 with a pendulum-like swing began the
demolition of the monopoly. Road haulage was removed from the BTC with the exception
of 7,000 lorries retained by British Road Services. In striving to replace inland transport
on a competitive basis the Act abolished some of the railways' restrictive obligations
although its freedom in charging remained in practice incomplete. Most importantly, the
1953 Act facilitated competition between road and rail at a time when changing transport
demands markedly favoured road transport rather than the railway service then available.
The result was not surprisingly a growing contrast in the share of inland transport handled
by the two media and it was in the aftermath of the 1953 Act that the Beeching retrenchment proposals for the railways were worked out and progressively implemented in the
early 1960s.

The statutory framework for the 1960s, at least until 1968, was mainly provided by
four Acts: The Road Traffic Act 1960 was a consolidating Act incorporating little change;
the Civil Aviation (Licensing) Act 1960 allowed BEA's monopoly of major internal air
routes to be challenged; the Transport Act 1962 reorganised the nationalised undertakings
and, while removing further restrictions from rail operation and also giving a measure of
protection to coastal shipping (from the railway), the Act says very little in general about
the relationships between the media; the Pipeline Act 1962 (in direct contrast to the
approach in the Civil Aviation and Transport Acts) assumed that pipelines are a natural

monopoly to be protected against duplication and excess capacity.[17]

The Transport Act of 1968 embodied several signal advances, some of which have seemingly survived a change in government. Container traffic on road and rail was to be integrated through the National Freight Corporation. Perhaps even more significant, in principle, the Minister of Transport was empowered to subsidise named transport services (road and rail) which were making a financial loss but were considered to be socially neces- sary to retain population or to encourage new industries in Development Areas. The Act also provided for Passenger Transport Authorities, subsequently established in Birmingham, Liverpool, Manchester, Newcastle and Glasgow, on the 1933 model of the London Passenger Transport Board. It should be noted that an important aspect of the 1968 Act, the quantity licensing provision which was intended to direct all goods traffic over distances in excess of 100 miles (161 km) and in vehicles of over 16 tons onto the railway, has not been implemented. In other respects, however, it does seem that after much delay and doctrinaire controversy a substantial measure of policy agreement may have been reached. Nonetheless there is no doubt that the political pendulum of the years since the Second World War has had a seriously debilitating effect on the transport system. It has been a major inhibition and frustration to the operation and staffing of transport undertakings that in general terms almost half of the period since 1945, about 14 years, has been spent mainly in waiting for major new legislation or reorganising to meet the requirements of the latest statute.

II   INLAND TRANSPORT BETWEEN CITIES AND REGIONS

II.1   Traffic Flows

In general terms the traffic flows of the UK form three distinctive but interconnected systems: the flow of raw materials and passengers from abroad and the return movements of passengers and manufactured products through the ports and airports; the flow of freight and passengers between the major conurbations and regions within the UK; local movements of people and goods to and from work, school and shops; also the collection and distribution of freight within towns, between neighbouring towns and in rural areas.

The majority of traffic movements can be assigned to one of these three broad cate- gories (in fact the vast majority of movements are local) but the detailed picture contains many complications. Passengers and goods may pass from local origins to distant desti- nations without passing through regional interchange points or using major through- routeways. Seaports, which specialise international traffic, also handle coal and oil- products moving from one part of the UK to another. The transport system of Northern Ireland is a discrete sub-system of that of the UK, only making connection with British transport through sea and airports, but it has strong historical ties and contemporary land links with the transport system of the Irish Republic.

These and many other complexities do not invalidate a general analysis of UK traffic flows at international, interregional and local levels. The urbanisation of the country has led to growing concentration of population in conurbations and large towns, separated by rural areas of much lower population density. Many of the changes in transport geography during the post-war period have resulted from increasing concentrations of traffic passing through a limited number of nodes. Each mode of transport has attempted to adjust to these developments but has been hampered by the legacy of its past, when traffic flows were more diffuse and did not fit so clearly into the three broad flow systems described above. To change the pattern of the network has not only required capital investment beyond the resources of the transport industries themselves but has required changes of attitude among management, trades unions, government and the general public, the abandonment of long-established services and widespread redundancy of employment. This section is concerned with the effect of these changes on the pattern of transport networks but continual reference must be made to the institutional framework and economic circumstances within which they have occurred.

Table 5.4 describes the UK transport system in 1950 and compares it with those of France, West Germany and Italy, as neighbouring countries with similar population and/ or area. The UK railway network was closely comparable to that of West Germany in all respects although the West German road network as defined was much smaller. Unlike the UK, France or Italy, West Germany already possessed 1,323 miles (2,130 km) of motorway and the capacity of much of the West German waterway system was considerably higher than that of the UK or France. France and Italy had smaller railway systems in relation to their area or population although the French road system was commensurate with the area of France and relatively high in relation to population.

TABLE 5.4

Transport Networks, Four European Countries, 1950

	UK	West Germany	France	Italy
Area (th. km^2)	244	248	551	301
Population (millions)	50	49	42	47
Road length (th. km)	317	128	716	173
Railway route length (th. km)	32.3	30.7	41.3	21.6
Inland waterways in use (th. km)	2.8	4.6	8.4	—
Road length per 100 km^2	1.3	0.5	1.3	0.6
Road length per 100 inhabitants	6.3	2.6	17.0	3.7
Railway per 10 km^2	1.3	1.2	0.8	0.7
Railway per 10,000 inhabitants	6.5	6.3	9.8	4.6

Source: National Statistical Abstracts

The density of the UK transport network was lowest in the uplands of Atlantic Britain where few canals were found and railways and some roads were single track. The network was distinguished from that of European neighbours by its high capacity in regions of moderate population density (100-500 per sq mile/50-200 km^2) where many railways were double-tracked and roads had durable asphalt surfaces. There were, however, no motorways and only one 46 mile (74 km) high-capacity inland waterway.

The Irish transport system evolved when the island was part of the UK but the establishment of a 5ft 3 in (1.6 m) gauge on the Irish railways in 1846 precluded the subsequent development of train ferries and the through-working of rail wagons between Ireland and Britain. The county boundaries which were hastily chosen to form the boundary between the Irish Free State and the UK in 1921 bore no relation to the road and rail networks of the island. The intricate net of country roads crossed by the sinuous boundary has been a source of political and military embarrassment to both governments. The 1921 Treaty would have preserved the unity of the Irish railway system under the jurisdiction of the Council of Ireland. Attempts to develop the Council were abandoned in 1925 but the Great Northern Railway (Dublin to Belfast and to Londonderry) was brought under the control of the Ulster Transport Authority only in 1953, and finally partitioned in 1958. The Government of Northern Ireland was responsible for transport within its six counties from 1925 until 1972 and the Transport Act (Northern Ireland) of 1948 contained similar provisions for the nationalisation of the transport system to those of the British Transport Act of 1947.

Figure 5.1 (adapted from Maps 8 and 9, *The Development of Major Railway Trunk Routes*) shows the general pattern of interregional inland traffic flows in Great Britain about the middle of the period under discussion.[18],[19] As the data on which figure 5.1 is based relate to weight and not value, fuel- and ore-traffic play an important role. Thus the average freight flow between adjacent conurbations or regions was of the order of 7.5 million tons, but this was exceeded in flows to or from all coalfield areas. Higher value goods generally travelled further than minerals. Figure 5.1 must be seen as representing a particular stage reached in a process by which coal was being partially replaced by oil. The oil travelled somewhat longer distances from the major refineries by rail, road and pipeline than did rail-borne coal. The decline in the use of local iron ores and the building of four large ore terminals in the early 1970s has reduced the distances of iron ore flows.

Figure 5.2 (adapted from Maps 10, 11, 12 in reference 18) shows that the flow of passengers is much more evenly spread than the flow of freight, but it should also be noted that passenger traffic in the Greater London area, including traffic to Sussex and Kent, has been excluded from the interregional map although it provided one-third of the railway passenger mileage in Great Britain.[18] While figure 5.1 may record up to 80 per cent of interregional freight movements, figure 5.2 does not show passenger movements by private car; these formed 62 per cent of the total in 1961. As a result figure 5.2 almost certainly under-represents week-end passenger movements of 50 to 100 miles (80-160 km) from inland towns to the coast and also summer holiday traffic, especially to western Wales and South West England.

These patterns of traffic flow are fairly longstanding. Sherrington [20] showed, for instance, that in 1865 the average annual flow of mineral traffic was 6,000 tons per route mile but that the railways of Scotland and North East England carried over 10,000 tons of minerals per route mile and those of the northern English coalfields over 7,000, whereas the railways of eastern and southern England carried under 1,000 tons. General freight was more evenly distributed among the companies, averaging 3,000 tons per route mile, but ranging from 9,000 tons per route mile on the Lancashire and Yorkshire Railway, 5,000 on the Midland, Great Northern, Great Central and South Eastern Railways to 2,000 tons per route mile on most other railway companies. Average passenger flow per route mile was 20,000, ranging from 54,000 on the railways linking London with the South West to 48,000 on the Lancashire and Yorkshire system, with a minimum of 10,000 in South West Scotland. Although it is not possible to be derived exactly from company figures, the proportion of British passenger traffic in the Greater London area appears to have been about the same as in 1965. Changes in patterns of traffic flow during the 1960s and 1970s therefore must be seen as marking the end of a long period of relative geographical stability.

II.2   Trunk Road Development

During the 1920s the roads emerged from their earlier role as feeders to :ail transport and traffic began to grow most rapidly on roads which could be used as through-routeways.

In 1918 the British road network of 180,000 miles (288,000 km) was classified by the newly-established Ministry of Transport into class I 'main traffic arteries', class II 'routes of lesser importance' and 'unclassified' roads. A similar scheme was adopted for the 13,700 mile (21,900 km) Northern Ireland network. In 1930 the Ministry began to provide grants for the improvement of class I and class II roads, a network of 66,800 miles (107,000 km). Their general maintenance was transferred from the 2,000 local authorities to the 177 county councils. In 1936 the Ministry became directly responsible for 4,505 miles (7,280 km) of trunk roads to which a further 3,700 miles (5,960 km) was added in 1948. In 1970, 8,332 miles (13,406 km), 4 per cent of the total road network in Britain was classi-

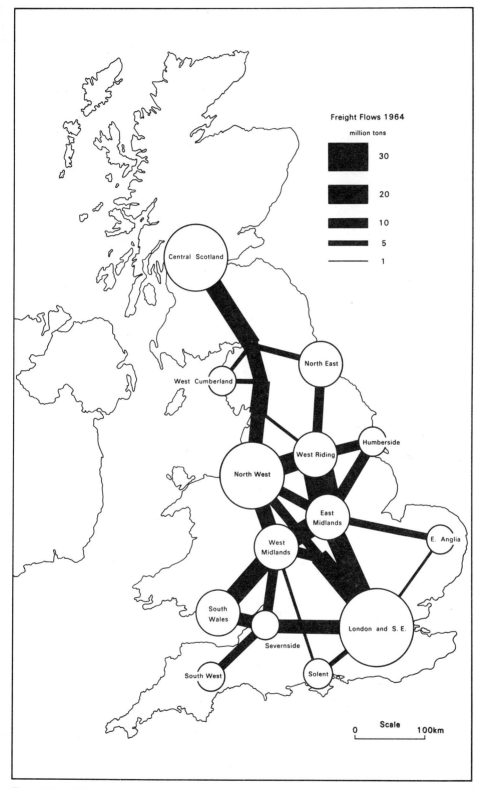

Figure 5.1   Major interregional freight flows, GB, 1964

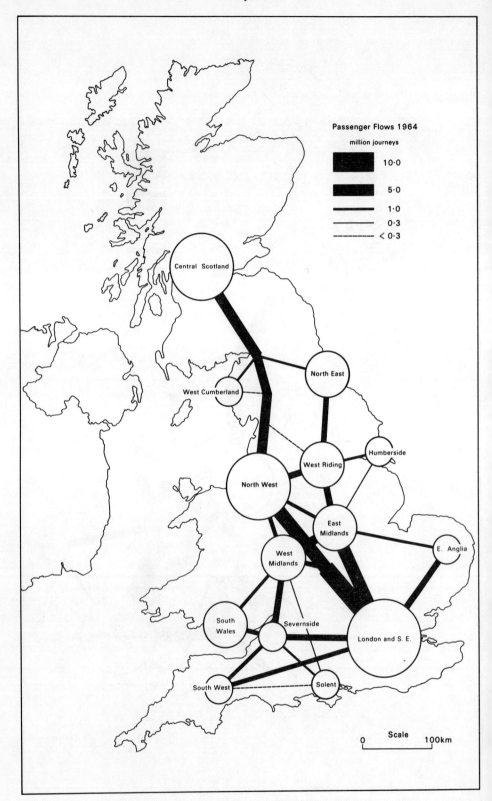

Figure 5.2   Major interregional passenger flows, GB, 1964

fied as trunk road, and 10 per cent (20,245 miles; 32,742 km) as principal (including former class I and II) road. In Northern Ireland 7 per cent of the network is classified as 'A' road. The improvement of classified and trunk roads made slow progress before 1955. Some roads radiating from London to the major cities and a few cross-country routes were rebuilt under the Trunk Road Reconstruction Programme of 1924 and new roads were built between Liverpool and Manchester, Edinburgh and Glasgow. There were some urban radial and ring roads built during the 1920s, but the Trunk Road Programme of 1929 was aborted by the financial crisis of 1931 and a new programme drawn up in 1939 by the Second World War. Dyos and Aldcroft[21] point out that total road mileage only grew by 4 per cent between 1899 and 1936. It grew by a further 5 per cent 1936-55 and by 11 per cent between 1955 and 1970. British roads remained the most crowded in the world with 62 vehicles per mile (39 per km) of road in 1970, compared to 51 vehicles per mile (32 per km) in West Germany.

An important feature of the road construction programme after 1955 was the replacement of the estuarine ferries by bridges and tunnels in order to reduce the distance and time from London and the Midlands to South Wales, Hull, South East Northumberland, West Cumberland, the Vale of Leven, Fife and North East Scotland. Each of these areas was actively seeking new industries which relied largely on road transport.

In a major bridge-building programme costing £82 million, ten high level bridges were built across the Tamar (1961), Medway (1963), Manchester Ship Canal (1960 and 1963), Forth (1964), Severn (1966), Wye (1966), Tay (1966) and Clyde (1971). Tunnels were completed under the lower Thames (1963), Clyde (1964), Tyne (1967) and Mersey (1970). The completion of the Humber bridge is scheduled for 1976 but a scheme for a barrage carrying a high capacity road across Morecambe Bay has been dropped in favour of a controversial road to West Cumberland across the Lake District (A66).

A regional element in priority planning was re-introduced in 1963 on the recommendation of the White Paper (Hailsham Report) on economic conditions in North East England and an equivalent Report on Central Scotland.[22] As the tide of post-war prosperity and reconstruction began to ebb in the late 1950s the depressed areas of the 1930s began to re-emerge as shoals and islands of unemployment and deprivation in the economic geography of the country. During the 1930s roads had been built in public works programmes to relieve unemployment including the road over Mynydd Llangeinwyr from Cwmamman to the Rhondda Valley, and the Durham, Chester and Birtley by-passes in North East England.

The 1963 government policies for Development Areas advocated road building in order to improve the environment of these areas and also as an element in growth zone policy to enable factories established on the coast or trunk roads and railways to draw on a wider labourshed and so relieve unemployment in upland areas where the staple industry of coal-mining was unlikely to be replaced by manufacturing or service industry.[23] Thus road schemes within these areas were accelerated and were not subject to the capital spending cuts imposed on the rest of the country during economic recessions in the late 1960s. Under these priority schemes the three-lane 25 mile (40 km) 'Heads of the Valley' road was built in 1966 along the North Crop of the South Wales coalfield to within 9 miles (14 km) of a dual carriageway route to the West Midlands. In North East England the Durham motorway linked Darlington to Gateshead and, via the Tyne Tunnel and a network of new roads in South East Northumberland, gave Morpeth and Blyth continuous dual-carriageway routes to London and the West Midlands. There can be little doubt that rebuilding of the Swansea-Cardiff, Manchester-Liverpool-Preston, Tyneside-Teesside, Greenock-Edinburgh and Glasgow-Stirling roads will enable the outer industrial areas of the UK to concentrate investment in industrial plant, ports, airports and New Towns in most favourable locations within each area, alleviating local unemployment, facilitating longer journeys to work in the short-term and redistribution of population in the longer-term.

In 1938-9, £1.5 million was spent on new construction and major improvement of trunk roads and £8.8 million on class I roads. By 1947-8 these expenditures had fallen to £1.0 million and £1.6 million respectively, only 4 per cent of the total spending on public roads in Great Britain in that year. From 1949-54 major improvement and new construction expenditure on trunk roads remained at just under £2 million per annum but rose on class I roads to £4 million. After 1954 expenditure on major improvements rose rapidly, on trunk roads to £12 million in 1957, £32 million in 1958, £68 million in 1962 and £201 million in 1969. By 1969 total expenditure on new construction and major improvements on all roads was £373 million representing 63 per cent of the total expenditure on all roads. The share of this expenditure devoted to trunk roads rose from 9 per cent in 1938 to 22 per cent in 1954 and 51 per cent in 1970. New construction included the extensive provision of dual-carriageways between towns and the separation of fast and slow traffic on hills by provision of three lanes.

Many roads of all classes were improved to higher capacity by widening and re-alignment, for the increasing flow of traffic created more and more 'bottlenecks' where the flow of traffic exceeded the capacity of the road to carry it except at greatly reduced speeds. In 1961, 15 per cent of the trunk roads of England and Wales, including some of the most heavily-used routes, were carrying traffic beyond their design capacity. County road authorities in particular sought to eliminate the worst of these bottlenecks, especially as many of these stretches of overcrowded road had high accident rates, but the removal of individual bottlenecks by road widening often merely creates another bottleneck further along the road. This is particularly likely if expenditure on road-widening schemes does not keep up with the overall growth of traffic in the area. The rapid growth of numbers of vehicles on the British roads, from 3.1 million in 1946 to 6,9 million in 1956, called for more radical measures.

II.3 The Motorway Network

The concept of high-capacity interregional roads with only limited access to the local transport network was outlined by Porsche in 1924, thus extending to the road system the principle of the separation of fast long-distance from the slower local traffic, which had led to selective quadrupling of rail track between 1890 and 1914. Porsche's motorway concept was as eagerly adopted as his 'beetle' design for the 'people's car' when the National Socialist party seized power in Germany in 1933. 1,330 miles (2,140 km) of this motorway system, built under the direction of railway engineers, was inherited by West Germany at the partition of the Reich in 1945.

Motorways appeared on the American scene as long-distance turnpikes between the major conurbations of the north-eastern United States after the Second World War and were only later extended across the continent, partly for defence purposes, under the Federal Interstate Highway System.

The planning of a national network of trunk roads in Britain between the wars was inhibited by the low status of transport among the Ministries, its limited administrative powers over the county councils, who were responsible for the initiation of schemes until 1936, and the subordination of national capital investment to problems of unemployment and international trade. The need for selective investment in the road network became more apparent as more detailed road censuses were taken. In 1964 the trunk roads in Great Britain were carrying 2,000,000 vehicle miles per road mile, the classified roads 600,000 and the unclassified roads only 100,000. Thus 1 per cent of the total road length carried 25 per cent of the traffic, with an average flow of 15,000 vehicles per day; a further 9 per cent of the road length carried a further 40 per cent of the traffic and the remaining 35 per cent of the traffic was spread over 90 per cent of the road mileage, half of which was carrying only 500 vehicles per day, a figure well within the capacity of a two-lane road.

The British motorway plan announced in 1957[24] comprised 1,000 miles (1,600 km) of motorway and a further 1,000 miles (1,600 km) of dual carriageway route to be completed by the early 1970s. The motorway network is shown in figure 5.3; the most important of the dual-carriageway routes was the 274 mile (435 km) A1 road from London to Newcastle.

The 1957 plan was designed primarily for the benefit of internal freight traffic, since it linked the main industrial areas by the shortest feasible network. As Appleton[25] has pointed out, London was linked to four conurbations by only one motorway as far as Watford Gap, where the Leeds (M1) and Carlisle (M6) roads diverged; a similar solution had lasted on the railways only between 1847 and 1860. There were no direct links from the urban periphery of tidewater conurbations to their docks and no motorways were planned to Harwich, the Channel Ports or Southampton, despite the increasing orientation of British overseas trade towards the European continent. There was no specific provision of motorways on routes linking conurbations with scenically attractive areas, which carried heavy private car traffic, despite many examples of such roads in North America. Some of the most overcrowded and dangerous roads in the country led into Devon, Cornwall and the Lake District, as holidaymakers deserted the express train in favour of their own cars for annual holidays and weekend outings.

There were delays in completion and changes of priority during the implementation of the motorway plan. The main delays were occasioned by the thirty-one legal stages required in order to purchase land to satisfy statutory planning procedures, which gave local inhabitants and other interested groups the right to challenge motorway routes and local alignments.

The first short stretch of motorway was opened in 1958 and the St Albans to Rugby section of the M1 in 1959. As the rural sections were completed first, the full benefit of the network only began to be felt when the motorways from London, Carlisle and Bristol to the West Midlands were linked at Gravelly Hill (Birmingham) in 1972. This link completed the 1957 motorway plan and allowed average speeds of 50 mph (80 kmph) for cars and 30 mph (48 kmph) for heavy goods vehicles between the major conurbations. In Northern Ireland a 55 mile (83 km) motorway has been built. M1 extends from Belfast to Dungannon and further motorways to the north-west of Belfast are under construction; a Belfast urban motorway is planned.

The British motorway building programme was more modest than that of her neighbours. In 1970 Great Britain had 670 miles (1,076 km) of motorway compared with 2,800 miles (4,460 km) in West Germany, 2,450 miles (3,900 km) in Italy and 970 miles (1,553 km) in France. In historical perspective the first fifteen years of railway building 1830-45 produced over 2,000 miles (3,200 km) of line.

The motorway plan, however, led to new methods of trunk route network planning which were as significant to the geography of the UK as the motorways themselves. The Ministry of Transport developed its research organisation and collected more detailed traffic data, enabling the formulation of long-term strategies for British roads. More sophisticated car ownership prediction models were made[26] and studies of early motorway statistics[27] helped to elucidate the extent to which motorways generate traffic by providing a facility which did not exist before, as well as in diverting traffic from existing roads.

The comprehensive Survey of Road Goods Transport of 1962, of which the geographical results were published in Ministry of Transport Statistical Paper 6,[19] showed the extent to which traffic flow was concentrated onto a limited number of roads with the rest of the network but thinly used. This and other surveys provided the basis for the construction of interaction models which could, on given assumptions on population and vehicle ownership, predict the future increase in traffic flow over specific routes. These predictions have been related to the proposals of the regional economic planning councils for the develop-

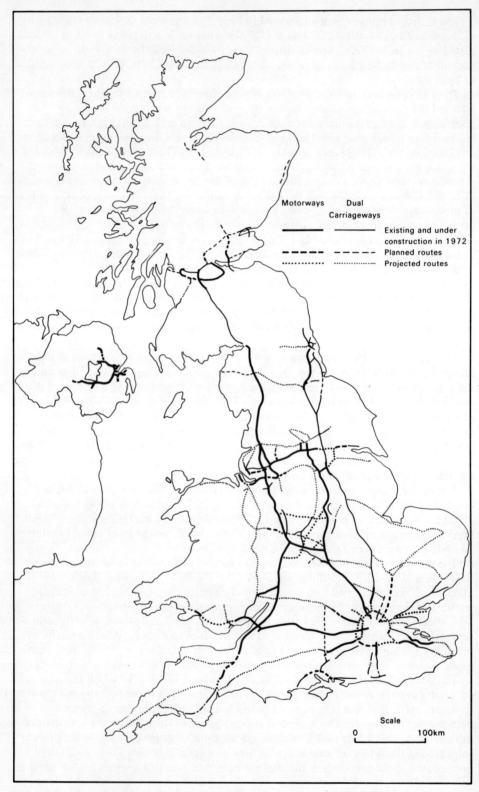

Figure 5.3   Development of motorways and strategy for trunk routes, UK, 1972

ment of New Towns and the prospective location of other major traffic-generating installations, such as green-field industrial plants, seaports and airports.

The new road-planning concepts were expressed in a Green Paper (1969)[28] and a White
Paper (1970).[29] These plans are based on the expectation that traffic will increase at 5
per cent per annum 1970-5 and thereafter at 4 per cent pa until the early 1980s, eventually
doubling in volume by the year 2000. The 1970 plan (figure 5.3) looked forward to a network of 2,000 miles (3,200 km) of motorway and 1,500 miles (2,400 km) of dual-
carriageway by 1982. The West Germans plan to have 8,200 miles (13,000 km) of motorway by 1984 and the Dutch 1,875 miles (3,000 km) of motorway by 1985. The UK network would cost £3,400 million up to 1990 and included a much more extensive network
of high-capacity routes than the 1969 Green Paper. The 1969 strategy routes gave a more
even areal coverage of Britain but the 1970 plan was more closely related to existing and
prospective traffic flow. Strategy routes which have not yet been given a place on the
current road plan are indicated on figure 5.3 as 'projected routes'.

The 1970 Plan suggested priorities in expenditure, without predicting how much money
would be forthcoming in any one year. Cost-benefit studies were applied to those stretches
of trunk road where predictions forecast the heaviest development of traffic, but the Plan
is to be re-assessed frequently in the light of new information derived from local traffic
censuses. By 1982 every town of over 80,000 people will be within 10 miles (16 km) of a
dual-carriageway or motorway trunk route. Figure 5.3 shows the distinction between planned
roads for which there is already a construction plan and 'projected' roads where there is
a long-term objective to build a high-capacity trunk road to a particular place without the
exact route yet having been fixed. The rate at which roads are constructed depends on
national investment priorities. The rate at which roads move from the 'projected' to the
'planned' stage in any region depends on consultation with county authorities and regional
economic planning councils.

The main additions to the original motorway plan include a Liverpool-Hull motorway
(M62) which has been completed between Manchester and Leeds. A second motorway
(M56) from Manchester south of the Mersey to Birkenhead is partially completed

In Scotland, the M8 (Edinburgh-Glasgow-Greenock) is completed between the outskirts
of Edinburgh and the Clydeside conurbation; within the conurbation it forms sections of
the Glasgow urban motorway system. Roads from Edinburgh to Perth via the Forth
Bridge, also from Edinburgh and Glasgow to Stirling are being built to motorway standards.
Similarly the London-Newcastle trunk road has been built to motorway standards through
part of Hertfordshire and County Durham, as has the London-South Wales road in the
Swansea area.

Under existing plans the major ports will be linked to their more distant hinterlands.
Spurs from the projected London Urban Ringway will serve Tilbury and Maplin airport.
Harwich has a trunk road to London but the A45 direct route to the Midlands is only
'projected'. Dover is now linked to London by a partially-completed motorway/dual-
carriageway route but must rely on the projected London Urban Ringways for direct links
with the rest of the country. A motorway/dual-carriageway route (M3) from London to
Southampton is almost complete, but the improvement of the southern 23 miles (37km)
to motorway standard is only projected. There is no projected direct dual-carriageway link
between Southampton and the Midlands, 128 miles (206 km), although dual-carriagways
are projected for most of the 65 miles (104 km) between Southampton and Oxford. The
strategy route of 1969 from Oxford to the West Midlands, 63 miles (101 km), is not on the
current road programme. Neither the 1969 nor the 1970 plan suggested a Southampton-
Bristol link. Similarly the route from Hull to Doncaster, 42 miles (67 km), and to Leeds
55 miles (89 km) is dual-carriageway for only 12 miles (19km), with motorways only
'projected'. The Teesside-Tyneside dual carriageway (A19) is virtually complete as is the
southern link from Teesside to the A1. With their Freightliner service the railways there-

fore continue to give a more direct access to ports than is provided by the national trunk highway system.

There are a series of important projected links between the Midlands and southern Pennine conurbations. A Manchester-Preston motorway has been built and dual-carriageways are projected to link with Sheffield. The existing dual-carriageway link from Sheffield and Leeds to Birmingham consists of a dual-carriageway via Derby and Burton. Projected motorways from Nottingham to Birmingham, Leicester to Nuneaton and Loughborough to Stoke-on-Trent will greatly improve the overall connectivity of the national motorway system. The A48 between Newport and Port Talbot is projected, to be augmented by a motorway extending as far west as Llanelli.

Private car traffic is now recognised as having importance in the trunk road programme, but many of the improvements are 'projected' and not yet planned in detail. The M5 from Bristol to Exeter, 75 miles (120 km), an extension of the original motorway programme, is under construction, with dual-carriageway building proceeding for a further 42 miles (67 km) to Plymouth and projected thence to Penzance. These motorways will combine the London to Pembroke, Devon and Cornwall traffic as far as Bristol, an arrangement which lasted on the nineteenth-century railway system for only sixteen years (1844-60). The direct London-Exeter A303, 170 mile (275 km) route, already motorway (M3) for 50 miles (80 km) to Basingstoke is only 'projected' beyond that point although other dual-carriageways are built or under construction from Basingstoke almost as far as Bournemouth. Similarly the A55 route along the heavily-populated coastline of North Wales is, apart from a few miles of by-pass, only 'projected'. A further motorway is projected from Preston to Blackpool. Dual-carriageways are projected to Norwich from London, Birmingham and Sheffield, from London to South Wales via Oxford and Cheltenham, and from Merseyside to South Wales via Shrewsbury.

The Lake District and Grampian Highlands have both tourist attractions and actual and potential industrial areas beyond them. A dual-carriageway (A66) is therefore planned to cross the Lake District from Penrith on the M6 via Keswick to Workington, 33 miles (53 km). The Perth to Inverness road (A9), 115 miles (184 km) has been given accelerated priority for improvement, owing to the expected economic development in the far north of Scotland as a result of North Sea gas and oil discoveries. This difficult route will, however, only have short stretches of dual-carriageway. The developing industrial region around Inverness and the Cromarty Firth will have a dual-carriageway as its main internal link.

II.4   The Modernisation of the Railway System

The British railway network reached its maximum extent just before the First World War, when 23,440 route miles (37,500 km) formed an intricate web of lines over England, Wales and Central Scotland. The only villages not served by rail or rail-steamer services lay in western Kintyre and along the northern coast of Scotland between Lochcarron and Thurso.

There was a decline in route mileage to 20,181 (33,800 km) in 1938 and to 19,694 (31,400 km) in 1950, a 16 per cent reduction on the 1914 figure. Northern Ireland had 478 route miles (721 km) in 1950. This UK network included 10,000 route miles (16,000 km) of double track and a further 1,500 miles (2,400 km) of quadruple track. Electrified track however amounted to only 1,300 miles (2,100 km), a low proportion in comparison with neighbouring European countries. With the exception of three lines radiating from Manchester and the Tyneside loop, the electrified lines were concentrated in the London region, Sussex and Kent. Rapid services of passenger and express freight trains were facilitated by the low gradients on the majority of main lines and the high axle loadings permitted by the track (figure 5.4).

The economic problems of the railways became apparent between the wars due to declining demand for coal, accentuated during periods of economic recession, a declining demand for mineral and steel traffic during the depression years of the early 1930s, and the location of many new industries in the Midlands and South of England where distances were shorter and road transport provided a more suitable service for many of their needs. Coal traffic comprised 60 per cent of railway freight in 1913, but fell from 226 million tons in that year to 113 million tons in 1970 (55 per cent of total freight). As coal was the only freight traffic which yielded a small margin of profit by 1961, the decline in this traffic had serious implications for overall railway finances. Other freight traffic fell from 139 million tons in 1913 to 78 million tons in 1967, but rose again to 93 million tons by 1970.

Falling general revenues made it difficult for the railways to effect expensive modernisation policies in order to win new traffic. In times of economic recession they were discouraged from raising charges by governments fearing the threat of inflation. The same governments were very reluctant to provide grants or loans for capital replacement and new investment. It is in this context that economies were sought by reducing the system and especially the extent of the network (table 5.5)

TABLE 5.5

The Changing Railway System, GB, 1950-70			
	1950	1970	Index 1950 = 100
Route mileage	19,694	12,037	61
of which electrified	1,300	2,203	170
Stations	8,487	3,114	37
of which passenger-handling	6,500	2,692	41
of which freight-handling	6,595	646	10
Staff	606,000	257,000	42
Locomotives	19,736	4,449	22
Freight wagons	1,122,215	371,000	33
Freight wagons capacity (tons)	14,417,000	6,420,000	44
Passenger coaches	42,218	7,699	18
Passenger coaches seating capacity	2,506,000	1,155,000	46
Passenger miles (million)	20,177	22,144	109
Freight ton miles (million)	22,135	16,394	74
of which coal and coke	10,182	6,247	61

Source: Annual Abstracts of Statistics (HMSO)
These figures include British Rail and London Transport
services but exclude railways in Northern Ireland

The 20,000 mile (32,000 km network) which, as table 5.4 shows, was of similar density to that of West Germany and France (when differences in the area of France are taken into account) had been built under the influence of four main factors. First, was the real need during the nineteenth century for improved transport between coalfields, ports and factories; city centres and dormitory suburbs; and between the main population centres. Secondly, companies frequently built lines in anticipation of needs which were not subsequently justified by the traffic generated. Thirdly, the competitive structure of the railway industry in its early years led to duplication of routes, in order to share potential traffic with rival companies or to forestall their access to particular markets for transport. Fourthly, the technical advantages for all purposes of the railway over other forms of transport led to its ubiquitous coverage of the UK. The extensive use of small private wagons, especially the ten-ton coal wagon, required a high ratio of track to traffic especially in the numerous marshalling yards.

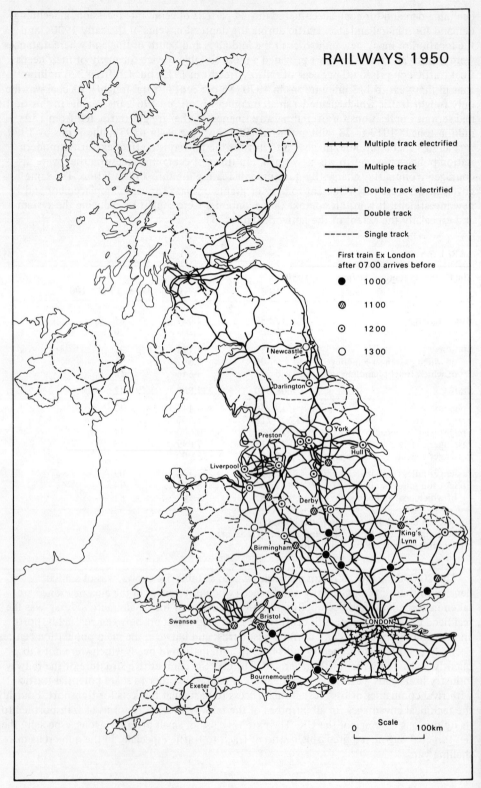

Figure 5.4   Railway network, UK, 1950

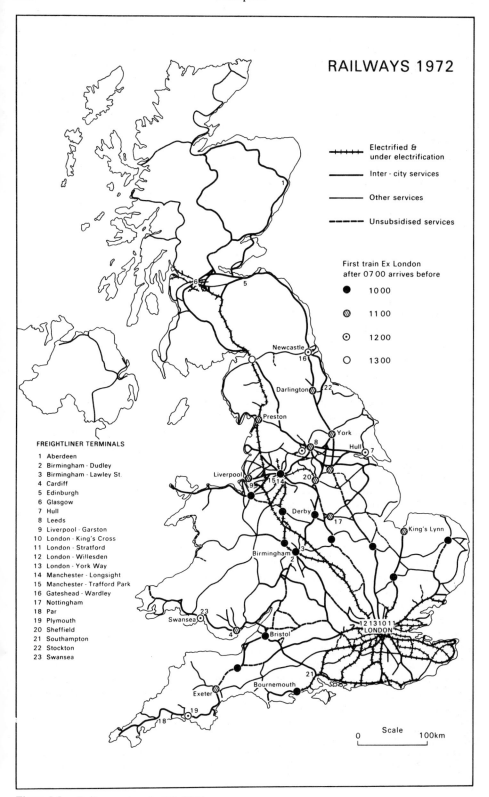

RAILWAYS 1972

Electrified &
under electrification

Inter - city services

Other services

Unsubsidised services

First train Ex London
after 07 00 arrives before

●   10 00

◍   11 00

◉   12 00

○   13 00

FREIGHTLINER TERMINALS

1   Aberdeen
2   Birmingham - Dudley
3   Birmingham - Lawley St.
4   Cardiff
5   Edinburgh
6   Glasgow
7   Hull
8   Leeds
9   Liverpool - Garston
10   London - King's Cross
11   London - Stratford
12   London - Willesden
13   London - York Way
14   Manchester - Longsight
15   Manchester - Trafford Park
16   Gateshead - Wardley
17   Nottingham
18   Par
19   Plymouth
20   Sheffield
21   Southampton
22   Stockton
23   Swansea

Newcastle
Darlington
Preston
York
Hull
Liverpool
Derby
Birmingham
King's Lynn
Swansea
Bristol
LONDON
Bournemouth
Exeter

Scale
0   100km

Figure 5.5   Railway network, UK, 1972

By 1950 the demand for railway services between coalfields, factories and ports had lessened, owing to declining coal and other traffic, inter-railway competition had ceased and road transport was much better equipped technically to meet the needs of thinly-populated and remote areas. Much railway traffic in these areas depended on the common carrier liability of the railways to accept traffic on which road hauliers could see no profit.

Although land freight transport grew between 1952 and 1962 from 41 to 46 thousand million ton miles (65 to 74 thousand million ton/km), the railway share fell from 22 to 16 thousand million ton miles (35 to 42 thousand million ton/km), the rest being handled by road. The share of C licence hauliers, firms carrying their own goods, rose from 25 per cent in 1952 to 35 per cent in 1962; that of haulage companies, including the nationalised British Road Services in 1952, from 20 per cent in 1952 to 30 per cent in 1962.

Sample surveys conducted in the West Midlands in 1953 by Walters[30], confirmed earlier findings by Walker[31] that the service provided by road transport was considered superior to that of rail by many manufacturers in terms of reliability, avoidance of damage in transit and also in speed. He found that the average transit time for rail parcels was 5.3 days against 3.8 days for road parcels and that average transit times for other traffic were longer on rail than road by 70 per cent to other parts of the Midlands, by 37 per cent to Wales and by 22 per cent to London. Only on journeys to Scotland was the average rail haul (5.3 days) shorter than the average road haul of 6.4 days. It is significant that none of the average rail hauls to the regions stated was less than 4 days. Rail charges were, however, lower than road charges on both short (less than 75 miles – 120 km) and long (over 100 miles – 160 km) journeys.

To the disadvantage of rail services for traffic in general manufactured goods and components were added others, associated with the decline in coal production and use and nationalisation of the steel industry. The railways were inherently ill-equipped to respond to rapid changes in the economics of their customers. In 1953 the tonnage of coal loaded onto the railways, their most profitable traffic, began to fall, followed in 1958 by a fall in receipts from coal traffic, from £142 million to £96 million in 1970.

Railway companies had traditionally cross-subsidised loss-making traffics and routes from profitable ones. The amalgamation of the twenty-three British railway companies into four companies (one of which had a financial stake in the Belfast-Coleraine-Londonderry route in Northern Ireland) in 1924 had sought to achieve cross-subsidisation of routes on a national scale, but the whole exercise depended on a general level of charges which provided substantial profits on certain railway services. In 1938 the railways had pressed for a 'square deal' to prevent road carriers cutting too deeply into their profits. Under threat of nationalisation in 1946 the then private haulage and railway companies moved towards a common policy designed to limit the competition of road services in this respect. Unfortunately the degree of cross-subsidisation of individual routes and services was not clearly known and the progressive amalgamation of the twenty-three companies into one led to less data being collected.

Although the railway route mileage was cut by 1,700 miles (2,700 km) between 1948 and 1961, the main effort of the railways was devoted to making good the capital investment which had been largely suspended during the Second World War and to increasing the capacity of the most heavily-used routes.

The first electrification scheme primarily designed for freight traffic was completed from Wath and Sheffield to Manchester, via the rebuilt Woodhead tunnel, to ease the flow of coal from South Yorkshire to Lancashire. In South East England the electrification of the passenger lines from London to Southend and Chelmsford, turned down in the 1920s, was completed. The Southern Electric system reached the Channel ports in 1962 and Southampton and Bournemouth in 1967.

The attempt to integrate rail and road transport under the provisions of the Transport Act of 1947 was abandoned under the Transport Act of 1953, which gave much greater freedom to private road hauliers and led to the reduction, but not the elimination, of the nationalised road haulage fleet. The railways were, however, largely freed from common carrier liability by the Freight Charges Scheme of 1957, but were not entirely free to dispense with uneconomic traffic by raising charges. In fact this freedom was used in an attempt to keep marginal traffics threatened by road haulage since the railways were unwilling to abandon their traditional obligation to carry all types of traffic and specifically not to raise charges on mineral traffics[32]. Gwilliam[33] gives a more detailed appreciation of this situation. Only in 1962 were the railways given complete commercial freedom; the jurisdiction of the Transport Tribunal was, however, retained in the London area.

The problems of road competition and the opportunities made available by a freer-charging policy led the railways to plan a major national scheme of railway modernisation for the years 1954-69.[34] This £1,200 million plan aimed to revolutionise the railway service 'not only by the full utilisation of modern equipment, but also by a purposeful concentration on those functions which the railways can be made to perform more efficiently than other forms of transport'.

The prime objectives of the plan were to increase the speeds of express freight and passenger trains to 100 mph (160 kmph) on main lines, the fitting of continuous brakes to wagons, the replacement of steam by diesel locomotion, the electrification of main routes from London to the West Midlands and Lancashire (achieved in 1966), and to Leeds and York (not yet begun).

The railways agreed to play a major role in the reorganisation of public transport on Clydeside by the electrification of 130 route miles (208 km) focusing on Glasgow. The electrification of the route from Lancashire to Clydeside was agreed and will be completed in 1974. Thus the route miles electrified increased from 1,300 miles (2,080 km), 7 per cent of the network in 1955, to 2,203 miles (3,520 km), 18 per cent of a reduced network in 1970. The increase of track capacity also involved extensive resignalling, the institution of centralised traffic control and the virtually complete rebuilding of the line from London to Crewe, one of the busiest railway routes in the world.

The 1955 Modernisation Report[34] marked a high point of optimism concerning the future role of the railways in the British transport pattern and was issued in a year which some economists now see as a turning point of British economic fortunes, between the period of post-war reconstruction and economic expansion and the first of many cuts in public investment which began in 1956.[35] Rail traffic had been stabilised at 22 million freight ton miles (35 million ton/km) and 20 million passenger miles (32 million passenger km) per annum since 1949, but the Modernisation Report foresaw the transfer to road of freight and passenger services outside the conurbations and inter city routes 'unless they could be made reasonably economic' (pp 7-8).

The railways paid their way until 1952, but in 1954 the surplus on operating account failed to meet capital charges. In 1955 working expenses equalled gross receipts for the first time and there was no surplus on operating account. By 1962 working expenses exceeded receipts by £100 million. These financial problems led to a reappraisal of the Modernisation Plan in 1959[36] and a financial reconstruction of the railways in 1960.[37] Many experts now accepted that capital expenditure under the Modernisation Plan could not achieve revenues sufficient to offset the downward trend in many traditional traffics. The Prime Minister suggested that 'the railway system must be remodelled to meet current needs and the modernisation plan must be adapted to this new shape'. The railways undertook an extensive research programme under the chairmanship of Beeching. The Beeching Report did not hazard a guess as to how much of the railway network could ultimately be made to pay but put forward proposals for shaping the system to provide rail transport for that part of the national pattern favourable to railways. The Report considered its proposals to be conservative with regard to closures and restrainedly speculative about new developments. An analysis of the nature of the traffic and revenue on railway routes showed small profits on parcel, mail and coal traffic. Passenger services accounted for 56 per cent of the deficit, to which express trains contributed 12 per cent, commuter services 14 per cent and other stopping trains 30 per cent. Wagon load merchandise accounted for 30 per cent of the deficit, sundries 12 per cent and mineral traffic 2 per cent.

Half the railway route mileage carried only 5 per cent of the freight ton-miles and only 4 per cent of the total passenger miles. This route mileage earned £20 million but cost £40 million to operate in that year. Of the 4,300 passenger stations on the British railway system, the 95 busiest yielded 48 per cent of total passenger receipts, but the 3,000 least-used stations produced only 6 per cent of the receipts (figure 5.6).

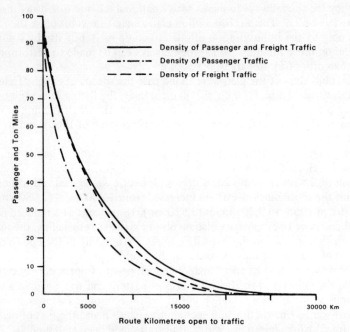

Figure 5.6   Cumulative distribution of traffic, British Rail, 1961

Inter-city passenger services ran on 7,500 route miles (12,000 km). These included large numbers of special weekend and summer holiday trains for which 66 per cent of the total coaching stock was maintained. It was recommended that these services should be abandoned and further agreed that economically-viable stopping train routes must carry at least 17,000 passengers per week where there was no other traffic, but might be viable down to a level of 10,000 passengers per week if there was sufficient freight on the line to absorb a share of the route costs. The withdrawal of services handling less than 10,000 passengers per week was recommended also on routes where freight or express passenger services continued to run. In fact passenger and freight revenue supported each other to viable levels on about 9,000 miles (14,000 km) of the railway network.

A further Survey[18] suggested the abandonment of duplicated routes between conurbations and cities. This report [p7] suggested that the 1,400 route miles (2,250 km) of three- and four-track railway were only being used to 42 per cent of their capacity and that the 6,100 route miles (9,800 km) of double track to 31 per cent of capacity. On the basis of forecast traffic flows for 1984, fully documented in the Report, it was concluded that the 7,500 route miles (12,000 km) of the 1963 proposals could profitably be reduced to 3,000 route miles (4,800 km), one-sixth of railway route mileage in 1961.

In Northern Ireland the Benson Report[39], having traced the decline of the railway network in the six counties from 1,200 route miles (1,940 km) in 1914 to 297 route miles (475 km) in 1962, suggested its further reduction to 75 route miles (120 km) as a commuter service from central Belfast to Larne, Bangor, Portadown (for Craigavon New Town) retaining the line south from Portadown to the Border for as long as CIE wished to retain a through rail service from Dublin to Belfast. This line was partitioned in 1958 and has been retained as the only rail service linking the UK with the Irish Republic where, as early as 1957,[40] a reduction of railway route mileage from 1,918 (3,060 km) to 850 (1,360 km) had been recommended.

In Britain, closures under the Beeching Plan were relatively slow and in 1966 when there were still 13,721 route miles (22,000 km) in operation, the government agreed with the British Railways Board that the network should be stabilised at 11,000 route miles (17,700 km)[41] including main Inter-city routes, major feeder lines to them, intensive passenger commuter services and rural services 'essential to the life of remote areas'. A further 2,500 route miles (4,000 km), although not recommended for future development, might be maintained for specialised freight services.

The modernisation of many main lines during the 1960s allowed British Rail to take the initiative in the land movement of the large modern containers which began to arrive at British ports, initially from America. These containers, unlike the existing railway-owned containers which had been introduced in 1926, were up to 30ft (9.2 m) long, 8ft (2.4 m) wide with a capacity of 1,650 ft^3 (47 m^3). The containers, whether covered, open, insulated, curtain-sided, owned by railways, shipping companies or private firms, were assembled into full trains travelling at high speed on standard daily schedules. The first of these services was launched between London and Glasgow in 1959 and, beginning in 1965, Freightliner services were extended to the seven conurbations, also Aberdeen, Edinburgh, Teesside, Hull, Sheffield, Nottingham, Cardiff, Swansea and Southampton, and to the container ports of Felixstowe, Harwich, Tilbury, Fishguard and Holyhead. Inland Customs depots were set up in each of the conurbations.

The railways partially replaced their declining coal traffic with oil products, whose traffic was doubled between 1963 and 1966, possibly forestalling a more extensive network of pipelines. The coal traffic itself was rationalised and many power stations were adapted to take permanently-coupled 'merry-go-round' trains operating out of the larger collieries. The rail haul of domestic coal was concentrated at central depots. 'Company' trains provided regular transport between different branches of the same firm, notably the major car companies or between producers and wholesalers as in the case of whisky.

The railways returned to the holiday traffic, which they had abandoned, in the form of holiday special passenger trains in 1963, by motor-rail services, which began in 1965 and were carrying 70,000 cars on 22 routes in 1970. Inter-city express passenger services, have been introduced on 4,250 route miles (6,850 km) of main line. The increased speeds of inter-city trains from London to major provincial centres are illustrated on figure 5.5 and a progressive improvement on existing schedules will lead to considerable acceleration on the Lancashire-Glasgow services when the electrified line is opened in 1974 and in London-Edinburgh services where the High Speed Train will begin operations in the mid-1970s and the Advanced Passenger Train, newly designed in order to reach 155 mph (234 kmph) on existing track, will be introduced in the early 1980s.

By 1969 the results of the modernisation policy were beginning to show. Passenger receipts rose by 70 per cent in 3 years on the London-Midland-Lancashire electrified lines and it was generally found that each 1 per cent increase in speed on Inter-city produced a 2 per cent gain in passengers. Inter-city passenger services now provided 19 per cent of total railway revenue, commuter services in the South East 18 per cent and other passenger services 5 per cent, but grants for rural and commuter passenger services accounted for a further 12 per cent. Freight revenue (46 per cent) was divided equally between train load and wagon load. The railways had increased their share of London-Manchester passenger traffic to 50 per cent and already held 48 per cent of the London-Newcastle services.

Coordination of inter-city transport, dormant since the Transport Act of 1953, was revived in the Transport Act of 1968, which was preceeded by four explanatory White Papers.[42] Under the Act, a National Freight Corporation (NFC) was formed to carry general merchandise, sundries and 40 per cent of the parcels traffic on rail and road. The NFC came into possession of containers, with their warehouses and depots, and also the former British Road Services. The NFC cooperates with British Rail in the actual operation of freightliner trains through a jointly-owned company, Freightliners Ltd.

The National Bus Company was established to operate inter-city passenger road-coach services in England and Wales, with the Scottish Bus Group performing a similar function in Scotland. In Northern Ireland Ulsterbus was already integrated with the provincial Transport Authority. These companies also operate road services in replacement of rail services which have been withdrawn. British Rail still faces the problem of obtaining sufficient capital to continue the modernisation of the system, which alone can develop new traffic and retain existing customers. Such developments include extended freightliner services and the Advanced Passenger Train which, using the Channel tunnel, could provide as fast a city-centre to city-centre service between London and Paris, Brussels, Newcastle and Manchester as air travel.

Under the Transport Act of 1968 the British Railways Board was required to maintain a network of about 11,000 route miles (17,500 km) providing passenger, mineral and some general merchandise services and to pay its way, apart from Government subsidies for specified services. These grants are due to be drastically curtailed in 1973 and, although the railways under their new financial organisation made small profits in 1969 and 1970, investment had fallen from £120 million in 1968 to £94 million in 1970. The country is still faced with the question which was first posed in the 1920s' whether to maintain a highly specialised but intensively-capitalised Inter-city network of railways, or to rely on an accelerated trunk road improvement programme for moving Britain's goods and passengers.

III   LOCAL TRANSPORT

Just as inland transport between the regions and cities of the UK has been increasingly taking place by road since the First World War, local transport has come to be dominated by private car movements. Table 5.3 shows that private car transport now accounts for 77 per cent of total passenger mileage. Local surveys suggest that the proportion of passenger mileage on local journeys made by car is considerably greater. The numbers of people per car in the UK has fallen from 20.6 in 1951 to 4.7 in 1970 and this rapid growth in the number of private vehicles has revolutionised local transport within two decades.

III.1   The Coordination of Urban Transport Systems

The 1969 Green Paper[28] forecast: 'Plans for interurban roads must make allowance for the increasing need for road improvements in urban areas'. In fact 75 per cent of the road space occupied by traffic is used by private cars. Private car traffic, which increased from 42 thousand million vehicle miles (66 thousand million km) in 1960 to 100 thousand million vehicle miles (166 thousand million km) in 1970, is predominantly used in and around the urban areas in which 80 per cent of the population lives and in which many of the remainder work or shop. Major traffic pressures began to build up in the larger towns in the late 1950s and the towns responded by abolishing tramways, widening radial approach roads, building circumferential by-pass routes or merely by diverting traffic through residential streets adjacent to the city centre or forming a viable through-routeway.

The Buchanan Report (1963)[43] proposed a sophisticated approach to urban traffic problems, depending on the size of towns and their street layout. Attention should be given to the 'primary distributors', major roads which carried traffic into and round towns, in the hope of creating pedestrian precincts and low density traffic zones between them. Where the volume of traffic reached a point when the primary distributors and their extensive interchanges become so large as to dominate the visual environment and displace large numbers of dwelling houses, schemes for the restricting of traffic by limiting parking, licensing or road pricing should be considered. Accessibility must be balanced with environmental preservation when the environmental deterioration caused by enlarging the major roads would no longer be acceptable. Public transport systems would then have to play an increasing part in moving people to work and to shop. The Report recommended planned coordination between transport systems developed through the medium of a statutory development plan which took into account predictions of size and direction of traffic flows.

The Beeching Report[38] also advocated the subsidisation of the suburban railways of London, Birmingham, Glasgow, Manchester, Liverpool, Leeds, Newcastle, Edinburgh and Cardiff as the cheapest solution to the problem of moving the numbers of people travelling to work in the central areas of those cities. The Beeching Report further noted that the railways, though overcrowded within 20 miles (32 km) of their central London termini, had the facilities and spare capacity to bring passengers into London from a radius of 20-100 miles (32-160 km). These facilities have subsequently been increased by the electrification of lines to Southampton, Reading, Rugby and Colchester.

The concept of 'total social cost', involving a full consideration of the costs and benefits of all possible transport systems, separately and in combination, so that each mode serves those routes for which it is technically and economically most suited, had been current for some years and was particularly expounded by Foster.[44]

The expertise in the formulation of combined traffic and land use surveys, which had been accumulated in studies of the North American conurbations during the 1950s by several firms of international consultants began to be applied to British cities, with the firm backing of the Ministry of Transport and to a slightly less enthusiastic extent by local authorities;[45] even in 1970 only two county boroughs combined highway and land use planning under the control of the same committee. The Teesside Survey and Plan (1969)[46] is a good example of such studies.

Only five years after the publication of the Buchanan and Beeching Reports the Transport Act of 1968 made provision for the establishment of coordinated transport schemes in the larger conurbations. Inspired by the example of the London Passenger Transport Board of 1933, large Passenger Transport Authorities (PTAs) on which local authorities were strongly represented, were set up in London, Greater Manchester (SELNEC), the West Midlands, Merseyside and Tyneside. These authorities took control of bus services within their areas and received grants to cover their commuter rail services, which in the case of London extended as far as Cambridge, Bletchley and Bournemouth. Outside London these grants are intended to cease in 1973, when several routes may be transferred from British Rail to the PTAs. The Passenger Transport Authorities are also grant-aided by the government, in respect of rural buses and the building of transport interchanges, and it is intended that local government, the metropolitan counties after 1974, will subsidise urban bus and rail services so that they are operated at prices which will minimise the total social and environmental costs of providing the services.

In most PTA areas, and in the larger cities, large-scale traffic management schemes and central pedestrian precincts are being introduced. Improved urban bus services and/or new electric light-railway systems are planned. With the largest population and most complex bus, railway and underground system, London[47] has the largest schemes and the highest proportion (54 per cent) of journeys to work on public transport. Improved underground services include the Victoria line, the first new underground line since 1907, planned in

1949 and opened in 1969, and the Fleet line, approved in 1971 with a 100 per cent govern-ment subsidy for its central London traverse. The London Transport Executive plans to spend £500 million at current prices on extending and renewing its underground railways and £200 million on buses and their routeways. British Rail hopes to be able to invest either £150 million on its surface commuter services, up to 1980, in order to maintain present standards, or £220 million to improve them.

An urban motorway scheme was first presented in 1967 in order to complement jour-neys from one suburb to another by express buses, delivery vans and private cars. The number of these journeys is growing as the city centre loses population and there is a limited decentralisation of offices. The circumferential ringways will also link the national motorways with the port and airports of London and the main roads to Europe.

The London Plan[48] includes a motorway box (ringway 1) surrounding the central 60 sq miles (155 km^2) of the city, a motorway/dual-carriageway linking the inner suburbs (ringway 2) lying 1-4 miles (2-6 km) outside ringway 1 and a motorway/dual-carriageway route at the fringe of the built-up area (ringway 3) 12-15 miles (19-24 km) from central London. The original plan would have cost £850 million between 1970 and 1985 which is roughly equivalent to the costs of investment schemes in public transport over the same period described above. The plans for these roads are arousing increasing opposition. Delays caused by statutory objections are increasing the eventual cost of the schemes and recommendations have already been made by leading consultants which would improve the standard of the motorways while doubling the original predicted costs. The completion date for the scheme has already been postponed into the 1990s and it looked less likely in 1972 than in 1970 that the full scheme will ever be carried out.

Similar schemes on a smaller scale have been proposed and opposed in the other British conurbations. Differing approaches by local councils and their planners and traffic engineers, changes in political control and in the date of initial plans are likely to bring about a situ-ation in which the British conurbations will look less like each other as the century advances, as each imposes a different balance between private and public transport on an already varied urban or physical morphology. Thus the Glasgow inner motorway ring[49] is scheduled for completion before the Passenger Transport Authority will be established and will obli-terate the original medieval High Street of the city. In Edinburgh, little road-widening has taken place; the Newcastle central area was replanned before the traffic and land use study but the Passenger Transport Authority was established before the urban ring motorway was built.

So far, urban transport has relied on the coordination of transport modes which were all invented by the end of the nineteenth century. There is considerable experimentation in mini vehicles for individuals, maxi-taxis available on request, moving pavements, light elevated busways and central control of traffic. It is difficult to see how further growth in the traditional transport vehicle fleets can be accommodated in many British regional capitals for much more than a further decade.

III.2 The Changing Pattern of Rural Transport

Rural transport is defined here in its widest sense as local transport outside towns. The rural railways were built in the mid-nineteenth century and rural bus services established in the 1920s. Further development of private car ownership during the 1950s created a total supply of transport well in excess of the ability of rural populations to pay for it.

The rural transport situation varies with rural settlement geography and four character-istic patterns may be distinguished:

(a)   Areas within 50 miles (80 km) of conurbations with population densities of over 250 per sq mile (100 persons per km^2). In Southern England and in rural areas within 20 miles (30 km) of conurbations and coalfields in the rest of the UK, the rural population has been swelled by an adventitious population of retired people and commuters who own at least one car per family, while enjoying higher average incomes than those working in local agriculture and other rural industries, and wish to combine the advantages of rural life with access to urban facilities.

(b)   Prosperous agricultural areas with population densities of over 250 persons per sq mile (100 persons per km²) and a village settlement pattern with most people living in communities of 3000 or over. Many coalfield areas conform to this pattern. Such areas lent themselves to bus transport and had inherited rail services from the nineteenth century.

(c)   Areas of dispersed rural settlement in hamlets, as in South West England, the Welsh Borders and Northern Ireland, or in strings of valley-bottom houses separated by uninhabited interfluves as in Central Wales or the Pennine Dales.

(d)   The NW Highlands and Islands of Scotland with a total population of 420,000 present the special problem of linear coastal settlements separated from each other by seas and from Central Scotland by extensive tracts of uninhabited upland. There is a considerable literature on the transport problems of the NW Highlands.[50] Since 1745 successive UK governments have provided, or paid for, roads, canals, harbours and railways in this area. Payments for postal services have effectively subsidised the operation of MacBraynes bus and steamship services. Air services to the islands have been cross-subsidised by BEA.

The need for rural transport has grown steadily since the Second World War. As employment in agriculture and mining has declined the medium-sized towns have increasingly supplied employment for rural inhabitants. Economies of scale in medicine and education have favoured the development of the relatively-large district general hospital of 800-1,000 beds and the secondary school of 500-1,000 pupils. Primary schools, maternity and geriatric hospitals are more frequently dispersed, but if the rural population wish to participate in rising national standards of living and welfare they are increasingly forced to travel to urban service centres in order to obtain these benefits. The introduction or retention of manufacturing or mining industry in rural areas has frequently required road improvements or the extension or maintenance of rail services.

The pattern of rural transport from the 1920s to the 1950s was of road and railway passenger services supported by cross-subsidisation from urban and inter-urban services. Many road freight services were provided by manufacturers operating their own vehicles under C licences or by wholesale and retail companies whose transport operations were inseparable from the rest of their business. The Transport Act of 1947 enabled British Road Services to cross-subsidise rural routes if they so wished. Thus the supply of the commodity needs of the rural population, the sale of farm products and the movement of fertilisers could be accommodated in the private sector of the road transport system relatively easily. The pattern of bus routes about 1950 was analysed by Green.[51]

Car ownership is normally higher in rural than in other areas. In 1952, for instance, when there were 16 people per private car in Great Britain, there were 10-12 in the counties of Mid-Wales, and in 1971 when there were 4·7 people to the car in Great Britain some rural areas had reached levels of 3·6.[52] Swedish studies have suggested that when car ownership passes the level of one car per 7 people public transport begins to have economic difficulties. This figure was reached in some rural areas in 1960, in Great Britain in 1963 and in Northern Ireland in 1965. Pilot studies of transport in rural areas of Devon and West Suffolk,[53,54] carried out in 1971 for the Department of the Environment, demonstrated the unsuitability of train and bus services for their irregular and scattered needs. Only 3 per cent of journeys made by people who owned cars were on public transport; three-quarters of all households had one car; in one-third of households at least two people had full use of a car. As many journeys were made in the form of 'lifts' as on stage bus services. The level of car ownership among men was double that for women, three times as high among the upper two social classes as in the lowest two classes, and three times as high among the under 45s as among the over 65s. The actual numbers of people relying solely on public transport, non-driving mothers with young children, the elderly and handicapped, had become relatively small, their needs being largely catered for by lifts. Only 6 per cent of all trips took place on public transport including 7 per cent of journeys to work and 13 per cent of shopping trips. Half the population never used public transport.

The concept of total social cost assumes that certain levels of welfare must be available to all members of the rural community. It is then possible to consider to what extent a concentration of transport on a limited number of routes or modes will provide access to minimum welfare, or whether subsidies will be necessary in order to maintain the rural population in their present geographical distribution.

The Devon and Suffolk studies showed that the purposes of rural journeys were fairly evenly divided between shopping and business (25 per cent) leisure (24 per cent) work (22 per cent) and school (18 per cent). The remainder of the journeys did not fit these classifications but it seems apparent that between a half and three quarters of journeys are to a larger urban centre.

These findings clearly call into doubt the future role of rural railway and conventional bus services. Transport facilities often outlast their need and the withdrawal of public transport has lagged several years behind the growth in car ownership. Rural rail lines began to be abandoned in the 1920s and by 1952 the Minister of Transport[55] had announced that railways were no longer obliged to retain uneconomic stations or branches; however, the rate of closure up to 1962 was slow.[56]

The publication of the Beeching Report[38] led to a notable public outcry over the proposed closure of rural rail lines, although there were few suggestions as to how the rural railway services might be made economically viable. The subsequent closure of many lines took place under the provisions of the Transport Act of 1962 necessitating public enquiries, discussions with Transport Users' Consultative Councils and, after the 1968 Transport Act, with Regional Economic Planning Councils. Closures rose from a rate of 2 per cent per annum of the existing route miles between 1958 and 1962, to 8 per cent per annum between 1965 and 1968 but fell away to 2 per cent per annum in 1969 and 1970 (see also Aldcroft).[57] The route mileage had fallen by 34 per cent in 9 years but remained half as large again as that recommended by the 1963 Report and four times as large as that recommended by the 1965 Report.[18] Among railway lines to be maintained in the 1966 'Network for Development'[41] were included 'services which, although they may never pay their way commercially, have an economic or a social value to the community as a whole which outweighs their money costs. These include . . . some rural services where alternatives would be impracticable or excessively costly.'

Although the 1963 Beeching proposal of 7,500 route miles (12,000 km) and the 1965 proposal of 3,000 route miles (4,800 km) were extended to 11,000 route miles (17,500 km) in 1966, there are differences in the shape of the network. Several routes recommended for retention in 1963 have been closed while many recommended for closure have been retained. These variations show how appreciations of the relative value of specific railway lines have changed within the British Rail administration as its accounting procedures become more sophisticated, and they also show the effects of local pressure exerted though members of Parliament, the Press, the Transport Users' Consultative Councils and the Regional Economic Planning Councils.

Under the provisions of the Transport Act of 1968 many rural railway services, including branch lines and stopping services on inter-city routes, have been retained under annual or biennial government subsidies (figure 5.5). The frequent reviews which must be undertaken before subsidies are renewed give rise to considerable uncertainty about the future of the services. Grant-aided services were operating on 90 per cent of the railway route mileage outside the areas of the PTAs and the London area (Bournemouth-Reading-Bedford-Cambridge-Ipswich) in the years 1968-72, but only generated 19 per cent of the annual passenger mileage.[58] The grants to these services totalled £32 million in 1971 and £31 million in 1972. A British Rail estimate in 1971 suggested that 130 of the grant-aided services were rural and that these grants were equivalent to 1·4 p per passenger. Only 76 of these services have so far been promised grants for 1973 and it is clear, as the Secretary of State for the Environment pointed out in 1971, that rural trains costing £1 per mile to run are much less economic than rural buses which may cost from 10-25 p. These figures have been confirmed by the National Bus Company in respect of the Carlisle-West Cumberland-Barrow route which they claim to be able to operate with a grant only one-tenth as great as that provided to British Rail.[59]

The decline in profitability of rural bus services came later than that of the railways and was more complex in its effects. Besides the regional bus companies, formed under the Transport Act of 1930, there were a large number of small operators who provided stage carriage, coach and charter services between villages and market towns until the late 1950s. Television dealt a fatal blow to most of these local companies by reducing the demand for evening coach trips to urban cinemas,[60] since contract work accounted for 50-65 per cent of their gross revenue. The viability of small firms was further weakened by rising costs of petrol, replacement vehicles and more stringent safety standards. During the 1960s, as their urban routes became less economic, the regional bus companies found cross-subsidisation of their rural routes less viable. They ceased to take over the routes of small operators when the latter suspended services and increasingly sought permission from the Ministry of Transport to abandon routes or to reduce or 'rationalise' services.

The number of passenger journeys on rural buses rose from 5·7 million in 1950 to 6·0 million in 1955 but then began to decline slowly to 3·7 million in 1970,[61] by which time half the mileage run by the National Bus Company failed to cover costs. Rural bus services were particularly affected by inflation since wages formed up to 60 per cent of operating costs and operational economies by the reduction in mileage or frequency of service may do nothing to lower wage, depreciation and terminal costs. On the Western National services, for instance, which cover a large sector of rural South West England, the number of passengers halved between 1955 and 1970, but the vehicle mileage only fell by 20 per cent.[53]

The National Bus Company and Scottish Bus Group, established under the 1968 Transport Act to run inter-urban-rural services, saw their initial profits become a combined loss of £9·9 million by 1970. In the same year the Highland, Island and coastal services of David McBrayne and the Caledonian Steam Packet Company lost £405,000.

The National Bus Company therefore proposed withdrawal of unremunerative bus services unless local authorities were prepared to grant-aid them under the provisions of the 1968 Act. In 1970 only £1 million was being spent on grants to bus services (shared 50:50 by local and national government) against £30 million in grants to railway services. The government also paid 12½ p per gallon to subsidise fuel costs and is pledged to contribute half of the cost of new buses until 1980. Local subsidies to rural buses from County Councils, either to compensate losses or giving fixed mileage studies, had been suggested by the Jack Committee in 1961,[62] but they considered that the concentration of school, post, parcels and other luggage transport on one vehicle would only offer limited solutions to specialised problems. Further studies produced little action until the amendment of the vehicle licensing regulations under the 1968 Transport Act enabled mini-buses to be run by the Post Office and by private individuals for public carriage. Several dial-a-bus schemes by which potential customers book seats on a vehicle or divert it from its standard route if they require a service, are now in an experimental stage.

The statutory obligation of local education authorities to provide bus or taxi services for children living more than two miles from a scheduled service to school was extended under the Transport Act of 1968 to allow local authorities to subsidise services within their areas which had become uneconomic. Few such services have yet been provided, but the 1968 Act allows school buses, which already accounted for 60 per cent of all bus journeys in the rural areas studied in 1971[53] to be used by other passengers. The Post Office may carry passengers on mail services and 4 such services are now in operation. Private hire operators may be allowed to pick up separate fares en route, and works contract buses covered 6 per cent of the journeys to work in the areas studied, almost as high a proportion as for those travelling to work on public buses. Thus ways are now being sought, under the pressure of rising costs, to meet the welfare needs of rural inhabitants without access to private car transport in one way or another. A strict operation of tests of economic viability at any time in the near future would virtually eliminate public rail and road transport services from the rural areas of the UK.

IV   AIR TRANSPORT

IV.1   Traffic

This section concentrates on the role of air transport within the UK, including traffic to the Isle of Man and the Channel Islands. Internal air transport was experimental during the 1920s with the present services tracing their origins to 1932. Dyos and Aldcroft give a full history of inter-war domestic aviation[63] and show that almost all the routes in use today, with the exception of London-Manchester, were in operation immediately before the Second World War. The number of passengers carried had reached a peak in 1937 of 161,000 compared with 5·3 million in 1970. In 1946, when services were fully resumed, domestic passenger mileage was three times as great as in 1938. Passenger mileage has doubled about every 4 years since 1946, until, in 1970 (table 5.6), 1,238 million passenger miles (1,950 million passenger km) were flown on domestic routes. The size of the UK tends to restrict the average length of flight which was 164 miles (262 km) in 1970. This distance is less than the most economic flying sector of most medium-range modern aircraft, and contributes to the problems of air-passenger transport in competition with land transport in Great Britain. The average distance between airports serving the conurbations and major cities of the UK is 163 miles (262 km) and the average distance between adjacent major airports is only 100 miles (160 km).

Figure 5.7 shows the main domestic routes and Table 5.7 illustrates the two main services provided by airways within the UK. Routes between the London airports (Heathrow, Gatwick, Stansted and Luton) and the more distant major cities carried 48 per cent of the domestic passenger traffic in 1970, including 23 per cent from Glasgow and Edinburgh, 10 per cent from Belfast, 8 per cent from Manchester and Liverpool, 5 per cent from Newcastle and Teesside and 2 per cent from Leeds-Bradford.[64]

Short sea-crossings to Northern Ireland, the Isle of Man, Channel Islands, Hebrides, Orkneys and Shetland accounted for much of the traffic at provincial airports. Traffic from Britain to Belfast accounted for 20 per cent of total domestic passenger traffic, to the Channel Islands 21 per cent and to the Isle of Man 7 per cent.

The Highlands and Islands services of BEA form an essentially separate network linking Glasgow, Edinburgh and Aberdeen with Campbeltown, Inverness and Wick and with the island airports of Islay, Tiree, Barra, Benbecula, Stornoway, Kirkwall and Sumburgh. Like other rural transport services these links are cross-subsidised within BEA and provide, among other things, direct access to the business centres and medical services of the mainland. A BEA helicopter service provides a similar link between Penzance and the Scilly Islands. Passenger traffic between British provincial airports only accounted for 13 per cent of total domestic traffic in 1970.

TABLE 5.6   Air Traffic, UK, 1946 and 1970

Domestic flights	1946	1970
Aircraft miles flown (million)	5·4	24·8
Passengers carried (million)	0·4	10·6
Passenger miles (million)	30·1	1,237·8
Freight ton/miles (million)	0·1	13·6
Foreign flights		
Passengers carried (million)	0·2	21·8
% of total	45	67
Freight handled (thousand tons)	3·7	204·3
% of total	81	77

Percentage of oversea journeys by air		
	1960	1970
Total	*47*	*65*
Irish republic	34	50
Europe	46	59
North America	74	97
Other continents	47	97

Source: *Annual Abstracts of Statistics,* (HMSO)

Of the 32·4 million passengers using UK airports in 1970, 21·8 million (68 per cent) were flying to or from foreign airports. Of the 10·8 million passengers leaving the UK 37 per cent were bound for neighbouring countries (France, the Low Countries, Germany and the Irish Republic), 30 per cent for more distant European countries (Spain, Italy, Switzerland and Scandinavia) and 16 per cent for North America.[65] Table 5.6 shows the extent to which air transport had captured the overseas traffic on these services, for in 1960 the near neighbours had accounted for 57 per cent of the air traffic, the more distant European countries 19 per cent and North America 13 per cent. The traffic to Spain, which has grown fourteenfold in 10 years, accounts for most of these differences.

Table 5.6 shows that the growth in freight transport since the Second World War has

TABLE 5.7   Domestic Air Passenger Traffic, UK, 1971 and Percentage Distribution 1970

Airport	Domestic traffic 1971 (thousands)	London	% distribution 1970 Belfast and British Islands	British Mainland
London	3,298	-	33	67
Glasgow	1,359	56	18	26
Belfast	1,063	50	3	47
Manchester	693	48	32	20
Edinburgh	592	83	6	5
Liverpool	308	31	53	16
Newcastle	271	77	17	6
Birmingham	235	19	59	22
Southampton	228	-	90	10
Leeds-Bradford	211	49	40	11
E. Midlands	163	2	67	31
Blackpool	124	-	99	27
Bristol and Glamorgan	95	1	72	27
Teesside	60	82	15	3

Source: DTI, *Business Monitor,* CA2 (March 1972)

% Distribution derived from *Business Monitor* CA6 (1971)

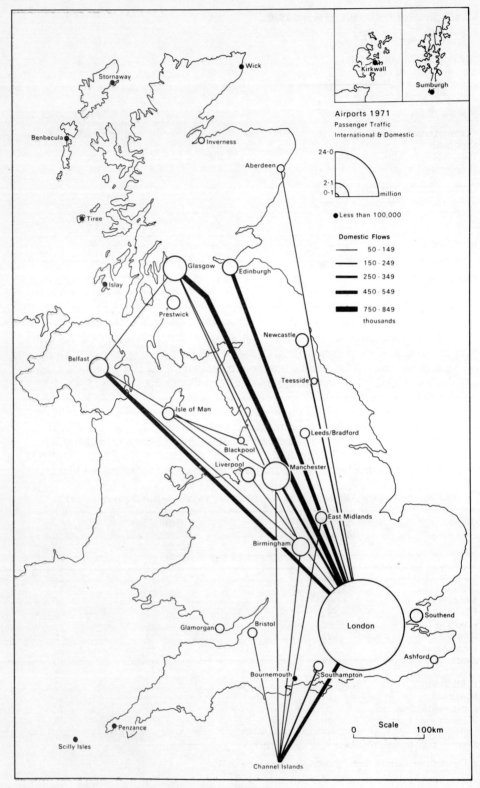

Figure 5.7   Airports and domestic air traffic, UK, 1971

been twice as rapid as that of passenger traffic, and that the growth of foreign freight traffic has been greater than that of domestic freight, which amounted to only 17 per cent of the total in 1970.[66] Under these circumstances it is not surprising that the London airports and Southend together handled 75 per cent of all freight in 1971 (Heathrow is the third port in the UK in terms of the value of goods passing through it); followed by Manchester and Liverpool (9 per cent) Glasgow and Prestwick (5 per cent) Belfast (3 per cent) and the Channel Islands (2 per cent).[67]

IV.2 The Location and Development of Airports

Figure 5.7 shows the foreign and domestic traffic handled by the airports of the UK with Heathrow, Gatwick and Luton aggregated as 'London' airports. The distribution pattern of provincial airports is inherited from the 1930s, when accessibility by surface transport was relatively restricted. Few people owned cars and airports were generally located within 20-45 minutes by airport bus of major railway stations. The trunk road network and faster Inter-city rail services of the 1970s would, in theory, enable both current and potential traffic to be handled by a smaller number of airports, each large enough to attract a wider variety of services than are now operated. Many provincial airports are now eccentrically located in terms of the load centre of their present traffic, and in some cases their sites restrict present traffic[68] or its predicted growth.[69] In the absence of any national airport plan, municipally-owned airports compete with each other and with the nationally-owned airports at London, Edinburgh and Prestwick for the traffic of their region.

In Central Scotland, for instance, an airport located between Stirling and Falkirk would have access to three million people living or working within 45 minutes travelling time by existing railway and motorway routes. There are, however, three airports. Prestwick, established in 1945, has an excellent, virtually fog-free site on the cost of the Firth of Clyde providing minimum noise pollution. It was established, like Shannon and Gander, at a time when piston-engined aircraft required to refuel before attempting the North Atlantic crossing with full payloads and has since been maintained under the ownership of the British Airport Authority and with the patronage of BOAC which operates direct flights to Canada. Passengers totalled 500,000 in 1971 and freight 11·7 millions tons. Prestwick is 30 miles (48 km) south-west of Glasgow and 70 miles (112 km) by road from Edinburgh. Glasgow Corporation bought a site for a new airport 1·5 miles (2·2 km) west of the city centre on the Edinburgh to Greenock motorway in 1958. This airport is now used for internal and short sea services. It handled 1·7 million passengers in 1971 and 15·2 million tons of freight. Edinburgh airport, now owned by the British Airport Authority, lies 6 miles (10 km) west of the city, 2 miles (3 km) from the motorways to Glasgow and Stirling. It had 690,000 passengers and 2·0 million tons of freight in 1971. The investment already made and the administrative responsibility for these three airports suggests that they will serve Central Scotland for the rest of this century. Yet if airport investment could have been centrally located at an early stage the area might have attracted better services from Europe. If Scotland had been free to accept more through services from Scandinavia instead of London, such a location might well have provided much better links with North America. A similar story of local rivalry could be told of North East England where Newcastle and Teesside airports lie 40 miles (64 km) apart, one to the north and the other to the south of the major settlements. In North West England, Manchester and Liverpool airports are only 27 miles (43 km) apart.

In 1971 the London airports handled 72 per cent of the air passenger and, if Southend is included, 75 per cent of the air freight of the UK[70] Taafe[71] has studied the extent to which large airports, once established, may absorb the potential air traffic of areas within 100-200 miles (160-320 km) radius. In 1968[72] and 1969 26-31 per cent of non-business passengers travelling abroad through south-eastern airports (including Luton, Southend and Southampton) came from other regions of Britain. The dominance of the London airports in the UK air traffic depends on several factors. London is a world business centre, the largest British conurbation and the chief single focus of land communications in Great Britain. In the early, formative years of air transport, London generated most of the official passenger and mail traffic which then formed a major component of airline business, and became the headquarters of the national and most of the charter and private airline companies. Although business passengers are not so numerous as leisure passengers, who comprised 60 per cent of the British passengers at London airports in 1969, their journeys are not seasonal and form the base load of regular demand for air transport. Leisure travel, on the other hand, is expected to grow to 80 per cent of the total of British traffic by the end of the century[73] and the number of foreign visitors is expected to grow markedly. At the present time almost all foreign tourists visit London and 85 per cent go nowhere else in Britain.

The Roskill Report[74] lists income, family composition and age as the chief factors affecting people's choice of air travel for holidays. Sealy[75] points out that the rapidly growing leisure air travel is strongly related to discretionary income, i.e. the amount of money available after basic needs for food, housing, clothing and taxation have been met. This discretionary income is higher in the South East and rises, as a proportion of total income, ahead of that of the other regions so that, apart from the fact that European travel is marginally cheaper from the South East than from more distant regions, the amount of money available for it is greater and therefore the South East generates more leisure travel. The proportion of retired people is also greater in the South East than in other regions.

The site of the first large airport for London was chosen in 1943 at Heathrow, 15 miles (24 km) west of the metropolis. When Heathrow came into full operation in 1954 the pre-war airport at Gatwick, 26 miles (41 km) south of London had been chosen as London's second airport.[76] Heathrow has continued to serve the majority of scheduled international flights and is preferred by business travellers because of its relatively short surface journey to Central London. Gatwick has concentrated on charter flights, which contributed 67 per cent of its traffic in 1967. Since 1960 Luton municipal airport has developed charter flights which here amount to 90 per cent of the passenger traffic. In 1957 it was realised that Heathrow and Gatwick, with or without help from Luton, would have sufficient capacity to handle traffic after 1980[77] when the numbers of air journeys to and from the London area might reach 56 million.[78] Subsequent growth has been forecast up to 2006 when 260 million journeys are expected, of which 35 per cent will be made by foreign visitors for business or leisure, 47 per cent by British tourists and 18 per cent by British businessmen.

The volume of traffic approaching Heathrow and Gatwick from the west and south precluded a third airport for London in these quadrants and determined that London's third airport should lie somewhere in an arc between Oxford and the Isle of Sheppey. The first choice in 1961 was Stansted, a large airfield 34 miles (55 km) north-east of London on the railway and projected motorway to Cambridge. The Inspector's Report after the statutory planning enquiry in 1966 and the Government's reaction to it[79] in 1967 led to the establishment of the Roskill Commission which, at a cost of £1·2 million, investigated 78 sites. Most attention was given to Foulness Island, north of the Thames estuary, 10 miles (16 km) east of Southend airport and 50 miles (80 km) from Central London, and three sites about 45 miles (72 km) north of London near Milton Keynes (Cublington), Bedford and Royston respectively. The Committee reported in 1970 producing seven volumes of evidence and a majority decision in favour of Cublington.[80]

The government rejected the majority findings of the Report and began negotiations to build London's third airport on Foulness Island, to be called Maplin. The layout of Maplin airport and its potential juxtaposition to a seaport and/or industrial development area has not yet been decided, nor has the route of a projected motorway and railway to London. The British Airport Authority considers[81] that the airport will take two years to plan once the scheme is activated, and a further five to build.

The Roskill Report has however made notable contributions to the study of the location of transport interchanges in the limited space of the UK. The development of cost-benefit (Appendices 15 and 20) and gravity model (Appendices 17-19) analyses in particular have given rise to lively controversy.[82] The fourteen-year search for a suitable location for London's third airport has illustrated the political powers which can be wielded by local but influential and educated communities (in this case the residents of Stansted and the three northern sites short-listed by the Roskill Commission) on a decision of national planning policy.

The Confederation of British Industry have suggested that a national freight airport might be built in the Midlands[83] to help to deal with air freight which has been growing at a rate of 13 per cent per annum. Passenger traffic may grow fourfold or sixfold by the end of this century. As the rate of development of short or vertical take-off and landing (STOL or VTOL) aircraft for passengers appears to be slow,[84] it is doubtful whether the degree of concentration of traffic at specific airports will be very different in 2000 from the pattern of the late 1930s. Air transport is the most capital-intensive and commercially-regulated of all transport media, but investment decisions have been taken independently at each stage by a large number of authorities and never within the framework of a national review of the air transport needs of the UK.

V   SEAPORTS AND WATER TRANSPORT

V.1   The Hierarchy of Seaports

With the exception of the English Midlands all of the main UK concentrations of industrial urbanism are directly connected in some measure with seaport functions. The status and functions of the major ports are of fundamental importance to the UK economy, so heavily dependant as it is upon overseas trading and industrial production. These seaports are major transport nodes, the points of interchange between sea and land transport, sometimes points of break of bulk but increasingly for non-bulk cargoes, the pivot of a through-transport link. These seaports are also almost invariably important industrial centres, perhaps industrial *complexes* in the sense of interrelated industrial production, for which the seaport location is, or has been, crucial. Some industry, however, is related to the needs of the population grouping itself and the central place functions, the regional or metropolitan role, which the settlement has come to support.

The distribution and hierarchy of major seaports is always related to some extent to the physical environmental basis for port development.[85] The potential of both water-site and land-site influence port development and indeed these influences have been reasserted, albeit indirectly, as the requirements of modern vessels and of port industries have become more exacting. Indirectly reasserted, because clearly these are not rigidly limiting influences but advantages to be utilised or disadvantages to be overcome and appear accordingly in the cost-benefit analysis of port development. Thus port growth and development may be influenced by the physical conditions of *site* but are commonly influenced more fundamentally by the economic conditions of *situation* − the potential to develop hinterlands and forelands.[86] The hierarchy of seaports emerges from a continual reappraisal of physical and economic circumstances. For most major seaports this is a long and complex historical process very often given its initial stimulus by a conscious declaration of intent, a political act in the granting of trading and market privileges or in the declaration of a sphere of interest.[87] Once firmly established the commitment and complex interrelationships of land, labour and capital in a major port are such that momentum and/or inertia ensure that 'there is not a rapid fluctuation in the relative status of these major ports' (Bird 1963, p.23). This remains, certainly in the short-term, a valid, suitably qualified generalisation but the contemporary reappraisal in terms of the striking technological developments in transport within recent decades has significantly modified the rank-order of the major UK seaports and will continue, perhaps increasingly, to do so.

Unfortunately there is no simple definitive method of establishing a hierarchy of seaports. The two most generally acceptable indices, although each has limitations, are the Net Registered Tonnage (NRT) of vessels and the value of cargo handled. The NRT of vessels *arriving* (or *departing*) with cargo and in ballast provides a measure of all traffic using a port. This does not reflect precisely the cargo handled as, quite apart from the unspecified tonnage in ballast, the figures do not recognise that some vessels will discharge only a part-cargo. Note also that it may be considered that NRT figures are in any event restricted, perhaps increasingly so, in their ability to reflect the trade and traffic of a port for two reasons. First, the NRT figures may be greatly inflated by a limited number of calls by massive bulk-carriers, especially super-tankers. Secondly, the much greater efficiency in break-bulk cargo handling following from unit-load cargo, and especially from containerisation and cellular vessels, means that the volume of cargo handled may increase significantly without a concomitant increase in NRT. Since neither of these issues affect all ports equally the rank-order may change and certinly NRT figures cannot be so appropriately used, as commonly in the past, to suggest secular trends in port development. The value of cargo handled provides a more uniformly consistent measure at a given time although trends are impaired by the rise and fall of prices and in the long-term by the change in value of money. The use of value figures clearly accentuates the status of the main break-bulk cargo ports. Conversely, NRT figures cause the bulk ports, or the bulk elements of any port, to be overstressed. Compare, for example, the rankings in the first instance of Hull and in the second of Milford Haven. A comparison of the rankings by NRT and by value gives the most acceptable approach to a hierarchy of seaports (tables 5.8 and 5.9).

The NRT figures are subdivided between coastwise and foreign but value figures are available for foreign trade only.[88] In a British context, although it was not so in the past, coastwise trade now rarely makes a main contribution to the status of major ports. Only in the case of Belfast, a reflection of the distinctive economic relationship between Northern Ireland and the rest of the UK, does NRT coastwise comprise as much as 70 per cent of the total NRT. For Swansea petroleum products and for the Tyne the remnant of the formerly large coastwise coal trade ensure that coastwise NRT is commonly about one-half of each port's total. For the Clyde about 30 per cent coastwise NRT includes the Irish trade and the particular requirements of the Highlands and Islands. In general the major ports are also major coastwise ports but apart from these particular examples coastwise traffic is of limited relative importance. Thus London is the leading coastwise port by NRT, exceeding Belfast, although coastwise tonnage comprises only about 18 per cent of the total NRT of London. However not all major ports have an important coastwise component. It is insignificant at Dover and Harwich reflecting the distinctive packet-boat/ferry-style functions and the lack of the time-honoured traditional basis which is a feature of some coastwise trade; it is unimportant for reasons of access at Manchester and limited in volume at Hull as other Humber ports have more importantly assumed this role. In contrast to the relative concentration of foreign trade the very nature of coastwise trade, its structure and operation, mean that a large number of ports are significantly involved (48 handling over 100,000 NRT 1970) and the major ports handled only 57 per cent of the total coastwise NRT.

A comparison of the rank-order of the 15 leading ports by total NRT with a rank-order

TABLE 5.8 The Hierarchy of UK Ports (Rank Order 1-15), by Value of Foreign Trade; Exports (including exports of imported merchandise) and Imports, Annual Averages for the Three-year Periods, 1936-8; 1958-60; 1968-70

	1936-8			1958-60			1968-70			
	£ million	% UK total		£ million	% UK total		Exports	£ million Imports	Total	%UK total
1. London	556·2	37·8	1. London	2,605·6	36·2	1. London	2069·7	2,003·4	4,073·1	30·8
2. Liverpool	320·1	21·8	2. Liverpool	1,656·5	23·0	2. Liverpool	1,137·8	1,029·3	2,167·1	16·4
3. Hull	89·1	6·1	3. Hull	411·0	5·7	3. Hull	390·7	385·3	776·0	5·9
4. Southampton	66·7	4·5	4. Manchester	386·6	5·4	4. Harwich	382·2	337·5	719·7	5·4
5. Manchester	62·9	4·3	5. Southampton	310·5	4·3	5. Southampton	271·6	333·9	605·5	4·6
6. Glasgow	60·3	4·1	6. Glasgow	295·2	4·1	6. Manchester	207·7	368·7	576·4	4·4
7. Bristol	31·5	2·1	7. Bristol	194·5	2·7	7. Felixstowe	216·1	233·5	449·6	3·4
8. Newcastle	28·6	1·9	8. Harwich	124·7	1·7	8. Dover	177·1	197·9	375·0	2·8
9. Harwich	27·4	1·9	9. Swansea	112·1	1·6	9. Clyde	174·7	198·4	373·1	2·8
10. Swansea	21·3	1·5	10. Dover	109·8	1·5	10. Grimsby	117·2	234·2	351·4	2·6
11. Grimsby	19·0	1·3	11. Newcastle	106·6	1·5	11. Forth	151·3	130·2	281·5	2·1
12. Leith	16·7	1·1	12. Middlesbrough	83·8	1·2	12. Bristol	45·2	230·7	275·9	2·1
13. Cardiff	15·6	1·1	13. Grimsby	71·2	1·0	13. Tees	108·5	152·0	260·5	2·0
14. Goole	14·4	1·0	14. Belfast	66·7	0·9	14. Milford Haven	37·7	165·9	203·6	1·5
15. Belfast	13·9	0·9	15. Goole	66·5	0·9	15. Swansea	60·9	88·4	149·3	1·1
		91·4			91·7					87·9
Total UK	1,469·9		Total UK	7,192·5		Total UK	6,124·8	7,104·1	13,228·9	

Sources: Annual Statement of Trade of the United Kingdom, vol. IV, Supplement (1938 and 1962); *Digest of Port Statistics*, (1969-71 inclusive); J H Bird, *The Major Seaports of the United Kingdom* (1963)

N.B. Glasgow (Clyde 1968 onwards) includes Greenock, Grimsby includes Immingham, and Forth (from 1968 onwards) includes Leith, Granton, Grangemouth, Burntisland, Kirkcaldy and Methil. Tees (1968-70) incorporates Middlesbrough.

TABLE 5.8 The Hierarchy of UK Ports (Rank Order 1-15), by Net Registered Tonnage (NRT) of Vessels arriving with Cargo and in Ballast in Foreign and Coastwise Trade. Annual Averages for the Three-year Periods, 1936-8; 1958-60; 1968-70

	1936-8			1958-60			1968-70			
	NRT thousand tons	% UK total		NRT thousand tons	% UK total		NRT thousand tons			% UK total
							Foreign	Coast	Total	
1. London	30,965	16·7	1. London	42,279	20·1	1. London	35,773	7,957	43,730	17·1
2. Liverpool	17,467	9·4	2. Southampton	24,816	11·8	2. Southampton	19,566	6,270	25,836	10·1
3. Southampton	13,366	7·2	3. Liverpool	19,743	9·4	3. Liverpool	16,043	5,548	21,591	8·5
4. Glasgow	9,899	5·4	4. Glasgow	9,499	4·5	4. Milford Haven	12,667	3,677	16,344	6·4
5. Newcastle	9,066	4·9	5. Manchester	8,118	3·9	5. Dover	12,587	257	12,844	5·0
6. Belfast	7,561	4·1	6. Newcastle	7,555	3·6	6. Glasgow	7,708	3,156	10,864	4·3
7. Cardiff	7,269	3·9	7. Belfast	7,448	3·5	7. Belfast	2,424	7,269	9,693	3·8
8. Hull	6,178	3·3	8. Bristol	6,017	2·9	8. Middlesbrough	6,758	1,576	8,334	3·3
9. Plymouth	5,908	3·2	9. Hull	5,919	2·8	9. Harwich	8,202	111	8,313	3·3
10. Manchester	3,941	2·1	10. Dover	5,694	2·7	10. Grimsby	5,906	1,997	7,903	3·1
11. Bristol	3,782	2·0	11. Middlesbrough	5,090	2·4	11. Hull	5,373	1,011	6,384	2·5
12. Swansea	3,464	1·9	12. Swansea	4,977	2·4	12. Tyne	2,817	3,042	5,859	2·3
13. Harwich	3,135	1·7	13. Harwich	3,736	1·8	13. Manchester	5,571	275	5,846	2·3
14. Newport	2,344	1·3	14. Cardiff	3,336	1·6	14. Bristol	3,015	1,732	4,747	1·9
15. Grimsby	1,969	1·1	15. Grimsby	3,008	1·4	15. Swansea	1,876	2,381	4,257	1·7
		68·2			74·8					75·6
Total UK	184,900		Total UK	210,314		Total UK	173,263	81,745	255,008	

Sources: *Board of Trade Journal* (1938-9 and 1958-61): National Ports Council, *Digest of Port Statistics* (1969-71 inclusive); J H Bird, *The Major Seaports of the United Kingdom* (1963).

N.B. Glasgow includes Greenock and Grimsby includes Immingham. Tyne (1968-70) is comparable to Newcastle in earlier periods according to value of foreign trade (in each case on the basis of annual average figures, 1968-70) confirms the pre-eminence of London as the leading UK port and clearly identifies the *major* ports in that thirteen ports appear in both rank-orders. Belfast and Tyne occur only in the NRT ranking and Felixstowe and the Forth occur only in the ranking by value. Such discrepancies now or at earlier times may be due to a combination of varied reasons, for example, the inclusion in the NRT of a considerable coastwise element (Belfast, Tyne); the fact that the value figures refer to Customs ports or a group of such ports which may cover an extensive area (Forth — although this is now one Port Authority); or to the very nature of an important element of the cargo, for example, high bulk, low unit-value (Tyne coal) or vice versa (Felixstowe container traffic). There is no particularly clear reason why 15 ports should be listed in each ranking. A critical break has often seemed to appear at different times somewhere between 11th and 15th in both NRT and value rankings. An extension to 15 ports in each ranking, involving in total 17 individual ports, gives a basic distribution of the main port activity of the UK (figures 5.8 and 5.9). Perhaps the only area which may seem undervalued in this distribution is South Wales and specifically by the omission of Cardiff. This distribution of major ports represents a considerable measure of concentration which is more pronounced in terms of value of cargo than in NRT, since the necessity to keep land transport costs to a minimum ensures that a larger number and a more widespread distribution of ports are importantly involved in handling cargoes of low value per unit weight. In the value rank-order the 2 leading ports (London and Liverpool) handle 47 per cent of the total, 4 ports (Hull and Harwich added) handle 59 per cent and the 15 major ports comprise 88 per cent of the total UK foreign trade by value. 4 ports (London, Southampton, Liverpool, Milford Haven) handle 42 per cent of the total foreign and coastwise NRT and the 15 major ports by NRT comprise 76 per cent of the UK total. The present hierarchy retains the signs of a long evolution but it also reflects the impact of recent technological developments in transport. Such developments have provided new opportunities, which are available and implemented to varying degrees, to modify the hierarchy of ports. The opportunities are broadly two-fold; first, to develop the ports' function of cargo-handling and, secondly, to enhance the port as a centre of industrial investment.

V.2   Seaports and Cargo-handling

One of the most striking economic developments of the post-Second World War period, a result of increased economic interdependence, has been the very rapid increase in the tonnage of international sea-borne cargo. The pre-war maximum, following the trough of the depression, was not greatly changed from that of 1929. In the post-war recovery a similar level was again reached in 1949 (about 500 million tons) and then within twenty years there was a remarkable four-fold increase. The vast rise in cargo has been outstandingly of bulk cargoes. Of the world total cargo handled in 1969 of 2,308 million tons, more than half (1,271 million tons) was of oil and more than 75 per cent of the total weight was of oil and dry bulk cargoes (i e of oil and of iron-ore, grain, sugar, coal, fertilisers and so on). The secular trend in cargo-handling at UK ports differed only in detail. It is true that the total of 84 million tons in 1948 was 31 million tons less than a decade earlier, due to the radical and irretrievable decline in coal exports, but thereafter the growth rate was close to that of world trade as a whole with total of 244 million tons of foreign cargo in 1970. The expanded UK trade moreover was structured similarly to the international trade with crude oil imports as the main growth point.

The general structure of sea-borne cargo is basically a response to the changing pattern of world trading and, in particular, to the changes in this pattern which relate to Europe's needs for energy and raw material resources in the economic development of the post-war period. Important major flows have developed, often over long distances, linking the areas

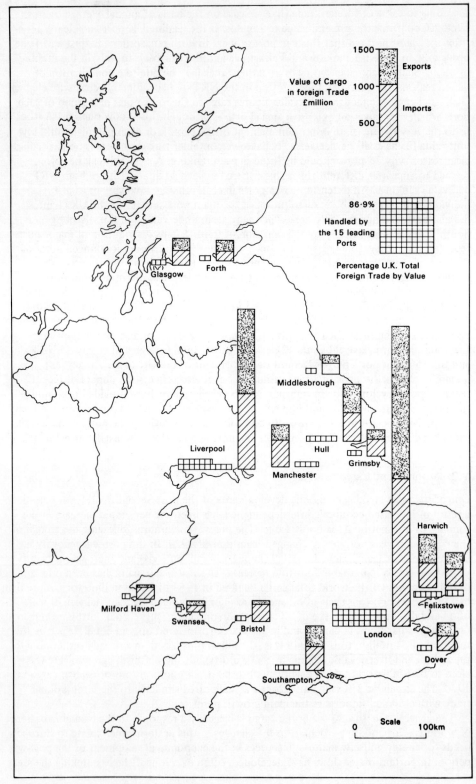

Figure 5.8   Hierarchy of ports (rank order 1-15), by value of foreign trade, UK, 1968-70

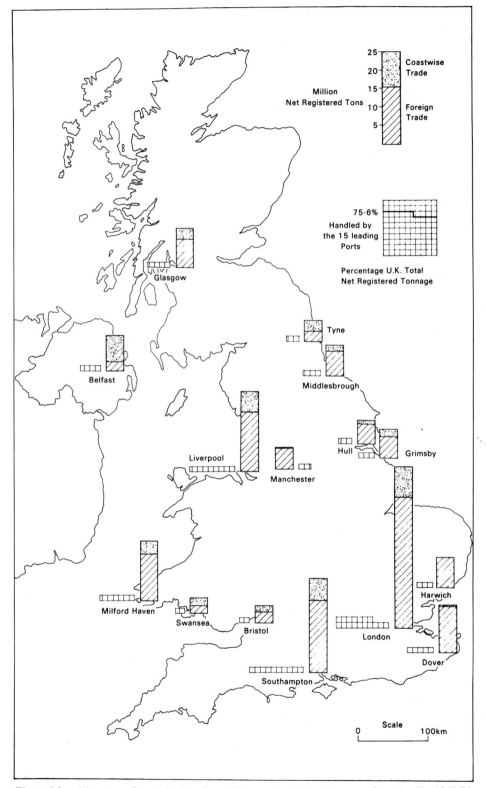

Figure 5.9   Hierarchy of ports (rank order 1-15), by net registered tonnage of vessels, UK, 1968-70

of economically advanced industrial urbanism in north-west Europe (and also in north-east USA and Japan) with mineral primary producers. These are often asymmetrical trade flows and the probability of sailing one direction in ballast, a reflection not only of the areas linked but also perhaps of the specialised vessels involved, has required the economies which large vessels allow.

A rapid growth of new tonnage and an increased size of vessel were the most general developments in maritime transport interrelated with the expanding and changing pattern of trade. These were often developments involving specialised and faster vessels and perhaps incorporating more advanced cargo-handling techniques. The increased size of vessel has been most obvious in the development of massive bulk-carriers to handle the greatly increased volume of movement of oil and to a lesser extent of ores. There are important general economies related to size of vessel but the main concern in this present context is that increased size has made vessels increasingly discriminating and demanding in terms of their depth requirements and the facilities they need.[89] Port costs in terms of dredging, facilities and installations rise with increasing ship size and may at some stage offset the economies of larger vessels. The increase in tanker size has meant that fewer ports are involved in handling the imports of crude oil and more oil is being moved by pipeline. Only 2 oil terminals, Clyde (Finnart, 95 ft 29 m, depth) and Milford Haven (68-70 ft 20-21 m, depth) can handle tankers in the 250-275,000 dwt range fully laden. There are 6 other terminals (Humber, Thames, Southampton Water, Medway, Mersey and Tees) which offer depths of 45 ft (13·7 m) or over. It is a distinctive and important characteristic of oil cargoes that a variety of berthing systems, for example, using jetties or hose, may potentially be used. 4 ports handle more than half of the total petroleum traffic, Milford Haven (19·6 per cent, 1970), London (14·1 per cent), Southampton (12·2 per cent) and Medway (11·4 per cent). In fact since the Second World War oil has been a significant item in the trade of most major UK ports and its distinctiveness is shown more obviously where it comprises a high proportion of total trade (Milford Haven 99·9 per cent, Southampton 93 per cent, Medway 90·1 per cent) and/or when it is linked to refinery capacity (see table 5.10 and section 5.V.3). An important element, about one-third, of all sea-borne petroleum movements is in coastwise trade, a result of the transfer of crude stocks and of the distribution of refined products.

Iron-ore vessels are less demanding in terms of depth but they do require conventional berths with specialised handling equipment. Until 1969, when the new facilities at Port Talbot came into operation, the Tyne with 30 ft (9·1 m) LWOST and able to handle vessels of 37,000 dwt provided the deepest available ore-berth. Port Talbot with a tidal harbour (29 ft, 8·8 m, tidal range) is now able to handle vessels of 100,000 dwt. It is provisionally planned to deepen to allow 150,000 to be handled although the berth already shows in some measure the high costs of some deep-water facilities in that it is estimated that dredging costs will be about £220,000 per annum. Ore-handling facilities for vessels of 100,000 dwt are also planned for Newport (Uskmouth), Redcar (Tees), Immingham and Hunterston (Ayrshire). The 22·4 million tons of ores and scrap imported in the foreign trade in 1970 showed a similar measure of port concentration to the petroleum traffic and indeed a more pronounced concentration if estuarial groupings are considered (table 5.10). Of the total imports, 62·5 per cent is handled in the three estuaries (Severn, Tees and Clyde) associated importantly with the steel industry and almost 30 per cent of the total is handled by South Wales ports. The ore trade is focused mainly on the leading industrial seaports (see section 5.V.3) although it has been in the past, and is likely to be increasingly in the future, influenced by available depths of water and the available or projected handling facilities. Ores are not a main item of most major ports' trade as is petroleum and the three South Wales ports (Port Talbot, Cardiff and Newport) in particular, and also the Tyne, are distinctive in the high proportion of ores in their total foreign imports.

TABLE 5.10   Major Bulk Cargoes, Leading UK Ports, 1970

Petroleum (total traffic)

Port	Petroleum traffic million tons	% total petroleum traffic	Total traffic of port million tons	Petroleum as % of total
Milford Haven	40·6	19·6	40·6	99·9
London	29·3	14·1	56·1	52·2
Southampton	25·3	12·2	27·2	93·0
Medway	23·6	11·4	26·2	90·1
Liverpool	14·2	6·8	28·9	49·1
Immingham	13·8	6·7	21·6	63·9
Tees	13·0	6·2	22·2	58·6
Clyde	8·5	4·1	14·6	58·2
Forth	4·2	2·0	8·1	51·9
Total GB	206·9	100·0	346·6	59·7

Ores and scrap (foreign imports)

Port	Ores and scrap million tons	% total ores and scrap	Total foreign imports of port million tons	Ores as % of total
Tees	4·3	19·2	15·9	27·0
Port Talbot	3·3	14·7	3·4	97·1
Clyde	3·0	13·4	11·2	26·8
Immingham	2·1	9·4	13·6	15·4
Liverpool	1·7	7·6	19·7	8·6
Newport	1·7	7·6	2·2	77·3
Cardiff	1·6	7·1	2·4	66·7
Tyne	1·4	6·3	2·3	60·9
Total GB	22·4	100·0	193·1	11·6

Source: National Ports Council, *Digest of Port Statistics* (1971)

None of the other bulk cargoes are of comparable volume or have shown a similar rate of increase in traffic in recent years. The coastwise coal trade of about 13 million tons in 1970 is very largely the lingering special relationship between the ports of North East England and the Thames. Coal has never regained its pre-Second World War importance in the foreign export trade and a volume of 4·3 million tons in 1970 (mainly from Immingham and Swansea) was surpassed by imports of unmilled cereals (7·8 million tons – notably London, Liverpool and Bristol); timber (5·4 million tons – London, Liverpool and Hull); and equalled by crude fertilisers and crude minerals (4·3 million tons – Immingham and Manchester). The remaining main traffics were in pulp and waste paper (3·8 million tons – Medway, London and Manchester) and sugar (2·6 million tons – Liverpool, London and Clyde). Most of such bulk imports are related to industry within the ports.

Important though the developments associated with bulk handling have been, there is no doubt that in the long-term the development of various forms of unit-load handling has more revolutionary and widespread implications for both trade and seaports. The general results of unit-load cargo have been discussed elsewhere (see section 5.I.2 and 5.VI.1), more specifically in relation to ports. The developments concern the spread of handling techniques and specialist vessels which are transforming the mode and patteɪ of general-cargo movement with important effects on traditional port functions. Unit-load refers to a variety of forms used to *consolidate* general cargo and has its full expression in containerisation. Often initially unit-load was associated with roll-on operation (where the road vehicle is carried on the vessel) and this is still favoured for some traffic and for particular routes. More importantly unit-load relates to various forms of palletisation and particularly to the use of the standard metal container. It involves, in varied measure, the use of special cranage and of converted or specially designed vessels. Not all operators are convinced that full containerisation should be developed wherever possible. It is pointed out that palletisation requires less costly equipment on both ship and berth. There is, of course, no dispute that unit-load, of whatever kind, reduces handling costs and thus in respect of through-transport costs the greatest gains are achieved on short-sea routes where terminal charges form a greater proportion of the total. It was on the short-sea routes to Europe that the new techniques were first developed by UK shippers but they have had an increasingly widespread effect on the hierarchy and functions of UK ports and thus the location of unit-load facilities has been very important in the growth and development of ports within the last decade.[90]

The development of unit-load facilities has taken place in the piecemeal unplanned and potentially wasteful fashion which has characterised so much of British transport history. There was very little government influence and no positive planning and control over the proliferation of unit-load facilities (see section 5.V.4). In 1962 there were 21 berths which could be classified as unit transport berths and this number had increased to 91 by 1969 when there were 9 further berths under construction. In fact roll-on or lift-on facilities with some form of container crane tended to become a *sine qua non* for most ports, not even just major ports (figure 5.10). This is far removed from the theoretical concept of the way in which these new handling techniques, if they are to be fully efficient, must concentrate general cargo handling. The initial development and the widespread distribution were related mainly to the short-sea trade. Some of the berths were used in more than one trade but only 10 of the berths handled some deep-sea trade, 28 berths handled coastwise and the largest number, 71, were concerned with the short- and near-sea trades, and particularly with traffic to France, Belgium, Netherlands and West Germany. Of course not all of these berths were handling standard-sized containers with transporter cranes from cellular vessels. This was more likely to be the case in the deep-sea trade but even here only a limited amount of concentration of traffic has occurred. It does appear that a focusing of activity has been achieved in the UK-Australia trade in which Associated Container Transportation (ACT) and Overseas Containers Limited (OCL) operate weekly services exclusively from Tilbury using 9 vessels of about 30,000 dwt and a capacity of $1,300 \times 20$ ft (6 m) containers each. No such accord has been reached in terms of the North Atlantic traffic in which a large number of UK ports vie for trade. At least seven UK ports are significantly involved in unit-load transport on the North Atlantic (Grangemouth, Greenock, Liverpool, Manchester, Felixstowe, Tilbury and Southampton) suggesting a clear excess of tonnage capacity.

One of the important implications of unit transport berths is that some of the traditional functions in handling, sorting and distribution are lost to the port. It is an essential characteristic of unit-load operation that the berth should be used for tran-shipment only and that Inland Container Depots (ICDs) are established to perform all other functions including Customs. Fifteen ICDs have been built and operate on a 'common user' basis although in most instances involving British Rail (figure 5.10). There is no compelling reason why ICDs should be near the ports. It is in retrospect perhaps unfortunate that two of the earliest and most publicised ICDs at Orsett (near Tilbury) and Aintree (Liverpool) should have been so near the port area in each case as to provoke industrial unrest by the apparent usurpment of what is traditionally considered to be dockers' work.

V.3   Seaports and Industry

The link between seaports and industrial development was forged in early medieval times in areas on or near the coalfields and was well established on many British estuaries

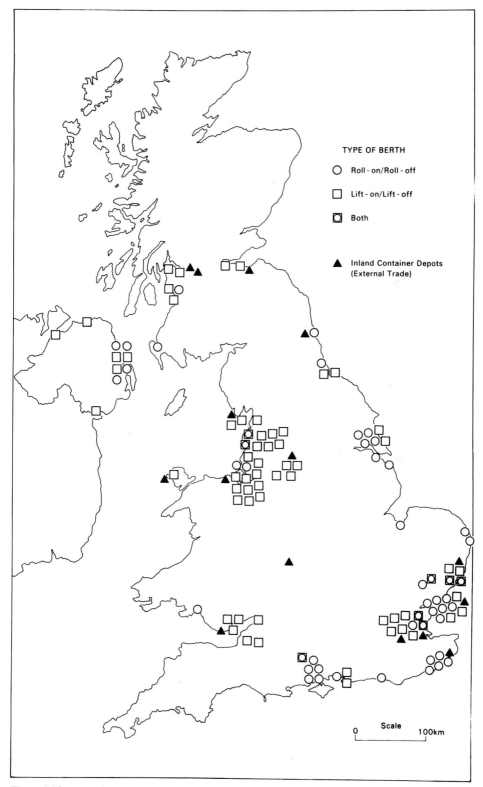

Figure 5.10   Unit transport berths and inland container depots, UK, 1970

by the mid-eighteenth century. There are traditional and continuing influences which promote industry in and around port areas. The attractions of a port location include: the cheap assembly of varied raw materials, especially those of high bulk and low value per unit weight, which in the past were unable to stand the costs of inland transport; the ability to utilise direct water access as in shipbuilding and repairing, or merely in the shipment of the end product; the ability to develop associated industries, cognate or ancillary to the main undertakings, and thus contribute to the interrelated complex of industrial production which is characteristic of most major ports.[91]

The secular decline of some heavy industries, especially in this context coal, ship-building and to a lesser extent textiles, allied with the depression of the 1930s obviously influenced ports and the level of port industries. On the other hand, the move of the iron and steel industry to the coast was one of the most important changes in economic patterns in the UK within this century and, progressively, particularly within the last twenty-five years, the development of the oil and petrochemical industries has markedly enhanced the significance of tide-water sites. Indeed, the recent past has seen a powerful restatement of the assets of port locations for industrial development. There is no doubt, for example, that the greatly increased size of vessel markedly enhances the asset of low-assembly costs for raw materials. It is true that not all ports can take advantage of these possibilities since clearly the requirements of such vessels are more exacting and equally the industries may be more discriminating in their locations. There is a 'sense' in which physical environmental considerations are reasserted in port growth and development, and outstandingly in the growth of industry within ports. This is a matter of both land-site and water-site. Major modern industrial development in ports requires extensive areas of level land or perhaps the ability to reclaim such land. The handling of the massive bulk-carriers requires considerable depths of water preferably at all states of the tide. In recent years it might be considered that deep water, in the right place, is one of the scarcest industrial resources. The Upper Clyde and the Tyne epitomise the industrial ports of the mid-nineteenth century associated with the interrelationship of coal and cheap water transport which produced a distinctive, specialised and vulnerable industrial structure. Their inadequacy has been increasingly apparent since the Second World War and the industrial future may lie with the Humber, the Tees and Severnside.

Undoubtedly the economic and technical changes of the period since 1945 have been conducive to major industrial development in seaport locations. It would appear, however, that the attitude of British port authorities to industrial growth has not undergone an equally felicitous transformation. With the notable exception of the Manchester Ship Canal Company, no British major port has pursued industry in a methodical and sustained fashion. British ports have suffered from a lack of local interest in them as poles of attraction for industry. This lack of interest is the more surprising in view of the preoccupation with regional development since the war and the role which estuaries can play within this. Many British major ports are Trust ports in which the controlling bodies are dominated by port-users whose main concern has been to keep port charges low and uniform rather than to develop an adventurous and adaptable commercial policy. It is true that continental rivals of the UK have been aided by local and central government subsidies but they have also pursued much more enterprising and flexible development policies that very clearly demonstrate the new potential for industrial investment characteristic of port locations in recent years. These ports show equally that a main emphasis in that growth has lain with the oil-refinery industry and associated petrochemical developments, and to a lesser extent with the development of the steel industry. Significantly perhaps, neither of these industries is inevitably tied to port locations. The fact that in the recent past they have been attracted overwhelmingly to coastal sites may serve to stress the particular contemporary assets offered by such locations. Moveover, these industries are of particular importance in that either or both may form the focus for an industrial complex of interrelated industries.

Major demands for large acreages of level land with deep-water access have been made by the oil industry. Direct water access is not inescapable for either refinery capacity or any associated petrochemical developments but the balance of locational advantages has tended to retain such industrial growth on coastal locations and may well continue to do so. Certainly it would seem that refinery capacity is likely to increase because the gap between such capacity and the demand for refined products continues to widen. UK refinery capacity in 1972 stands at about 121 million tons (about 2·5 million tons of crude oil was refined in Britain in 1947) with notable concentrations on the Thames Estuary, at Milford Haven and on Southampton Water. The oil industry has certainly focused attention on deep-water access and proposed developments will continue to do so. It is noticeable, however, that a variety of other issues may influence proposed developments. Such developments may, for example, be a part of comprehensive development proposals, they may be influenced by environmental issues or their location may be affected by nearness to the oil resources. Development plans, including the oil industry as a main element within them, have been proposed for the Clyde and notably for the Hunterston site where they are linked in the first instance with an iron-ore quay, a steel works and a power station. Thus far, however, only the iron-ore quay has firm planning approval. A wide-ranging development plan, within which the oil industry has some part, is a proposal for Foulness which could provide the first custom-built industrial port within a complex including London's third airport. A further proposal for the Clyde, the Murco refinery planned for Bishopton, 10 miles (16 km) from Glasgow, was in 1970 the first major economic development in Scotland to be rejected on planning grounds, mainly on the environmental argument of the potential threat of air pollution. The refinery proposal for Hunterston remains controversial. Environmentalist pressure groups have also succeeded in impeding if not as yet preventing the commencement of an off-shore terminal and on-shore storage for oil on Anglesey to feed the large and expanding refinery on the Mersey at Stanlow. Although seemingly an unlikely consideration when a commodity so eminently transportable as oil is involved, there is no doubt that the location of oil resources has importantly influenced developments on the east coast of Great Britain in the recent past. The working of British Petroleum's Forties Field, 110 miles (177 km) east of Aberdeen, is planned to increase considerably the throughput of the Grangemouth refinery to which oil will be sent by sea- and land-pipe, and a new *island* terminal is planned downstream of the Forth Bridges to handle the export of surplus crude and perhaps of petroleum products. Perhaps less predictable and again explicable mainly in terms of relative position, it now seems possible that the Philips' Ekofisk petroleum field, on the Norwegian continental shelf but separated from the mainland by the major gash of the Norwegian Trench, may be most easily worked by sending the oil westward to the nearest effective British estuary, the Tees. It is estimated that this would more than double the crude oil (10 million tons) at present handled by the two Teesside refineries and require a further refinery with deep-water berths.

According to the extent of processing of the petroleum feedstocks and natural gas, petrochemical production may take place within the refinery or on a separate, often adjacent, site. The refinery might commonly produce raw materials (for example naphtha) and intermediates (for example propylene). Finished products such as plastics would be more commonly produced on a separate site and this need not be adjacent to the refinery. Petrochemical feedstock pipelines link ICI Wilton to Runcorn and the Stanlow refinery (77 miles, 125 km) with off-shoots to

Partington (near Manchester) and Fleetwood. Fawley is linked by a similar pipeline to the petrochemical developments at Severnside (43 miles, 70 km). Whether within refineries or not, petrochemical industries have in recent years made a major contribution to industrial investment in ports and have grown at an appreciably faster rate than the national economy. These are highly capital-intensive industries but nonetheless petrochemical development greatly increases employment as compared with the oil refinery alone.

Also of increasing importance in focusing industrial investment in seaport locations in the period since the Second World War has been the steel industry. The British steel industry has come to rely increasingly upon imported ores. Measured by iron content, imported ores account for about three-quarters of the steel made in 1970 compared with about one-half in the immediate post-war years. Indeed total ore imports into the UK have increased from 5 million tons in 1945 to 19·9 million tons in 1970. Since commonly more than half the cost of steel is accounted for by the delivered cost of production materials it is not surprising that there has been an increased emphasis upon seaport locations. The assets of such locations were enhanced by the increased size of ore-carrier developed although this was a development of which the British steel industry was very slow to take advantage.

With a dispersed and fragmented pattern of production, a legacy from the nineteenth century, the British steel industry has been increasingly conscious in the postwar period of its limitations in equipment and size of plant compared with its continental rivals. A programme of rationalisation has aimed to concentrate production and, especially in recent years, to concentrate it in modern Basic Oxygen Steelmaking (BOS) plants. In this, the established coastal locations play a major part, notably South Wales (exemplified by the Llanwern works at Newport and the new dock and BOS developments at Port Talbot) and the South Teesside group.

Not surprisingly, some of the most notable recent developments of industry in seaports have related to the increasing assets of the cheap assembly of raw materials made possible by the increased size of bulk carrier. Although the size of production unit involved may not seem to have fully exploited the advantages of bulk carriage, three new aluminium smelters came into production in 1970-1 at Holyhead (Rio Tinto Zinc), at Lynemouth near Blyth (Alcan) and at Invergordon (British Aluminium). Both Holyhead and Invergordon can handle vessels of 50,000 dwt and the 22,500 dwt possible at Blyth is quite adequate to the capacity of the nearby plant. The scale of vessel in use in recent years has also stimulated development in the handling of grain and in flour-milling, one of the range of food industries; sugar-refining is another, processing imported raw materials. Recent developments at London, Liverpool and Glasgow to handle the larger vessels of 50,000-60,000 dwt which may now be used in the grain trade have reaffirmed flour-milling as a port activity and in the case of Tilbury have attracted one large new flour mill.

Although the very varied port industries demonstrate differing measures of interrelationship and differing degrees of dependence upon the trading functions of the port, these industries do show a common reliance upon the basic infrastructure of the surrounding area and more specifically a reliance upon the port facilities and the navigable channel of the port. In 1967 the UK government commissioned an enquiry into sites suitable for maritime industrial development. This was not published but was broadly interpreted in the National Ports Council's Progress Report of 1969.[92] The report notes that size of ship and the extent to which direct water access is critical are problems of varying degree according to the particular requirements of specific industries. It is clear also that the search for potential industrial sites is made more difficult by the fact that most obvious sites are already in use while others are remote and/or have a high amenity value.[93] The criteria suggested for suitable sites provide an interesting comment on the present interrelationships of ports and industry and upon the potential pattern of future activity. It is suggested that MIDA (Maritime Industrial Development Areas) require first, to be near to deep water (now seen as 50-60 ft (15-18·5 m) mean high water neaps without excessive dredging), secondly, to have a minimum of 5,000 acres (2,200 ha) level land, although this may be obtainable if necessary by reclamation, and thirdly, to be near main population concentrations and have good transport links inland. Only 3 sites were considered to meet all these requirements, Humberside, Thames-Medway and Cardiff-Newport. 8 further sites met some of the requirements and were considered possible MIDAs, namely Cromarty Firth, Firth of Tay, Clyde Estuary, Upper Firth of Forth, Tees Estuary, Lune Estuary, The Wash and Weston Super Mare-Clevedon (figure 5.11). In fact no such major developments have ensued. It may well be that the emphasis laid upon long-term views and optimum solutions, involving expensive investment projects unlikely to be implemented in the immediate future, has impeded development which might perhaps have proceeded had attention been given to less ambitious projects using existing facilities. As Hallett and Randall[93] conclude (1970, p. 108), decisions on the location of maritime industry have frequently been determined on a too restricted basis which frustrates the type of coordinated development which in the long-run would be desirable from the viewpoint of both industrial efficiency and amenity. The interrelationships of seaports and industries are, however, only one sphere of activity which may suggest that the broad *strategic* decisions on infrastructure have not received the attention they deserve in national policy-making.

V.4   The Changing Status and Functions of Seaports

The outstanding technological developments in transport in the last decade, which will achieve their full potential in the 1970s, were the catalyst producing the changing status and functions of ports. Important developments have occurred already but, in general, it is still true to say that the initiative lies firmly with the ports, and that major changes must ensue if the full advantages of modern transport are to be reaped. In the recent past, UK ports have not been noted for providing facilities in advance of a demand and this has sometimes led to the criticism of port authorities as providing too little and too late.

Port developments are basically related to changes in the volume and pattern of trading and the effects which these changes produce in port facilities and in the structure and operation of the merchant fleet. In more specific detail, the changes in ports relate to the interrelationships between land and sea transport. In the past, the high costs of inland transport, and also the small size of vessels in use, produced a dispersed pattern of ports. Inland transport costs may still be relatively important, often as an expression of time delays, and there is, in a general sense admittedly, some tendency to use the nearest port, and ports develop some measure of monopoly hinterland (see Martech Survey).[94] However, developments in inland transport have allowed widespread accessibility and lower costs so that, in theory, the possibilities of competition between ports, for containerised general cargo for example, are greatly enhanced. It might thus be considered that these recent developments would suggest the retention of a dispersed pattern of ports. There is no doubt that such a pattern would be uneconomic and undesirable if ports are to take full advantage of the technological possibilities of efficient and effective operation. Moreover, it has been true in recent years that, because of its striking technological advances, the more compelling component of the sea and land transport relationship has been sea transport. This certainly would suggest a concentration of activity since the ports can now be technically more efficient and handle much greater volumes of cargo and theoretically reduce shipping costs through

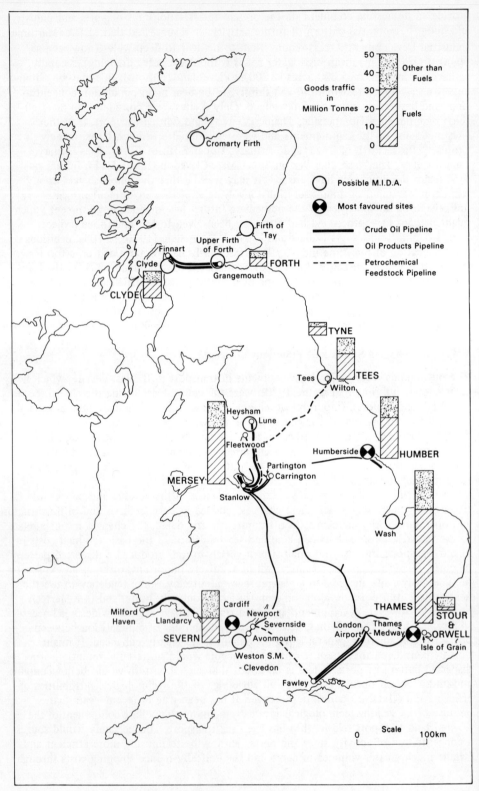

Figure 5.11   Main estuaries and MIDA sites, UK, 1970

the use of large vessels. Such economies may then be more important than inland transport costs. However, while in the recent past it would seem that sea transport has been able, in some measure, to shape port developments and land transport networks to meet its needs, it is as well to remember that since the volume of goods in foreign trade is so small a proportion (about 10 per cent) of the total goods moved in the UK, the needs of foreign trade are unlikely to dominate inland transport developments.

Port developments have occurred and will continue to take place within certain broad limits related to physical conditions and to economic and political influences upon port operation and administration. That is, port developments continue to be influenced by considerations of *site* and of *situation*. Neither are static influences and require to be reappraised continually in the light of technical and economic changes. At most levels of operation the increased size of vessel has meant that depth limitations have had some influence on port development. Clearly, however, this has been rigorous only in the case of the exacting requirements of tanker operation and only a small proportion of the world's merchant tonnage is ever likely to be of the massive dimensions of the modern super-tanker. The most appropriate size of vessel and the ultimate limits of vessel size will vary in different trades. Also the rate and extent of the acceptability and operation of larger vessels may vary from trade to trade. All such issues influence the extent to which depth is an important guiding factor in port development. Note also that any limitations in this respect of the UK ports may be less obvious and less restrictive if the trade route links areas of less sophisticated port facilities; for effective operation a similar level of facilities must be available at *both* ends of the maritime route. In terms of site, particularly if the industrial potential of the port is involved but also for container operations, the nature and extent of the suitable land-site may be of as great importance as the depth of the navigable channel. Despite these variously qualified comments it may well be that physical environmental conditions of site, in so far as they affect the status of UK ports, have been reassessed rather more rigorously and to greater effect than have the economic issues of situation. In this there is a considerable measure of inertia. The commerical connections of an established port are not readily set aside. There must be a considerable momentum in the traffic flows of major UK ports outlined by Bird, although hinterlands and forelands are being reshaped in terms of the new potentials of both land and sea transport.[95] Equally they are continuing to be shaped by particular initiatives of port authorities, by the actions of trading companies and shipowners and perhaps, almost indirectly, by public policy.

At least in theory, investment decisions may be seen as subsuming in varying measure a wide range of physical, technical, economic and political influences upon port development. Many UK ports are being faced with difficult investment decisions and, at the level of capital provision required, it seems probable that everywhere, although in varying degree, the government will be increasingly involved, if only in an attempt to avoid uneconomic duplication and ensure the best use of scarce resources within a national framework. In fact, as yet, the UK Government's direct involvement has been very limited. Concern over the lack of investment in British ports was one reason for the establishment of the Committee of Inquiry which reported in 1962 and did stimulate the level of investment.[96] In 1964, £20 million was invested and from 1965-9 a total of £200 million was invested in UK ports. This was still not high by north west European standards and Government aid was discontinued in 1971 in line with the Government's concern that port authorities should be encouraged to be independent and self-financing. As previously noted, largely because of the make-up of the controlling boards of most British ports, the investment record in the recent past has not been good and doubts have been expressed about the level of managerial skills and their competence to pursue the required aggressive and forward-looking policy. The recent financial problems of the Mersey Docks and Harbour Board underline a more widespread problem.

Clearly there is competition for investment or for State approval of investment plans which will achieve the differentiation between ports, facilities and schedules; that is, the difference in the *services* upon which competition between ports is based. Although there has been central control over major investment, in fact the tendency, with few exceptions, has been to encourage *all* ports. There has been no overall national plan clearly defined but nonetheless the status of ports is changing. Such changes are continually underway as the ports react variously to the new possibilities of growth and development. Thus the Tees, with developing chemical, steel and oil industries associated with major reclamation schemes, typifies the impact of the new industrial potential in ports. The Tees has 39 Conference Lines using the port and a total of 24 deep-sea and 60 short-sea sailings per month. It was acknowledged that the quality of the services available and particularly the quality of labour and of labour relationships caused the UK West Africa Line, which has a near monopoly of the British export trade to West Africa, to announce in November 1970 plans which could increase Teesside's share of Britain's total export trade to West Africa from the present 3 per cent to about 25 per cent of the total by value. Felixstowe exemplifies the impact of the new transport technology in cargo-handling, having increased its trade from about 60,000 tons in the 1950s to 2·2 million tons in 1970. Felixstowe and Harwich together are now listed by the NPC for statistical purposes among the estuarial groupings as the Stour and Orwell estuary (the Haven Ports). It is as yet uncertain to what extent such changes involve an overall concentration of activity and a refining of the pattern of ports in the UK. It may be that developments will produce dissimilar results in differing regional areas. The rate and diversity of growth of industrial port activities on Teesside in the last twenty years has certainly markedly changed the relative importance of the ports of North East England. The Tees has now outstripped all rivals. The Tyne has limited prospects and is likely to be shorn further of its bulk trades. The Wear and Blyth have no certain long-term viability and the small coal ports such as Amble and Seaham Harbour are declining and have no future. On the other hand, the growth of short-sea trading has revitalised some of the small ports of East Anglia which have increased their proportionate share of UK foreign trade. The concentration of activity has been pursued more markedly in respect of bulk cargoes and industrial activity rather than in relation to general cargo-handling. Moreover, in the recent past, the flow of general cargo at the major terminals has sometimes seemed particularly vulnerable to industrial disputes. This has encouraged small ports to operate outside the control of the National Dock Labour Scheme. Whitby and Scarborough are examples of ports, although seemingly within the shadow of the Tees and/or Humber, which have increased their foreign trade by virtue of low wage-rates employing non-union labour.

Change is clearly occurring although it may be questioned to what extent it is a directed and planned process. The planning procedure available to the Government is in essence a negative one. The Government has power to withhold investment approval but no more than this and therefore it is very difficult for the National Ports Council in its capacity as counsellor to the Minister of Transport to envisage and maintain a coherent plan. Very often developments have been approved (as most proposals have been) as economically appropriate to individual ports but it is at least doubtful if they were in the overall best interests of the nation. It was, however, on the latter grounds that the proposal to develop at Portbury (Bristol) was refused and the reasons for the Minister's decision produced a good analysis of the wider implications of an individual port's development.[97] The case for a planned approach to port development would seem a strong one. However, it is certainly valid to ask what kind of a dock system would have been inherited if our predecessors had had the benefits now available to us of a highly introspective economic theory with which to quench their vigorous acts of expansion on a speculative basis.[98] It is at least possible that the rate of change will be slower and certainly less ruthless as Government policy and public inquiry replace commercial initiative and this may not always be in the best national interest. The planned approach may be considered to be essential, for example, in so far as the implications of MIDAs go far beyond the port requirements, and must involve government in considering the potential of the port as an instrument in both regional and national planning.[99] Moreover, there is no doubt that in the re-shaping of the pattern of port activity there will be great redundancies of labour, services and equipment, and that the UK ports are faced in effect with a problem similar in kind, if not in scale, to the rationalisation process which faced the National Coal Board after 1948. Equipping the UK ports for the second half of the twentieth century may well be an exciting and challenging process but it will certainly be a painful one which requires a carefully planned and almost certainly governmental approach. There is also the quite basic general point that modern port technology is such that competition would be wasteful of capital resources. Given such technology ports are *natural* monopolies and quite positive national control should be exercised over their investment activities.[100]

It seems too often the case that an individual port development is viewed in relation to its investment profitability and too rarely placed in a context aimed at minimising the costs of the complete door-to-door transport system for flows of imports and exports for *the country as a whole.* Again, while not gainsaying the necessity for a national approach, it is sometimes questioned whether this is strictly an economic issue at all. Ports, it is said, should be constructed as a matter of policy and justified not in economic terms but in terms of the extent to which they are used. It is as yet too early to see the full implications of the impact of the contemporary revolution in transport technology upon the pattern of port activity but it is likely that in the long evolution of seaports the early 1970s may well appear as a period during which major decisions of long-term significance were taken.

V.5 Inland Waterways

The inland waterways of the UK now perform a very limited transport function (0·1 per cent of total UK freight ton-mileage) with most of the commercial traffic on rivers where the navigable channel has been regulated and locked. It is no longer appropriate to identify an inland waterways *network* for traffic purposes. The relevant stretches of waterway are in small separate sections mainly linked to major estuaries. The role of the waterways is now very largely that of a feeder to and from selected ports. The waterways demonstrate, in extreme form as far as transport is concerned, the focusing of activity upon restricted stretches of the traditionally available pattern.

The UK has never provided favourable conditions for the development of inland water transport. Even before the railway provided overwhelming competition, the effectiveness of coastal shipping in serving centres of population and industry, mainly located on tidewater, limited inland water transport. Equally fundamental, in most areas the relief of the country and especially the short distances involved are not conductive to efficient operation of this transport form. Historically the piecemeal development of canals with varing widths and capacities, and with fragmented ownership, did not encourage the functioning of a network over the longest possible distances. There has been also a secular decline in demand, quickening in the period since the Second World War, for the type of services which the inland waterways can supply. Watts points out (in a very useful concise appraisal with good maps[101]) that it is not common in the UK for distances to be long enough and for vessels to be large enough to counteract the disadvantages of high terminal charges. The present commercially operated stretches of waterway reflect these circumstances. The preferred distances are rarely available but the most effective waterways are those which are able to use the larger vessels and to do so with *direct* loading from ship or factory and thus keep terminal costs as low as possible. The traditional categories of waterway are narrow and wide (or broad) but since 1965 the British Waterways Board has recognised a two-fold division[102] into 'commercial waterways', totalling about 340 miles (547 km) and 'other waterways' with very limited traffic and with functions relating to water supply and/or especially recreation and thus of no direct relevance in this context. The commercial stretches are: the Weaver navigation, related especially to canal-side industry; the Lea navigation and the Lower Grand Union system, both concerned with distribution from the Port of London; the Severn system linking the Port of Bristol with the West Midlands; and the most extensive system, radiating from the Humber and including the Aire and Calder, the Sheffield and the South Yorkshire canals where the main traffic is coal, together with the Trent navigation from the sea to Nottingham, notably carrying petroleum inland.

These commercial waterways handle about 95 per cent of the traffic. The total of 5·4 million tons in 1971 was perhaps unduly low, being affected by hopefully non-recurring factors such as strikes and mechanical handling-equipment failure, but this total was little more than half that of 1953. There is no doubt about the secular decline in tonnage handled and in ton-mileage, especially in the 1960s (table 5.11). It seems

TABLE 5.11   Traffic British Waterways Board, 1953-71

	Million tons	Million ton-miles		Million tons	Million ton-miles
1953	10·3	184·3	1962	9·3	152·3
1954	10·1	174·8	1963	9·1	148·1
1955	10·5	183·7	1964	9·0	141·1
1956	10·5	183·8	1965	8·5	132·4
1957	9·9	175·2	1966	7·6	111·1
1958	9·3	166·1	1967	7·1	98·4
1959	9·0	163·8	1968	7·3	93·7
1960	9·6	163·8	1969	6·7	85·6
1961	9·3	163·7	1970	6·4	79·3
			1971	5·4	61·0

Sources: British Transport Commission, Annual Report 1962, (London 1963); British Waterways Board Annual Reports, (1963 to date)

likely that the average length of haul is now even less than the 16·6 miles (27 km) of 1953 which was already too low for effective inland waterways operation.[103] The traffic in 1971 was 62 per cent bulk fuels, being 37 per cent coal and coke, and 25 per cent liquids. The remainder of the cargo, classified as general merchandise, was largely grains, oil seeds and timber (table 5.12). Recent government attitudes and policies towards the waterways reflect, in general terms, the transport situation. The enquiries of 1955 and 1958 were still looking to commercial possibilities with a fairly widespread network and with an air of expectancy and development.[104] The reports of the 1960s made, from a

TABLE 5.12   Traffic Composition, British Waterways Board 1971

Commercial Waterways	Thousand tons	Thousand ton-miles
Coal, coke and patent fuel	1,898	17,746
Liquids in bulk	1,282	20,424
General merchandise	1,913	21,740
Total	5,093	59,910
Other waterways: total	289	1,047
Total Traffic	5,382	60,957

Source: British Waterways Board, *Annual Report 1971,* (London 1972)

transport viewpoint, a much more realistic appraisal of the prospects of commercial operation in limited separate systems and did so with an air of retrenchment and abandonment.[105] They led, however, to financial support for the Waterways Board's total commitment (although aimed especially at its non-commercial, cruising network). The grant-in-aid in 1971 was £2·5 million. The most recent proposals, for implementation in 1974, would seem to demote the transport function in an administrative framework which envisages control of waterways by 10 regional authorities based particularly on catchment and water-supply areas.

The still considerable dependance upon coal traffic is not reassuring for the future of the waterways. In 1971 the Gas Industry decided to terminate gas-coal movement by waterways because of the progress with North Sea gas and this means a loss of about 250,000 tons of traffic. Also, the liquids are threatened by pipeline competition as has already occurred on the Severn system north of Worcester. A main positive development has been the Board's introduction in 1971 of a push-tow fleet and its involvement in a BACAT (barge aboard catamaran) scheme to link the West Riding and the Rhine. Such developments, essentially similar to LASH (section 5.VI.1), may perhaps revitalise some limited sections of waterway with suitable capacity as the traffic between continental Europe and British east coast ports increases.

VI   RETROSPECT AND PROSPECT: SOME DEVELOPMENTS AND PROBLEMS

VI.1 The Transport Revolution

Technological developments have played an important role in changing transport patterns in the UK in the recent past. Within the last decade it has become commonplace to refer to a transport revolution in goods transport. Changes have been very rapid and although there were precursors (e.g. the London, Midland and Scottish Railway Co. was first to use containers in 1926 and they were used by the Ford Motor Co. to ship from Dagenham to Amsterdam in the 1930s) the main expression of the developments has been within the last ten years and the full implications are yet to be experienced. The revolution refers particularly to the changes in bulk movement and to the progressive spread of unit-load transport in increasingly integrated systems.

Important developments in bulk-handling, with widespread implications (sections 5. V.2 and 5.V.3), concern the greatly increased size of vessel. Both construction costs per ton and operating costs per ton decrease as the dwt of the vessel increases and operating costs do so at a faster rate so that the largest vessels are most effectively and efficiently used over long distances. More specifically and in detail the advantages vary according to the type of vessel.[106] Oil tankers have demonstrated the most striking rise in total tonnage and in size of vessel. In 1950 only 5 per cent of the world's tanker tonnage was of vessels over 20,000 dwt but in 1969 more than 19 per cent was of vessels of over 100,000 dwt and vessels 200,000-250,000 dwt were no longer uncommon. Although some larger vessels are already in operation (a vessel of 477,000 dwt was launched in Japan in 1972 and Shell have two vessels of 540,000 dwt on order in France), it is doubtful if any main economies are to be gained by tankers of over 250,000 dwt. In the case of ore-carriers it seems probable that the main advantages have been reaped by the time the size of vessel has reached 90,000 dwt and that the large specialised ore-carriers may remain predominantly at about 100,000 dwt although some combined function carriers (especially the OBOs, Ore/Bulk/Oil) are already operating at above this size. In any event, apart from the economies of scale becoming less apparent after a certain point, there are other even less advantageous aspects of operating very large vessels which may curb the size to which they will commonly develop. Quite specifically in the case of oil-tankers the hazards of potential pollution and destructive explosions, although clearly not restricted to supertankers, are of greater impact the larger the vessel and the greater the capital risk. Doubts from these sources about supertankers are reinforced by the increased insurance premiums which have been charged following pollution claims and, especially, following the three tanker explosions of December 1969. For the tanker of 250,000 dwt insurance premiums form more than half the running costs.

A more recent and as yet restricted development which increases the flexibility and adaptability of bulk movement is the LASH (Lighter Aboard Ship) technique. In this a mother-ship carries barges (a vessel with 73 of 400 tons each is in service on the North Atlantic and one of 18 × 140 tons on the short-sea route to Europe) which are handled by the ship's own gear and proceed independently as required at the assembly and dispersal ports. Obviously this is a system which is most effective if there is an extensive and efficient inland waterway network at one or both ends of the trade route. In an elementary sense this is an intermodal system. Of much greater importance to the development of intermodal transport and central to the *transport revolution* is the container or some less formal type of unit-load transport. Commonly in the past each element of a transport chain has been concerned almost solely with its own sphere of activity although it has long been true that developments in one link of the chain tend to have implications and to promote change elsewhere. Containers presuppose a through-transport system. It was necessary that one element amongst those involved should have an overall view and take the initiative in imposing the system. For the most part this has been done by the shipowners and appropriately so because of their pivotal position and capital resources. Nonetheless a major part of the working-out of the system, and very often its chance of success, rests with the land-based components.

An investigation of total transport costs for non-bulk cargoes from inland point to inland point between North America and Western Europe suggested that 62 per cent of total cost related to sea freight of which about half was the cost of loading and discharging, 28 per cent to inland freight and 10 per cent to port charges and dues.[107] Containerisation is already modifying this costing. It would appear that the ports have the most to gain and certainly in the maritime section of the trade route the results of unit-load operations can be pronounced. A considerable increase in tonnage can be handled over a single berth. Although estimates vary a total of about 100,000 tons per annum over the conventional berth is considered to be increased about 5 times by roll-on operations and by at least 10 times by full containerisation.[108] It also follows that there is a considerable decrease in the number of vessels required for a particular traffic (9 specialised container vessles on the UK-Australia run begun in 1969 will replace about 80 smaller conventional vessels), that there is a decline in the requirement for port labour, that the costs of general cargo handling may well be decreased (and reflected in lower charges at least on short-sea routes where conference agreements are not involved), and that finally a speedier and more efficient service will be provided. In short, this is one of the best indications that merchant shipping has become, and seaports *must* become, increasingly capital-intensive. Although containerisation has been widely developed it is not without opponents in some circumstances and certainly not without problems. The costs of conversion from conventional operation to palletisation are relatively small when compared with a fully containerised system and thus palletisation may be preferable on lower density routes and on shorter routes.[109] Moreover a greater proportion of general cargo can be palletised than containerised. An average load is pallet-sized (1-1·5 tons) and only 4 per cent of non-bulk dry cargo consignments weigh 10 tons or more (about 10 tons being the preferred full – 30 ft, 9 m – container-load). Equally basically, effective container operation requires comparable facilities and access inland for containers at *both* ends of the trade route and outstandingly it requires a suitable *two-way flow* of cargo (at present about one-third of all containers travel empty).

Containerisation has not only given reality to a through-transport system between sea and land transport but also has potentially made feasible a much greater integration between rail and road transport. Containers are not new to the railway but the main development followed the Beeching proposals with the formation of the Freightliner system. The first Freightliner ran from London to Glasgow in November 1965. The Freightliner system in external trade linking the regions with Inland Container Depots (ICDs) and the ports has been referred to earlier (5.V.2). A largely separate network, necessary as the ICDs involve HM Customs and the goods are in bond, handless inland trade with 23 Freightliner terminals sharing between them about 32 two-way services linking the main centres of population.[110] Road transport of containers is involved at the terminals and is directly in competition for container traffic over the shorter distances, perhaps to about 150 miles (241 km). Even in the limited period to date there has been some readjustment in the competitive relationship between rail and road although Freightliner has not as yet developed as British Rail forecast. It clearly shares some of the same problems discussed in terms of maritime container routes. There is, however, some evidence of integration in, for example, the road hauliers' use of Freightliner for the trunk haul operation. Air transport is not excluded from the transport revolution or from intermodal developments but air freight, especially domestically, has relatively a very small volume. Specialised freighters have increased in speed and capacity. However, while standard containers are handled, more common is the pallet-stye *igloo* shaped to the cross-section of the fuselage for easy and efficient loading.

VI.2 Pipeline Development

Pipelines, although an inconspicuous, indeed usually concealed, element of the transport system, have been extended rapidly in the last decade, mainly in relation to the transport of energy. The separateness and exclusiveness of the pipeline network is to some extent deceptive. From tanker to pipeline is clearly intermodal transport and there is competition between pipeline and coastal shipping and more directly between the pipeline and the railway. Pipelines undoubtedly have an increasing role in UK transport, but it must be noted that this is a role limited not only by the particular characteristics of the pipeline as a transport medium but also quite specifically limited by the size and shape of the country. The dimensions of the UK are such that the main asset of pipelines, bulk movement over long inland distances, cannot be fully exploited. Moreover there are no inland refineries, thus tankers can commonly provide equally cheap movement of oil, and so there are few demands for crude oil pipelines.

Any pipeline has certain specific characteristics and a distinctive competitive potential. Both influence the involvement of pipelines in the total transport system. Most obviously pipelines are a restricted medium because of the rigidity of the route and especially in the limited range of commodities which can be transported, mainly oil, gas and some solids as slurry. Pipes are able to handle greater gradients than any other media but although they involve continuous movement at a constant rate they are invariably slow, perhaps 3-5 mph (5-8 kmph). Pipelines are a high capacity media and to operate effectively need a consistent even demand (since unlike other media capital costs completely dominate pipeline transport) and preferably a high level of demand (since with increased diameter, capacity increases at a faster rate than costs).[111] Pipelines have the asset of being able to be used for large volume storage if needed, and have a very low labour requirement. Pipeline transport costs, when appropriate comparisons are possible, are usually assessed at about equivalent to those of water transport and thus perhaps, in comparable situations, no more than one-quarter the cost of rail transport. Pipes may offer increasing competition to the railway for the movement of coal or ore as slurry, although the limited distances involved and the fact that a railway hungry for traffic will often be available must limit development.

A remnant of the extensive wartime network to supply airfields is still in use but the effective present-day pipeline network is almost entirely a product of the 1960s. Developments after the Pipeline Act 1962 (applicable to all pipelines over 10 miles (16 km) in length) took advantage of a much simplified, although still strictly controlled, procedure which previously required a private Bill in Parliament. There are three short stretches conveying gaseous oxygen and one moving chalk slurry for the Portland Cement Co. from Dunstable quarries to Rugby but most pipelines are in two broad categories; oil, indeed mainly oil products and gas.[112] With water transport so all-embracing there is usually little demand for crude oil pipelines. The first in the UK linked the incomparable depth advantages of Finnart on Loch Long with Grangemouth refinery in 1951 (figures 4.3 and 5.8). Three further lengths of crude oil pipeline have been laid to feed refineries at Llandarcy, Stanlow and Heysham where depth limitations prevent the use of large tankers. The petroleum products pipelines, the main network, include stretches of the wartime network linking the Isle of Grain refinery to Walton on Thames (and subsequently to London airport) and linking Stanlow to industrial Severnside. The developments of the 1960s were essentially of similar links to meet the needs of transport and industry, for example the pipeline from Fawley to Staines and London airport in 1963 and the longest stretch of 317 miles (510 km) completed in 1969, linking the Thames and Mersey with short Midlands off-shoots. In preference to linking Fawley with the Thames-Mersey pipeline the Esso Company decided to adopt the rail 'liner-train' method of distribution. Petrochemical feedstock pipelines linked Fawley to Severnside (1962) and interconnected two further main concentrations of the petrochemical industry, the Tees (Wilton), and Lancashire and Cheshire (Fleetwood, Partington, Runcorn and Stanlow) by 1968.

Oil pipelines may seem largely removed from the intermodal transport system but clearly competitive situations can arise. It is less easy to envisage such situations in respect of natural gas. However, that there can be some link with other transport media is shown by the first main length of the present natural gas pipeline system completed in 1962 from Canvey Island (Thames) to Leeds to carry Algerian methane gas brought as a refrigerated liquid by tanker. The situation was soon to be transformed by North Sea gas. In 1967 the West Sole well was linked to Easington (near Hull) and to Sheffield and the Leeds pipeline. The following year the Leman, Hewett and Indefatigable fields feeding to the coast at Bacton (Norfolk) were joined to the distribution grid at Rugby. The grid continues to spread into North and South Wales, into the South West peninsula and into eastern Scotland, then arcing west ultimately to end near Glasgow (Glenmavis).

Pipelines, already restricted, seem further limited in the UK context although interestingly the dimensions over which they can operate have been stretched into the North Sea by gas and soon by oil. It is possible, although unlikely, that the distance restraints of insularity could be removed by under-Channel links. Nonetheless pipelines are not without the potential to re-shape some economic distributions and could certainly do so to the detriment of industrial seaports, although perhaps in most instances the advantages of the coastal site would continue to prevail.

VI.3 Complementary or Competitive Transport Media?

The UK transport situation has been always basically competitive; the media compete for traffic and thus none of them works to capacity. The costs involved, in fact the costs of having a choice of modes, are considered justified by the efficiency which the competitive situation is thought to promote. Theoretically, in this context, no control is needed to ensure that each medium operates in the most appropriate sphere. Alternatively it may be argued that the excess capacity could be avoided by rigorous planning of networks and of modal choice, embodying, for example, a decision that all heavy traffic will go by rail. Such an approach may attempt to ensure that each media handles the traffic for which it is technically and economically most suited but it fails to cater for a choice which is related not so much to costs as to the quality of service, which may indeed be unfavourably affected by such plans. This approach might well also prove unduly rigid, inimical to technological change, and not necessarily more efficient than a competitively based one. It would aim 'to ensure that the required transport services are provided with the minimum call on the real resources of the nation'.[113] The position of the transport system at any given time on the continuum between competitive and complementary extremes has tended in the period since the Second World War to be a political issue reflected in policies (see section 5.I.3). On balance, and over a much longer period, the prevailing view has been that competition is necessary but there has invariably been a failure to effectively pursue comparability of charges to ensure effective competition and informed choice. A basic issue in the approach to transport is often the provision of so-called *essential services*. A failure to provide such services may be adjudged to occur with either broad approach but the decision to deliberately and directly subsidise particular groups or areas is more likely to occur following a political decision aimed at a complementary approach.

The general spheres of operation of the different transport media are fairly well established. Water transport (together with pipelines) and air transport lie at opposite ends of both cost and speed scales. While they may intrude competitively into the *middle-ground* in particular circumstances, this area is pre-eminently that in which the interrelationship of rail and road has produced the most intractable transport problems of the last fifty years. It is realistic to reaffirm at the outset that since 1945 the dominance of road transport in the UK has been confirmed largely by reason of its increased economy and reliability, its ability to provide low volume transport and especially because it provides the quality of service in demand.[114] There is, of course, some measure of interdependence between road and rail in the extent to which the road still serves as a feeder to the rail network. It may seem also on occasions that the competition is more apparent than real. Rail freight is in some measure distinctive, a high proportion being coal, iron-ore and other minerals which form a very small part of road freight. Even more obviously than in the past, rail is now the transport medium of the heavy industries. To that extent its declining freight traffic is related more to changes in the national structure of industry and in the particular transport needs of heavy industry rather than to any switches in modal choice. Of course there is no doubt that the rail lost some of its most lucrative traffic to road transport in the 1930s but in the 1950s, when road freight first achieved clear dominance, modal changes of freight were not an important issue. The respective roles of rail and road have been more clearly defined in the period since 1950. However, in recent years the attempt of the railway to regain lost traffic by Freightliner operation may again widen the scope of effective competition, although it seems unlikely to affect importantly the growth of road traffic. In part confirming a modal split by the nature of the commodity, Baylis and Edwards[115] found that, while there was no conclusive influence upon choice between rail and road haulier, consignment weight was most important in explaining the distribution of traffic between these two modes. They note also, however, that 'ready availability and speed' were considered important and both increased the probability of carriage by road haulier. If the modal choice included the firm's own transport then length of haul was very clearly the main explanatory factor. There is equally evidence of a generalised split between rail and road based mainly on their most effective operating distances. Gwilliam in 1964 gave the average rail haul as about 70 miles (113 km) and the average road haul as about 25 miles (40 km).[116] Of the traffic of British Road Services over 70 per cent is over distances of less than 150 miles (242 km) and it is estimated that at about 150 miles (242 km) the *direct* costs of road and of rail Freightliner are equal and that rail offers a slight saving over this distance.[117]

The competitive basis between rail and road is continually changing. After the Second World War the railway was poorly equipped to meet intensified road completion, one ιe aspect of the declining demand for its services which by the mid-1950s had seriously impaired British Rail's financial position. British Rail's subsequent retrenchment and reorganisation has once more improved its competitive position and there is some evidence in the 1960s of increased tonnages of freight and of increases in the average length of haul, although these may not necessarily affect the long-term trend.[118] Electrification has undoubtedly strengthened the passenger carrying role although notably here in competition with air transport which the railway would now claim to have checked to distances above about 250 miles (403 km). This may be modified further by the work, already well forward, on the Advanced Passenger Train capable of 155 mph (250 kph) on existing tracks. No development by the railway, except perhaps in particular circumstances in urban areas, can hope to compete with the personal transport of the private car, especially with the owner's usually quite unrealistic costing of the car as, in effect, do-it-yourself transport. The attraction of the private car has been importantly enhanced now that the motorways allow sustained speed but so also have the advantages of the long-distance bus. The cost advantage of the inter-urban bus is reasonably accurately reflected in the price per mile paid by passengers which is about half that of the train. The bus journey, however, typically takes about 50 per cent longer than an express train on the same route. Road transport is the only transport form at present subject to direct legislation within the EEC although there is a declaration of intent to *harmonise* the various media. The competitive position of road transport in the UK is likely to be immediately influenced by regulations controlling driving hours and daily mileages, for international journeys from January 1973 and for domestic journeys from January 1976. An increase in the maximum weight of road goods vehicles is also in prospect following the UK's entry into the EEC.

Transport policies have contributed to the changing relationships between the media although rarely positively and comprehensively facing the problems. The 1968 Transport Act, although emasculated by the change of government in 1970, perhaps gives a more effective base than previously available from which to achieve an effective coexistence. In a sense it contributes something to both the complementary and competitive approaches. In the rural areas, where bus services have been in decline since the early 1950s, any unprofitable routes considered to be socially necessary can be submitted to the local authority as candidates for subsidy before being withdrawn. Local authorities, however, are not eager to take up the opportunities for subsidy, only about £1 million being spent in 1971. The bus companies have been ordered to operate profitably so cuts and changes in services will be made and it is likely that public road transport will become quickly worse. British Rail was similarly empowered so that, especially in the peripheries of the network which are still under threat, named services could be offered to the government for direct subsidy. Such grants for social reasons totalled £65 million in 1971. In theory both public road transport and British Rail should be able to operate more effectively and competitively as a result of these developments but the Act does not ensure that the competition is any more nearly on a basis of true costs.

VI.4 The Rationalisation of the Ports

If the ports of the UK are to take full advantage, both in cargo handling and in industrial investment, of the technological advances in maritime transport and if also they are to compete more effectively with the ports of the north-west European interface especially from within the EEC, then a rationalisation of facilities is an urgent need. Such a move raises difficult decisions of investment, of choice of sites and of integration. As has been shown to have occurred, or to be necessary, in so much of UK transport, a more intense use and development of selected sections of the system is required.

The traditional problems of a port authority in seeking to initiate major capital schemes are markedly exacerbated by the present tempo of technological change in transport. A new vessel can be built within a year and the conversion of a vessel carried through in half of this time. However, to plan, build and equip a dock may take at least three years. There is, moreover, the perpetual problem that the infrastructure of a port is much longer-lasting than the life of a merchant vessel. Major mechanical equipment such as cranes and loading bridges may be written-off within twenty-five years but for quay walls and port works a period of fifty years would be more normal. It is clearly unlikely that a period of fifty years, calm will be available to port authorities to accommodate this rate of depreciation. For both these reasons the port authority must not only attempt to forecast future developments but also provide a design which is sufficiently flexible to meet unforeseen changes. Informed and planned choice of sites for development is therefore critical and this is difficult to envisage without positive government oversight, especially since government will undoubtedly be involved in the provision of capital. In contrast to the Belgian and French governments' practice of paying respectively 100 per cent and 80 per cent of port infrastructure costs, the UK government's contribution has been limited to 20 per cent of certain restricted types of port investment. This low level of direct government financial involvement has often been considered a disadvantage of the UK ports compared to their continental rivals and notably, for example, with Antwerp and Rotterdam which have demonstrated so forcibly the benefits of a vigorous planned investment policy.

The choice of sites to be emphasised raises many problems. There is no lack of candidates. In terms of industrial development the government enquiry (see section 5.V.3), although acknowledging other influences, paid most attention to the physical characteristics of the sites. In fact it must always be acknowledged that the established major ports with possibilities of reclamation near the sea or off-shore, will have a real and justifiable advantage. New deep-water locations to meet the exacting requirements of modern vessels are unlikely and will certainly be few. Does this mean that the list of proposed MIDA sites can be sifted and sorted; and that perhaps (in terms of their site, situation and current achievement) the Thames-Medway, Humber and Tees have a distinctive potential for industrial development possibly allowing a special place for the Cardiff-Newport location to meet the unlikely event that the depth limitation of the English Channel will ever become a serious inhibiting influence? In cargo-handling the commercial initiative of ports has given a more positive lead to influence developments and concentrate activity. This is seen clearly in the case of Southampton. Atlantic Container Lines' decision to base its transatlantic operations in the port, followed by Southampton's nomination by ACT and OCL as the premier port for the Far East and Elders and Fyffes' decision to group all their banana and cargo operations in the port, are of main importance to the future development of Southampton. Similarly, a measure of increasing concentration has occurred through the nomination of particular ports by shipping lines for their container traffic, for example British Rail's decision to concentrate its container movements to the continent through Harwich and those to Ireland through Holyhead. These commercial initiatives require, of course, the cooperation of the port authority and ultimately, as major finance is almost invariably involved, the imprimatur of public policy through the approval of the Minister of Transport.

One important development, in part government stimulated and in essence no more than a restatement of a long-standing feature of British port activity, has been the focusing of attention upon estuarial groupings. The Rochdale Report focused ideas of reorganisation upon the estuaries and subsequently the National Ports Council recommended amalgamations. Between 1966 and 1968 reconstituted authorities on the Clyde, Tees and Forth assumed such comprehensive estuarial responsibilities and the new Port of Tyne Authority was a similar, although incomplete, reorganisation (British Railways

Board Dunston Staiths remained independent). In a more limited sense, in those areas
where several major undertakings are operated by the British Transport Docks Board,
e g the Severn, the Humber and Southampton Water, more formal and more positive
cooperation has enhanced the estuarial focus. The Ministry of Transport working documents which served as a basis for consultation leading up to the White Paper, *The
Reorganisation of Ports* (1969), proposed the development of 8 regional port authorities
with wide independence. However it had begun to seem that this suggestion was unlikely
to be implemented even before the entire proposals, which were in effect a ground-plan
for nationalisation, were put aside at the change of government in 1970. Given Britain's
preoccupation, albeit with sporadic enthusiasm, with regional development since 1945, it
is strange that the ports have not played a more positive role. It has long seemed likely
that the most appropriate development would be to create some formal link between the
estuarial ports and the authorities concerned with regional development in their area.
It seemed possible that the schemes for the reorganisation of Local Government Areas
would provide a renewed opportunity for such associations. In fact such potential
remains fairly limited. Although it preceded the main reform programme for England,
the new Teesside local government area does potentially allow such an association and,
equally, the South East region in the Wheatley proposals for local government in Scotland
allowed the possibility at least for the Forth Ports Authority to deal with a single administrative unit in the promotion of the regional development of the area but have now been
amended to establish the unity of Fife.

Apart from integrating the port activities fully with a developing regional economy the
aim of these estuarial amalgamations is to rationalise the services and in so doing to specialise
and to concentrate activities in a smaller number of ports to enable the full advantages of the
technological advances in both land and sea transport to be achieved. Some concentration
of activity is seen as critical to the achievement of an acceptable efficiency. A smaller
number of ports are required to exploit the possibilities of larger vessels and of modern
cargo handling. It follows equally that trans-shipment as a port operation will grow in
importance. Some ports will require to settle for a function as *feeder* ports rather than
as *pivot* ports in a re-shaped trading pattern. It is sometimes suggested that if an adequate
concentration cannot be achieved otherwise, then it might be necessary statutorily to
designate ports or estuaries to handle particular geographical trading areas and in this
way concentrate traffic. In whatever way concentration is achieved there are clearly
political problems to be faced at both the regional and national levels in the selection
of a limited number of favoured ports. That some measure of concentration of activity
might be appropriate to the rigours of competition within the EEC is perhaps suggested
by the fact that the UK has about 15 major ports while Germany, Belgium and the
Netherlands have about 3 each.

REFERENCES

1. W Smith, *An Economic Geography of Great Britain* (London 1949).
   C I Savage, *An Economic History of Transport* (London 1961).
   H J Dyos and D H Aldcroft, *British Transport, an Economic Survey from the
   Seventeenth Century to the Twentieth* (Leicester 1969).
2. J H Paterson, *Land, Work and Resources* (London 1972).
3. J H Appleton, *The Geography of Communications in Great Britain* (London 1962).
4. A J Brown, 'Surveys in Applied Economics: Regional Economics, with Special
   Reference to the UK', *Economic Journal,* **79** (1969), pp. 759-96.
5. S L Edwards and B T Baylis, *Operating Costs in Road Freight Transport*
   (Department of Environment 1971).

6. W Owen, *Strategy for Mobility,* The Brookings Institution (Washington DC 1964).
7. M Chisholm, 'Freight Transport Costs, Industrial Location and Regional Development', in M Chisholm and G Manners (eds.), *Spatial Policy Problems of the British Economy,* (Cambridge 1971), p. 240.
8. A Marshall, *Principles of Economics,* vol. I (London 1890), pp. 718-19.
9. M Chisholm, 'Geographical Space: A New Dimension of Public Concern and Policy', in M Chisholm and G Manners (eds.), *Spatial Policy Problems of the British Economy,* p. 5.
10. *Royal Commission on Canals and Waterways, Final Report,* Cmnd 4979 (1909).
11. D Munby (ed.), *Transport, Selected Readings* (Harmondsworth 1968), p. 7.
12. A Patmore, 'New Directions for Transport', in M Chisholm (ed.), *Resources for Britain's Future* (Harmondsworth 1972), pp. 50-61.
13. Owen, *Strategy for Mobility,* p. 33.
14. C Sharp, *The Problem of Transport* (Oxford 1965).
15. K M Gwilliam, *Transport and Public Policy* (London 1964).
16. Gwilliam, *Transport and Public Policy,* p. 96.
17. Gwilliam, *Transport and Public Policy,* pp. 224-32.
18. British Railways Board, *The Development of the Major Railway Trunk Routes* (British Railways Board 1965).
19. Ministry of Transport, *Statistical Paper 6, Survey of Road Goods Transport 1962, Final Results, Geographical Analysis* (HMSO 1966).
20. C E R Sherrington, *The Economics of Rail Transport in Great Britain,* (London 1928).
21. Dyos and Aldcroft, *British Transport,* p. 370.
22. Scottish Development Department, *Central Scotland, a Programme for Development and Growth,* Cmnd 2188 (HMSO 1963).
    Secretary of State for Industry Trade and Regional Development, *The North East: A Programme for Regional Development and Growth,* Cmnd 2206 (HMSO 1963).
23. R Lawton, 'The Journey to Work in England and Wales', *Town Planning Review,* **29** (1959), pp. 241-57.
    G Humphrys, 'The Journey to Work in Industrial South Wales', *Transactions, Institute of British Geographers,* **36** (1965), pp. 85-96.
    B Fullerton and M Bullock, *Accessibility to Employment in the Northern Region,* Papers in Migration and Mobility, **10** (Department of Geography, University of Newcastle upon Tyne 1968).
24. *Hansard* vol. 536, col. 1095 (1957).
25. J H Appleton, *The Geography of Communications in Great Britain* p. 222.
26. B V Wagle, 'A Statistical Analysis of Car Ownership in Great Britain and a Forecast for 1975', *Journal of the Institute of Petroleum,* **54** (1968), pp. 44-9
    J C Tanner, 'Car and Motorcycle Ownership in the Counties of Great Britain, 1960', *Journal of the Royal Statistical Society,* Series A, **126** (1963) pp. 276-84.
27. M E Beesley, T M Coburn and D J Reynolds, *The London-Birmingham Motorway, Traffic and Economics,* Road Research Laboratory Technical Paper 40 (HMSO 1959).
28. Ministry of Transport, *Roads for the Future – New Inter-Urban Plan* (HMSO 1969).
29. Welsh Office, *Wales – The Way Ahead,* Cmnd 3334 (HMSO Cardiff 1967).
    Scottish Office, *Scottish Roads in the 1970s,* Cmnd 3953 (HMSO Edinburgh 1969).
    Ministry of Transport, *Roads for the Future – The New Inter-Urban Plan for England,* Cmnd 4369 (HMSO 1970).
30. A A Walters, *Integration in Freight Transport,* (Institute of Economic Affairs 1968).
31. G Walker, *Road and Rail,* (London 1947).
32. D H Aldcroft, *British Railways in Transition,* (London 1968), p. 142.
33. Gwilliam, *Transport and Public Policy,* pp. 169-81.

34. British Transport Commission, *Modernisation and Re-equipment of British Railways,* (BTC 1955).
35. J and A M Hackett, *The British Economy – Problems and Prospects,* (London 1967). Ministry of Transport, Select Committee 254. *Re-appraisal of the Plan for the modernisation and re-equipment of British Railways,* Cmnd 813 (HMSO 1959).
37. Ministry of Transport, *Re-organisation of the Nationalised Transport Undertakings,* Cmnd 1248 (HMSO 1960).
38. British Railways Board, *The Reshaping of British Railways* (HMSO 1963).
39. Govt. of Northern Ireland, *Northern Ireland Railways,* Cmnd 458 (HMSO Belfast 1963).
40. Govt. of Ireland, *Report of the Committee of Inquiry into Internal Transport* (Irish Stationery Office 1957).
41. Ministry of Transport, *British Railways Network for Development* (HMSO 1967).
42. Ministry of Transport, *Transport Policy,* Cmnd 3057 (HMSO 1966). Ministry of Transport, *Public Transport and Traffic,* Cmnd 3481 (HMSO 1967). Ministry of Transport, *Railway Policy,* Cmnd 3439 (HMSO 1967). Ministry of Transport, *The Transport of Freight,* Cmnd 3470 (HMSO 1967).
43. C D Buchanan, *Traffic in Towns* (HMSO 1963).
44. C D Foster, *The Transport Problem* (London 1963).
45. London Transport Executive, *London Travel Surveys* (LTE 1950, 1956). A G Wilson, A F Hawkins, G J Hill and J Wagon, 'The Calibration and Testing of the SELNEC Transport Model,' *Regional Studies,* **3**(1969), pp. 337-50. W Solesbury and A Townsend, 'Transportation Studies and British Planning Practice, *Town Planning Review,* **41** (1970), pp. 63-80.
46. *Teesplan,* Teesside Survey and Plan (HMSO 1965).
47. *Economist* (14.8.71) reporting a paper prepared for the European Conference of Ministers of Transport, October 1971.
48. Greater London Council, *Greater London Development Plan* (GLC 1969).
49. City of Glasgow, *Greater Glasgow Transportation Survey* (1967).
50. Scottish Dept. of Agriculture, *Report of the Highland Transport Board on Highland Transport Services* (HMSO Edinburgh 1967). D L Munby, 'Transport Costs in the North of Scotland', *Scottish Journal of Political Economy,* **1** (1954), pp. 75-95. D Turnock, Hebridean Car Ferries, *Geography,* **50** (1965), pp. 347-8. D Turnock, *Patterns of Highland Development,* Ch. 7 (London 1970). Scottish Office, *A Programme of Highland Development,* Cmnd 7976 (HMSO Edinburgh 1964). Highlands and Islands Development Board, *Annual Reports,* 1957 onwards, (HIDB Inverness). D C Thomson and I Grimble, *The Future of the Highlands* (London 1968). A C O'Dell, 'Highlands and Islands Developments', *Scottish Geographical Magazine,* **82** (1966), pp. 8-16.
51. F H W Green, 'Urban Hinterlands in England and Wales. An Analysis of Bus Services', *Geographical Journal,* **116** (1950), pp. 64-88. F H W Green, 'Bus Services in the British Isles', *Geographical Review,* **41** (1951), pp. 645-55.
52. Ministry of Transport, *Rural Transport Surveys* (HMSO 1963). Council for Wales and Monmouthshire, *Report on the Rural Transport Problem in Wales,* Cmnd 1821 (HMSO 1962). D St John Thomas, *The Rural Transport Problem* (London 1963).
53. Dept. of the Environment, *Study of Rural Transport in Devon: Report by the Steering Group* (HMSO 1971).

54. Dept. of the Environment, *Study of Rural Transport in West Suffolk: Report by the Steering Group* (HMSO 1971).
55. *Hansard,* vol. 501, col. 490 (1952).
56. J A Patmore, 'The Contraction of the Network of Railway Passenger Services in England and Wales, 1936-62', *Transactions, Institute of British Geographers,* **38** (1966), pp. 105-19.
57. Aldcroft, *British Railways in Transition,* p. 201.
58. Rural District Councils Association, *Rural Transport; What Future Now?* (London 1971).
59. *Economist,* (10.6.71).
60. W R Snaith, S E Robinson and D Mennear, *The Rural Transport Problem in Mid-Northumberland,* Northumberland Rural Community Council, (Newcastle 1957).
61. *Annual Abstract of Statistics,* table 244 (HMSO 1971).
62. Ministry of Transport, *Report on Rural Bus Services* (HMSO 1961).
63. Dyos and Aldcroft, *British Transport,* pp. 373-88.
64. Dept. of Trade and Industry, *Business Monitor,* CA 2 Air Passengers March 1972 (HMSO 1972).
65. *Annual Abstract of Statistics* (HMSO 1971), table 267.
66. *Annual Abstract of Statistics,* 1971, table 258.
67. Dept. of Trade and Industry, *Business Monitor,* CA 3 (HMSO 1972).
68. The extension of the Leeds-Bradford airport runway was refused by the Dept. of the Environment on local planning grounds in 1971.
69. *Report of the* (Roskill)*Commission on the Third London Airport,* Appendix 6, p. 192 (HMSO 1971) comments on Manchester Ringway airport in relation to future potential traffic.
70. Dept. of Trade and Industry, *Business Monitor,* CA 3 (HMSO 1972).
71. E J Taafe, 'The Urban Hierarchy, an Air Passenger Definition', *Economic Geography,* **38** (1962), pp. 1-14.
    E J Taafe, 'Air Transport and United States Urban Distribution', *Geographical Review,* **46** (1956) pp. 219-39.
72. *Passengers at London's Airports* (HMSO 1970).
    Report of the Commission on the Third London Airport, Appendix 6 table 7, p. 192 (HMSO 1971).
73. *Rept. of the Commission on the Third London Airport,* appendix 6, table 5, p. 191.
74. *Rept. of the Commission on the Third London Airport,* appendix 6.
75. K R Sealy, 'The Siting and Development of British Airports', *Geographical Journal,* **133** (1967), p. 157.
76. Ministry of Civil Aviation, *London's Airports,* Cmnd 8902 (HMSO 1953).
77. *Report of the Commission on the Third London Airport,* gives a short history of these developments in ch. 1, pp. 1-5. See also K R Sealy 'London's Airports and the Geography of Airport Location', *Geography,* **40** (1955), pp. 255-65.
78. *Report of the Commission on the Third London Airport,* table 10.1, p. 96.
79. K R Sealy 'Stansted and Airport Planning', *Geographical Journal,* **133** (1967), pp. 350-4.
80. *Report of the Commission on the Third London Airport,* ch. 13, pp. 130-46 and a Note of Dissent by Colin Buchanan, pp. 149-60.
81. *Report of the Commission on the Third London Airport,* table, 5.4, p. 24.
82. J G U Adams, 'London's Third Airport', *Geographical Journal,* **137** (1971), pp. 468-505.
    J G U Adams, 'Westminster, the Fourth London Airport?' *Area,* **3** (1970), pp. 1-9.
    P G Hall, 'Roskill's Arguments Analysed, *New Society,* (28.1.71).

E J Mishan, 'What is Wrong with Roskill?', *Journal of Transport and Economic Policy,* **4** (1970), pp. 221-34.

P Self, 'The Roskill Argument', *New Society* (4.2.71).

83. *Commission on the Third London Airport,* Public Hearings vol. 1 p. 44 (HMSO 1970).

84. *Report of the Commission on the Third London Airport* 5.18-5.19, p. 26.

85. L R Jones, *The Geography of London River* (London 1931).

J H Bird, *The Major Seaports of the United Kingdom* (London 1963).

86. N R Elliott, 'The Functional Approach in Port Studies', in J W House (ed.), *Northern Geographical Essays* (University of Newcastle upon Tyne 1966), pp. 102-18.

N R Elliott, 'Hinterland and Foreland as Illustrated by the Port of Tyne', *Transactions, Institute of British Geographers,* **47** (1969), pp. 153-70.

87. J H Bird, *Seaports and Seaport Terminals* (London 1971).

88. *Digest of Port Statistics,* National Ports Council, annually.

Annual Statement of the Trade of the United Kingdom, HM Customs.

89. E Hunter and T B Wilson, 'The Increasing Size of Tankers, Bulk Carriers and Containerships with some Implications for Port Authorities', *Research and Technical Bulletin, National Ports Council,* **5** (1969), pp. 180-224.

90. *Containerisation: Its Trends, Significance and Implications,* Report by McKinsey and Co. Inc. to the British Transport Docks Board, 1966.

Containerisation: the Key to Low-cost Transportation, Report by McKinsey and Co. Inc. to the British Transport Docks Board, 1967.

Containerisation on the North Atlantic: a Port-to-Port Analysis, Report by Arthur D. Little Ltd. to the National Ports Council, 1967.

Transshipment in the Seventies – a Study of Container Transport, Report by Arthur D. Little Ltd., to the National Ports Council, 1970.

Final Report on Containerisation, Universities of Glasgow and Strathclyde, 1970.

91. N R Elliott, 'Tyneside, a Study in the Development of an Industrial Seaport', *Tijdschrift Voor Economische en Sociale Geografie,* **53** (1962), pp. 225-37 and pp. 263-72.

92. *Port Progress Report,* National Ports Council, 1969.

M H Preston and R Rees, *Maritime Industrial Areas: a Preliminary Report,* National Ports Council, 1970.

93. G Hallett and P Randall, *Maritime Industry and Port Development in South Wales* (University College Cardiff 1970).

94. *Britain's Foreign Trade: A Summary of the Report prepared for the Port of London Authority by Martech Consultants Limited covering Britain's Overseas Trade* (Port of London Authority 1966).

95. J H Bird, 'Traffic Flows to and from British Seaports', *Geography,* **54** (1969), pp. 284-302.

96. *Report of the Committee of Inquiry into the Major Seaports of Great Britain,* Cmnd 1824 (HMSO 1962).

97. *Portbury: Reasons for the Minister's Decision not to Authorise the Construction of a New Dock at Portbury, Bristol* (HMSO 1966).

98. G A Wilson, 'The Effect on the Land Transport System of Ports and Water Transport', *The Dock and Harbour Authority,* **45** (1965), p. 90.

99. H Jurgenson, 'The Regional Impact of Port Investments and its Consideration in Port Investment Policy', in R Regul (ed.), *The Future of the European Ports,* vol. 2 (Bruges 1971), pp. 576-602.

100. H C Garnett, 'Competition between Ports and Investment Planning', *Scottish Journal of Political Economy,* **17** (1970), pp. 411-19.

L H Klaassen and N Vanhove, 'Macro-economic Evaluation of Port Investments', in R Regul (ed.), *The Future of the European Ports,* vol. 2 (Bruges 1971), pp. 603 et seq.

101. H D Watts, 'The Inland Waterways of the United Kingdom', *Economic Geography*, **43** (1967), pp. 303-13.
102. *The Facts about the Waterways,* British Waterways Board (London 1965).
103. *Canals and Inland Waterways,* British Transport Commission (London 1955) p. 31.
104. *Canals and Inland Waterways* (1955).
    Report of the Committee of Inquiry into Inland Waterways, Cmnd 846 (HMSO 1958).
105. *The Future of the Waterways,* British Waterways Board (London 1964).
    The Facts, BWB (1965).
106. G Hallett and P. Randall, *Maritime Industry and Port Development in South Wales* (University College Cardiff 1970), Ch. 3.
    F S McFadzean, 'The Economics of Large Tankers', *Strathclyde Lecture, March 1968,* Shell International Petroleum Co. Ltd. (London 1968).
    E Hunter and T B Wilson, 'Increasing Size of Tankers, Bulk Carriers and Container Ships with some Implications for Port Authorities', *Research and Technical Bulletin, National Ports Council,* **5** (1969), pp. 180-224.
    R O Goss and C D Jones, 'Economics of Size and Dry Bulk Carriers', *Government Economic Service Occasional Paper* **2** (1972).
107. *Ocean Freight Rates as Part of Total Transport Costs* (OECD 1968).
108. *Containerisation on the North Atlantic: a Port-to-Port Analysis,* Report by Arthur D. Little Ltd. to the National Ports Council (1967).
109. N I Turner, 'For and Against: Containers, Pallets and Roll-on, Roll-off', *The Dock and Harbour Authority,* **49** (1969), pp. 389-90.
110. *Final Report on Containerisation,* Universities of Glasgow and Strathclyde (1970).
111. G Manners, 'The Pipeline Revolution', *Geography*, **47** (1962), pp. 154-63.
112. R T Foster, 'Pipeline Development in the UK', *Geography,* **54** (1969), pp. 204-11.
113. Gwilliam, *Transport and Public Policy,* p. 214.
114. Owen, *Strategy for Mobility,* p. 99.
115. B T Baylis and S L Edwards, *Industrial Demand for Transport,* Ministry of Transport (1970).
116. Gwilliam, *Transport and Public Policy,* pp. 123 et seq.
117. *Final Report on Containerisation,* para 6.12.
    Transport Holding Company, Annual Report (London 1968).
118. M Chisholm, 'Forecasting the Generation of Freight Traffic in Great Britain' in M Chisholm *et al.* (eds.), *Regional Forecasting,* Colston Research Society, **22** (1970), pp. 431-42.

6

In Conclusion

I AN ASSESSMENT

This geographical interpretation of the economic, social or political conditions affecting and affected by the UK space since 1945 has been concerned with the changing balance of forces, the spectrum of trends, the ensuing problems, and the shifting public and private policy mix over almost three decades. Even in terms of public policy overall coherence of spatial objectives has been lacking, much has been piecemeal in character, and indeed public recognition of the importance of a spatial perspective in national affairs has been both tardy and grudging. This situation has scarcely been helped by the lack of sophistication in regional or other spatial analytical methods in all social sciences until very recent years, whilst the persistent lack of adequate and comparable regional data is only now being remedied.

The needs are thus for clearer and more comprehensive spatial management objectives, to be operated through the regional and/or urban networks, and with an ordered sequence of priorities for the use and safeguarding of natural resources, including land, distribution or deployment of people and work, harnessing and harmonising of energy sources and industrial strength, with full exploitation of the potential offered by the great increases in mobility of people and commodities. There is no optimal geographical solution to the arrangement of the UK space but the range of options is becoming more fully defined. Increasingly in a democratic society, and almost as a counterweight to the centralising tendencies of a complex urban and industrial economy, there is a rising emphasis upon nations and economic regions as the first stage breakdown of the UK, and a viable level for enhanced decision-taking. Indeed the conferment of powers and channelling of initiatives at this regional level may ultimately contain the key to the hitherto elusive problem of growth without inflation in the post-war UK.

The economic and social record of the UK since 1945 has been steady rather than spectacular, lacking in 'economic miracles' and with progress forward, but on any criterion somewhat slowly and irregularly. By the time of entry to the EEC the UK had achieved a major post-war transformation, a redefined and reduced world role. What is henceforth economically and socially possible in UK planning, what can be afforded and what is seen to be desirable will need to take EEC perspectives into account, though not exclusively so. The difficulties in balancing internal UK forces with externalities in an interpretation of post-war changes in the UK space have become apparent in succeeding chapters. The externalities are likely to be even more important in the future, but the problems of public management of economy and society are not likely to become less by virtue of an increase to the European-scale perspective in the short-term.

Problems facing UK planners are substantial and complex. Whatever the forward projection of population there will be a sizeable increase and it will accelerate towards the end of the present century. The distribution of the industrial and urban population reflects an Industrial Revolution heritage, changed in degree rather than kind in the twentieth century. Physical planning in the UK has made giant strides since 1945 but coherent regional planning is still in its infancy, both conceptually and in reality on the ground. The debate on optimum population size is mounting, to rival that on the possibilities and risks of unrestrained economic growth. Arguments for greater social justice command increasingly wide assent and the need for greater decentralisation in decision-taking is the more stridently proclaimed as economic and administrative forces seem to favour ever more rationalisation and concentration to achieve economies of scale and of unit costs.

Confident forward projections for the UK space are hard to justify, except in very general terms, in face of the complexities and uncertainties of both the immediate and the longer-term future. Furthermore the ability to predict ahead varies with the discipline being used: reliable manpower forecasts rarely go beyond a few years, land allocations in physical planning up to fifteen years, and broad regional strategies may set up options to the end of the century. Predictions will also be conditioned by political beliefs and intentions, by an assessment of the likely and desirable courses of change of economy and society, as well as of polity.

At the base of all forecasting, in the light of the evidence of this book, lies the prime need to evaluate and rank the forces which are tending to polarise, centralise or concentrate, on the one hand, and those which are tending in the opposite direction, to disaggregate, disperse or breakdown concentration or congestion. The aggregating forces have been strongly and increasingly detected through the chapters of this book, notably the range of market forces leading to concentration at fewer, larger sites in: energy output, manufacturing or commercial plants or firms, transport nodes, major recreation centres or water storage sites. To these forces the centralising tendencies in government, banking, insurance and finance may be added, in the search for administrative efficiency or convenience. Spatially interpreted, these forces tend to the strengthening of the centre against the periphery, of more affluent against less prosperous regions, in short the growth regions against the development regions (see section 1.IV.1).

On the other side of the argument, and together these forces may prove decisive, must be listed: the desirability of greater regional balance in the economy and society of the UK, for the satisfaction of component national and regional aspirations, but also from the common-sense points of view of reducing congestion in growth regions; diminishing the sources of inflationary pressure there and spreading social justice and better prospects for economic growth throughout the UK space. Regional policies by successive UK governments have recognised the validity of this thinking, but the means provided have not yet permitted the desirable ends to be realised.

II   THE REGIONAL PROBLEM

Perhaps even more than hitherto since 1945 the UK regional problem will in future be affected by externalities, in the short-term the stimulus from entry to the EEC, in the longer-term by further accommodation to shifts in the balance of world and European economic forces. In the first instance, the GNP of the UK will set the limits to effective government action on the problems of regional imbalance, but EEC decisions on regional policies and locational priorities may increasingly take precedence and promote solutions different in nature and timing from those responding to national objectives from within the UK.

There is likely, however, to be coincidence of views on the desirability of diffusing prosperity into the outer margins of the EEC and of seeking greater equalisation of regional economic opportunity, though without detriment to the growth momentum of the EEC as a whole and without permitting uniquely protective national solutions to work against the European interest. The UK and the EEC share a common preoccupation to further industrial re-structuring in UK development regions to the point of achieving self-sustaining economic growth there and, thereafter, with a transformed employment structure, a competitive position within the EEC.

Differences of view might emerge on how such 'take-off' is to be achieved, how quickly and with what appropriate level of governmental or supranational aid. With adequate overall growth momentum, both in the UK and the EEC, the self-sustaining stage for the development regions may be reached during the 1980s. By then pressure of a growing population on national resources will be more apparent and the role of underutilised reserves of labour and land in the UK development regions will be an even greater asset than today. Even now the merits of capitalising upon such assets may make a very useful spatial contribution to diminishing the UK inflation, which traditionally has flared up and been fuelled in affluent regions of land and labour scarcity.

Accepting that the regional problem in the UK development regions owes its persistence more to unfavourable economic structure than to the effects of marginal location, though both are certainly ingredients, the reconversion problem is the more capable of solution. It requires government aid, and perhaps more aid than at present, in the short-term, but diminishing thereafter. Both manufacturing and service industries will have a role in the reconversion process and regional planning, through management in particular of urbanisation, infrastructure and job redistribution by public policy, will be increasingly important.

From within the regions and constituent nations of the UK there is a rising sense of identity and purpose, even of resolution for greater and more effective devolution of powers from the centre. The Commission on the UK Constitution may, and desirably should, define new levels of autonomy for Wales, Scotland, Northern Ireland, or even for the provinces of England. The birth of a more appropriate local government structure for the UK in 1973-4 is likely to make local as well as regional aspirations more coherent and realisable, even though new concepts of Euro-region may later bu superimposed on the UK administrative structure.

The regional initiatives and central government allocations likely to be consolidated from the current set of definitive economic regional strategies, in spite of their present diversity of presentation or stage of formulation reached, will provide the acceptable frameworks and preferred options for growth and change first to 1981 and, thereafter, in more general terms to the end of the century. The recognition and accommodation of regional aspirations and their harmonisation with national or European objectives is perhaps the greatest problem and challenge UK governments are likely to have to meet in the immediately foreseeable future.

III   POPULATION TRENDS

The stagnation and, possibly, fall in population numbers expected from pre-1939 trends, especially the level of births, have not transpired (chapter 2). Higher birth-rates than anticipated from the mid-1950s — due in part to earlier and more universal marriage and to increased illegitimacy-rates, together with a further reduction in infant mortality and general death-rate — reflected in a gradual increase in expectation of life, have led to higher natural growth rates: net immigration gains from overseas in the late 1950s and early 1960s have further assisted a steady increase in population in the UK. Estimation of future population levels on the basis of past and current trends is a hazardous business for they depend on assumptions which may be invalidated by changing social and economic circumstances. Successive revisions of population estimates for 1990, have led, for example, to estimates varying between 53 million (based on 1955 assumptions) and 67 million (1964-based); these wide differences are due largely to alternative assumptions concerning birth-rate.

Whatever their precise level, however, all estimates from the mid-1950s agree in predicting growth into the 1990s and it is unlikely that the recent downturn in birth-rate will change this trend, though if continued through the 1970s it would certainly reduce the relatively modest growth rates of some 0·7 per cent per annum that were made on the basis of the 'moderate' 1968-based estimate. But many people now challenge the ability or desirability of growth in such a populous and, in some urbanised industrial regions, already overcrowded country. Hence, in the last few years, the debate has been joined over what is regarded as an optimum population for the UK, a debate which reflects a growing awareness of the significance of population trends and distribution for all aspects of national life — demographic, [1] social, economic and environmental.[2]

An optimum population is not capable of a single, precise definition since it depends upon many variables, each of which is dynamic: population, resources, land, the level of expectations, and consumption. The first official government investigation (1971) considered these problems in an appropriately wide context, and gathered evidence from a very wide range of viewpoints,[3] but did not emerge with any general consensus, though it did make a number of recommendations which amounted to a possible population policy for the UK.

It would be foolish to speculate over precise future population totals in view of the fluctuating trends in population of the last 25 years. But it *is* possible to indicate the sort of problems which must be taken into account in any analysis of the spatial and environmental implications of population. In terms of food and natural resources the UK would certainly be regarded as over-populated already, if we depended upon indigenous supplies alone, for we do not support anything like our present population. Indeed a suggested maximum of 40 million people, made some years ago by the then President of the British Association, is not unrealistic in this context.[4] However, neither on the basis of present nor any envisaged population trends is such a target likely to provide the basis of a practical policy, at least in the forseeable future.

Population is, moreover, an economic asset, both now and in the future, arguably the most important which the UK, as a technologically-advanced society, possesses. Over the past two centuries a numerous, vigorous and inventive people have proved capable of enlarging the economic capacity and population potential of our islands at a rising standard of living for an increasing proportion of our people. They may be capable of doing so into the future, though certainly not at the rate which characterised rapid nineteenth-century growth. Furthermore, decreasing demand for manpower, in terms of numbers, as against skills, which has already been reflected in at least some of the structural component of unemployment in the past few years, sheds some doubt on our capacity to absorb the potentially larger labourforce even of the 1980s.

One of the most powerful factors behind the growing concern over population growth in the UK, as in other parts of the developed world, has been an increased awareness of the enormous environmental impact of a large and closely-packed population in a modern industrial and urbanised society. Pressures on basic resources such as land and water, as well as on food and raw materials, are reflected in growing problems of over-use, e.g for recreation, and of problems of waste disposal, both of human wastes (sewage) and non-recoverable wastes (such as plastics or poisonous chemicals), and in problems of excessive pollution of air, water and, in places, also land.

While undoubtedly many such difficulties are due to misuse of the environment and past irresponsibility by industry, commerce and private individuals, they are exacerbated by high population numbers and concentrations. Loss of land to building and communications is not likely to pose insurmountable problems over the next thirty years, but it will undoubtedly add to pressures which are already severe in some large urban areas. It may well be that some more stringent curbs will need to be introduced on further industrial, commercial, housing and transportation growth in some of our over-congested regions.

Seen thus, a critical aspect of the UK's population problems, now and in the future, is that concerning regional distribution and trends. While the UK could probably accommodate a population of up to 80 million by the second quarter of the twenty-first century, it could do so only if a satisfactory regional balance of population can be achieved in relation to land, resources and communications. Seen in this context, population policy is not a separate target for national planning but rather a key aspect of regional planning policy. Any major problem of regional planning today illustrates this point: the dispersal of homes and people from overcrowded cities; the location of employment in both industry and services; the provision of adequate transportation; access to land for recreation; environmental control and restoration.

Without appropriate and integrated regional planning policies, especially for land-use and industry, it will be impossible to relieve population pressure in the overcrowded areas. Yet in some of the less prosperous regions additional jobs, homes and people could be easily accommodated. It is unlikely that, left alone or subjected to the limited and intermittent regional planning policies of the 1950s and 1960s, future regional population trends will differ much from those of the post-war period. Although regional population estimates are as yet subject to much uncertainty, the maps of projected population change at subregional level (figure 6.1) is very similar to that of the 1951-69 period (figure 2.5). Migration gains are likely to be mainly in the arc from the South East through the Midlands but the greatest increases are still likely to occur in the environmentally vulnerable area between London and Birmingham, and, to a lesser extent, between the West Midlands and North West England. If a British megalopolis stretching from Greater London is to be avoided, more people must be retained in and indeed must be attracted to the hitherto less prosperous regions, some of which have more land for housing and industry and most of which are nearer to good recreational areas on the coast, in highlands and in national parks. In such areas investment in urban renewal could be an act of population policy as well as of economic, social and regional planning. But to retain or attract population there and redress the imbalance of the last seventy years, capital will be needed to rectify the many deficiencies in housing, education and amenities (social as well as physical).

If we do not more fully utilise the resources of the whole of our islands, further population increases will inevitably bring greater and perhaps intolerable pressures to the present over-crowded regions. In recommending that a special government office should be set up to deal with these problems the Select Committee (1971)[3] urged that it should take account not only of population but also of 'such major issues as food supplies, natural resources, economic growth and the environment'. But at the core there undoubtedly lies a population/resource problem, the outcome of which will be a key factor in the social, economic and regional geography of the UK in the late-twentieth century.

IV   ENVIRONMENT AND LAND USE

Environmental management will become increasingly important as pressures for space increase with the need to optimise the available resources, in the interests of all land users. The apparent conflicts between these users are no doubt a result of lack of liaison hitherto rather than intention and can only be adequately resolved by adopting conservation or management policies which take all potential users into consideration. While short-term decisions may be satisfactorily made by subjective means, in the long-term it would appear necessary to have complex models where evaluation of land-use policies can be fully tested. For this, continued data collection and research into the relationships between

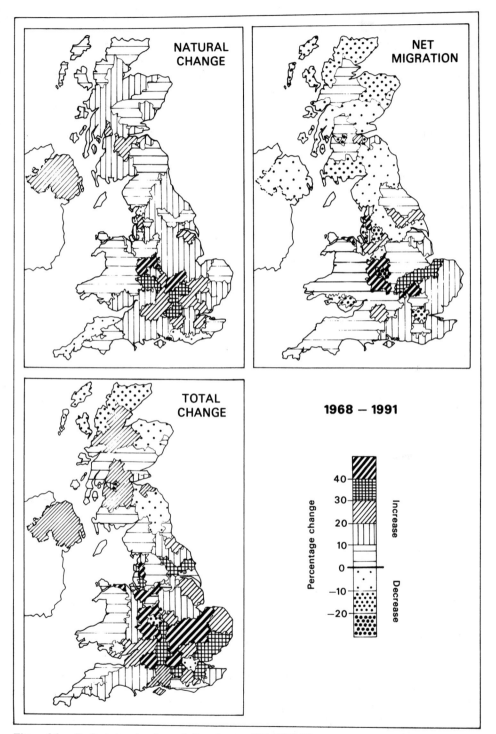

Figure 6.1   Projected regional population changes, UK, 1968-91

land use and environment is an urgent need. However, there is clearly a dilemma, for land use requires field observation and is therefore both costly and slow and the more detail required the longer it will take. Stamp's land use survey was kept simple and was thus completed within a short time. The more detailed second land use survey is of necessity a much slower operation and its value as an inventory of land use on which to base planning decisions is greatly reduced, particularly on a regional or national scale.

Land classifications have a similar problem but the complexity of the environment makes it essential for the classification to consider the potential user of the map so that no universally satisfactory classification can be produced. Because of the variety of users more classifications are needed in the future, and the task facilitated by data storage and retrieval systems, though the problem of interpretation of environmental factors for the specific purpose remains. Modelling of land-use systems, at present being developed for uplands where the conflicts between agriculture, forest, urban water-supply and recreation are relatively simple, must be extended to include the much more complex problems of the heavily populated lowlands.

Many aspects of measurement of the physical environment can be improved and, in particular, the closing of the wide gap which exists between the macroclimatic scale of standard meteorological records, which exist over a long period of time, and the microclimates which so clearly affect human activity. The development of studies of local climates must again be problem-orientated. This however involves the isolation of the parameters important to production, particularly the commercial yields and potentials of living things such as agricultural plants and forest trees. Equally important to production are the physical conditions permitting work to be carried out, e.g. in certain farming operations water may be critical, or in building operations wind and temperature could be limiting. The accurate prediction of these conditions will enable industry or agriculture to project production and to make more efficient use of human resources. However this will only be possible by improvements in the long-term forecasting of these parameters.

Environmental pollution will change in its nature and effects so that continual monitoring is necessary. Water pollution and land pollution will become a matter of river basin management and can be more effectively controlled under the administrative reorganisation proposed for 1974 in England and Wales. Conservation must imply continuance, though not necessarily maximisation of production, rather than just preservation, so that here too industrial and agricultural land-use must be evaluated in terms of the long-term effects on the environment. On occasion there may be a major conflict between the desire to attract industry (or allow it to grow) and priorities in conservation. Studies of industrial and urban pollution must not remain a UK problem in isolation. Entry into Europe brings with it an opportunity to achieve a measure of environmental control over the atmosphere and the seas of Europe which could not be envisaged before.

It is as yet too early to state with confidence that environmental constraints will eventually set limits to economic growth, but it is already clear that increasing numbers of citizens are prepared to evaluate, take into account, and even give precedence to environmental implications arising from excessive preoccupation with growth.

V   DISTRIBUTION OF ECONOMIC ACTIVITY

By the early 1970s the main trends in the changing distribution of economic activity within the UK space through to the end of the next decade have already been firmly established. They were determined by the operation of the factors discussed in chapter 4: further increases in the proportion of the labourforce in services, continued centralisation of control in industry, allowing rationalisation and increasing size of units to achieve economies of scale, and reduction in effective economic distance between major centres through transport improvements. All these tend to increase the attractions of market locations at the national and regional levels, modified only marginally at present by government action influencing some of the more flexible manufacturing and service activities. Within individual regions, however, these same trends help to create greater flexibility of locational choice, with manufacturing and services now able to disperse farther out from the main centres. These trends determine that the largest increases in the labourforce, in absolute numbers, will continue to occur where the largest concentrations of people were in 1970. The regions benefiting (or suffering, depending on your point of view) most will be the South East and the Midlands. Within all regions of the UK, most of the expansion of industries and services will continue to take place within the hinterlands of the largest urban concentrations.

Apart from UK government or EEC action on the UK regional problem (Chapter 6-I), modification of these trends could result from three new circumstances: a government decision to assume full responsibility for the location of public sector economic activity, planning decisions at the national level to develop the potential of Humberside, Severnside and Tayside, and the market implications of the entry of the UK into the EEC. The government has enormous potential for influencing patterns because of the proportion of the labourforce now employed in the UK in public sector activities. These range from coal-mining and Forestry Commission operations in the primary sector, to the steel industry and minor engineering and food processing in the manufacturing sector, and to a whole range of services from education and health to transport and communications, and the utilities of gas, electricity and water. Between them these activities account for 25 per cent of employees, most of them in the now dominant service sector of the economy. Only recently has the government begun to recognise both the importance of services in influencing the location patterns of economic growth, and the flexibility of much service activity, but no government has yet accepted full responsibility for coordinating the location decisions taken by public sector services at the national and regional level. It is unlikely that any British government would assume such responsibility and apply wide-ranging powers within the context of a policy for the proper distribution of economic activity in the UK. If this did occur the trends outlined earlier would be modified, with more dispersion of employment nationwide, to the peripheral regions and intraregionally to smaller places, than could otherwise be expected.

The effect of developing the estuarine areas of Humberside, Severnside and Tayside with million-plus populations, would be to add three major city regions to the industrial map of the UK. The growth here would be somewhat at the expense of other, perhaps adjacent, regions, which would accordingly grow by that much less. These centres based on extensive industrial sites with nearby dock complexes, would be most attractive to industries processing imported raw materials and also to export-based manufacturing. The areas which could be most adversely affected by this would be South Wales, the North East, the North West, and West Scotland which traditionally have concentrated on raw material import-processing, and the West Midlands which has strong engineering industries supplying exports.

The effect of UK membership of the EEC will be to strengthen the market trends operating in the early 1970s, unless they are deliberately counteracted by a stronger or more comprehensive regional policy for marginal areas (chapter 6-I). The larger markets available encourage further centralisation of control into fewer hands in some industries, and more rationalisation to achieve economies of scale. Indeed such developments appear to be essential in some industries if they are to remain competitive with industries on the mainland of Europe. Entry into the Community has also reinforced the attractions of eastern and southern locations within the UK, at the expense of the west and north. On the economic potential map of Britain (figure 4.13) the South East, already in 1966, had

the highest figures. For the enlarged EEC the area with the highest economic potential is
the 'golden triangle', bounded by lines joining Cologne-London-Amsterdam-Cologne. With
market attractions increasingly important, industry serving the wider markets of Europe
would clearly have an advantage in being close to this area; in the UK this means the coasts
in the south-eastern quadrant of the country. Even before the creation of the enlarged
community, mainland Europe including the USSR, provided over 40 per cent of UK
imports and took over 40 per cent of its exports, and these proportions will continue to
rise. Proximity to the sources and destinations involved in this trade attracts activity to
the south and east of the UK in the same way as proximity to the axial belt (London-
Midlands-Merseyside) was attractive in the past.

These comments leave little doubt that the considerable changes in the patterns of
economic activity within the UK space between 1945 and 1970, described in chapter 4,
were much greater than the differences which can be expected to occur between 1970 and
the end of the century. The former was a period when the Victorian mould of Britain's
economy and geography, which had survived to 1945, was at last structurally adapted to
the needs of the mid-twentieth century. The latter will be a period when the new patterns
which emerged from these transformations are being consolidated and developed.

VI TRANSPORT

The outstanding period of transport developments, beginning soon after the Second World
War, is not yet complete. Some developments are yet to be fully implemented and further
important technological advances have not been used commercially. If the technological
possibilities are to be fully exploited then certain recent features of the UK transport
systems will be accentuated in the years ahead. There will be a further concentration of
activity into a limited number of nodes such as the major ports and an increased intensity
of working in limited sections of the transport networks, as has so obviously ensued in the
rail and inland waterways networks. Transport also will continue to become increasingly
capital-intensive and within the next decade both the railways and, outstandingly, the
ports will face difficult problems of labour redundancy. The systems will continue to be
shaped mainly by demand. It will be a demand which increasingly involves the quality of
service and thus presumably, in inland transport, reinforces the dominance of road
transport. However it is likely that transport, and road transport in particular, will be
subject to environmentalist pressure groups and arguments about the 'quality of life'
which may well influence the relationships of road and rail media over long hauls and the
status of the road within urban areas.

The immediate future is likely to see a fuller development of intermodal transport and
this will assuredly be an influence upon the investment decisions to be made concerning
motorway mileage and the rationalisation of the ports. The development of the Advanced
Passenger Train (APT) and of vertical take-off and landing aircraft (VTOL) promises more
radical change. On present showing the APT is the firmer and more immediate prospect.
It may well equalise the distance over which the railway is competitive for passengers with
air transport to include the Anglo-Scottish services before the VTOL aircraft cause a
reversion perhaps to inside the present competitive limits of about 250 miles (403 km).
However, while there are clearly technological advances to bring to fruition, it may be
that after a period dominated by technological issues the transport systems of the third
quarter of the twentieth century will be influenced notably by the reassessments of
scale and of space relationships which follow from membership of the EEC. In some
respects the insularity and limited dimensions which have been a feature of UK transport
will be modified although only directly if a Channel tunnel is dug. More immediately the
activities of a wider community will inevitably thicken the transport concentration in

South East England, accentuate the problem of circumnavigating London or perhaps lead to an increasing volume of traffic avoiding the problem by using East Anglian ports. Indeed, in general, it seems likely that the eastern seaboard of Britain will assume a relative importance unapproached since the advent of trans-oceanic trade.

VII   A FINAL NOTE

During the remaining years of this century the UK space may well not be further transformed as fully as it has been since the Second World War.[5] Entry to Europe will surely confer the expected economic benefits of the larger market and thus hopefully provide for the scale of sustained economic growth necessary to complete the adjustments to the UK economy and society begun in 1945. If the UK regional problem cannot be solved in the sense of balance and equilibrium of living standards or job opportunity in all regions equally, it can certainly by the 1980s be so improved that all regions can move to self-sustaining economic growth and a more competitive position in a European future. To achieve this the mobilisation of regional and national forces on the grand scale will be needed, but the verdict of this book must be that the target is technically and geographically realisable. There will, however, be continuing and extremely difficult reconversion problems for some regions over the next decade, and the necessary further management of the UK space, through more effective and coherent regional planning, will not be feasible without widespread, and, in the shorter-term, greater and more decisive public intervention to channel market forces in the national interest.

REFERENCES

1.   See, for example, *Towards a Population Policy for the UK,* Population Investigation Committee, LSE (London 1970).
2.   L R Taylor (ed.), 'The Optimum Population for Britain' *Institute of Biology Symposium,* **19** (London 1970).
3.   *First Report of the Select Committee on Science and Technology. Session 1970-1 Population of the UK,* (HMSO 1971).
4.   Sir Joseph Hutchinson, 'Land and Human Populations', *The Advancement of Science,* **23,** 111 (1966), pp. 241-54.
5.   C Leicester, *Britain 2001 AD,* (HMSO 1972).

Index